THE CHALICE AND THE BLADE IN CHINESE CULTURE

Gender Relations and Social Models

Chinese Partnership Research Group

Min Jiayin
Editor-in-Chief

China Social Sciences Publishing House

Published by China Social
  Sciences Publishing House
Gulou Xidajie Jia 158
  Beijing 100720,P.R.China
© 1995 by China Social
  Sciences Publishing House
Printed by Zhao Chen
  Printing House
ISBN 7−5004−1741−1 ∕ C · 30
CIP (95)13106

Translated by
Cover Designer:Mao Guoxuan

Partnership entails cooperation and respect among people. It involves joining, linking and working together in peace and harmony for the common good of all. The partnership way is a unifying principle, defined by affiliation rather than violence-based ranking that spreads into the mainstream of society.

Partnership requires fairness, consensus, and mutuality, utilizing democratic, participatory decision-making; necessitates active listening, empathic sharing, collective support and encourages growth. It is inclusive and seeks to unify people. In partnership settings, people feel valued, genuinely cared about and safe. True partnership leads to empowerment and self-actualization.

ADVISORY GROUP

Honorary Advisors:

Ru Xin — Executive vice-president of Chinese Academy of Social Sciences

Riane Eisler — Co-Director, Center for Partnership Studies, U.S.A.

David Loye — Co-Director, Center for Partnership U.S.A.

Advisors:

Wang Junyi — Deputy editor-in-chief of the China Social Sciences Publishing House

Wang Xingjuan — Director of Beijing "Women's Hot Line"

Wang Baoxuan — Research fellow, Institute of Philosophy, Chinese Academy of Social Science

Wu En — Executive deputy director, Institute of Archaeology, Chinese Academy of Social Sciences

Liu Bohong — Director, Theoretical Section of the Women Research Institute, All-China Women's Federation

Li Xueqin — Director, Institute of History, Chinese Academy of Social Sciences

Song Zhaolin — Research fellow, Museum of Chinese History

Chen Yunquan — Director, Institute of Philosophy, Chinese Academy of Social Sciences

Chen Yiyun — Director, Beijing-Toronto Family Center

Zheng Bijun — Director, Center for Women's Studies, Beijing University

Cao Dawei — Associate professor, Department of History Beijing Normal University

Meng Peiyuan — Director, History of Chinese Philosophy Section, Institute of Philosophy, Chinese Academy of Social Sciences

Jing Tiankui — Director, Section of Marxist Philosophical Principles, Institute of Philosophy, Chinese Academy of Social Sciences

CONTENTS

PREFACE

Ru Xin

The book, **The Chalice and the Blade in Chinese Culture: Gender Relations and Social Models**, written jointly by scholars of the Chinese Academy of Social Science and other academic institutes is off the press, which is a great event in the Chinese academic field. As far as I know, there are very few monographs which present such a systematic study and exploration of the historical changes in relations between men and women and of women's status in Chinese society. Its publication will be conducive to promoting the study of women's issues in China.

The book is characterized by a close combination of historical examination and theoretical research and it studies women's issues by taking into account the entire process of development of Chinese society. The book, therefore, does not proceed from abstract human rights concepts to discuss Chinese women's status and rights, but tries to relate women's issues with the development and changes in the economy, politics, culture, society and family life in China in order to provide a scientific explanation of the evolution of Chinese women's social status. Based on ancient mythology, archaeological discoveries, a vast amount of historical records and rich anthropological data collected by contemporary scholars in the course of field-work among ethnic minority inhabited areas of the country, the authors of the book present a vivid historical picture depicting Chinese women's conditions from ancient times to the present. The historical changes in Chinese women's social status not only reflect the universal laws governing human social development, but also the unique characteristics of Chinese society itself. I believe that all those readers who care for Chinese women and who are interested in women's issues will obtain reliable information from this work, and thereby have a better understanding of the history and present conditions of Chinese women.

Historically, Chinese women had a splendid past. On Chinese territory, as in other places in the world, matriarchal society existed over a long period of time, in which, as the ancient philosopher Shang Yang observed, "people knew they had mothers, but did not know they had fathers", females enjoyed high status and prestige, and were the masters of the society. With the emergence of slave society and patriarchy, male dominance was established gradually and the concept of man being superior to woman began to become the main theme in gender relations. In feudal society, women's status lowered further and women were subjected to various forms of cruel oppression and restrictions. Since China's feudal rule endured over an especially long period of time, feudal ideology was especially fully developed and the feudal ethical code represented by a Confucian school of idealist philosophy of the Song and Ming dynasties further bound Chinese women with heavy ideological shackles. Only with the upsurge of the modern anti-feudal enlightenment movement did Chinese women begin awakening and put the task of female emancipation on the agenda. However, it was not until the Chinese revolution thoroughly overthrew the semi-colonial, semi-feudal old system and the People's Republic of China was founded that the realization of the liberation of Chinese women became possible in real terms. Today, Chinese women, described as "half of the sky," are playing an important role in all realms of social life and have become a decisive force in building a socialist modernized country with Chinese characteristics. In the millennia old historical development process, Chinese females who once enjoyed the status of masters were reduced to being the accessories of males. Now, they have finally risen from their enduring humiliation and have regained their full rights as masters of the society. Of course, this recovery of rights can never be the return of the rights women enjoyed in ancient times, but all social rights and obligations women now share with men on the basis of the new and totally equal gender relations. Dialectically, this may be termed "the negation of negation." As early as the beginning of the last century, people with advanced ideas set women's liberation as one of the goals of social progress. The outstanding utopian socialist François Marie Charles Fourier pointed out explicitly, "the degree of women's liberation is the natural criterion for judging liberation in general". Now the great ideal of this socialist ideological forerunner is being realized in China. If Fourier knew of this, surely he would acclaim it?

As the publication of the book coincides with the Fourth World Conference on Women to be held in Beijing, readers should regard this book as one contribution of Chinese scholars to the conference.

FOREWORD

Riane Eisler

In the Preface to the Chinese edition of my book **The Chalice and the Blade: Our history, Our Future**, I expressed the hope that Chinese archaeologists, folklorists, historians, and other scholars will probe the roots in Chinese culture of the two basic types of social organization that my work identifies: the partnership and dominator models.

I wrote that I could only speculate about whether, as appears to have been the case in the West, there was in China also "a time before the force-backed domination of man over woman and over other men became 'normal'." I pointed to suggestions of this in writings such those of Laozi emphasizing the essential need for balance between yin and yang. I also pointed to the continuing veneration in China of female deities as beneficent life-giving and compassionate goddesses. I noted the persistence of much that is stereotypically considered feminine in Chinese culture—all the way from the strong aesthetic sensibilities to the very strong valuing of community, affiliation and piety, which are in the West generally associated with a feminine ethos. And I suggested that perhaps much of early Chinese tradition was in a partnership rather than dominator vein, with the eventual blend of the two models resulting in what has often been described in the West as the "paradox" of Asian culture.

I never dreamed that my hopes that Chinese scholars would investigate these suggestions would be so quickly, so thoroughly, and so elegantly realized. When, following the publication of

The Chalice and the Blade: Our History, Our Future in China in 1991, the Partnership Research Group was formed, I realized that this was an important step in this direction. But this book, by members of the Chinese Partnership Research Group, exceeds my expectations.

I therefore want to begin by thanking the seventeen scholars from the Institutes of Philosophy, Archaeology, and History, the journal, and the Center for Documentation and Information of the Chinese **Social Sciences in China** Academy of Social Sciences, Beijing University, Beijing Normal University, China University of Political Science and Law, Tianjin Normal University, and Zhengzhou University whose research and writing are represented in this book. I also want to express my appreciation to all those who have given their support to this project, including the Chinese Academy of Social Sciences Publishing House, the Threshold Foundation, Elinore Detiger, Robert Graham, and the Board of the Center for Partnership Studies, particularly Dr. David Loye. I especially want to thank Professor Min Jiayin, who has been so instrumental in bringing the Chinese Partnership Research Group together, as without his unflagging efforts this book would not have come into being.

The Chalice and the Blade in Chinese Culture: Gender Relations and Social Models is a major contribution to our understanding of the interconnection between the organization of gender relations and the larger social structure. It expands our understanding of history by drawing from a data base that includes the two halves of humanity: women and men. It sheds important new light on the past and present of the hitherto largely ignored female half of humanity. Perhaps most important, it highlights that the way gender relations are structured in both the so-called private and public spheres plays a key role in matters vital for our future: whether a society is more peaceful or warlike, more creative or destructive, more egalitarian or exploitative.

The Chalice and the Blade in Chinese Culture traces that relations between women and men in connection with changes in social and ideological organization in China from prehistoric to contemporary times. On the basis of Chinese fairy tales and legends, and archaeological studies of the life style of some ethnic minorities in the south-western mountainous areas of China, it points to the conclusion that in prehistoric China there was a period which may be symbolised by the Chalice rather than the Blade. More precisely, it presents evidence that, as in Western prehistory, there appears to have been in Chinese prehistory a time of Goddess worship and partnership between men and women. While Chinese archaeologists have not been able to find signs of massive intrusions by nomadic groups such as those who in Europe brought with them male dominance, warfare, and strong-man rule, there are indications that the semi-farming and semi-nomadic Han people in the north may have at a certain point shifted to this type of social organization, and that it was through the cutting edge of their blades that the earlier culture was eventually replaced by a more dominator-oriented social and ideological organization.

In short, **The Chalice and the Blade in Chinese Culture** shows that (as I and others have found happened in Western history), the social status of women in China gradually declined over a period of several thousand years, as warfare and autocratic dynasties that ruled primarily by the blade—that is, by the power to dominate and destroy, rather than by the chalice, the power to give, nurture, and illuminate life—gained ascendancy. It also shows other important parallels between Western and Chinese history. For example, it indicates that the Confucian philosophical classics played a role similar to that of the Judeo-Christian Bible in Western history in justifying the ideology of "man is superior to woman" on ostensibly moral/ethical grounds. Similarly, it shows that symbols of the regenerative powers of nature, such as the snake (which periodically sheds and regrows its skin, and which was in Western prehistory associated with the worship of the Goddess), were also in Chinese history associated with a partnership ethos—as still illustrated in a rubbing from a Han dynasty (206-220 BCE) tomb that shows the first Chinese ancestral couple, Nü Wa and Fu Xi, as intertwined serpents.

Although most of the contributors to this book agree with my conclusion that there was an earlier more peaceful and agalitarian age, there are differences on one important point of interpretation. This relates to the term to describe these earlier societies.

Since my interpretation is that the earlier societies where a Goddess Creatrix was venerated were societies with a high degree of gender equality, with neither women nor men considered the sexual property of the other, I have proposed that the term gylany (symbolic of the linking of woman or gyne and man or andros) is more descriptive than the term matriarchy. Indeed, I note that semantically matriarchy and patriarchy are two sides of the same dominator coin.

Others, however, following the anthropological tradition of Lewis Henry Morgan and Friedrich Engels, prefer the term matriarchy. Of these there are also two schools. Some see a somewhat lower status of men, while others see matriarchy as describing a society where women and men have equal rights and status.

This question of terminology is far from resolved. For example, the archaeologist Marija Gimbutas uses the term matristic. But she also describes the old civilization of Europe with my term gylany, emphasizing that this was not a system of autocratic rule by women, but rather a structure in which the sexes are more or less on equal footing. Similarly, in the Goddess-worshipping Indus Valley cultures of India and Pakistan, before these areas were overrun by Aryan or Indo-European male dominant and warlike invaders, the evidence points to an equal valuing of male and female.

This is still an area in the pioneering stages of intensive

research using what I call a gender-holistic methodology. Adding further complexity is that cross-culturally there may be significant regional variations. Nonetheless, what we are learning—and what **The Chalice and the Blade in Chinese Culture** also amply documents—is that the long-accepted view that human history always has been male-dominant and chronically warlike is erroneous.

But **The Chalice and the Blade in Chinese Culture** not only provides invaluable materials for all those interested in a clearer view of our past; it is also a source of hope for our future. For it shows that in China, as in the West, the modern struggle against domination and exploitation—be it man over woman or man over man—is rooted in very ancient traditions from a time when society oriented more to a partnership rather than dominator model.

So it is particularly appropriate that this book's publication coincides with the Fourth United Nations World Conference on Women hosted by the People's Republic of China in September of 1995. For the interconnected goals of the World Conferences on Women, beginning with the First United Nations Decade for Women of 1975-1985, are equality, development, and peace —the key configuration of a partnership rather than dominator model of social and ideological organization.

I think this book will be of use to all those who are today in our world working to realise these goals—not only for women, but also for men and children of both genders. It brings still further support for two of the key points of my cultural transformation theory: that the way a society structures the relations between the female and male halves of humanity is central to all aspects of women's and men's lives in both the private and public spheres, and that in this time of social ferment we have the opportunity for completing the shift from domination to partnership as the guiding organising principle in human relations.

Moreover, **The Chalice and the Blade in Chinese Culture**

does this by offering us a veritable feast of information about one of the most ancient and fascinating cultures in the world: a culture that to this day venerates female deities such as Ma Zu, Avalokitesvara, and Guan Yin (Kwan Yin), and has during this 20th century, particularly since the Revolution, made great efforts to reinstate woman to her rightful place of equal rights and status with men.

As the author of **The Chalice and the Blade: Our History, Our Future**, as co-director of the Center for Partnership Studies, the U.S. organization which has supported the work of the Chinese Partnership Research Group presented in this book, and as a woman deeply committed to work for a more peaceful, equitable, and sustainable future, I again thank all those who have participated in the creation of this important work.

May 1995

INTRODUCTION

Min Jiayin

This book, compiled by members of the Chinese Partnership Research Group, is a comparative study made under the influence of the book **The Chalice and the Blade: Our History, Our Future** by Dr. Riane Eisler. The Chinese edition of this book is titled 阳刚与阴柔的变奏 and **Variations of Yanggang and Yinrou** would be an accurate, but mystifying, word-for-word translation of the Chinese title. The English edition of the book is therefore simply titled **The Chalice and the Blade in Chinese Culture: Gender Relations and Social Models**. In this introductory discussion, I will, however, discuss the key concepts used in the Chinese title.

1. Riane Eisler and **The Chalice and the Blade**

(1) General Exposition

Riane Eisler was born in Vienna, the capital of Austria, in 1931, and when she was seven years old she experienced the great calamity caused by the Nazi Anschluss of Austria. Her family fled Europe to Cuba by ship, and she migrated to the United States at the age of 14. The war, the Holocaust, three different countries and three cultures made her, from her childhood, concerned with the destiny of humanity and caused her to ponder these questions: Why do human beings slaughter each other? Why are human beings so cruel and brutal to their own kind? Why is the world so full of man's oppression of man and of woman? Are women born inferior to men and destined

1

to remain in a subordinate status forever?

She studied sociology and anthropology at the University of California, obtained a Juris Doctor (J.D.) in its College of Law, and then taught cultural anthropology at the University of California and Immaculate Heart College. The destiny of women and the issue of equal rights between men and women have been the focus of her study and writings. On these subjects she has already published four works: **Dissolution** (1977), **The Equal Rights Handbook** (1978), **The Chalice and the Blade** (1987) and **The Partnership Way** (1991).

Eisler spent 15 years working on **The Chalice and the Blade**, reading hundreds of books on the relationship between the sexes, making systematic studies on the history, current conditions and the future of gender relations from the wide perspective of cultural anthropology and making findings of universal importance. The dust jacket of her book carries the evaluation that this is "the most important book since Darwin's **Origin of Species**", a comment of Ashley Montagu, the noted anthropologist from Princeton University. The English edition of the book was reprinted 15 times in the first two years after it was published. In the book reviews published by U.S. newspapers and magazines, the book was hailed as "the most significant work published in our lifetimes", "a key to our survival", and "a very important picture of human evolution". Over the past few years the book has been translated into a score of languages and published world-wide. It has been widely read and discussed. The author has been invited to give lectures on her new cultural transformation theory on the international circuit and to attend international academic seminars and give TV interviews. Her book has inspired films, TV programs, poems, operas and the formation of. The Center for Partnership Studies and the International Partnership Network. A World Partnership Conference organized by the former First Lady of Greece was held on the Mediterranean island of Crete (October 4-11, 1992), with representatives from 40 countries participating. Riane Eisler has been acclaimed as a highly creative thinker, a modern Renaissance woman, and a leading advocate for equal rights between men and women.

So what is the nature of **The Chalice and the Blade**? And why has it won such acclaim and exerted such a great influence?

To put it briefly, archaeologists in Europe made a startling discovery by unearthing many human cultural remains belonging to the pre-historic age in Europe and bringing to light the conditions of matriarchal society which were previously unrecorded and buried underground. Through its investigation of the archaeological remains of matriarchal society and a critical analysis made by combining the two major roots of recorded Western patriarchal culture—the Bible and the culture of Christianity, as well as ancient Greek and ancient Roman culture, the book demonstrates that Western society has had two different models of society. One model is based on gender equality and partnership; the other is a dominator model in which men oppress women and other men. The former is symbolised by the chalice in the hand of the Goddess worshipped in matriarchal society, which could bring about peace, harmony, economic prosperity and a flourishing culture, while the latter is symbolised by the blade in the hand of the esteemed warrior of patriarchal society, which could bring about violence, wars, suppression and destruction. Western civilisation, from such a perspective, can be summarised as the tortuous path of development of a five millennia old dominator model of society. It was a civilisation created by a hierarchical dominating society which was established after the fairly developed civilisation created by matriarchal society was wiped out by many massive invasions and after the "chalice" was smashed by the "blade" of the Kurgans and Achaeans, nomadic people who lived in the border areas, who worshipped force and who practised patriarchy. The typical Westerner (Indo-European) who is tall, blond haired, with a high nose bridge and deep eye sockets we see today was actually not the original resident of the European mainland but the descendant of the Kurgans. The single male deity worshipped by Christianity—the awe-inspiring and brutal Jehovah—is merely a representative in heaven of the patriarchal and hierarchical dominating society established on earth. Of course, such global problems as the population explosion, ecological damage, shortage of resources, armament race and violence and pornography, which have resulted from Western civilisation and the expansion of its social model, are all directly related to the social model. Therefore, in order to solve these problems, a more fundamental problem, the relationship between men and women—the twin components of the human race—must be tackled first of all. The patriarchy with men dominating and women being oppressed should evolve into the new type of system typified by equality between men and women. The violence and oppression in society and the crude destruction of nature can only be further eliminated, first of all, by eliminating suppression and violence within families and building partnerships between husbands and wives.

It can be seen that **The Chalice and the Blade**, beyond the level of love, marriage and family life, discusses the relationship between men and women from the higher perspective of human civilisation's evolutionary history and contemporary global problems, and indicates that women's liberation and the efforts to achieve equal rights and rebuild the partnership between men and women are not secondary problems, but major problems that should not be solved finally but first of all.

(2) Remains of Matriarchal Society: The Archaeological Bombshell

The existing textbooks on world or European history state that the earliest human civilisation appeared in ancient Egypt around 3000 BC and that around 2500 BC Sumerian and subsequent cultures began to emerge in the Euphrates and Tigris river valleys. The culture of the European mainland, it is also stated, was introduced from outside and it was not only much later than the above-cited cultures, but also much later than the cultures of ancient China and India. Many articles by Western scholars venerate Oriental civilisation, and they maintain that Europeans were still wandering around wrapped in animal skins when the ancient Chinese were already living civilized lives in palatial housing.

However, this picture of early European history is being revised in the light of more than 100 remains of the Palaeolithic and Neolithic periods discovered near the Mediterranean and as the unearthed relics were precisely dated by means of the radioisotope C-14.

The remains tell us that as early as 30,000 BCE, residents of the European mainland were in the Palaeolithic period, then entered the neolithic stage around 10,000 BCE. Between 7,000 and 3,500 BCE, the early civilisation of ancient Europe flourished in the south-eastern part of the continent. This culture featured civilized farming, settlement villages, a developed architecture even featuring two-storey temples, and an advanced pottery technology and art. Many painted pottery figurines and wall paintings remain from that period. These artistic articles reflected the worship of females, mothers and a Goddess in the culture of matriarchal society, rather than the "primitive fertility cult" or prurient sexual interest as some earlier scholars maintained from a perspective of the culture of patriarchal society. For example, the Palaeolithic remains of vagina-shaped cowry shells, the red ochre used in burials and the "Venus" figurines found all over prehistoric Europe reflect an important concept of primitive people: the female body as the source of life and the divine chalice that has the power to transform death into life. For this reason, such articles were often located in a central position in the excavated chambers while, in contrast, the masculine symbols occupied more peripheral positions.

The neolithic remains at the towns of Çatal Hüyük and Haçilar excavated in the 1960s by British archaeologist James Mellaart, who directed the excavations for the British Institute of Archaeology at Ankara, demonstrated how the above-mentioned concept had evolved into Goddess worshipping cultures and religions. There were large quantities of excavated plaster reliefs and Goddess figurines made of clay, many altars and shrines dedicated to the Goddess. In sites in the Balkans there are figures of Goddesses and the modelling of water, bird and snake images as incarnates or symbols of a Goddess. In a word, "God was a woman".

Archaeologist Nicolas Platon excavated the island of Crete in the Mediterranean for 50 years, the site of the legendary culture of Minoan Crete. Vast multi-storied palaces, villas, farmsteads, districts of populous and well-organized cities, harbour installations, networks of roads crossing the island from end to end, organized places of worship and planned burial grounds were brought to light. Excavated also were viaducts, paved roads, look-out posts, roadside shelters, water pipes, and reservoirs. In the late period of the culture of Minoan Crete, bronze ware was used and living conditions were extraordinarily "modern": "all the urban centres had perfect drainage systems, sanitary installations, and domestic conveniences." The scripts in use, and the large quantities of frescoes, sculptures, vases and carvings all embodied a lively and joyful artistic style. All these were developed in the 4,000 years after the neolithic civilisation of the European mainland spread to the island of Crete in 6,000 BCE. Its advancement in farming and water conservancy, its excellent architectural and handicraft skills and developed arts and religions "dumbfounded archaeologists".

In contrast to later Indo-European civilisation, so-called Western culture, what is notable in neolithic remains is the absence of caches of weapons, military fortifications, dominating chieftain burials and remains of those buried with the chieftains. In neolithic art there are no images of warriors, nor scenes of battles. In Minoan Crete, in the remains of the great palace, a figure of the Goddess or her high priestess stands at the center while two approaching processions of men bear tribute to her. The religions were embodied in every aspect of life, and everywhere various kinds of figures of the Goddess were worshipped.

Even though the masculine principle as represented by the head and horns of the bull, as well as by priests, was also an important part of the religious imagery, it seems that the culture of Minoan Crete was female and priestesses and female heads of clans played major parts as representatives of power and widom. However, power then was merely responsibility and maternal love. Families then were evidently matrilineal and property was inherited in the mother's line, but there was no "matriarchy" like the later "patriarchy": women did not dominate and suppress men. On the contrary, men and women maintained an equal co-operative relationship and partnership. In families and society there was no pyramid-like hierarchic system of domination. People and nature maintained harmonious relations. Therefore, the basic factors of human civilisation in later generations were already created in a society typified by partnership.

(3) The Rerouting of Civilisation: Barbarians Smashed the Chalice with the Blade

The Indo-European or Aryan language-speaking stock as it is now termed, or the pure European race which was idealised and praised by Friedrich Nietzsche and Adolf Hitler as the only fine race, is, in fact, not the original European race, but a group formed by warlike nomadic peoples ruled by priests and warriors who invaded Europe and settled there from the Asiatic and European northeast. They came down in many bands: Kurgans in eastern Europe, Achaeans and later Dorians in Greece, Hittites and Mittani in Turkey and Aryans in India, as well as a Semitic people we call the Hebrews in Canaan (Palestine).

They herded horses, lived in small villages formed by semi-subterranean houses and practised the male patriarchal system. The chieftains ruled within fortifications, pursued a social model in a hierarchic structure and held in esteem violence and military expeditions. They used metallurgical technology (for copper, bronze and finally iron making) originally used to make tools, utensils and ornaments, to fashion all kinds of weapons of slaughter, which played such a critical part in what Engels termed "the world historical defeat of the female sex".

The strong cavalrymen led by male warriors destroyed the peaceful and prosperous farming society established by partnership, which can be precisely described in the figure of speech "smashing the chalice with the blade". This process took place between 5000 BCE and 3000 BCE. For instance, the Kurgans invaded eastern and south-eastern Europe and migrated in three waves respectively in 4300-4200 BCE, in 3400-3200 BCE and in 3000-2800 BCE. Wherever they intruded, villages and temples were burned, farmland laid waste, fine handicrafts and art objects either destroyed or looted, written records burned and a large number of original residents, men in particular, were slaughtered, with the surviving women and girls becoming wives and concubines of the warriors. The disaster of war and the tremendous social changes over these 2,000 years were even worse than the later collapse of the Roman Empire, the darkness and pestilence of the Middle Ages, and the two world wars.

By the year 1100 BCE the world had changed beyond recognition. The Goddess with the Chalice raised high in her hand and her attendants were replaced by stately male deities with sharp blades in their hands and female deities were reduced to wives, concubines or paramours of male deities. The physically strong, insensitive males occupied all dominator positions in the social hierarchic structure. Whether in the family or in society, power was privilege, domination, ease and comfort, oppression and plundering. We now see polygyny burying the living with the dead, slaves, male figures, pottery warrior figures, defence works and arsenals. The finest technology was that for making weapons and the most developed trade was that for weapon manufacturing. History became a unilinear male history and a record of expeditions and invasions. Art objects were often odes to war or descriptions of brutality.

At this juncture occurred the origin of Western civilisation described in the beginning of history textbooks and in the stories told in the Bible, one of the major sources of Western culture.

Worshipped as the highest holy scripture and set of statutes by the Western world and by the Catholic, Eastern Orthodox and Christian world, the Bible was actually rewritten by Hebrew priests on the basis of ancient myths, historical stories and laws after the suppressive rule by the male half of humanity over the other female half was established. The endeavour, which re-created male deities and made the false appearance of male dominance seem holy and eternal, was to last thousands of years.

Subsequently, the only chief god we read of in the Bible is already a man—the God Jehovah. He is an almighty father and monarch who can send down calamity and grant blessings. One single man, Jehovah created the world in just six days. After he rested for a day, Jehovah took some of the dust of the soil, and moulded it into a man called Adam and placed him in the Garden of Eden. As Man was alone, Jehovah took a rib from Adam's body and out of it created Eve. Thus, woman was destined to be inferior to man and must attach herself to man from the very beginning. In order to blaspheme the Goddess and her leading symbol of the serpent and to warn all women that they must be subordinated to the male God and their husbands, a story of the metaphorical crime of the first ancestors (original sin) who were driven from Paradise was invented in an extraordinarily painstaking effort. The serpent, the most crafty of all creatures in the fields, induced Eve not to listen to Jehovah's warnings, but Eve ate the fruit picked from the tree of knowledge and gave it also to Adam, thus committing a monstrous crime. As a result, they both were banished into the world. Jehovah made the woman and serpent enemies pitted against each other for all time, placed all women under the control of their husbands forever and made all women suffer when they are pregnant and give birth.

In the following pages, we can read legally and morally correct stories about fathers or husbands who handed over their own daughters or wives to be raped, beaten and killed. Jehovah did not show indignation over nor did he condemn such acts; on the contrary, he sometimes granted special blessings to such men. This indicates how undisguised the Bible was and is in safeguarding the male dominator model of society.

(4) The Path of Growth and Decline of the Two Models of Society

When European written history began, the social model, with the blade as the symbol and with male domination and oppression of the female as the general feature, replaced the prehistoric unwritten partnership model of society, with the chalice as the symbol and with equal involvement between men and women as the general feature. However, following the "historical defeat", the female and her cultural features did not disappear totally, and the related model of society was not wiped out completely. We can still recognise the path of the struggle between and the growth and the decline of the two social models.

Another major root of the Western culture is ancient Greek culture. In classical Greece, women by and large had no civil rights and were excluded from Athens' democratic politics so highly spoken of by later generations. However, the well-known Homeric Epics recorded the memory of many Goddesses. For example, Odysseus was detained by the nymph Calypso, who rules the island of Ogygia. When, after the intervention of the Goddess Athene, Odysseus finally gets to leave Ogygia, there is a storm, and he is saved from drowning by a veil that the Goddess Ino gives him. In the Greek pantheon, the Great

1   伏羲和女娲（汉代南汉画像石刻）

     Nüwa and Fuxi

     (stone relief, Han dynasty, Nanyang)

2   天帝同伏羲和女娲在一起（汉代山东画像石刻）

     God of Heaven together with Nüwa and Fuxi

     (stone relief, Han dynasty, Shandong)

3   牛河梁女神头像

     Head of a goddess from Niuheliang

4   东山嘴陶塑孕妇（1）

     A pottery pregnant woman from Dongshanzui(1)

5   东山嘴陶塑孕妇（2）

     A pottery pregnant woman from Dongshanzui(2)

1	2	3
4		5

6 案板的陶塑孕妇

A pottery pregnant woman from Anban

7 柳湾的人像陶壶

A pottery vase shaped after a woman from Liuwan

8 大地湾的人头口彩陶瓶

A pottery vase with the mouth in the shape of a human head

9 商代的后母戊鼎（妇妌墓出土，875 公斤）

Houmuwu tripod of the Shang dynasty

（Lady Jing's tomb，875kg）

| 6 | 7 |
| 8 | 9 |

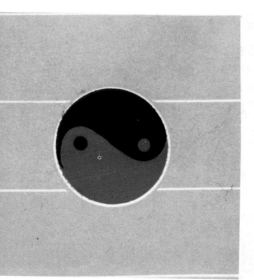

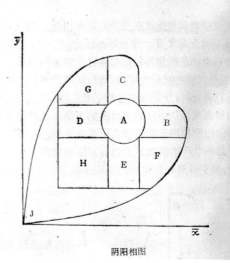

阴阳相图

10 商代的被铐裸体女陶俑（左，正面；右，背面）
A pottery shackled nude woman of the Shang dynasty
(Left, front view, right, back view)

11 商代带枷陶俑（左，女俑正面；右，男俑背面）
Pottery shackled man and woman of the Shang dynasty
(left, woman from front, right, man from behind)

12 阴阳平衡（明代绘画）
Yin and Yang in balance
(painting, Ming dynasty)

13 阴阳和谐
Yin and Yang in harmony

14 阴阳相图
Phase diagram of Yin and Yang

10	11	12
13	14	

15　老子造像(在福建泉州,依天然巨石雕成)
　　Laozi(carved out of a huge stone,
　　Quanzhou,Fujian)

16　孔子石刻像
　　Confucius(engraving)

17　中国的400毫米等降水线示意图
　　Map of 400mm isoheyt of China

中国湿润带与干燥带示意图
以四百毫米等降水线为界,其东南为湿润带,其西北为干燥带。

18 战争——男人的事业(秦始皇墓兵马俑)
   War--men's task
   (Terra Cotta army near Qin Shi Huang's tomb)
19 汉高祖墓出土的骑兵兵马俑(在陕西咸阳)
   Pottery cavalry from the First Emperor of
   the Han dynasty(Xianyang,Shaanxi)
20 晋竹林七贤(今人傅抱石作)
   "Seven Gentlemen of Bamboo Grove"
   (by Fu Baoshi,a modern artist)

21 87神仙卷（局部）（唐　吴道子作）
"Eighty-seven Deities"(detail)(bv Wu Daozi,Tang dynasty)

22 女皇武则天像
Empress Wu Zetian

23 武则天母亲杨氏墓前的石狮
A stone lion guarding the tomb of the empress Wu Zetian's mother

21	
22	23

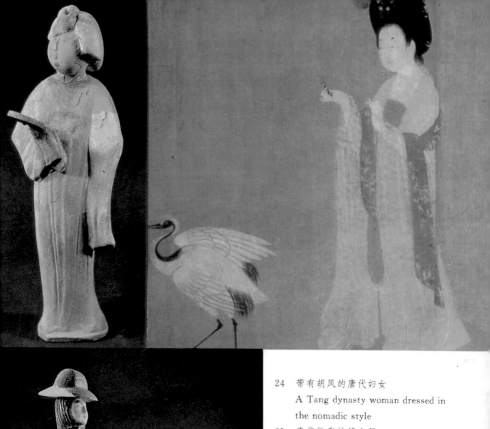

24　带有胡风的唐代妇女
　　A Tang dynasty woman dressed in
　　the nomadic style
25　唐代粉彩持镜女俑
　　Woman holding a mirror of the Tang
　　dynasty
26　唐代仕女画像
　　A Tang dynasty noble woman

25	26
24	

27 韩熙载夜宴图卷（局部）
 （五代 顾闳中绘）
 "Night Banquet at Han Xizai's
 Home" (detail)
 (by Gu Hongzhong, Five dynasties)

28 韩熙载夜宴图卷（局部）
 （五代 顾闳中绘）
"Night Banquet at Han Xizai's Home"
(detail)
(by Gu Hongzhong, Five dynasties)

27	
28	

Goddess—in such forms as Athene, Hera, and Aphrodite, is still enshrined, but is now subordinate to Zeus, the top male God. What is most interesting is that the Goddess Athene was remoulded into a goddess of war, complete with helmet and spear, her chalice now a shield. Historical records show that philosopher Pythagoras received most of his ethical lore from a priestess Themistoclea. The teacher of Socrates was also a priestess and Socrates was sentenced to death in old age for his heresies that included the advocacy of equal education for women. Moreover, according to the records, all Greek political leaders went to Delphi to hear from a priestess suggestions on the most important social and political issues of their times. In Plato's **Republic,** we read, on the one hand, of a strictly hierarchical country, and, on the other, of a system similar to humanitarianism and communism and conforming to equal and fair principles, of which the latter is obviously close to the model of society with the chalice as its symbol. Moreover, some women had their own school of philosophy which stood for establishing a "world in which there would be neither masters nor slaves". These facts show that ancient Greek society and culture contained factors echoing strong partnership between men and women, which contended with the principal dominator model of society.

As described above, the first half of the Judeo-Christian Bible, the Old Testament, although containing traces of the earlier system and important partnership teaching, is the heavenly portrayal of the male dominator model on earth. However, in the second half of the Bible, the New Testament, we read that 2,000 years ago a young Jew called Jesus denounced the ruling classes of his time, preached universal love and the spiritual equality of all, and told followers, "there is neither Jew nor Greek, there is neither bond nor free, there is neither male nor female: for you are all one in Christ Jesus". He instructed that the meek, humble, and weak would some day inherit the earth. He mingled freely with women and cared for orphans and widows. A woman called Mary Magdalene, presumably a prostitute, whom he treated with respect and caring, became a leader of the early Christian movement after Jesus died. In a word, Jesus was a sincere teacher and advocate of partnership between men and women. This may have been because he was aware that the "masculine" values of dominance, inequality, and conquest he saw all round him were debasing and distorting human life, and he advocated a softer and more "feminine" set of values based on compassion, responsibility, and love. Therefore, he has been recognized by many men and women as one of the greatest spiritual figures of all time.

However, the ancient Roman culture which inherited the ancient culture adopted a typically androcratic and militaristic bloodthirsty model of society. After the enormous empire it established in Europe by means of strong armed force collapsed, amid the dark chaos, an originally minor mystery cult, Christianity, which had been subjected to persecution since it was spread to Rome from the Middle East, flourished on the vast ruins of Rome, but metamorphosed into the Gospels which safeguarded the hierarchic androcratic model. As an orthodox ideology contrary to the spirit of Jesus, it pursued a stringent religious hierarchical system, barred women and was violence based. The officially approved Christianity and the Holy Roman Empire established a system combining church and state. It pushed the ancient male dominance to new brutality and cruelty by waging religious wars, destroying pagan temples, shrines, and idols, closing academies and burning books, and persecuting progressive public figures. In the dark 1,000 years of the Middle Ages, women in Europe were defined as sexual tools and reproduction machines. The grave consequence of this was the stagnation of society as a whole.

Between the late 13th century and the middle of the 16th century, Europe experienced the Renaissance. In terms of its surface forms, this progressive cultural revolution re-discovered and advocated classical learning written in ancient Greek and

Latin, while in terms of its spiritual contents, it re-discovered people and advocated the theory of human nature, individualism and humanism, thus relieving people of the pressures of the theology of Christianity. Women remained at the bottom of society, but gained liberation to some extent in the spring of this human liberation, but the liberation was limited only to upper-class women who obtained good education. These women obtained higher status in families so that they were able to be in charge of household affairs, and even sponsor salons, and tried to display their talents in poems, paintings and music. It was the overture for the recovery of the partnership model of society. The work that could best embody the revival of the female spirit was Sandro Botticelli's The Birth of Venus, in which a naked, slender and golden haired Venus rises again from the sea in a seashell amid the spring sunshine.

(5) The Reality of Male Dominance and the Feminist Movement

The modern feminist movement first flared in the 19th century. A great number of feminists wrote hundreds of works, which effectively promoted the movement and improved the status of women in European and American countries. Domestically, these "mothers" of modern feminism liberated women from laws that sanctioned wife beating. Economically, they helped free women from laws that gave husbands control over their wives' property. They opened up professions like law and medicine to women and won women access to higher education.

A number of progressive male ideologists also advocated modern revolutionary ideas such as freedom, equality, universal love, progress and liberation which ran counter to the androcratic relationship model. The British philosopher Thomas Hobbes proved that nature had made men equal in the faculties of body and mind. Jean-Jacques Rousseau wrote that not only were men born free and equal, but that this was a "natural right" that entitled them to "sever their chains". The British ideologist

Mary Wollstonecraft asserted that this "natural right" belongs to women as well as men. The French utopian socialist Charles Fourier pointed out that the degree of emancipation of women is an index of the degree of a society's emancipation. Karl Marx, in part influenced by the first discoveries of the pre-androcratic era, wrote of a classless society in which "the free development of each is the condition for the free development of all". With the victory of the bourgeois revolution, republics replaced monarchies, secular schools replaced religious ones, and less autocratic families replaced rigidly male-dominated households. And technical and industrial progress created increasing opportunities for women to emerge from the narrow family circle and become career women.

However, Eisler maintains that because capitalist society emphasises individual acquisitiveness, competitiveness, greed (the profit motive), and hierarchism (the class structure), and continues its reliance on violence (e.g., colonial wars), it remains fundamentally androcratic. The former socialist Soviet Union advocated equality between men and women in line with the theories of Marx and Engels in its early period, but, under Stalin it massively regressed to its reliance on violence and authoritarianism and failed to bring about a change in patriarchal relations within the family.

Eisler wrote that there were also those like Arthur Schopenhauer and Friedrich Nietzsche who were squarely and unabashedly androcratic. They even deemed the Judeo-Christian tradition represented by the Bible as not sufficiently androcratic because it contained an "effeminate" "slave-morality". They wanted to restore the force-valuing tradition of Indo-European warriors (Aryans and Kurgans) and realise the dream of ruling the world by pure Aryan men. Although fascism met with crushing defeat after it inflicted frightful destruction on humanity during World War II, the current revival of neo-Nazism in some European countries indicates that fascism did not completely step down from the stage of history. Now fundamentalism of all forms forces women to return to their traditional subservient place by making women reinstate the veil, imposing laws on sexual segregation, banning freedom of speech and the press, executing "heretics" and launching a "holy war". Even in the United States which flaunts the banner of "liberty" and "democracy", the American Christian fundamentalist New Right represented by Jerry Falwell, a good friend and spiritual advisor of President Reagan, also openly opposed a women's legal right to reproductive freedom of choice and the equality between men and women.

Most of the world's women still live in misery. As the United Nations State of the World's Women in 1985 points out, globally women are half the population, perform two thirds of the world's work in terms of hours, but earn one tenth as much as men earn, and own one hundredth the property that men own. In many developing countries women do most of the food growing, and also take care of children and prepare the food, but they are the last to eat. As a result, 55 percent of them suffer from nutritional anaemia. Moreover, in books, newspapers, magazines, films and videos there is a barrage of hard-core pornographic descriptions and presentations and enormous publicity for humiliation and violation against the female sex and the use of the female sex only as a tool for male sexual pleasure.

A major ideology that resists totalitarianism and authoritarianism, violence and wars, suppression and exploitation of women, and the actual conditions of rampant pornography, all caused by the androcratic model, is the feminist movement that flared up again in the latter half of the 20th century.

Although many people laid theoretical foundations for feminism long ago, this term was not articulated until July 19, 1948, at Seneca Falls, New York at a conference on women. Here, Elizabeth Cady Stanton made a pivotal statement, saying that "among the many important questions which have been brought before the public", "there is none that more vitally affects the human family than that which is technically called 'Women's Rights'". After that thousands of women's organizations were established in Europe and America, and these worked hard to create a more fair and peaceful society in harmony with the ecosystem. Many national women's organizations also appeared, ranging from the official All-China Women's Federation to the National Women's Studies Association and the Older Women's League in the United States. Later a United Nations Decade for Women was set up. It has set three goals—sexual equality, development, and peace—and sponsored world conferences on women. In addition, a large number of feminist philosophers, writers, artists, theologians, scientists and activists working for feminism emerged. Feminism may become one of the overarching ideologies in the historical changing process in which the partnership model of society is replacing the dominator one.

(6) The Partnership Concept and the Theory of Cultural Shift

Riane Eisler and her husband and partner in work David Loye are members of the General Evolution Research Group. This is an international transdisciplinary research group organized by systems philosopher Ervin Laszlo, a member of the Club of Rome and scientific advisor to the United Nations Educational, Scientific and Cultural Organization. UNESCO Secretary-General Frederico Mayor, Nobel Prize winner in chemistry Ilya Prigogine and Nobel Prize winner in medicine Jonas Salk are all honorary members and the remaining twenty members are all leading scholars in their own fields. The research group aims to sum up new human achievements in such fields as astronomy, astrophysics, non-imbalance thermodynamics (dissipative structures theory), chaos theory, sudden change theory, molecular genetics, biological evolution theory, human cultural study and historical study, and to study the general laws that run through the process of universal, material, biological, social and ideological evolution so as to solve the world problematique facing humanity as described in many reports of the Club of Rome, and to lead humanity to "produce conscious evolution from evolutionary consciousness" (Salk) and smoothly proceed to the branching point where a sudden change of the global system draws increasingly near.

In **The Chalice and the Blade**, Eisler convincingly proved that from 5000 to 3000 BCE, many massive invasions by the bloodthirsty and force-valuing nomadic Kurgan people completely destroyed the life of European society, and as a result, the whole social system fell into chaos. The new order out of the darkness was the patriarchal social system ushered in by the Kurgans. Male deities replaced female deities, the blade replaced the chalice, and men's hierarchical domination replaced the partnership between women and men, thereby causing the whole of society to complete a cultural shift. After that, the conflict between the partnership social model and the leading dominator social model, as two types of attractors in the dynamic change of social systems, still lingered on, but the latter could not be replaced after all. Currently the male dominance social model is coming to an end, since the world problematique such as the armaments race, war threats, the population explosion, shortage of resources and environmental pollution all have profound internal links with an irrational social model, and since the social model, which highly values the power of the blade and operates by relying on violence and war machines, takes women as reproductive machines and rapaciously plunders and unrestrainedly destroys nature. The solution of all these global problems lies in the replacement of the dominator social model. When the world system reaches an irreversible branching point for a sudden change, it will face many choices in its path of evolution. The best choice is not the establishment of global totalitarian and hierarchical domination, but the partnership social model. However, there will never be the old fashioned matriarchal society or a new feminism with the female oppressing the male. There should be a new partnership society, with equality between men and women and with corresponding major changes in the social structure and ideologies. This will be a new cultural shift for humanity.

Then, what is partnership? I once asked Eisler about this and she sent this explanation to me, which reads:

"Partnership entails cooperation and respect among people. It involves joining, linking and working together in peace and harmony for the common good of all. The partnership way is a unifying principle, defined by affiliation rather than violence-based ranking that spreads into the mainstream of society.

"Partnership requires fairness, consensus, mutuality, utilises democratic, participatory decision-making, necessitates active listening, empathic sharing, collective support and encourages growth. It is inclusive and seeks to unify people. In partnership settings, people feel valued, genuinely cared about and safe. True partnership leads to empowerment and self-actualization".

Thus it can be seen that "partnership" contains rich and profound connotations. It is appropriate to use it to describe the relations between men and women in prehistoric matriarchal society and in the future society with equal rights for men and women. Moreover, in a broader sense, it can be a basic concept in handling relations among companies, groups and countries.

The most impressive slogan advanced by the women's movements in modern and contemporary times is "equality between men and women." However, what are relations between men and women and between husbands and wives like when men and women are equal? "Partnership" is probably the appropriate wording. In an ideal happy family, the couple should be partners in daily life, spiritual life and sexual life, partners in bearing and raising children, and partners in study, work and career.

For Chinese people, "partnership" is a new concept, but it is not difficult for it to find identity in our culture. Chinese people have always described a devoted married couple as "twin lotus flowers on one stalk" and "mandarin ducks" and they often swear: "in heaven we are like a pair of lovebirds and on earth we are like trees whose branches interlock". These are surely vivid metaphors for partnership?

In the revolutionary ranks under the leadership of the Chinese Communist Party, equality between men and women has long been materialised. Many married couples customarily term their relations as "relations between comrades" and "relations between comrades-in-arms". Don't they contain the meaning of revolutionary partners? In the new period of reform and opening up, people often describe women as "half of the sky" and "the other half of man." Is it not fair to say that women are the equal partners of men?

Therefore, the "partnership" concept elaborated by Eisler in her book **The Chalice and the Blade** can surely take root, blossom and bear fruit among Chinese people and in Chinese culture.

2. The Concept of *Yin* and *Yang* and Gender Relations

(1) The Original Implications of the Concept of *Yin* and *Yang*

The concept of *Yin* and *Yang* is basic and unique to Chinese philosophy and culture, and it has been introduced into other languages and cultures, even functioning as a loan-word in English. From the perspective of philology, the ancient Chinese character *Yin* is written " 侌 " or " 霒 ", and is a glyph of associative compounds, in accordance with which the meaning of a character is suggested by the significant combination of two or more pictographs. The ancient character signified "the sun hidden by clouds". The character *Yang* " 昜 ", is also a glyph of associative compounds, signifying "the sun shining over the land". In the earliest Chinese dictionary *Shuowen Jiezi*, an etymological dictionary compiled by Xu Shen (58-147) of the Han dynasty, two picto-phonetic characters " 陰 " and " 陽 ", with one element indicating meaning and the other sound, replaced the earlier associative compounds. On the left part of the new character for *Yin* is the radical " 阝 ", a pictograph " 阝 " indicating two mountains. Therefore, the original meaning of *Yin* (陰) is the "northern slope of a mountain" or "the southern bank of a river", which do not receive direct sunshine, while the original meaning of *Yang* (陽) is the "southern slope of a mountain" or "the northern bank of a river" which, in contrast, are bathed in sunshine. In line with such primitive implications, the program for simplified Chinese characters introduced in the 1950s by the People's Republic of China created the two simpler and clear characters for *Yin* (阴) and *Yang* (阳) used today. The composition of the modern characters for *Yin* suggest "the mountain slope bathed in moonlight" while *Yang* suggests "the mountain slope bathed in sunshine".

The modern Chinese reformer and ideologist Liang Qichao made a statistical study of the two characters *Yin* and *Yang* in four of the oldest classics of the Confucian school, i.e., *Yi Jing* (The Book of Changes), *Shu Jing* (the Book of Ancient Documents), *Shi Jing* (the Book of Songs) and *Yi Li* (the Book of Rites). His study showed that *Yi Li* does not use the characters *Yin* and *Yang*; *Shi Jing* uses the character *Yin* eight times and *Yang* 14 times and both *Yin* and *Yang* once; *Shu Jing* uses *Yin* three times and *Yang* also three times; and *Yi Jing* uses *Yin* once in the explanations of diagrams for divination of the second ninth gloss of the Kung Fu (Central Sincerity) Hexagram. Liang's conclusion was that in these classics "*Yin* and *Yang* are merely superficial and insignificant phenomena in nature with no profound significance".[1] The natural phenomena he refers to here are cloudiness and clearness, brightness and darkness, the north and south slopes of a mountain, and north and south banks of a river, which are the primitive meanings of *Yin* and *Yang*.

(2) The Expansion of the Concept of *Yin* and *Yang*

During the Spring and Autumn period (722-468 BCE), *Yin* and *Yang* were frequently used with much broader connotations in two contemporary histories *Zuozhuan* (Zuo Qiuming's Commentary on the Spring and Autumn Annals) and *Guoyu* (Discourses on the States).

Zuozhuan records that in the 16th year of Xi Gong (644 BCE), meteorites fell to the ground in the state of Song and seabirds flew backwards over the capital of Song. Song Xiang Gong asked Shu Xing whether these were good or ill omens. Shu Xing told Song Xiang Gong that these were good omens, but privately told others, "The King phrased the question incorrectly. These are *Yin* and *Yang* phenomena not produced by good or ill fortune"[2]. Here *Yin* and *Yang* have become synonyms for natural phenomena.

In the 1st year of Zhao Gong, discussing the causes of diseases, Yi He said that there are six forces in nature, i.e., *Yin*, *Yang*, wind, rain, darkness and brightness, and these can cause diseases if there is a surfeit of any one of them. In the human body "an excess of *Yin* causes 'cold illnesses' and an excess of *Yang* causes 'heat illnesses'". Here *Yin* and *Yang* are regarded as

---

[1] Liang Qichao, "Origin of *Yin* and *Yang* and Five Elements", in *Gushi Bian* (Analysis of Ancient History), (Shanghai Classics Publishing House, 1982), vol. 5; Quoted from Xie Songling, *Tianren Xiang: Yin Yang Wuxing Xueshuo Shi Daolun* (The Symbol of Heaven and Man: Introduction to the History of the Theory of Yin and Yang and Five Elements), (Shandong Literature and Art Publishing House, 1989), p. 19.

[2] Quoted from Yang Xuepeng, *Yin and Yang*: **Forces and Variables**, (Science Press, 1993). In the following paragraphs several more quotations from this work appear, but they are not separately acknowledged.

two kinds of body forces, described as "cold" and "heat".

In the 9th year of Ai Gong, Zhao Yang of the state of Jin divined to determine whether he should fight a war. The divination read: "Water flows to fire". Shi Min explained this divination to mean "that *Yang* will be subdued, so you can dispatch troops". Fire is *Yang* and water is *Yin*, and so when fire meets water, fire will be subdued. Therefore, Zhao Yang could dispatch his troops and win the war.

In another example, in the 15th year of Xi Gong when Qing Zheng was describing a timid horse on the eve of a battle, he said the horse was "affected by the *Yin* blood in its body". In the 7th year of Zhao Gong, when Zi Chan was discussing "ghosts and spirits", he said, "The man who has just died is called the soul, and the soul, a type of *Yang* force, is therefore called the spirit". This shows a further extension of the concept, whereby people regarded blood as *Yin* and spirit as *Yang*.

In these two history works we can see that *Yin* and *Yang* had begun to be used as two opposite concepts to explain various kinds of natural phenomena and that these two concepts began to have philosophical overtones.

According to *Zuozhuan*, in the 21st year of Zhao Gong, a solar eclipse occurred. A senior official called Zi Shen explained that when a solar eclipse takes place in the summer or winter solstices, or in the vernal or autumnal equinoxes, there will be no disasters, but at other times, there will. The cause of solar eclipses was interpreted as the inability of *Yang* to subdue *Yin* and, as a result, floods usually occur.

In the 28th year of Xiang Gong, the winter was uncommonly warm, with no ice throughout the season. Zi Shen explained that the reason for this was that "the *Yin* force was unable to exclude the *Yang* force".

"The Discourse on the State of Zhou" in *Guoyu* contains a passage relating how the Zhou Taishi (Grand Preceptor), Boyang Fu, explained that the cause of earthquakes was that "the *Yang* force is concealed and suppressed by the *Yin* force, so that the *Yang* force cannot produce normal movement, and as a result an earthquake occurs".

"The Discourse on the State of Yue" in the same work quotes Fan Li as saying that when *Yang* goes to the extreme, it will turn into *Yin* and when *Yin* goes to the extreme, it will turn into *Yang*. This phenomenon parallels that of sunrise following sunset, or the full moon being inevitably followed by the crescent moon.

(3) The *Yin* and *Yang* Concept and Various Ancient Schools of Thought

The late Spring and Autumn and the Warring States periods (770-221 BCE.) were the golden era of Chinese philosophy, generally described as "the contention of the hundred schools of thought". Philosophers of all schools discussed *Yin* and *Yang* in their works and it can be said that a consensus regarding *Yin* and *Yang* was reached. *Yin* and *Yang* were used to explain the relationship between heaven, earth and man, thus elevating *Yin* and *Yang* to be the basic category of Chinese philosophy and culture.

In this, the most influential theoriser on *Yin* and *Yang* and the person who elevated it to the highest category was Lao Zi, the founder of Taoism (Daoism). In the 42nd chapter of his **Lao Zi** we read: "Dao (the Way) gave birth to One, One gave birth to Two, Two gave birth to Three, and Three gave birth to all the myriad things. All the myriad things carry *Yin* on their backs and hold *Yang* in their embrace, deriving their vital harmony from the proper blending of the two vital Breaths". This is the Taoist theory regarding the origins of the universe. *Yin-Yang* had now become a philosophical category second only to the "Way (*Dao*)". Everything in the universe contains opposite *Yin* and *Yang* forces which clash with each other. The normal relationship between, and the perfect standards for, *Yin* and *Yang* are "harmony".

Another Taoist philosopher Zhuang Zi (Chuang Tzu)

shared the same viewpoint and wrote: "When *Yin* and *Yang* are not in harmony, and cold and heat come in untimely ways, all things will be harmed". ("Yufu", *Zhuang Zi*) And: "When the two have successful intercourse, things will be produced". ("Tian Zi Fang", *Zhuang Zi*)

The Moist school deemed the law of the movement of *Yin* and *Yang* to be objective, and unchangeable even by a sage. "Anything that roams between heaven and earth and that is contained within the four seas is the product of the combination of heaven and earth and contains the harmony of *Yin* and *Yang*. Even the Sage cannot change it". (*Mo Zi*)

The Legalist philosopher Guan Zi maintained, "The principle *Yin* and *Yang* is the highest principle of heaven and earth". And: "The man who holds a position establishes himself on *Yin* and because *Yin* is in a static state, if the man moves he will lose that position". ("Xin Shu, Pt. A", *Guan Zi*)

The school of Military Strategists also used the *Yin* and *Yang* category when they discussed strategic opportunities and favourable geographical positions. In *Sun Zi* we read: "Opportunity refers to *Yin* and *Yang*, cold and heat, and opportunity and endeavour". And in **Sun Bin's Art of War** we read of a similar principle: "The general principle of the earth is that *Yang* is the outside and *Yin* the inside".

The Eclectics (Zajia) also maintained that "the harmony between *Yin* and *Yang* does not promote the growth of one category; and sweet dew and timely rain do not have partiality for any one particular thing". ("Guigong", *Lüshi Chunqiu* or Master Lu's Spring and Autumn Annals). "Everyone and everything is transformed from *Yin* and *Yang*". ("Zhifen", *Lüshi Chunqiu*)

The Confucian philosopher Xun Zi in his later period also touched upon *Yin* and *Yang*. He wrote that "all stars revolve together, the sun and the moon shine in turn, the four seasons proceed in succession, the blending of *Yin* and *Yang* forces produces all things, wind and rain benefit all things, and all things come into being through the proper joint operation of all natural conditions and grow from their nourishment". ("Tian Ji", *Xun Zi*)

It is worth noting the fact that philosophers of all schools maintained that the Way of *Yin* and *Yang* lies in harmony and, wherever there is disharmony, disasters or diseases will occur. Zhuang Zi provided an example: "Zi Yu was ill... He was stooped, he had five ulcers on his back, his face was lowered to his navel and his shoulders raised above his head, while his neck craned forward. All this resulted from the disorder of *Yin* and *Yang* forces". ("Da Zong Shi", *Zhuang Zi*).

(4) The *Yin* and *Yang* Philosophical System

To sum up, after a long historical process, by the Warring States period (475-221 BCE), the two concepts of *Yin* and *Yang* were elevated to embrace two opposite, but complementary, basic categories. First, they refer to two substances with opposite natures, such as heaven and earth, the sun and the moon, water and fire, etc. Second, they also refer to *Yin* and *Yang* forces, but the concept of "force (*Qi*)" is the vague intuitive experience of the ancient Chinese on invisible efforts and on the invisible, intangible flow of matter, energy and information. Finally and most importantly, they refer to opposite natures, such as cold and heat, dryness and wetness, and motion and rest. The final reference makes *Yin* and *Yang* opposite variable states derived through the application of the dialectical concept of one dividing into two. For example, Zhang Jingyue, a famous Chinese medical scientist of the Ming dynasty, gave the following definition: "*Yin* and *Yang*, one divides into two". ("*Yin-Yang* Lei", *Leijing*). Such a conception of the *Yin* and *Yang* concept had symbolic functions, such as 1 and -1, or 1 and 0, in modern binary mathematical language.

In the Warring States period, apart from those philosophers of various schools who widely adopted the *Yin* and *Yang* concept, other philosophers also established independent philosophical schools featuring the *Yin* and *Yang* category, such as Zou Yan, who founded the *Yin-Yang* and Five Elements School. Unfortunately his works were lost in the calamities and wars that marked the late Qin and early Han dynasties.

On the other hand, as we mentioned, the earliest classics of the Confucian school do not contain *Yin* and *Yang* as a philosophical concept. *Yi Jing* compiled in the Yin and Zhou dynasties, which came to be regarded as the most important Confucian classic and indeed a book of divination, in particular does not contain either the *Yin* and *Yang* concept or systematic metaphysical ideas. In the book the concept of "*Yin*" only appears in the following sentence: "The crane cries out in her hidden retirement, and her young ones respond to her". Here, the word "*Yin*" is a phonetic loan character for "retirement".

However, this does not necessarily mean that *Yi Jing* is free from more concealed concepts of *Yin* and *Yang*, as in the notions of the two divinatory symbols "—" (unbroken line) and "--" (broken line). There are many explanations of the origin of these two symbols and the most satisfactory and credible maintains that the symbols derived from the appearance of the reproductive organs of the two sexes. This explanation is based on a paragraph in *Lao Zi* and two paragraphs in "The Great Appendix" of *Yi Jing*.

In the sixth chapter of *Lao Zi*, we read: "The Spirit of the Fountain dies not. It is called the Mysterious Feminine. The Doorway of the Mysterious Feminine is called the Root of Heaven-and-Earth. Lingering like gossamer, it has only a hint of existence; and yet when you draw upon it, it is inexhaustible". This paragraph means that the reproductive organ of the female is the inexhaustible source of heaven and earth. The paragraph has been annotated as follows: "The hollow changes, which never cease, are the mysterious mother principle. The doorway of the mysterious mother principle is the source of heaven and earth. It exists like endless gossamer and is itself inexhaustible".[3]

In "The Great Appendix" of *Yi Jing* we also read: "There is *Qian*. In its [individual] stillness it is self-absorbed [like a ball]; when exerting its motive power it goes straight forward; and thus is its productive action on a grand scale". The character *Qian* is formed by six "☰" (unbroken lines) symbols and the latter two sentences describe the movement of the reproductive organ of the male. Another passage in the same work describes the movement of the female reproductive organ: "There is *Kun*. In its [individual] stillness, it is self-collected and capacious [closed]; when exerting its motive power, it develops its resources [open], and thus its productive action is on an expansive scale". The trigram *Kun* is composed of six "☷" (broken lines).

Thus it can be seen that the natures and dynamic states of the two basic symbols used in *Yi Jing* are opposite and are described as the inexhaustible source of heaven and earth, thereby describing the symbolic reproductive functions of *Yin* and *Yang*. This point was understood by scholars in the Warring States period, who began to explain *Yi Jing* in terms of *Yin* and *Yang*. In *Zhuang Zi*, there is the sentence which reads: "*Yi Jing* is the explication of *Yin* and *Yang*".

By introducing into *Yi Jing* the Taoist *Yin* and *Yang* concept generally accepted by philosophers of all schools, Confucians interpreted *Yi Jing* and transformed it into a complete philosophical system with *Yin* and *Yang* as its basic category. The work was not finished until the Western Han dynasty (206-25 BCE), when *Yi Jing* was re-named *Zhou Yi*. At the end of the text were appended ten articles called "The Appendices" ("Yi Zhuan") explaining the principles of *Yin* and *Yang*. "The Appendices" state: "The *[Zhou] Yi* is a book of wide comprehension and great scope, embracing everything. It encompasses the way of heaven, the way of man, and the way of earth. It then

---

[3] Chen Guying **Explanation and Appraisal of Lao Zi**, (Zhonghua Book Company, 1984), p. 86.

takes [the lines representing] those three powers, and doubles them so that they total six. What these six lines [i.e. the hexagrams] then show is simply the Way of the three powers". ("The Great Appendix")

In another appendix titled "Shuo Gua" (Remarks on the Hexagrams), this is explained in greater detail: "In ancient times, when sages created the *[Zhou] Yi*, it was with the design that [its diagrams] should be in conformity with the principles underlying the nature [of man and things], and the ordinances [for them] assigned [by Heaven]. In accordance with this view, they exhibited [in the diagrams] the Way of Heaven, designating [the lines] *Yin* and *Yang*; the Way of Earth, designating [them] the weak (or soft) and the strong (or hard); and the Way of Man, being benevolence and righteousness. Each [trigram] embraced [those] three powers; and, when repeated, the trigrams [of three lines] formed hexagrams [of six lines]. A distinction was made in [the positions assigned] to the *Yin* and *Yang* lines, which were variously occupied by strong or weak forms, thus completing the configuration [of each hexagram]".

These two passages explicitly describe how the interpretations outlined in "The Appendices" transformed *Yi Jing* into a philosophical system explaining the way of heaven, way of earth and way of man, namely, the unity of nature and society. They also explain that in this system, another basic category, apart from *Yin* and *Yang*, was introduced, i.e. "the weak and the strong" (*Rou* and *Gang*). "The Appendices" explain the laws governing changes in astronomical phenomena and official positions, by employing the twin categories of *Yin-Yang* and *Rou-Gang*, as well as similar dialectical categories such as movement and rest, advance and retrogression, going and coming, closing and opening, cold and heat, stretching and bending, superior and inferior, good luck and bad luck, gain and loss, disturbance and peace, the noble and the mean, and far and near. These natural laws are demonstrated by changes in the *Yin yao* (broken lines, corresponding with "weakness") and the *Yang yao* (unbroken lines, corresponding with "strength") which make up the hexagrams, each of which consists of six lines in three pairs, upper, middle and lower, and which, according to "The Great Appendix" represent "the successive movement of *Yin* and *Yang* (or inactive and active operations) which constitutes the course (of things), the Dao". Moreover, "the strong lines and the weak lines displace each other, and hence the changes [in the diagrams] take place".

(5) Hard *Yang* and Soft *Yin*: Gender Temperament and Relationships in Chinese Culture

The *Qian* and *Kun* hexagrams in **Yi Jing** are the basis of all the other hexagrams and so are placed in the first and second places. The *Qian* hexagram is formed from six unbroken horizontal lines. The "Tuan" section of "The Appendices" provides the following explanation of the *Qian* hexagram: "Vast is the 'great and originating [power]' indicated by *Qian*! All things owe to it their beginning. It contains all meaning belonging to [the name] heaven". The "Xiang" section of "The Appendices" elaborates: "Heaven, in its motion, [gives the idea of] strength. The superior man, in accordance with this, strengthens himself for ceaseless activity".

The *Kun* hexagram, ☷, is formed by six tiered broken lines. The "Tuan" section of "The Appendices" provides the following explanation of this hexagram: "Complete is the 'great and originating [capacity]' indicated by *Kun*! All things owe to it their birth. It receives obediently the influences of Heaven". The "Wenyan" section of "The Appendices" elaborates: "Yes, what gentleness characterises the Way of *Kun*! It receives the influences of heaven, and acts at the proper time".

The "Great Appendix" of "The Appendices" further links the male and female principles with the *Qian* and *Kun* hexagrams. "*Qian* represents what is of the *Yang* nature (bright and active); *Kun* what is of the *Yin* nature (shaded and inactive)". "The attributes expressed by *Qian* constitute the male; those expressed by *Kun* constitute the female". In accordance with this, the status and nature of the male and female are determined: "Heaven is lofty and honourable; earth is low. [Their symbols], *Qian* and *Kun*, [with their respective meanings], were determined [in accordance with this]. Things low and high appear displayed in a similar relation. The [upper and lower trigrams, and the relative position of individual lines] as noble and mean, had their places assigned accordingly. Movement and rest are the regular qualities [of their respective subjects]. Hence comes the definite distinction [of the several lines] as the strong and the weak". "The *Yin* and *Yang* unite according to their qualities, and thence comes the embodiment of the result by the strong and weak [lines]. In this way the phenomena of heaven and earth are visibly exhibited, and we can comprehend the operation of spiritual intelligence". Since then, in Chinese culture, the male has been equated with *Qian* and the female with *Kun*; similarly, the male is identified with heaven and the female with earth. The male principle is *Yang* and the female *Yin*. The male is regarded as noble and the female as base. The male is always in motion, and the female is always at rest; the male is strong and the female is weak. If interpreted into mathematical language, the male is 1 and the female is -1; or the male is 1 and the female is 0. This is what is described as the general principle of heaven and earth and the operation of spiritual intelligence.

Finally, the authors of **Yi Jing** expounded on a gender relationship in which males were superior to females defined through the analogy with heaven and earth, and this accorded with the hierarchical arrangements of patriarchal society. "Heaven and earth existing, all [material] things then acquired their existence. Once all [material] things acquired existence, male and female emerged. From the existence of male and female emerged the existence of the husband and the wife. From the husband and the wife came the father and the son. From the father and the son came the ruler and his minister.

From the ruler and the minister came the social hierarchy, and once [the distinction between] high and low had its existence, arrangements of propriety and righteousness emerged". Once this Confucian social view had been formulated, Chinese culture held that the relationship between husband and wife is replicated by that between father and son and that between ruler and minister. In society, the female thus came to be in a submissive position in relationship to the male, and in line with such a view it was regarded as right and proper for the male to rule and oppress the female, and the female could only meekly submit to this oppression.

Liang Shuming, one of the representatives of 20th century Neo-Confucianism, once pointed out that one of the characteristics of Chinese culture is that "philosophy has taken the place of religion". The Confucian philosophy in Chinese culture is equivalent to Christianity in Western culture, while the Confucian classics are the equivalent of the Bible. The Chinese "heaven" can be equated with the Christian "God", and Confucius was in some senses a cultural equivalent of Jesus. The superior position of males to females in patriarchal society was established in the name of "heaven" through the Confucian interpretation of **Yi Jing**, chief among the Confucian philosophical classics, and "The Appendices" were ascribed to Confucius himself.[4] The Confucian social order closely resembles that established by the Hebrews on the basis of the Bible ascribed to Jehovah, and while the cultural approaches differed the ensuing results were remarkably similar.

(6) Methodology Questions

This book systematically studies and describes the evolution of gender relations and social models from prehistoric through to contemporary China with reference to the study of the

---

[4] (4) Modern scholars, on the basis of textual research, believe that **The Book of Changes** was written by Confucian scholars in the Warring States period and the Qin and Han dynasties.

evolution of gender relations and social models in the Indo-European world undertaken by the U.S. cultural anthropologist Prof. Riane Eisler in her book **The Chalice and the Blade**. This book is intended to trace the evolution of male-female partner-ship in matriarchal society, male dominance over females in patriarchal society and the new model of partnership between men and women that has emerged in contemporary Chinese social history, by examining what constitutes femininity and masculinity within Chinese culture, and by providing a chron-ological reference for the evolution of China's social models, culture and gender relations.

The Chinese edition of the book is titled **Variations of Yanggang** and **Yinrou**, because in the 2,000-year Chinese culture, "strong *Yang*" has been the synonym for the male and mascu-linity while "weak *Yin*" has been the synonym for the female and femininity. The concept of *Yin* and *Yang* has been gradually accepted by other nations, and through this book, we hope that the two derivative concepts of "strong *Yang*" and "weak *Yin*", which have a long history and profound meaning in Chinese culture, can take their place among the world's cultural con-cepts. The use of the word "variations" in the title is intended to indicate the complex and tortuous nature of the evolution of Chinese gender relations and social models. Through the indi-vidual studies that make up this book, we hope that these variations will shed light on the main symphonic themes.

This book is the first research project completed collective-ly by members of the Chinese Partnership Research Group. The group was formed by Chinese philosophers, archaeologists, historians, cultural historians, women's historians and folklor-ists, in response to the call made by Riane Eisler in the preface of the Chinese edition of her **The Chalice and the Blade**.

It would have been deceptively easy for a research team composed of 17 men and women scholars in various fields to present alternative perspectives on our subject matter, and so in order to co-ordinate a multi-disciplinary approach, to enlarge the perspectives of the work, and to ensure the academic and scientific authenticity of its contents, we invited a dozen Chinese and foreign scholars of high-level academic attainment to serve as our advisors, and most have participated in the discussion and examination of the drafts of this book, and have contributed their well-informed suggestions.

We have always stressed that this is a comparative study made independently by Chinese scholars and that we must adhere to a scientific and down-to-earth attitude in viewing historical materials and historical facts. We indicate when our findings are in conformity with the evolution of gender relations and social models in Indo-European cultural history described in **The Chalice and the Blade**, and when they are not.

The co-authors of this book are experts in their own particular fields and they have discussed their research results in three rounds of heated debate, reaching a consensus on basic major viewpoints, but reserving the right to differ on many details. As members of the Chinese Partnership Research Group, it was of course necessary to establish an academic partnership within the group, and so we have attached great importance to academic democracy. During discussions intense confrontations often occurred, but every contributor was ultimately responsible for his or her own contribution. The editor-in-chief stressed repeatedly that no one was allowed to impose his or her own viewpoint on another, and no one was allowed to abuse their official power to force a co-author to change his views. Therefore, readers may occasionally hear musical variations in this book which are not completely in harmony.

CHAPTER ONE
MYTH AND REALITY:
THE PROJECTION OF GENDER RELATIONS IN PREHISTORIC CHINA

Cai Junsheng

Prehistoric civilisation in China goes back to ancient times, and gender relations in the prehistoric period also underwent a process of evolution. In this chapter we will explore the social conditions informing prehistoric gender relations by analysing prehistoric myths and data drawn from ethnological surveys. Due to limits of space, in the early section devoted to "myth" we begin by examining myths about N Wa, while in the latter "reality" section we will examine the matriarchal system of the Naxi nationality in Yongning county, Yunnan province, where the most complete example of a matriarchal society in the contemporary world is to be found. Such ethnological data can, of course, only echo genuine prehistoric society, nevertheless they still vividly reflect social situations that once prevailed.

1. Nü Wa and Her Partners

Nü Wa is the most important and ancient mythological female figure handed down from the prehistoric age. The achievements of Nü Wa and her partners reflect the changes in gender relations through the entire prehistoric period. However, due to the elimination and misinterpretation of information during the subsequent long period of patriarchal society, available data are very limited. Consequently, in order to view the past as completely as possible, our analysis must be based on a broader historical background.

(1) Nü Wa

Nü Wa, the most ancient "heroine" of north China's Central Plain region, was long regarded by the Chinese as the creator/creatrix of the world. As early as the Warring States period (475-221 BCE), Qu Yuan, a poet of the state of Chu, in his epic poem "Tian Wen" (Questioning Heaven), posed the question: "Nü Wa has a body. [But] who created her?"[1] Wang Yi of the Eastern Han Dynasty annotated this line of poetry and made the following comment regarding Nü Wa's "body": "It is said that Nü Wa had the head of a human being but the body of a snake and she gave birth [*hua*, a word simultaneously encompassing the concepts of creation, transformation and change] to seventy offspring on one day."[2] Prior to Wang Yi, Xu Shen, in his **Shuowen Jiezi** (An Etymological Dictionary of Chinese Characters) glossed [Nü] Wa as an "ancient goddess (*shenshengnü*) who gave birth to all living things on earth." *Shenshengnü* may also be interpreted as "female sage". Until the Han dynasty, Nü Wa continued to be regarded as the creatrix and female sage with the head of a human being and the body of a snake. From Qu Yuan's time on, however, the question of "who created her" has continued to be asked. Today we can approach that question in the light of modern scientific knowledge.

Nü Wa should not be regarded as a specific individual but rather as an archetype of the great feminine spirit of the matriarchal age that once prevailed across the Central Plain. According to studies of prehistoric social development the matriarchal age encompasses the periods in which later palaeo-

---

[1] "*Tian Wen*" (Questioning Heaven) in **Chu Ci** (Elegies of Chu).
[2] Ref: Wang Yunwu ed., **Chu Ci: Wang Yi Zhangju** (Elegies of Chu, as Edited by Wang Yi).

lithic clan communes and neolithic matriarchal commune systems both prevailed. Palaeolithic society was one of hunters and gatherers organised into both clans and communes which were co-extensive in terms of population, and the extensions of both, moreover, coincided. Communes were units of production and life, while the clans constituted a social system based on exogamous group marriage. This was a period in which, according to the ancient philosopher Shang Yang, "people knew they had mothers but did not know they had fathers."[3] During the neolithic age, farm production began on the Central Plain and individual marriages occurred alongside group marriage. At that time, women were the mainstay of farm production and so the females of the clan "acquired" (*qu*) their husbands from their allied marriage clan and set up a commune in which they would subsequently work and live together, while the males of the clan "married" (*jia*) into the commune of the allied marriage clan. Clan and commune were thus interconnected. Genealogy, however, was still determined in accordance with the matriarchy, the clan and commune both remaining matriarchal.

Every clan had a totem, usually an animal, as its symbol in the periods when the clan and matriarchal communes held sway. At that time, people had a concept of direct recognition of the totem and believed themselves to be the totem and the totem to be themselves. Their souls, or spiritual phenomena, were imbued in the totemic animal. The blood coursing through their veins was that of the totem animal. This was totemic consciousness. Every success in their collective activities was regarded as the success of the totem, and every setback was believed to be caused by poor co-operation between the totem and themselves. People would decorate their bodies and don attire to resemble their totem at the outset and termination of all socially significant activities, and in such ceremonies dancing

---

[3] Ref: "Kai Sai Pian" ("Chapter on No Prohibitions") in **Shang Jun Shu** (The Book of Lord Shang).

and chanting played an important role. In fact, all actual behaviours were regarded as their own totemized sorcery. This totemized way of thinking and mode of action constituted the mythicization of the people themselves.[4] In this "mythic age" people mythicized themselves by creating their history and myths in the name of their own totem. Although mythology was the product of this historicizing process, people's actions reversed the relationship, firstly, by regarding this mythological history as the real history of their semi-human and semi-animal totem ancestors, and then by regarding their behaviour and achievements as the norm for all behaviour in everyday life and as the basis for traditional customs and habits. This self-mythicization was realised through mythic history. In the past, many groups practised a ceremony whereby an individual was initiated into adulthood, and the ceremony persists among many ethnic groups today. The ancient form of the initiation ceremony was one of totemization, and in the course of initiation the young were instructed in their people's mythic history and in the norms of behaviour and incantation.[5] Those who went through the ceremony became mythicized human beings, just like their totemic ancestors. Therefore, in the age of myth, not only was myth regarded as real history, but living people were themselves also mythicized. These were the two major features of the age of myth.

This realisation concerning the age of myth enables us to reassess the image of Nü Wa, with "the head of a human being and the body of a snake". She was clearly the mythicized ancestor of clans who regarded the snake as their totem. Initially, possibly only one or several clans adopted the snake as their totem, but these matriarchal clans reproduced and split up to

---

[4] Ref: Cai Junsheng, **The Formation of Human Society and the Form of Primitive Society**, [Beijing: China Social Sciences Publishing House, 1988], pp. 300-321.

[5] Ref: Cai Junsheng, **The Leap of Civilization**, [Wenhui Publishing House, 1992], pp. 136-7.

form many "daughter" clans. As viewed from the Chinese glyphs for various ethnic groups in the south of China during the ancient period, "Man" (蛮) and "Min" (闽) contained the radical "*chong*" (loosely glossed as "insects", but embracing various vertebrate and invertebrate classes of animal, including "reptiles"). The "Nanman" (南蛮 , Southern Man) and "Yuemin" (越闽 , Distant Min) regions in the lower and middle reaches of the Yangtze River were possible places where the snake totem was concentrated. In addition, such classic texts as *Shan Hai Jing* (The Book of Mountains and Rivers) contain references to images of totemic ancestors which spread from the time of the Nü Wa myth, or a little later. These include totemic birds, beasts, insects and various kinds of fish, featuring either a human head, human torso, or a body combining the features of different animals. These semi-anthropomorphic images were clearly the depiction of totemic ancestors. In this context, the image of Nü Wa was not isolated.

By "giving birth to seventy offspring daily", Nü Wa clearly constituted the basis for many social standards and traditional customs of the matriarchal age in the Central Plain, but it is a pity that today we have only scanty knowledge of this mythology, encompassing the legends concerning Nü Wa's creation of humankind, her repair of the skies (*bu tian*), and her establishment of the institution of marriage.

The myth of Nü Wa as creatrix first appeared in *Fengsu Tongyi* (A Comprehensive Discussion of Customs) authored by Ying Shao of the Eastern Han dynasty. In this extant work we read that in ancient times, there were no human beings between heaven and earth. Nü Wa "was rolling yellow clay into a human being" at the side of a pond but she regarded this method as too slow. She then hit upon a new method using a rope to dip into the mud slurry and toss the mud. Each dollop of mud she tossed would become a discrete human being. This myth described the origins of mankind.[6] This folklore spread widely and many details were added. For example, Nü Wa was regarded as not only the creator of mankind, but also of other living things. She created chickens on the first day, and dogs, pigs, sheep, horses, cattle, human beings, grains, fruits and vegetables respectively during the subsequent nine days. The first ten days of the first month of the lunar calendar designate these various origins.[7] It was also said that Nü Wa separated males from females while creating human beings, and subsequently allowed them to marry and reproduce.[8]

The myth of her "repair of the skies" (bu tian) is recorded in the chapter titled "Lan Ming Pian" (Travelling in the Netherworld) of **Huai Nan Zi**: "In ancient times, the sky collapsed on one occasion and the earth cracked, a conflagration spread far and wide, and floods embraced the earth; beasts of prey devoured man and vicious birds consumed the carrion. The people suffered from unprecedented disasters. At this juncture, Nü Wa fashioned coloured stones to patch up the sky, and amputated the four limbs of giant terrapins to prop up the four sides of the sky. She then slaughtered the malevolent black dragon and saved the people of the Central Plain. She stemmed the swelling flood-waters with reed ash. Thus did she enable her children and grandchildren to lead peaceful lives".

The author of **Huai Nan Zi** commented: "She contributed to the sky and earth and was well known to coming generations and her achievements shed brilliance on all living things." "Yet, she did not mention or speak of what she had done; she

---

[6] Only ten of the original thirty fascicles of **Fengsu Tongyi** are today extant. This quotation is drawn from a fragment contained in fasc. 78 of the ancient encyclopaedia **Taiping Yulan** (The Taiping Imperial Encyclopaedia).

[7] Ref: Yu Fei and Gui Qing, **Folk Customs**, [Beijing: Social Scientific Documents Publishing House; 1990], p. 41.

[8] Ref: Tao Yang and Zhong Xiu eds., **Chinese Myths**, [Shanghai: Shanghai Literature and Art Publishing House; 1990], pp. 126-130.

maintained the virtue of a sage and let all living things develop in their own way." The author highly praised the merits, virtue and noble character of this great female ancestor.

In the "Liu Yi Le" (Brief Introduction to the Six Arts) passage in the *Yi Wen Zhi* (Records of Literature and Art) section of *Han Shu* (the History of the Han Dynasty) we find the story detailing Nü Wa's invention of the *shenghuang*, an ancient instrument with a bottle-gourd base and thirteen pipes inserted into its upper section. The reeds inside the pipes resonate when the pipes are blown. A similar instrument, simply called the *sheng*, is still played today by southern China's Lahu, Lisu, Dai, Va and Dong nationalities. *Sheng* in Chinese is a homophone for "giving birth", and the bottle gourd from which the *sheng*'s base was fashioned is regarded as a reproductive symbol, viz. a big belly with many seeds. Traditionally, the *shenghuang* was often used as an instrument on occasions when males and females discussed trysts. Today's musical instrument has that very function. In the context of the Nü Wa myth, this reference to her invention of the *shenghuang* has links with sexual love and human reproduction.

Nü Wa's association with the establishment of the marriage system may also be found in Ying Shao's *Fengsu Tongyi*: "Nü Wa prayed to the god of the temple to act as the female match maker and therefore she established the marriage system (*hunyin*)". "Later in every state, Nü Wa was worshipped as a great match maker".[9] This passage demonstrates that after patriarchal society was ushered in, the status of the female declined. The "marriage system" (*hunyin*) referred to here was the patriarchal marriage system, but importantly, in the matriarchal age, Nü Wa was credited with establishing the marriage system among the clans. After the patriarchal age followed the disintegration of the matriarchal clan, Nü Wa appointed herself the female "match maker", becoming the god of the sub-urban temple

---

[9] Luo ping ed., *Lu Shi Hou Ji*.

(*jiaomei*), and in ancient times memorial sacrifices to this god were performed. A platform was erected at the temple on the city outskirts and the "*tailao*" ceremony, in which the three major domestic animals, pigs, cattle and sheep, were offered as sacrifices,[10] was carried out in the second month of spring each year. During the ceremony, young men and women from various areas would gather to dance, sing and engage in various entertainments. Those who found each other congenial could leave the gathering and sleep together freely in the great outdoors.[11] Married males and females who wanted to have male offspring could also participate.[12] This was clearly a practice derived from the custom of group marriage handed down from the matriarchal age, and demonstrating that after Nü Wa was deified, she still upheld the marriage customs of the matriarchal age. It was, therefore, rational to describe Nü Wa as the creator of the marriage system in the matriarchal age.

Among China's minority nationalities, there are also many folk tales like that of Nü Wa. For example, the Yao nationality have a legend concerning a mythical female called Milotou who used her master's rain cap to create the sky, his limbs to prop up the four corners of the sky, and his torso to prop up the sky and earth in the middle, and then she created mountains and rivers, grasses and trees, birds and animals, insects and fishes. Discovering that bees were industrious, united, well organized and disciplined, Milotou decided to create human beings from bees. She placed a swarm of bees in a box and trained them three times by day and three times by night. Nine months later, the bees became little babies and she raised them by breast-feeding these first humans.[13] The Hani nationality have a legend concerning a woman called Taporan who descended from a crack in the sky to the earth where she was to be the only woman. She

---

[10] "Yueling" (Monthly Ordinances), in *Li Ji* (The Book of Rites).
[11] "Mei Shi", *Zhou Li* (Book of Rites of the Zhou Dynasty).
[12] "Sheng Min" and "Zhuan", *Shi Jing* (Book of Songs).
[13] Ref: Tao Yang and Zhong Xiu eds., idem, pp. 91-93.

lived in a mountain cave, foraged to survive, and conversed with animals. One day when she was seated against a tree and dozing, a strong wind roared by and she felt very cold. Her belly subsequently grew steadily larger and she had to eat increasing quantities of food. After seven months, she could feel movement in her belly and detect legs, arms, feet and fingers inside her. When nine months had passed, many living things emerged from her one night, and when these things dropped to the ground, they became different creatures, such as tigers, boars, sparrows, snakes and eels. In the course of the night, she gave birth to seventy-seven offspring before dawn and designated them as various nationalities Hani, Yi, Bai and Han, to name only a few.[14]

According to Manchu mythology, Abukahehe, Banajiemu and Woladuomama were three sisters who created the universe. Abukahehe turned the paste she had rubbed from her body into the goddess Hehemanni who picked up a piece of the blue sky as her drum and a high mountain as her whip. As the earth trembled with the beating of her drum, she gave birth to mankind and all the living things.[15]

These are all examples of female ancestors revered by different ethnic groups in China. Other examples are husband and wife teams, such as Zhepama and Zhemima of the Achang nationality and Busangga and Yasangga of the Dai nationality, who in partnership created all the living things in the universe including mankind.[16] These legends resembling those concerning Nü Wa are of great antiquity.

(2) Mythicized Females in the Age of Patriarchal Clans

Between the matriarchal age in which Nü Wa served as a totem and the patriarchal age in which Nü Wa became trans-

---

[14] Idem., pp. 148-149.
[15] Ref: Yu Fei and Gui Qing, idem., pp. 51-52.
[16] Ibid., pp. 46-7 and pp. 49-51.

formed into a deity presiding over the sub-urban temple, was an intermediary age of patriarchal clans. Patriarchal clans emerged in two ways.

In pastoral areas, the taming and raising of livestock were activities mainly conducted by males, and from the very beginning, males "married" (*qu*) wives from the allied marriage clan or seized them, and together they would form communes. The females of this clan would then "go to be wives" of the commune which belonged to the allied marriage clan. Thus, genealogies began to be calculated in accordance with the paternal rather than the maternal line, and clans gradually became patriarchal clans while communes became patriarchal communes. In agricultural areas patriarchal clans came into being with the use of heavier implements in farming which then came to be practised by males. Therefore, males of the patriarchal clan would not go to the commune of the allied marriage clan and marry there. Instead they married wives of the allied marriage clan within their own clan and formed a commune. Females of the clan would marry into the commune of the allied marriage clan. Thus, clans in agricultural areas changed from matriarchal to patriarchal clans and communes also changed into patriarchal communes. In both pastoral and agricultural areas, the change from the maternal side to the paternal side was a long and gradual process. This change entailed the calculation of clan genealogy, but the clan totem and other social norms of clan society remained unchanged. Self-mythicization persisted in this continuing mythic age.

Many mythicized male figures emerged at the time of the patriarchal clan in the Central Plains. These include Yan Di, Huang Di, Chi You and Dongfang Dadi Jun, literally Jun Great Lord of the East, who invented new skills, such as ploughing, the use of ships and vehicles in communications and transport, the development of a herbal pharmacopaeia, and the improvement of skills in making earthenware. These myths reflect progress made in material production. The size of social organizations increased and strong tribal alliances emerged. All these mythic figures became leaders of tribal alliances. Yan Di, for example, was the leader of the agricultural area. These mythic leaders engaged in large-scale wars among themselves, fighting for control of the Central Plain. The Banquan Campaign, for example, was fought between the Yan Di group and the Huang Di group with the latter defeating the former; the Zhuolu Campaign was fought between the Huang Di group and the Chi You group with the former defeating the latter. Thus, Huang Di finally became supreme commander of the Central Plain.

The above-mentioned mythicized figures were all males, and therefore, two questions need to be asked: (1) What is the relationship between Nü Wa and these mythicized figures of the time of the patriarchal clan? and (2) What were the status and achievements of the mythicized females during the time of the patriarchal clan?

At the time of the patriarchal clan in China, Nü Wa's activities seem to cease, and she "died". But the deaths of mythicized figures often signal the phenomenon of birth. In the case of Nü Wa, she went on to give birth to other mythicized figures. Two examples of this are recorded:

(1) In the "*Shuo Lin Pian*" chapter of **Huai Nan Zi** we read: "Huang Di gave birth to *yin* and *yang*, Shang Pian to ears and eyes, and Sang Lin to arms and hands, events which were among the seventy transformations of Nü Wa." The classical commentator Gao Xiu notes that Shang Pian and Sang Lin were the names of gods. According to research by the scholar Yuan Ke, *yin* and *yang* in this passage is a reference to male and female genitals.[17] What is meant here is that Huang Di, Shang Pian and Sang Lin were all included within Nü Wa's seventy transformations (*hua*). In other words, Nü Wa, or a part of Nü Wa, gave birth to Huang Di, Shang Pian and Sang Lin, who in turn gave birth

---

[17] Ref: Yuan Ke, **Notes to Selected Ancient Myths**, p. 17.

to mankind, *yin* and *yang*, ears and eyes, arms and hands.

This passage clearly records a myth which emerged at the time of the patriarchal clan as males sought to be admitted into the pantheon of mankind's progenitors and reflects changes in the social status of both genders at the time of the patriarchal clan. Nevertheless, the myth still does not deny Nü Wa's role in giving birth to all living things. Some modern scholars have interpreted the mythological record to suggest that Huang Di and Nü Wa were contemporaries who together created mankind, but such a view fails to explain the phrase "events which were among the seventy transformations of Nü Wa". Nü Wa clearly pre-dated Huang Di and others if she gave birth to them.

(2) In the "Da Huang Xi Jing" chapter of *Shan Hai Jing*, we read: "Ten mythicized figures who were born out of Nü Wa's intestines stand in the wilderness of Liguang, blocking the passage through." The fact that Nü Wa's intestines had turned into "ten mythicized figures" showed that Nü Wa had already "died". The "ten mythicized figures", like the other mythicized figures in *Shan Hai Jing*, were not gods in a religious sense. This passage has, however, not been fully explained to date.

Apart from Nü Wa, at the time of the patriarchal clan there were other female mythicized figures, such as Xi He, Chang Xi, Yao Ji and Jing Wei. All were involved with male figures, and the phenomena of their transformations and disappearances were directly connected with birth and death. Xi He, for example, was the mother of the sun and wife of Dongfang Dadi Jun, with whom she procreated and gave birth to ten suns. Xi He lived in the state of Xi He which was beyond the Eastern Sea and among the Gan Shui. She helped her ten offspring suns bathe at a place called Tanggu where the water was always very hot. In the centre was a tall Fusang tree and in its branches the ten suns perched, one always in the uppermost branches and the rest among the lower branches. As soon as the uppermost sun went forth to illuminate the earth with its rays, another sun would take its place among the uppermost branches and when the travelling sun returned it would rest among the lower branches. The suns journeyed on a three-legged crow, variously titled "handsome crow" (*junwu*), "sun crow" (*yangwu*) or "golden crow" (*jinwu*). The three-legged crow was also regarded as the soul of the sun.[18]

Chang Xi was said to be the mother of the moon and another wife of Dongfang Dadi Jun, with whom she gave birth to twelve moons, whom she also helped bathe.[19] The myth does not record whether the moons similarly lived in a tree, but according to "Hei'an Zhuan" (Records of Darkness) in the popularly transmitted work **Shennongjia**, the moons lived in a very large tree located on the Central Plain and called the Suoluo tree, a word that today designates the species common reevesia, and these moons also seem to have patrolled singly.

Yao Ji was a younger daughter of Yan Di, Great Lord of the South, but she died before getting married. According to the "Zhong Ci Qi Jing" section of **Shan Hai Jing**, her body was buried on Mount Guyao and later turned into a yaocao plant with overlapping leaves. Its flowers are yellow and its fruit resembles dodder. Eating the fruit confers beauty. Another myth concerning Yao Ji relates how Yan Di felt sorry that she had died unmarried, and so appointed her the goddess of clouds and rain. She was "buried on the southern slope of Mount Fushan". While travelling through the Gaotang area, King Huai of the state of Chu had a day-dream in which he saw her "declare herself the female sage of Mount Fushan". The emperor then made love with her, and later constructed a temple for her "called Zhaoyun". A later king of Chu, King Xiang also dreamed he saw her while travelling through the Gaotang

---

[18] Ref: "Da Huang Nan Jing" in **Shan Hai Jing**.
[19] Ref: "Da Huang Xi Jing" in **Shan Hai Jing**.

region and made love with her.[20] This myth demonstrates that females still had sexual rights and freedom in the age of the patriarchal clan.

Jing Wei was another younger daughter of Yan Di and her name was Nwa. She drowned while swimming in the East China Sea. Her soul turned into a bird "with a tattooed head, a white bill and red legs". It was called Jing Wei and lived on Mount Fajiu in the north. Everyday, she would carry small pieces of stones and wood from Xishan, the Western Mountain[s], in her bill in an attempt to fill the East China Sea and she never ceased doing so.[21] Another myth concerning Jing Wei relates how she married a petrel in the East China Sea and the male bird they gave birth to resembled a petrel, while the female bird they gave birth to resembled Jing Wei. She vowed not to drink the water of the East China Sea, thus earning her the name "pledging bird" (*shiniao*), "justice bird" (*yuanqin*), and "ideal bird" (*zhiniao*). The common people called her "bird of the emperor's daughter" (*dinque*).[22]

The above myths reveal how in the age of the patriarchal clan the social status of males was improving. Not only were they in charge of public affairs but they were also responsible for producing offspring and raising children. The social status of females remained very important. Their mythicized representative could be the mother of the sun and the moon. These mythicized figures had marriages, enjoyed sexual freedom and had the ability to join with male mythicized figures in giving birth to all living things. The age of the patriarchal clan was, therefore, still a society in which males and females were equal, although males formed the mainstay of society.

(3) Nü Wa and Fu Xi

After people entered civilized society following the disband-

---

[20] From "Gaotang Fu" in *Wen Xuan*.
[21] Ref: "Bei Ci Shan Jing", in *Shan Hai Jing*.
[22] Ref: *Shu Yi Ji* (Accounts of Marvels).

ing of the clans, a spouse was found for Nü Wa in order to create an ancient origin for monogamy, and the spouse was Fu Xi. The plot of the marriage between brother and sister, as in the case of Fu Xi and Nü Wa, had ample historical grounds and this should be viewed as another component of the mythology concerning Nü Wa.

Fu Xi was a very ancient mythicized figure and was well-known as one of the "three emperors"[23] and he came to be as well-known as Nü Wa. He also had the head of a human being and the body of a snake. He "taught people how to hunt"[24] and how to weave fishing nets.[25] He invented cooked food, invented the *se*, a musical instrument similar to the zither, and composed a melody named Jia Bian.[26] These details demonstrate features of the matriarchal clan, but other features of the myth, such as his fashioning of marriage dowries and his use of high-grade felt as gifts,[27] and his formulation of the Eight Trigrams[28] based on his observation of heavenly and terrestrial changes and of all living things, show elements of patriarchal clan society. Like Nü Wa, Fu Xi "died" and was reborn, and, in common with many mythicized figures, his achievements after his rebirth were listed under his own name, or one of his other five names. Fu Xi can be regarded as a transitional mythicized figure from the period when the matriarchal age gave way to the patriarchal age.

Documents from before the Qin and Han dynasties show that Nü Wa and Fu Xi were originally two individual mythicized figures with no inter-relationship. Only in the Han dynas-

---

[23] The phrase "three emperors" first appears in **Zhou Li**.

[24] See **Shi Zi-Jun Hua** ("Ruler's Living—Analects of Master Shi Zi").

[25] Ref: "Xi Ci Xia Zhuan" in **Zhou Yi** (Book of Changes of the Zhou Dynasty).

[26] Ref: "Da Zhao" (Summoning the Soul) in **Chu Ci**.

[27] Luo Ping, op. cit.

[28] "Xi Ci Xia Zhuan" in **Zhou Yi**.

ty is there reference to Nü Wa being a female emperor (*yindi*) who assisted the ruler.[29] Portraits of Nü Wa and Fu Xi are to be seen in many stone and brick carvings of the Han dynasty. Above the waist, they have human bodies with Fu Xi wearing distinctive headgear and Nü Wa wearing a gown, while below the waist they have intertwined snakes bodies suggestive of copulation. Some carvings depict Fu Xi holding a carpenter's square, while Nü Wa holds a pair of compasses; other carvings show Fu Xi holding a sun in his hand with a golden crow inside the sun and Nü Wa holding a moon with a toad inside it; still other carvings include a child between them with one of his two hands in each of their sleeves. Such carvings imply that the two were partners in marriage. Holding a carpenter's square and a pair of compasses represented their inexhaustible wisdom and inventiveness, and might possibly also represent the establishment of monogamy. Holding the sun and the moon further illustrated their status as *yangdi* (the masculine or the male) and *yindi* (the feminine or the female). In these carvings the sky is generally dotted with colourful clouds. They were clearly the creator and creatrix of mankind, on whom they conferred various life norms and skills of living.

It was not until the Tang dynasty that a comparatively complete set of tales concerning them appeared in Li Rong's **Du Yi Zhi** (Annals of Marvels): "At the beginning of the universe, there was Nü Wa and her brother on Mount Kunlun and there were yet no people on earth. It was said that they were husband and wife and they themselves felt shy. The brother and his sister then went to live on Mount Kunlun, chanting: 'If they send us down as husband and wife, the smokes of the two fires will merge, and if not, the smoke will disappear'. The smokes of the fires merged and the sister came to the brother. They made fans of grass to cover their faces". This is the earliest record of the inter-marriage between brothers and sisters and there is no

---

[29] Ref: Gao Xiu annot., "Lan Ming Pian", **Huai Nan Zi**.

mention of the legendary deluge. But Chinese popular legend does tell of a deluge, and, according to one version, in ancient times, the rivers overflowed their banks and drowned mankind and only the sister and brother pair, Nü Wa and Fu Xi, remained. They wanted to marry to perpetuate mankind, but this depended on the will of Heaven. They then went to Mount Kunlun and each made a fire and the smoke of their fires merged; they then each carried a millstone to the top of the mountain and let the millstones roll down and the two millstones merged. They then married and re-created mankind. This legend was popular not only among the Han nationality, but also among the Zhuang, Yao, Buyi and Gelo nationalities.[30]

What does the intermarriage of Fu Xi and Nu Wa, brother and sister, signify and how did the two become the ancestors of mankind in the Central Plain region? These questions must be examined in light of the period when the legend about intermarriage between brother and sister emerged, which was the age when the patriarchal clan was disintegrating. The terms "brother" and "sister" are references to men and women of the same generation of the same clan. As we all know, in such social historical conditions when group marriage existed between clans, kinship nomenclature was one of categories with every kinship term referring to a category or group of persons. "Mother", for example, designates one's own mother and her elder and younger sisters. Therefore, within the same clan, all the people of the same generation were brothers and sisters regardless of their blood relationship. Because of the original ban on intermarriage within the same clan, such brothers and sisters were originally forbidden to have sex, let alone intermarry, during both the periods of the matriarchal and of the patriarchal clan. However, as private ownership emerged, the

    [30] Ref: Tao Yang and Zhong Xiu, op. cit., pp. 181-183; and, Ancient Documents Collation Group of Minority Nationalities of the Central Institute for Nationalities comp., **Collection of Myths of China's Minority Nationalities**; Stories About the Deluge.

patriarchal clan and commune began to disintegrate. Brothers and sisters of the same clan but not born of the same parents began having sexual relations and they demanded individual marriages. This was a serious challenge to the preceding tradition, directly threatening the existence of the clan itself. Therefore, it met with stubborn resistance from the forces of tradition. Within the mythic tradition many stories record this struggle to realize "intermarriage between brothers and sisters." Brother-sister intermarriage originally referred to brothers and sisters of the same clan but not born of the same parents.[31]

Once we have a clear understanding of the historical authenticity of brother-sister intermarriage, the symbolism of the flood episode in the mythic tradition also becomes clear. There were at least three torrential floods in the Central Plain region referred to in the mythic record: the flood which occasioned Nü Wa to patched up the sky; the flood in which the God of Water Gong Gong and the God of Fire Zhu Rong fought a mighty battle; and the flood which caused Gun and his father Yu to regulate the rivers. In recent decades, many scholars studied the occurrences of great floods in the prehistoric and historic periods for evidence of some mighty deluge of the scale described in the myths, but such investigations have produced nothing. The flood episode in the context of myths of brother-sister intermarriage was only symbolic, signalling an important turning point in the history of mankind, namely, the disintegration of the clan system, the monogamous breakaway from

---

[31] In his writings, Lewis Henry Morgan once regarded the consanguineous marriage and the family represented by the Malay type of kinship as a phase in the develoment of the most ancient married family and he placed it before clan society. This view has been overturned by ethnological data discovered later. Therefore, Chinese scholars should revise their interpretations about the legend of brother-sister intermarriage based on Morgan's views. For comments on his viewpoint and the question on the historical authenticity of consanguineous marriage and family, see Cai Junsheng, **The Development of Human Society and the Formation of Primitive Society**, pp. 30-40, and pp. 41-50.

group marriage norms, and the change in the kinship system prevailing in clan society from the category type to the type based on monogamous marriage. The myth records the social need to seek the antecedents for single spouse marriage.

In the Central Plain, another myth recording brother-sister intermarriage is that of Pan Gu and his sister. Pan Gu makes a late appearance in historical texts and we read of him for the first time in Xu Zheng's *San Wu Lieji* (Histories of Prehistoric Legendary Tribal Leaders), a Three Kingdoms period work. Pan Gu, also called Pan Hu, is sometimes identified with Fu Xi.[32] The references, however, provide no other details of Pan Gu's marriage.

Among China's minority nationalities, there are large numbers of legends about brother-sister intermarriage. The Bai nationality have a legend about the intermarriage between the brother and sister Xiang Liang and Xiang Mang. Another legend relates how Lao Bian fought Lei Gong, and in the struggle Lei Gong brought down a flood to drown Lao Bian, and finally only Lao Bian's son and daughter remained and so they married. Apart from the legend of the marriage between Fu Xi and his sister, the Buyi people have a number of brother-sister marriages, such as those between Fu Xiong and Xi Mei, Di Jin and Di Yi, as well as Tian Rui and his sister. The Mulao nationality have a legend concerning the marriage between Ah Rang and his sister.

The Tujia nationality have a legend in which Nü Wa appears in the context of brother-sister intermarriage: A widow prayed to Nü Wa and ate an immortal peach. The widow then gave birth to eight sons and one daughter and the youngest son married the daughter. The legends of various other nationalities also record marriages between brothers and sisters: Dong nationality (Jiang Liang and Jiang Mei), Lisu nationality (Le Shan and Shuang Shan), She nationality (Pan Ge and Yun Nan), Nu

---

[32] Ref: Yuan Ke, op. cit, p. 7.

nationality (La Pu and Ya Niu), and Dulong nationality (Bo He Nan and his sister). The Hani, Li and the Sani people of the Yi nationality have similar legends, while marriages between sisters and younger brothers occur in legends of the Jingbo and Tibetan nationalities.[33] This points to a universality of legends concerning brother-sister intermarriage.

When we look again at earlier Han dynasty versions of the legend of Fu Xi and Nü Wa, we find two characteristics: (1) Fu Xi and Nü Wa retain the bodies of snakes, the totem; and, (2) there is no reference to a flood. The retained totem indicates that the two were regarded as being in the kinship group of siblings within a clan of the same totem, while the absence of a flood episode shows that this was a later interpolation. These two characteristics show that earlier versions of the myth were closer to the historical reality, and, in historical terms intermarriage between brothers and sisters of the same clan but not born of the same parents should occur in the pre-Xia or early Xia period. Monogamy subsequently broke the rules governing marriage outside the clan and stories about brother-sister intermarriage began to spread. Until the Han dynasty there was a need for images of the ancestors who established monogamy, and Fu Xi and Nü Wa filled this need. At the time the myths were created, the "brother" and the "sister" in the brother-sister intermarriage stories were not misinterpreted as brother and sister born of the same parents. By the time Li Rong wrote his account of the story in the Tang dynasty the original myth was greatly distorted with the aim of changing the "re-creation of mankind" into the "creation of mankind" to better serve the contemporary monogamous marriage system based on the authority of the husband.

Every age in fact produced its own myths regarding the origin of mankind. When the matriarchal clan prevailed, women were regarded as the creators and this was transformed into the

---

[33] Idem.

myth that related how Nü Wa fashioned human beings from clay. During the age of the patriarchal clan, human beings were created by men with the aid of women, and this was expressed in the myth relating how Huang Di and several others created human beings with the aid of Nü Wa's soul. With the disappearance of the clan and group marriage and the establishment of monogamy, this was given mythic expression in the legend about the brother-sister marriage of Fu Xi and Nü Wa designed to recreate mankind. The historical changes in the myth of Nü Wa reflect the gradual decline in the social status of females in the long course of Chinese historical development, but this should not obscure the resilient image of Nü Wa as the most ancient female ancestor of the Chinese.

2. Traces of the Age of Group Marriage

When the areas inhabited by the Han nationality in the Central Plain entered the period of male-ruled civilized society and after the form of marriage became monogamy, many nationalities in the area remained at the stage of matriarchal clan society or patriarchal clan society, and group marriage between clans still prevailed. These nationalities would undergo a long and tortuous process to make the transition to civilized society and the monogamy marriage system, and for many peoples this process has extended into the second half of the 20th century. Within these nationalities, group marriages and individual marriages within the group marriages of the clan coexist as the clans disintegrate, while pre-marital and extra-marital sexual freedom remain as residual traces of group marriage after the clan disintegrated and monogamy was established. Here, we will examine three sets of evidence documenting this process: textual records describing the social situation in the border areas of the Central Plain in prehistoric times as reflected in the recorded myths of Xi Wang Mu (Queen Mother of the West); the reality of a pristine type of matriarchal society, viz. the matriarchal system of the Naxi nationality in the Yongning area; and group marriage vestiges among other nationalities.

(1) Xi Wang Mu

Xi Wang Mu was originally the representative of the matriarchal clan society in China's western border area. In the "Da Huang Xi Jing" section of *Shan Hai Jing*:

> To the south of Xi Hai and at the border of the desert, at the back of Chi Shui and in front of Hei Shui, there is a mountain called Kunlun. There, there is a god with the face of a human being and the body of a tiger. It has a totemic face and a tail with white dots. The mountain is surrounded by a river called Ruo Shui, and out of the river is a flaming hill and anything thrown at it will be burned. There, you see a human being wearing headgear. The human being has teeth resembling those of a tiger and a tail like that of a leopard. It lives in a cave and its name is Xi Wang Mu. All things can be found on that mountain.

In this passage we find a totemic image "with the face of a human being and the body of a tiger" as well as a human being closely resembling the totem with "headgear" (*sheng*). This headgear was originally worn by women in the Han dynasty, and the name of the human, possibly a chieftainess, was Xi Wang Mu (Queen Mother of the West). However, while the name might be the direct title for the female chief, it might also be a title for a group of humans, their totem and their place. Since Xi Wang Mu's place, Kunlun, had a totem and totemized people represented by a female, we can interpret this a vestigial myth of matriarchal clan society.

Shan Hai Jing was completed in the Warring States period, and the contents of certain sections of the work, such as "Da Huang Jing", are even more ancient. There were also textual references to contacts between Xi Wang Mu and the Central

Plain. *Zhushu Jinian* (The Bamboo Annals) contains the following passage:

> In the 9th year of Emperor Shun, Xi Wang Mu came to meet the emperor with a white ring and a piece of jade.

And:

> In the 17th year of his reign, Emperor Mu of the Zhou dynasty went to the Kunlun mountain in the west to see Xi Wang Mu. The following year, Xi Wang Mu came to the imperial court to meet the emperor as his guest in Zhaogong.

There are more detailed records in *Mu Tianzi Zhuan* (Biography of Emperor Mu) about the contacts between Emperor Mu of the Zhou dynasty and Xi Wang Mu:

> In the *renhai* year, Emperor Mu came to the State of Xi Wang Mu. On the day of *jiazi*, the emperor went to meet Xi Wang Mu as her guest bearing a large piece of white jade and a large piece of black jade. The emperor presented her with 100 *cun* of silks and satins (about 1,333 meters). Both were very happy. The emperor then presented her with a further 300 *cun* of silks and satins (about 4,000 meters). Xi Wang Mu accepted them and expressed her thanks. On the day of *yichou*, the emperor asked Xi Wang Mu to drink with him at Yaochi and Xi Wang Mu sang the emperor a song: "There are white clouds in the sky and hills on earth. We are far from each other, separated by mountains and rivers. We may come here again if there is an occasion." The emperor replied by singing her a song: "I shall go back to the Central Plain and rule all the states there well. When all the people are equal, I'll return to see you. After three years of governing, I'll return to your place." Xi Wang Mu said to the emperor: "Xi Tu prevents me in the west, I must remain with the tigers, leopards and birds. My fate is not fortunate, and I can only regard you

as the emperor. Your people are good, so how could they let you come. When I saw you off amid the playing of the *sheng* and *huang* last time, I was feeling very vexed. You are a good son of your people and the hope of Heaven." The emperor drove to the Hesheng Mountain and carved the details of their meeting on the stones of the mountain and planted many Chinese scholar-trees on both sides of a rock in which he carved a new name for the mountain: 'Mount Xi Wang Mu'.

These records show that Emperor Mu met the chief of the State of Xi Wang Mu and that the chief was female. *Zhushu Jinian* is universally regarded as a reliable historical text. From the 9th year of Emperor Shun to the 17th year of Emperor Mu of the Zhou dynasty, the female chief of the State of Xi Wang Mu would have changed many times. The fact that they "came to the imperial court" twice shows that matriarchal society existed on the western borders of the Central Plain.

On the Central Plain the totem image of Xi Wang Mu was constantly Han-ized, and this process is recorded in two relatively late entries in *Shan Hai Jing*:

> Mount Yu was where Xi Wang Mu lived. Xi Wang Mu resembled a human with a leopard's tail, tiger's teeth and an ability to roar. With long hair and distinctive headgear, Xi Wang Mu was in charge of Li and Wuchai.[34]

And:

> Xi Wang Mu sat on a high platform with distinctive headgear and a stave. There were three green birds from the south who would obtain food for her from the lands north of Mount Kunlun.[35]

Mount Yu, literally Jade Mountain, was another name for Mount Kunlun, a place abundant in jade. Xi Wang Mu com-

---

[34] Ref: "Xi Ci Shan Jing", Shan Hai Jing.
[35] See "Hai Nei Bei", in ibid.

bines a totem image and the image of an actual human being now transformed into a deity resembling a human being. Now we find that Xi Wang Mu is in charge of Li and Wuchai, the names of two constellations of ill omen, a task which identified her with the immortals of the Han nationality. The detail about the three green birds fetching food for her is also a later interpolation, presenting a picture of Xi Wang Mu quite different from that of *Mu Tianzi Zhuan* or "Da Huang Xi Jing". These are two later Han dynasty interpolations which convey the Han conceptions of a deity. By the time of the Wei, Jin and Northern and Southern dynasties, Xi Wang Mu has discarded her totemic decorations and donned the headwear of noblewomen of the Han dynasty, and she is set among the world of sages. In *Han Wu Di Nei Zhuan* (The Inside Stories of Emperor Wu Di of the Han Dynasty), attributed to Ban Tu, we read that she visited Emperor Wu Di from the south-west by "riding on purple clouds and six-colour dragons and accompanied by fifty goddesses. She was wearing a golden gown, colourful, yet solemn and respectful. She tied a 'Feiling' silk belt about her waist from which a 'Fenjing' sword hung. She had a 'Taihua' hair style and was wearing a crown and a pair of blue jade shoes patterned with a phoenix. She was about thirty years old, of medium height, slim and graceful, and was the most beautiful goddess." By the time of the Ming dynasty, she had become apotheosized into the wife of Yuhuang Dadi, the Jade Emperor.

The textual references to Xi Wang Mu show two tendencies in the Central Plain's attitudes to nationalities living in the border areas. One was that these texts were imprinted with the intrinsic feudal viewpoint of the people of the Central Plain. The other was that the historical facts about the nationalities in the border areas were treated as exotica and in the process of transmitting them, the imagination of the people of the Central Plain was imbued in them and they were finally raised to the level of being fantastic tales. A good example is the apotheosis whereby Wang Mu became an emperor's wife. This was also the case with records in documents of various dynasties concerning the sexual behaviour of nationalities in border areas. Among border nationalities, especially those which were pre-literate societies, the social status of females was generally higher than that of females in Han nationality areas and they had greater autonomy in matters of sexual freedom and sexual choice. In the Central Plain this gave rise to folk tales concerning lands of women, where there were no males, where women got pregnant by facing into the wind or by taking a shower at a well, where women only gave birth to daughters or to sons destined to die young, or where women were amazons and were sexually rapacious if they captured males.[36] Such legends were perpetuated, but they nevertheless provide evidence, confirmed by genuine historical data, that forms of group marriage existed among matriarchal border nationalities, especially in the west and south-western border areas where the Xi Wang Mu legends were located.

Among the reliable historical documents is the "Xinan Yi Zhuan" (Account of the Southwest Yi Nationalities) in *Hou Han Shu* (the History of the Later Han Dynasty) where various "Jun and Kunming tribes" of today's southern Sichuan and northern Yunnan were to be found:

> In a vast area of several thousand *li*, there was no recognized chief. People wore their hair in braids, moving at will with the domestic animals.

In the northeast of this area was the state of Ran Mang, where people "were either local residents or nomads moving with their domestic animals." Moreover, "there were six ethnic groups in the east, seven in the south and nine in the west, and they each had their own tribes. Their chief was a learned man and imposed strict laws. Women were very noble and were organ-

[36] Ref: "Dong Yi Zhuan", *Hou Han Shu; Taiping Yulan*, fasc. 395; Zhou Qufei, *Lingwai Daida* (Replies From the South); and, Zhou Zhizhong *Yiyu Zhi* (Annals of Outer Regions).

ized in accordance with the matriarchal side".

The "Dong Nü Guo" (Eastern Women's Kingdom) section of *Jiu Tang Shu* (The Old History of The Tang Dynasty) contains the following account:

> Dong Nü Guo was an affiliate of the Xi Qiang and lay in the middle of Xi Hai. Its chief was a woman,.... It took nine days to travel from the east to the west of the state and 20 days from south to north. The state had more than 80 large and small cities and the chief lived in the city of Kangyan-chuan traversed from north to south by a river called Rushui River (i.e., the Yalong River in today's southern Sichuan). They use ox hides to fashion coracles. The population consists of more than 4,000 households and more than 10,000 warriors scattered in mountains and hills. ... People respected women and looked down upon husbands.

And:

> Rushui Wang was the Rushui tribes at the beginning the state of Nü, ... and the largest tribe had 2,000 to 3,000 households.

In the "Dong Nü Guo" section of *Xin Tang Shu* (The New History of the Tang Dynasty) the following passage occurs:

> [In Dong Nü Guo] "people looked down upon men, and noblewomen had servants with long hair and green faces. The tasks of the servants were fighting and farming. Children took their mothers' surnames.

Speaking of the Luoluo nation, the Yuan dynasty writer Zhou Zhihong had this to say in his *Yiyu Zhi* (Annals of Outer Regions):

> Luoluo was the state of the Gubo people who were of Panhu origin. When speaking, the sound came out of their noses. They were ferocious and not afraid of death. They were fond of eating things raw. Their hair was as long as one *chi* (about 33 cm), they could stand on their heads, and

they wore felt. Their leader was a woman, and mothers were in charge of everything. A noblewoman had as many as one hundred husbands. They had strict discipline and orders were issued by carving them on small pieces of wood.

These accounts all show that since the Han and Tang dynasties and down to the present day, in southern Sichuan and northern Yunnan, there have existed tribal societies "without recognized chiefs", featuring a matriarchal system in which "children took their mothers' surnames", and there was group marriage in which "a noblewoman had as many as one hundred husbands". To enquire more specifically into such societies we will turn to examine the results of surveys of the matriarchal system of the Naxi nationality in the Yongning region conducted by ethnologists in the 1950s and 1960s.

(2) The Matriarchal System in the Yongning Region

The matriarchal system of the Naxi nationality in the Yongning region of the Ninglang Yi Autonomous County of China's Yunnan Province may provide us with modern examples of matriarchal society and group marriage between the clans.

Scholars generally maintain that the ancestors of the Naxi nationality were a branch of the ancient Qiang people who later moved to the Yongning region on the border of Yunnan with Sichuan. According to the Naxi people's own legends, they migrated here from the north. Their legends also describe the organizational situation of the ancient clan society of the Naxi nationality, and as Professors Yan Ruxian and Song Zhaolin have commented:

Legends say that the ancestors of the Naxi nationality moved here from the north. They had six matriarchal clans when they first arrived at the Lugu Lake in the Yongning region. These six ancient matriarchal clans originally lived in Sibuahnawa on the north of the lake. And later they moved to the south in three groups; Xi Er and Hu Er were in one group, Ya Er and E Er in one group and Bu Er and Cuo Er in one group, and they followed the practice of intermarriage.[37]

This research provides a vivid picture of the intermarriage between two clans. Elsewhere the two professors wrote: "Although these matriarchal clans have long since disintegrated, most people and households know which matriarchal clan they once belonged to."[38] The two researchers statistically surveyed all the old clans of the people in the local five townships.[39] Evidence of this knowledge of matriarchal clans is provided by Naxi funeral services, when the people would ask a wizard, Daba, to chant scriptures in order to make a path for sending off the soul. Daba would describe in detail the route along which the ancestors moved to the south and then the soul of the departed would be sent to where the ancestors came from along the same route. The most ancient clan or Er later gave birth to many daughter clans or Siris as the Naxi people called them, and these were still identifiable prior to the democratic reform of 1956. The two researchers describe these:

The matriarchal clan lived by gathering together on the basis of the Er at the beginning and later on the basis of the Siri. Before the democratic reform, some villages composed of consanguineously linked Siris still existed in Wenquan Township. ... Although many changes later took place later, the traces of this shift were still quite clear... As for the number of people constituting the Siri, the Wahu, Wala and Sada in Wenquan Township were the largest according to statistics compiled before the democratic reform, all standing at around one hundred, and other places in the township had more than fifty

---

[37] Ref: Yan Ruxian and Song Zhaolin, **The Matriarchal System of the Naxi Nationality in Yongning**, [Yunnan People's Publishing House, 1981], p. 31.

[38] Ref: Ibid., p. 31.

[39] Idem.

or sixty Siri members... [In the Naxi language] the Siri meant a 'human being with one piece of bone' or 'a plateful of rice and meat', and the latter derived from the practice whereby a public plate used in making sacrifices was offered up by the Siri members when commemorating their ancestors, and when one ancestor's name was mentioned by the Daba, rice and meat would be placed on the plate. This showed that the Siri was also a unit of production and consumption.[40]

As a clan commune, the unit of common production and consumption, the Siri existed at the time of the Yuan dynasty or even earlier. According to the first draft of **The Joint Edition of the Simplified History and Annals of the Naxi Nationality** and **Investigative Report on the Naxi Nationality Society and its Matriarchal System in Yongning, Ninglang Yi Autonomous County** (Set 1), in 1253 Hubilie (Kublai Khan) or Emperor Renzong of the Yuan dynasty brought his armies here while driving towards the south and recruited the chief of the Yongning Naxi nationality (it is also said that the Naxi people fought together with Kublai's armies and rendered meritorious service) and established the system of appointing hereditary headmen.[41] From that time on, the Yongning region was placed under the command of the central authorities. The policy of the Yuan dynasty toward the minority nationalities here was that "provided they accept the command of the central authorities, hand in tribute and taxes and allow their headmen to be appointed by the higher authorities, all the rest would remain unchanged."[42]

[40] Ibid., p. 35.

[41] Ref: Nationalities Institute of the Chinese Academy of Sciences eds., **The Joint Edition of the Simplified History and Annals of the Naxi Nationality** (first draft), [Beijng; 1963], p. 27; Yunnan Nationalities Investigative Group of the Nationalities Institute of the Chinese Academy of Sciences and the Yunnan Provincial Nationalities Institute eds., **Investigative Report on the Naxi Nationality Society and its Matriarchal System in Yongning of Ninglang Yi Autonomous County** (1963), p. 1.

[42] Shen Chen, *Yunnan Jiwu Chao Huang*, ref: "Renzong Benji" in *Yuan Shi* (History of the Yuan Dynasty).

However, "all the rest" here could only mean the customs covering production and life in the clan communes as grass-roots social units, but in other social organizational forms the tribes lost their original position due to the establishment of the appointment of hereditary headmen. Therefore, in the Yuan Dynasty, only the Siri existed as grass-roots units.

By the Ming and Qing dynasties, the Siri further shrank with the introduction of comparatively advanced farm production skills. The clan commune also disintegrated into matriarchal groups composed of brothers and sisters born of the same mother in the same clan, whom the local people then called Yidu ("households").[43] Thus, the Siri existed as a matriarchal clan but lost its nature as a commune. At the same time, with the development of the economy, the system of feudal lords was introduced, and the ranks of society began to be broken up into grades, namely, Sipei, Zeka and Er, equivalent to nobles, common people and peasants attached to large estates. But the Yidu as grass-roots social units firmly remained in place, their external structure resembling "peasant households", but within an economy dominated by feudal lords. The internal structure did not resemble that of a family, but only the tributaries of the matriarchal clans, and because they functioned as the smallest production and life units, they were simultaneously tributaries of clan communes. Because of the firm existence of the matriarchal Yidu, many social customs of the matriarchal clan period, including the marriage form, were retained. The matriarchal Yidu had the following four basic features:

(1) The genealogy was calculated on the maternal side. The members were brothers and sisters born of the same mother, fifteen to twenty in all, with the mother or the eldest sister as the head or Dabu, as termed in the local language. The matriar-

---

[43] The word Yidu literally means "residence", referring to people living in the same residential quarters. Therefore, it is often interpreted as "household", but actually it refers to the relatives on the matriarchal side.

chal Yidu itself was often named after its Dabu.

(2) Property was publicly owned. The farmland the Yidu used was originally conferred by the clan commune (Siri) and later it became the "share" in the feudal economic system. Apart from the farmland, the Yidu's residence, domestic animals and labor tools were public property. The Yidu followed the principle of collective labor and common consumption and had public warehouses. All property was inherited in the maternal line.

(3) Exogamy was practised. Although, in principle, the Yongning Naxi nationality followed the system of exogamy, as a tributary of the Siri, the Yidu was obviously an exogamous collective. Internally, the Yidu strictly prohibited sexual relationships, and especially marriage relationships.

(4) There were public graveyards. The graveyards originally belonged to the Siri and were later split up into the public graveyards of the Yidu. The Naxi nationality followed the custom of cremation and the ashes of the dead were placed according to the principle of older and younger generations with females on the right and males on the left.

It is clear that the four features were still the basic features of the clan communes in the period when the matriarchal system prevailed.

With the matriarchal Yidu as the basis, the marriage form here still retained the group marriage of the period of the matriarchal system. The adult women lived in "guest-houses" built by the matriarchal Yidu with one room for each woman. The woman's spouse (usually a male of another Siri) would come to stay in the woman's "guest-house" at night and return to his own Yidu for production and living during the day, thereby leading a married life which entailed "visiting" the female companion at night and going back in the morning. The local people referred to this marriage relationship as *Ah Xiao*, meaning "living friends", a special term for sexual partners. Such relationships were easy to establish and renounce, and *Ah Xiao* relations could in fact be established at any time provided they were within the scope of intermarriage. A male need only say to a female: "Shall we have *Ah Xiao* relations?" If he received an affirmative reply, he could visit the female at night and stay with her. *Ah Xiao* relations among the Yongning Naxis had the following features:

1. Marriage outside the clan. In earlier times, a system of marriage outside the Er prevailed. Males and females of the same Er (clan) were not allowed to establish *Ah Xiao* relations and only the males and females of different Ers were allowed to have *Ah Xiao* relations. If this rule was disregarded, the offenders were regarded as being "less than pigs or dogs". With the disintegration of the Er, a system of marriage outside the Siri emerged, and only males and females of different Siris could establish *Ah Xiao* relations. In the past century, although Siris frequently split up, few males and females of the matriarchal systems separated by only four or five generations established *Ah Xiao* relations, although there were some exceptions. Everyone knew from his or her mother and uncle when very young who were the people "belonging to the same piece of bone" and that he or she must maintain serious relations between males and females. Therefore, marriage outside the clan was perpetuated.

After society broke up into hierarchical groups, the marriage form was not restricted by those groups. "In Zhongshi village, there were 9 households (Yidu) of the Er grade, and in the village, out of 50 *Ah Xiao* females, 14 led an *Ah Xiao* life. Their gradated groups were: 38 belonged to Er, 4 belonged to Zeka, 3 belonged to Sipei, and 5 belonged to other nationalities. There were 9 males who led an *Ah Xiao* life, with 21 female *Ah Xiao* and of them, 6 belonged to Er grade, 4 belonged to Zeka and 1 belonged to Sipei, and the rest were of other places."[44] The Er-grade *Ah Xiao* could be seen in every grade of the society. This demonstrates the existence of the matriarchal

---

[44] Ref: Yan Ruxian and Song Zhaolin, op. cit., p. 102.

Yidu.

2. The principle of voluntariness and making one's own choice. It was entirely up to the males and females themselves to establish *Ah Xiao* relations, and although the opinions of mothers and uncles carried some weight, they usually would not take the initiative to interfere. After the adulthood initiation ceremony[45] which was held at the age of 13, the male or female child had the capacity to make *Ah Xiao* friends, but generally they would begin establishing these relationships two years later when sexually mature, around the age of 14 or 15 for females and 17 or 18 for males.

At the beginning of the *Ah Xiao* life, the males generally secretly visited the females, the females having already moved into the "guest-house". Some young people spent their "first night of married life" in a grass-roofed hut, in the fields or in an outside place. After a period of contacts, if both were willing to maintain the relationship and the parents of the female were not opposed to the relationship, the male could openly take his luggage and move to the female's "guest-house". He would go back to his own Yidu during the daytime to engage in production and other activities and return to stay with his female *Ah Xiao* at night. "At this time, the female would wear the clothes and other decorations her male *Ah Xiao* gave her, and openly declare that she now had her own long-term *Ah Xiao*"[46] Henceforth, the *Ah Xiao* relationship enters its public stage.

In terms of the entire *Ah Xiao* relationship of a person, it could be divided into two categories: the long-term *Ah Xiao* relationship and the temporary *Ah Xiao* relationship. The long-

---

[45] The adulthood initiation ceremony of the Naxi is also referred to as a ceremony of putting on skirts and trousers. The Naxi young people, whether boys or girls, wear linen gowns and no trousers. On the eve of their 13th birthday, a ceremony is held in the central hall of the matriarchal Yidu, at which boys put on trousers and girls put on skirts. Ref: Yan Ruxian and Song Zhaolin, op. cit., pp. 141-149.

[46] Ibid., p. 118.

term *Ah Xiao* was the major spouse and the temporary *Ah Xiao* was the supplementary spouse. There were three differences between the long-term *Ah Xiao* and the temporary *Ah Xiao*: (1) The long-term *Ah Xiao*s should give gifts to each other. It was the custom that every year, the male should give the female one skirt, a pair of shoes and one bamboo hat. The female should give the male one pair of linen trousers in return, and those who were better off could return more if they wished to do so. There was no such custom in the case of the temporary *Ah Xiao*s. (2) The long-term male *Ah Xiao* could move his own bedding to the "guest-house" of his female *Ah Xiao* and place it together with hers. Once the female *Ah Xiao* moved the bedding of the male *Ah Xiao* out of the "guest-house" or the male *Ah Xiao* himself took his bedding away, the long-term *Ah Xiao* relationship ended. There was no such provision in the temporary *Ah Xiao* relationship. (3) The long-term *Ah Xiao* relationship was public and was recognized by society and therefore it had sexual priority. The temporary *Ah Xiao* relationship usually only filled a temporary sexual need, sexual love or sexual feelings and was "just for fun", as expressed in the language of the Naxi. If both of the temporary *Ah Xiao*s had their own long-term *Ah Xiao* partners, or one of the temporary *Ah Xiao*s had a long-term *Ah Xiao*, they were encouraged to concentrate on the long-term relationship. The temporary relationship did not have sexual priority. The long-term relationship could continue for two to three months or even decades, while the temporary relationship was not stable.

Naxi people, when young, tended to have more temporary *Ah Xiao* relationships and in some cases no long-term *Ah Xiao* relationships, thereby enjoying greater sexual freedom. When they grew older and especially after the female *Ah Xiao* gave birth, they would aspire to enter into stable long-term *Ah Xiao* relationships. In short, the *Ah Xiao* relationship, whether long-term or temporary, was established or revoked on the basis of the entire voluntariness of the two parties, and no one party had the right to force the other to enter into such a relationship.

3. Non-economic principles. Male and female *Ah Xiao* partners lived and worked in different Yidu (households) and generally they had no economic ties apart from offering courtesy gifts to each other. This made it possible for the *Ah Xiao* marriage relationship to shake off the restrictions of economic ties and to be based purely on the sexual love of both the male and female partners.[47] In the choice of partner, both male or female *Ah Xiao*s took appearance, age, health and individual capability into consideration. It was easy for the young, capable and attractive persons to find *Ah Xiao* persons, but it was difficult for those regarded as unattractive or for those who were handicapped. The key, however, was regarded as being of good moral character. Once affection faded from an *Ah Xiao* relationship, the couple would inevitably separate. The following is a surveyed example:

> Jia Ah was the adopted daughter of the old man, Si Ge, of the Bazhu village and she called him uncle. "She was very pretty when she was 16 and 17 and had many *Ah Xiao* friends." Later, Jia Ah became pregnant and her *Ah Xiao* friends left her, because they "did not have the duty to take care of her". After Jia Ah gave birth to a baby, Yi Shi of Xiaoloshui village "came to see her with eggs, rice wine and pork". "Jia Ah thought Yi Shi had affection for her and was a good-hearted guy. From then on, the two became long-term *Ah Xiao* friends.[48]

---

[47] Engels maintained that no such thing as individual sexual love existed before the Middle Ages, and that throughout antiquity, marriages were arranged by parents, ("the little conjugal love was not in any way a subjective inclination, but an objective duty; not a reason for but a correlate of marriage"). (See: **The Origins of Family, Private Property and the State, in Collected Works of Marx and Engels** [People's Publishing House, 1972], vol. 4, pp. 72-73). This statement cannot apply to *Ah Xiao* marriage.

[48] Ref: Yan Ruxian and Song Zhaolin, op. cit., p. 115.

This example showed that sexual love was not the only factor in *Ah Xiao* relationships, and that the moral character of an individual played a key role.

Another point that deserves attention in examining the choice of sexual partner in the *Ah Xiao* marriage of the Yongning Naxi nationality is that the mother was always very much concerned with the physical quality of her daughter's male *Ah Xiao*. The mother's opinions or suggestions about her daughter's choice of *Ah Xiao* mainly stemmed from such a concern. The reason was that the offspring of *Ah Xiao* marriages stayed with the female side and were the members of the Yidu (household) of the female side. Such a concern was thus a concern about the physical conditions of the members of the third generation of her own Yidu. This was a eugenic concern perpetuated over generations and the physical quality of the Naxi people in the Yongning region has been generally good. This was also the result of what can be seen as a non-economic principle.

4. Equality between male and female, with the female as the mainstay. The above-mentioned features already demonstrate that the male and female enjoyed equal social status, but the mode of sexual integration with the male "visiting" the female illustrated that the female was in the position of host, and the male in that of guest.[49] The female side was responsible for bringing up the children and the uncle (mother's brother) replaced the father. Therefore, the female was responsible for all duties in the *Ah Xiao* marriage and therefore she was given greater autonomy and initiative. Viewed from the perspective of society, in such a marriage the female was the mainstay. This is reflected in the Naxi language. Yongning's Naxi people "even today still say 'females and males' rather than 'males and females'; they call big trees 'mother trees' and small trees 'male

---

[49] In some areas inhabited by people of the Han nationality, men call their wives Tangke, meaning "visiting resident". This is obviously quite different from the *Ah Xiao* marriage of the Naxi nationality in the Yongning region.

trees', while big baskets are 'mother baskets' and small baskets are 'male baskets'. They still regard females as senior."[50] Obviously, these linguistic features are the products of the matriarchal system.

We mentioned earlier that during the period of the clan commune in the matriarchal age, group marriage existed among clans. The *Ah Xiao* marriage of the Naxi nationality in the Yongning region provided a vivid example of group marriage. Although the clan communes here had disintegrated into the matriarchal Yidus, the matriarchal Yidus were still the outer marriage production and life units composed of the same Yidu members. With this as the premise, the marriage form here fully retains the basic content of the group marriage of the clan commune period and every one of the four features of the *Ah Xiao* marriage is a current illustration of the group marriage of the clan commune period. The concept of "group marriage" originally referred to marriage among the clans. The fact that the Naxi people in Yongning may have several *Ah Xiao* friends accords with the rules of group marriage, and no concept existed here of "illegally living together" or "living in sin". Group marriage did not rule out the existence of individual marriages which accorded with the rules of the group marriage. On the whole, the *Ah Xiao* marriage here was a part of group marriage among clans.

Prof. Riane Eisler raised the social mode of equal partnership between male and female in her book **The Chalice and The Blade**. She stated that in such situations "social relations are primarily based on the principle of linking rather than ranking. In this model—beginning with the most fundamental difference in our species, between male and female—diversity is not equated with either inferiority or superiority."[51] The above-mentioned features of the *Ah Xiao* marriage of the Naxi nationality in the

---

[50] Ref: Yan Ruxian and Song Zhaolin, op. cit.

[51] See: Riane Eisler, **The Chalice and The Blade** (Chinese edition), [Social Sciences Document Publishing House, 1993], p. 6.

Yongning region demonstrate that the difference between male and female was "not equated with either inferiority or superiority" and that both *Ah Xiao* partners find their relationship is "primarily based on the principle of linking rather than ranking." If we leave the *Ah Xiao* relations and have a look on the relations among the individuals inside the matriarchal Yidu, such as the relations between the Dabu (chief of the genealogy) and other members, the relations between the male members and the female members, and the relations between the older generation and the younger generation, we find that property was publicly owned and "the Yidu followed the principle of collective labor and common consumption". These relationships too were "primarily based on the principle of linking rather than ranking". This is to say that social relations whether inside the Yidu or among the Yidu were all practical and lively partnerships. Professor Eisler also mentioned that "the original direction in the mainstream of our cultural evolution was toward partnership."[52] Since the social relations that took shape on the basis of the matriarchal Yidu of the Naxi nationality in Yongning were the legacy of the matriarchal age in history, "the original direction" is here confirmed.

The Xi Wang Mu State at the time of the Yin and Zhou dynasties, as we mentioned earlier, is an example of a matriarchal society with the tiger as its totem. The totem of the ancestors of the Naxi nationality in Yongning was also the tiger, and the Naxi nationality has the custom of forbidding the hunting of tigers. In the Naxi language, *La, Ah* and *Luo* mean tiger and the surname of the hereditary headman was tiger. Many mountains, lakes and villages were named for the tiger, such as Nala Mountain, Ahla Mountain and Ladazhai Mountain. Lugu Lake was also called Lagu Lake. In the names of villages, Lawa means "tiger village", Lakua means "tiger claw" and Lake means "tiger elbow". People hung paintings of tigers

---

[52] Idem.

on the lintels of the doors and regarded the tiger as the deity capable of eliminating evil. Amulets made of tiger skin were decorated with paintings of figures with the head of a human being and the body of a tiger, evoking the totemic image.[53]

However, these are mere vestiges of the "self-mythicized humans" of the matriarchal age. The present-day social life of the Naxi nationality in the Yongning region, including the matriarchal Yidu and the *Ah Xiao* marriage, has been customized. People no longer regard themselves as belonging to the same category of tigers. You can no longer see today the totemized images like those who dressed like the tiger totem in the Xi Wang Mu State. What remains are the legends concerning the worship of a goddess. This change is reflected in the history of Mount Ganmu, formerly called Ladazhai Mountain.

Mount Ganmu and Lugu Lake beneath it symbolize the Yongning region. Mount Ganmu is also called Shizi (Lion) Mountain today, perhaps following Buddhism's introduction into the region.[54] As late as the Yuan dynasty, Mount Ganmu was still called Ladazhai (Tiger) Mountain. Beginning from the Ming dynasty, it was renamed Mount Ganmu, Heidi Ganmu in Naxi, Heidi meaning Yongning, Gan meaning "mountain" and Mu meaning "female".[55] The change from "tiger mountain" to "female mountain" shows the transition from the totemized symbol to the symbol of goddess, and this reflected a change in people's beliefs. Today we can still find the following legend concerning the Ganmu Female Mountain:

In ancient times, the Yongning area was a smooth terrain and a fertile grassland, and in the center of the grassland was a lake called Lugu lake. At that time, there were two

---

[53] Ref: Yan Ruxian and Song Zhaolin, op. cit., pp.189-193.

[54] In the Ming and Qing dynasties, Tibetan Buddhism gradually entered the region. Since late modern times, every Yidu should send a male to serve as a lama, but a lama could make *Ah Xiao* friends, which signified an amalgam of traditions.

[55] Ref: Yan Ruxian and Song Zhaolin, op. cit., p. 195.

gods, one male and one female. The female god was called Ganmu and lived on the north bank of the lake; the male god was called Hawashan and lived on the south bank of the lake. They became *Ah Xiao* friends, lived in a cave and led a wild life. Once, the male god invited Ganmu to meet him at the lake-side, but Ganmu arrived late. It was already dawn when they began chatting and were seen by the God of the Sun, violating the rule that they could only meet at night. So the God of the Sun ordered them to stay for ever in the mundane world and forbade them returning to Heaven. Thus, Ganmu became a mountain, standing on the north bank of the lake, and her *Ah Xiao* friend became Mount Hawashan on the south bank of the lake.[56]

There was another legend which goes like this:

The female god Ganmu not only had Hawashan as her *Ah Xiao* friend. Her first *Ah Xiao* friend was Warubula, a mountain in Qiansuo, Sichuan. Her second was Zezhi, a mountain at the back of Zhongshi village. Once Warubula happened to see the female god sleeping with Zezhi, and Warubula spliced Zezhi's sexual organ with a knife. It was said that the low hill near Dapo village was Zezhi's cut sexual organ. The female god also had *Ah Xiao* relations with the snow-capped Hedibigu mountain in Qiansuo. She wanted to go there, but was stopped by the strong Warubula. In the end, none of her four male *Ah Xiao* could approach her and could only walk around her.[57]

The goddess Ganmu was the highest ranking protective deity of the Naxi nationality in the Yongning region, and her history and life were undoubtedly the religious reflection of the matriarchal system. The ceremonies of the Naxi people in Yongning in which they offered sacrifices to Ganmu were most solemn. On the 25th day of the seventh month every year,

[56] Ibid., p.196.
[57] Ibid., pp. 197-198.

people would put on their holiday best early in the morning and take food and wine with them as they proceeded to Ganmu Mountain on horse-back or on foot in groups of two or three. Many *Ah Xiao* friends would make the journey. They gathered at the foot of Ganmu Mountain, where they would chat and laugh. The ceremony was held on the basis of Siri or Yidu and was usually presided over by the Dabu or by a lama (every Yidu had its own lama). They made a fire of pine branches, and offered sacrifices, sprinkling wine and throwing flowers onto the fire, to which they then performed obeisance. The ceremony itself was very pious and was intended to secure a good harvest and the safety and flourishing of the people and their domestic animals. At the end of the ceremony, the participants would tour Ganmu Mountain and Lugu Lake. The ceremony would last one to two days. During the day, they held horse races, enjoyed picnics and danced, and at night they slept where they were in the open. This was a good opportunity for making *Ah Xiao* friends. Naturally, old and new *Ah Xiao* friends enjoyed these events and some would sleep together at this time. This was the annual celebration of the Naxi nationality in the Yongning region.

This sacrificial ceremony has much in common with the sub-urban sacrifices of ancient China mentioned earlier. This is not a coincidence. Ganmu was the Nü Wa of the Naxi nationality in the Yongning region. The form of the female god Ganmu, her character and function illustrated once again the process of how ancient China's Nü Wa was gradually transformed from the totemized female ancestor to the sub-urban temple god.

(3) Vestiges of Group Marriage

The form of group marriage governing gender relations among the Naxi nationality in the Yongning region was not isolated. Vestiges of prehistoric group marriage still persist among many nationalities of China's border areas, and these take different forms:

1. Group marriage of the age of the matriarchal clan.

The Ahmei people who live in the Conggu area on the eastern seaboard of Taiwan island and along the coastal areas of the island are an affiliate of the Gaoshan nationality. Until the mid-20th century, the Ahmei people still kept the fairly complete social system of the matriarchal clan age. They had well-organized social institutions such as clans, full brother clans, tribes and tribal alliances. These organizations followed the typical primitive democratic system, and chiefs at various levels had great prestige. Geographical villages were called She, which were originally matriarchal communes, but which later became matriarchal communities which served as production and life units. These were historically later than the matriarchal kin clans of the Naxi nationality in the Yongning region. In other words, the elder and younger sisters of the Ahmei's matriarchal kin clans, like those of the Yongning Naxi nationality, had taken their own "long-term *Ah Xiao*" or married them, and they then worked and lived together, forming the matriarchal commune with the matriarchal clan as its nucleus. These matriarchal communes, through disintegration, became the matriarchal communities.

The economic life of the Ahmei people mainly consisted of farming, hunting and fishing, with women doing the farming, and men the hunting and fishing. In sexual relations, the Ahmei people's individual marriage followed the practice of living with the wife. At the same time there was pre-marital and extra-marital sexual freedom, because group marriage among the clans still existed.[58]

Other Gaoshan nationality groups in Taiwan include the Pingpu people who lived in the plains and at the foot of the

---

[58] Ref: Xu Guoliang and Zeng Siqi, **Customs of the Gaoshan Nationality**, (Publishing House of the Central Institute for Nationalities, 1988), pp. 30-63 and pp. 102-105.

mountains. They were also originally a matriarchal clan society, but were later Han-ized. The Beinan people of the Gaoshan who lived to the south of the Beinan river and north of the Zhiben river still lived in the stage of matriarchal society. The Yamei people of the Gaoshan nationality lived on Lanyu island and several small islands around it, which are 45 nautical miles southeast of Taiwan island. They lived by fishing. Lanyu island features beautiful scenery, characterized by towering old trees, wonderful exotic flowers and fantastic rocks born out of vol- canic slurry. The Yamei people lived in "caves they dug them- selves, and wore simple clothes. Usually, males wore a T-shape cloth belt and females only tied a square cloth between breast and waist. In choosing spouses, it was always the female who took the initiative to choose a male. When a girl decided to choose a boy, the boy could go to the girl's family and live with the girl. ..."[59]

2. Group marriage of the age of the patriarchal clan.

The Dulong nationality who live in the Dulong river valley in Gongshan County, northwest Yunnan Province, retained the patriarchal clan system until the democratic reform of 1956. The marriage system there was a mono-directional outer-clan marriage system, whereby the female of clan A went to clan B and married male there, and the female of clan B went to clan C and married a male there. Wives went to live with their husbands. This form of marriage actually already existed in the age of the matriarchal clan and the only difference was that the male married out and lived together with the wife. When males became the main farm laborers, "living with the wife" gave way to "living with the husband" and hence the mono-directional outer-clan marriage system emerged. Among the Dulong na- tionality, family seniority divisions in marriage were not strict, and if a female's husband died, she then became the wife of her

---

[59] Wu Cunhao, **Marriage Customs in China**, (Shandong People's Publishing House, 1986), pp. 221-222.

husband's elder or younger brother, or even of her father-in-law or son, and the male, if he was rich, could simultaneously marry his wife's elder or younger sisters, and even aunts and female cousins. Every Dulong village had a "public house", where the young people could sing, dance and chat and meet friends, and even have sex. These activities were all approved by the society, although the young people had to abide by the marriage rules governing clans. Therefore, pre-marital sexual freedom existed but extra-marital sexual freedom was restricted because wives were bought.

In the Dulong language, marriage is called *pumawang*, meaning "to purchase a wife". The betrothal gifts usually consist of two head of cattle, one wok, one three-legged iron stand, iron knives, table salt, linen and woollen blankets. These must be presented before marriage. If the fiancee died after their engagement, the fiancee's younger sister must marry the fiance. If the female initiated a divorce or disengagement, the female must return all the engagement money. If the husband died, the widow should marry her husband's brothers or cousins on the parental side. If her husband's brothers or cousins on the parental side already had wives, they were also allowed to marry the widow. The male side did not have to give any betrothal gifts when the widow shifted to another husband in the male clan. If the widow did not shift husband and returned to live in her own parent's home, the female side had to return all the engagement money.[60] Here the social status of the female was obviously lower than that of the male.

The Li nationality on Hainan island still practised a patriarchal system before the democratic reform, and in areas that followed the "joint land system" (public ownership of the land) there were patriarchal family communes. In sexual relations, the Li nationality followed the Fangliao pairing system, meaning free integration in line with the principle of outer-clan

---

[60] Ibid., pp. 427-8.

marriage. Every village had a special house called *bulong gui*, and these were reserved for brothers and for sisters. Usually it was the males who took the initiative to look for a Fangliao friend. When dusk was approaching, the young men would go to the sisters' *bulong gui* of other clans in the group and if they found each other congenial, they would offer gifts to each other and live together. This was permitted by society, and it was normal for married women to receive male friends at her own parents' home. On festive occasions, men and women, in their holiday best, would venture out to gather and make friends. This included having sexual relations, as was permitted by local custom, and this was, moreover, not restricted only to unmarried young people. We read in one account:

> The Li nationality in Yaxian and Lingshui counties "have fasting days" after relatives die, unmarried or married young men and women could look for their friends and even have sex. Even if the husband or wife was present they could go their own way and nobody would interfere. On the very day when the wedding ceremony was held in the Li nationality of Baoting county, the males of the various villages of the bridegroom's Dong [Dong is equivalent to a 'district' or 'township'] could dine together with the females who accompanied the bride to the Dong. They could toast each other over dinner, sing songs in antiphonal style, and enjoy themselves. After dinner, they could talk of love and romance and even sleep together and no one will criticize them.[61]

Pre-marital and extra-marital sexual freedom thus also existed here.

The Li nationality followed the individual marriage custom of living with the husband but did not develop the practise of staying at the husband's home. The bridegroom and the bride did not sleep together on the wedding day. Early on the morning

---

[61] Ibid., p. 186.

of the following day, the bride would go back to her own parents' home after meeting the parents-in-law. She then lived in her own room and led a monogamous life. In the busy season, the bride would go to her husband's family and work for several days; her husband would go to his wife's family and work for several days and stay there for three or five nights. This went on for two to five years. The wife would stay with her husband's family only after she gave birth to a baby. The wife still belonged to her parents' family even if she stayed with the husband's family, and only the children belonged to the husband's family. After the wife died, she could be buried in the grave which belonged to the clan of her father and the funeral was handled by her parents' family. This shows that male and female social status among the Li nationality was comparatively equal.

In northeast China, the patriarchal clan, patriarchal families and vestiges of group marriage can be found to differing extents among the hunting Olunchuns, the nomadic Ewenkis, and the fishing Hezhes, as well as among the Taiya and Bunong people of Taiwan's Gaoshan nationality. Among these nationalities, the social status of the females was close to that of the females of the Li nationality, and not as low as that of the females of the Dulong nationality.

3. Inter-clan marriage in the period in which the clan was disintegrating.

As we mentioned earlier, the historical period during which "brothers and sisters" married and "created" mankind was the period when the patriarchal clan was disintegrating. The youth of the Jinuo nationality who lived in the Jinuo mountains in Jinghong county, Xishuangbanna, Yunnan province, and its surrounding areas in the period before the democratic reform would undergo an adulthood initiation ceremony when they were 15 or 16 years old. Following the ceremony, they would join two social organizations, *Raokao* (boys' organization) and *Mikao* (girls' organization) to find partners of the opposite sex.

Every village would set aside a "public house" for the young members of the *Raokao* and *Mikao* to go to find love and romance. In love matters, the young Jinuo people went through a clear three-step process: *Bapiao*, a secret love period in which they chose a partner; *Babao*, a public love period after having chosen a partner; and *Bali*, a period of love and romance and sleeping together. What warrants attention is that the Jinuo people's love affairs were conducted within the same village, and among boys and girls of the same age within the same clan. This broke the ancient rule that sexual relations were forbidden among boys and girls of the same clan. But formal marriages were still criticized because of the existence of the outer-clan marriage system. This could create a dilemma. The Jinuo nationality's love song titled *Bashi*, meaning "people of the same clan", vividly illustrates the dilemma inherent in allowing people to have romantic affairs but not permitting them to marry. One observer has written that "when the love song *Bashi* was sung within the clan, not only did the eyes of the middle-aged men and women fill with tears, but leading singers over sixty years of age would choke with sobs when they sang the touching words, and they would have to stop and wait before continuing to perform".[62] Nevertheless, in practical life certain social rules took shape with regard to marriages within the clan. For example, boys and girls of the same clan in Baka village, if determined to get married, could do so after gaining the approval of the village head and holding a ceremony to offer sacrifices to the ancestors.[63]

Yunnan's Nu, Bulang and some Lisu groups also all retained the form of the patriarchal clan but the exogamous marriage system was not so restrictive.

4. Classified kinsfolk system and pre-marital sexual freedom.

[62] Ibid., p. 464.
[63] Idem..

Alhough the system involving marriage outside the clan was broken at the time the clan was disintegrating, the marriage form of the clan period did not disappear even after the clan disintegrated. This was because, on the one hand, the sexual relations and intermarriage rules stipulated by the classified kinship system continued, and, on the other, because the special living quarters, customs, habits and holiday activities for realizing group marriage among clans were traditions which provided the young people with the basis for pre-marital sexual freedom. In addition, the custom of "not living with husband's family" also helped prolong sexual freedom.

For example, in kinship terminology, the males of Yunnan's Jingbo nationality called their children and the children of their brothers "my children", and the females called their children and the children of their sisters "my children", regardless of the closeness or otherwise of their relationship. In the marriage relationship, the husband would call his father-in-law and mother's brothers by the same designation, and his mother-in-law and the wives of mother's brothers by the same title, while the wife would call her father-in-law and the husbands of her father's sisters by the same title, as well as her mother-in-law and her father's law.[64] These were all features of the classified kinship terminology at the time of the clans, because then children or grandchildren of a brother and a sister or of sisters were born as potertial husbands and wives. In fact, the Jingbo nationality retained mono-directional marriage, that is, the daughters of mother's brothers were born as the daughters-in-law of father's sisters, while the daughters of father's sisters would not marry the sons of mother's brothers but would marry the sons of father's sisters of the daughter of her father's sisters. Therefore, clan A was forever what is called in Chinese the *zhangren zhong* ("father-in-law species") of clan B and clan B was forever the *guye zhong* ("son-in-law species") and the *zhangren zhong* of

---

[64] Ibid., p. 257.

Clan C, etc. In love and romance, the young people of the Jingbo nationality would first of all ask whether they were in line with the rules of *zhangren zhong* and *guye zhong*. This was exactly the same as the mono-directional outer-clan marriage system of the Dulong nationality, while the husband-shifting and unequal family seniority marriage systems both existed.

The Taluzhi of the Yi nationality in Yongsheng County, Yunnan Province, had a Nichama relationship in marriage form, which was similar to the *Ah Xiao* relationship of the Naxi nationality in Yongning region. When the girl was grown up, the seniors would set up a "girl's room" next to their residence and from then on, the girl could make Nichama friends with males who had affection for her and who did not belong to any branch of her family (her family branch could be regarded as the extension of the patriarchal clan). The girl's Nichama friend could come to the "girl's room" to live with the girl and go back in the morning, leading a monogamous life. The girl could either marry or not do so. If the girl did get married, her children belonged to the male's family and in the future could acquire their portion of the family property if the family was divided up.

The Ahxi people, another branch of the Yi nationality in Yunnan, had a public housing system similar to that of the Li nationality in Hainan. Every village designated two public houses, one for the girls to live in and the other for boys. Every evening, the boys of the village would go to the female public houses of other villages and hold parties with the girls, and the girls of the same village would stay in their house to entertain young men from other villages, and they were permitted to have sex.

The villages of the Hani nationality in Xishuangbanna and Lancang also had public houses. Some parents set up a special small house next to their bamboo houses for their unmarried girls to look for spouses in the evening. When dusk came, young men and women would gather in the public house, chatting or singing songs in antiphonal style. After the autumn harvest, young men would go to other villages in groups to "visit girls" and look for ideal partners. Lovers would date separately and express loyalty to each other and even have sex, and nobody would interfere. "Sleeping together was allowed by custom but girls could not become pregnant. If a girl did, she must marry the man she loved."[65]

Baikuyao in Nandan County, Guangxi, had the pre-marriage Wanbiao custom ("going for love and romance"). During holidays, wedding or funeral ceremonies, especially the traditional spring festival, young men and women in their dozens and hundreds, had a get-together, chatted and sang to each other softly. When a girl found an ideal young man, she would take him out of the gathering to run into the hills or to her home for the night. When the girl reached the age of Wanbiao, her parents would designate a special small house for the daughter to receive Wanbiao friends.

The Singing Festival of the Yao nationality of Dayao Mountain, Guangxi, and in Bapaiyao, northern Guangdong, was a special love festival. The festival, which was held by various villages in rotation, began on the 16th of the tenth lunar month and lasted three to nine days. The festival began with the offering of sacrifices to the ancestors which was followed by the singing of love songs. Young men and women of various villages gathered on a square outside the village. The young men took the lead in singing love songs to the girls who would carefully look at the boys and choose the friends they would pursue. After they made their choices, the girls would step forward and sing love songs to the young men. The girls and boys who had developed affections for each other during the singing, would leave the gathering and go to a quiet place on the hill in the evening and have sex. Those boys the girls did not pick up would come on the second day and sing love songs

---

[65] Ibid., p. 151.

one after another until the couples returned. The Yao nationality also had a custom called "opening the cowshed". From the 1st to the 3rd of the 1st lunar month each year, "those who were married or not and those who once had friends but were now separated from them could all sing love songs beside the villages or in the fields, and even have sex, without interference from anybody."[66]

Although there was not so much institutionalised pre-marital sexual freedom among some minority nationalities, there were still many traditional customs which provided ways for young men and women to engage in pre-marital sex, such as *chuan guniang* (Wa and De'ang nationalities), *gan tuozong* (Jingbo), and *ganba* (Dai nationality in Yunnan province), *zoupo* (Mulao nationality), *geyu* and *chuan zhai* (Zhuang nationality, Guangxi), *youfang, tiaoyue, zuomei* and *ganpo* (Miao nationality in Guizhou, Guangxi, Sichuan and Yunnan), *ganbiao* (Buyi nationality, southern Guizhou), *xingge zuoyue, youshan, taoconglan* and *kaizhongqin* (Dong nationality, southeast Guizhou).

The custom of "not living with the husband's family" did not preclude pre-marital sexual freedom among the Pumi nationality in the Zuosuo district of Yanyuan county, Sichuan province. There existed a custom of "three returns and nine home-comings" before a Pumi girl got married. Those who went to meet the bride must do so three times and each time the bride and bridegroom would not sleep together. Early in the morning of the second day, the bride was accompanied back to her parents' home. The bridegroom and the bride could sleep together on the fourth occasion when the bride was escorted to the husband's home but the bride would soon return to her parents' home. This would be repeated many times until the bride got pregnant. Public opinion maintained that the female was free to return back to her parents' home and continue her

---

[66] Ibid., p. 125.

free sexual life prior to pregnancy. In Zhenyuan and Baojing counties, Guizhou, the Dong girls, on the eve of their marriage, would sing songs in the antiphonal style for a whole night with the male friends they once had loved and farewell them before getting married. On the wedding day, the bride and bridegroom would not sleep together and the following day, the bride returned to her parents' home. Later, her mother-in-law and husband's younger sisters would come to take her home when the busy season came. The bride stayed for two to three days and then went back to her parents' home again. This would continue for three years. The bride would "put on whatever she did on the first occasion"[67] she was accompanied to her husband's home. The expression emerged, "Dong brides are new for three years".

Buyi girls in southern Guizhou have a custom of wearing a "fake shell" hat. After they get married, they do not stay with the husband's family for at least one or two years, or at most for three or five years, and even longer. The sisters-in-law and her husband's younger sisters must slip into her own parents' home and seize her by the waist while she is unprepared, and untie her braids by force and put the "fake shell" hat on her head. The hat was round across the brim and square at the back with the tail bending upward, and it was about 33 cm long and twined with a piece of black cloth. The bride would stay in her husband's home only when this had been accomplished. If the sisters-in-law and her husband's younger sisters failed to do so and the bride was able to free herself, they had to wait for the next occasion. They usually failed several times. The Yi, Zhuang, Miao, Yao and Hani nationalities all had the custom of "not living with the husband's family".

5. Pre-marital and extra-marital sexual freedom of the Tibetan nationality.

Before the democratic reform, the Tibetan nationality was

---

[67] Ibid., p.121.

a serf society of landed estates following a rigidly stratified marriage system within the social hierarchy. However, the marriage form and people's sexual lives were not contiguous. Many features of sexual relations and the form of marriage were due to the above social factors, but other aspects of the marriage system gave sons and daughters equality in inheriting family property, and there was flexibility in the matter of husbands going to live with wives' families, and vice-versa.

Young Tibetan women in Qinghai and Gansu participate in a ceremony called in Chinese *Daitiantou* ("getting married with Heaven") when they are 13 or 14 years old. After the ceremony, the girls can take boy friends home and live with them as though spouses. Any children born of the relationship are welcomed by society. Such girls can get married or stay at their parents' home for their whole life, together with their children, thus forming a matriarchal family.

Tibetan society was formerly divided into four grades and the form of marriage of every grade had its own features:

(1) *Geba* (feudal lords). They owned land, pastures and manors. Their family property and the "ancestors" were usually inherited by the patriarchal side. Males married one wife and maintained concubines, one of the major reasons for doing so being to have sons, and females were married out.

(2) *Chaiba* (bailiffs of feudal lords). They acquired portions of land different in size from their lords and paid taxes on their holdings accordingly. Apart from a few cases of monogamy, in most cases one wife would have several husbands or one husband would have several wives. The reason was to avoid the division of family and property, because after divisions of family and property, they must pay taxes on the basis of new family units and the amount of tax would increase greatly. If they could not pay their due taxes, their portion of land would be taken back by the lords and hence they would be downgraded to the status of *Duiqiong* (bankruptee). Therefore, if they had several sons, they would choose a virtuous and capable girl

within the same social echelon to be their wife. At the Tibetan wedding, the mother-in-law would give the key to the house to the bride, indicating that the mother-in-law delegated power to the daughter-in-law.[68] Public opinion maintained that one wife could harmonize several husbands and take good care of the family, and therefore should be praised and respected. Moreover, if there were only daughters and no son, a male would be chosen as the husband for their daughters. In both cases, weddings were, by and large, of the same format.[69] The son-in-law and the son had the same status in the family and they could inherit the family property and the "ancestors". Moreover, there were cases of mother and daughter sharing the husband, and the father and son sharing the same wife of the middle-aged deceased. In the former case, the marriage would be in the name of the mother and in the latter case, the marriage was in the name of the eldest son. These practices were all permitted by society.

(3) *Duiqiong* (landless serfs). Marriage rules governing this group were basically the same as those governing *Chaiba*. The only difference was that the marriages of *Chaiba* were mostly arranged by parents. *Duiqiong* did not face the risk of "dividing property", and therefore parents listened to their children and those concerned could choose their spouses within the same grade of their own accord.

(4) *Langsheng* (family serfs of *Geba* with no personal freedom). This group had no freedom in marriage, and were subservient to their masters.[70]

The above-mentioned forms of marriage could continue for long periods also because of the existence of extra-marital

---

[68] Ref: Yu Dingxian, **The Marriage Customs of Various Nationalities in China**, (Northern Women's and Children's Publishing House, 1988), p. 597.

[69] Ibid., pp. 588-595.

[70] Ref: Wu Cunhao, op. cit., pp.23-6; and, Chilai Qoiza, **Customs in Tibet**, (Tibetan People's Publishing House, 1982) pp. 190-197.

sexual freedom. For example, in the case of several sons sharing a wife, it was not difficult for the wife to look for a lover because the sons were out herding most of the time. "The ratio of males to females in Tibet was about 48 to 52",[71] meaning there were more females than males. Moreover, Yellow Hat lamas were not allowed to get married and one female could have several husbands. Therefore, many females led lives without formal husbands, and this conversely supported extramarital sexual freedom.

The marriage forms in Tibet took shape under special historical conditions and the author of this article maintains that they are not vestiges of prehistoric group marriage. However, the Daitiantou custom and the various possibilities for sexual contact between males and females would seem to be vestiges of prehistoric adulthood initiation ceremonies. Premarital and extra-marital sexual freedom were also a perpetuation of prehistoric sexual relations. The custom whereby sons and daughters were equal in inheriting the "ancestors" could also date back to the matriarchal-patriarchal system of the transitional period from the matriarchal clan to the patriarchal clan. All these should still be regarded as prehistoric vestiges.

Pre-marital and extra-marital sexual freedom also existed among the Mongolian and Yugur nationalities in China's pastoral areas. The Mongolian people of the Alashan Banner of today's Inner Mongolia have the custom of "appointing an object as a daughter's husband". When the daughter grows up, her parents appoint an object as her husband or marry her to an honorary husband, and henceforth, the daughter can sleep with other males. But usually she cannot formally marry again.

If a rich family of the Yugur nationality has no son or daughter, it can adhere to the custom of "acquiring a daughter-in-law without a son". The family can choose a girl from among the poor herdsmen, and when the girl reaches an odd-numbered

---

[71] Chilai Oiza, op. cit., p. 193.

age, such as 15 or 17, a ceremony is held in which she is "married to Heaven", and a grand banquet is held on this occasion. Henceforth, the girl becomes the daughter-in-law of the family and can receive males at home, lead a spousal life and inherit the "ancestors". It is thus evident that pre-marital and extra-marital sexual freedom had been always popular in non-Islamic pastoral areas of China.

CHAPTER TWO
GENDER RELATIONS IN PREHISTORIC CHINESE SOCIETY: ARCHAEOLOGICAL DISCOVERIES

Jiao Tianlong

Prehistory was the age when no textual records were made. The passage of time ensured that the cultural remains of prehistoric man were sealed underground by heavy earth, over which only puzzling myths and legends flickered as survivals into history, so dimly and mysteriously that even the ancient thinker Confucius (551-479 BCE) sighed when confronting the uncertainty of remote antiquity.

Now, the dense fog veiling prehistoric times is being cleared by modern Chinese archaeology with its unremitting field work conducted over more than seven decades. Archaeological excavations have uncovered dwelling remains, tombs and countless cultural relics that inform us about prehistoric man's life, productive activities and mental pursuits. From the damp caves of Peking man to the massive city-walls of the Longshan culture, from the crude stone tools of Yuanmou man to the exquisite jade objects of the Liangzhu culture, prehistoric Chinese society underwent a developmental course from lower to higher levels and from simpler to more complex forms. This process involved the constant advance of culture, as well as the continuous evolution of various social relations, among which gender relations played an important role comparable to that of a melody in harmonised music.

I. Settlement of Chinese Gens Communities

(1) To Begin with Banpo

Prior to the 1950s, Banpo was a small little-known village beyond the eastern outskirts of Xi'an City. Since 1954, when the Institute of Archaeology of the Chinese Academy of Sciences undertook the first of five seasons of large-scale excavation here, this locus has become world renowned because of the substantial prehistoric remains unearthed at this site which now constitute a vital chapter in Chinese prehistory.

The excavations at the Banpo site lasted for some three years, in the course of which 10,000 sq. m in total were examined. More than 40 rather complete house foundations, more than 200 tombs of various types, and nearly 10,000 tools of production and domestic implements were discovered. The most important discovery, however, was the clarification of a gens residential area measuring some 30,000 sq. m.

This settlement area is encircled by a large ditch about 5-6 m in both depth and width, and occupies a roughly spherical patch of territory wider from north to south then from west to east. Dwelling houses, stock pens, children's urn burials and ash pits are clustered in the centre. To the north of the settlement is a common cemetery; to the east, pottery making kilns. A small ditch 1.5 m deep and 2 m wide divides the residential area into two section. Each section contains a large house surrounded by small dwellings, with the doors all facing roughly in the same direction, largely to the south or south by west.

Banpo was the first Neolithic settlement site extensively excavated by Chinese archaeologists, and in its layout one can detect the organic principle of the gens community. Archaeologist Shi Xingbang, director of the Banpo excavations, believes that the Banpo settlement was the dwelling place of a matrilineal gens community, and that the two sub-areas at the site "may have belonged, respectively, to two groups or economic communities within the gens." The large houses were the gens heads' residences and also the gens members' meeting places.[1] Archaeologist Yan Wenming maintains that the inhabitants of the Banpo settlement probably lived in an organization of three grades, i.e. "the residents of a medium-sized house and several small ones constituted a household, those living in the houses of each large group separated from the other by the small ditch may be a community based upon a gens; and those of the whole settlement, presumably a phratry community formed of several gentes".[2]

The excavation at Banpo was a great event in the history of Chinese archaeology, yielding the first batch of reliable archaeological material which provided a picture of life and production in a prehistoric Chinese gens community. The Banpo people led a rather stable sedentary life, grew foxtile millet and other crops, and often engaged in hunting and fishing. They organized themselves into a large collective bound by blood relationships and living together in a village. Although their houses were different in size, small dwellings generally lay near a large building, which was largely the place for the gens members' common activities. Such differentiation reflected blood relations, but not a hierarchical disparity between gens members. The gens possessed a common burial ground and shared a pottery-making kiln cum workshop. The whole settlement displayed strong cohesion, and emphasised collectivism and equality. All gens members had no conception of either private property or differentiation between rich and poor.

The Banpo settlement is a type site of the earlier Yangshao culture, and the particular cultural complex it represents has been denominated by archaeologists the "Banpo type" and assigned to the absolute date 48-4300 BP according to radiocarbon-dating. Archaeological data indicate that, as early as 1,800,000 years ago, prehistoric man had already begun to

---

[1] **The Encyclopaedia of China** (Archaeology Volume), p. 34.

Yan Wenming, **Studies of Yangshao Culture**, (Cultural Relics Publishing House, 1989), p. 232.

create cultures in China's territory. During the very long pre-historic period, the model of social relations changed with the development of culture. The gens relations mirrored in the Banpo settlement merely constituted one link in the chain of prehistoric social development, and only against the vast background of Chinese prehistory can its position be understood in its full sense.

(2) The Periodisation of Chinese Prehistory

Prehistory in China, as generally accepted, refers to the long time span of time of ca. 1,800,000-4,000 BP that can be divided into four major stages, i.e. the Palaeolithic, Mesolithic, Neolithic and Chalcolithic Ages.

Palaeolithic

It was the childhood, as well as by far the longest period, of China's history. According to archaeological data recorded so far, Palaeolithic culture appeared in China some 1,800,000 years ago and it lasted from then on to 20,000-10,000 BP, chronologically roughly corresponding to the Pleistocene geo-logical period. This was the slowest and most arduous span of human history. Man encountered grim nature with its violent storms and fierce beasts when he finally "stood up" and his first priority was the struggle for subsistence, in the course of which our ancestors unceasingly reformed their bodies, undergoing the physico-evolutionary stages from early and late Homo erec-tus and early and late Homo sapiens; at the same time, they created a rich and varied culture.

Chipped stone tools were the essential implements of pro-duction for Palaeolithic man, and gathering, hunting and fish-ing became the basic means of living. In the light of cultural developments, environmental changes and other indicators, the Palaeolithic Age in China is divided into lower, middle and upper stages. The first goes back to c. 800,000-150,000 BP, when Peking man, Yuanmou man, and Lantian man walked the earth. The second stage, c. 150,000-35,000 BP, is represented by the cultures of Dingcun man in Shanxi, Dali man culture in Shaan-xi, and others. The third stage, c. 35,000-20,000 or 10,000 BP, has upper Shandongding man culture as its representative.

The archaeological data available at present are still not enough to reflect the then social structure. As inferred from the general developmental trend of prehistoric society, the primitive horde might have been the human social formation of the lower and middle Palaeolithic Age, while at its upper stage the gens organization probably emerged.

Mesolithic

This was the transitional stage from the Palaeolithic to the Neolithic and it occupied the geological post-glacial Holocene era. The archaeological research on Mesolithic China carried out up to the present have largely been limited to surveys, with no substantial discoveries, and inadequate type sites. The period is still subject to dispute. Generally speaking, the Mesolithic Age began 10,000 years ago and it varied in duration in different regions, with peripheral areas detained for relatively long periods. Its principal characteristics are as follows: chipped stone tools were still used as the main implements of production, with microliths being the most prevalent; polished artefacts were rarely made; and, pottery was not yet introduced. Gathering, fishing and hunting remained the chief human economic activities, while farming and stock-breeding did not emerge.

Neolithic

This period was characterised by agriculture, animal husbandry, pottery making and stone tool polishing. Henceforth, man began to turn to exploiting nature rather than depending on it. The foraging economy of fishing, hunting and gathering became less important, while the productive economy began to meet the needs of human life. With the development of the latter, culture flourished and human social relations were rapidly transformed.

The inception of the Neolithic Age in China was around 10,000 BCE, and it went through its early, middle and late evolutionary stages. The Chalcolithic Age subsequently began around 3500 BCE. Within the territory of Neolithic China, there was a considerably dense distribution of population. In more advanced regions, such as the Yellow and Yangtze river valleys, Neolithic sites have been discovered with almost as great a frequency as the occurrence of modern villages. Year after year, various populations lived relatively stably in certain areas different in natural environments, and the creations of past generations were inherited by successive ones that in turn made progress on the basis of old traditions, thereby forming different archaeological cultures.

Early Neolithic

Approximately 10,000-7,000 BCE. The sites known so far are mostly distributed in South China and represented by Zengpiyan at Guilin in Guangxi, the Spirit Cave at Wannian in Jiangxi, etc. Presently, in the Yellow River valley a few early Neolithic sites have also been recorded, such as Nanzhuangtou, Xushui county, Hebei province.

Middle Neolithic

7,000-5,000 BCE. Among the representatives are the Beixin, Peiligang and Laoguantai cultures in the Yellow River valley, the Pengtoushan, Chengbeixi and Hemudu cultures in the Yangtze valley, and the Xinglongwa and Zhaobaogou cultures in the Liaohe River valley.

Late Neolithic

5,000-35,000 BCE. Represented by the earlier Yangshao and earlier Dawenkou cultures in the Yellow River valley, the Majiabang and earlier Daxi cultures in the Yangtze River valley, and the earlier Hongshan culture in the Liaohe River valley. The Banpo settlement site belongs to this stage. It was a period when culture made great progress, and, with the further development of agriculture, population increased markedly, and settled villages of a rather large size came into existence in various places.

Chalcolithic

This was the transitional stage from the Stone Age to the Bronze Age. Although copper objects were introduced, their material was usually pure copper, and the techniques used in their manufacture were quite primitive. Typologically, most of them were small-sized artefacts, such as the awl, chisel, knife, ring and bell. Stone tools remained the main implements of production.

The Chalcolithic in China extends from 3,500 to 2,000 BCE. Outstanding achievements were obtained in agriculture, handicrafts and architecture. Social wealth sharply accumulated, the disparity between the rich and the poor became more and more striking, people's social positions tended to polarise, and their diversity in property and status increased continuously.

The Chalcolithic Age is divided into two stages:

Early stage

Dating from 3,500-2,600 BCE, and represented by the later Yangshao, later Dawenkou and Majiayao cultures in the Yellow River valley, the later Daxi, Qujialing and early Liangzhu cultures in the Yangtze valley, and the later Hongshan and Xiaoheyan cultures in the Liaohe valley.

Late stage

Dating from 2,600-2,000 BCE and including the Longshan, Central Plains Longshan, late Liangzhu, Shijiahe and Qijia cultures. It is designated the Longshan period in some archaeological literature.

(3) Evolution of the Prehistoric Settlement and Social Relations

In the long period of development from the Palaeolithic to the Chalcolithic, prehistoric Chinese settlements underwent corresponding stages of development. A settlement was the sum total of a prehistoric village and related buildings, such as the burial ground and handicraft workshop. It must have reflected the then social relations in the functions and manner of combination of its different houses, as well as its general layout.

Palaeolithic

Few dwelling remains of the lower and middle Palaeolithic have been discovered up to the present, because man migrated unceasingly or lived in caves. Presumably the social organization during this period was a small primitive horde with few members.

In the upper Palaeolithic, owing to the improvement in skills of subsistence, man built temporary camps and simple, crude houses in valleys and by lakes. At the Yanjiagang site outside Harbin city, two bonfire-making or temporary camps of upper Palaeolithic hunters, some 40 m apart, have been documented. One is an oval enclosure built by piling up more than 200 animal bones, measuring 4 m from west to east and 3 m from north to south; the other, a semicircle formed of above 300 bones. The bones are arranged in order and are mostly bear bones with man-made traces of chopping. Ashes were found within the structures. At Jigongshan, Jiangling, Hubei, a floor site has been found with vestiges of production coming from 50,000-40,000 BP, including five circles formed from pebbles. Nevertheless, upper Palaeolithic man still used natural caves as his major form of dwelling. That was the case, for example, with upper Shandingdong man who was quite culturally advanced; other evidence comes from the Xiaogushan site, Liaohai city, which is also a cave site.

These cave dwelling sites and water-side residential remains are all that remain of the earliest settlements in prehistoric China. They were very small in size and limited in the number of inhabitants they could accommodate, which implies that, although the gens organization had come into being, it was still tiny. Within the gens there must have been equality and mutual aid between the members, who struggled together against immense odds in order to subsist.

Early Neolithic

The sites of this period are usually rather small, about 10,000-20,000 sq. m for the largest and only several hundred sq.

m for the smallest. In South China, cave and midden sites account for the majority. Hunting, gathering and fishing remained the main economic activities, which restricted the growth of population, and obstructed the formation of large-sized settlements. At the Spirit Cave site, Wannian, Jiangxi, 22 fireplaces have been recorded, and a similar picture emerges from the Zengpiyan site, Guilin, Guangxi. These might reflect the appearance of organizations of different grades. If the whole cave was the dwelling of a gens, then this had split up into several small households, each having a fireplace of its own and not sharing a fireplace with others.

Middle Neolithic

The sites at that time were much larger than those in the early period, generally measuring over 20,000 sq. m. The Cishan site at Wu'an, Hebei, as large as 80,000 sq. m, is already a village of considerable size; the Jiahu site at Luohe, Henan, also covers a vast area of 50,000 sq. m. As for the general layout of the settlements in the Central Plain, we have no conception yet owing to the limited coverage of excavations. The available unearthed data only show that people largely lived in small semi-subterranean houses, and the residential quarters were separated from the common cemetery.

In North China, however, a rather complete settlement has been recovered by archaeologists in Inner Mongolia the Xinglongwa site within the territory of the Aohan Banner. Six seasons of extensive excavation, uncovering a total area of nearly 20,000 sq. m, have revealed a prehistoric village going back to c. 5,500 BCE. The village was built according to a unified plan and well-conceived layout. It was surrounded by a circular ditch, which measures at present 2 m in width, 1 m in depth and some 68 m around the perimeter. Within the ditch are 10 parallel rows of buildings, each comprising 3-7 houses arranged from northwest to southeast. The houses are semi-subterranean and generally cover 50-80 sq. m, the largest measuring 140 sq. m. Usually a house has an earth-pit fireplace, and pottery, stone and bone artefacts, animal bones and stoneware have occasionally been found in the rooms. The pottery includes jars, bowls and other vessels for daily use, showing that the houses served as dwellings for a semi-dependent productive and consuming unit. To the northeast of the village are densely distributed storage pits regular in both shape and arrangement, obviously left over from a repository shared by the villagers. West of the ditch, are two burials in side-by-side earth pits, suggesting that there was a common cemetery belonging to the whole village.

Unique among the villages known from prehistoric China in having houses built in rows and encircled with a ditch, the site has been named the Xinglongwa settlement model by its excavators. Concerning its social organization, archaeologist Yan Wenming infers that each house must have been the dwelling of a pairing family, each row of houses would have constituted the living place of a household, and the whole settlement may have belonged to a community based upon a gens.[3]

The gens community consisting of pairing families and households must have been the universal form of mid-Neolithic social structure. Its members were organized into a whole by blood relations, shared common property, and were buried in the same cemetery after death. There was no differentiation between rich and poor, nor was there hierarchical social stratification, and human relations seem to have been governed only by the principle of equality.

Late Neolithic

Settlement sites from this time are more plentiful, and several have been fully excavated, including the famous Banpo site, as well as the Jiangzhai site, Lintong county and the Beishouling site, Baoji county, both in Shaanxi province, the

---

[3] Yan Wenming, "Research on Settlement Patterns in Neolithic China", **Schriftfest in Celebration of Su Bingqi's Fifty-fifth Anniversary in Archaeology** (Cultural Relics Publishing House, 1989).

Dadiwan-A site in Qin'an county, Gansu, and the Beizhuang site in Changdao county, Shandong.

These settlements share with Banpo the characteristic of being relatively independent and self-contained, while the residential quarter, production area and burial ground were closely combined and at the same time distinctly demarcated. Every settlement was a self-contained and self-sufficient economic unit. The buildings within it were arranged according to a unified plan, and all houses, tombs, pottery-making kilns, storage pits and stock pens were organically linked in a well-conceived design, which made the whole pattern coherent and internally oriented. The most representative is the layout of the Jiangzhai settlement.

The Jiangzhai settlement site lies in today's Lintong county, Shaanxi province, closing to the Weishui River in the north, to Lishan Mountain in the south and to the Linhe River in the west. It consists of a residential quarter, a pottery-making workshop and a burial ground. In toto, it has an oval plan with a minor axis of 160 m from north to south and a major axis of some 210 m from west to east, covering about 33,600 sq. m. The arrangement of its houses strikingly demonstrates that its inhabitants were in a large, densely populated collective. The houses are clustered into five complexes, each comprising a large building and several medium and small ones. These complexes roughly form a circle, all doors facing onto the central open space of the settlement. The small houses generally have an area of 10 sq. m or so, and contain a fireplace in the centre and implements for daily use placed to the left and right. Occasionally there is a low earthen bed on one side of the door. This sort of house was suitable for 2-4 persons to dwell in, and probably housed a small-sized pairing family lacking economic self-sufficiency.

The medium-sized houses measure 24-40 sq. m, and also contain a fireplace, implements for daily use and one or two low earthen beds. They were capable of accommodating 5-10 persons. Around them there are always several closely-arranged small houses. Their inhabitants must have been organized into a relatively stable household managing its own economy. The residents of the medium house were probably the seniors of the household, as well as its old and young unmarried members.

The big houses usually cover 53-87 sq. m, the largest measuring 128 sq. m. Inside the door of these is a double fireplace at the centre and an earthen bed on either side, showing that the house served a residential purpose, and at the same time fulfilled a common use function as the room between the beds must have been a place for public activities and meetings. Formed of a large and several medium and small houses, the complex may have represented a gens grade organization, with the large house serving as the residence of the gens head. The five complexes at Jiangzhai represent five gentes who lived in the same village, and the whole settlement belonged to a phratry higher than the gens.

This phratry community possessed a strong primitive communist character in the allocation of wealth. The pottery-making workshop by the river obviously belonged to the whole settlement, and pottery production was organized by the phratry community. All large houses and stock pens were collective property. Grain storage pits were distributed around the complexes, each generally having 3-4 groups, the largest cluster comprising 13 pits. These repositories evidently did not belong to particular small houses, and their stores were gens-owned.

Since the pairing family had little property, there cannot of course have been a disparity in wealth. This is also revealed by the shape of tombs and the number of funeral objects. The Jiangzhai tomb is a rectangular earth pit in general only capable of holding one corpse, and its grave goods consist of merely a few pottery vessels for daily use and implements of production. Little difference between graves can be detected.

These features of the Jiangzhai settlement are very like those displayed at Banpo, as well as at the Beishouling and

Beizhuang sites (see above). Such a universal settlement structure suggests that society in the late Neolithic was still fairly egalitarian, and people, tied by blood relations, lived together, jointly took part in production, and shared wealth equally.

Early Chalcolithic

This was a turning point in social evolution of prehistoric China. Distinct changes were brought about in settlement patterns, which reflected the fact that prehistoric social relations stepped into a new epoch. Differentiation emerged within the settlement. There was clear diversity in the quality and dimensions of houses: some sites have been discovered to have houses immense in size and of elaborate construction. At the Dadiwan-B site, Qin'an, Gansu, for example, a large house covering some 290 sq. m has been revealed. It was partitioned into an anteroom, a back room and two siderooms. In the anteroom are massive columns, with a diameter of 87-90 cm, and a very large fireplace 2.5 m in diameter. The floor was lined in many layers, then laid with a sort of concrete mixture of clay and pottery fragments, and its surface finally polished. In front of the house was an open space with two rows of post-holes, fronting a high-level public centre. Nevertheless, most houses were still simple, small and semi-subterranean or earth-and-timber surface buildings.

Moreover, changes also appeared in architectural design. At some sites, double and even seven- to eight-roomed houses have been unearthed, each for a family far more complex than those in single-roomed dwellings. The partitioned residence indicates that the family living there may have included more than one married couple. At the same time, there was still the single-roomed house, its inhabitants probably being a pairing family. This co-existence shows that the family institution was diversifying.

The disparity between rich and poor is distinctly displayed in burial practices. Three grades of tombs appear in late Dawenkou culture. The large tomb was equipped with a coffin and chamber and could contain some hundred funeral objects, all products of the highest technological level of that time, including white pottery vessels, burnished and painted wares, ivory articles, and jade artefacts. At some sites, large tombs are arranged in a row or concentrated on a single plot, which seems to indicate the appearance of a rich family group. Among the medium-sized tombs only a few have coffins and they contain one to several dozen grave goods. The small tomb is so tiny it can only contain the corpse of the deceased without a coffin and a few simple mortuary objects or even none at all.

Settlements also show a diversity in size, with central settlements coming into existence often with small-sized settlements clustered around them. The larger central settlement was prominent not only for its higher developmental level, but also for its vast area. For example, the Dawenkou site in Tai'an county, Shandong province, covers an area of more than 800,-000 sq. m, the Dadiwan site at Qin'an in Gansu 360,000 sq. m, while ordinary sites measure only several ten-thousand or even less than ten-thousand sq. m. This difference reflects a change in social relations. Equal, undifferentiated society was gone, and a gap between rich and poor had appeared and gradually widened. Rich and powerful persons emerged at some central settlements. The large-, medium- and small-sized tombs of the Dawenkou culture show that the gens members were differentiated into various ranks. The initial ruling authority in ancient China may have been formed in this period.

The diversity between settlements also marked the emergence of ruling relations. Economically and culturally more advanced large settlements conquered small ones around them by force of arms and subjected the inhabitants of the latter to their rule. From tombs of that time have been unearthed a large number of weapons, including the stone *yue* battle-axe, often entombed with the deceased as a symbol of military leadership, mirroring the ascendancy of warfare in people's minds. Plundering warfare resulted in the rapid concentration of wealth in the hands of a few military leaders and the acceleration of social polarisation between the rich and the poor.

Late Chalcolithic

This period was most typified by the appearance of the early city and castle, which indicates that prehistoric settlement had developed to the stage of differentiation between town and country. The gap between the rich and the poor continued to widen and this ushered in serious class oppression and antagonisms.

In the Yellow and Yangtze river valleys, more than ten cities and castles have so far been documented. These are widely diverse in area, ranging from 10,000 to 200,000 sq. m. At the Chengziya site, Longshan township, Zhangqiu county, Shandong province, a city site has been discovered surrounded by rammed earth city walls, which enclose an area of more than 200,000 sq. m. The construction of such a large city required not only unified planning, but also the organization of an enormous labour force.

Public facilities and residential houses in cities were also constructed on elaborate lines. At the Pingliangtai site, Huaiyang county, Henan province, a city of the Longshan period has been unearthed. It features underground pottery drainpipes in the middle of a city gateway, stretching from inside the city to the exterior, along the lines of the drainage that was a feature of later cities. Excavations within the city have revealed more than ten houses built of adobe and partitioned into rooms, with tamped earth platforms and corridors, features absent from ordinary settlement sites.

The differentiation between town and country accelerated that in social rank: the gulf between rich and poor widened and social stratification into aristocracy, common people and slaves emerged. The deceased of different ranks were often buried in various plots as shown, for instance, in the cemetery of the Longshan culture at Xizhufeng, Linqu county, Shandong Province, where large tombs lie to the south-west and small ones to the northeast, forming two burial grounds 180 m apart. The former were reserved for the burials of persons of extremely high rank and feature not only a coffin and chamber, but also side and foot partitions for grave goods. The surface of the coffin and chamber were decorated. Funeral objects were many and of exquisite workmanship. These include jade *yue* battle-axes, knife and crown emblems, "egg-shell" black pottery goblets, *lei* pots and *gui* tripods.

A similar picture has been brought to light in the Liangzhu culture, where the tombs of aristocrats are also separated from those of common people. The former are generally situated in enormous artificial tumuli several tens of thousands of cubic metres in size, while the latter are located near settlements, with the pits capable of holding only the deceased. The aristocratic graves usually contain large numbers of fine jades, and lacquer and pottery articles, among which the jade *cong* and stone *yue* attract the greatest attention. The *cong* was a sacrificial ritual object, while the *yue* served as the symbol of military leadership. Some examples of the two types are incised with complete figures of mythical beings in big crowns and leather body armour, riding fantastic beasts and conveying a sense of power and grandeur. Evidently the tomb-owners qualified to possess these objects must have been kings with great spiritual and military power.

In contrast to the above, slaves of lowly rank appeared. At Bianxianwang, Shouguang county, Shandong province, in the tamped-earth foundation-ditch of a city wall, a pit for the foundation-lying ceremony has been found to contain the skeletons of a pig, a dog and a human being. The human was buried with the pig and dog as a sacrificial victim to be offered up at the ceremony commemorating the construction of the city wall. In the Liangzhu culture, immolated slaves have also been discovered in a few aristocratic graves.

Prof. Yan Wenming believes that the Chalcolithic roughly corresponded to the earliest recorded dynasties and that its late stage may have been the age of Yao and Shun.[4] This was the time when prehistoric Chinese society was ending, and the early Chinese state was emerging in some advanced regions, ushering in an epoch of class oppression and violent domination.

II. Burial Institutions and Prehistoric Gender Relations

Relations between the sexes constitute a component part of social relations. During prehistoric times, the development of gender relations was synchronous with the evolution of prehistoric society, and so the marriage patterns, the division of labour and social ranks, and other relations displayed features characteristic of the social formation where they were practised.

Among the relevant archaeological data, the layout of settlements and the structure of houses reflect to a certain extent the changes of the prehistoric marriage and family pattern, and, similarly, gender relations are represented in the burial institutions. However, it should be pointed out that, as archaeological data are static and one-sided, our research cannot be comprehensive and we can only make inferences regarding prehistoric gender relations in the light of available evidence. At the same time, the burial institution was restricted by a number of complex social factors, not only the influence of contemporary life, but also the effects of historical tradition and religious belief, and so it reflects to some degree contemporary social relations but cannot be a complete expression of them.

(1) The Tomb of Multiple Burial and Matrilineal Gens Society

In 1958-1959, an archaeological team from Beijing University excavated the cemetery of the Yangshao culture at the

---

[4] Yan Wenming, "A Brief Discussion of the Origins of Chinese Civilisation", in *Wenwu* (Cultural Relics), 1992:1.

Yuanjunmiao site, Huaxian county, Shaanxi province, and uncovered 57 tombs, including 28 of mixed multiple burial. This
rather unusual form of entombment aroused immense interest
in academic circles, and many researchers have published papers on the social system it reflects. It is generally recognized
that, following the excavation at Banpo, the discovery provides
another piece of important evidence in Chinese archaeology,
suggesting that Yangshao culture was at the stage of matrilineal
gens society. The most representative view belongs to Prof.
Zhang Zhongpei, who prepared the report on the excavation of
the Yuanjunmiao site. He maintains that "the Yuanjunmiao
cemetery belonged to a tribe comprising two gentes", whose
grass-roots organization was "the matriarchal household" and
that "the society was a matriarchy". Based upon his analysis of
the burial institution and the number of funeral objects, he
concludes that in the gender relations in this gens-tribal society
"woman played the leading role in production", "social position
of females was generally higher than that of males, and that of
girls higher than that of the boys. Mothers already had the
conscious need to distinguish their own daughters and pass
property on down to them; moreover, relying on her privileged
position, she could confer full adult status on the most favoured
daughters".[5]

Since the excavation at Yuanjunmiao, similar joint burials
have successively been discovered by archaeologists at a dozen
Neolithic sites in Gansu, Shaanxi, Henan and Shandong, enabling researchers to more comprehensively discuss their origins,
distribution and formal variety, as well as the gender relations
they reflect.

Available evidence indicates that multiple burial was largely
practised in the Yellow River valley. It first appeared in the
Laoguantai and Beixin cultures of the mid Neolithic Age,

---

[5] Archaeology Teaching and Research Section of the History Department at Beijing University, **The Yangshao Cenetery at Yuanjunmiao**,
(Cultural Relics Publishing House, 1983).

prevailed at the early stages of the Yangshao and Dawenkou cultures, and then almost disappeared. This burial custom was therefore prevalent in the Yellow River valley during the middle and late Neolithic. It should be emphasised that even at the sites with this burial as a popular practice, single burial tombs still existed in a number of places simultaneously, which is an important phenomenon that cannot be overlooked in research into gender relations mirrored in joint burials.

The multiple burials can be classified into same sex and mixed sex burials; most feature secondary entombment. Same sex burials are common in the cemetery of the Dawenkou culture at the Wangyin site, Yanzhou county, Shandong province. For example, in Tomb No 2240 22 individuals are buried, and those that are identifiable are all males. This type of tomb is also present in the Yangshao culture as demonstrated by the Yuanjunmiao cemetery, where three adult males are jointly buried in a single tomb.

Mixed sex burials are, however, more common, and tombs containing mixed burials often hold a large number of persons of both sexes and various ages. At the Yuanjunmiao site, of the 28 joint burials 15 belong to this category, such as Tomb 405 which contains 12 human skeletons 6 adult males, 3 adult females, 2 children and 1 young person. In adult tombs of mixed sex joint burial, the two sexes are extremely disproportionate in number, as for example, in Joint Burial 6 at the Shijia site, Weinan county, Shaanxi province, where the remains of 28 have been identified as 24 males and 4 females, and in Tomb 456 at the Yuanjunmiao site, which contains 7 skeletons-6 males and 1 female.

Scholars have advanced different explanations for the above phenomena. A large number believe that joint burial reflected close blood relations in the gens system, with the single sex tomb burials belonging to brothers, sisters or other similar blood relatives, while the mixed sex burials, judging from the distinct quantitative unevenness between males and females, represents the natural state of gender proportions in the household or gens, and these groups were also blood relatives.

Nevertheless, there is a remarkably wide divergence of opinion on the question of whether these burials represent a system of matrilineal or patrilineal descent. Zhang Zhongpei, quoted above, maintains that the society did not necessarily belong to the matrilineal gens system. On the basis of a great deal of ethnographic material, he argues that these joint burials merely represented a burial custom in gens society, which could be either matrilineal or patrilineal or even bilinear, and the multiple burial tombs of the Yangshao culture did not represent matrilineal households.[6] Prof. Yan Wenming in turn cautiously points out that the Banpo type of Yangshao culture developed in the gens community period, when the community was generally a three-grade organization formed of the household, gens and phratry, and "blood relations may chiefly have been matrilineal, especially in regions with developed agriculture. But this does not preclude the possible existence of the patrilineal system in some areas; it was no essential prerequisite that this system be matrilineal".[7]

Descent in prehistoric society was a very complex phenomenon difficult to fully examine from fragmented archaeological data. For research into prehistoric gender relations, descent, of course, is of great significance, and even greater importance is attached to the findings from settlements and tombs that mirror the gender' social positions. Moreover, joint burial was only a burial custom in certain regions during certain periods, and the gender relations it represented could not be separated from the developmental stage of the society of the time.

---

[6] Wang Ningsheng, "A Study of the Burial Customs and Social Organisation of Yangshao Culture: A Discussion of the Theory of Yangshao as a Matrilineal Society and its Methodology", *Wenwu*, 1987:4.

[7] Yan Wenming, "Burial Institutions and Social Systems of the Banpo Type", **Studies of Yangshao Culture**, (Cultural Relics Publishing House, 1989).

In the discussion of settlement patterns we have seen that prehistoric Chinese society in the mid and late Neolithic was one of equality and collectivity, without differentiation between rich and poor, and no hierarchic oppression. There might have been some division of labour between the sexes, but their relations were based on equal partnership. Since joint burial prevailed in this period, the gender relations it reflected must have corresponded to the then socio-developmental stage.

Tombs of joint burial reflect just such an equal, collective social principle. Each tomb of this sort has the deceased numbering up to dozens, while the funeral objects it contains are few, and these were shared as collective property. This would suggest that the concept of private ownership had not yet appeared, and there was little concern for wealth. The female's centrality cannot be detected in the burial manner, because the overwhelming majority of the joint burials occur in tombs of secondary burial, with the human skeletons moved from other places and placed together in a disorderly fashion. Some tombs contain female remains of primary burial, and male tombs of that type have also been found. In fact, joint entombment was merely a burial custom with no direct connection between those buried and their social position during their lifetimes.

A similar picture emerges when single burials co-exist with joint burials. According to statistical data, in Banpo Type cemeteries with mainly single burials, pottery vessels of the male average 2.43 pieces a tomb and 2.09 pieces per person, which includes 17 persons having above 5 pieces each, accounting for 13.9% of the total of the deceased males covered by the statistic, and the maximum for one person being 11 pieces. For females, the average is 2.84 pieces a tomb and 2.17 pieces a person, with 16 persons having more than 5 pieces each. The latter 16 account for 19.8% of the total of the deceased females. The average number of pottery accompaniments of the females exceed those of the male, but the maximum for one female is only 9 pieces, less than that of several males. If we combine this with the fact that in terms of the number of other mortuary implements of production the males slightly exceed the females, then it should be recognized that the sexes in the Banpo type cemeteries were roughly equal in terms of tomb furniture holdings.[8]

Tools reflect the roles of the sexes in productive activities. In Banpo type cemeteries, "deceased females have far fewer implements as burial accessories than do males,... For both sexes, handicraft implements constitute the main type of burial accessory implying that both sexes often took part in manual labour, including spinning". A statistical analysis of mortuary farm implements also indicates that "both sexes participated in agricultural production, and there is no evidence that woman were the main farm labouring force".[9]

Therefore, gender relations in middle and late Neolithic China were characterized by equality, and the sexes worked together and shared wealth. Perhaps lineage in most regions was matrilineal, but there was no matriarchy, no rule and oppression of man by woman.

(2) The Tombs of Mixed Sex Double Burial and Patrilineal Gens Society

The joint burial of one male and one female first appeared in the late Neolithic Age, increased in number during the early Chalcolithic, and gradually disappeared in the late Chalcolithic in all areas except for the Gansu and Qinghai regions of the Qijia culture. Obviously it was also a distinctive burial custom of a specific prehistoric period.

Such burials were more common in Dawenkou culture and have so far been recorded at a dozen or so sites, when they first appear in the earlier strata then becomes very common in the middle period of the site. The male is invariably laid in the tomb

---

[8] Ibid.
[9] Ibid.

on the left while the female is on the right. This uniformity clearly had specific meaning, and scholars have variously explained the phenomenon.

Prof. Tang Lan writes: "In the Dawenkou joint burials, the funeral objects are mostly placed on the side of the male, suggesting the subjection of the female,... some women may have been forced to be buried as sacrifices to their patriarchs".[10] He argues further that the Dawenkou culture saw the advent of the patriarchal family and the initial formation of slave society.

Most archaeologists, however, do not agree with this view, believing Dawenkou tombs of this type simply represent the joint burial of a couple, not of a husband with his immolated wife. They infer that mid Dawenkou culture witnessed the beginning of the transition from the matrilineal to the patrilineal gens.[11]

A third view argues against the simple identification of the joint burial as the tomb of a couple or of a male with an immolated woman, and insists that the mid Dawenkou culture was the transitional stage from pairing marriage to monogamy, and that the joint burial tomb was simply a reflection of the special circumstances denoting that transitional stage. After the end of the Dawenkou culture, this type of tomb vanished, and, with the establishment of patriarchy, couples were separately buried in single tombs.[12]

What the above theories all have in common is that all of them regard the adult male and female jointly buried in the double burial tomb to be a couple and interpret this as an indicator that the patrilineal gens or patriarchal society had

[10] Tong Lan, "The Beginnings of Slave Society in China 5000-6000 Years Ago", **Papers on Dawenkou Culture**, (Qilu Shushe, 1981).

[11] Cai Fengshu, "On the Nature of Society in the Dawenkou Culture Period", in **Wen Shi Zhe** (Literature, History and Philosophy), 1978:1.

[12] Lu Bo, "On the Origins of Private Ownership in China in the Light of Dawenkou Culture", **Wenwu**, 1976:7.

emerged. Interpreting the gender relations this burial custom reflects calls for a comprehensive approach, taking all relevant archaeological data into account. It should first be pointed out that in the period of Dawenkou culture, such tombs only constitute a very small proportion of the total number of burials. Of the 133 tombs excavated in the cemetery at Dawenkou, only four sexually-identifiable burials belong to this category, while at the Yedian cemetery site in Zouxian county, Shandong province, only 6 of 80 are of this type. A roughly similar picture emerges at other cemeteries of the Dawenkou culture. Thus this burial custom was rare, single entombment remaining the most prevalent burial institution, and in large, rich tombs co-burial is absent.

What this says about the subjugation of women is therefore unclear, because even though the burial accessories were often placed on the male side this does not indicate that the items were not shared. In some tombs, mortuary articles are put mainly on the side of the male, as is seen in Yedian Tomb 47, where 68 objects are close to the male, while the female has only two hair-loops and four perforated stone knives, in other tombs, however, the burial objects placed on the female side are rather more numerous than those on the male side. For example, in Yedian Tomb 31, on the side of the female are 42 articles, while the male has only an ivory spear-head and six strings of neck ornaments.

It would seem, in fact, that the sexes were rather equal in social position, and there was no subjugation of the female by the male. Although differentiation between the rich and the poor had appeared in society, it was disparity between different strata but not between the sexes. Some women retained high rank as exemplified by the cemetery at Dawenkou, where the largest, richest tomb belonged to a woman, who was provided with not only an elaborate coffin and burial chamber but also more than 180 burial accessories, including a number of exquisite artefacts rarely seen in Dawenkou culture.

Nevertheless, the entombment of two adults of opposite sex in the same pit is still of great importance, and it probably reflected a change in the marriage pattern and probably suggests that the monogamous marriage model was gradually emerging in the middle Dawenkou culture period.

According to the numbers of implements of production used as burial accessories in the single burials of the middle Dawenkou culture period, the sexes then began to differentiate in terms of their labour roles. In the cemetery at Dawenkou, of the 17 male tombs identified, 14 contain implements of production, while among the 14 tombs identified as those of females, only four have such grave goods. The Dawenkou burial ground at Dadunzi, Peixian county, Jiangsu province, has 14 tombs containing tools as burial accessories. 11 belong to males, accounting for 78.6% of the total, and 3 to females, merely 21.4%. These data seem to indicate that the male's role was tending to rise, even though both sexes took part in labour.

The middle and late Dawenkou culture belonged to the early Chalcolithic Age. The change in marriage patterns and the increase in the male's role in labour may have mirrored the fact that the patrilineal gens community began to be the principal social formation. This inference, naturally, does not exclude the possibility that the matrilineal system survived in some regions.

In the Qijia culture of the late Chalcolithic Age, there were also a number of mixed sex adult double burials, where the deceased are buried in a regular manner, i.e. the male lies in an extended supine position, while the female lies on her side, with the limbs contracted and facing the former. Hence most researchers believe that the male held a dominant position in society while the female was subordinated, and that patriarchy had already appeared in the culture.[13]

This is a misinterpretation. The burial institutions of the

---

[13] Xie Duanju, "Qijia Culture in the Upper Yellow River Valley", **Archaeological Discoveries and Research in New China,** (Cultural Relics Publishing House, 1984).

Qijia culture were considerably complex. Single burial remained most prevalent, and joint burial was only practised in rare cases. Among the tombs of the latter type, apart from mixed sex double burials, there are also joint burials of adults with children or babies, as well as multiple burials. Therefore, mixed sex double burial was only one burial custom.

The female's burial lying sideward with flexed limbs should not be regarded as a manifestation of her subordination, because flexed burials have been quite commonly recorded in Qijia culture, even in tombs of single burial. Moreover, in the mixed sex joint burials, both sexes have funeral objects, giving no obvious sign of a relationship between principal and subordinate.

In the Qijia culture period, prehistoric Chinese society approached its end, and class antagonism distinctly sharpened, which resulted in the appearance of female immolation with the deceased. In Tomb 76 at the Huangniangniangtai site, Wuwei county, Gansu province, two adult skeletons of the opposite sex have been discovered, the male's complete, while the female's has no skull. In Tomb 314 in Liuwan county, Qinghai province, a male skeleton lies supine in a coffin, while a female's is in a flexed position outside the coffin and with one leg beneath it. Evidently these women were immolated maidservants.

Judging from the above, gender relations became more complex in the period of Qijia culture. On the one hand, both sexes of the same stratum remained rather equal, with no indicators of relationships of oppression or slavery, signalling no lowering in the female's position; on the other, in terms of different strata, males of higher status seem to have also enslaved females of lower rank, and social differentiation developed synchronously with the worsening of the female's position.

This status of gender relations revealed in the Qijia culture seems to demonstrate the general character of gender relations overall at the end of Chinese prehistory.

III. The Prehistoric Goddess World: Chinese "Venuses"

Prehistoric female figures have attracted great interest in academic circles. From the beginning of the 20th century, there have been successive discoveries in Europe and West Asia of Palaeolithic and Neolithic nude female statuettes, called Venuses by archaeologists and students of art history. They provide valuable material for research into prehistoric religious beliefs.

Among the archaeological data known so far from Palaeolithic China, there has as yet been no report of such female figures, but at Neolithic and Chalcolithic sites, clay and stone female sculptures have been brought to light in recent decades. These Chinese "Venuses" form a rich and varied world of goddesses and indicate that the worship of goddesses also prevailed in prehistoric China.

(1) Goddess Altars at Dongshanzui

In 1979 and 1982, Liaoning archaeologists carried out two seasons of excavation on a terrace north of Dongshanzui, a small village on the western bank of the Daling River in Kezuo county, Liaoning province, and revealed a group of stone altars and two clay nude female statuettes. This was the first time Chinese archaeologists discovered prehistoric "Venus" figures, and the discovery caused a sensation in the academic world.

In all three altars were unearthed. They were rectangular, round and multi-circular respectively and arranged roughly along an axis from north to south. The rectangular one covers a larger area than the other two, measuring 11.8 m from west to east and 9.5 m from north to south; the wall-foundations on its four sides are built of wrought stone blocks and have a remaining height of 0.15-0.40 m. Within them are stones in three clusters, the largest of which are pointed, flat-bottomed sandstone blocks slanting to the northeast. 15 m from them stands a round altar, measuring 2.5 m in diameter. Its base is a loess stratum 50 cm thick, encircled with rectangular stone flakes and supporting a layer of pebbles of much the same size. Of the multi-circular altar only three connected circles now remain, two of them having a clearly defined outline and enclosing a layer of pebbles.

Two small clay statuettes of pregnant women and twenty-odd relics of large-sized human figures have been recovered from near the round altar. The former were both unearthed with the head and right arm missing. They are 5 and 5.8 cm in height respectively (Plates.4 and 5). They represent nude women in a standing position, belly distended and with steatopygous hips, the left hand placed on the upper belly, and genitalia indicated by an incision. The remains of large human figures are mainly incomplete upper and lower torsos, approximately half life-size. From the remaining details it can be inferred that the original works must have been seated representations in frontal view, legs crossed and arms intersecting at the belly, but the sex of the figures is unidentifiable. These findings suggest that a large group of idols was placed on the Dongshanzui altars.

The pottery shards unearthed at the site indicate that the altars belonged to people of the later Hongshan culture living c. 5,000 BP.

The discovery has excited Chinese archaeologists. Scholars unanimously recognise that the Dongshanzui relics are important data for research into the social system and religious belief of the Hongshan culture. Prof. Zhang Zhongpei says that the size of the Dongshanzui sacrificial site is a demonstration of the then complex religious system in which goddesses held a lofty position, and that "the religion with the goddess as the major divinity was associated with matriarchy". Prof. Yu Weichao believes that the clay female sculptures on the round altar were idols worshipped by the Hongshan people, symbolising fertility and agricultural goddesses, while the rectangular altar was a platform for sacrifice to the Earth Mother symbolised by the group of standing pointed stones.[14]

(2) The Goddess Temple at Niuheliang

Niuheliang is a hilly ridge on the boundary between Ling-yuan and Jianping counties, western Liaoning province. In 1983-1985, archaeologists discovered over ten sacrificial sites and tomb groups of the Hongshan culture, among which a goddess temple with clay female statues is another important discovery following the excavation at Dongshanzui. The temple consists of a multi-roomed major building and a single-roomed house, lying on an axis from north to south respectively, 2.05 m apart from each other. The former is 18.4 m long from north to south and 6.9 m from west to east, and has a main room and several connected siderooms, antechambers and a rear chamber, forming a complex structure. The latter measures 6 m in length and 2.65 m in width. Judging from the unearthed structural remains of the main building, its walls were built of timber and daub and painted on the surface with bright designs in red, yellow, white, and other colours.

The images of the deities in the temple have been shattered by collapsing roofs, leaving the floor heaped with fragments. Among these are the remains of anthropomorphic figures, as well as some animal figurines. The former include fragmented heads, shoulders, arms, breasts and hands. The arms and shoulders are fine and smooth, exhibiting feminine features; the broken breasts vary in size and shape, and clearly characterise the female form. The most conspicuous fragment is an almost complete human head, roughly life-sized, with a plump face, red in colour and having long, smoothly contoured ears, a slightly raised nose-bridge and bright and piercing eyes with shallow sockets and eyeballs represented by inlaid round jade pieces. Every detail distinctly displays feminine characteristics. On the crown is a looped head-dress (Plate 3).

---

[14] "A Seminar on the Dongshanzui Site", *Wenwu*, 1984:11.

The unearthed fragmented clay sculptures belong to about 5-6 individuals and show no male features, strengthening the view that these were goddess images. These figures vary in size, the smaller being life-sized, the larger two or three times life-size; in age, there are older as well as younger females depicted. In posture, they either have arms akimbo, outstretched hands, bent elbows and clenched fists, all vividly represented. In short, we have a group of goddess idols around a central image and arranged on different levels.

In association with the broken figurines, clay pig's lips and giant bird's claws have been unearthed, presumably remains of the animal deities worshipped along with the goddess images. This pantheon dates back more than 5,000 years. A majestic goddess oversees this pantheon in the sacred temple, and serves as the supreme deity in the minds of the Hongshan culture people.

A recent archaeological discovery suggests that there may be another, still larger temple at Niuheliang. In the middle of the ridge, a vast platform has been found measuring 159 m long and 175 m wide. It has stone walls on all sides, with some fragments of the wall surface brought to light, suggesting that it might have been the foundation of a large religious building. The goddess temple described above, standing in an inferior position in both size and location, must have been auxiliary to the building represented by the platform. In the deposits of burnt clay found north of these remains, a large clay human ear, evidently remaining from a deity figurine, has been discovered.

900 m south of the goddess temple, another altar of the Hongshan culture has also been discovered. It has a round plan and was surrounded by a wall formed of light red granite stakes; at present there remains a platform in three tiers.

Around Niuheliang and over an area of 1.5 sq. km, there have been discovered six groups of stone tombs, but no remains of residential settlements. The tombs lie on small hills surrounding the goddess temple located roughly at the centre. The tombs are built of stone, enclosed with stone walls and covered with stones, and have a square or rectangular plan. In general, the burials contain fine jade objects, implying that the tomb-owners must have been influential figures of their time.

The goddess temple, sacrificial altars and stone tombs constitute an organic cluster, which, combined with the absence of dwelling remains in the vicinity, indicates that this area was exclusively used as a holy site. Here, the goddess temple co-existed with the graves of the nobility where the Hongshan people buried their deceased ancestors and offered sacrifices to their ancestors and to the goddesses in the temple. The excavators, including Sun Shoudao and Guo Dashun, believe that these goddesses were regarded by the Hongshan people as their remote ancestors and worshipped them as such.[15]

(3) The Stone Sculptures of Pregnant Women from Houtaizi

The Houtaizi site is located at Jingoutun township, Luanping county, Hebei province. In 1983, stone female figures were excavated by workers in a brickyard in the course of obtaining clay with a bulldozer. The local administration of cultural relics undertook a salvage excavation at the site and discovered that the finds belonged to the Zhaobaogou culture of the middle Neolithic.

At this site six stone female sculptures were unearthed. With the exception of two broken figurines, they were fairly intact. They are fashioned from gabbro, mixed rock and diabase, imperfect in shape and simple in workmanship.

---

[15] Sun Shoudao and Guo Dashun, "The Discovery and Study of the Heads of Hongshan Culture Goddess Images from Niuheliang", *Wenwu*, 1986:8.

Among them are five statuettes of naked pregnant women in sitting positions, with distended bellies, swollen breasts, and hands on their bellies, and some feature defined genitalia. The most complete three measure about 32 cm in height (Plates II-9).

These are the most complete and representative stone "Venuses" discovered to date by Chinese archaeologists. Their original location is unknown owing to the serious damage of the site, but the presence of a lower base suggests that they must have been set upright somewhere on the site.

In 1989, archaeologists recovered a stone goddess at the Baiyinchanghan site in Linxi county, Inner Mongolia, providing evidence for inferring the location of the Houtaizi sculptures. The site is the remains of a settlement dating from more than 7,000 BP, where a stone goddess 35.5. cm high stands near the fireplace of a semi-subterranean house. She is depicted as a pregnant woman with a swollen belly and projecting breasts. Her hands are placed on her belly and the legs are bent in a squatting position. A number of ruined houses have also been excavated at the Houtaizi site, and so it is inferred that the stone female figures unearthed there must also have been set in a house.

Furnishing houses with goddess images similar in shape, size and posture was a manifestation of the goddess's high position in the religious beliefs of the times. Representing the goddess as a pregnant woman must have ensured more descendants and conferred blessings on the growing family. Some specialists maintain that the Houtaizi stone female figures were images of a fertility goddess and may have served as protective deities of the home.

(4) Female Figures in the Plastic Arts of Northwest China

Among the pottery artefacts recovered from sites of the Yangshao and Majiayao cultures in Gansu and Qinghai provinces, a common feature was the modelling of clay human heads at the mouths of vessels. Artistic potters, by making full use of the characteristics of the vessel form and by applying various sculptural and coloured, painted design techniques, created elaborate human representations, including masterpieces with distinct female features.

One of the representative works is a late Yangshao painted pottery bottle with a human head at its mouth unearthed from the Dadiwan site in Qin'an county, Gansu. It is 31.8 cm high and is topped with a sculpted human head, with a round hole made through the centre as the vessel mouth. The hair is long at the back and on both sides and cut short across the forehead. The face is plump, the nose prominent, the eyes and mouth feature open-work, and the ears are perforated for wearing ornaments. The belly of the vessel is painted black with three groups of elaborate. The entire vessel resembles a pregnant woman in an elaborate. She is sedate and graceful, and stares into the distance with a slightly open mouth as if she is about to say something (Plate 8).

This bottle could have had a practical function, but, as its wall is perforated by the mouth and eyes, it does not seem likely to have been an ordinary vessel for daily use. The traces of a break and restoration on its upper belly dating back to the time of its use suggest that the bottle was extremely treasured. This leads to the inference that it might have been a ceremonial vessel used only in grand sacrificial activities.

On a painted pottery vase unearthed from the Majiayao culture cemetery at Liuwan, Qinghai province, not only the head but also the body of a human figure is represented. The vessel measures nearly 34 cm in height, the human head was sculptured and attached to the neck of the vessel, the hair is draped over the shoulder, the nose is slightly raised, and mouth somewhat opened. Below, a naked pregnant woman is vividly depicted on the body of the vessel. Her hands are placed on her stomach and her legs are stretched apart. Two round lumps represent her breasts, and two black dots are painted to represent her nipples. Between the legs are exaggeratedly sculpted and painted female genitalia. The entire figure is a representation of a woman in an advance stage of pregnancy or about to give birth. Such a sculpture shrouds the vase in mystery. Evidently the vessel was not a purely aesthetic work but a sacrificial container embodying a desire for bumper harvest and an entreaty for fertility, and the naked pregnant woman was the goddess capable of bringing such felicity to her worshippers (Plate 7).

(5) Worship of the Goddess and Women's Status in Prehistoric Times

The above archaeological data indicate that at the latest in the middle Neolithic, the worship of the goddess made its first appearance in China, and in the early Chalcolithic, it developed to its full extent, represented by Hongshan culture.

From the middle and late Neolithic, female sculptures have been discovered. They are quite similar in shape, showing no obvious difference in size and height. For example, the more complete stone statuettes from Houtaizi are all about 32 cm high. This reflects that goddesses enjoyed an equality in position, and there was little differentiation between primary and secondary deities. This was a sacred world without ranking divisions.

Goddess images from that time, including those sculpted on pottery, have largely been found in ash-pits or ruined houses which implies that there were no specific temples built for them. The common people enjoyed ready access to them and they could readily express their wishes to their deities and pray for their blessing at any time.

However, by the early Chalcolithic the presence of deities in every home was no longer a phenomenon, at least in Hongshan culture. Goddesses were reverentially moved onto sacred altars in majestic temples, and thus they became separated from the residences of human beings. Moreover, in relatively large areas, common religious precincts were set far apart from residential villages, and were constructed exclusively for the worship of divinities and ancestors, as at the sacred site of Niuheliang. At the same time, differentiation of rank emerged among the deities themselves. The dimensional variety of the goddess images in the Niuheliang temple was a reflection of ruling relationships within the world of divinities.

The evolution of goddess worship in both form and content, as revealed by archaeological data, was apparently synchronous with the change in social relations in the human world. As we have seen, the beginning of the Chalcolithic marked a turning point in prehistoric Chinese development, and henceforth an egalitarian society was gradually replaced by an unequal one and the differences in status between human beings increased daily. This change is reflected in the changes in goddess worship.

Furthermore, as most researchers have pointed out, worship of the goddess represented esteem for woman and for the mother's fertility, and it demonstrated the high status of women in prehistoric times. This was especially apparent in Neolithic regions where agriculture was the main means of subsistence.

Although great transformations in social relations in prehistoric China began in the Chalcolithic, these represent a social stratum differentiation but not a fall in the position of women. On the contrary, as the majestic goddess images of the Hongshan culture display, respect for the mother and for female ancestry reached an unprecedented height. The changes in prehistoric Chinese social relations from equality to inequality caused some community members to lose social status, but this group comprised both women and men. The emergence of class society and the consequent formation of the state in China took place without a necessary concomitant decline in the overall social position of women.

CHAPTER THREE
THE SOCIAL RELATIONSHIPS
OF MEN AND WOMEN
IN THE XIA-SHANG ERA

Du Jinpeng

1. The Succession to the Throne under Patriarchy

The succession to the throne for Chinese written history's most ancient rulers (Tang) Yao, (Yu) Shun and (Xia) Yu, it is believed, took the form of *shan rang* (abdication in favour of a chosen successor). This is reiterated in the most ancient Chinese written historical and philosophical works, such as **Shang Shu** or **Shu Jing** (The Book of Documents), **Meng Zi** (The Works of Mencius), **Mo Zi** (The Works of Master Mo), and **Shi Ji** (Records of the Historian). Although both Yao and Shun took their own sons into consideration when searching for a successor, they eventually decided to choose men of ability rather than their own progeny. For example, in discussing the succession from Yao to Shun **Shi Ji** records: "Yao understood that his son Zidan was not worthy of the leadership, and so he conferred the leadership on Shun". This was later regarded as a commendable example of the judicious choice of a man of ability rather than of kin.

However, another set of historical documents are more sceptical and they attribute the accession to the throne among these sage kings as typified by the use of force. **Zhushu Jinian** (The Bamboo Annals), or the edition titled **Jizhong Zhushu**

Jinian (The Bamboo Annals from the Tumulus at Ji), record how when Yao lost his moral integrity, Shun threw him into jail and installed himself on the throne. This interpretation also appears in *Meng Zi* and *Hanfei Zi* (Works of Master Han Fei).

Despite the different views of ancient, and contemporary, historians on whether the throne was conferred or usurped, one thing is unquestioned: none of these ancient sages vacated their thrones in favour of their sons.

A change occurred in Yu's late years. According to *Meng Zi* and *Shi Ji*, Yu's first choice Gaotao died before him, so he made Yi his successor. After Yu's death, Yi abdicated in favour of Yu's son Qi, while Yi himself lead a reclusive life on Jishan Mountain. Qi enjoyed popularity, but Yi lacked political experience, and so if he were installed on the throne, his rule would not necessarily be guaranteed a smooth administration. The regional leaders all abandoned Yi and supported Prince Qi, whom they claimed to be their true lord. Qi's replacement of Yi therefore seemed to be a matter of course.

However, other sources give a different picture. In *Zhushu Jinian* we read that, "as Yi blocked Qi's access to the throne, Yi was killed by the latter".[1] It was also recorded in *Zhanguo Ce* that Yu made Yi his successor and Qi an assistant to Yi, but in his old age Yu discovered that Qi was not the right person to govern the country and so he accordingly conferred power on Yi. Qi and his followers later wrested the country from Yi. According to *Shi Ji*: "Qi's ascent to the throne was questioned by the Youhu people, and so Qi despatched a military expedition against the latter. The battleground was at Gan.... Qi defeated Youhu Shi and acquired the allegiance of the entire country". In this version, Qi's

---

[1] *Zhushu Jinian*, as quoted in *Kuodizhi* (A Comprehensive Geography) and "Wu Di Benji: Jijie" of *Shi Ji*.

succession to his father was quite gory. Qi inherited his father's crown, and so initiated the long Chinese tradition of 'rule by one family'. *Hanshi Yizhuan* (Han's Commentaries on the Book of Changes) neatly encapsulated this change in the following passage: "The Five Emperors regarded the country as belonging to everyone and so they found the ablest men to run it, whereas the Three Kings regarded the country as their own private property and so bequeathed it to their children".[2]

The royal genealogy of the Xia dynasty was as follows:

```
Yu---Qi---Taikang
 1    2    3
Zhongkang---Xiang---Shaokang---Yu---Huai---Mang---Xie
    4          5         6        7     8      9     10
Bujiang---Kongjia---Gao---Fa---Jie
   11        14      15    16   17
Jiong---Qin
  12     13
```

The horizontal sequence indicates father-to-son inheritance, while the vertical sequences indicate older brother to younger brother inheritance. This diagram thus demonstrates that thirteen kings left the throne to their sons, two to their younger brothers and one to his nephew. The royal succession was totally patrilineal, and no woman of the royal family ever ascended the throne.

The Shi Ji's account of the royal succession during the subsequent Shang dynasty is also corroborated by inscriptions found on excavated oracle bones. The royal line of succession reconstructed from these two sources again shows that royalty was patrilineal.

---

[2] Quoted in "Biography of Dongxi" in *Jin Shu* (the History of the Jin Dynasty).

2. An Analysis of the Marriage System in the Xia and Shang Dynasties

(1) Emperors and Their Wives and Concubines

During the Xia-Shang period, a king had one wife and more than one concubine. According to *Shang Shu* and **Shi Ji**, the founder of the Xia dynasty Yu married into the Tushan tribe. *Lienü Zhuan* (Lives of Honourable Women) recounts how "Qi's mother was a daughter of the Tushan tribe, and was married by Yu as his wife". *Shui Jing* (The Book of Waters) provided the same information in quoting from *Lüshi Chunqiu*. The Tushan woman should, therefore, be regarded as Yu's wife rather than as his concubine.

In *Zuo Zhuan* we read: "Once upon a time Jiao of the Guo people, after slaying Zhenguan, launched an attack on the city of Zhenxun. King Xiang of the Xia was killed, and his pregnant wife fled to her maternal tribe the Youreng Shi. There she gave birth to Shaokang, who on growing up held the position of Muzheng (Officer in Charge of the Royal Herds). Jiao sent Shu to assassinate him. Shaokang escaped to the Youyu people and there became Paozheng (Director of the Royal Kitchens). The Youyu people had respect for Shaokang as he was a descendant of the kings of Xia. They gave two girls named Yao to him in marriage as wife and concubine respectively".

In Qu Yuan's epic poem *Tianwen* from the anthology *Chu Ci* we read a set of questions which are posed to shed light on the status of women: "What did Jie obtain from his expedition against the Mengshan tribe? How evil was Weixi [i.e. Jie's wife]? And how did Tang fight them?" These questions were asked in response to an ancient legend, which is explained in *Zhushu Jinian* as follows: "Jie waged a battle against the Minshan (sic) tribe. The tribe presented Jie with two of its women, Wan and Tan. Jie married them, and inscribed their names on jade, while leaving his first wife Weixi alone in Luo".[3] It was also recorded that the Youshi tribe sued for peace with Jie of Xia by presenting him their daughter Meixi. Meixi won Jie's favour and destroyed Xia in conspiracy with Yiyin.[4] Apart from these references, it is also recorded that Jie fled to sea together with his concubines when he was attacked by Tang. After his death, his son "Xunzhou married his concubines, and fled to the remote north".[5]

The oracle bone inscriptions also contain many references to the wives of the Shang kings. The table below shows the "formal royal wives" (*zhengqi*), or in some scholars' terminology "legal spouses" (*fading pei'ou*), of the kings of the Shang dynasty based on the late Prof. Chen Mengjia's **Comprehensive Explanations of Oracle Inscriptions from The Ruins of Yin**:

King	Wife	King	Wife
Shiren	Bigeng	Qixin	Bijia
Shikui	Bijia	Qieding	Bisi & Bigeng
Dayi	Bibing	Xiaoyi	Bigeng
Dading	Biwu	Wuding	Bixin, Kui & Wu
Dajia	Bixin	Qiejia	Biwu
Dageng	Biren	Gengding	Bixin
Dawu	Biren	Wuyi	Biwu
Zhongding	Bisi & Bikui	Wending	Bikui
Qieyi	Bisi & Bigeng		

Of the seventeen emperors, thirteen had one legal spouse, two had two legal spouses, and one had three legal spouses. The question emerges: What social custom does this represent? Prof.

---

[3] *Zhushu Jinian* as quoted in *Taiping Yulan*.
[4] "Jinyu" in *Guoyu*.
[5] *Kuodipu*, as quoted in *Shi Ji*: Xiongnu liezhuan: Suoyin

Hu Houxuan's explanation many years ago was that "the Yin kings practised monogamy plus polygamy; they initially married one wife, and subsequently married others".[6] However, according to a more widely accepted hypothesis, the Shang kings married only one formal wife. The impression that polygamy was practised was created by some of these kings' re-marriage following their wives' death, or by the practice of "retro-conferment of title" (*zhuizun*), i.e. in the event of a concubine's son ascending the throne he would nominate his mother as his late father's formal wife. For example, one of King Wuding's three legal spouses, Lady Hao, died quite early. Because her son was already a "small king" or crown prince, Lady Hao retained her status as her husband's formal wife. The other two spouses obtained their titles either through re-marriage or "retro-conferment". According to **Shang Shu** and the exegesis of that book by the Han dynasty scholars Ma Rong and Zheng Kangcheng, Wuding's two sons, Zugeng and Zujia, were step-brothers. Both of them became kings, successively. Zugeng's mother succeeded Lady Hao, while Zujia's mother was granted the title by her monarchical son. This was why King Wuding had three legal spouses. King Zhongding had two wives, but only one son, Zuyi, who later became king, and so one of his wives must have died earlier. King Zuxin had two wives, but also had two monarchical sons. The third woman must have obtained her title through retro-conferment by her son King Zuding.[7]

The above table is limited to kings' legitimate spouses enjoying filial sacrifices, which, according to the late Prof. Guo Baojun, "serves as evidence of the contemporary practice of

---

[6] Hu Houxuan, **Essays on Oracle Bone Inscriptions and History of the Shang Dynasty**, Vol. 1.

[7] Li Yanong, **Social Life of the Yin Dynasty**, (Shanghai People's Publishing House, 1955), p. 20, f.n.

monogamy".[8] However, in addition to formal wives, monarchs also had concubines.

In general the sons of concubines could not succeed to the throne. *Shi Ji* contains the following passage: "King Diyi's eldest son Qi could not succeed to the throne because of his concubinary mother, whereas his younger brother Xin became a successor to the throne because his mother was queen". According to *Lüshi Chunqiu*, King Zhou's mother was a concubine when she gave birth to Weizi Qi and Zhongyan, but became the formal wife when she had Zhou. Zhou's parents wanted to make Qi the crown prince. The advisor argued that it was a ruling that a concubine's son could not accede to the throne, if the son of the king's formal wife was available. Therefore, Zhou acceded to the throne. There could have been a dispute if Zhou and Qi were blood brothers, but the fact that King Diyi had both a wife and concubine is beyond question.

According to *Shi Ji*, King Zhou, a lecherous drunkard, only heeded the advice of women, especially Daji, a beauty from the Yousu tribe. Later, Jiuhou presented his beautiful daughter to Zhou, but the woman could not abide Zhou's lascivious ways and so was put to death. Later when Zhou imprisoned Emperor Wenwang of the Zhou dynasty, Wenwang's people sought beautiful women and fine horses as exotic gifts to please Zhou, from which detail it is also clear that Zhou had more women than a single wife.

In the Shang dynasty, a king could have many consorts. The statistics provided by Prof. Hu Houxuan show that King Wuding alone had 64 women, including nearly thirty designated by the title Lady (*Fu*), a title used in the Shang dynasty to designate a king's consort. The names of eight of King Xiaoyi's consorts have appeared in oracle bone inscriptions, and they were given posthumous titles taken from the Heavenly Stem system of

---

[8] **China's Bronze Age**, (Shenghuo Dushu Xinzhi Sanlian Press, 1963), p. 193.

serial designation: Geng, Jia, Bing, Ding, Si, Xin, Ren and Gui.[9] It is quite evident from these facts that polygynous marriage was practised by the kings of the Shang dynasty.

There were four categories of consorts during the Xia-Shang period:

The first category roughly corresponds with what we today term "betrothal", and Yu's union with the daughter of the Tushan tribe is a good example of this category. However, I do not want to further discuss this category for the present.

The second was sororal polygyny (*yinghun*), and examples are provided by the practices of two kings, Shaokang and Jie. According to *Zuo Zhuan* and *Shi Ji*, as mentioned above, when Shaokang sought refuge with the Youyu tribe, the Youyu people provided him with two sisters named Yao in marriage. *Zhushu Jinian* records that when King Jie waged a war against the Minshan tribe, the latter presented him two girls called Wan and Tan. Sororal polygyny is further corroborated as a practice by the story of Shun. *Shi Ji* records that when Siyue recommended Shun to Yao as his successor, Yao married his two daughters to Shun and asked them to wait in attendance on Shun. The practice of marrying two sisters on one occasion can be seen as a remnant of the Pulunuan pattern of marriage or the harbinger of the later type of *ying* polygyny. The later *ying* polygyny was a marital bond characterized by concubines who came together with the formal wife, and these concubines were called *ying*. According to Prof. Hu Houxuan, "when an ancient emperor (*tianzi*) married, three other states of the same clan name would each marry a woman to him, and all three women were each accompanied by a 'sister' [or female cousin] designated as *zhi* and *di* respectively. Thus the emperor would marry twelve women at one time. If an enfeoffed *zhuhou* (ruling noble) married, two other states would similarly provide wives, and as a result the enfeoffed ruler might be the husband of nine

---

[9] Hu Houxuan, op. cit.

women at one time. A nobleman below an enfeoffed ruler in the hierarchy would marry one wife plus a *zhi* and a *di*, as he was not supposed to marry with those outside of his own state. This explains why Wuding had so many wives".[10] This sounds quite convincing. There are references in **Yi Jing** to this practice, and one passage relates how a "concubine returned to her parents with the *di* who had been married to her husband together with her", and another passage discussing Diyi's daughter relates how the husband's attire could not even compare with that of her *di*. Chinese history from the Yin dynasty·into much later times, as the late Prof. L Zhenyu pointed out, bears constant witness to such a marital pattern.[11] In fact, we can trace it back further, at least to the Xia period, as mentioned above. This system of polygyny was well developed during the Shang dynasty, and as the late Prof. Shang Chengzuo has pointed out the word " 娸 " in oracle bone inscriptions referred to the very marriage in question. The Zhou dynasty saw the full flowering of the custom. When the marquis of Han went to see Emperor Li, it was recorded, the latter married him to his sister "along with a vast number of *di* that reminded one of extensive clouds. The marquis was overwhelmed by the spectacular scene at the palace gate".

Ying polygyny had its origins in primitive group marriage. However, it served to continue to provide men access to more than one women and terminated women's earlier exposure to more than one man. Engels was right when he said that having more than one wife was a product of slavery. Only a minority of people in special positions were afforded this luxury. Engels was also correct when he asserted that monogamy, in the context of the system of slavery, only meant a single spouse for

---

[10] "Studies on the Systems of Marriage, Clan, Patriarchy and Child-bearing of the Yin Dynasty", in Hu Houxuan, op. cit.

[11] **Chinese Society in the Yin-Zhou Period**, (Shenghuo Dushu Xinzhi Sanlian Press, 1962), p. 107. The first edition of the book appeared in 1936.

women, never for men. Those Xia-Shang emperors and kings with their hosts of concubines, in addition to a wife, are an excellent example of this.

A third category of consorts were those provided by plunder. Jie's acquisition of a woman from the Youshi people, whom he had fought against, is a good case in point. His expedition against the Minshan tribe won him two more women, Wan and Tan. All three of Jie's women were loot of sorts. Quite a few wives of other Xia-Shang emperors and kings were prisoners of war. It is no coincidence that the character *qie* was used in oracle bone inscriptions to refer to both female slaves and late emperor's spouses. As Shang dynasty slavery was practised at the group level, captured men and women were a chief source of slaves. It is no surprise that some scholars have equated *qie*, as human sacrifices, with female prisoners of war. It is quite likely that the *qie* group, besides providing human sacrifices, also served emperors as a pool of candidate spouses. Otherwise, it is hard to explain why the same term is used for both groups.

The fourth category of consorts consisted of those received as tribute from lesser states. **Shi Ji** records how the Jiuhou tribe presented as tribute their beautiful women to Zhou, and details the Jiuhou people's quest for good-looking women and other treasures to present to Zhou in order to please him and secure the release of their leader Wenwang from imprisonment. Jie, the last emperor of Xia, was also believed to have been a great hunter of women. A considerable part of his collection, I would say, were gifts extorted from smaller states.

One question we need to answer in our discussion of the royal marriage system of the Shang dynasty is why are there oracle bone inscriptions about a certain emperor's having more than one father and mother. For example, the divinations by Wuding referred to Mothers Jia, Bing, Ding, Wu, Si, Geng, Xin, Ren and Gui, while those by Zugeng and Zujia cited Mothers Si, Geng, Xin, Ren and Gui. These were interpreted by Guo Moruo in the 1930s as evidence of polygynous practices. The plural fathers or mothers as recorded in oracle bone inscriptions, in Guo's opinion, suggests a plural sub-consanguineous marriage, which could help explain the practice of using the word "father" in reference to one's uncles. The bronze halberd inscribed with "plural fathers" unearthed at Baoding convinced him of "the evident existence" of this type of marriage in the late Shang dynasty.[13] Such a view, however, was questioned by such scholars as Lü Zhenyu[14] and Hu Houxuan[15] immediately it was published, and was rejected by Guo himself in the 1950s. Perhaps Guo Baojun was correct when he argued it was questionable that Wuding's use of the term "father" with reference to Yangjia, Xiaoxin and Xiaoyi, "should perhaps immediately be interpreted as remnants of the polygamy or pairing marriage among the forefathers of the Shang people". Instead, he subscribed to Engels' view that when the family came into being, kinship terminology remained ossified, and the latter continued as convention, while the former underwent change. When monogamy made its appearance, the term "father" continued to be used to refer to one's father's brothers, but by that time this was a linguistic fossil in kinship terminology harking back to the times when polyandric marriage was common.[16] However, some scholars have recently argued in favour of Guo Moruo's view of the 1930s that the early Shang marriage was at the Pulunuan stage, and that the change toward pairing marriage only took place in the late Shang, while the entire dynasty was dominated by the matrilineal lineage.[17] This point of view is subject to discussion, however.

---

[12] "Hanyi", in Daya section of **Shi Jing**.

[13] **Research into Ancient Chinese Society**, (People's Publishing House, 1977), p. 201.

[14] **Chinese Society in the Yin-Zhou Period**, (Shenghuo Dushu Xinzhi Sanlian Press, 1962), pp. 104-6.

[15] "Studies on the Systems of Marriage, Clan, Patriarchy and Childbearing of the Yin Dynasty", in Hu Houxuan, op. cit.

[16] **China's Bronze Age**, (Shenghuo Dushu Xinzhi Sanlian Press, 1963), p. 194.

The exogamy of the Xia people is well documented. Examples include Yu who married into the Tushan tribe, Xiang into the Youreng tribe, Shaokang into the Youyu tribe and finally, Jie whose first wife came from the Youshi tribe and two concubines, Wan and Tan, from the Minshan tribe.

This remained a practice of the Shang people. Tang, for example, married into the Youxin people. Among Wuding's over sixty wives or concubines, "Ladies Zhen, Zhou, Chu, Ji, Jiang, Lai, and Pang were all named after their tribes or states. It is also recorded that he 'married a woman of Zheng.' All are instances of exogamy".[18] Only Lady Hao shared the same surname with Wuding, suggesting an endogamous bond. However, some argue that what Wuding and she had in common was that they were of the same tribe, which actually consisted of two sub-tribes. Marriage between the two sub-groups was permissible[19] as it could be regarded as exogamy in its broad sense.

(2) Monogamy among Ordinary People

Engels wrote in **The Origins of the Family, Private Property and the State** that polygyny was definitely a product of slavery, as only few men in particular positions could afford to have many wives. While a nobleman of the Xia-Shang era might own more than one woman, an ordinary man could have only one. *Baihu Tong* (Comprehensive Discussions in the White Tiger Hall) contains the following passage: "Why are ordinary people called '*pi fu*'? *Pi* means 'pair.' A man and his wife constitute a pair, just as *Yin* and *Yang* are mutually dependent for existence. A family refers to a husband plus a wife. A wise ruler should never leave a grown-up person unmarried". The numbers of men and women in a society are basically the same. Unless there is a polyandrous adjustment, the more women one man marries,

---

[17] Chen Yunluan, "Change in the Lineage and Kinship of the Yin People", in **Journal of Hainan Teacher's College**, 1991:2.

[18] Hu Houxuan, op. cit.

the more bachelors that society will contain. However, the two systems have never been empirically encountered together within the same society.[20] The inference that monogamous marriage prevailed among ordinary people in the Xia-Shang period is therefore quite understandable.

Large numbers of small Shang graves have been excavated at the Yinxu site near Anyang. They are believed to be occupied by ordinary people. These graves, consisting of two pits containing a male and female respectively, are neatly planned and arranged. Their common features include an unvaried combination of a male and a female occupant (male on the left and female on the right), skulls pointing in the same direction, and only a short distance separating one tomb from the next. Statistics show that there are about 300 small tombs of husband-wife joint burial in the western and southern sections of the Yinxu site. Three pairs of these, all located east of Qijia village in the southern section, warrant further examination.

Tombs 256 and 259 are 0.85 m from each other, and cover 2 sq. m each. The heads of the corpses, in both cases, point to the south. Tomb 259, to the east of Tomb 256 and with a shaft 2.15 m deep, contains a wooden coffin covered in red lacquer. The tomb occupant, laid prone, is a male. The funeral objects include a pottery *gu*-cup, a *jue*-cup and a plate. Tomb 256, located a little behind Tomb 259, features a 4.6-m-deep pit. The female occupant lies on her back and tomb artefacts include a pottery *gu*-cup, a *jue*-cup, plate, a *gui*-food container and jade ornaments.

Tombs 233 and 234, are 0.7 m apart and each covers an area of 1.5 sq. m. Again, the heads point south. Tomb 234 is located to the east and a little behind Tomb 233. Its pit has a depth of 2.1 m. The red lacquered coffin contains a male in a prone posture. The funeral objects include a pottery *jue*-cup, a *gu*-cup,

---

[19] Zhao Lin's view is quoted in Jia Shiheng's "Several Aspects of Women's life of the Yin-Zhou Period", **Dalu Zazhi**, Vol. 60, No. 5, p. 9.

a plate and shells. Tomb 233 has a 2.3 m. deep pit and a red lacquered coffin containing a supine female. The funeral objects include a pottery *jue*-cup, a *gu*-cup, a plate and jade ornaments.

Tombs 211 and 212 are 0.3 m apart, cover an area of 1.5 sq. m each, and the heads of the corpses face north. The former is located to the west of and a little ahead of the latter. Tomb 211 has a 2.5-m-deep pit, and a red lacquered coffin containing a prone male without any funerary objects. Tomb 212 has a 2.9-m-deep pit and a red lacquer coffin containing a supine female also without any funerary objects.[21]

These small tombs would seem to provide a clear picture of the monogamy which prevailed among the ordinary people in the late Shang dynasty. However, some scholars argue that such burials only account for one third of the total number of tombs at the Yinxu site, and that the remaining tombs, because of their location, provide no clues regarding marital relationships. This majority of single burials can only be explained, they argue, either by lack of a stable spouse or by the failure to be interred together with spouses for some reason. Such scholars conclude that monogamy was still an embryonic, individual occurrence in the Shang period, and the more primitive, unstable pairing marriage or even hetairism dominated among the common people. Men and women who had no spouse sufficiently entitled to lie beside them after death were buried separately in tribal graveyards in the old manner. (Archaeologists note the presence of male graves separated from female graves at the Eastern Cemetery near Qijia village, Yinxu).[22]

Such an opinion, although not without empirical support, is at odds with the fact that the Shang emperors or kings were also buried separately from their legitimate spouses. Only em-

[20] **China's Bronze Age**, (Shenghuo Dushu Xinzhi Sanlian Press, 1963), p. 195.

[21] Meng Xianwu, "Report on the Excavation of Tombs in the Southern District of Yinxu", **Zhongyuan Wenwu**, 1986:3.

perors' or kings' tombs have been found in the western section of the royal graveyard at Yinxu. In the eastern section, one large tomb associated with the famous 'Si Mu Wu-ding' tripod is believed to have belonged to one of Wuding's spouses, but is not a joint burial of husband and wife. Another spouse of Wuding was buried within the palace area, but this was also set apart from the emperors' tombs. All this, I am afraid, undermines the belief in unstable pairing marriage and hetairism reconstructed exclusively from the separation of male from female burials.

3. The Legendary Genesis of the Founders of the Xia and Shang Peoples and Sexual Customs Mirrored in These Legends

(1) The Mythology

According to old literary data, Yü of Xia, Qi of Yin and Qi of Zhou, the respective forefathers of the Xia, Shang and Zhou peoples, were contemporaries who all accomplished great deeds in the Yü-Shun period. Their origins are veiled in the mists of mythology.

First let us examine the legends recorded concerning the birth of Yü of Xia. According to *Lunheng* (Discussions Weighted in Balance): "Yü's mother ate the plant *yi* (Job's tears) and subsequently gave birth to Yü".[23] This is provided as the reason why the Xia people were named Yi. *Wu-Yue Chunqiu* (Spring and Autumn Annals of the Wu and Yue States) provides a more detailed account: "Gun married Nüxi, the daughter of the Youxin tribe. Nxi did not get pregnant until one day she ate some Job's tears in the Dishan Mountains. Feeling strange, she found she was pregnant, and later cut open her rib cage to give birth to Gaomi (Yü)".[24] According to *Diwang Shiji* (History of

---

[22] Meng Xianwu, idem.

[23]*Shi Ji*: Xiabenji: Jijie, citing *Li Wei* (The Weft Book of Rites)'s reference to "Yu's birth after (Yu's mother's) eating Job's tears".

Emperors and Kings), Gun's wife watched a shooting star traversing the sky and after having accepted the star in the dream with her mind, ate magical beads and Job's tears, and from her chest gave birth to Yü". Despite minor disparities, the three sources have one thing in common: a plant rather than a man impregnated Yü's mother. In other words, Yü's birth had nothing to do with his father Gun.

The story about the birth of Qi of Yin is equally strange. Jiandi, Qi of Yin's mother, according to *Shi Ji*, was a daughter of the Yourong people and Diku's secondary wife. One day when having a bath with two other women, she found that a black bird had laid an egg. She ate it and became pregnant with Qi of Yin. Chu Shaosun's supplement to "Lineage of the Three Dynasties" in *Shi Ji* recounts the same story. *Huainan Zi* also maintains that Qi of Yin emerged from a bird's egg, and earlier documents also include the same legend.

The legend of the birth of Qi of Zhou, which first appears in *Shi Jing* recounts how Jiangyuan honored Heaven piously in order to ward off infertility. One day she stepped on a footprint left by Heaven, and felt wonderful. She became pregnant and gave birth to Houji. The account in *Shi Ji* is roughly similar: Jiangyuan went into the wilds and found a gigantic footprint on the ground. She experienced a delirious desire to touch it, and when she did so, felt pregnant and later gave birth to Qi of Zhou.

(2) Unveiling the Legends

Some historians have discounted these legends as sheer mythical nonsense. However absurd they may at first appear, they are shadows cast by historical realities, and it is possible, with a proper perspective and methodology, to derive a factual core in these legends.

The remote past, according to Zhuang Zi, was a time in which people knew who their mothers were, but did not know their fathers. *Lüshi Chunqiu* also described remote antiquity as a time when "there were no monarchs. People simply lived together, knowing their mothers, but not their fathers. There were no categories such as relatives, brothers, husbands and wives, or males and females". In *Lie Zi* this antiquity is depicted as a time of sexual freedom in which marriage was absent. Such matrilineal hetairism is associated with a knowledge of one's mother, not his or her father. The legends that ascribed Qi of Yin's birth to his mother's eating a bird's egg and Qi of Zhou's birth to Jiangyuan's touching a god's footprint, Guo Baojun once wrote, served to defend this agnatic ignorance.[25] Such an interpretation, quite convincingly, tends to put a matriarchal imprint on the age of the founders of the Xia, Shang and Zhou peoples. However, it is quite obvious from an abundance of historical and archaeological data that the mothers of these founders lived in a patriarchal society and were the legitimate wives of somebody. These genesis legends should therefore not be hurredly explained in terms of matriarchal hetairism as a marital system. They may in fact reflect certain sexual customs and concepts of fertility.

After our ancestors stepped across the threshold of civilisation, the new monogamy grew stronger. The old hetairism ceased to be the basis of a general sexual relationship, but continued for quite a time as a sexual custom limited to specific time and places. *Zhou Li* (The Rites of Zhou) records that "in the second spring month rendezvous would be organized for men and women. Those who are attracted to each other can have sexual intercourse if they so desire". Such a sexual gathering was even institutionalised as the Shangsi Festival. The *Shi Jing* provides a charming portrayal of this event in a poem, which according to one Han dynasty exegesis, talks about "husbands and wives who go out separately when stimulated by spring and have sexual liaisons under the guise of collecting

---

[24]*Xiben*, as quoted in *Shiji*: Xiabenji: suoyin ("Gun married the daughter of Youxin called Youzhi, who gave birth to his son Gaomi".)

flowers... On leaving they exchange flowers to preserve the memory of the encounter". The famous Song dynasty neo-Confucianist Zhu Xi also saw the poem as a story about a man and woman having a sexual liaison. Confucius, according to *Shi Ji*, himself had such a sexual encounter with a woman named Yan in the wilds. Mo Zi, a Warring States philosopher, once observed that "Zuze in the state of Yan, like Sheji in the state of Qi, Sanglin in the state of Song and Yunmeng in the state of Chu, are designated venues for sexual rendezvous". These references, as well as the record in *Zhouli* quoted above, were interpreted by Guo Moruo as descriptions of sexual coition in the wilds.[26] Therefore, we can conclude that in the Zhou dynasty an orgiastic custom was observed every spring, which permitted women to have sanctioned sexual intercourse outside marriage, and it was impossible to associate any child resulting from these liaisons with a specific father. Such was the historical context in which the legends mentioned above emerged.

The ancient Chinese may have realised that pregnancy was the result of coitus, but they also regarded it as a blessing from the gods, and believed that a woman and a man alone could not produce a child without such a blessing. Married couples needed to ask the gods to bestow such a favour.

Li Ji (The Book of Rites) recorded a ceremony of mid-spring, when the "black bird" returned, and animal sacrifices were made to Gaomou, the god of fertility. The rite was attended by the emperor and all of his women. According to a Tang dynasty scholar, Gaomou should be read as '*jiaomou*', a term open to several interpretations, apart from being the god of fertility. The Han dynasty exegete Zheng Xuan simply identified Gaomou as Gaoxin's wife, because according to legend she conceived after observing the black bird and eating its egg, and later emperors as a result of this regarded her as auspicious

---

[25] **China's Bronze Age**, (Shenghuo Dushu Xinzhi Sanlian Press, 1963), p. 192.

and set up shrines in her honour. Another interpretation sees 'gaomou' as a kind of sacrifice, but this is contradicted by other documents. A third view is that the characters should be read Jiaomou, and that this was a place-name. Zheng Xuan's exegesis of *Shi Jing* states that "in ancient times a ceremony used to be held at Jiaomou for child-bearing purposes. On the day of the advent of the black birds, animal sacrifices were made at Jiaomou, and the emperor and all his wives attended the ceremony". *Zhou Li* also records that the emperor and his wives "made sacrifices to the gods to protect themselves from infertility". *Zhou Li* also states that "in mid-spring, men and women are encouraged to make rendezvous, and there are no bans on sexual activities. Thus, sacrifices were made in the suburbs to the gods endorsing such practices. This was called *jiaomou*". Despite this difference, two things seem clear about the ceremony. One is that its purpose was securing fertility. The second was that the venue of this ceremony was the city outskirts, the sub-urban area. The detail about the black bird's appearance is also difficult to explain. Zheng Xuan in his exegesis of *Li Ji* provided the following explanation: "The black bird is the swallow. It arrives in the productive season, and builds nests under people's eaves where it rears its young, a sign of fertility. Therefore, the officer in charge of marriages would arrange to celebrate them on the day of the swallows' arrival". Kong Yingda expressed the same view in his exegesis of *Shi Jing*.

Men and women would attend this carnival knowing there were no prohibitions on sexual activity. It was said, moreover, that "those who had no good reason but did not go would be punished". Such a rule should perhaps be understood in terms of population policy. The often cited "random sex" among the people of the state of Zheng also took place in the city outskirts in spring-time, so it too should fall under the same category as the carnival or ceremony described in *Zhou Li*. Guo Moruo also wrote about such mid-spring orgies described as follows in *Li Ji*: "In this month, when the black birds arrive, the farmers have little work to do in their fields, and so they renovate their houses and temples. They abstain from military expeditions that would thwart their agricultural affairs". Guo Moruo wrote: "Gaomou was of the same order of activity as *chizu* and *guanshe*, which even emperors and their wives must attend. The 'agricultural affairs' referred to in *Li Ji* were a reference to sexual activities, but this was re-phrased euphemistically by 'civilized' people of later times. The ancients did not see this as a shameful activity but rather as a task of national significance. They would even punish those who did not attend without good reason.[27] Now that we understand the function of the ceremony, that of inaugurating a sexual carnival, the legends concerning the births of the founders of the Xia, Shang and Zhou dynasties no longer remain an enigma.

In the legend of the birth of Qi of Yin the black bird figures prominently. This dovetails neatly with the account of the ceremony held at the time of the arrival of the black birds from their migration, with the imperial attendance at the ceremony and with the ceremony designed to eliminate sterility. Zheng Xuan's explanation of the poem titled "Black Bird" (*Xuanniao*) in **Shi Jing** is really insightful: "When the black bird came in mid spring, Jiandi from the Yourong tribe was married to Emperor Gaoxin, and the couple went to Jiaomou to attend a ceremony, after which they begot Qi. It was later surmised that Heaven had sent the black bird to impregnate the woman". The pregnancy resulting from the eating of the bird's egg can be seen as an adapted version of the mid-spring sex rites which took place at the advent of the migrating birds.

The legend of Qi's mother's receiving the egg during her bath, it seems, can also be traced back to the *jiaomou* ceremony. There is evidence that bathing in the spring waters was a part of the ceremony. According to Zheng Xuan's exegesis of **Zhou**

Li, "the ancient annual custom of purging oneself of malign dirt is quite similar to today's Shangsi festival which takes place by the water's edge in the third month and in which people clean themselves with soaked aromatic straw". The flirtation between a man and a woman described in the *Shi Jing* occurred beside the Qin river, the waters of which were experiencing the spring thaw. Cai Yong wrote in his *Yueling Zhangju* (Commentaries on Yueling) that "bathing in the Yi river in late spring, as recorded in *Lunyü* (The Analects), was a universally practised custom in the old days, and this laid the origins for today's Shangsi ceremony which takes place on the waters". In *Jin Shu* (History of the Jin Dynasty) we read: "By the time of the Han dynasty, officers and ordinary people offered sacrifices on the streams flowing east in late spring time". All these references serve to authenticate the ancient custom, which even has echoes in the custom today in some areas of bathing in water in which peach blossoms float. This tradition, some believe, began with Jiandi.

The legend of the pregnancy of Yü's mother can also be interpreted in the light of what we know about the *jiaomou* festival. This daughter of the Youxin tribe had an infertile marriage and so she went to Dishan to attend the sacrifice to the god of fertility, where she had sex with somebody and became pregnant. Her eating of Job's tears evokes the exchange of flowers between the man and woman on the Qin River described in *Shi Jing*.

In the legends about the mother of Qi of Zhou and her participation in the *jiaomou* ceremony, the detail concerning her touching the giant's footprints in the wilds would seem to be a reverence to her engaging in sexual intercourse at the ceremony.

We can conclude that ceremonially condoned female engagement in pre- or extra-marital sex for the purposes of procreation is the historical fact that lies at the core of the legends concerning the births of the founders of the Xia, Shang and Zhou dynasties.

(3) Old Customs from a New Perspective

That sexual freedom was permitted under certain conditions is an established fact in the pre-Xia and Zhou eras. It is hard to imagine that the practise was suspended during the intervening period, just as it is unreasonable to hypothesise its total demise after the Zhou dynasty.

According to *Bowu Zhi* (Records of the Investigation of Things), "in the time of Jie of the Xia dynasty, a Palace of Eternal Night was built in the depths of a valley to house promiscuous men and women. It kept Jie away from his office for seventy days". The last emperor of the Yin dynasty also "built a pond of wine and a forest of meat where naked men and women played together, and drank all night". The practices of these tyrants have been subsequently condemned by generations of Confucian moralists, however, they may be based on a misunderstanding of the historical reality. The episodes may not have been instigated by Jie and Zhou, but may have been an old rite organized by the government similar to the spring ceremony and the accompanying sexual activity designed to increase the population. The 'jiaomou' ceremonial was attended by emperors and their wives. In fact, everyone was required to attend and extra-marital sex was permissible.

Let us examine more closely the legend of Yu's marriage with the Tushan woman and the birth of their son Qi. *Shang Shu* reports that Yu told Qi that four days after his marriage with the woman, Qi came crying into the world, but that Yu had to ignore his duty as a father and serve his people devotedly. Other sources of literature also referred to Yu's impatient departure for his greater tasks. However, this birth of his son so promptly after his marriage was questioned by later commentators. Sima Zhen, a Tang dynasty scholar of early literature, insisted that the account in *Shi Ji* in which Yu became the father of Qi only two days after his marriage was absurd, but Sima Zhen was only reflecting the sexual taboos of the Tang period.

Yu's time was different, and he must have had sexual relations with the Tushan woman before their marriage. *Chu Ci* asked: "Why did Yu take a break from his fight with the flood to meet the woman of Tushan, and have an affair with her at Taisang?" It is evident that Yu impregnated the Tushan woman before their marriage. According to *Wu-Yue Chunqiu*, Yu arrived at Tushan, and rushed into marriage with a woman call Jiao for fear that he was getting a little too old.[28] In another source Yu had already known the woman before their marriage, as he had tried in vain to arrange a covert meeting with her before his journey to the south (*Lüshi Chunqiu*). Their pre-marital relation testifies to the sexual freedom of the time, an impression reinforced by ethnographic data and folk literatures.

As a folkway, extra- and pre-marital sex outlived the Zhou dynasty for quite some time. For example, in *Hou Han Shu* (A History of the Later Han Dynasty), we read that an annual spring gathering on the water was followed by sexual behaviour, which prompts our memory of the earlier custom. A Song dynasty geographical work, *Taiping Yülan*, refers to a local custom of the Nanyizhou region: In the middle of each month, young men and women gather together and frolic in the moonlight. At midnight they pair in the open and then disperse. The Qing dynasty work *Xü Taiwan Wuzhi* (Supplement to Records of Taiwan) reports that young native Taiwanese sang and played music in the mountain, and those who were attracted to each other would have sex.

The custom can even be encountered occasionally in modern times. One example is reported from Sichuan, where a local women's festival is celebrated every year from the end of the twelfth month through to the following third month of the lunar calendar. During the long carnival held around bonfires,

---

[28] According to *Shang Shu* and *Shi Ji*, Yu was given the job after his father had failed in it, and so had to succeed at all costs. It must have been for some very special reason that Yu took four days off to marry a woman.

young men and women sing and dance, discuss love and find sexual partners, culminating in coitus in the open. The second example comes from Lintong, Shaanxi. Every year on the third day of the third month people attend a ceremony and worship the Goddess Nüwa at an ancestral temple, and wash themselves with water containing peach blossoms. Women who have not given birth hold cloth baby dolls to their bosoms, pick up attractive men and take them into the nearby woods.[29] The same custom is also illustrated in the archaeological record. Rock paintings from Xinjiang and Guangxi, as well as painted bricks of the Han dynasty unearthed in Chengdu, Sichuan, all depict scenes of coitus in the wild.

Extra- and pre-marital sexual freedom outlived, in certain cases, the Yao-Shun era and continued through the Zhou dynasty, a period that saw the establishment of monogamy. We can possibly interpret the practice as a compensation for women's, especially upper-class women's, sexual loss in a polygynous period.

4. Women's Professions and Social Status

(1) Ordinary Women's Professions

Previous research on this topic took a palaeographic approach. For example, the sexual division of labor in early times was interpreted in the light of the principle governing the etymology of the Chinese characters for 'male' and 'female'. 'Female' in its early form 㑋 pictographically represents a woman on her knees doing some manual task at home, while male in its early form 㓁 portrays the idea of manual labor in the fields. The pattern of men ploughing and women weaving

---

[29] Song Zhaolin, **Fertility and Sexual Witchcraft**, (Cultural Relics Publishing House, 1990), p. 152.

was manifested in the characters created as such.[30] Another character for female, which is derived from the 'broom', indicates the type of work socially assigned to women.[31] Such an approach, although quite interesting, tends to oversimplify things, as the Xia-Shang society's women's labor roles varied greatly according to socio-economic grouping.

In 1969-77, archaeologists excavated 939 tombs of ordinary people in the western district of the Yinxu site. Of these tombs, 166 yielded weapons, indicating that their occupants had served in armies. Judging by their dispersal in different clan cemeteries, the soldiers were drawn from the ordinary people. All of the tomb owners interred with weapons were male, according to physical anthropologists.[32] Going to war was an exclusively male business at least those who fought on the battleground were not women from the ranks of commoners. Ordinary men in their young and robust years also did farm work when there was no war. It was said that when Tang gathered his people for the expedition against Jie of Xia, many complained that Jie knew only fighting and that Jie but had no concern for their farm work. During the Shang dynasty, recurrent wars drained manpower resources, leaving farm work, in addition to other 'female tasks' such as weaving, to the women. According to the scientific examination of skeletal remains from tombs of commoners at the Yinxu site, the average life expectancy of males was 34.8, while that of females was 30.3. Considering the fact that the average male life expectancy should be lower than that of females because of repeated wars, the reversed ratio implies how hard life was for ordinary women.

According to archaeological records, female commoners

---

[30] **The Decipherment of Oracle Bone Inscriptions**, (The Institute of History and Philology, Central Academy, Taibei, 1965).

[31] Zhao Lin's view is quoted in Jia Shiheng, "Several Aspects of Yin-Zhou Women's Life", **Dalu Zazhi**, Vol. 60, No. 5.

[32] "The 1969-77 Excavation of Tombs in the Western District of Yinxu", **Kaogu Xuebao**, 1979:1.

were usually buried in very small tombs with an area of 1.5-2 sq. m. The tomb furniture usually included a wooden coffin, several pottery utensils and a few small jade ornaments. Poor women were buried with no funeral objects. Although enjoying personal freedom socially, they had to struggle hard to survive, and this determined the broad range of work they engaged in from farming to handicrafts, from animal husbandry to housework.

(2) Noblewomen's Tasks

What did noble women do on a daily basis? Some scholars have tried to answer this question by examining oracle bone inscriptions, and have found that the major activities of upper-class women included warfare, divination, preparing bones or turtle shells for augural purposes, and agricultural management.

In oracle bone inscriptions we often encounter the inscription to the effect that Lady So-and-So has prepared so many parcels of turtle shells. For example:

帚   示   屯

The character 示 means "divination", according to Prof. Hu Houxuan, who maintained that the Yin people who obtained turtle shells and bull scapulae would hold a ceremony before using them for augural purposes.[33] The character 屯 has been deciphered as "parcel" by Guo Moruo.[34] Some interpret the whole sentence to read: "Lady (name) paid honour to (number) parcels of turtle shells for augural use". However, the late Prof. Chen Mengjia disagreed with such an interpretation, arguing that the character 示 was written as 际 or 眿 in archa-

---

[33] "Some Remarks on Five Recorded Inscriptions of the Wuding Period", in **Essays on Oracle Bone Inscriptions and the History of the Shang Dynasty**.

[34] **Sequel to A Collection of Ancient Inscriptions: Studies on Bone Inscriptions**.

ic Chinese, which means processing turtle shells in a certain way before using them in formal divination.[35] There is, however no question that these inscriptions document the participation of royal wives in such tasks. One inscription tells how Lady Jian and a minister jointly prepared seven sets of bull scapulae, and a task shared with a minister could not have been regarded as being as trivial as housekeeping.

Another interpretation of the above inscriptions identifies these royal women's tasks as a form of archival work. The Yin people regarded divination as a serious business, and they attached great importance to the preservation of oracle inscriptions. The job required literacy, so those females who participated in this work were well-educated, civilized intellectuals like their male colleagues.[36]

Some royal wives also participated in military activities. In one divination it was asked how Lady Jing's expedition against the enemy state of Longfang would eventuate. There are a number of divinations about the military activities led by Lady Hao, including details of her expedition to the enemy state of Longfang, her recruitment of soldiers from the Pang tribe, the number of captives she would bring back, and of her expeditions against the Eastern Yi people, the Tufang people in the northwest, and the state of Bafang in the south.

Eminent women also presided over important ceremonies. Many excellent examples are again provided by oracle bone inscriptions concerning Lady Hao. Questions such as these were asked of the augurs: Let Lady Hao watch over the sacrifice? Let Lady Hao offer sacrifices to the late mother? And with wine? Do not let Lady Hao watch over the ceremony of burning fuel? Do not let Lady Hao offer a sacrifice? Let Lady Hao sacrifice the captives to late Mother Gui? Do not let Lady Hao attend the sacrifice offered to Late Mother Gui?

---

[35] **A Comprehensive Study of Oracle Bone Inscriptions from the Ruins of Yin**, (Zhonghua Shuju, 1988), p. 117.

[36] Li Yanong, op. cit.

According to some researchers, there were female augurs called *si* in the Shang court. The '*si* fish' and '*si* sheep' in oracle bone inscriptions and the '*si* rabbit' in bronze inscriptions were references to female augurs in charge of those sacrificial animals respectively. Lady Hao once served as a '*si* bull'.[37]

Besides warfare and augury, royal wives were also required to supervise the farming in their fiefs, and the diviners asked related questions: Will Lady Jing have no good harvest? Will Lady Jing have a good harvest in millet? Will Lady Hao have a good harvest? Will Lady Jing have a good harvest?

(3) Royal Wives' Tombs and the Hierarchy

Those noblewomen who enjoyed wealth and prestige during their lifetimes and after their deaths, present a striking contrast with commoners. In 1938, a Shang dynasty bronze tripod was found by villagers at Wuguancun at the Yinxu site. This doubling-ring rectangular vessel rested on four cylindrical feet and was covered with *taotie* designs. Measuring 1.32 m in height and weighing 875-kg, it is the largest ritual bronze discovered so far in China. Three characters inscribed on it have led to a dispute concerning interpretation but all agree that the owner of the tripod was a noblewoman with the title Wu. The vessel is believed to have been unearthed from a medium-sized tomb of the Shang dynasty. Located in the eastern section of the royal mausoleum precinct, the tomb lies at a distance of 40 m from Royal Tomb No. 1400 to the north, and is adjacent to stretches of human-sacrifice pits. Its occupant must have been a female member of the royal family, or more precisely, an emperor or king's wife. According to scholars' studies of the oracle inscriptions, three royal wives who had the title 'Wu' were respectively spouses of Wuding, Zujia and Wuyi. Since the tripod was made in Wuding's period, its owner should be Lady Jing or late

---

[37] Cao Dingyun, "Remarks on 司 癸 母 ", **Huaxia Kaogu**, 1992:4; "On the Relationship between Lady Hao and Xiaosi", **Zhongyuan Wenwu**, 1993:3.

mother Wu.'[38] Tomb robbers have ensured that nothing remains of the tomb, but the wonderful tripod suggests a once brilliant cache, which would not pale beside the tomb of Lady Hao that yielded thousands of funeral objects.

In 1950, a Shang dynasty tomb with two tomb passages was excavated at Wuguancun near Anyang. There, archaeologists found seventy-nine human bodies including thirty-four skulls and forty-five intact skeletons, as well as twenty-eight horses and eighteen monkeys, deer and other animals.[39] Due to repeated robberies, the tomb furniture was scanty but did include some twenty bronze pieces of different types a tripod, *gui*-container, *you*-jar, *gu*-cup, *jue*-cup and dagger-axe, and some white pottery ware *you*-jar, *lei*-jar, and a plate. A stone bell with a tiger design was also discovered. Some believe that the tomb dates to the late Wuding reign, and its occupant was a member of the royal family who came next to the emperor hierarchically. Among the victims buried in the tomb, archaeologists have identified two of Emperor Wuding's close courtiers, whose names have appeared in oracle inscriptions. So, the tomb owner should be Wuding's spouse called 'late mother Gui'.[40] The likelihood of its belonging to a royal wife is reinforced by the fact that it is paired with Royal Tomb No. 1400 which lies 30 m away in the same eastern section of the royal mausoleum precinct, as well as by its contiguity to sacrificial pits.

In 1976, archaeologists excavated the tomb of Lady Hao, Emperor Wuding's famous wife, at Xiaotun village, Yinxu. Apart from sixteen human victims and six sacrificial dogs, the

[38] Yang Xizhang et al., "The Human Victims of the Shang Slave Society as Reflected in the Sacrificial Pits", *Kaogu*, p.14; Du Naisong, "Chronological Studies on the Simuwu Tripod", *Wenshizhe*, 1980:1.

[39] Guo Baojun, "Excavation of Yinxu in Spring 1950", *Zhongguo Kaogu Xuebao*, No.5; The Anyang Archaeological Team of IA, CASS, "Excavation of the Southern Passage of the Large Tomb at Wuguan Village, Yinxu", *Kaogu*, 1977: 1.

[40] Cao Dingyun, "Inquiry into the Ownership of the Large Tomb at Wuguan Village, Yinxu", *Zhongyuan Wenwu*, 1988:3.

tomb yielded 1,928 beautiful funeral objects made of bronze, stone, pottery, bone and ivory, agate and crystal. Among the 468 bronze vessels is a set of about 200 vessels and more than 130 weapons. The ritual bronzes include such rare treasures as a rectangular tripod, a *zun*-vessel in the shape of a bird, a wine cup in animal shape, a double square *yi*-vessel, a big *jue*-cup and a triple *li*-vessel. A bronze battle-axe with a length of 39.5 cm and a weight of 9 kg is a splendid example. Four bronze mirrors with ring-knobs are the earliest examples of their kind from the Central Plain region. Jade and ivory carvings with beautiful designs are also highly-prized finds.

Many bronzes bear inscriptions, and most, those on more than one hundred pieces, contain references to Lady Hao, while many others contain the inscription 'Si Mu Xin'. It is for this reason that scholars believe the tomb occupant to have been Lady Hao, and that 'Mu Xin' ('Mother Xin') was a term used by Emperor Zugeng to refer to his mother. The latter was Lady Hao's posthumous title.

The discovery of Lady Hao's tomb verifies the record in the oracle bone inscriptions of her tasks: her participation in grand ritual ceremonies and her participation in warfare, as exemplified by the bronze battle axe that was symbolic of military power.

The above data all attest to a stratification of the female population into a rich, powerful aristocracy and a lower class living in poverty.

5. The Superior Male and Inferior Female: The Origins of the Later Theme

(1) The Gender of God

The unequal relationship between men and women during the Xia-Shang period was not only manifested in the male monopoly of the throne, but was mirrored in many other things.

The sex of God (Shangdi) is one example. In the eyes of the Shang people, God was a male. In the oracle bone inscriptions there is a word referring to 'God', the supreme authority governing nature and mankind, and exerting magical force. A divination for Wuding is concerned with whether God would marry Lady Hao. Another divination also asked whether Tang or Taijia or Zuyi would marry Lady Hao. A male God was a projection of the secular patriarchy into the religious domain.

(2) Other Manifestations

Since Shang emperors had many women, they also had many children. Oracle inscriptions contain a lot of references to sons, and many of these princes had fiefs. For example, a disaster in the east was reported to Emperor Wuding from Prince Hua, which implies that the prince was enfeoffed to the east.[41] According to Prof. Hu Houxuan, another prince, Zong, was an enfeoffed duke.[42] Hu also points out that Wuding had other sons enfeoffed to the north, such as Sujia. Therefore, a royal son who had no chance of becoming overlord of the entire country could rule over a part of the country. Both **Shang Shu** and **Shi Ji** mentioned Wuding's enfeoffment in a local region before his accession to the throne. There is no reference to princesses, not to speak of female enfeoffment.

Sexual inequality also found its way into the Shang people's preference for having boys rather than girls. Having a boy was considered a sign of luck, whereas the birth of a girl was regarded as inauspicious. Some divinations pronounced that it would be propitious if a baby were to be born on such and such a day, and inauspicious if a birth took place on another day because it would be a girl.

Divinations for Emperor Wuding showed great concern for his wife's future baby. Questions regarding the future sex of the

---

[41] "Studies on the Feudalism of the Yin dynasty", **Essays on Oracle Bone Inscriptions and the History of the Shang Dynasty**, Vol. 1, p. 4.

[42] Idem, p. 6.

child were constantly asked, and these serve as evidence for the bias for male offspring in the Shang dynasty.[43] The bias damaged the natural balance between the sexes through the brutal practice of "extending congratulations on the birth of a boy and killing a girl when she comes", as is recorded in *Hanfei Zi*. References to female infanticide are corroborated by archaeological discoveries. The scientific examination of 172 human skeletons from the Shang tombs at the Yubei Textile Factory, Anyang shows that 95 of them are male, 43 female and 43 unidentified, with a sex ratio of 2.2 : 1,[44] regardless of the unidentified group. Twenty-seven human skeletons from controlled excavations in the western section of the Yinxu site in 1969-1977 included 17 male, 9 female and 1 unidentified skeleton, with the sex ratio being nearly 2 : 1.[45] Data obtained from the Taixi site, Gaocheng county, Hebei province, included 15 male tomb occupants, and 7 female tomb occupants, the sex ratio being 2 : 1, as well as 8 male victims, 1 female victim and 1 unidentified.[46] The numbers obtained from the 1950-53 excavations at Anyang and Huixian together reveal that of 80 human skeletons, 61 were male and 19 female, with the sex ratio being 3.7 : 1. Excavations during the Republican period of sacrificial pits at Xibeigang, Yinxu, yielded 319 male and 51 female skulls out of a total of 370 skulls.[47] In 1976, large numbers of human skeletal remains were unearthed from the excavation of sacrificial pits in the eastern section of the royal mausoleum precinct at the Yinxu site. Of the 715-718 skeletons examined, 339 were

[43] "On the Systems of the Marriage, Clan, Patriarchy and Childbearing of the Yin Dynasty", **Essays on Oracle Bone Inscriptions and the History of the Shang Dynasty**, Vol. 1, p. 23.

[44] **Examinations of Skulls from Yinxu, Anyang**, (Cultural Relics Publishing House, 1985), p. 51-3.

[45] "The 1969-77 Excavation of Tombs in the Western District of Yinxu", *Kaogu Xuebao*, 1979:1.

[46] **The Taixi Site of the Shang Dynasty at Gaocheng**, (Cultural Relics Publishing House, 1985), p. 110.

[47] As f.n. 1, p. 149.

male, 35 female and the rest unidentified.[48] The foregoing statistics show an unbalanced sex ratio. However, the "victim group" may invite question about its representativeness as a sample.

Ordinary burials may provide a better sample of the population. The sex ratio of the whole population obtained in that way seems to be in the neighbourhood of 2 : 1. The natural sex ratio at birth is roughly equal, with the female portion exceeding the male by a small amount. The high adult imbalanced sex ratio of the Shang dynasty population must, therefore, be due to some man-made reason. This demographic fact might conform with a bias in favour of male children in the Shang dynasty and the record of female infanticide in later periods.

Infant mortality also warrants attention. During the 1958-61 season of excavation at Yinxu, 123 infant burials (the real number should be larger, because some urn burials have not been taken into account) were found beside 302 adult ones. According to some scholar's estimates, "the infant mortality rate was more than thirty percent".[49] Apart from dystocia and disease, infanticide must have been a major reason for the high infant mortality rate.

(3) Men and Women: Social Status and Life Expectancy

Mention should also be made of male and female life expectancies. Our discussion of the life expectancy at that time will disregard sacrificial victims and concentrate on occupants of medium- and small-sized tombs. The following table shows results from a scientific examination of 172 skeletons excavated from medium- and small-sized Shang tombs at Yinxu during 1950-70.

---

[48] Ibid, p. 109.
[49] Yang Shengnan, **The Economy of the Shang Dynasty**, (Guizhou People's Publishing House, 1992), p. 24.

Age group	Male	Female	?	Total
13 and below	4	2	16	22
14-23	17	13	5	35
24-35	28	16	9	53
36-55	35	11	3	49
56 and above Adult	7			

The average male age at death is 34.8, for females 30.3, revealing a difference of 4.5 years. The female mortality in the 14-35 year age group was higher than the male counterpart. Few women lived into middle age, while no old women were found at all. This difference in life expectancy serves as an indicator of women's lower social status in Yin-Shang slave society.[50]

The table below is based on 22 Shang tombs excavated at the Taixi site, Gaocheng county, Hebei province, and shows men's and women's ages at death.[51]

Age at death	Male	Female
14-23	2	3
24-35	4	4
36-60	6	
Unidentified	3	
Average age at death	36.9	24.8

The 12-year difference in the average age of men and women suggests an even lower status of women outside the capital.

---

[50] **Examination of Skulls from Yinxu, Anyang**, pp. 51-53.
[51] **The Taixi Site of the Shang Dynasty at Gaocheng**, p. 110.

(4) The Husband and Wife Relationship among Commoners and Royals

To inquire into the husband-and-wife relationship among ordinary people, we need to look at those smaller tombs at the Yinxu site. Commoner couples were buried in the same graves but separate chambers. Husband and wife burials were roughly similar in terms of the size of the tomb chamber and the amount of funeral furniture, indicating the partners' equal status in the family. However, the subtle difference in the location of the couple's tomb chambers implies a dominant/submissive relationship.

In 1985 two lesser noblemen's tombs of the Shang dynasty were excavated at Jingjie village, Lingshi county, Shanxi province. Sets of bronze ritual vessels and weapons were found in them, beside human victims. In Tomb 1, the wooden coffin chamber included three coffins in juxtaposition each containing one skeleton. The man in the middle coffin lay on his back, while the women in the remaining two lay on their sides facing the man. In the case of Tomb 2, the male tomb owner lay on his back in the middle of the chamber, with a woman lying on her side facing him.[52] This unmistakably reflects a pattern of male domination over females. Judging by the evident conjugal relationship between the men and women, and the vertical shaft which means that the dead were interred at the same time, women were most probably placed there to serve their men in the after-life. Such a suttee-like practice attests to how patriarchal late Shang dynasty society had become in some areas.

We mentioned the eminent position of royal wives, but it should be stressed that their eminence was eclipsed by that of their monarchical husbands. An empress' status was far above that of commoners, but it was always below that of a male.

Exclusive control of the throne by male members of the

---

[52] "The Shang Tombs at Jingjie Village, Lingshi, Shanxi", *Wenwu*, 1986:11.

Xia-Shang royal family was a basic aspect of the royal couple's conjugal relationship. An empress did enjoy enviable wealth and political power, but she was a subject of her sovereign-husband.

A major service these women offered their husbands was bearing their children. Many of Wuding's divinations, for example, express concern about whether the queen is fertile, whether she can still bear his child, whether his late mother will bring disaster to the baby the queen is carrying, whether she will die in pregnancy, when the birth would take place, and the day for an auspicious boy or an inauspicious girl. The queen or empress was thus clearly intended to produce princes.

The royal marriage sometimes also contained a political factor, such as an alliance. An example is provided by Shaokang who sought refuge among the Youyu people, who, feeling grateful to the Xia people, presented him with two of their women in marriage. Another example is Jie's expedition against the Minshan people, who sought to delay him by presenting him with two women. According to legend, Tang of the Shang people heard there was an able person called Yiyin living among the Youxin tribe. He asked the Youxin people to send Yiyin to him but was refused. Later, he made a request to marry a Youxin woman and to include Yiyin in the bride's retinue. This time he succeeded. Yiyin served Tang as a highly capable prime minister, and did an excellent job in helping him to overthrow the Xia dynasty. The woman in this account was, in fact, only of political consequence.

Among Wuding's wives were Lady Qin, Lady Zhou, Lady Ji, Lady Jing, Lady Zhu and Lady Chu. The names following 'Lady' indicate the states from which these women came, and so Wuding's marriages with them were largely a set of alliances binding their states with his. The Shang empire, a great power in Wuding's time, won for its monarch many offers of women from those lesser states who were seeking the patronage of Shang. Wuding's commitment to broadening his territory required the assistance of those smaller states, and so, like other Shang emperors and kings, he married women from and to them. *Yi Jing*, for example, mentions Diyi's sister who came home from her husband and whose attendant maiden's clothes were better than his. In such a marriage, the woman usually served as a political tool.

Royal wives, when no longer attractive, would leave the palace. Wuding's Lady Jing and Lady Hao did so by going to war. Those who had fiefs were required to pay tribute to the emperor. For example there is a record in the oracle bone inscriptions of Lady Hao sending fifty turtle shells as tribute. In divinations, Wuding was often concerned whether Lady Hao had a good harvest. The larger the harvest, the more tribute he received.

To put it in a nutshell, an emperor means a sovereign as well as husband to his wife during the Xia-Shang period. Patriarchy dominated the relationships between men and women within the same social group or class.

6. Class and Gender

(1) Prisoners' Sex

The slave society of the Xia-Shang period was characterized by a drastic class conflict. The whole of society can be broken down into three parts: the powerful ruling class, free people as its basis and slaves with no guarantees governing their physical existence. Each class consisted of men and women, and so gender was never independent of class. The following is an analysis of the interplay of the two.

There is a character 囝 in oracle bone inscriptions, depicting handcuffs. The whole character means an enclosure with instruments of tortures, that is, a jail. Another character, 圉 , depicts a shackled man inside an enclosure. The existence of prisons and prisoners at that time is clear. In 1937, the

15th season of excavation at Yinxu uncovered three pottery yoked figurines. The man's hands were shackled behind his back, while the woman's hands were shackled at her front (Plate 11).[53] The Yinxu site has also yielded a pottery figurine of a naked woman with her hands shackled at her belly (Plate 10).[54] Some see these figures as prisoners while others believe them to be slaves, but the borderline between a prisoner and a slave was never clear-cut in the Shang dynasty.

(2) The Gender of Human Sacrificial Victims

Shang slaves, mainly captives, were often killed by their owners as offerings to their gods or ancestors. According to Prof. Hu Houxuan's calculation, oracle bone inscriptions include over three thousand items concerning human sacrifice, of which two thousand provide the number of victims and these total 13,000 people. The number of victims varied for different kinds of sacrifices, from several up to five hundred.[55] The sacrificial victims were of both sexes. Oracle bone inscriptions, for example, record that on one occasion at dusk thirty male slaves and thirty female servants were slaughtered as sacrificial victims for the emperor's wife, and on another occasion thirty male slaves and thirty female servants were offered to late royal wives.

Evidence of this brutal custom of sacrificing human beings in the Xia-Shang period is also to be found in the archaeological record. A city site of the late Longshan culture unearthed at Wangchenggang, Dengfeng county, Henan province, is contemporary with the early Xia dynasty and is believed by archaeologists to have been the early Xia city of Yangcheng where the

---

[53] Zheng Zhenduo, **An Illustrated Literary History of China**, Vol. 2, Figs. 3, 8, 9, 10 and 11.

[54] **Yinxu: A Miniature of Slave Society**, (Cultural Relics Publishing House, 1976), p. 40, Fig. 28.

[55] "On the Human Tomb Slavery and Human Sacrifice in China's Slave Society", **Wenwu**, 1974: 8.

legendary Yu had his residence. Here archaeologists have not only found city walls, but a series of pits containing human victims (sacrifices offered prior to the construction of large-size buildings) of both sexes and all ages. Pit 1 yielded seven bodies including three children and two young men and two young women.[56] At the Hougang site near Anyang a round pit 2.2-m in diameter and 2.8-m in depth has been discovered, and in it a total of 73 victims were buried in three layers. In the first layer were found 25 bodies, 9 male and 16 sexually unidentified; in the second, 29 bodies, 8 male and rest the unidentified; and, in the third, 19 altogether, 5 male adults, 3 young women, 4 children and 2 infants, with the rest of them unidentified.[57]

The excavations conducted in the eastern royal mausoleum precinct at Yinxu between 1934 and 1976 brought to light thousands of sacrificial pits full of human bones. These pits were all earthen ones of a rectangular plan, and were aligned in a north-south direction in most cases. A majority of victims, all young males, were beheaded. Most of the pits had eight to ten victims. Those pits with a west-east orientation contained female adults and children, who, although not beheaded, were buried alive with hands bound.

The archaeological reports concerning these skeletal finds can be condensed as follows. A total of 389 skulls were collected during the archaeological excavations at Yinxu in the 1920s and 1930s. These included 370 adults, 319 male and 51 female, the remainder being too damaged to be identified. Of this batch of findings, 337 skulls were unearthed from 99 sacrificial pits in the eastern section of the royal cemetery at Xibeigang, Yinxu.[58]

The 1976 season of excavation of 191 sacrificial pits at the

---

[56] **Wangchenggang at Dengfeng and Yangcheng**, (Cultural Relics Publishing House, 1992), p. 39.

[57] **Excavation of Yinxu**, (Cultural Relics Publishing House, 1987), pp. 265-269.

[58] **Examinations of Skulls from Yinxu, Anyang**, (Cultural Relics Publishing House, 1985) p. 29.

eastern section of the royal cemetery yielded 1178 human skeletons. Of the 715-718 skeletons examined, 339 were male, 35 female and the rest unidentified. The average age of male victims came anywhere between 15 and 35, while that of females was between 20 and 35.[59]

At the Taixi site of the Shang dynasty, a sacrificial pit was found in front of Building 3. This 1.5-m-long pit of a rectangular plan contained three human skeletons, two male adults and one boy. Judging by their postures, they were buried alive after being bound and thrown into the pit. At the corner of Building 2 was found a skull of a young woman, also a sacrifice offered at a foundation laying ceremony.[60]

Excavation of a sacrificial site at Qiuwan, Tongshan county, Jiangsu province, yielded 20 human skeletons together with twelve skeletons of dogs, all sacrificial offerings. The human victims consisted of males and females of young and early middle age. They were buried in a kneeling position with hands bound behind them.[61]

The majority of human sacrifices of the Xia-Shang period were male adults, with female victims only accounting for a small portion of the total.

(3) The Gender of Tomb Slaves

The Xia-Shang period witnessed a brutal sutteeism whereby slaves were murdered on their owners' deaths so as to continue to provide their services underground. The number of tomb slaves depended on a slave owner's status. Archaeologists have encountered many cases of immolation. The most important sites include Yinxu, the Shang city at Zhengzhou, Panlongcheng at Huangpi, Taixi at Gaocheng, and Sufutun at Yidu. The

---

[59] Ibid., pp. 109-111.

[60] **The Taixi Site of the Shang Dynasty at Gaocheng**, (Cultural Relics Publishing House, 1985), pp. 20 and 25.

[61] "Excavation of the Qiuwan Site at Tongshan, Jiangsu", *Wenwu*, 1973: 2.

following is a brief account of the discoveries at several selected sites.

Large numbers of skeletal remains of human victims have been found in royal tombs of the Shang dynasty at Yinxu. A tomb coded HPKM1001 contained nearly one hundred tomb slaves. The corpses of nine young men were found at the bottom of the tomb. Each was holding a bronze or stone dagger-axe and must have been a royal bodyguard. Ten victims with small funeral objects were found, in coffins or not, skirting the coffin-chamber of the tomb owner. These must have been the tomb owner's personal attendants. 75 tomb slaves, most headless, were found in the tomb tunnel, including 61 corpses without heads and 73 skulls. In addition, archaeologists excavated 22 sacrificial pits containing a total of 68 tomb slaves.

Among the small tombs excavated during 1969-1977 in the western section of Yinxu, 11 yielded a total of 15 tomb slaves, including three men in youth or middle age, one woman and five adults of unidentified sex. Five medium-sized tombs equipped with a tomb passage yielded altogether 22 tomb slaves, mostly children, with some adults of unidentified sex.[62]

In a large tomb at Wuguancun, Yinxu, were found 79 tomb slaves, 17 of whom, mostly males, were on the eastern secondary platform, and 24, mostly female, on the western platform.

16 tomb slaves were found in Lady Hao's grave, including 4 male and 2 female and 10 sexually unidentified skeletons, among which were two children.

Tomb 4 of the Shang dynasty excavated at Laoniupo near Xi'an is a small-scale burial. The tomb owner, a young man, lay extended on his back in the middle of the tomb pit. A young woman lay bent on her side beside him. In Tomb 10 was found a tomb slave, a man in his fifties. The tomb owner was sexually

---

[62] "The 1969-77 Excavation of Tombs in the Western District of Yinxu", *Kaogu Xuebao*, 1979:1.

uncertain.[63]

The tomb slaves of the Shang dynasty display a heterogeneity of background. A majority of them must have been slaves and captives, since they were often beheaded or dismembered. Some were body guards, and some were tomb owners' personal attendants, or what were called "lesser courtiers and lesser concubines" in oracle bone inscriptions. These people would have a relatively higher social status, as is demonstrated by the presence of coffins, tomb furniture and attendants, but they were nevertheless slaves, and had to die at the time of their owners' demise.

(4) Conclusion

The evident male dominance over females in the Xia-Shang period does not mean that any man was socially higher than any woman. Male domination is mainly exhibited among members of the same group in the social hierarchy, and principally between husband and wife, and between male and female family members. The ruling group that headed the social pyramid consisted of both sexes, while those toiling at the lowest stratum of society naturally also included males and females. The same is true of prisoners, and sacrificial victims. Deities of either sex could enjoy the offering of human sacrifices of either sex. A noblewoman could enjoy, just as her male counterpart, a retinue of underground tomb slaves of both sexes. All this tells that in comparison with class, gender was a lesser determinant of social status.

---

[63] "The Excavation of a Shang Dynasty Cemetery at Laoniupo near Xi'an", *Wenwu*, 1988:6.

CHAPTER FOUR
THE RISE AND FALL OF THE ZHOU RITES; A RATIONAL FOUNDATION FOR THE GENDER RELATIONSHIP MODEL

Du Fangqin

The Zhou dynasty is an important turning point in the history of the development of Chinese civilisation. It is also the important period for the founding of Chinese institutional civilisation and spiritual culture. In gender relations, the Zhou dynasty also established the fundamental structure and the model of Chinese sexual culture. The rites and philosophy of the Zhou, the other temple cultures and popular cultures of that time, and the relevant sex norms and values of the various philosophical schools in the late Zhou all exerted a far-reaching influence on later ages.

1. The Rise of the Zhou Rites: The Founding of the Institutional Civilisation of the Gender Order

(1) The Rise of the Zhou Tribe and its Cultural Origins

Historians generally refer to the period before the elimination of the Shang by the Zhou as the pre-Zhou period. They also periodise the Zhou into the Western and Eastern Zhou, demarcated by the date when the king Pingwang moved Zhou's capital eastward. According to archaeological findings and documentary sources, the Jizhou tribe which lived in present-day Shanxi province originally derived from the mainly agricultural Jiangyan culture. The relationship between the Jizhou culture and Jiangyan cultures can be traced back to Jiang Yuan, the ancestress of the Zhou people, and her son Qi (Ji). The poem "The Birth of the People" (*Shengmin*) in the "Daya" section of **Shi Jing** recounts the origins of the Zhou people, praising the unusual nature of Ji and his mother Jiang Yuan. The line of Ji's father was unknown. A legend recounted how his mother had stepped onto the footprint of a giant and become pregnant. Ji was abandoned several times because he was fatherless, and so was originally named Qi, meaning "abandoned". His unusual experiences, however, finally moved Heaven and he was also accepted by his mother's family. He learned farming skills, and so the respected name Ji, meaning "millet", was conferred on him. His mother was also ardently worshipped as the earliest ancestress of the Zhou people was Jiang Yuan.

Born and raised by the farming Jiangyan tribe, Ji later went to the Huangdi tribe which had the surname Ji. He and his descendants worked successively under Yao, Shun and Yu as "nongguan" (officials in charge of farming). Archaeologists maintain that Yao was active in what is today Shanxi, where the ancestors of the Zhou also lived. Some scholars maintain that Jizhou culture was a branch of Guangshe culture which in turn derived from the Longshan culture of Taiyuan. Pottery excavated in Shanxi, Shaanxi and Henan provinces bears the symbolic marks of the *Tian* (Heaven) clan, a major branch of the Zhou tribe. The surname of the Tian clan was Ji, which, according to **Guo Yu**, the ancient documentary text, only four of the twenty-five branches of Huangdi's descendants could acquire, and the

Tian clan was one of them.[1] In the Tian clan examples of the tribal insignia of Tianshou (Heavenly animals) have been recovered. These consist of the Chinese character "*tian*" above various animals, such as tigers, "*pi*" (a mythical wild animal), bears, pigs and foxes. These tribal insignia were probably inherited from the totems of the tribes under Huangdi.[2] The Zhou people adopted the surname Ji because they identified themselves with the orthodox descendants of Huangdi. In the late Xia dynasty, these descendants lost their positions as "nongguan". They wandered between the Rong and Di tribes and adopted their nomadic customs. It was only after Gong Liu became leader that the Zhou people moved to Bin and "restored Hou Ji's cause, practised farming and used the land in a proper fashion". And so, "subsequently, the institutional civilisation of the Zhou people began to prosper".[3]

During the time of Gugong Danfu, most of the Zhou people were forced to leave Bin and move to Qixia because of the invasion of the Di people of Guifang. "Gugong then abandoned nomadic customs, built houses within walled precincts, and settled in villages and wards". In other words, under him the nomadic lifestyle of the Rong and Di was abandoned in favour of a settled life. The Zhou people established matrimonial relations with a surnamed Jiang from the north-west. (Archaeologists maintain that this tribe was a branch of the Qiang tribe of the Xindian and Siwa archaeological cultures period, a little later than Qixia culture). Gugong married Tai Jiang, and the Jizhou culture merged with the Jiangyan culture once again. The poem titled "Mian" in the "Daya" section of *Shi Jing* recounts the history of this period.

---

[1] "Jin Yu" in *Guo Yu*.

[2] For the relations of Guangshe culture and the Tian clan with Zhou culture and the descendants of Huangdi, see Zou Heng, "Lun Xian-Zhou Wenhua", in *Xia Shang Zhou Kaoguxue Lunwen Ji*, (Cultural Relics Publishing House, 1980).

[3] "Zhou Benji" in *Shi Ji*.

The Zhou tribe subsequently increased in grew stronger, and moved its centre of rule firstly to Feng and later to Hao. It established close commercial and even matrimonial relations with Shang, a large state to its north. Gugong's younger son Gong Ji married Tai Ren of the Ren family of the Shang tribe; Gong Ji's elder son Ji Chang married the daughter of Di Yi who was the king of the Shang. From these examples, the strong influence of Shang culture on Zhou culture can clearly be seen. It can, therefore, be said that Zhou culture was influenced by Jiangyan, Yin-Shang, Rong, Di and other cultures of the Central Plain, but it had its own characteristics. For example, Zhou's mode of production was based on the natural economy represented by the peculiar division of labour, a settled existence in which men engaged in farming and women in weaving. Moreover, the matrimonial family, in which the male was in the dominant position, was formed by his marrying a spouse with the different surname. These cultural characteristics fixed the gender relationship structure of the Zhou dynasty, and established the basic living model and gender relationship structure and conceptions of the Chinese people.

(2) The Zhou Rites: The standard of dual hierarchic system of class and sex

The Rites (*li*) was a system, a ruling order consciously established by the dominant class after it developed to a certain stage; it was further standardised and systematised by this class for the purpose of ruling. Naturally, the establishment of a particular institutional civilisation is always backed by an ideology with the particular values and ethical views as its core. 'The Zhou rites' are the earliest Chinese institutional and behavioural norms we now know of, and they became the standard for Chinese civilisation. The historical legend of the Duke of Zhou devising the Rites was a natural outcome of the principle of 'patriarchy' developed by the Zhou people on the basis of patriliny. The marriage of spouses of the same surname was strictly forbidden. The wife's eldest son was sole heir. Males were responsible for matters outside the home while women were responsible for domestic matters. The sexual division of labour saw males farming and females weaving. People led settled lives. All these elements strengthened paternal power, encouraging the sense of it and giving rise to a social consciousness. Paternal power could be extended to all other realms of power in society and families. A man's dominance over other states and individuals was of his highest success of his highest success.

The legend concerning the Duke of Zhou devising the Rites also reflected the history of the Zhou people who, after overthrowing the Shang, summed up the lessons of the collapse of the Shang people who were described as "given over to drinking and female beauties, listening to women's words, not worshipping heaven and the ancestors, drifting away from kith and kin and making use of distant persons".[4] These words stress the view that self-adjustment and restraint is important in establishing paternal domination. Moreover, in the relationship between Heaven and human beings, the Zhou people paid more attention to 'human affairs' than did the Shang. They co-ordinated their belief in spirits and gods with an emphasis on human affairs. Hence, the Zhou nobility laid a special stress on worldly order, i.e. the establishment of the Rites.

The core and essence of the Zhou rites was hierarchy, which classified individuals according to their classes, ties of blood and sex. The Rites defined the relationship between upper and lower stations, and the dominant and the dominated were assigned their proper place ("*mingfen*") in the hierarchy. The positions, rights and obligations of each level (or individual) were represented through their mutual connections and comparisons. There were no independent individual rights and obligations. Here I try to use the concept of a dual hierarchy of

---

[4] "Mushi" and "Taishi" in **Shang Shu**; "Zhou Benji" in **Shi Ji**.

class and sex to explain the essence of the Zhou rites in gender relations. The word 'dual' here specifically refers to the complex parallel and intersecting forms expressed in the hierarchic relations of classes (strata) and sex. Specifically speaking, in the vertical division of upper and lower classes, the Zhou rites divided men into several levels according to their social status and position. The common saying that "men are divided into ten levels, like the ten suns in the sky" realized the principle that the upper dominate the lower, and the lower submit to the upper, level by level. This was well expressed by Wu Yu from the state of Chu, who is quoted in *Zuo Zhuan*: "The Son of Heaven rules the universe, the feudal lords rule in their own fiefs.... There are ten suns in the sky and ten levels of human beings. This is the reason why the lower serve the upper and the upper worship the gods. For this reason, the king is served by the lords, the lords by their ministers, the ministers by the "shi" (gentlemen)....[5]

In the Zhou rites system which strictly adhered to the principle of "rites remote from the commoners", male aristocrats' positions, status and power relations were determined according to their ties of blood and fiefs. Wang Guowei summed up the essence of the Zhou rites in its four principles>honouring the honourable, loving the close and the beloved, respecting the virtuous, and discriminating between man and woman. These principles were expressed in three systems: the system of inheritance by the wife's son, the system of ancestry worship and the marriage system.[6] The first three principles were applied to rule the state and maintain the clan (i.e. to maintain the rule by patriarchy and king's power). "The Zhou people derived the norms of honouring the honourable and loving the close and the beloved to offer sacrifices to the ancestors, to regulate descendants and to care for brothers; and

---

[5] "Yigong qinian" in *Zuo Zhuan*.

[6] Wang Guowei, "Yin Zhou Zhidu Lun" in *Guantang Jilin*, (Zhonghua Shuju) vol. 10, pp. 477, 453-4.

derived norms from the principle of respecting the virtuous in order to govern the state."[7] Discrimination between man and woman was a principle derived from blood ties designed to implement the practice of marrying a spouse with a different surname. Under the guidance of these four principles, the Zhou had three basic systems which were different from those of the Shang.

The first was the system of inheritance by the wife's son, and from it came the patriarchal clan system and mourning system, and then the system of feudal descendants, and the system whereby the king ruled over the feudal lords. The second was the system of the ancestral temple. The third was the system of marriage among families of different surnames. All these practices were designed to govern the state by means of specific bonds and relationships, bringing all within the same set of ethics, and incorporating the son of Heaven, feudal lords, ministers, ranking officials, shi and commoners into one ethical group.[8]

When analysing further the influence of these four principles and three systems on the hierarchic order of the nobility, one finds that: (1) The system of inheritance by the wife's son in the power transfer defined in the Zhou rites abandoned the remnants of the principle of "loving the close and the beloved" in the Yin dynasty inheritance system and implemented the notion of "using the principle of honouring those in honourable positions to govern the principle of closing up to those closer in terms of blood ties". The rule that the heir was the eldest son of one's wife's, regardless of whether the eldest son were virtuous or not was designed to obviate struggles among sons of the one wife. This was the hierarchy of power inheritance, and with it came the patriarchal clan system and the mourning system. The patriarchal clan system was also a system of

---

[7] Ibid., p. 472.
[8] Ibid., pp. 453-4.

inheritance used by the aristocrats below the ministers. It was used to regulate the sacrifices to the ancestors, clan ceremonies and the incorporation of clans according to seniority and distance of the line. It was this also an organizational law of the nobility enabling the maintenance and development of the interests of the paternal line and the patriarchal families. The inheritance law and the patriarchal clan law were used within specific bonds and relations to maintain relationships among the living, while the mourning system was used by the living to reinforce hierarchic clan relationships. Again, the underlying principles were the distinction of sons of the wife from sons of the concubine, honouring those in the honourable positions, creating closer bonds with those related by closer blood ties, and keeping those who are distant in line and at a distance. The origin of the feudalism of the Western Zhou was the distinction of sons of wives from sons of concubines. The heir to the throne was the oldest son of the king's wife, and the other sons, whether of the wife or concubines, were all granted with fiefs. According to the hierarchical principle, they were ranked as dukes, marquises, earls, viscounts and barons. Thus the system whereby "all the lands are the territory of Zhou, and all people are Zhou's subjects' was formed. (2) The ancestral temple system was established according to the principle of closeness with those closer in blood ties. The Shang people offered sacrifices to all ancestors and former kings, and "the principle of closeness to those closer in blood ties of blood over-rode govern the principle of honouring those in the honourable positions in the ancestral temple system", while "the principle of honouring those in the honourable positions governing the principle of being close with those closer in blood ties was used to found the system of distinguishing sons of wives from sons of concubines".[9] (3) The Zhou dynasty was the period when exogamy emerged in China. The Shang dynasty still preserved

---

[9] Wang Guowei, op. cit., vol. 10, p. 468.

the form of marriage within the clan. Wu Ding's wife, for example, had the same surname. The principle of discrimination between male and female in the Zhou rites was at first not aimed at limiting women to the home, but at distinguishing between the surnames of men and women. Only through this distinction could marriage between spouses of different surnames be implemented. Even after a hundred generations, there could be no marriage of persons with the same surname. This principle originated with the Zhou people.[10] This principle was implemented not merely to proliferate descendants, but more importantly for the need of adjusting the order of power. Only by restricting the marriage of those of the same surname could the discrimination between the noble and the humble, and between the close and the distant according to paternal blood ties become possible. Moreover, the absolute authority of patriarchy and kingly power could be realized in the paternal system through the installation of heirs, the worship of gods and ancestors, enfeoffment and the conferral of ranks and titles. In this sense marriage was the foundation of the Rites.

Although the Zhou rites did not clearly define levels and ranks for woman, in the rites concerning patriarchal clan and family the gender hierarchy is revealed to some extent.

Firstly, women belonged to paternal families and to men. Before marriage, a woman obeyed her father; after marriage, her husband. "*Gui*" (returning) meant marrying off one's daughter, so that the only place she could return to was her husband's home after marriage. Moreover, the married woman's status was incorporated into her husband's rank and level: the king's wife was the queen ("*hou*"), the lord's wife was the lady ("*furen*"), the minister's wife was the "*ruren*", and the "*shi*"'s wife was the "*qi*". The woman from the aristocratic family was qualified as one's legal wife. The status of the concubine who came with one's wife to the family or was adopted by the man

---

[10] Ibid.

at another time was inferior in status to the wife. In short, woman's hierarchic position in society and the family was determined through marriage by the man's position.

Secondly, within the nobility, the gender hierarchy was expressed in the practice of "internal and external tasks" ("*nei-wai fenju*") and in the special form of the division of labour according to gender. In various ancient documents we read how a woman's place is in the home ("*nei*", lit. "internal") and how involvement in public affairs ("*wai*", i.e. "external) is inappropriate for women. For example: "Zhou's law cannot be bright if women participate in politics". And: "Women cannot participate in politics, nor can they cease to raise silkworms and weave". Moreover, "if the hen takes charge of crowing in the morning, the family will decline".[11]

The Zhou rites strictly forbade woman to play a direct role in politics, although she could be a good wife or mother and assist her husband or son in politics. This sexual discrimination in politics is expressed in the ancient cautionary comment that a "woman's words cannot be adopted". Political activities were exclusively the preserve of male aristocrats. In the economic activities, the form of the division of labour whereby men engaged in farming and women in weaving was set and strengthened by the Zhou rites which outlined the "jitian" ceremony performed by the king and his feudal lords and which was designed to promote farming, and the "gongsang" ceremony performed by the queen and designed to encourage sericulture. The "jitian" ceremony took place in the first month of spring, and in the course of the ceremony the king and his feudal lords would ritually farm their private estates ("one thousand "*mu*" for the king and one hundred "*mu*" for each feudal lord"). They would carry farming implements and lead their officials to

See *Guo Yu* ("Zheng Yu"), *Shi Jing* ("Daya: Zhanyang") and *Shang Shu*// ("Mushu"), respectively.

witness them personally cultivate their lands.[12] The corresponding female activity was the ceremony of encouraging sericulture attended by the queen and her ladies. In the last month of spring, after fasting, the queen and the imperial concubines would proceed to the eastern outskirts of the capital to plant mulberry trees. All women were required to attend, and female officials were appointed to encourage the raising of silkworms. These exemplary religious ceremonies of the imperial house were a propaganda call to the Zhou people. After the founding of the Zhou dynastic, this economic model continued throughout the entire period of dynastic China typified by the natural economy model. In these religious ceremonies, the division of ranks and levels, the discrimination of man and woman and the strict division of their tasks were clearly defined. In the Zhou dynasty, the most important affairs of state were the offering of sacrifices and participation in warfare. The offering of sacrifices to gods and ancestors served to publicise filial piety, mediate disputes, govern the state peacefully and stabilise the population. As time went on, the qualifications of the chief worshippers (those qualified to communicate with the ancestors and gods), the scope and objects of the worship in the ceremonies, and the times and procedures of the ceremonies were made increasingly hierarchical and standardised. For example, the king could offer sacrifices to all gods, the feudal lords to Heaven and Earth, celestial bodies, and the mountains and rivers, while the "*shi*" and commoners could only offer sacrifices to their ancestors.[13] Males, as masters of the state and the family, were naturally the chief worshippers, and their wives could only act in minor roles or as assistants. While the king or the feudal lords offered "*sansheng*" (the pig, cow and sheep used as sacrifices), the queen and her ladies could only offer grains prepared by themselves. While the king personally officiated at

---

[12] "Yueling", *Li Ji*.
[13] "Chu Yu", section 2, *Guo Yu*.

the sacrificial rites, his queen was required to prepare the garments he wore in the ceremonies in order to demonstrate her reverence for the gods and ancestors. During the Shang dynasty, sacrifices were offered only to the king's deceased mother, but in the Zhou dynasty this practice was changed, and the sacrifices were extended to the ancestors as well as to the dead mother. However, in the seven temples of the king or in the five temples of the feudal lords, the rites of offering sacrifices were all mainly intended for the ancestors, and the rites for one's deceased mother were only secondary. The Zhou broke with the practice of exclusively offering sacrifices to deceased mothers.

The discrimination between males and females among the aristocrats in their political, economic and religious lives led to the acceptance of the conception that males were in the superior position and females in the inferior position. The male aristocrats were the future masters, the lords and kings who could continue the lines of families and clans and have distinguished. They were cared in every possible way after birth, while women were the wives of other families after marriage, and were destined to take charge of serving food and making clothing for men. They were despised from babyhood. There is a description of this phenomenon in *Shi Jing*:

> If the baby is a boy,
> he can sleep upon the bed,
> is dressed in finery,
> and can play with jade "zhang".
> He can weep and wail,
> and is dressed in crimson when he grows up.
> We will serve as an official, lord or king.
>
> If the baby is a girl,
> she can sleep upon the ground,
> is wrapped in cloth,
> and can play with weaving weights.

> She cannot express her views,
> and must serve the food and drinks.
> She will bring only trouble to her parents.

Significantly, according to the Zhou rites, a man could have one wife and several concubines. Under this system, the ranks and levels of the various women of an aristocrat were also clearly defined. The system of one wife and concubines and its derivations, the patriarchal clan system and mourning system, divided women into levels of the noble and humble, and the close and distant. This system of one wife and concubines placed relationships within a framework in which a son's status was determined by that of his mother and vice versa. A mother's status directly determined her son's future. The status of the wife as mother was superior to that of the concubine and father's concubine as mother. Even among the concubines there were several levels of gradation. The patriarchal clan system consolidated women's subordinate status, as well as their ranks and levels. It was based on the paternal lineage of male domination. A woman, as wife, became a member of her husband's clan through marriage, and her status and seniority in the family followed that of her husband. "If her husband is the father of the family, she is the mother; if he is the son, she is the daughter-in-law".[14] In temple worship and in the mourning system women were similarly assigned rank. For example, according to the relevant rites, the wife could be worshipped and buried together with her husband and could also be worshipped with her mother-in-law. Even the rites of burial were strictly hierarchical among women. There were three major distinctions. Firstly, if a king's wife died, obituaries would be sent to the feudal lords. Secondly, after the dead wife was buried, the husband could mourn behind the ancestral temple, but the concubine was not accorded this privilege. In addition, there were also distinctions between the wife of the heir of the middle

---

[14] "Dazhuan", *Li Ji*.

level aristocrat and the wives of his other sons in the patriarchal clan system, and distinctions between father and son, mother and son, and between husband and wife in the mourning system. All these distinctions represented a strict gender hierarchy. This dual hierarchic system of class and sex was founded by the Zhou rites.

(3) The sex relationship and woman's position in the matrimonial family

1. The marriage between the spouses with different surnames and the practice of following the husband as mentioned above, as well as the formation and consolidation of the marriage between the spouses with different surnames, stemmed from the need to maintain the stability and continuity of a paternal family. This kind of marriage was different from the marriage between the spouses of the same surname, and was based on the interests of the males in the paternal line. It divided the two sides in the marriage into two parts: "*nei*" (inward) for males and "*wai*" (outward) for women; a man married his wife into his family, and married his daughter out of his family.

The aim of marriage was to acquire good fortune and avoid misfortune. "Marriage is the step to either good fortune or misfortune. If the marriage is in the interests of "*nei*" (man), good fortune will follow; if it is in the interests of "*wai*" (woman), misfortune soon follows".[15] For example, the marriages between Wang Ji and Tai Ren, Wenwang and Tai Si, Tai Wang and Tai Jiang, Wuwang and Yi Jiang, and Tai Ji and Hugong were all held to be models of "benefiting '*nei*" (the husband's family) and establishing felicitous matrimonial relations". The marriage between the spouses of different surnames and the practice of the wife following her husband emphasised

---

[15] The words of Fu Chen, minister of Xiangwang of Zhou, in "Zhou Yu", *Guo Yu*.

the woman's contributions and obligations to her husband's paternal family and her own; but they were not equal. She should first consider the interests of her husband's family, then those of her father's family. One of the attributes of a woman which was constantly emphasised was her ability to bear descendants, especially sons. Such poems in *Shi Jing* as "Linzhi", "Jiaomu" and "Peiyi" all bestow blessings and pray for the good fortune to have many sons. To have many descendants was regarded as an act of filial piety to the ancestors. As the Shi Jing expressed it: "Boundless is filial piety; it serves always as the example for people to emulate". And: "Gentlemen's causes last ten thousand years; they always are provided with good fortune and descendants".[16]

The second of woman's emphasised contributions was her part in maintaining and co-ordinating human relations within the paternal family and in making clear the status between father and sons, and among brothers and among clan members, in order "to have a happy relationship between husband and wife that is like harmonious music, to enable the brothers to live in a friendly atmosphere, and to have all in the family live in a harmonious environment...".[17]

The third contribution was the expectation that through marriage she forges the relationship between the paternal family and society. "Through ordinary marriage, a wife's relatives can become ranking officials even though they are not virtuous and talented".[18] And: "A wife's brothers, nephews and uncles are never the same as others".[19] The marriage not only established the matrimonial relationship with the wife's clan, but also linked in closely with the uncles and nephews on the mother's side. All these were outcomes of marriage which could consolidate and extend male power by also marrying one's daughter

---

[16] "Daya: Jizui", *Shi Jing*.
[17] "Daya: Tangdi", *Shi Jing*.
[18] "Daya: Jienanshan", *Shi Jing*.
[19] "Xiaoya: Kuibian", *Shi Jing*.

into the other family. For example, the king of the Zhou established matrimonial relations with Jiang's family for consolidating his power, and Wuwang of the Zhou married his elder daughter to Duke Yu Hu, the first feudal lord of the Chen, also in order to extend his power.

2. The Husband-Wife Unit: One Man with Several Woman, Dominant Husband and Submissive Wife.

In **Shang Shu**, there is an injunction to "not injure or do violence to the innocent, and to care for orphans, widows and "*shufu*" (dependent wives)".[20] "*Shufu*" belonged to their husbands, who had the obligation to protect them from violence; the wife in turn was controlled and watched over by her husband. In the "Jiaren" section of **Zhou Yi**, there are statements referring to "watching over one's own wife" and to the effect that "the wife should not misbehave; she should take charge of food and drink". These are real descriptions of the "*shufu*"'s status. Male aristocrats could have several wives and concubines according to the Rites: the king could have twelve women, the feudal lords nine, and other aristocrats less according to their rank. There is a vivid description in **Shi Jing** of the marriage of an aristocrat who had many concubines:

Marquis Han was married to the woman who was the niece of Xuanwang of the Zhou and the daughter of Jue Fu. Marquis Han went to Jue Fu's native place to meet the bride. Each of a hundred carriages was drawn by four horses, and the bells on the carriages rang like music. It was a grand parade and Marquis Han was in the limelight. So many concubines and ladies followed the bride that one could hardly count. The marquis looked right and left, and was radiant with joy.[21]

In the family where man was in the dominant position and had several wives and concubines, there was a system of rota-

---

[20] "Zhoushu" and "Zicai", **Shang Shu**.

[21] "Daya: Hanyi", **Shi Jing**.

tional "sexual favours" ("dangxi-zhi"). There is an oracle in
Zhou Yi which pronounces that "providing sexual favours in
turn to each wife and concubine in the palace benefits the ruler
himself".[22]

The relationship between husband and wife in the aristocratic family as defined by the Zhou rites was somewhat contradictory. This came from the pragmatic need to protect the
sexual interests of the dominant class. The wife was required to
observe the demands of the husband's family on the one hand,
while there were also suggestions that the husband and wife
were in equal positions, and that a man should respect his wife.
"In the ancient Xia, Shang and Zhou dynasties, the wise rulers
had to respect their wives. This was not without reason. The
wife bears her husband's heirs, so why would he dare neglect
her?"[23] In the marriage ceremony, the Rites were emphasised
and the bridegroom, with the exception of the king, was requested to meet his bride himself. If the bride's parents had high and
noble positions, she could enjoy power and a higher position in
her husband's family, as did the women of the Ji and Jiang
families after marriage.

3. Respecting Mothers and Observing Filial Obedience

Respecting mothers was the residue of maternal society.
In paternal-patriarchal society, respecting mothers was condi-
tioned by the mother's duty to produce an heir and descendants
and by her contributions to the family. She was no longer
worshipped as the goddess as in maternal clan society, but was
judged in accordance with whether her role in the family
conformed to the norms of patriarchy. For example, Tai Si, the
mother of Wuwang, was referred to by her son as "one of the
ten able ministers governing the state", not only because she
assisted her husband and son ably, but also because she had
given birth to ten sons and one daughter and was respected as

---

[22] "Bogua", **Zhou Yi**.
[23] "Aigong Wen", **Li Ji**.

one of "the three mothers of the Zhou". Yi Jiang, the mother of Wuwang, was also the more respected because she had given birth to Chengwang and Shu Yu. After the Duke of Zhou instituted the Rites, bearing descendants and governing the family had become the special duties of a mother. Because of a mother's industry and her special contributions to the family, the Zhou rites laid special emphasis on the connection between "respecting one's mother" and "displaying filial duty to one's parents". The Rites entailing the display of filial obedience to one's parents stressed the principle that if the parents were alive, the descendants should show filial obedience to them, and if they were dead, offer sacrifices to them. But this practice took place was under two sets of conditions:

1. The son waited upon his mother because he wanted to show filial obedience to his father. In this situation, the father was respected but not close and the mother was close but not respected. 2. The mother was required to be virtuous and abide by the Rites, otherwise even though she had given birth to princes and was the honourable queen, she would be blamed and punished like others. Bao Si, Youwang's wife, was regarded as "the chief culprit" in causing the state confusion because she had intervened in political affairs, and was not respected even though she had given birth to sons.

4. The Principal Ideologies and Sexual Norms

The Zhou rites included the superstructure of whole institutions for the aristocratic domination and the principal ideologies which played the guiding role in society. The principal ideologies consisted of the hierarchical conceptions of the Rites system of the Zhou, the *Zhou Yi* philosophy and the idea of the integration of Heaven and Man expressed in the "Hongfan" section of *Shang Shu*. They directly and indirectly influenced the sexual norms and conceptions of that time. Here I will focus on the idea of the positions of "*qian*" and "*kun*" in *Zhou Yi* and of the division of "*yin*" and "*yang*" in "Hongfan" to discuss the prototype of the sexual philosophy that prevailed under the Chinese patriarchal system, and from the temple culture of the Western Zhou (using identifiable sources of the Western Zhou in *Shi Jing*, *Shu Jing* and *Li Ji*) to analyse the penetration and representation of this sexual philosophy, ideas and conceptions.

. (l) "Hongfan" and *Zhou Yi*: The interaction of Heaven and Man and the sexual philosophy of dual elements

"Hongfan" is a chapter of *Shang Shu*, and was written by Ji Zi, according to the legend, but it was actually a tool used by the Zhou nobility as the deity's 'self-warning' and as a 'warning to the people' to adjust the human order. It stressed the integration and interaction of Heaven and Man. The nine categories of phenomena, such as the five elements and the others, included the relations and norms of nature and human affairs, dominated by the Lord of Heaven (*Tiandi*) and carried out by rulers on earth. Rulers, ministers and subjects all had their respective representations in Heaven (such as the sun, moon and stars). Their behaviour and ethics directly influenced the operations of nature.[24] During the reign of Xuanwang of the Zhou, Bo Yangfu's explanation of the relationship between earthquakes and ill omens is a reflection and continuation of this idea. He maintained that the earthquakes and river blockages were the results of the disorder of yin and yang.[25] The *Shi Jing* also records eclipses of the sun and moon, earthquakes and avalanches that happened during the reign of Youwang of the Zhou, terrible phenomena which people could not explain and so paid homage to Heaven and laid the blame for these events on human beings such as Bao Si and wicked ministers at court.[26] "Hongfan" is a political philosophy imbued with mysticism, the essence of which was is to construct and prove the order of Heaven and Man, specifically emphasizing that human power and the ethical order are controlled by and interact with the

[24] "Song Weizi Shijia", *Shi Ji*.
[25] "Zhou Yu", I, *Guo Yu*.
[26] "Xiaoya: Shiyue Zhijiao", *Shi Jing*.

order of nature. It, therefore, provided the theoretical grounds for the human hierarchy and the domination order.

The **Zhou Yi** constitutes a philosophical model in which the world is in the form of the dual order system. It overlaps the symbols and on three levels to form eight different arrangements ("*gua*") representing eight different objects or phenomena as follows:

Names of *"Gua"*   *"Qian" "Kun" "Zhen" "Xun"* *"Kan" "Li" 'Gen" "Dui"*
Forms
Representations Heaven Earth Thunder Wind Water Fire Mountain River

These eight basic forms were arranged and grouped into sixty-four changes to include all things and phenomena in the universe in order to explain the changes of nature, society and human affairs and further to predict fortune and misfortune.

Before **Zhou Yi**, there had already existed the oracle books in the Xia and Shang dynasties (such as Lianshan and Guizang), and a Shang oracular work titled Kun-*qian*. The placing of "*kun*" before "*qian*" in this title shows the fact that more remnants of the matriarchal system existed in the Shang. **Zhou Yi** reverses that order, placing "*qian*" before "*kun*", and stresses the world outlook of the separate positions of the dual elements and of two integrating into one, while the conception of "*yin*" and "*yang*" in "Hongfan" stresses the idea of the interaction of Heaven and Man and its corresponding methodology. The merger of the doctrine of "*yin*" and "*yang*" and that of "*qian*" and "*kun*" and their corresponding relations with nature then constitute the following pattern:

"*yang qian*" heaven sun ruler   man father husband........
"*yin*" "*kun*" earth moon minister   woman son wife ....

The merger of these two doctrines suited the need of the dual hierarchical systems of class and sex in the Zhou. The philosophical essence, once brought into the realm of gender, formed the gender patterns for "determining the positions of "*qian*" and "*kun*" and "fixing the characters of "*yin*" and "*yang*".

(2) Fixing the positions of "*qian*" and "*kun*" and fixing the characters of "*yin*" and "*yang*": the essence of the sex philosophy

In the Western Zhou, the Yi Jing had already established the conception of fixing positions in the hierarchical order which divided the dual elements into noble and humble, inside and outside, and principal and subordinate. At some time in the Eastern Zhou, the conception of "*yin*" and "*yang*" corresponded to the doctrine of "*qian*" and "*kun*", and had a tendency to merge with it. **Zhou Yi** states: "*Dao*" (truth, principle) is the existence of "*yin*" and "*yang*". And: "*Yi*" (change) is the interaction of "*yin*" and "*yang*" and their proliferation".[27] It was maintained that the basic content of "*yi*", the theory of the formation of the universe, was the interaction of "*yin*" and "*yang*" which were divided from "taiji" (the traditional mystical diagram used to explain things and phenomena of the universe) into two, and then the two were divided into four, and four into eight. From "*yin*" and "*yang*", there emerged the conception of "gang" (vigour) and "rou" (tenderness), and "*yin*" and "*yang*" were bestowed the characteristics of "rou" and "gang" respectively. It was the interaction of "*yang*-gang" and "*yin*-rou" that caused changes in things. Some even held that the characters of "gang" and "rou" determined the positions of noble and humble, and of superior and inferior in the two elements ("*qian*" and "*kun*", "*yin*" and "*yang*"). This is described in the "Yizhuan" section of **Yi Jing**:

> Heaven is high and in the noble position; earth is low and in the humble position, hence the positions of "*qian*" and "*kun*" are determined. Once the natures of the noble and the humble are clear, their positions are also fixed; there are the regularities in movement and stillness, hence the na-

[27] "Xici", I, **Zhou Yi**.

tures of "*gang*" and "*rou*" are clearly distinguished....[28]

And:

Qian evolves into man; *kun* evolves into woman.[29]

And again:

"Qian" belongs to "*yang*" and "*kun*" belongs to "*yin*". "*Yin*" and "*yang*" have the virtue of harmonious integration; "*gang*" and "*rou*" belong to "*yang*" and "*yin*" respectively....[30]

And:

"*Kun*" has the character of utmost tenderness but is vigorous when in movement. It also has the character of utmost stillness and is virtuous and dignified.... "*Kun*" is so tender ... it represents earth, wife and minister....[31]

And:

"*Qian*" is the most vigorous in the world; "*kun*" is the most tender in the world.[32]

From these quotations can be derived the following antithetical pairs:

"*Qian yang*" heaven king man husband superior noble movement vigour robustness....

"*Kun yin*" earth minister woman wife inferior humble stillness tender obedience....

So in the gender order and their value, the characteristics of superior and inferior, noble and humble, movement and stillness, and vigour and tenderness were inherently given to man and woman, and husband and wife. From these characteristics, we can also discern a number of dual standards for man and woman, such as principal and subordinate, and inside and outside. In sum, these entail fixing the positions of "*qian*" and

---

28 "Xici", I, *Zhou Yi*.
29 Ibid.
30 "Xici", II, *Zhou Yi*.
31 "Jian: Wenyan", *Zhou Yi*.

"*kun*" and also of "*yin*" and "*yang*".

The idea of fixing the positions of "*qian*" and "*kun*" derived from the doctrine of "*qian-kun*" in which "*qian*" represented king, father, man and husband, and "*kun*" represented minister, son, woman and wife. The domination of "*kun*" by "*qian*" was regarded as natural and reasonable because it was extended from the principle of "noble heaven and humble earth". Specifically speaking, the symbol of "*qian*" was the "flying dragon", the male dominator or the king, while the symbol of "*kun*" was the strolling mare which acted only in accordance with her master's orders.[33] In the sexual relationship, a woman could only wait to be married, and a wife could only wait for her husband's favours in order to bear children. The vertical relationship of noble and humble derived from fixing the positions of man and woman was extended to the division between inside (domestic) duties and outside duties; a man was engaged in his career outside, a woman was responsible for cooking, weaving and bearing children. The outside career was regarded as important and noble, while the inside duties were trivial and humble. If a woman did not do her "cooking and weaving" and participated instead in political affairs, she would be blamed for ruination of the state.

The idea of fixing the characters of "*yin*" and "*yang*" came from "Hongfan" and *Zhou Yi* in which "*yin*" ("*kun*") and "*yang*" ("*qian*") were given the characteristics of stillness and movement respectively. Hence "*qian*" ("*yang*") had the character of vigour and robustness, and "*kun*" had the character of tenderness and weakness. The conclusion was further drawn that woman (wife), imbued with the characteristic of tenderness, should be governed and controlled by man, with the characteristics of vigour and robustness, and should abide by the ethics of observing chastity all her life. "If she does not abide in virtue, shame will soon come". And: "To abide in virtue constantly is

---

[32] "Xici", II, *Zhou Yi*.

conspicuous for woman and ominous for man".[34] Such maxims were intended to rationalise the dual standards for man and woman. Certain prognostications in **Zhou Yi**, such as "*Gou*", "*Jian*" and "*Guimei*", all referred to such subjects as "*rou*" encountering "*gang*" and "a woman waiting for a man to join her in marriage", the assumption being that marriage and serving a husband were the final destination of woman. The married woman still had to be "supervised" because a woman's virtue had its dual nature. Firstly, a woman was easily tempted to depart from virtue because of her tenderness. Secondly, a woman could not be straight and upright because of her tenderness, and so she needed to be guided by her master. Therefore, a woman needed to retain her tenderness.

The harmony of "*yin*" and "*yang*"

The sexual philosophy of "*yin-yang*" and "*qian-kun*" not only had the character of discriminating between "*yin*" and "*yang*" and emphasizing the change in "*yin*" and "*yang*", but also the effect of encouraging the harmony of "*yin*" and "*yang*". The discrimination was thus designed to achieve harmony. The theory of discriminating between the sexes by fixing the positions of "*yin*" and "*yang*" was intended to attain a harmonious life and the integration of husband and wife; the theory of "*gang*" and "*rou*" in fixing the characteristics of "*yin*" and "*yang*" was intended to achieve a gender division of labour and the mutual complementarity of their qualities. The principle of suppressing "*yin*" and strengthening "*yang*" was intended to achieve harmony and mutual complementarity.

(3) **Shi Jing**, **Shu Jing** and **Zhou Yi**: Temple Cultures: Sexual Norms and Pan-moralism

In the establishment of the domination system which integrated families and state, the Zhou nobility defined the ethical norms for woman step by step. Among the prevalent injunctions was: "To set a good example for the queen, and even for the

---

[33] "Henggua", **Zhou Yi**.

brother, is of benefit in governing the state". Male aristocrats were required by the Rites to set good moral examples for their wives and concubines in order to rule the state and govern their families, although in governing families, a model women was required, and hence virtuous wives and good mothers made their appearance. Tai Jiang, Tai Ren and Tai Si were designated "the three mothers of the Zhou" in later ages, and were praised as the earliest exemplars of virtuous wives and good mothers. There were three criteria for a good mother in the Zhou dynasty. Firstly, she should assist her sons' careers and causes. Tai Si had many sons and assisted Wuwang in eliminating "the mighty Shang". Secondly, she must be a "virtuous wife" above all else. Although having sons and being honoured as queen, Bao Si was, nevertheless, blamed as the chief culprit in "the ruination of the state" because she could not abide by the norms expected of a wife and woman. Finally, a good mother was required to work industriously for her family. There are passages praising a mother's industry and diligence in *Shi Jing*: "My father supported me, my mother raised me; They took care of me from childhood to manhood. Even now they still give me consideration".[35] Also: "Mother works diligently ... mother performs invaluable services".[36] Clearly, the duties and diligence of a mother were emphasised and deified by later generations, and these ethical principles served to guide women to devote their lives to their families.

There were three standards for a "virtuous wife". Firstly, she should assist her husband correctly, without over-reaching her power, in the same way in which Tai Jiang had assisted Gugong Danfu and Tai Si had assisted Wenwang. Secondly, she should take charge of governing the family and preparing food and beverages. Finally, she should remain faithful to her husband all her life. During the Western Zhou, when the patriarchy

---

[34] "Daya: Siqi", *Shi Jing*.
[35] "Xiaoya: Liao'e", *Shi Jing*.

was only recently established, the rites and ethical norms for women were not as strict as those in the later ages. The ethical demands on women were relatively tolerant. There is an instance in *Shi Jing* in which a "husband and wife are on bad terms", and so the wife leaves her husband, who in turn takes in a concubine who already has a son already. This set of events is not censured.[37]

However, the later prevailing theory that women were the source of disaster was the direct outcome of women becoming the instrument for male sexual gratification in patriarchal society. In the "Xiashu" section of *Shang Shu*, there is a warning that "disasters from within are the outcome of an infatuation with "*se*" (beauty / beauties)". *Shang Shu* contains the advice that "a king should not indulge himself in "*sheng*" (song and music) and "*se*". The exegist Kong Yingda was of the opinion that the idea that women were what was intended by the word "*se*" in the classics was a profound observation.[38] Beautiful women, together with wanton music, dogs and horses, came to be regarded as the luxurious trappings of entertainment. Beautiful woman, it was later held, had not only infatuated the ruler, but had also participated and intervened in political affairs. The image had made its appearance of the beautiful wife with the glib tongue, often proffering bad suggestions and advice, and who at times could even precipitate national political crises. "The glorious Zhou dynasty was destroyed by Bao Si!"[39] The Zhou nobility bitterly attacked Bao Si as an ominous "owl" and as a woman who had ruined the nation:

> The clever men built the city walls;
> the clever women brought them down.
> Such women were just like owls.
> The women with glib tongues

---

[36] "Beifeng: Kaifeng", *Shi Jing*.
[37] "Dinggua", *Zhou Yi*.
[38] Kong Yingda, annotation of "'sehuang'" in *Shisan Jing Zhushu*.

were the roots of disaster.
Disasters did not stem
from Heaven, but from women.[40]

The theory that "women occasioned disaster" and the norms for a "virtuous wife and good mother" both originated in the Zhou dynasty, and women were subsequently subjected to such pan-moralism.

5. The Rites Remote from Commoners: Popular Gender Relations

During the Western Zhou when the Rites were just established, they tended to be remote from commoners and functioned as the privilege of society's upper strata. Therefore, a considerable number of antique traditions of human relationships, including those between husbands and wives, still remained. Tolerance, peacefulness, happiness and harmony were the characteristics among the common people at that time.

The **Shi Jing** contains many passages which extol the gentle virtues of marriage:

"To live with a soft and amiable wife is like playing harmonious music".

And:

"A couple of water birds sing on the islet in the river, the kind and beautiful girl is the ideal spouse of a gentleman".

And:

The peach trees flourish
and the peach blossoms fascinate;
this girl is going to be married,
how fortunate her husband's family!"[41]

Longing for a harmonious and warm family life between husband and wife was not only the desire of the nobility, but

---

[39] "Xiaoya: Qiaoyan", **Shi Jing**.
[40] "Xiaoya: Sangrou", **Shi Jing**.

also the heartfelt desire of ordinary people. The folk song sections of **Shi Jing**, such as "Zheng Feng", "Wang Feng" and "Qi Feng", also describe the harmonious and happy connubial life:

> The wife says: 'Now the cocks crow, it's time to get up.'
> The husband says: 'It's early, go out and observe the sky, there are many bright stars in the sky.
> After daybreak, I'll go
> shoot some wild ducks and geese,
> and bring them with some drinks with you.
> We'll play the lute and zither (lit., "qin" and "se")
> and remain devoted couple till the end of
> our lives. What harmonious and happy lives we have![42]

> My husband is in a joyful mood.
> He holds the "sheng" (a kind of wind instrument)
> in his left hand and beckons me
> into the bedroom with his right hand.
> How happy we are![43]

ll these songs present vivid images of happy married lives, and from these documentary sources we can see that there was a tradition from the Zhou dynasty onwards that encouraged husbands and wives to live together and lead peaceful and happy lives in a stable society. However, the social order of that time dictated that individual and family interests must be subordinated to the interests of state, the king of Zhou and the feudal lords. Military conquests, corvee and other public services inevitably cast their shadows over calm and united families. The laments of separated couples in **Shi Jing** became a common theme of the period, and during the invasion of the Xianyun (Xiongnu), we hear the voices of soldiers who lament campaigning and having to leave their wives, and who express their longing to return home.

---

[41] "Xiaoya: Tangdi", "Zhounan: Guansui", "Daoyao" in **Shi Jing**.

Collecting "*wei*" [a kind of vegetable], collecting "*wei*".
They are sprouting once again.
Expecting to be home by winter,
but this year will soon be over.
Leaving wife and leaving home,
all because of the invasion of the Xianyun.
Unable to live a stable life,
all because of the invasion of the Xianyun.[44]

The above poem, "Dongshan" in the "Bin Feng" section of
Shi Jing expresses, in plain language, the feelings of a man
thinking of his wife while he is campaigning. A man from
Guanxi, the speaker in the poem was conscripted to fight in an
eastern expedition not long after his marriage. He has kept
thinking of the wedding ceremony and his beloved wife for
three years. There is also a corresponding poem expressing the
anxiety of a wife expecting her husband to soon return from the
expedition:

The trees are growing taller and they flourish.
Too frequent is the king's corvee and
I am so sad. The more flourishing,
the plants and flowers, the more sad this wife.
Come back soon, my husband.[45]

External factors were not always responsible for the destruction of the cosiness of the family. *Shi Jing* contains instances of domestic friction: "The wheels and spokes part,
husband and wife are on bad terms"[46] Even an affluent family
could not avoid the tragedy of disintegration:

Although the house was large and extravagant,
when peeping in, it was cheerless and empty.
Nobody had lived there for three years.

---

[42] "Zhengfeng: Nuyuejiming", "Qifeng: Jiming", *Shi Jing*.
[43] "Wangfeng: Junzi Yangyang", *Shi Jing*.
[44] "Xiaoya: Caiwei", *Shi Jing*.

Ominous.[47]

In *Shi Jing* there are also instances of wives leaving home and husbands being unable to find them:

Surrounded by rocks
and punctured by vines,
the man came home and
found that his wife had disappeared.[48]

All these examples drawn from *Shi Jing* show that families were loosely organized when the patriarchy was first established, especially during the period when the Rites were remote from commoners. However, all dominant ideologies are those of the ruling classes. As the superstructure and ideology serving the interests of male aristocrats took hold, the patriarchy naturally provided more privileges and conveniences for males. In the Western Zhou, the husband had the right to control and govern his wife, and to ask her to wait on him and his parents. People at that time, moreover, accepted the view that a marriage between the old husband and young wife was more propitious than one between an old wife and young husband:

The withered poplar sprouts,
the old man has a young wife.
This is propitious.[49]

The withered poplar flowered,
the old lady was married to a young man.
Though not ominous,
it was not propitious.[50]

The instances of husbands finding new lovers and neglecting their wives were common in *Shi Jing*. In the poem titled

---

[45] "Xiaoya: Didu", *Shi Jing*.

[46] "Xiaochugua", *Zhou Yi*.

[47] "Fenggua", *Zhou Yi*.

[48] "Kungua", *Zhou Yi*.

"Huangniao" in the "Xiaoya" section of that work, a woman is rejected because she is on bad terms with the members of her husband's family:

> The people here cannot treat me well,
> so I return to my mother's home
> to be a member of my original clan.

Rejected women had different personalities and found themselves in different conditions. Many were unyielding:

> You don't receive me,
> so I'm returning to my clan.
> I won't think of my ex-husband
> but will try to find a new spouse.
> I don't want him to be rich,
> but I want him to be uncommon.[51]

There is an evident self-confidence in this poem.

Economic life and sex

The kings of the Zhou distributed lands to aristocrats as fiefs, while most people were reduced to being landless serfs and peasants. Compared with the strict division of labour in which a man worked the farm while the woman took care of household duties and weaving, peasants more clearly represented the model of gender relationships of mutual dependence and the division of labour in economic life. In large-scale slave collective farming and in individual farming,[52] the model of the division of labour, whereby men worked the land and women delivered meals and engaged in weaving, was always present. In the poem titled "Zaishan" in the "Zhousong" section of *Shi Jing*, we read descriptions peasants gratefully gobbling down their meals brought to them by their wives; some of the women lean close by their husbands, while others test if the plough blades are sharp enough. It is the beginning of the farming year. This is a

---

[49] "Gugua", *Zhou Yi*.
[50] "Dagua", *Zhou Yi*.

warm and tender scene of serfs labouring while their wives deliver meals to them, which contrasts with a depiction of husband and wife working a private plot in close cooperation:

> To live with wife and children
> in the hut within our the plot,
> to cultivate the land
> and to have meals delivered everyday.

The poem titled "Qiyue" in the "Binfeng" section of *Shi Jing* contains a description of peasant couples in the Western Zhou period living mutually dependent lives under the yoke of class oppression and exploitation. The men farm the land and the women weave; the men plant mulberry trees and the women raise silkworms; the men hunt and the women toil. This must be a genuine portrait of the daily working lives of commoners in the Zhou dynasty.

The worship of shamanism

According to documentary sources, male shamans emerged and began to flourish in the time of Zhuan Xu, one of the Five Legendary Emperors at a time when religion and politics were said to be integrating. Originally, shamans and priests, shamans and healers, and shamans and historians were one and the same. The magic forces were invoked by shamans to bring propitiousness and avert disaster, to prevent droughts and floods, and to exorcise and heal disease. Shamanism was so prevalent in the Shang dynasty that statesmen at that time regarded it as a social pollution. *Shang Shu* defined shamanism as "dancing and singing without restraint in order to please the gods".[53]

Zhou's institution of the Rites defined the difference between temple shamanism and popular shamanism. There was an official post designated "*siwu*", and the distinction between male and female shamans was defined in the "*Chunguan*" section of Zhou Li. The female shaman was called "*wu*", loosely translated as "witch", and the male shaman was called "*xi*". The "*xi*"

---

[51] "Xiaoya: Woxingqiye", *Shi Jing*.

officiated over sacrificial ceremonies and healing, while the "*wu*" conducted prayers for good fortune and for averting disasters and danced for rainfall in times of drought.[54] This gender distinction can be observed in the ancient dictionary titled Shuowen: "*Wu*", the woman who prays, the woman who can serve gods and ask them to descend to earth by means of dancing.... . "*Xi*", the man who serves gods by means of fasting and by paying homage to them. The woman who performs such duties is called "wu".[55]

From this explanation it would that the female shaman communicated with the gods through dance, while the male shaman served the gods through fasting and piety. In the Zhou dynasty temple shamanism and popular shamanism co-existed, and popular shamanism, moreover, varied because of regional differences. The most distinctive characteristic of shamanism in different regions was its focus on reproduction, as in the "Minggui" section of *Mo Zi*: "Yan's ancestry is equivalent to the territory of Qi, the mulberry groves of Qi and the Yunmeng lake of Chu; all these are places to offer sacrifices to gods and ancestors, and for men and women to frolic and make rendezvous". Shamanism was very prevalent in the states of Chen and Chu, and Yunmeng was a place where Chu's nobility worshipped the gods of reproduction. The Chu people, self-styled descendants of Zhuan Xu, had a long tradition of shamanism, and the natives of neighbouring Chen, located in present day Huaiyang, saw themselves as descendants of Tai Hao. Wuwang of the Zhou enfeoffed Gui Meng, a descendant of Shun, in the state of Chen, as Hugong of the Chen. Wuwang also married off his elder daughter Tai Ji to Hugong, which indicates that the women in the state of Chen women were regarded as noble. Tai Ji liked the ceremonial and sacrifices, and attached importance to official historians and shamans, which was said to be why

---

[52] "Zhousong: Zaishan", "Xiaoya: Xinnanshan", *Shi Jing*.
[53] "Shangshu: Yixun", *Shang Shu*.

shamanism was prevalent in Chen.[56] In the "Chen Feng" section of **Shi Jing**, there is a verse describing the professional witches dancing to amuse the gods:

> The daughters of Zi Zhong dance under the trees.
> Women do not weave
> but are fond of dancing
> just to please the gods.[57]

This enthusiasm for amusing the gods was even extended to "dancing while beating drums, and not caring if it were winter or summer".[58]

The shamanism of the states of Song and Wei inherited the tradition of spirit worship of the Shang dynasty. Dancing and rendezvous under the mulberry trees and wandering along the banks of the Zhen and Wei rivers, as recorded in **Shi Jing**, were remnants of ancient shamanistic worship and travelling traditions, as well as of the arts of shamanistic reproduction. The magic power of shamanism sometimes extended to the powerful elite.

During the reign of Liwang of the Zhou dynasty, the king used shamans as spies among the population specifically to detect slander against him.[59] Qi's shamanism inherited the tradition of the Dawenkou and Longshan cultures of Shandong. The Qi people wanted their elder daughters not to marry but to become witches. In the "Dili Zhi" section of **Han Shu**, Ban Gu maintains that these customs began with Huangong of the state of Qi, but this is probably incorrect.

6. The Fall of the Rites and Degeneration of Music: the Challenged Sexual Order and Its

---

[54] "Chunguan Zongbo", **Zhou Li**.
[55] **Shuowen Jiezi**, "juan" 50.
[56] "Dili Zhi", **Han Shu**.
[57] "Chenfeng: Dongmen Zhifen", **Shi Jing**.

Self-grouping

At the end of the Western Zhou, because of the extravagant and dissipated lifestyles of the kings, and the rise and fall of the power of feudal lords and alien tribes, the exile of Youwang and the short "republican" period of united aristocratic government (841-28 BCE) prevailed. The latter is called the period of "the restoration of Xuanwang". Although the king's power was restored and the political situation stabilised, the rule of kings was unstable. The deposition of the queen by Youwang violated conventional rites and norms. Youwang is described in the histories as having "favoured the new and kept the old at a distance", having deposed Shen and making Bao Si queen in her stead. The former queen sprang from the Jiangshen family which had matrimonial relations with the king's house for generations, while the latter was from conquered state of Bao. This action caused indignation at court and throughout his kingdom.

The Zhou collapsed because of internal disorder and external invasion. Yi Jiu, Youwang's son, with the assistance of feudal lords, moved the capital to Luoyang and founded the Eastern Zhou.

In the Eastern Zhou, the Zhou rites met a greater challenge and test. The aristocratic dictatorship based on the Rites contained its own potential crises, which sprang not from alien tribes and "disasters caused by women", but from the conflicts of interests, desires and rites of the male aristocratic power holders themselves. The weakening of the Zhou imperial house, the annexation of weak feudal lords by those that were powerful, the growth of the states of Qi, Chu, Qin and Jin, government under the control of a chief feudal lord, and the release of orders "in the name of the Zhou king" were naturally serious challenges to the Zhou ritual order. Moreover, among the court and the feudal lords, the rite system was often eroded and disintegrated by the extravagance and dissipation of incumbents.

The primogeniture affecting power transfers became the focus of conflicts which were presented as secret and open struggles and the entanglements among women and between men and women in families, which later developed into political crises surrounding the succession to the throne.

(1) Crises: Challenges from Within the Nobility

"Two queens, two crown princes, two internal governments and strong, hostile countries on the outside are the roots of political disorder".[60] This relatively sober-minded aristocratic commented by the author of *Zuo Zhuan* notes four factors causing political chaos, two of which relate to women. In the three centuries from the collapse of the Western Zhou to the Spring and Autumn period, there was continuous confusion caused by installing queens ("*hou*" or "*furen*") as heirs. According to *Zuo Zhuan*, from the times of the kings Zhuangwang, Huiwang and Xiangwang, there were incessant wars because of problems of deposition and installation, and as a result, the feudal lords grew stronger in the name of the king and determining master, while the imperial house of Zhou became weaker.

In the disorder among the feudal lords, Wu Jiang, the mother of Zhuanggong of the state of Zheng, demanded to assert her mother's power and depose her elder son in favour of the younger. This action initiated a war between the brothers (743-721 BCE). At almost the same time, a rebellion broke out in the state of Wei. It was led by Zhou Yu, son of a favourite concubine of Zhuanggong of Wei. He killed his elder brother, Huanggong, and declared himself king of Wei. After Zhou Yu was killed in turn and Xiangong acceded to the throne, thirty-one years (718-688 BCE) of political chaos ensued, precipitated by incidents such as incest, the forceful seizure of another's

---

[60] "Huangong shibanian", *Zuo Zhuan*.

wife, the installation of concubines and the deposition of the legal wife. Xiangong of the Jin deposed the crown prince Shen Sheng and banished other princes because he favoured his concubine Li Ji and tried to install her son on the throne. Further internal disorder broke out and this lasted a further twenty years (655-636 BCE). There is a detailed record of these events in *Guo Yu*. Even in the state of Lu, the fief of Zhougong who founded the institutions of the Rites and Music, crises of installation and deposition also existed. These crises were also connected with "dubious sexual affairs". For example, Huangong of Lu's death in the state of Qi was the result of his wife's adulterous relations with her elder brother Xianggong of Qi. She flagrantly violated the Rites and returned many times to Qi to meet Xianggong. After discovering this secret, Huangong was killed by an assassin sent by Xianggong.

After succeeding to the throne in 694 BCE, Zhuanggong of Lu also violated the Rites and secretly promised Meng Ren that he would make her his wife. This action caused Qing Fu to kill Ban, Meng Ren's son, and install Mingong. Qing Fu also had an adulterous affair with Zhuanggong's wife, Ai Jiang. Ai Jiang, in trying to install her lover Qing Fu, became involved in a secret plot to murder Mingong. Finally, Xigong (661-659 BCE) succeeded to the throne. He was the son of Zhuanggong's concubine Cheng Feng. The large eastern state of Qi was also experiencing great unrest. Xigong treated his nephew Gongsun Wuzhi in the same way as the crown prince Xianggong, and, as a result, Gongsun killed Xianggong and installed himself as king. Gongsun himself was killed too, and this incident led to the struggle between Prince Jiu and Xiao Bai (Huangong). The struggle resulted in Xiao Bai's victory. But in his later years, Huangong who had been the overlord among the feudal lords in the Spring and Autumn period could not avoid "favouring beautiful women", many of whom he "adopted". Conflicts finally broke out among his sons and concubines, and as a result he died in prison of hunger.

Such incidents of violating the Rites and norms spread like an epidemic among the upper strata in the various states. Faced with this situation, sober-minded people who insisted on the Rites among the nobility made every effort to prevent such incidents before they occurred or to proffer sound advice when such incidents happened. For example, minister Fu Ren warned Xiangwang of the Zhou not to violate the Rites because the latter "favoured the new and kept the old at a distance", and not to depose Shen Lu and install Di as his queen, in order to avoid offending the feudal lords in the Central Plain. Shi Que, Wei's minister, advised Zhuanggong of the Wei not to confuse "*liu shun*" (the six norms) with "*liu ni*" (the six offences). The six norms required that "the king issues orders properly, ministers implement orders faithfully, the father treats his sons kindly, the son treats his parents filially, the elder brother cares for the younger brother, and the younger brother respects the elder brother". The six offences referred to actions whereby "the humble stand in the way of the noble, the junior offend the senior, the distant drive a wedge between those who are close, the newly favoured sow the seeds of discord among the elders and senior ministers, small states overshadow large states, and the improper overrule the proper".[61] Shi Que's action was the most authoritative interpretation and steadfast protection of the Zhou rites at that time. Similarly, Shen Xu, minister of the state of Lu, advised Huangong not to go to Qi to attend a "*she*" ceremony in order to comply with Wen Jiang's wishes. Li Ke, minister of the state of Jin, advised Xiangong not to install the younger son born by his concubine and depose the elder son born by his wife. All these actions were conscious attempts to protect the Zhou rites, but this reasonable advice could seldom restrain the privileged who were eager to seize power. However, there were exceptions, and sometimes rulers attempted to restrict violations of the Rites. The famous Kuiqiu conference (651

---

[61] "Yingong sannian", **Zuo Zhuan**.

BCE) was one of the important events in which Huangong of the state of Qi pledged oath of allegiance when he formed the alliance giving him domination over the Central Plain. The oath included "*wu wu*" (five prohibitions): "Not to block rivers; not to stop storing grain; not to change the installed son and heir; not to promote his concubine to be his wife; and, not to let women intervene in state affairs".[62] The last three prohibitions directly related to women, which demonstrates the prominence and prevalence of such concerns.

The words of advice, admonition and oath increasingly failed to prevent violations of the Rites. On the contrary, the process of the fall of the Rites and the degeneration of Music accelerated because of the weakening of the imperial house, the loss of political control and the tyranny of officials. Events of the late Spring and Autumn period testify to this. For example, Linggong of the state of Chen acted licentiously, together with his minister, towards Xia Ji, Xia Zhengshu's mother, and so was killed by Xia Zhengshu (598 BCE). After the death of Dinggong of the state of Lu, the minister Xiang Zhong killed two sons of Dinggong's wife Ai Jiang, and installed the son of Dinggong's concubine as king (Xuangong of the state of Lu) (608 BCE). Mu Jiang had an adulterous relationship with the minister Shusun Qiaoru, and they plotted unsuccessfully to depose Chengong and install Shusun as king (575 BCE). Pinggong of the state of Song adopted a concubine and promoted her to be his wife (574 BCE), while Pinggong of the state of Jin "loved beautiful women above all else" and adopted four women surnamed Ji to be his wife and concubines, violating the rites that no marriage could be formed among families with the same surname (ca. 550-32). In the state of Lu from the reign of Zhaogong onwards, political power was in the hands of by three aristocrats and the powerless Zhaogong was forced to live in other states in exile. During the reign of Dinggong, Yang Huo,

---

[62] "Xigong jiunian", *Chunqiu Guliang Zhuan*.

an official of the Jisun family, controlled politics and was despised by Confucius. Jinggong of the state of Qi installed his son Tu born of his concubine on the throne, while his other sons fled to Wei and Lu.

The coming of the Warring States period was initiated when the Chen and Tian families took the place of the Jiang and Lu families and was signalled by the division of the state of Jin into three. These events not only presented the Zhou rites instituted by Zhougong with their greatest crisis to date, but it also presaged a favourable turnabout for the Rites. I call it crisis because it was the end of feudalism and the seeming existence of the Zhou dynasty, but favourable in that the aristocratic hierarchy and the patriarchal clan system, after some internal self-adjustments and institutional changes, could still operate as before. These internal self-adjustments of the aristocratic ruling mechanism began when this mechanism was challenged. This fact can be explained by the warnings and advice issued by the aristocrats who stressed the Rites and by the oaths of alliance among the feudal lords. However, up to the late Spring and Autumn period, violent killing, exiles and imprisonment were often used to solve tense situations and crises at upper levels. Such events can be found continuously in the historical records. Even Sima Qian, the historian, was perplexed by these events: "Father and son kill each other, and elder and younger brothers try to destroy each other. How could this happen?"[63]

Another effective way to restore order was to strengthen education in the Rites. There were many educated and sober-minded aristocrats, such as Zi Chan of Zheng, Shu Xiang of Jin, Yan Ying of Qi and Confucius of Lu, and they felt deeply about the worsening situation for aristocrats brought about by the collapse of Rites and the degeneration of Music. They spared no effort to use their position and knowledge in an attempt to influence society and people in the fields of politics,

---

[63] "Wei Kangshu Shijia", *Shi Ji*.

diplomacy, culture and education. Some wrote books, explained classics and trained disciples; some strengthened family education and governed their families with the Rites and norms; some with the status of official historians recorded historical events in order to praise virtue and condemn evil. Confucius and his followers regarded "restraining oneself and restoring the Rites" as their main task.

As demonstrated by facts, the reinterpretation of the official classics of the Western Zhou and the dissemination of them had a positive social effect. Almost all official documents were reinterpreted and annotated. *Zhou Yi*, *Shi Jing* and *Shang Shu* were compiled as books, annotated and distributed among the nobility and commoners. I would like to select some cases related to gender issues which reflect the change which took place with the use of education to adjust the rites.

From the change in "*yixue*" (the doctrine of change), we can see that *Zhou Yi* was possibly popular among noblewomen in the Spring and Autumn period. Mu Jiang, the wife of Xiangong of Lu was very familiar with practising divination and "*yixue*". The *Zhou Yi* was augmented with "*Gua Ci*" and "*Yao Ci*" (two oracular texts), and ten appendices of interpretation of "*yixue*", called *Shi Yi* (The Ten Wings). By comparing the texts of the hexagrams "*Jiaren*" and "*Heng*" with their interpretations in these various appendices, we can see how the original meaning of *Yi Jing* was modified by these various Appendices.

In the "*Yao Ci*" gloss of the trigram "*Heng*" we now read: "Six five. Keeping constant is a virtue, maintain sexual morals, propitious for woman, ominous for man". The "*Xiang Ci*" Appendix comments on the same trigram: "Woman pure and chaste, propitious, this means constancy until the end; man defines principle, to submit to a woman is dangerous".

The hexagram "*Jiaren*" is similarly reinterpreted in the new "*Gua Ci*" gloss: "Favourable to woman". The "*Tuan Ci*" appendix reads: "Hexagram *Jiaren*, keep women in the proper place within, keep men in the proper place without. The proper places of men and women, the proper division of labour is the most important principle in the universe. There must be ruler-like authorities in families; they are parents. If father, son, brothers, husband and wife keep their proper places respectively, the family order and atmosphere will be right and proper, and the universe will be peaceful and stable". The "*Yao Ci*" comment on the same hexagram reads: "Ninth, watch one's own wife, no regret". The "*Xiang Ci*" Appendix comments: "Watch one's own wife to see if she has been unchaste and inconstant". The "*Yao Ci*" comment on one line is "*Jiaren*" is: "Six-two: not to satisfy one's wife's wishes, order her to take charge of food and drink, propitious". The "*Xiang Ci*" comments on that same line: "These words in six-two correspond to "*shun*" (submissive) in the "*sun*" trigram". Another line the "*Yao Ci*" glosses as follows: "Nine-three: strictly control the wife and children in the family, propitious even though there are complaints; wife and children act loosely, misfortune comes in the end". On which the "*Xiang Ci*" elaborates: "Wife and children complain because of the strict control, but still the proper order and atmosphere of the family is kept; the wife and children act loosely, family norms will degenerate".

The *Qian* and *Kun* trigrams undergo a similar reinterpretation. These are new interpretations of **Zhou Yi** made after the beginning of the Spring and Autumn period. In gender relations, more attention was now paid to the aspect of domination in gender relations. Not only the **Zhou Yi**, but other classics controlled by aristocrats, such as **Shi Jing**, **Shang Shu** and **Li Ji**, were propagated widely, and the aristocratic women were often the major recipients of education in these classics. The training of "model women" depended on the inculcation of the doctrines of the classics and training in daily norms, such as **Nei Ze** which lists the rules and norms that women must abide by. In the Spring and Autumn period, although there were women who violated the rites like Wen Jiang, Ai Jiang (the wife of Zhuang-gong of Lu), Mu Jiang and Xia Ji, "model women" who observed the Rites conscientiously were more common. Madam Xi, for example, was praised by later generations for not serving her second husband and keeping a vow of silence in repentance; the concubine of Gongbo of the state of Song remained a widow after her master's death, and was burned to death because her woman teacher was absent and she refused to leave the place. Her mother Mu Jiang had been an adherent of the Rites, but she was imprisoned in the eastern palace because of her participation in an abortive plot with Shusun Jiaoru. She practised divination and was told to "abide by the hexagram". She preferred to repent her past and die in the palace than escape:

> As a woman, I took part in the activities,
> to plunge the state into disorder.
> Under the king,
> I ungratefully worked to depose him
> and so cannot say I have the virtue of "yuan".
> To plunge the state into chaos
> I cannot have the virtue of "heng".
> To do some foolish things
> at the expense of my own interests
> I cannot say I have the virtue of "li".
> To abandon the noble position of wife and mother of rulers
> to please my lover

I cannot say I have the virtue of "zhen"....[64] She reflected deeply and castigated herself, using the Rites and ethical standards of male aristocrats. This instance shows clearly woman's piety to the orthodox rites at that time. Another example is that of Zhong Zi, the concubine of Linggong of the state of Qi, who ran counter to contemporary practice and was opposed to moves to install her own son as crown prince.[65] Jing Jiang, the mother of Wenbo of the state of Lu, was a model mother and

---

[64] "Xianggong jiunian", *Zuo Zhuan*.
[65] "Xianggong shijiunian", *Zuo Zhuan*.

was praised as "a female sage" in the Spring and Autumn period. She insisted on observing the discrimination between man and woman prescribed by the Rites. Even when she talked to her nephew, she still did not cross the threshold. Although she was a noblewoman she still diligently practised her weaving and never behaved wantonly and idly. She was a widow, but acted with strictest propriety. She taught her sons and daughters-in-law to ensure that her descendants did not suffer the bad reputation of "being deeply attaching to their wives". When she mourned for her husband and son, she did so in accordance with the Rites by mourning her husband in the daytime and crying for her son at night, insisting that the Rites prescribed that "a widow never cries for her husband at night". Confucius highly praised her model behaviour.[66]

These facts indicate that the rites and ethics representing the interests of the male aristocrats under the aristocratic hierarchy were accepted by these model women. They implemented the Rites and ethics faithfully and became their true protectors and steadfast guardians. These facts also show the true vitality of the Zhou rites and their corresponding ideologies, and are important factors determining why these system, laws and conceptions of gender relationships could last several thousand years.

(2) Power and Sex: Gender Relations in the Warring States Period

In the Spring and Autumn period, the feudal lords struggled for hegemony and launched armies undertaking military conquests. The Zhou rites collapsed and even the institutions were eliminated. "The feudal lords launched military conquests and were not submissive to the king of Zhou. They hated the Rites and Music for being restrictive and abolished the classics

---

[66] "Lu Yu", *Guo Yu*.

and institutions. Then, seven major states emerged."[67]

During the Warring States period, pragmatism dominated the hierarchy and personal ambitions destroyed the Rites and norms. The ruling class wished to realise their desire to dominate a united country, and so during the more than two centuries of annexation and resistance, all states struggled to recruit "talented men" to serve their own interests. They recruited advisers, diplomats and men versed in the martial arts. The system of inherited ranks and titles broke down. The rulers of different states were now not only served by aristocrats, who were themselves divided. These capricious men brought eloquence into full play and manoeuvred among the various states. As such men gradually came to be trusted by a ruler, he would be accorded high position, a handsome salary and glory. The chaotic situation and the elevation of diplomats and advisors gradually encouraged the growth of a worldly tendency which emphasised interests, power and influence. People strove to break from the confinement of the Rites, and profit and loss became the yardstick for evaluating society and man. The effect of this social mood on gender relations directly led male powerholders to indulge their sexual desires and advocate utilitarianism and demoralisation in matters of sex, while women accept this utilitarianism and the conception of regarding women as the sexual tools on the other hand.

Marriage and Beauty: Political Deals

In the Warring States period, the principle of "*li nei*" (benefiting the state and family) in marriage was not emphasised; women to be married off to other states were no longer praised as "women representing their states". The states attached more importance to scheming, and were eager for quick successes and immediate benefits. The inter-marriages among feudal states were now no more than acts of mutual political collaboration and the means to subvert hostile states.

---

[67] Xu Shen, **Shuowen Jiezi**.

The matrimonial conspiracy between the states of Qi, Wei and Qin became evident when Meng Chang lost his post as prime minister, and subsequently fled to Wei. The Wei people divorced their wives from Qi on order to sever their relations with Qi. Advisor Han Chun persuaded Zhaowang of the Qin to immediately marry a woman from Qi and form an alliance with Qi to attack Wei.[68] In another example, Zhang Yi used a beauty as bait to entice the king of Chu, and at the same time sowed discord between the king and his queen, Nanhou. As a result, Chu severed its relations with the states allied against Qin and so was finally defeated.[69] Su Qin also once advised Xuanwang of the Qi not to overlook the inter-marriage between Yan and Qin, but to attack Yan when it was weak.[70]

The weak states increasingly needed to "export" beauties to establish matrimonial relations with other states for self-protection. After its defeat at Changping, the state of Zhao "acted humbly, expended wealth generously, and sent women to the states of Yan, Wei, Qi and Chu to befriend them. It tried every means to avert an attack from Qin".[71]

Sometimes even the legality of marriage was abandoned. The weak states simply sent beauties to the rulers of stronger states. Wei, for example, sent a beauty named Zheng Xiu to Chu for subversion.[72] Moreover, Han tried to bribe Qin in order to protect itself, but, lacking gold, "Han sold off beautiful women, but the prices were too high for other feudal lords to purchase them. Qin purchased them with three thousand units of gold, and then Han also gave this amount to Qin, so that Qin obtained both the gold and the beauties".[73]

Politicians and speculators also used beautiful women in

---

[68] "Qin Ce", IV, *Zhanguo Ce*.
[69] "Chu Ce", I, II, III, *Zhanguo Ce*.
[70] "Yan Ce", I, *Zhanguo Ce*.
[71] "Zhongshan Ce", *Zhanguo Ce*.
[72] "Chu Ce", IV, *Zhanguo Ce*.
[73] "Han Ce", III, *Zhanguo Ce*.

their grab for power and interests. In addition to the political strategists like Su Qin and Zhang Yi who manoeuvred among the various states, Li Yuan and Lu Buwei were more representative. Li Yuan from the Zhao presented his sister to Huang Xie, Lord Chun-shen of Chu. After she was pregnant, these three persons plotted together to present her to King Kaolie of Chu. Then Li's sister became queen, and her son became crown prince, later succeeding to the throne. Li Yuan then killed Lord Chunshen for keeping it secret.[74] Lu Buwei, a rich merchant, spent a huge amount of money on befriending Yi Ren, a son of Qin Zhaowang's concubine then acting as a hostage in Zhao, in the hope that Yi Ren would struggle for the position of crown prince. Lu adopted a concubine from Handan, and when she was pregnant, Lu presented her to Yi Ren. This investment got a favourable return. Lu was given the title of hou and a fief of one hundred thousand households, and became the prime minister of Qin.[75]

In Qi, the Chen (Tian) family, which had replaced the Jiang family, benefited from making use of woman's beauty to seize power and consolidate its position after it acquired power:

Tian Chang selected several hundred women from Qi who were all over seven chi tall for his rear palace. Some of his guests and hangers-on could enter the rear palace without restriction. After his death, Tian left more than seventy sons.[76]

Tian Wen, Lord Mengchang, emulated his grandfather, and also allowed a hanger-on to have illicit relations with women in the rear palace. Someone reported this matter to Meng Chang and asked him why he did not kill this hanger-on. Meng Chang said: "It is natural because when they both saw each other they fell in love. Just keep

---

[74] "Chu Ce", IV, *Zhanguo Ce*.
[75] "Shihuang Benji", "Lu Buwei Liezhuan", *Shi Ji*.
[76] "Tianjing Zhongwan Shijia", *Shi Ji*.

silent!"[77]

This excused hanger-on served Tian Wen at the critical moment in return for Tian's generosity.

The widespread use beautiful women demonstrates that women were used as things, objects and tools of political aims. When the restrictions of norms and ethics no longer existed in society, such a demoralisation also brought misfortune to women. Moreover, these phenomena did not mean that women could be unchaste. They still faced yet another oppression.

Man-centred dual standards for woman

On the one hand male aristocrats indulged themselves in beauties and drinking, and "surrounded themselves with concubines and young women". Speculators purchased beautiful women as assets for future promotion and fortune, while women were required to abide by dual ethical standards in order to fulfil male demands. The story of "the man of Chu with two wives" provides a vivid picture of this double standard:

A man from the Chu had two wives. Someone tried to seduce the older wife, but she resisted. He then seduced the younger wife and succeeded. Not long after the man from Chu died. A man asked the seducer whom he would select among the two women. The answer was the older woman. The man asked: "The elder castigated you and the younger one was willing. Why do you try to adopt the older wife?" The seducer replied: "When she was another man's wife, I wanted her to be willing, but if she were my wife, I would want her to resist".[78]

As a seducer, man wanted woman to be wanton and submissive; once he became a husband, he wanted his woman to be chaste. Only consideration of the male position counts.

Public opinion regarding a woman's virtues and conducts seemed more important than regarding a man's. Remarried

---

[77] "Chu Ce", IV, *Zhanguo Ce*.
[78] "Qi Ce", III, *Zhanguo Ce*.

women were, however, clearly not despised at that time. If a divorced woman could remarry nearby and quickly, she was held to be a good woman.[79]

Woman's acceptance and submission

The buffeting waves whipped up by the quest for power, position, influence and interest were soon accepted by women who were already in the submissive positions. They wanted to be patronised and supported, and exchanged their moral qualities, dignity and freedom for patronage and support. An example is provided by the humble and snobbish conduct of Su Qin's wife and sister-in-law. When Su was in dire straits, "his wife was reluctant to do sewing for him, his sister-in-law was reluctant to go to the kitchen for him, and his parents were unwilling to talk to him". After a meteoric rise to success, "his wife dared not look him in the face, his sister-in-law bowed deeply when walking before him and made four prostrations to express her gratitude". She openly stated that she acted humbly, "because her brother-in-law is now noble and wealthy".[80] Women's acceptance of power and position was greatly developed and encouraged by men's desires to possess these things.

The fortunes of women who acted as the roles of sex tools varied because of their different conditions. Some were sold; some were treated as gifts; some were the objects of political deals. Among the beauties of Zheng who were the victims of the slanders of Zheng Xiu, or Han's beauties sold to Qin, or the numerous other women sent here and there as gifts, some were themselves collaborators in political schemes like Li Yuan's sister and the concubine from Handan, some were victims and some were "winners" in political struggles like Zheng Xiu, the queen of Huaiwang of Chu, who made a point of slandering other beautiful women.

7. The sexual conceptions of the pre-Qin philosophers

The Spring and Autumn and the Warring States were periods when the society of the aristocratic rites was just founded and was

---

[79] "Qin Ce", *Zhanguo Ce*.
[80] "Zhao Ce", *Zhanguo Ce*.

seriously challenged, and the times when the Chinese society made important changes. The ideologies were active and vigorous at that times. They offered the opportunities to the thinkers of various classes and strata to attack the current abuses, to suggest the ways to save the world and country, and to develop free arguments. There emerged various schools to propagate their won doctrine. The spokesmen of various interest groups wrote books, founded doctrines and travelled to various states to persuade leaders of their views and to propagate their ideas. The academic and ideological atmosphere was active and intense. Of a dozen or more philosophical doctrines summarised by the later generations, the most influential were Confucianism, Mohism, Taoism and Legalism. We will now examine the sexual conceptions of these three most important schools.

(1) Confucianism

Using the Rites to establish correct ethics and to restrain desires, Confucius was the founder of Confucianism. The Confucian "five classics" include **Shang Shu**, **Zhou Yi** and **Li Jing** which was written by Zhougong are the documents of the Western Zhou. Confucius studied and arranged these classics. The other two, **Shi Jing** and **Chunqiu**, were written and compiled in the Spring and Autumn period. From the Western Zhou to Confucius's time, the idea of rites, using the Zhou rites to correct human ethics and to restrain desires, developed continuously.[81] Confucius epitomised the thoughts of these classics.

Confucius lived in the late Spring and Autumn period (551-479 BCE). He felt deeply that his times were facing a serious

---

[81] See the above-mentioned "*liu shun*" and "*liu nie*" by Fu Chen and Shi Que respectively. Also "*ba li*" (the eight virtues) outlined in **Guan Zi** ("*Wufu*"). "*Ba li*" includes injunctions that the "ruler should be impartial and selfless; the minister should be loyal and not form cliques; the father should be kind and diligent in education; the son should be filial and respectful; the elder brother should be lenient and kind; the younger brother should be respectful and obedient to the elder brother; the husband should be kind, tolerant and constant; and the wife should be diligent and chaste."

crisis occasioned by rampant human desires, class disorder, the collapse of the Rites and the degeneration of Music. He advocated "restraining oneself and restoring the Rites". In order words, the people of the upper levels of society should restrain their personal desires and act according to the Zhou rites. He regarded "the setting of proper places and status" as the key to restoring the Rites and as the most urgent task in government. When Jinggong of Qi and Zi Lu asked Confucius about governing a country, he immediately answered that it was important to set the proper place and status of "ruler, minister, father and son".[82] This "setting of proper places and status" meant to play one's part in society and the family according to the Rites and norms, and to accept the share of one's corresponding rights and obligations. On sexual relations, Confucius recognized only the proper places and status of men and women within each hierarchic level and set corresponding ethical norms for these. The principle of "respecting one's mother" was further specified by Confucius as "showing obedience to one's parents" and "sparing no effort to wait upon one's parents".[83] The concept of "zhongqi" (paying attention to the wife) required that the husband attach importance to a wife's ethical qualities and to her contributions to the family, and so "value virtue instead of appearances".[84] He blamed those aristocrats who "are more fond of beauty than of virtue".[85] He appreciated very much those virtuous wives and good mothers who act according the rites and he highly praised women such as Jing Jiang, Ji Sun's wife. On the other hand, he despised such behaviour as being infatuated with beauty or confusing one's ruler's decisions by meeting him privately. He maintained that "a woman's words can have an upright man dismissed, and a private meeting with a woman can cause him to perish".[86] Confucius despised

---

[82] "Yan Yuan", "Zi Lu", *Lunyu*.

[83] "Xue'er", *Lunyu*.

[84] Ibid.

[85] "Wei Linggong", *Lunyu*.

[86] "Kong Zi Shijia", *Lunyu*.

women indiscriminately, and placed women and "*xiaoren*" (mean persons) into the same category: "Women and "*xiaoren*" are hard to deal with, and when one is close to them, they will act excessively, and when one keep them at a distance, they will complain".[87]

More than one century after Confucius, Mencius (c. 372-289 BCE), confronting growing social contradictions, fiercely attacked current abuses such as destroying the Rites and abolishing institutions, as well as the rampancy of human desires and the looseness of the ritual line between man and woman. He despised the man who "climbs the wall into his neighbour's house and embraces the virgin there". He objected to miscreant men and women who "without their parents' permission and a matchmaker's introduction, drill holes to peep through and climb walls to meet", behaviour not condoned "parents and countrymen".[88] Mencius also defined the principle that "a man and woman cannot give and receive things directly" as a "rite" of discrimination between men and women:

Chunyu Kun asked: "Man and woman cannot give and receive things directly. Is this in accordance with the Rites?" Mencius answered, "Yes". Chunyu asked: "Can a man help himself when his sister-in-law falls into the river?" Mencius answered: "When the sister-in-law falls into the river and the man stands by, he is a beast. Man and woman cannot give and receive things directly because this is regulated by the Rites, but when the sister-in-law falls into the river and the man goes to help, this is to act according to particular circumstances".[89]

Therefore, in Mencius' view the sexual desires which could not be restrained by the self must be handled by keeping men and women apart and using the Rites to suppress the desires, as can be seen in the example of giving and receiving, but in the instance where the sister-in-law falls into the river, the man should lend a helping hand. This is the famous "theory of the

---

[87] "Yanghuo", **Lunyu**.
[88] "Gaozi", **Meng Zi**.
[89] "Lilou", **Meng Zi**.

flexibility and expediency" of the Rites.

On sexual desires, Mencius maintained that in addition to the restraints from outside, "to cultivate the mind" and "to lessen desires" through self-cultivation were more important. Mencius elaborated on the theory that man's original nature is good to extend it to argue that humans have innate goodness. A gentleman, he continued, should "maintain goodness in his mind", and when a person loses his kind heart ("*fangxin*"), he can retrieve it ("*qiu fangxin*") by way of mental cultivation ("*yangxin*"). "The best way to cultivate one's mind is to lessen one's desires", the less one desires, the kinder one's heart. It does not matter if a man in a high position likes beautiful women; if he can put himself in the place of another, and allow every man and woman to have a spouse, he would have done a great deed.

Mencius paid special attention to the principle of human ethics in gender relations. He proposed the famous "*wu lun*" (five relations) affection between father and son, righteousness between ruler and minister, discrimination between husband and wife, order between senior and junior, and faithfulness among friends. Compared with the ethics governing relations between husband and wife in Confucius' theory of "setting the proper places and status", one can see that the times had changed. Relations between husbands and wives in the Warring States period were facing the challenges from social demoralisation and there was a need to define the behaviours of husband and wife by setting proper human ethics. Moreover, relations between husbands and wives in the Warring States period were more unequal than in the Spring and Autumn period, and male-centred ideas were growing in strength. The decline of the woman's position in family clan be proved by Mencius' attitude towards his wife (he intended to dismiss her on the grounds that she did not know the Rites), his attitude towards utilizing women and his treatment of women as tools. He believed that "the purpose in marrying a wife is to have descendants" and "for perpetuating the family line". "There are three offences against filial conduct, and the first is the offence of having no descendant". He also regarded "favouring wives and neglecting parents" as one of "the five offences against filial obedience".

Not long after Mencius, Xun Zi (c.313-238 BCE) completed the transfer from the Rites system to the idea of ruling with law. His doctrines, Confucianism in name but Legalism in reality, advocated that "the original character of the human being is evil. A person's good character is artificial". He also argued that one's conduct can accord with the Rites and norms only after one has been educated and reformed. He therefore stressed not only the Rites and law, but also education. His idea of "emphasizing the Rites" actually also included some concept of ruling in accordance with laws.

(2) Taoism: Respecting the mother and worshipping tenderness; touching on ethics lightly and lessening desires; complying with nature.

Lao Zi thought that the Tao (Dao) was "the mother of universe", "the profound female character" and "the mother of everything and the beginning of heaven and earth". Tao had the character of utmost tenderness. According to the principle of "tenderness prevailing over vigour", female tenderness was invincible.

Unlike the Confucian conception of gender which emphasised proper ethical places and status, duties and obligations, Taoism only touched lightly on family ethics, and instead stress complying with human nature, restoring one's true nature and quality, and awakening man's innate and pure conscience. It sought harmony among the people originating from below, rather then using the Rites and righteousness to bind social and family relations from above. In the matter of husband-wife relations, the famous Taoist teacher Zhuang Zi sat and sang while beating his bowl after the death of his wife. He thought that a man's death was analogous to completing the change of "lying down and sleeping in a big room"; the factors causing quarrels between one's mother and wife are that "the house is not empty", and that people have too many duties and obligations.

Because the character of Taoism was held to be "compliance with nature", the Taoists' basic attitude towards human desires is to seek to purify the mind and lessen desires. The Taoist conception of sex called for refraining from beauty and sexual desires. Lao Zi said: "The Five Colours will dazzle one's eyes, and the Five Notes of music will deafen one's ears". Thus, beauty and music were regarded as harmful to one's health and one's original nature.

The Taoist attitude towards "beauty" entailed both an ultra-utilitarian attitude and a purely spiritual aesthetic standard, and these were used to judge women. Taoists regard the integration of "quande" (perfect virtue) and "quanxing" (perfect form) as the highest standard of woman's beauty. "Quande" is the Taoist spirit of purifying mind and lessening desires, and of retaining calmness, emptiness and modesty. "Quanxing" is perfection of form and quality, and it entails refraining from artificial measures such as binding the waist and piercing one's ears in the quest for natural beauty. If a woman cannot have both, then "quande" was regarded as being more important than "quanxing". The "Caomu" section of **Zhuang Zi** records a story about an inn-keeper praising his ugly wife and despising his beautiful concubine. The ugly wife is conscious of her ugliness and modest ("the ugly wife is self-conscious, and so I do not think that she is ugly"); the beautiful concubine is conscious of her beauty and arrogant, ("the beautiful one is self-satisfied with her beauty, so I don't think that she is beautiful"). Taoists attach more importance to the long-lasting spiritual innate beauty than to external beauty which occasions transient pleasure. This aesthetic judgement which emphasises a woman's spiritual beauty had a positive influence in later ages.

(3) Legalism: The attitude of regarding woman as tool and the principle of punishment

Han Fei's view of woman as a tool drove the utilitarian attitude toward woman to the maximum. He advocated "using woman as a trap and calculating the effects" using beautiful woman to subvert hostile states, to overcome political opponents, to get information and to solve mysteries. In almost all political struggles, she was a very effective means to win victory. But he also warned that when using a beautiful woman as a trap, the plotter should not act in compliance with his favoured woman's opinion, and should guard against "private requests" of his wife or concubine. He further reminded rulers to guard against the woman "in the same bed", and to be on the alert against beautiful women who "cause disasters". Legalists advocated ruling the state with severe punishments and draconian laws, and to carry out the principle of punishment in dealing with family ethical relations. Han Fei thought that the kind and benevolent morality of Confucianism was not dependable; husbands and wives had different interests; they were two parties always on opposite sides; man should guard against a woman's intrigue, betrayal and disloyalty; a man should use the authority as "the master of the family" to control his wife and concubine in order to make them obey him unconditionally. Han Fei clearly proposed the norms governing "the minister serving the ruler, the son serving the father, and the wife serving the husband". He maintained that "if these three relationships are in order, the world will be governed; if in disorder, the world will be in confusion". This idea led to the theory of "san gang" (the three bonds) in the Han dynasty.

Regarding the relationship between husband and wife, Han Fei maintained that a wife should be submissive to her husband, unconditionally; there should not be two dominators in a family; the husband governed the home and the wife carried out the husband's orders; and, the husband should keep close watch over his wife to monitor wanton conduct and divulging secrets. His doctrine thoroughly destroyed the mild tenderness of Confucian family ethical relations and plainly exposed the interests-oriented relations of a family.

In sum, the Rites (including the institutions, behaviour norms and values) were founded in the Zhou dynasty, and gender relations were confined within the hierarchical civilisation based on the male-centred and paternity-dominated clan order with blood-tie relationships. According to the norms of the Zhou rites, men and women divided their labours in the interests of their families, states and universe. The rites defined the order of the noble and the humble, the levels of the close and the distant, the symbols of vigour and tenderness, and the discrimination of inside and outside. When the Rites were first founded, these distinctions and classifications were practised only among the aristocrats, but during the time when "the Rites became remote from the commoners", there still existed some remnants of the antique sexual tradition. After the struggles for hegemony in the Spring and Autumn period and the annexations in the Warring States period, the social order was thrown into confusion and the classes were divided and re integrated. The Zhou rites experienced the process of decline and the ritual Music degenerated. However, the gender order did not break down but developed, after the conscious regrouping of the dominant class and sex, and its reinterpretation. It became the standard of the gender culture which dominated for more than two thousand more years.

CHAPTER FIVE
ORDER AND CHAOS:
THE SOCIAL POSITIONS OF MEN
AND WOMEN IN THE QIN, HAN AND
SIX DYNASTIES PERIOD

Sun Xiao and *Pan Shaoping*

The eight centuries from the unification of China by the Qin dynasty in 221 BCE until the founding of the Sui dynasty are traditionally designated by historians as the Han-Wei-Six Dynasties period. The establishment of a centralised autocratic political system in the Qin and Han profoundly changed society. Unlike the pre-Qin patriarchal clan system, the centralised autocratic system abandoned the dual administrative system based partly on regions and partly on blood ties, and divided the administrative regions on the basis of prefectures and counties. People at that time became citizens of the country in a new sense. As Dr Michael Loewe points out, the ideology of the people in the Qin can be distinguished as four main attitudes of mind, among which the most important are man's concern with the order of nature and the peculiar position of man.[1] People freed themselves from the old patriarchal clan system based on

---

[1] Cf. Denis Twitchett and Michael Loewe eds., **The Cambridge History of China**, Vol. 1, (Cambridge University Press, 1986). Dr Loewe holds that four dominant attitudes of mind may be known in what is known of the intellectual history of Qin and Han. They were centred respectively on the order of nature, the peculiar position of man, the needs of government, and the call of reason.

blood ties, and were regrouped and administered by the state through registered households and governing subjects. The member of the clan now became a member of the state, a citizen.

The centralised autocratic system also changed people's personal lives. The theory of man's dominance and the conception that the Way will not change since Heaven does not change freed people from the confines of blood ties and reset them within a new hierarchical relationship. In the Han dynasty, Dong Zhongshu, the founder of the Confucian idea of "unification" (da yitong), drew inspiration from the Yin-Yang school of philosophers of the pre-Qin period in order to formulate his view that there is integration in everything. As a result, upper and lower appear, and "lord and minister, father and son, and husband and wife are all part of the Way of yin and yang". He further argued that within this hierarchy, "a minister is subordinate to his lord, a son to his father, and a wife to her husband".[2] Hence, under the centralised autocratic political system, the unequal relationships among people, and the dominating and dominated roles in gender relations, which prevailed from the Qin on, did not essentially change; what did change was the force of the dominance within this relationship.

In this context there are several questions which we need to examine. After the founding of the Qin and Han, was there any essential difference between the new centralised autocratic system and the old patriarchal system based on blood ties? Was there any subtle relationship between autocracy and patriarchy? How did the Confucian ethics of "bonds and virtues" explain the inequality between man and woman?

1. The Ethics of Bonds and Virtues in an Autocratic Age

[2] Dong Zhongshu, "Jiyi", **Chunqiu Fanlu**. (String of Pearls on the Spring and Autumn Annals)

(1) The Goddess in the Qin-Han Mentality

To understand the autocracy of the Qin and Han, one must clarify the meaning of patriarchy. In a specific sense, the patriarchal clan system based on blood ties and autocracy were extensions of patriarchy, which is sometimes also called the "patriarchal clan system", the latter designation signifying that the primitive basic units of society were formed from the blood ties of the father. This system constituted the second phase of clan communes after the demise of the matriarchal clan system. Patriarchies were, and are, spread widely throughout the world. The Dawenkou site, excavated in 1959, provided evidence of the early existence of patriarchy in China. Early patriarchal society did not depend on unequal gender relations, however social inequality and the appearance of relationships characterised by dominance should be regarded as products of patriarchy. In this context it is worth mentioning the reinterpretation of social models by Riane Eisler, who uses the terms partnership and domination relationship to replace the traditional conceptions of patriarchy and matriarchy, and infuses them with new meaning and spirit. As Eisler points out[3], "for a more precise term than patriarchy to describe a social system ruled through force or the threat of force by man, I propose the term 'androcracy'." We always treat new terms favourably and cautiously; favourably because "we are now at the point where for both clarity and economy of communication, we need more precise terms than those offered by our conventional vocabulary";[4] and cautiously, not only because these terms, once understood, will result in childish mistakes, but also because we must consider if these terms can be properly applied to the special subjects we are researching. According to Riane Eisler in **The Chalice and the Blade**, there are two different models, the partnership model and the domination model. The former appeared in history as

---

[3] Cf. Riane Eisler, **The Chalice and the Blade**, Ch. 8.
[4] Ibid., p. 105.

the matriarchal community, with maternal lineage but without maternal power, with leaders but without a developed hierarchical structure. Male and female members of the community were partners, and they participated in activities in equal positions. This partnership model is the matriarchal society of which we usually speak. But this new term is more precise than the term "matriarchy". We often regard matriarchy as the system with maternal power, and emphasise the contrast between maternal and paternal power. This view seems problematical. From the myth that "sages had no fathers, and their mothers became pregnant through interaction with Heaven", and from the ancient records that tell how "people knew their mothers but not their fathers"[5], we can vaguely trace the matriarchy that emphasised the lineage on the maternal side. From the present discovery of stone depictions of Fu Xi and N Wa from the Han dynasty, we can see the vividness of this partnership model. It is said that Fu Xi and N Wa were brother and sister, as well as husband and wife.[6] The portraits of the pair are mostly seen on illustrated stones of the Han dynasty. Some portraits were carved on two corresponding stones, and some

---

[5] For details of myths of this kind, see: Sun Xiao, **A Brief History of Chinese Marriage**, (Guangming Chubanshe, 1988), Ch. 2. Examples include: Hua Xu bore Fu Xi after stepping on a giant's footprint; An Deng bore Shen Nong after an encounter with a mystical dragon; N Deng bore Huangdi after an encounter with the Plough constellation; N Deng bore Yan Di after an encounter with a mystical dragon; N Jie bore Shao hao after an encounter with a meteor; N Shu bore Zhuan Xu after an encounter with rainbow light; Qing Du bore Yi Qi (Yao) after interaction with a red dragon; Qi's mother bore him after steeping on the footprint of a giant; N Xi bore Yu after swallowing Job's tears; Jian Di bore Xie after swallowing a swallow's egg; and Jiang Yuan bore Hou Ji after stepping on the footprint of a giant.

[6] Records and popular legends contain various versions of the relationship between Fu Xi and N Wa: 1, they were brothers; 2. they were brother and sister; 3. they were husband and wife; they were first brother and sister, and later husband and wife. Ref: Wen Yiduo, "Fu Xi kao", **Wen Complete Works of Wen Yiduo.**

were carved together on one stone and were depicted with their serpent bodies intertwined. Could the worship of Fu Xi and N Wa as remote ancestors of man reflect the Han people's recall of the partnership model of man and woman that had come down from remote antiquity?

This bold supposition may be justified. In the Han dynasty, people's imaginative worship of Xi Wang Mu (Queen Mother of the West) also represented another form of spiritual consolation for those who lived under an autocratic system. Legends concerning Xi Wang Mu were quite popular in both the Western and Eastern Han. She was said to live on Mount Kunlun and was the object of worship for all strata from the emperor down to commoners. The Han people also regarded the God of Mount Tai (Taishan) as Dong Wang Gong (King Father of the East), who was said to be married to Xi Wang Mu.

There are many legends concerning brother-sister intermarriage circulating among China's ethnic minorities. In Yunnan province alone, the flood myth can be found among nearly twenty ethnic groups, and in these legends the theme of a brother and sister who marry either before or after the flood occurs.

The lifestyle of the Mosuo people, now living in Yongning, Ninglang county, in north-western Yunnan is also a living form of the partnership model described by Eisler. In accordance with Mosuo custom, people call men and women of the same generation brothers and sisters, and they trace the lines of brothers and sisters back to one single ancestress. Blood lines are maternal, and property is inherited by descendants in the female line. Surnames are also adopted from the maternal line. Work and earnings are distributed equally. Significantly, the Mosuo also worship a supreme goddess. Spouses are freely chosen and are regarded as "friends", and the term for this form of partnership in the Mosuo language is Azhu. The existence of this form of Azhu marriage means that mercenary or arranged marriages do not exist, nor do problems associated with abandoned children, children born out of wedlock, orphans or unwanted widows.[7]

(2) From the Ethics of the Patriarchal Clan System to the Ethics of the Autocratic System

Eisler's second model is the model of the domination relationship. This model was specifically represented by the hierarchy of military organisation and the religious hierarchy. Under the autocratic system, male dominance pervaded practically every level of society, while the female was in the position of subordination and obedience. To introduce the model of the domination relationship into research into ancient Chinese history has a deeper meaning. We tend to regard institutional research as the foundation of historical research, but we never go beyond institutional history to examine the function and meaning of the institutions as a means of oppression. In the Qin-Han autocracy, institutions were represented by personified forms. We link state (*guo*) and family (*jia*) together, and so designate the nation guojia, while local officials are called fumuguan (lit. "parent officials"). The reality of cruel oppression was covered by a veil of tenderness. However, by using the model of the domination relationship, we discover more about the relations between the patriarchal clan system and the patriarchy and about the relations between the centralised autocratic system and the patriarchal clan system. We may also explain more clearly the origins and practical functions of the old ethics of bonds and virtues.

The patriarchal system of the pre-Qin period was a variation of the administrative rule of the primitive clan connected by blood ties. By conscientiously surveying the documentary sources of ancient Chinese history, we find that the administrative rule of a united country was often no more than the

---

[7] Ref: Sun Xiao, op. cit.; also, **History of National Minority Marriage in Yunnan**.

extension of the administration of primitive clan tribes. In the vast territory of a country, it was very difficult, however, to maintain the integrity of the state in chaotic times of war.

The theoretical core of the patriarchal clan system was the Rites. The Rites laid emphasis on distinctions of rank and level; moreover, they focused attention on the discrimination between noble and humble, elder and younger, and on the conception of blood ties. The Rites stressed the discrimination of ranks and levels, and this often began with gender discrimination. We read: "The discrimination between man and woman is a significant matter within a country"[8] To stress gender discrimination was to maintain the order of patriarchal clan society in which males were in the dominant position. When discrimination was first made between men and women, the oppression of women was considered to be the fundamental step in establishing the model of the domination relationship. In the chapter titled "Hunyi" of *Li Ji*, we read: "The discrimination between man and woman bestows meaning on the roles of husband and wife, then on the affection between father and son, and then on the correct relationship between lord and minister". The essence of the code of the Rites was to establish a social order within the patriarchal clan system which adhered to the principle of respecting the noble and elder and loving the beloved, by playing down the position of women. In the context of marriage, the Rites ostensibly enjoined man and woman "to share sorrow together and to be equal in social position", but the actual conditions were quite different. "Woman is subordinate to man. She obeys her father and brother when young, her husband after marriage, and her son after her husband's death. ... Husband and wife share sorrow together and are in equal social positions. A woman therefore has no rank of nobility, but must follow her husband's rank and social position".[9]

---

[8] "Zhuanggong ershisi-nian", *Zuo Zhuan*.

[9] "Jiaodesheng", *Li Ji*.

After their unification of China, the Qin dynasty adopted the theory of the Legalist philosophers on social order, as the old patriarchal clan system collapsed and the new centralised autocracy was established. But, as mentioned above, these two systems were no more than two forms of the same model of social domination. The establishment of the centralised autocratic system only changed the relationship in which the individual was dominated by the community based on ties of blood to one in which the state became the only force which dominated families and the individual. The conception of discrimination against women grew steadily, and the centralised autocratic system, with the emperor and high-ranking officials at the centre, became the most complete symbol of male domination. In the Legalist conception of law, the system of collective responsibility was very important in strengthening agriculture and weakening commerce, as well as in achieving social control.[10] In the specific explanation of collective responsibility, the inclination to discriminate against women was obvious. In a legal text titled "Fal Wenda" (Questions and Answer on Law) found on bamboo slips excavated from a Qin dynasty tomb at Shuihudi, we read: "When the husband commits a crime, the wife must give herself up to the authorities, and she will be exiled with her husband". This Legalist conception was developed more fully in later ages. Cases of the legal inequality between males and females in the Qin dynasty abound. For example, a wife could be flogged one hundred times for hitting her husband, but her husband could not be punished if he hit her".[11]

The Chinese political system based on centralised autocracy only fully emerged after the Han took the place of the Qin. The

---

[10] Derk Bodde and Clarence Morris, **Law in Imperial China**, (Harvard University Press, 1973).

[11] There are these provisions in the Ming and Qing legal codes. See Ch' T'ung-tsu, **Law and Society in Traditional China**, (Paris and The Hague: Mouton; 1961).

Han rulers seriously summarised the lessons learned from the Qin's early demise after only thirteen years in power and attributed the Qin collapse to "its appointment of cruel officials and its application of draconian laws". For this reason, they turned more readily back to the Rites of the patriarchal clan system of the pre-Qin period, synthesised these with Legalist ideas, and created a new socio-ethical system which integrate the Rites with Law. In the "Li" (Rites) section of his *Xin Shu* (New Writings), Jia Yi of the Western Han period wrote: "The tenderness of a wife makes her dignified and gentle, the kindness of the mother-in-law makes her obedient, and the obedience of the wife makes her gracious. This is the essence of the Rites". The new social order, devised with the new code of Rites, was still based on such conduct, but it was different from the pre-Qin Rites of the patriarchal clan system. In the Qin and Han dynasties, the families of individual peasants broke away from the traditional clans, and became independent social units and the foundation of centralised autocratic rule. Rule in accordance with the Rites (*li zhi*), which defined the hierarchical levels of society in the time of the patriarchal clan system, gradually evolved into rule in accord with filial piety (*xiao zhi*). The filial piety of the family became the core of that which maintained social order, and by means of the principle of transforming filial piety into loyalty, a complete system of political ethics was founded. The transformation from *li zhi* to *xiao zhi* was a clear sign distinguishing autocracy from the patriarchal clan system. In the new social system with filial piety at its core, the social position of women had still not fundamentally improved, but this ethics of filial piety seems a little more humane, and the hierarchy composed of filial son, kind father, chaste wife and virtuous mother was even more misleading.

During the period when the centralised autocracy became increasingly complete, the philosophical system in which ethics served the autocracy was also increasingly systematised in theory. Dong Zhongshu of the Western Han played a very important

29　宋代妇女塑像（山西晋祠）
A clay woman of the Song dynasty
(the Jinci Temple, Shanxi)

30　女神观世音像
Avalokitesvara as a goddess in the Chinese
Buddhism

31 女神妈祖像
    Goddess Mazu
32 明代妇女画像(剧本《西厢记》插图)
    Women of the Ming dynasty
    (illustration in Story of Western
    Chamber)

	31
	32

33 唤庄生（明代绘画）
   "Waking up Zhuangsheng"
   (porn of the Ming dynasty)

34 狎戏（明代绘画）
   Porn
   (the Ming dynasty)

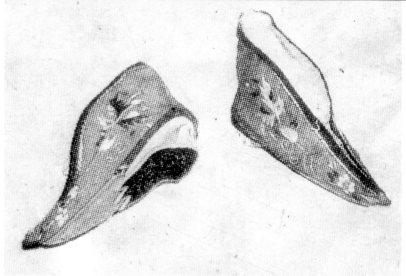

35　清代京华辞岁图

"At the Turning of the Year"

36　清代妇女的小鞋

A pair of small shoes for bound feet of the Qing dynasty

37 38

39

40 纳西族母系大家庭
   A matrilineal family of the Naxi people

41 男女伙伴在跳竹竿（流行于西南少数民族）
   Men and women in "Bamboo Jump",
   a dance popular among ethnic groups in
   Southwestern China

42 富有阳刚气质的中国武术
   Martial art exhibiting Yanggang

43 富有阳刚气质的陕北农民腰鼓
   Northern Shaanxi Peasants in their Yangga
   "Waist-drum Dance"

40	4
42	
43	

	44	
		45
46		

44　北大纪念五四运动 65 周年大会会场（1984 年）
A meeting commemorating the 65th anniversary
of May Forth Movement in Beijing University in
1984

45　中国当代男女大学生（北大图书馆一角）
Contemporary male and female college students
(in the Beijing University library)

46　当代中国男女青年
Contemporary young men and women

47 中国首届妇女内衣大赛（1994年）
   A lingerie show in 1994

48 谢军——国际象棋世界冠军
   Xie Jun, winner of World Chess Champion

49 中国女排——连续五个世界冠军的获得者
   The Chinese National female volleyball
   team consecutively winning world champions

	47
48	
	49

胜利的喜悦——中国女排在第23届奥运会上战胜美
The Reptures over the Victory—after the
Chinese Woman Volley Ball Team Best its
American Counterpart during the 23rd
Olympic Games.

role in this work. He regarded the maintenance and consolidation of centralised autocracy as the most important task, and his philosophical system of ethics drew widely from the ideas of the Yin-Yang philosophical school and from the Legalists. Unlike the Yin-Yang school, he did not use their theories to explain nature, but used the concept of yin-yang to explain human relationships, and develop further the theories of the superiority of yang and the inferiority of yin, and of the correspondence between Heaven and Man. Unlike the Legalists, he did not strictly follow the provisions of Law, but used the Confucian idea together with Law as the essence of Legalism to devise the theory of "the three bonds and five virtues" (*sangang wulun*), as well as his theories arguing for the necessity "to pass death sentences in spring and autumn".

Dong Zhongshu maintained that "Heaven has two characters, and these are exercised through the Way of yin and yang".[12] From the conception of yin-yang, Dong Zhongshu further elucidated the view that "there is integration in everything, and hence the upper and lower side appear". "Lord and minister, father and son, and husband and wife are all the Way of yin-yang".[13] From his theology, he maintained that the husband was bonded with the wife, the father with the son, and the lord with the minister. These were the three bonds (*san gang*) in which wife, son and minister were completely subordinate to husband, father and lord. He also defined *ren* (benevolence), *yi* (righteousness), *li* (the Rites), *zhi* (wisdom) and *xin* (faith) as the fundamental principles to adjust these relationships or bonds. Like Heaven and Earth or yin and yang, this social order could not be changed, and was established completely by the Will of Heaven. He pointed out that "the three bonds of the kingly way can be found in Heaven".[14] This of course means that they can be neither found nor proved. With "the three

---

[12] Dong Zhongshu, "Dongcha Minghao", **Chunqiu Fanlu**.
[13] Dong Zhongshu, "Jiyi", **Chunqiu Fanlu**.
[14] Ibid.

bonds and the five virtues" forming the core, the social order of autocracy, the deified law of the universe and the mysterious universe itself also became a part of the model of the domination relationship. The artificial hierarchical differences under autocracy were elevated to the supreme position of the law of "God". Unlike the pre-Qin Confucianists who had deducted the Rites from their daily lives, Dong's theory was extended on the basis of the unity of heaven, earth and yin-yang, so that it has a kind of theological touch. For this reason, it is not an exaggeration to say that Dong Zhongshu reformed Confucianism as theology, and was the founder of the teleological theory supporting the autocracy.

There are specific elucidations on woman's position in the eternal laws of "the discrimination between superiors and inferiors" and of "the superiority of yang and the inferiority of yin" devised by Dong Zhongshu. He stressed that "the husband being of yang and the wife being of yin, she is destined to assist".[15] The wife was required to be obedient to her husband absolutely, and "if the wife were disobedient, she would be severed of the matrimonial relation", because "she did not serve and obey heaven, and so deserves it".[16] Dong Zhongshu went on to define further the position of a woman within the family. The positions of wife and concubine, above all, cannot be out of order.[17] This also completely conformed with the social order of autocracy. Although this seems unimportant at first glance, it helped precipitate a series of bloody tragedies, as wives and concubines contended for favours from husbands.

Dong Zhongshu's theoretical system of autocracy was further enriched and developed in the Eastern Han dynasty. In 79, the government held a conference at Bohu-guan (White Tiger Hall) which was designed to unify the ruling dynasty's

---

15 Ibid.
16 "Shunming", op. cit.
17 "Wuxing Shunni", in ibid.

social ideology[18] At this conference, Dong's theory of the three bonds (*san gang*) was developed into the theory of "the three bonds and the six relations" (*sangang liuji*). In ***Baihu Tongde Lun*** (Universal Discussions at the White Tiger Hall) there is a definition of this new concept: "What are the three bonds? They are the bonds of lord and minister, father and son, and husband and wife. The six relations referred to are those of fathers, brothers, clan members, uncles, teachers and friends". These strict hierarchical relations were another new means of autocratic domination. The maintenance of male power and the oppression of women were the most fundamental steps in this kind of domination. The "Yixu Guanzhuan" chapter in *Baihu Tongde Lun* states that "man and woman are prior to husband and wife, husband and wife are prior to father and son, father and son are prior to lord and minister". This formulation is also designed to fix the social hierarchy in which superior dominated inferior, and noble dominated humble. ***Baihu Tongde Lun*** also maintains that the Chinese written characters *fu* (husband) and *fy* (wife) also embody the meaning of discrimination between superior and inferior: "What are the meanings of *fu* and *fy*? *Fu* (husband) means to support with the hand, and in this context it means to support with means of the Tao. *Fy* (wife) means to submit, or, in other words, to submit to the Rites".[19] The wife's fate was determined by her husband. "If the wife is out of favour with her husband, she cannot leave him, just as the earth cannot part from the heavens".[20]

From xiao zhi to Dong Zhongshu's theory as expressed in ***Baihu Tongde Lun***, the ethical system of bonds and virtues

---

[18] The ostensible purpose of the Bohu-guan conference was to co-ordinate the differences between the Ancient Text and the New text classics, which had emerged since the unification of the Western Han. The historian Ban Gu took full notes on the proceedings and later wrote ***Baihu Tongde Lun***.

[19] "Sangang Liuji", ***Baihu Tongde Lun***.

[20] "Jiaqu", ibid.

remained the fundamental theory of the centralised bureaucracy. Underlying the ethic of bonds and virtues was the view that man's oppression of woman was the truth of heaven and earth and that the hierarchic relations between father and son and between lord and minister were the law of the universe. The aim of these ethical views was to seek justification for the model of autocratic domination, in order to serve the centralised autocracy.

The theory exercised a great influence on later ages. Even in the subsequent war torn and divided Wei and Jin dynasties, this theory still held a firm position, and in the post-Qin centralised autocratic society the partnership life of male and female (if there were any) was the stuff of myths and legends, and the memory of remote antiquity was no more than spiritual consolation in the face of reality. The broken chalice was once again broken, and its fragments, scattered in the gloomy forest, teasingly refracted the bloody light of autocracy.

2. The Conception of Female Chastity and Instructions to Women (*Nüjiao*)

(1) The Solemnity and Breadth of the Conception of Female Chastity

Female chastity is an essential question in any discussion of gender issues during this period of autocracy. At the time of the patriarchal clan system, female chastity was a social issue and a woman, as a complete person, lost her freedom and rights and became a part of the property of the clan and family. Marriage was often an economic behaviour. The ancients mention that Fu Xi sent *lipi* (a type of deer skin) as a marriage gift. Skins were used as currency in ancient times, and to send lipi as gifts in marriage was a mercenary operation of sorts. In the "Shi Hunli" section of *Yi Li*, we read of "the use of black animals, bundled silk and lipi as matrimonial gifts". Two ancient terms, fei for imperial concubine and tang meaning wife, have an economic basis in that the former originally signified "bundled silk" and the latter "golden coins".[21] Underscoring the fact that marriage had its mercenary side is the fact that we read in ancient records how women, as men's possessions, were sometimes "stolen" by bandits.

This connection is also revealed by a study of the etymology of the word "marriage" (*hunyin*), which closely connects with word hun meaning "evening".[22]

Women were treated as the personal possessions of males, and so a woman's chastity was a part of that possession. In the "Yan Ce" section of *Zhanguo Ce*, we read that "if a virgin has no match-maker, she will not get married, even growing old. To introduce herself without a match-maker, she will not succeed". Marriage without a match-maker was sneered at by society, even if the woman was suspected of not being chaste. "If a woman wants to be married, she must do so through a match-maker; without a match-maker, she will be sneered at and suspected". And so, "the married woman who does not use a match-maker is not glorious or trust-worthy".[23]

However, pre-Qin patriarchal clan society still preserved most of the customs of clan society, in which a woman's chastity was not an issue; on the contrary, the attitudes of early societies to chastity appear to be radically different from later views. Song Yu's poem "Zhao Hun" (Summoning the Soul) describes how in the state of Chu "men and women sat together without discrimination". The customs of the state of Qi were, however,

---

[21] ***Shuowen Jiezi***.

[22] There is a close connection between the concepts of "marriage" and "evening". In the "jiaqu" section of ***Baihu Tongde Lun*** we read: "What is marriage? It is the ceremony held in the evening. So we call it hun". Why was the marriage ceremony held in the evening? According to the "Yaoci" section of ***Yi Jing***, this was because robberies happened at night. Ref: Sun Xiao, ***Zhongguo Hunyin Xiaoshi***, ch. 3.

[23] ***Guan Zi***.

quite fascinating:

> At local meetings, men and women mix freely. They drink, gamble and play games. They hold hands and stare into each other's eyes not fearing censure. The jewels drop here and there. When the sun sets and night comes on, the men and women sit on the mats together, their shoes discarded in a pile, and the wine cups and dishes scattered after feasting. When the lights in the hall are extinguished, the silk coats are untied, and a mild fragrance fills the air. So, it is said, a drunken frolic causes indiscreet behaviour.

Even the *Zhou Li* suggests that administrative means be devised to encourage such folkways:

> In mid-spring men and women are ordered to rendezvous, although elopement is not permitted. Persons who do not attend the gathering without good reason are punished. The order instructs all unmarried people to attend ... the private indiscreet behaviour that takes place is beyond description.[24]

Attitudes to chastity in such a society were clearly relaxed.

After the establishment of centralised autocracy, the Qin and Han attached more importance to female chastity because its control was an important component in the government's attempt to implement a social hierarchy and stabilise society. The First Emperor of the Qin (Qin Shi Huang) paid great attention to the issue and pointedly referred to it on several occasions in stone stele inscriptions, as for example in this inscription on Taishan Mountain:

> Set the Rites concerning men and women in order, so that they carry out their respective duties, the inside and the outside are separated, and everything is pure and clean.

After its founding, the Han dynasty inherited the institutions of the Qin and encouraged chastity all the more. The Han,

---

[24] "Xuandi Ji", *Han Shu*.

for example, made great efforts to follow the example of honouring the Baqing widow in Qin. In 58 BCE, Emperor Xuan issued a decree bestowing silk on chaste and obedient women. Such dubious honours and awards later became common.

In the early years of the Western Han, the concept of chastity was different from that in later dynasties, especially the Ming and Qing. Although the concept that men were superior to women was to remain unchanged, women's physical chastity was not excessively demanded. At that time, a woman was only asked to obey *li-fa* (rites and laws), but the practice of only living with one husband throughout a woman's life was not earnestly encouraged. "The Biography of Kuai Tong" in *Han Shu*, for example, records how Kuai Tong asked Xiao He: "There are two women. One was married three days after her husband's death, the other remained a widow and never stepped out her door. Whom would you prefer to marry?" Although Xiao He answered that he would prefer to marry the latter, the fact that a woman could remarry three days after her husband's death was not regarded as untoward.

In the late Western Han, the demand that women maintain chastity became very strict. In *Lien Zhuan* (Biographies of Honourable Women) by Liu Xiang[25] the major theme encourages women to retain their chastity, the most fundamental expression of which was not remarrying after a husband's death. In the "Zhenshun Zhuan" section of that book is the story of a woman of Song who was married to a man from the state of Cai. After their marriage, the man suffered from a serious illness, and her mother asked her to remarry. However, the woman of Song answered: "Now that I have married him, I can never change". Liu Xiang praised her greatly, commenting: "The people of later times praised her for her chastity and

---

[25] Liu Xuan (77–6 BCE), styled Zizheng, was originally named Geng Sheng. He was an active writer during the reigns of Emperor Yuan and Wang Mang, and his most famous works include *Xinxu, Shuoyuan* and *Lien Zhuan*.

obedience".

The Eastern Han placed a greater emphasis on female chastity. In the 1970s mural paintings of that period discovered in tombs at Holingol in Inner Mongolia were narrative works in praise of chaste women, such as Zhao Yuezheng of Chu, Madam Zhao of Dai and the wife of Qiu Huzi.[26] Contemporary stories also reflected the filial piety of women, such as Yewang Dinglan. The Eastern Han philosopher Wang Fu[27], in his *Qianfu Lun*, reiterates the view that a woman cannot remarry. In the "Duansong" chapter of that work, he wrote:

> The essence of a woman's behaviour is purity and cleanliness. Now she is re-marrying, she feels ashamed to enter her late husband's door. The local official determined, however, that she should re-marry, but such a decision can neither teach the citizens to control the root of chaos nor does it encourage chastity and purity. A chaste woman should be firm and never change her mind. And so, there have been poems in praise of firmness. They urge women to neither misbehave nor encourage grudges. They praise the virtue of not forgetting one's origins. Once a woman makes a promise, she should never change her mind. This is the way to encourage chastity and purity, and to console and calm her father and brother.

Wang Fu was the first to make purity and cleanliness the yardstick of ethical standards for women.

From the Eastern Han on, the concept of chastity was no longer a conception limited to moralists and theorists, as it gradually spread through popular culture. Xu Shu's "Wei Shishu yu Xiongdi" (An Oath to My Brothers) reflects this

---

[26] Ref: Gai Shanling, **Murals of the Han Tombs at Holingol**, (Inner Mongolian Publishing House, 1977).

[27] Wang Fu (85-163), styled Bei Jie, is the author of **Qianfu Lun** in 36 juan, a work which is still extant.

change.[28] Xu was from Longxi, and her husband was a Huang-menlang (Gentleman of the Palace Gate). After her husband's death, she was forced to re-marry by her brothers, but she refused them by taking an oath, in which she announces: "A man should guide with virtue and correct with Rites. Hence an upright man has unswerving will, and a chaste woman cannot remarry".

During the Six Dynasties period, because of the chaotic political situation and frequent wars, the concept of chastity in society was somewhat weakened. The government sometimes forced widows to re-marry in order to strengthen the country by increasing the population more rapidly. For reasons of political expediency, autocratic rulers began to neglect the demands of *li* and *fa*. In the Three Kingdoms period, the Wei Kingdom even ordered prefectural governors to send widows to soldiers who had performed meritorious service. This practice was even sometimes extended to married women. In "Du Ji Zhuan" (Biography of Du Ji) in **Sanguo Zhi** (The History of the Three Kingdoms) an annotation cites **Wei Le** as follows:

At first, Hetong prefecture was ordered to seek widows. At that time, widows from other prefectures had been forced to remarry. The widows were rounded up in accordance with the issued order. The women wept as they stood along the road. Du only chose widows, and so he did not send women in great numbers. However, after Zhao Yan replaced Du, more women were sent. Emperor Wen asked Du about the sudden increase in numbers. Du replied: "The women I sent were widows, but Zhao is now sending married women". The faces of the emperor and his attendants paled.

Such incidents also occurred later. The Northern Qi dynasty, for example, sent 2,600 "widows" from Shandong to the army, and twenty to thirty per cent of these were, in fact,

---

[28] See Du Yu, "Nji", **Taiping Yulan**, juan 4431.

married women.

The concept of chastity during the Qin, Han and Six Dynasties evolved from one which was tolerant to one which was harsh, and then the social mood swung back again. This process reflected a society moving from unification to division, and then from order back to confusion. However, in terms of the domination relationship, the specific content of which was autocracy, the concept of chastity, be it tolerant or harsh, revolved around the axis of autocratic domination. When the concept was strictly held, women were deprived of more freedom; when it was more tolerant, such events as the conscription of widows for army "service" would occur and so women would be deprived of their rights completely. Under male autocratic domination, it was impossible for a woman to determine her own fate. The severity or tolerance with which the conception of chastity was held was completely determined by the autocratic political system, and the concept served the autocracy in carrying out its political aims.

(2) The "Female Sage" Ban Zhao and Her **Instructions to Women**.

With the strengthening in this period of the concept of chastity based on the theory of autocratic "bonds and virtues", sets of instructions or handbooks for women providing women with educational standards became popular. Such handbooks had very early origins in China. The "Nei Ze" chapter of *Li Ji* records that a woman must learn the Rites and norms before marriage. She must rise at daybreak, wash and comb her hair, put her hair up into a bun, and don full attire with a belt. In the morning she must first wait on the elders and ask what they would like to eat. Once the elders had partaken of breakfast, she would have to return to her room. If the elders wanted to eat, she would have to cook for them. In the "Quli" chapter of *Li Ji*, a woman is asked "to listen and observe without expression, not climb high places or approach deep holes, not spread slander, and not act frivolously. She must stand graciously, listen attentively, answer quietly, and act diligently". After marriage, the demands were even more diverse and complex. For example, when in the residence of her parents and elders, she "must respond enthusiastically when given an order, receive ·people undiscriminatingly, and curtsey wherever she goes; she must not contradict her elders, stretch herself, look askance, or shout". There were an extraordinary number of taboos to memorise. However, *Li Ji* was considered to be one of the Confucian classics in later ages, so one can imagine the restrictions placed at that time on a woman's life.

The Qin-Han period is very important in the formation of Chinese traditions, and the instructions to women written at that time formed the basis for the compulsory education of women. The subjects in *Lien Zhuan* cited by Liu Xiang became norms set for women.[29] In discussing these handbooks of instructions to women of the Qin, Han and Six Dynasties, there is one work that warrants detailed study and that is *Nüjie* (Instructions for Women) written by the "female sage"· Ban Zhao. She was the younger sister of the renowned Eastern Han historian Ban Gu. Born into a well-educated family, she· "behaved circumspectly, often fearing the disgrace of being dismissed and so bringing shame upon her parents". The conception of the male as superior had been formed in her mind at an early age. After the death of her husband, Cao Shishu, she was summoned to the palace by Emperor He to serve as tutor to the empress and other palace ladies and so was called "Great Scholar Cao" (Cao Dajia). Before the appearance of her *Nüjie*, there were already various theories concerning the marriage bond, including those of Liu Xiang, but most were unsystematic and superficial. Liu Xiang limited himself to historical examples. It was not until the appearance of *Nüjie* that the traditional

---

[29] Seven chapters of *Lien Zhuan* are now extant, and each contains fifteen biographies.

instructions to women were systematised, and they were to exercise great pressure on women.

Nüjie, the entire text of which runs to about 1,600 Chinese characters, consists of seven chapters"Beiruo" (Humility and Weakness), "Fufu" (Husband and Wife), "Jingshen" (Respect and Conscientiousness), "Fuxing" (The Conduct of Women), "Zhuanxin" (Concentrating the Mind), "Qucong" (Submission and Obedience), and "Shumei" (Relations with Cousins). In the preface, Ban Zhao clearly states her purpose in writing the work:

> I am so worried about those girls who are about to marry but who do not feel a sense of shame after receiving their instructions. They know nothing about the Rites of women. I fear that they will bring disgrace to their families and shame to their clans. I am now seriously ill, and may die at any time. I am so sad when I think of them, so I am taking my time and writing these seven chapters.

The essence of the work was thus an elucidation of the principle that the male is superior and the female inferior, which she specifically explains in the first chapter aptly titled "Humility and Weakness":

> In ancient times, three days after a girl was born, she was placed under the bed beside the tiles and bricks. It was a blessing to be placed there, because she would learn that she was lowly and weak, and destined to be subordinate; being beside the tiles and bricks, she would grow accustomed to labour, and be destined to be diligent and hard-working.

Ban Zhao asked women to understand their position and value in society as early as childhood, and to realise that when they grew up they should be all the more careful and prudent, willingly playing the role of a slave of society. Throughout their lives, women should be modest and respectful, place the interests of others before their own, and never make good deeds known, nor apologise for their bad conduct. Women should restrain their anger, keep silent, and act cautiously. This is the conduct of the humble and the weak.

In the chapter "Jingshen" we read:

> *Yin* and *yang* are of different characters, and a man's conduct differs from that of a woman. Vigorousness is considered to be the virtue of *yang* and tenderness to the use of *yin*. Man values strength and a woman considers a weakness to be beauty.

The use of the *yin-yang* formulation to justify the domination relationship was a standard theoretical ploy in ancient China. As man and woman, and superiority and inferiority were defined as yin and yang, the principles underlying Chinese autocracy and its domination order were seen to be self-evident. In discussing the relationship between husband and wife, Ban Zhao used the *yin-yang* doctrine as a foundation:

> The Way of a husband and wife can likened to that of *yin* and *yang*. It communicates with the divine, and is faithful in its comprehensive meaning of Heaven and Earth. It is an important virtue in human relations. So the Rites value the relationship of a man and a woman, and affection becomes the theme of poetry.

A husband could remarry but a wife could not, because "a husband is Heaven and cannot be escaped from; hence a husband cannot be disobeyed". The difference between a husband and wife was that like between heaven and earth. The husband was the master, and the wife could not argue with him, regardless of whether she were right or not. In advising a woman to be a good wife, Ban Zhao, in the chapter titled "Jingshen" states that a husband and wife should live together all their lives. To achieve this, a woman should not cause her husband to lose his temper, and this was achieved by not making fun of him. She clearly needed to consider herself subordinate.

More unreasonably, Ban Zhao even regarded the relationship of a husband and wife as a relationship conferred as a favour. This idea seriously poisoned women of later ages. Many women were unable to win favour from their husbands, but nevertheless clung to them because they had been shown kindness at one time. Even casual sexual relations in the open in archaic times were considered to be a favour bestowed by the male. This may be the main reason why many couples lived without love, but with the woman feeling a sense of gratitude under the model of the domination relationship.[30]

Ban Zhao in *Nüjie*, moreover, establishes general principles for women on the basis of the cardinal idea that the male is superior. These are called "the four virtues" (*si de*), which are *fude* (a woman's virtue), *fuyan* (a woman's speech), *furong* (a woman's appearance) and *fugong* (a woman's work), and these are explained in *Nüjie* as follows:

A woman's virtue is not necessarily learned. She simply needs to be quiet and dignified, to preserve chastity and good order, to remain aloof from disgraceful behaviour, and to practise conduct in line with norms.

A woman's speech is not necessarily eloquent or loquacious. She simply needs to speak with proper terms, to not speak viciously, to speak at the right time, and to not say things that disgust people.

A woman's appearance is not necessarily colourful. She simply needs to clean the dirt off herself, to dress in plain clean clothes, to bathe regularly, and to keep the body clean.

A woman's work is not necessarily so skilful. She simply needs to concentrate the mind on weaving, to not cavort around, to do the cleaning and to prepare sumptuous feasts for guests.

Ban Zhao gave concrete expression to the three bonds and

---

[30] Ref: Sun Xiao, "The Morality of Marriage in Qin-Han Society", in *Xinzhai Wenxue Ji*, (Tuanjie Chubanshe, 1993).

the five virtues which upheld the centralised autocracy, and she created the theory of the three obediences and the four virtues to educate women. Her development of the concept of male superiority had a great influence on later ages. She was subsequently elevated to the status of a "female sage" and her theory became normative for women. As a teaching text, *Nüjie* became a genre model for later writers, and, together with Song Ruohua's *Nü Lunyu* (The Woman's Analects), Empress Xu's *Neize* (Domestic Principles) and Wang Xiang's mother's *Nüfan Jielu* (Account of Female Norms), it was a part of *Guige Sishu* (The Four Books for Women). These works were as popular as *Qianjia Shi* (The Poetry of a Thousand Poets) and *Sanzi Jing* (The Three Character Classic).

As a woman, why did Ban Zhao create such models of female inferiori-ty? In a society where the domination relationship reflected autocracy, it could be construed as natural for men to oppress and restrict women, but why did women have the same idea at that time? Why did Ban Zhao write this guide for women? Perhaps the centralised autocracy alienated women and distorted their thinking, heightening any sense of inferiority they may have had to the extent that they could neither reflect on their own innate character or on freedom.

In the Qin, Han and Six Dynasties periods, another major instructive work for women appeared *Yanshi Jiaxun* (The Family Instructions of Yan). This most influential work was written by Yan Zhitui of the Northern Qi dynasty.[31] Yan encouraged a woman to maintain her correct place:

> A woman is responsible for the rites of serving food and for attire; she is forbidden to participate in politics. The family forbids her to create confusion. If she has talent and wisdom, and knows of things past and present, she should

---

[31] This view is expressed by a number of scholars including Wang Sanpin and Yuan Zhong.

assist her husband. Otherwise, disaster will ensue.[32]

Under the model of the autocratic domination relationship, a woman had no independence in the family, not to mention social rights or position.

3. Woman's Position in Social Life

(1) The Restrictions Placed on Women by Autocratic Ethics

In the societies of the Qin, Han and Six Dynasties periods, the specific form of the model of the domination relationship was autocracy. The centralised autocracy was the only dominator of families and individual lives. The formation of the autocratic social order in which there were clear distinctions of superiority and inferiority and of the noble and humble may have benefited in some sense from society's success in oppressing women. As we have seen, the establishment of the system with hierarchic divisions and strict order, and the emergence of the theory of three bonds and five virtues came, step by step, with the development of the distinction between man and woman, father and son, and lord and ministers. Hence, it may be said that the cruel oppression against women was one of the deeper inner characteristics of autocracy.

After the collapse of the pre-Qin patriarchal clan system, large families with ties of blood disintegrated gradually, and the newly emerging small peasant families appeared and these became the basic social units of the Qin, Han and later dynasties. The centralised authorities organised the small peasant families through a household registration system through which administration was exercised. During the Six Dynasties, although the patriarchal clans in some senses seemed to reappear, these clans were essentially different from the pre-Qin patriar-

---

[32] "Zhijia", *Yanshi Jiaxun*.

chal clans because the small families had become independent units. The social domination order after the Qin and Han changed compared with the pre-Qin order, but the social position of women did not change, because the model of the male-centred domination relationship had not changed at all. We can prove this conclusion by surveying woman's position in matrimonial life at the time.

The ancients maintained: "Husband and wife are integrated as one".[33] This means that after a man and woman marry, they should share legal and moral obligations, and organise an integrated family together. However, there was absolutely no quality in their "integrated" lives. A wife was required to obey her husband in all matters and she had no independence. Obedience was held to be the nature and duty of a wife, and everything was determined and arranged by the husband. A wife was required to obey her husband "just as a hen obeys a rooster". The change in a wife's designation also indicates a change in the mode of "integration". The pre-Qin woman had no given name (*ming*). Although a woman in the Qin, Han and Six Dynasties had a surname and given name (*xing-ming*), it was not used after marriage, when she was referred as "the wife of XXX", or her name was replaced with her husband's surname. Sometimes a woman was designated by putting her husband's surname with her own. These three nomenclature changes all reflect a shift in the relative positions within the matrimony.

There were other inequalities in matrimonial life in the Qin, Han and Six Dynasties. Firstly, a woman's inferior position was reflected in the theory of centralised autocracy. Women were required to be in a submissive and tender position, in no way opposed to man. According to the text accompanying the "Heng" (Constancy) Hexagram:

Woman is formed by *kundao* (the way of *kun*, i.e. *yin*), and man is formed by *qiandao* (the way of *qian*). They are

---

[33] "Sangfu Zhuan", *Yi Li*.

not the same in nature.... Woman belongs to *kun*, her nature is of tenderness; so she should follow yang and remain in the position *yin*. ... *Yin* always submits itself to *yang*, that is woman's auspiciousness; if man always submits himself to woman, that is man's ominousness.[34]

It was therefore regarded as natural that a woman obey a man. A woman was not only asked to be tender in her disposition, but also to be physically weaker than a man. There is an oracular text in the "Hungua" hexagram of the *Yi Jing* which states:

If *yin* is the dominator in a family, then a man becomes an outsider and the Way runs in a contrary direction; therefore yang will become weak and *yin* will become strong. ... If you meet a woman who is physically stronger than you, do not accept her.

Sturdiness in a woman was, therefore, regarded as a terrible thing.

Under the model of the autocratic domination relationship, a woman could not participate in various activities and was required to be completely submissive to men. In *Chunqiu Guliang Zhuan* completed in the Western Han dynasty, there is an entry for the second year of Yingong's reign which reads:

A woman's marriage to a man is called gui (return), while a woman's return is called laigui. This means she is subordinate to man. A woman is controlled by her father at home, by her husband after marriage, and her son after her husband's death. She is not independent and must follow males.

Women had no position in socio-political activities, and as the ancients said: "No woman is mentioned in public places".

Secondly, in male-dominated societies, the position of husband and wife in popular social conceptions is not equal.

---

[34] "Henggua", *Yi Jing*.

However, in etymological terms, husband and wife were held to be equal, because the character denoting wife was interpreted as *qi*, meaning "alike". In the **Baihu Tongde Lun**, we find the following passage: "Wife means *qi* (alike), and she enjoys the same position as her husband in the system. This principle is applied to lord and commoner alike". Zheng Xuan, the great Confucian thinker of the Eastern Han, explained why a wife was thus defined as *qi*: "A wife is designated as *qi*, because when asked about the Rites, she is in the same position as her husband".[35] Moreover, the word *qi* (wife) in ancient times was written in the form *gui* (meaning "valuable") with the radical for "woman" on the left. This written form elevated woman. Although husband and wife were thus equal in terms of the written characters denoting them, the wife was in fact required to be submissive to her husband, to hang on his every word, and to never remarry after his death. The ancient Chinese character *fu* (also meaning "wife") was written in the form of a woman kneeling and holding a broom. In **Shuowen Jiezi**, the ancient Chinese etymological dictionary, we read that "fu (woman, wife) means fu (submission)". Submission was, thus, a woman's duty. In the "Jiaoteshen" section of **Li Ji** this is further explained: "When going out the door, woman follows man;, hence the meaning husband and then wife emerges". **Baihu Tongde Lun** further explains: "Husband means support, supporting with the Way; wife means submission, submitting with the Rites".

The autocratic social theory also devised this "integrative" matrimonial relationship, and this can be seen in the legal code. If a husband committed a crime, a wife must share in the punishment. In Qin law the practice existed of killing the wife's clan if the husband committed a crime. Although this law was abolished in the Han dynasty, if a man committed a particularly heinous crime, his wife, parents and children were publicly executed, and his concubines were not exempted. In the reign

---

[35] Zheng Xuan annot.,"Neize", **Li Ji**.

of Emperor Ming of the Jin dynasty, the law was somewhat modified, and some women began to be exempted. Punishments, however, became stricter again in the Tang. While the "integrative" notion would seem to indicate that husband and wife share honour and disgrace equally, this could hardly be the case if the independence of the woman was completely denied and the wife was completely subordinate. This is delicately expressed in a poem titled "Guafu Shi" (Song of the Widow) by the Northern Wei poet Ding Yi:

> I leave my parents to return,
> To serve my husband and do chores;
> A vine clinging to the pine tree,
> Duckweed floating on the pond.

Thirdly, the positions of men and women in family life were extremely unequal. In the Han, Wei and Six Dynasties period, the birth of a girl was not considered to be of any importance. The birth of a boy was termed "obtaining a jade" (longzhang), while the birth of a girl was "getting a tile" (*longwa*), the objects in question also serving as metaphors of the later difference in social position of the genders. The practice of female infanticide was also well documented, and this practice was earlier described in the "Liufan" chapter of **Han Fei Zi**: "Parents treat their children differently. When a boy is born, they congratulate each other. When a girl is born, they kill her. Although they both spring from the same womb, they are treated differently, in view of the later advantages and benefits they will bring".

Within the family, the father was absolutely dominant. Prior to marriage, a woman has no personal belongings and her marriage is determined by her father. In "Gaodi Zhuan" (Biography of Emperor Gaodi) in **Han Shu**, we read how Lü Gong married his daughter to Liu Ban. Lü's wife complained that she had not been consulted, but her husband told her that this was not a matter in which women should be involved. Moreover, after marriage, a woman, as daughter-in-law, should still have no possessions, and this is justified in *Li Ji* as follows: "The daughter-in-law should neither have personal possessions, nor dispose or give away property without permission. ..."[36]

Family life in this period was like a microcosm of the social order under autocracy its clear distinctions of hierarchy. In the Eastern Han dynasty writer Cui Shi's *Siyue Shiling* (Songs of the Season) we find a vivid description of family life. On the spring festival the patriarch of the family leads his wife and children to pay their respects to their ancestors, but the daughters-in-law and grandchildren, in turn, pay their respects to the patriarch.

Fourth, man and woman were not equal in marriage at this time, as we have seen. The dominant role of the husband can be seen in the model marriage between Liang Hong and Meng Guang described in the *Hou Han Shu*. After Meng Guang married Liang Hong, Liang wore her hair in a bun, dressed in plain clothes, and worked diligently. Liang was delighted: "This is a wife who can serve me well!"[37]

Concubinage also underscores women's inferiority in the model of the autocratic domination relationship. Concubinage was a very common contemporary practice, and it was not limited to the emperor who had dozens of palace women and concubines,[38] but extended also to commoners. In the "Neichu" section of *Han Fei Zi* there is an illustrative anecdote:

A couple from the state of Wei made wishful prayers, and the woman prayed for one hundred bundles of cloth. The man asked her why she requested so little, and she replied that if she were to pray for more, he would use the wealth to buy a concubine.

In the Qin and Han there were various terms for concubine —*qie*, *xiaoqi*, *xiaqi*, *xiaofu*, *shaofu* and *weifu*, but in the Six

---

[36] "Quli", *Li Ji*.
[37] "Duxing Liezhuan", *Hou Han Shu*.
[38] "Hunyi", *Li Ji*.

Dynasties concubinage became regulated by social status and so the number of concubines decreased. During the reign of Emperor Xiajing of the Eastern Wei, Yuan Xiaoyu submitted a memorial requesting to adopt a concubine. Yuan was the great-grandson of Toba Tan, and he had inherited the title of Prince of Linhuai from his elder brother. In his memorial he stated his reasons for wanting a concubine:

> This is to establish instruction for women, and to have many descendants. To have many descendants accords with filial piety and establishing instruction for women accords with the Rites. The present dynasty has abandoned these practices. Many ministers and generals have married princesses, and kings and lords have even married women of the empress' clan. It might be natural for them to not have concubines, but women today are unfortunate because men cannot adopt concubines and must have one wife only.[39]

There was some support for Yuan's complaint: "It is my desire that the adoption of concubines will make the descendants of king and nobles multiply and keep the dynasty eternal".[40] In the subsequent Jin dynasty the emperor issued an edict ordering men to have many concubines.

While men could have concubines, women could not have more than one husband, considered in the ethical code of the autocratic society to be a heinous crime. In some districts, such as Yan and Zhao, in the Han dynasty, polyandry did persist, but when such practices were detected the punishment was severe. The trial superintendent Fan Yanshou tortured any such miscreants he discovered:

> Fan made the judgement that this conduct violated human ethics and he compared it with a bestial act. These women's sons were placed under their mothers' care, and

---

[39] "Wudi Wuwang Zhuan", *Wei Shu*.
[40] Ibid.

the men were publicly executed.[41]

Fifth, in the mourning period, the rites observed by husband and wife were different and unequal.[42] A wife had to observe the mourning rites conscientiously in the mourning period after her husband's death, and even though a husband would grieve, "he could grieve privately without showing any emotion publicly".[43] After his wife's death, Wang Gong observed the mourning rites for his wife scrupulously with his sons, and he was ridiculed for doing so by his contemporaries.[44]

Finally, in the matter of divorce, we also see the dominant role of the male. In this period there were seven pretexts on which a man could divorce his wife, and these were called *qi* chu (the seven expulsions). The "Benming" section of the *Dadai Liji* (Recorder of Rites Compiled by Dai the Elder) writes:

> The seven [reasons for] expulsion are: disobeying the parents-in-law; acting contrary to virtue; having no son and so severing the line; wantonness and causing confusion within the clan; untidiness; serious illness preventing the wife from serving meals; speaking out of turn and so sowing the seeds of discord among relatives; and stealing, which violates righteousness.

He Xiu's annotations of *Gongyangzhuan* in the Eastern Han cite a different set of *qi* chu: having no son; wantonness; not serving the elders; speaking out of turn; stealing; jealousy; and, serious illness. Jealousy replaces untidiness or sloth. Although the contents of the seven might change, they were excellent justification for males to behave in a fickle manner.

(2) The Relative Independence of Women in Married

[41] *Hou Han Shu*, cited in *Taiping Yulan*, juan 231.
[42] Ch' T'ing-tsu, **Law and Society in Traditional China** contains an excellent discussion of this question.
[43] "Qianli", *Fengsu Tongyi*.
[44] "Wang Can Zhuan", *Sanguo Zhi*. See note citing Zhang Fan, *Han Ji*.

Life

It is undeniable that in this period people's memories of a remote antiquity when the partnership relationship prevailed had some influence on social life and women had relative independence. In the late Western Han, society was in chaos and peasant armies were in rebellion, and among them was a rebellion led by Mother L. Rule by filial piety (*xiao zhi*), although based on hierarchic differences, tended to prevail over rule by the Rites in the Western Han and *xiao zhi* tended to be milder. Moreover, most of the anecdotes recording instances of filial behaviour from the Western Han tend to be stories about children caring for their mothers, such as the story of Yang Zhen caring for his mother, Yu Yi caring for his grandmother, and Jiang Ge carrying his mother to safety on his back.[45]

Women could also initiate divorce under certain circumstances. An interesting historical anecdote is that of the wife of Zhu Maichen who divorced and remarried. Zhu was a poor wood-cutter, and because he could not support his wife, she asked for a divorce. Zhu told her that he would be rich at the age of fifty and at that time would repay her for her long suffering, but his wife left and remarried. The tables turned when Zhu later became an official and invited the couple to his home. After a month, the ex-wife felt remorse and committed suicide.[46]

During the Six Dynasties, the restrictions of autocratic bonds and virtues were again somewhat relaxed. Women had more independence in matters of divorce, but in the main, males remained the dominators in society, and many marriages were inflexible and lacked vitality. Two historical anecdotes demonstrate this. A man named Xue Changxu would have to send a maidservant to his wife's room to first inform her whenever he

---

[45] Ref: "Filial Piety and the Han Dynasty Family", *Zhongguo Shi Yanjiu* (Chinese History Research), 1988:4.

[46] "Zhu Maichen Zhuan", *Han Shu*.

wanted to speak with her, and he had to make an appointment in advance if he wished to sleep with her. A fangshi or necromancer of the Eastern Han period named Fan Yin fell ill and his wife sent a maid to express her regrets in accordance with the Rites. This excessive propriety reduced marriage to a purely social obligation in which emotion could not play a part.

The story of Zhang Chang who lived during the reign of Emperor Xuandi is even more revealing. Zhang was the governor of the capital in the Western Han dynasty. He lived harmoniously with his beautiful wife, whose eyebrows he would often paint. This latter detail was the subject of a public scandal and the emperor was notified of this practice by memorial. The emperor was furious and summoned Zhang to the palace for an interrogation. Zhang said to the emperor: "I have heard that the private affairs of men and women in the boudoir are more intimate than painting eyebrows". The emperor could only smile, but the anecdote is revealing in that such a private matter could be reported.

Shishuo Xinyu records a similar anecdote from the Jin dynasty. Wang Anfeng's wife often kissed him. Wang retorted: "Kissing one's husband does not accord with propriety, so don't do that again!" Wang's wife said: "I kiss you because I love you. If I don't, who else can?" Wang raised no further objections.

4. The Invasion of Alien Peoples and the Division of Culture

(1) The Division of Society and the Development of Female Jealousy

In the Qin-Han period the domination model of Chinese autocratic politics acquired its full form, and the consolidation of a unified political system and the emergence of a unified country led to the development of a new social order. The rule of the Han lasted more than four centuries and in that time

Chinas experienced one of its most flourishing ages. As the Eastern Han progressed, the division of ruling strata in the centralised autocracy, combined with such factors as the invasions of alien peoples and the introduction of Buddhism, caused the unified nation to disintegrate and society to lapse into unrest and chaos. Although the traditional autocratic bonds and virtues were still the mainstay of contemporary social ethics, they were influenced by various new social philosophies, customs and religious doctrines. Culture tended to fragment and divide.

In the late Eastern Han, the Yellow Turban rebellion fundamentally shattered the base of Han autocratic rule. The kingdoms of Wei, Shu and Wu emerged, and China was later briefly reunited by the Western Jin, but by the end of that period the ruling groups again split. A rebellion of eight princes which lasted for sixteen years not only destroyed the order of autocratic domination, but also provided the opportunity for invasions by minority peoples from the north.

The ancient historians ascribed these invasions to "the five barbarian groups", the ethnic Xiongnu, Jie, Di, Qiang and Xianbei. From the late Western Han onwards, the frequency of wars and the decrease in population had caused the southward migration of northern minorities to increase annually.[47] "The sixteen states of the five barbarian peoples" emerged against this background. From the time of the northern division until re-unification by the Northern Wei, the social order in the north was one of great confusion. In the south much the same situation prevailed. After the collapse of the Western Jin, the large clan families strengthened their control of society in the south. However, the corruption of these families caused the southern regimes to fall in rapid succession. After the Eastern Jin, four dynasties emerged, the Song, Qi, Liang and Chen. Social order was in complete disarray. The division of society

---

[47] Another important factor causing these southward population movements was the onset of a colder climate in the north. See: Zhu Kezhen, **Climate Changes in China Over the Past Five Millenia**.

in the Wei-Jin and the Northern and Southern Dynasties periods was the main factor in the cultural division which occurred.

Another major divisive factor for traditional Chinese culture was the introduction of Buddhism in the Eastern Han. At first, Buddhism was regarded as a kind of magical art.[48] The Buddhist doctrines began to be systematised by Dao An and Hui Yuan in the Jin. Buddhism was quickly accepted by commoners in the Six Dynasties when social order was in complete confusion. Groups of Buddhist monks appeared, and Buddhist temples proliferated. The Buddhist ideas gradually formed a strong intellectual current which could compete with orthodox autocratic ideas.

In addition to Buddhism, there was a metaphysical doctrine derived from the Taoism of Huangdi and Lao Zi, which had a strong influence on the literati. Metaphysics (*Xuanxue*) was the term for this new intellectual current which represented a synthesis of Confucianism, Buddhism and Taoism. Later it became the major intellectual trend of this period, in which the invasions of various alien peoples and the emergence of various doctrines meant that traditional culture had to find its own variations among different social strata and groups. Nevertheless, the autocratic ethics of bonds and virtues remained the main body of socio-intellectual thought. In his *Lao Zi Zhu* (Annotations of Lao Zi), Wang Bi, one of the leading Metaphysicians of the Jin period, wrote:

> The earliest institution was designed to educate people to become officials. The officials in that institution required ranks and levels to distinguish high positions from low, and so there was differing status in the earliest institutions.

---

[48] Ref: "Lihuo Lun", *Mou Zi*: "[Buddha's] words must be comprehended. He can change into various forms. His body can be spilt in its existence or non-existence, and become large or small.... He cannot be harmed by fire and blade, nor can he be defiled. He is safe when disaster comes. He will fly when he wants to walk and projects light when seated. This is why he is called Buddha".

Thus the aim of defining status was to maintain autocracy through hierarchical distinctions, and, in this process, maintaining the male oppression of females was a fundamental step.

We will firstly analyse the identity and continuity of the ethics of bonds and virtues in the Qin, Han and Six Dynasties period within the context of law, the most important political form in the centralised autocratic political system. In pre-Qin patriarchal clan society, there was no complete system of law. It was only after the completion of a unified empire that a systematic legal system began to emerge. Han law abridged Qin law, and was completely derived from the latter. As a means of exercising authority under the model of the domination relationship, the laws of Qin and Han strictly defined the positions of superior and inferior, and woman was in a very inferior legal position. This idea was inherited throughout the Six Dynasties. Jin law encouraged hierarchical distinctions and even "forbade the elevation of a concubine to the status of wife".[49] The laws of the Southern Dynasties were also "completed by abridging and enlarging Han law".[50] According to the law of collective responsibility, the most heinous crime would be redressed by punishing the clan on the wife's side.[51] Women were subordinate to males within the family and her legal position was totally dependent on that of her husband. The law of the Northern Dynasties did not differ from this, but because of the invasions of alien peoples and the emergence of intellectual currents, the orthodox positions of autocratic ethics was more or less shaken, and woman's position was somewhat elevated as a result.

Historical documents recording women's sense of jealousy became more common, which is an interesting phenomenon, because in this period it became difficult for men to adopt

---

[49] Xiao He and Zhang Cang abridged the law to formulate *Jiuzhangü* of the Han. Ref: "Xingfa Zhi", *Han Shu*.

[50] Ref: *Cheng Shude, Jiuchao Lü Kao* (the Laws of the Nine Dynasties), vol. 4.

[51] "Xingfa Zhi", *Sui Shu* (The History of the Sui Dynasty)

concubines. The above-mentioned Yuan Xiaoyou of the Eastern Wei asked to adopt a concubine, but his request was not granted. In the Eastern Jin we read the following account:

> Xie An was fond of music and singing and was often accompanied by prostitutes. Later he wanted to acquire a concubine, but his wife Madam Liu watched him closely. His nephews knew of his intention, and they asked Madam Liu, telling her that poems record how there were some kinds of birds and insects that had the virtue of not being jealous. Conscious of being satirised, Madam Liu asked: "Who wrote this poem?" They replied, "The Duke of Zhou wrote this poem". Madam Liu replied, "The Duke of Zhou was a man, but if his wife had written the poem, she would not write like that".

Xie An was a high-ranking official at court, but he was not able to acquire a concubine. This story appears in *Dufu Ji* (Records of Jealous Women) written by Yu Tongzhi in the fifth century. At that time, the princesses were extremely jealous, and Emperor Ming was very worried about this. He commissioned Yu Tongzhi to write this admonitory work. Emperor Ming's contempt for jealousy is highlighted by a number of incidents, e.g. issuing an order commanding Yuan Yan's jealous wife to die, and an order commanding Jiang Xiao to wrote a divorce notice. *Dufu Ji* records many such anecdotes, as do other works.

Anecdote 1

Princess Lingchuan, sixth daughter of Emperor Wen of the Song, was married to Wang Zao, governor of Dongyang. Wang loved another woman, and the princess jealously denounced him to the emperor, who had him arrested and executed. The princess then divorced Wang.[52]

Anecdote 2

Emperor Ming's secretary and chancellor Rong Yanyuan received favours from his master because of his skill in playing

---

[52] Ref: Zhao Yi, *Nianershi Zhaji*.

chess. Rong's jealous wife slapped Rong across the face, so the Emperor suggested that Rong should tame her. Rong agreed that he should, and so the Emperor gave Rong poison to kill her that night.

Anecdote 3

Liu Xi's wife was extremely jealous, so Emperor Ming presented Liu with a concubine and ordered that Liu's wife be flogged twenty times and made to labour in a small kitchen preparing street food.

Anecdote 4

Emperor Wu of Liang tried to cure the jealousy of his wife Empress Qie by feeding her food made from oriole flesh, which someone had told him cured jealousy. Her jealousy did abate, but spots appeared on her face if she ate too much.

An anecdote from *Youyang Zazu* (The Youyang Miscellany) is even stranger. It tells the story of "the jealous woman ford" (Dufujin):

It is said that in the third century, the wife of Liu Boyu of the Western Jin, nee Duan, was extremely jealous. Liu often read his wife *Luoshen Fu* (Prose-Poem to the Nymph of the River Luo), commenting: "I would have no regrets if I had married a woman like the nymph of the Luo River". Duan asked: "Why do you favour this water goddess and despise me? If I die I am sure to be a water nymph". Then she drowned herself that night. After seven days, Liu dreamed that his former wife was talking to him: "You like the goddess ,and now I am one too". After that Liu never forded the river. Whenever beautiful women in finery crossed the river, the waters would become stormy and turbulent, but ugly women fording the river did not make the goddess jealous, even if they were decked out in their finest attire. Whenever a woman crossed the river without encountering the turbulence, she imagined that she was ugly because the goddess had not been jealous and so she would put away her finery in order not to be ridiculed. The people of Qi later had a saying: "If you want a beautiful wife, just stand on the river bank and watch, because when women pass by there the beautiful are immediately distinguished from those who are ugly.

At that time jealously not only prompted women to keep their men away from other women, but also from young men. The Southern Dynasties writer Shen Yue has recorded this piece in *Sushuo* (On Customs):

Xun Jiezi was an inspector from Jingzhou who had an extremely jealous wife. Mr Huan was in Xun's study, and would close the blinds whenever guests arrived. One of Huan's friends who was an officer in the army visited Huan to discuss business. When the discussion was over, they remained in the study discussing trivial matters. Huan was young and handsome. Standing outside the study, Xun's wife bawled out: "Officer Huan, do you not know how to be a man? The discussion is over, so why don't you leave?" Huan left in an awkward manner.

In the Six Dynasties this jealousy could take untoward forms, as in this anecdote from *Song Shu*:

Princess Shanyin [the elder sister of Emperor Fei of the Song in the fifth century] once said to the emperor: "Your majesty and I, though of different sex, are both descendants of the late emperor, but Your Majesty has several hundred beauties in the rear palace, while I only have one husband. How can things be so unequal?" The emperor then presented her with thirty young men as lovers, but was still not satisfied. She requested the emperor send her Chu Tuan, an official of the Board of Personnel who was extremely handsome, but Chu steadfastly refused. The matter was not over for several weeks more.[53]

(2) Female Elegance in the Six Dynasties

Women in the Six Dynasties were regarded as being extremely elegant. "Xianyuan" in **Shishuo Xinyu** records that Wang Guang was being married to the daughter of Zhuge Dan called Gong Xiu. When the bride arrived, Wang joked: "The bride looks quite humble, not like Gong Xiu". She answered: "You are not equal to the outstanding, so why should your woman match the elite?"

Such anecdotes were prevalent in the Eastern Jin and are denoted as a literary genre called "pure talk" (qingtan). Xie Daoyuan, the talented and eloquent sister-in-law of the renowned calligrapher Wang Xianzhi, was praised in anecdotes for "her graceful charm and fluent eloquence. She spoke of family affairs frankly, then answered questions reasonably and without hesitation". She was also lauded for "looking bright and refined, and seeming aloof from politics and worldly considerations". Purity and clarity were also qualities praised in women.[54]

Female elegance, boudoir improprieties and the strong emphasis on female jealousy in the Six Dynasties all reflect the fact that a woman's position was elevated to some degree at this time. A woman was sometimes seen to be unwilling to be subordinate to a man, and sought to assert herself through these various means. All these phenomena were scorned by Chinese traditional moralists, but woman was struggling against the cruelty and darkness of autocratic ethics. The emergence of these phenomena can be explained by three factors. First, society was divided drastically in the Six Dynasties. Matrimonial relations connected the large and powerful families, and family background was very important in establishing marriages. "The

---

[53] "Feidi Ji", **Song Shu**.
[54] "Xianyuan", **Shishuo Xinyu**.

families of officials and the gentry should not establish matrimonial relations with those of craftsmen, dancers and singers, or with those of humble origin".[55] Because both parties to a marriage were from powerful families, a wife could make use of her family to control her husband. A vivid anecdote in the "Xianyuan" section of **Shishuo Xinyu** clarifies this:

> After the conquest of Shu by Huan Xuanwu, the younger sister of Li Shi was adopted by Huan as one of his concubines and she was greatly favoured by him. She often visited him in his apartments. At first Huan's wife did not know about this, but on discovering the matter, she rounded up a group of servant girls. Armed with knives they raided Lady Li's apartments. Lady Li was combing her long hair and was not frightened by the raid. She spoke calmly: "My country was eliminated and my family destroyed. I cam here against my wishes, It is my desire that you kill me now". Huan's wife felt ashamed and retreated.

Secondly, the period was a time of intellectual turbulence, and the system of autocratic theories founded in the Qin and Han was buffeted by Buddhism, Metaphysics and other ideologies, and as a result the ethics of bonds and virtues based on the oppression of women began to be shattered.

Thirdly, the influx of alien peoples had an effect in China quite different from that of the alien invasions of Western Asia and Europe described by Riane Eisler: "Now everywhere the men with the greatest power to destroythe physically strongest, most insensitive, most brutalrose to the top, as everywhere the social structure becomes more hierarchic and authoritarian. Womenwho as a group are physically smaller and weaker than men, and who are most clearly identified with the old view of power symbolised by the life-giving and sustaining chaliceare now gradually reduced to the status they are to hold hereafter: male controlled technologies of production and reproduction".

---

[55] Ref: Decree of 463 in **Wei Shu**.

As Eisler points out, after the invasions of the alien peoples, the chalice of partnership was broken. Women's positions fell drastically and the model of the male domination relationship was established. But in the Six Dynasties (and in other periods), the relative elevation of woman's position happened after the invasions of alien peoples. How can the difference between Chinese historical facts and Eisler's theory be explained? In my view, this is not very problematical. The northern ethnic groups were living in primitive and semi-primitive societies and they retained more memories and impressions of the partnership period than did people in the Central Plain. Their lifestyles retained customs regarded as corrupt by orthodox autocratic theorists. During their invasions they also brought some of their customs with them. When these merged with autocratic culture, they could possibly have played an active role in cultural division.

After mentioning these three factors, we should note that women's struggle against oppression by men mostly came from within the imperial household and the large and powerful families. They were by no means common social phenomena. The invasions of alien peoples caused cultural division, but the foundation of autocratic ethics was not shattered and it was able to incorporate some diverse elements. However, the struggle of women was very limited, as can be seen from the instances of jealousy. Emperor Ming, who we noted above, had Rong Yanyuan's wife flogged for jealousy, led quite a licentious life and would force his wife to watch naked dancing girls with him. When the empress refused to watch and covered her eyes with a fan, Emperor Ming became angry and asked: "Our relatives' residences are such cold and cheerless places. Now we are amusing ourselves, why don't you watch?" The empress answered: "There are many forms of amusement. But how can we amuse ourselves by watching naked women when my family visit?" The male domination relationship was firmly in place, and it was absolutely impossible to realise equality.

The Six Dynasties was a unique period in the development

of the traditional Chinese autocracy. The intellectual surges and the invasions of northern alien peoples had a great impact on orthodox autocratic culture. For this reason, Chinese intellectuals sought some forms of emancipation at that time, but the cultural division and the intellectual emancipation were only superficial phenomena. The centralised autocratic political system had not been destroyed at its core and "the three obediences and four virtues" and "the three bonds and five virtues" were still passed on from generation to generation. The hierarchy remained firm and the women's struggle failed, and was doomed to fail.

CHAPTER SIX
A FIXED STATE OF AFFAIRS AND MISPOSITIONED STATUS: GENDER RELATIONS DURING THE SUI, TANG, FIVE DYNASTIES AND SONG DYNASTY

Gao Shiyu

In no other dynasties than the Tang and Song can one find more mature and sumptuous cultural artefacts, and the same is true of the change and form of the ancient social formation as it entered a later stage. The Zhou and Han dynasties had seen the gradual establishment of the feudal ethical code of cardinal guides and constant virtues dominated by Confucianism, and the relations between venerable and humble, principal and subordinate, and masculine and feminine had become transformed into an unchangeable traditional fixity. This became increasingly stable with the maturity and prosperity of the ancient civilisation during the period from the Sui and Tang to the Song. From the Song dynasty on, with the emergence of Lixue or the Neo-Confucianist "idealist philosophy" and the flourishing of the Confucian ethical code, the traditional gender pattern became not only more stable but also further developed with the male's rights on the ascendant and the female's status in decline. The gap between men and women widened.

The Song Dynasty marked a transitional turning point in the history of gender relations, and some social changes in this period exerted a great impact on gender relations, bringing about disharmonies within an increasingly general trend of stabilisation.

I. Social Change and Gender Relations

During the period from the Sui and Tang dynasties to the Song Dynasty, two major historic changes affected and transformed the entirety of society. The first was the renewal of national composition. In the wake of the separatist regimes and the ethnic warfare which filled the three centuries of the Wei, Jin and Northern and Southern Dynasties, in the Sui-Tang period a unified multi-national country with unprecedentedly vast territory emerged. Many nomadic peoples from north China would absorbed into the nation, and this "fresh blood" helped renew society. As the cultures and customs of the various nomadic peoples and the traditional culture and custom of the farming Han people blended, Chinese civilisation became richer and more varied. The second change was in the social formation and structure itself. Unlike the ethnic infusion, this deeper social change occurred quietly and slowly, resulting in the gradual withdrawal of the old nobility from the historical arena and their replacement by new nobles originally from the lower strata of society. Moreover, the once insurmountable boundary between the old nobility and the would-be new nobility who sprang from obscurity was removed by official postings. National land ownership and manor serfdom were in decline, and were being replaced by the private ownership of land and a tenancy system, as well as by a new employment system. The status of labourers rose somewhat and personal dependence was comparatively reduced. The commodity economy developed in an unprecedented fashion and cities expanded on in scale. The urban population became a vital emerging force in society. These changes undermined the traditional hierarchy of "the four estates" and there was movement between classes, fragmenting the social structure and weakening the traditional rigid hierarchy. These two social changes penetrated all levels of social life and also exercised a great influence on gender relations and concepts, both directly and indirectly.

(1) The Shock Caused by the Customs of the Yi and Di Nationalities

If we say that is was the great unification during the Qin and Han dynasties that formed the Chinese nation into an indivisible large family, then the second great unification took place during the Sui and Tang dynasties when the Xianbei and other northern nomadic nationalities were encompassed within the nation. From the Western Jin Dynasty on, the nomadic nationalities in north China had begun migrating down to the Central Plain and participating in the Chinese political arena by founding a dozen or so small states and, then, powerful regimes during the Northern Dynasties. They and the Han people lived together so long that the two gradually assimilated each other. The unification of the country achieved by the Sui and Tang was one of ethnic fusion.

The dynasties of the Sui and Tang founded unified states on the basis of the Northern Dynasties of the Xianbei. Emperor Yang of the Sui dynasty and Emperor Li of the Tang dynasty, both founding emperors, were themselves of Hu extraction, and they rose to power and position from the ruling stratum of the national minorities of the Northern Dynasties, belonging to the military nobility of the Guan-Long areas (present-day Shaanxi and Gansu provinces). As a result, they had the deeply rooted culture and customs of the non-Han nationalities of the north and a tradition of military accomplishments. After the unification of the whole country, they inevitably brought with them the common practices and customs of the Yi and Di tribes of the east to the Central Plain.

Apart from these historical roots, during the three centuries of Sui-Tang, China was constantly influenced by alien cultures and customs. The Sui Dynasty was short-lived, but it was powerful and prosperous during its short span and its influence reached as far as the Western Region, the area west of Yumen-guan including the present Xinjiang and parts of Central Asia. In the later Tang dynasty, China was frequently visited by foreign diplomats and "the non-Han nationalities in the north and the Yue nationality in the east were one family". Emperor Taizong of the Tang Dynasty was even respectfully called "the Heavenly Khan". His celebrated dictum reads: "Ever since ancient times, the Chinese nation has been highly valued, while the Yi and Di nationalities have been despised, but I wish to see all nationalities treated equally".[1] This displays the boldness of vision with which the ruler of the Great Empire unified the country and his personal concern for both the Han and Yi nations. Owing to its vast territory and powerful national strength, the Sui and Tang dynasties adopted a policy of opening to other countries. As a result, interchange between China and other countries was unprecedentedly frequent and alien cultures and customs steadily flowed into the Central Plain. The common practices and customs of the non-Han nationalities in the north enriched the cultural atmosphere of the Sui and Tang dynasties before and after their establishment and this exerted a great influence upon the traditional culture of the Han people of the Central Plain. In this historical period, the influence of the non-Han nationality customs on clothing, food, shelter, transportation and cultural entertainment constitutes an attractive historical phenomenon.

Of all the non-Han nationalities in the north and the Yi and Di nationalities in the east, the most important culturally were the nomadic nationalities, even though their stage of social development was more backward than that of the Han people. In terms of gender relations, although they had established a

---

[1] Sima Guang, *Zizhi Tongjian* (Comprehensive Mirror for the Aid of the Ruler), juan 193.

male-centred marriage system based on monogamy, some primitive marriage-related customs of the matriarchy stage, in which
"children know their mothers only and not their fathers", persisted. Consequently, women in general had a higher social and
economic position in these nomadic societies, and in some
aspects of the system and customs women wielded greater
power. Moreover, marriage among the non-Han nationalities in
the north was freer and sexual relations were more promiscuous
than among the Han people. This is not only apparently among
such nomadic nationalities as the Xianbei, Tujue (Turk), Qidan
(Khitan) and Tuguhuan, but also it finds its reflection in
neighbouring countries such as Japan, Xinluo (present Korea),
Linyi (also called Zhancheng, present Vietnam) and Dongn
(present Sichuan) during the Sui and Tang dynasties. For example, in the flourishing Tang Dynasty, An Lushan, who originated among a minor nationality in the north and who was a
general who garrisoned a border region, prostrated himself first
before the highest imperial concubine and then before the
emperor, professing, "The non-Han nationalities in the north
rank the mother above the father".[2] "Some nationalities regard
women as superior to men".[3] Among the Xianbei and Tujue
nationalities women often held power. Primitive customs and
practices in sexual relations and marriage were even more
obvious. The Xianbei nobility in the Northern Dynasties was
notorious for its promiscuous behaviour, and prior to the
establishment of the Northern Wei dynasty, a decree was issued: "Men or women who do not practice proper sexual
intercourse shall be killed".[4] Nevertheless, in order to multiply
its population, the government of the Northern Wei dynasty
time and again issued imperial edicts, ordering men and women
to have sexual intercourse in mid-spring according to the ancient Rites and none were allowed to not partake. The Southern

[2] Ibid., juan 215.
[3] "Dongn Guo", *Jiu Tang Shu*.
[4] "Xingfa Zhi", *Wei Shu*.

Song dynasty of the Han people also chose to encourage population growth, but it did so through marriage.

Lifestyle also distinguished the women of the nomadic nationalities from the farming and weaving women of the Central Plain. The former excelled in horsemanship and archery, and went herding and hunting, galloping across the vast grasslands, and acquiring toughness and valour in the practice. With the founding of the Sui and Tang dynasties and with frequent contact between the nationalities, the common practices and customs of the Yi and Di nationalities constantly blew down to the Central Plain, buffeting the mode of traditional gender relations.

More importantly the Sui and Tang rulers with origins among the Yi and Di lacked a knowledge of Confucian ethics. After the establishment of their dynasties, they built up a powerful political system based on a centralised feudal empire, but failed to set up a single authority in ideology and culture, and they did not venerate Confucianism exclusively as had been the case in the Han dynasty. Instead, they adopted a syncretic policy embracing Confucianism, Buddhism and Taoism, which had in fact been taking shape since the Wei and Jin dynasties. The ruler of the Tang dynasty, Li Shimin, was surnamed Li as was Lao Zi (Li Er), the founder of Taoism, and so he regarded Lao Zi as his ancestor and devoted great efforts to encouraging Taoism with a view to adding its authority to his rule. As a result, Taoism was ranked above Confucianism for a considerably long historical period. The religious tolerance of the Tang rulers also saw Buddhism rapidly develop and enter its heyday.

In short, in the Sui and Tang period, the three religions in question basically kept pace with one another, and, as a result, Confucianism and its ethical code never succeeded in building up absolute authority and forming a powerful ideological force. It is worth noting that the ideological system of Taoism which was rooted in the vast land of China proper contained from its inception the connotations of advocating nature and venerating

femininity and the female. As an introduced religion, Buddhism, although gradually influenced by the Chinese traditional
culture, still retained the concept of all living creatures being
equal and it was therefore less discriminatory towards women.
Although Taoism and Buddhism gradually flowed together with
Confucianism in the concepts of ethics and gender relations as
a general trend, they both retained their own ideological characteristics and did not become totally subservient to Confucianism. Under such conditions, in which the three religions kept
pace with one another, it is no wonder that people's ideas and
concepts of morality appeared free and pluralistic.

As the customs of the non-Han nationalities made their
impact and the ideological sphere lacked authority, there was a
generally easy-going mood in society and feudal ethics were in
abeyance. Women had a higher position in society and the
family and were less trammelled by etiquette. Women also had
a certain toughness. When Wu Zetian became the concubine of
Emperor Taizong of the Tang dynasty, there happened to be a
fierce horse in the imperial court. Nobody dared train him, yet
Wu declared in the presence of all: "I can control him but I need
three things: an iron whip, an iron bar and an iron dagger. If I
can't bring him under control with the iron whip, I'll use the
iron bar. If he still refuses to be docile, then I'll cut his throat
with the iron dagger."[5] Emperor Taizong highly appreciated her
courage. Her performance contrasts dramatically with the gentleness and weakness of the traditional woman. In addition,
influenced by the nomadic nationalities, native women took to
soldiering and archery on horseback. They were often depicted
in murals in martial attire, galloping across the landscape with
bows and arrows drawn or hunting in the hills and wildernesses.
The status and conduct of women naturally affect gender
relations, and this lifestyle pounded at the traditional mode of
relations based on discrimination between the respectful and

---

[5] *Zizhi Tongjian*, juan 206.

lowly, the principal and subordinate, and the masculine and feminine between men and women. This point was clearly evident in social and family life during the Sui and Tang dynasties.

Men and women were free of many restrictions and had more freedom in sexual behaviour in this period. The moralist Zhu Xi once concluded that the Tang originated and developed from the Yi and Di nationalities, and it was no surprise that "discourtesy in the boudoir" was commonplace.[6] This "discourtesy in the boudoir" was seen by later ages as a female breach of the feudal ethical code and negligence in observing the laws and rites governing relations between men and women. For these reasons, the domination relationship between men and women in this period weakened and taboos for both sexes were not that strict.

(2) The Establishment of Civilian Rule and the Weakening of the Masculine Disposition

Civilian rule prevailed in the Song dynasty, but it began in the Tang. After conquering all quarters of the country, the ruler of the Tang lost no time in establishing civilian rule. Consequently, the imperial examination system began to prevail, and scholars graduated according to their literary talents. The jinshi was a successful candidate in the highest imperial examination which laid particular stress on poetry and descriptive prose interpreted through verse. The valuing of belles-lettres and the belittling of the martial arts became social trends. However, it was in the Song dynasty when the development of civilian government and the esteem for literature reached their zenith. In the Song dynasty the examination system was a socially dominant force. Warriors were overshadowed by gifted scholars seeking to become high officials.

The prevalence of civilian government in the Song dynasty

---

[6] ***Zhu Zi Yulei***, (Quotations from Zhu Xi) juan 136

has its historical background. In the two centuries from the late Tang to the Five Dynasties, China was torn apart and divided into rival principalities. The Song dynasty saw a reunited country different however different from that of the Sui and Tang dynasties. The Song dynasty was less vast in territory as the Sui and Tang dynasties, and was faced from the start with the threat posed by powerful regimes of minor nationalities in the north. These political regimes of nomadic nationalities include the Liao, Xixia and Jin, which were in the heyday of their rise and development. They had great military strength and a very powerful cavalry. Later the Mongol Yuan dynasty would rule an empire covering both Asia and Europe. Confronted by such powerful forces, the Song dynasty found itself in a precarious position.

Under such hard-pressed conditions, the Song dynasty rulers should have strengthened their military forces and maintained combat readiness, and yet they adopted the policy of valuing literature and belittling the martial arts and going in for civilian governing. Among other things, the Song refused to emulate the later Tang and the Five Dynasties and confer power on military governors who could later set up separatist regimes by force of arms. Emperor Taizu, founder of the Song dynasty removed the military leadership from persons who had rendered outstanding service and replaced them with generals with outstanding service, providing them with excellent pay and conditions. Hereafter, the Song dynasty took a series of measures ranging from politics to military affairs, devoting major efforts to strengthening centralism and the system of imperial despotism in order to weaken local power and the political, financial and military power of ministers. As a result, the strengthening of despotic system of the Song dynasty went far beyond that of the Sui and Tang Dynasties. Among these measures, the rulers energetically assigned Confucian scholars to posting, because they were too weak to constitute a menace to the central regime and hence scholars smoothly and successfully sought official positions.

Another reason for civilian government is because men of insight of the Song dynasty felt that there were only a handful of loyal and righteous officials in the Five Dynasties, and hence there was demoralisation in society which resulted in social upheaval. For example, Ouyang Xiu, a famous official and man of letters of the Song dynasty, once said remarked: "When I speak of the disorder of the Five Dynasties, I mean that the sovereign did not behave like sovereign, neither did father or son. As to brothers and husbands and wives, human relations were abominable, and Heavenly reason was almost eliminated".[7] In view of such social conditions, and beset with domestic trouble and foreign incursions, the Song dynasty tried desperately to boost civilian government in order to strengthen the traditional Chinese culture and moral principles and ethics in order to train righteous men who were loyal to the Song and to forestall the emergence of mutinous official who would surrender to invaders, as was the case in the period from the latter half of the Tang to the Five Dynasties. By consolidating the centralised rule of the Song dynasty both ideologically and culturally, it was hoped the Song could successfully resist the cultural incursion of other nationalities. It is worth noting that the situation of the Song dynasty was different from that of the Tang dynasty. The Tang dynasty, though confronted with national contradictions too, was the suzerain state over the four Yi nationalities for most of its span whereas the Song dynasty was always under great pressure from alien nationalities, to whom its rulers even had to pay tribute. Under such conditions, the Song dynasty was not in a position to adopt an open-door policy as had the Tang. On the contrary, it pursued a closed-door policy and assumed a defensive attitude. In terms of alien cultures, the Tang dynasty took in everything, without being concerned about any menace. We read for example: "The Han

---

[7] "Yi Xing Zhuan", **Wudai Shi**.

women married non-Han people and began to copy their fashions".[8] In the Song dynasty the spectre of invasion and conquest loomed: "The loyalists of the fallen Tang dynasty shed their tears in barbarian dust".[9] The Song felt hatred and fear in face of "barbarian customs" and naturally sought to strengthen the traditional culture of the Chinese nation to withstand it.

Because of the needs of civilian government, the imperial examination system prospered to an unprecedented extent. Compared with the Tang dynasty, the imperial examinations in the Song dynasty experienced many reforms and changes, and they were fully developed and perfected. As a result, not only was the number of recruitment increased tenfold, but the successful examinees more easily were recruited into the civil service. Moreover, the government took measures to stop illegal entry into the civil service, so that the system fairer, and the imperial examination system, as a result, attracted scholars all the more. People from all walks of life attempted to sit for the examinations and the numbers of literate males proliferated. At the same time, the implementation of the policy of encouraging learning led to an increase in the number of schools and academies of classical learning. Advanced techniques of paper-making and printing made block printing prosper and books became very popular. All this made the Song dynasty the heyday of civilian government and culture.

The stress on literature rather than the martial arts and the encouragement of civilian government had two main consequences. Firstly, while the Song dynasty had effective control of its subjects and territory, its military power was too weak to resist foreign invasion, and so China often found itself being attacked. On the other hand, the abandonment by a large number of fine men of military service in favour of literary practice tended to weaken males. On the whole, the chivalry and

---

[8] Yuan Zhen, "Faqu", *Xin Yuefu*.
[9] Lu You,

martial qualities of righteous men and warriors who yearned to render meritorious service on the battlefield in the Han and Tang dynasties were on the wane, whereas the habitual practices of the weakened men of letters were on the increase. The literati and officialdom increasingly revelled in writing in clichis without originality, "chanting poems or lyric verses while drinking from half-filled cup" or hankering after academic and cultural pursuits. That Songxue, Confucian idealist philosophy of the Song dynasty represented by the Cheng-Zhu and Lu-Wang schools, became a xianxue (celebrated teaching) proves this point. The weakening of males as a group was also a major cause of the decline in martial arts during the dynasty. Marco Polo, familiar with the social conditions of the Southern Song dynasty, wrote: "People here are far from being brave fighters.... In [the Emperor's] realm there are no herds of horses, and his subjects never practice martial arts, engage in military training or perform any military service. If only his people had engaged in military affairs, this nation would have never been conquered. It is because they refused to practice military arts that this nation was finally subjugated".[10]

His view is not necessarily entirely fair and equitable but it has some basis. Liu Zhizhen, a modern scholar, has also noted the gentleness and frailty of the Song dynasty people. He made a survey of the conditions of the Song imperial family after they moved south of the Changjiang River, and discovered that all officials rode in carriages or sedan chairs, and that none rode on horseback. Previously, high-ranking officials had rode on horses when going to court or undertaking a journey. Liu commented: "Comfort and ease in housing and travelling were much sought after, which accounts for the gentleness and frailty of men at that time".[11]

Of course, one cannot flatly negate the practices of valuing

[10] Marco Polo, **The Travels**.
[11] Liu Yizheng, **History of Chinese Culture**, ch. 16, pt. 2.

learning and belittling the martial arts. It is precisely owing to this trend that the splendid culture of Song culture so rapidly developed. Moreover, the civilian government deserves to be praised for its boundless merits and virtues, and for creating a level of civilisation higher than that brought about by the wanton engagement in military aggression and violence. A "masculine disposition" does not necessarily entail military service or the martial arts. An ancient Chinese scholar once said: "One should worry about one's nation before indulging in pleasure". One cannot fail to notice that in the farming-based Chinese nation which lacked bravery and "a masculine disposition", in comparison with nomadic nationalities, the civilian government tended to make the population even more gentle and frail. The perception of male gentleness and frailty and related values became the mainstream in society to an even greater extent after the Song dynasty. In literature of the Ming and Qing dynasties, most heroes and ideal figures for female love are almost all gentle and frail-looking scholars who are talented or handsome, mirroring the social mood.

(3) Re-building the Edifice of the Confucian Ethical Code

Having been hit by the whirlwind of the unorthodox beliefs of Metaphysics (*Xuanxue*) in the Wei dynasty, Taoism and Buddhism and by the customs of the Yi and Di nationalities, the edifice of the Confucian ethical code set up in the Han dynasty seemed to be tottering, but it could not collapse totally for it was rooted firmly in traditional society. In the mid Tang dynasty and thereafter, the restoration of the edifice was tentatively begun, and the Song dynasty saw its completion.

In the mid Tang dynasty, the ruling Li family had been influenced increasingly by the traditional culture of the Central Plain, and had lost much of its "foreign" flavour. They began to despise the "barbarian" customs of their forefathers and to admire instead the etiquette and family education of the old wealthy and influential clans of Shandong which had been so despised by Emperor Taizong, founder of the Tang dynasty. In the mid and late Tang, Emperors Dezong and Xuanzong constantly advocated law, discipline and the Rites, took pains to unite with the old wealthy clans and the new influential clans by marriage, and in particular, paid attention paid to restraining the unbridled and pampered royal daughters with law, discipline and the Rites. In the early Tang dynasty, the princesses gained notoriety for defying "boudoir precepts" and "women's principles", showing disrespect for their husbands, elders and superiors, and even for riding roughshod over their husbands and other family members. Emperor Dezong ordered the Rites officials to lay down rules of etiquette, stipulating that princesses shall adhere to the principles and codes governing women's behaviour, and the discipline and Rite of their husbands' families. Having been instructed and restrained, the princesses began to abide by law, discipline and the Rites, and some acquired a reputation as "virtuous women" for their courtesy, humility and kindness. The noble and influential official families followed the example of the old wealthy clans in managing their households with Rites. For instance, Prince Xiping Li Cheng was proclaimed an exemplar among high officials for stressing law, discipline and the Rites. He was married into a powerful gentry clan from Shandong, and he treated his daughter in strict accordance with the precepts of etiquette. In the first month of one lunar year when his daughter returned to her parents' home, he did not allow her to enter the house, but ordered her to go back to her husband's home to prepare food and wine for her mother-in-law. When his birthday was observed, his daughter came to congratulate him on his birthday, but he threw his chopsticks down in a fury, when he heard that his daughter's mother-in-law was not well and ordered his daughter to return immediately to attend to her mother-in-law. He himself paid a visit to the parents of his son-in-law to apologise abjectly for his failure to have managed his daughter.[12] All this action suggests a tendency to strengthen the Confucian ethical code and domestic discipline against women in the mid Tang dynasty and thereafter. At the same time, the literati and officialdom represented by Han Yu also advocated Confucian orthodoxy and began to make efforts to resurrect Confucianism.

However, it was in the Song dynasty that the real rejuvenation of the Confucian ethical code took place, symbolised by the rise of Lixue, Neo-Confucian idealism. Represented by Cheng Hao and Cheng Yi of the Northern Song dynasty and by Zhu Xi of the Southern Song, Lixue emerging as part of the emphasis on civilian government and the effort to re-build the feudal ethical code embodied in the three cardinal guides and the five constant virtues. The merits of the Lixue school lie in not only its rejuvenation of the Confucian ethical code which had been declining decaying for several hundred years but in its formulation of a philosophical theory justifying that code. Following the domination of Confucianism in the Han dynasty, Lixue pushed Confucianism to a new stage and became it once again became the dominant official philosophy school in the post-ancient society of China. After the Southern Song dynasty: "People said nothing which did not conform with Zhu Xi's interpretation of the Confucian classics; people conducted themselves in strict accordance with the family rites laid down by Zhu Xi".[13] Consequently, Master Zhu became the major figure in the Confucian "pantheon" after Confucius.

As is well known, in ancient China, it was the feudal ethical code chiefly based on the Confucian school that served as the most powerful weapon in maintaining the unequal status of men and women and the pattern of gender relations. The emergence of Lixue not only strengthened the endurance of the Confucian ethical code, but it also directly influenced the

---

[12] "Tang Yulin" (juan 1), "Li Cheng Zhuan", *Jiu Tang Shu*.

[13] Zhu Yizun, "Baoshu-ting Xu" (Preface to **Baoshuting Writings**) and "Dao Shi Lu Xu" (Foreword to **Collection of Taoist Poems**).

position of women and gender relations. Take Cheng Hao for example. On the subject of widows remarrying, he commented: "It is trifling when a widow is starved to death, but it is a very serious matter when she loses her chastity". When asked, "It seems unreasonable for a man to marry a widow. Do you think so?" Cheng answered, "Yes, I do. If you marry a widow, you have to be a match for her. If you marry a widow who has lost her chastity, then you must have lost your moral integrity". When asked again, "Can a widow who is poor and helpless marry again?" To which Cheng replied: "It is only because of the recent view that death from poverty or hunger is something to be feared that such an opinion has arisen. Nevertheless, it is trifling when a widow is starved to death, but it is a very serious matter when she loses her chastity".[14] Although a number of adages had been current condemning widows who remarried, it had never previously been suggested that widows should not marry again even if they were in danger of starving to death. Only in Lixue philosophy was the chastity of a woman regarded as something even more important than life itself. But one should be fair with Cheng Hao. While he held that women must not re-marry, he also insisted that men should not marry again, which was regretfully overlooked in later ages.

Zhu Xi later advocated and developed Cheng Hao's theory, personally advising people to preserve their chastity. These shocking views were to exercise far-reaching influence, and have dire consequences in later ages. In post-Yuan dynasty China, this drastic concept of chastity was to become socially dominant and to provide the most powerful theoretical basis preventing widows from being re-married. Fang Bao, a Qing dynasty Confucian scholar wrote: "The meaning of marriage was not clarified until Master Cheng presented his views on the relative values of starvation and chastity, after which even farmers in

---

[14] ///Henan Chengshi Yishu ///(Posthumous Writings of the Cheng Brothers from Henan), juan 22.

the countryside and children of the city were familiar with the view. Henceforth, men began to regard women's loss of chastity as a shame, and they hated and despised them for it, and this is why women are self-disciplined and exert themselves. Alas! After Emperor Qin Shi Huang issued his prohibitions, people preserved them through the ages, but few people were changed by them. Yet what Master Cheng said has shaken the world, and that is why human relations and courtesy in the sense of ethics have survived in later ages".[15] This demonstrates the influence Cheng Hao's sayings exercised on people in later ages.

As Song dynasty Neo-Confucianism became the dominant philosophy in later ages, it was venerated and elaborated upon by rulers and literati, and the status of women status dropped sharply. As a result, there was a great disparity between the status of the sexes and a man's control over a woman was more secure and cruel than ever before.

In addition, in the Song dynasty, a number of celebrated writings on family education made their appearance, such as *Jia Fan* (Family Norms) by Sima Guang and *Shi Fan* (Norms for the Age) by Yuan Cai, which re-affirmed the Confucian ethical code. *Jia Fan* stipulates that "the man administers external affairs, while the woman manages internal affairs." A number of precepts in that work were to be highly influential: "Women are not to peep at the entrance of the inner hall for any reason"; "The woman who goes out of the entrance of the inner hall for any reason must cover her face"; "The male servant should not enter the door of the inner hall unless he has to do a repair job or has major cause for entering; if he must enter, the women should artfully avoid him or cover their faces with their sleeves if they fail to avoid him quickly". Sima Guang also stressed that all communications between the inner household and outside were to be handled by the old and trusty servants. The appearance of writings on family education handed down to posterity

---

[15] *Fang Bao Ji* (Anthology of Fang Bao), juan 4.

also furnish us with information on the gradual restoration and re-building of the edifice of Confucian ethics. However, although the Confucian ethical code began to rejuvenate in the Song dynasty when *Lixue* emerged, it did not have a great immediate social impact. *Lixue* was viewed as a "pseudo study" (*weixue*) for a long time. Not until the Southern Song dynasty did *Lixue* attain some position, and begin to exert influence. Although women's status and gender relations in the Song dynasty are somewhat different compared with those in the Tang dynasty, and were interlinked in many aspects with those of the Tang, there is a much greater contrast with the Yuan, Ming and Qing dynasties when *Lixue* was to acquire a dominant position and the Confucian ethical code was in the heyday of its development. A number of scholars have noticed the time lag between the emergence of *Lixue* and its social influence. Having examined women's social status in the Song dynasty, some scholars stress that the Tang and Song dynasties were relatively lenient periods in the application of socio-ethical codes affecting women, even though the Confucian ethical code was intensifying. The conditions of women in the Ming dynasty when the *Lixue* philosophy of Cheng and Zhu came to dominate were much harsher.[16]

In late ancient society, the strengthening of the Confucian ethical code, the decline in the position of women and the increasing strictness of gender relations had, nevertheless, already become visible in the Song dynasty. The degree of freedom between in gender relations in the Song and Tang dynasties cannot be mentioned in the same breath. The female in particular, was much more reserved in marriage and gender relations than her counterpart in the Tang dynasty (this point will be dealt with later in detail). Women were also somewhat restrained from appearing in public and taking part in social

---

[16] Zheng Bijun, "The Confucian Ethical Code and Women in the Song Dynasty", **Selected Papers from the International Seminar on Song Dynasty Culture**, (Sichuan University Press, 1991).

interaction. The Song dynasty also saw a new practice that required to go out with their heads covered in gaitou, which resembled a large scarf generally made of purple or black silk, near translucent, silk which women used to cover their heads and half the bodies when they went out. The ancient Rites originally stipulated: "Women must cover their faces when they embark on a journey".[17] This point was also re-affirmed in Sima Guang's *Jia Fan*. During his time in office in Quanzhou and Zhangzhou, Zhu Xi, issued a decree that women must wrap their faces with floral scarves when they were away from home. This practice was very prevalent in the social environment in which the Confucian ethical code was being advocated and valued. City women covered their heads with scarves when they went out shopping, to see a doctor or to handle business. Even some farming women wore gaitou when they went out of the house.

It was the prevalent practice of foot binding that truly reflects the fall in female status and the strengthening of the confinement of women. It is by no means accidental that the notorious practice that cruelly injured women for hundreds of years began in the Song dynasty, and it is a symbol of the gradual change in gender relations. Opinion has greatly varied on when foot binding began. According to one view, the practice was initiated in the Five Dynasties period. According to some historical records, in the late Five Dynasties, Li Yu, the head of the Southern Tang state had at his court a maid of honour, named Yaoniang, who was an adept dancer. Li ordered that a golden lotus be fashioned and that Yaoniang bind her feet so that they became slender and bent enabling let her to dance on the golden lotus. Her dancing posture would then appear even lighter, nimbler and more graceful. It was said that women subsequently emulated her and that this became a common practice. Basing themselves on this account, later scholars main-

---

[17] "Neize", *Li Ji*.

tained that foot binding began at that time.[18]

Li Yu was on the throne in the period spanning the late Five Dynasties and early Northern Song dynasty. Although opinion varies on the date of the origins of foot binding and scholars are unable to decide which is correct, the present author holds that foot binding spread gradually in the Song dynasty and became a prevailing practice in the late Song, or Southern Song dynasty. In recent years, foot bound female corpses have been discovered in tombs of the Southern Song dynasty at De'an in Jiangxi province. From the historical records mentioned, we can see that from the very start, the operation of foot binding was originally performed to satisfy male aesthetic interest in the female body and posture. Females catered to this male aesthetic interest which expressed male fondness for female gentleness and weakness. As foot binding gradually developed into a custom and women were increasingly confined, people invested foot binding with greater significance. The Qing dynasty *Nü'er Jing* (Classic for Women) explains that foot binding is performed less for aesthetic reasons ("it is not because the feet look beautiful like a bow") but because "the husband fears that she shall walk away from home so lightly that her feet are bound with cloth, layer upon layer, to restrain her". Foot binding was quite clearly a form of bondage.

As foot binding spread and was adopted by women from all walks of life, foot binding became a pernicious custom that swept society in the Yuan, Ming and Qing dynasties. The development and spread of foot binding entirely paralleled the increasingly intensifying confinement of women by the Confucian ethical code, and it is in the Song dynasty that foot binding developed into a custom.

---

[18] Tao Zongyi, *Chuo Geng Lu* (Records Made When Stopping Ploughing), juan 10.

2. Gender Relations in Social Life

(1) "The Hen Crows in the Morning": Women in Politics

Ever since the pre-Qin period, China was a firmly masculine monarchical society based on imperial power, although there is a tradition of female exertion of political power. From the time of the Empress Dowager Xuan of the state of Qin on, the practice of women being at the helm of the state still persisted in the Han, Jin and Five Dynasties. This is quite surprising in the androcratic political system of ancient China, but the emergence of this phenomenon is not surprising. It is the very by-product of the androcratic monarchical political system and the family-domination system. The autocracy of imperial power demanded that power be absolutely concentrated in one man's hands, whereas family domination was designed to ensure that imperial power was handed down from generation to generation in one family with one surname. If the emperor suffered some misfortune, fell ill, or was too young to be enthroned, the emperor was substituted by the person closest and dearest to him to ensure that imperial power did not fall into the hands of others. The princes and dukes of the imperial clansmen, the prime minister and high-ranking officials, were likely to usurp state power regardless of how intimate and loyal they might appear to be, and so only a mother or wife could act in the emperor's interests and not replace him, ensuring that imperial power would not fall into the hands of others. The emperor himself had no other alternative than to trust his closest relatives. Moreover, ever since ancient times China has attached the greatest importance to filial piety, to a mother's loving kindness in bringing up her children and to advocating respect for mothers. As a result, the mother of the emperor or the emperor's heirs enjoys great prestige in the royal family, and this provides the emperor's mother and concubines, who have the status of mother and wife, an opportunity to participate in government and political affairs. That the empress or empress dowager could attend to state affairs at court from "behind a screen" thereupon became an unwritten law in ancient China, and this practice constituted the origins of female management of political affairs. Although from the Han dynasty on, it was found that there were still some drawbacks when the empress or empress dowager held court instead of the emperor in that it was not a guarantee that imperial power did not fall into the hands of others, because behind them stood other family clan relatives of the emperor on the side of his mother or wife, who more often than not seized imperial power because of the empress was in charge of state affairs. This historical phenomenon has been repeated time and again, however no better method of handling the problem was formulated. "Attending to state affairs from behind a screen" continued as before. It is worth noting that regardless of how powerful these empresses or empress dowagers in power might be, they were fulfilling the roles of mother or wife. In other words, they wielded power in place of the male sex with the status of the male's relative, not with status of the female sex per se. In that sense, they might be "principals" but they remained "subordinates", being subordinated to the male sex.

This state of affairs changed in the Tang dynasty when women played a role in politics unparalleled in any other period of Chinese history. A female emperor, Wu Zetian, even emerged. She changed her subordinate status as mother and wife and came into power as an independent female. Not content with attending to state affairs from behind a screen in the name of the male sex, she openly walked out from behind the screen, assumed the crown and changed the name of the dynasty. She ascended the throne as an individual. The assumption of the title of emperor (*huangdi*) was of inestimable significance, because this was the only instance in Chinese history when a woman reigned as a fully fledged emperor.

The emergence of Empress Wu was the outcome of a long period of development of females in politics and the product of her age, not unrelated to the influence of nomadic customs and the weakening of the Confucian ethical code. The ruling clique from which the Li-Tang dynasty came had the tradition of the female autocrat handling state affairs. The Northern Wei dynasty of the Xianbei nationality saw two famous female autocrats, Empress Dowager Feng and Empress Hu. In comparison with their counterparts in the Han and Jin Dynasties, they were visibly influenced by nomadic ethnic customs, and were tougher, more valiant and more unscrupulous. Similarly in the Sui dynasty, although no female autocrats openly wielded power, there were two empresses, whose vital status is recorded—Empress Wen Ji of the Sui dynasty, and Empress Dugu, who exercised near total influence over Emperor Wendi. They never failed to control court affairs, including the coronation of princes and official appointments. In reality, the monarchy during the reign of Emperor Wendi of the Sui was two-person regime, but this also laid the foundation for Wu Zetian to go one step further.

In the Tang dynasty, the common practices of ethnic nationalities in gender relations within the royal family directly helped Wu Zetian to climb to the summit of power. Wu Zetian was initially a humble concubine of Emperor Taizong, but she had an adulterous relationship with Crown Prince Li Zhi. It was, however, by this former affair that her circumstances improved and, after a period spent in a nunnery, she returned to the palace where she was dramatically appointed empress consort. If the Confucian ethical code had not been eclipsed at that time she could not have also had an affair with Prince Li Zhi. It is also quite remarkable that she became empress consort of the son after being the concubine of the father. In addition, the relations between Wu Zetian and Emperor Gaozong suggest a feeble husband by guided by a strong wife. Following the tradition of the Northern Dynasties, among the Tang royal family and nobility, wives managed the household and the a tradition of husbands "fearing wives" (*weiqi*) emerged. The same is true of the relations between Emperor Gaozong and Wu Zetian. It was because of this relationship that Emperor Gaozong entrusted his wife with state affairs when he was seriously ill and Wu Zetian was in a position to act arbitrarily, to force the emperor to do her bidding and to arrogate all affairs of state to herself, the emperor being reduced to "cupping one hand in the other before his chest" (*gongshou eryi*).[19]

It also has much to do with the atmosphere of the age that she dared to risk universal condemnation by dethroning two emperors, changing the name of the dynasty from Tang to Zhou, ascending the throne and assuming the reins of state, which she held firmly for over ten years. After she became empress of the Great Zhou dynasty, some members of the royal clan, and the old ministers, literati and officialdom who defended legitimism constantly abused and opposed her, and it was often said that "the hen crows in the morning". There were also rebellions to overthrow her. However, most officials were willing to serve her and her regime was quite stable. Armed rebellions generally failed because the generals and armies remained loyal to the empress. Although there was some male resistance, her regime was by and large supported.

Finally, Wu Zetian's tragedy was that there was no mechanism in place to legitimise her successor in traditional Chinese patriarchal society and she herself could not cast off the traditional Chinese patriarchal system and mother-son affection. In her late life she considered handing over power to her nephew in the Wu family, but was finally reluctant to sever the relationship between mother and son in the Li family, which indicated that power was destined to be restored to the male hereditary line. The empress and her Great Zhou were doomed to last only briefly. It is worth noting that when her daughter-in-law Em-

---

[19] *Zizhi Tongjian*, juan 201.

press Wei was in power, Princess Anle, the daughter of Empress Wei, worked out a way to remedy the succession tragedy of the empress, by repeatedly begging her parents to appoint her "crown princess" (huangtain). Later she poisoned her father in league with her mother, who wished to become empress. Obviously, Princess Anle was ambitious, but she was only woman who conceived of a female hereditary system in the millenia of patriarchal society in ancient China. Her conception simply failed to materialise.

Wu Zetian not only openly challenged the male-centred authoritarian society by declaring a new dynasty and proclaiming herself empress, but she also took advantage of the power in her hands to redefine the status of women. For example, for the first time she led the wives of governmental officials in commemorative ceremonies which had previously always been presided over only by men. She made it a fixed rule that the wives enter the imperial court to pay respects to the empress and empress dowager. She changed the ancient rite whereby a son should be in mourning for a father for three years but for a mother for only one year while the father was still living. She enforcement the rite that a son should be in mourning for a mother for three years when the father was still living. All this could not fundamentally change women's low position and the traditional pattern of sexual relations, but it shook traditional society in which men were revered while women were debased for thousands of years.

In this context, the essay titled "Yidu Neiren" written by Li Shangyin, a contemporary of Wu Zetian, is worth examining. The essay describes how Wu Zetian had too many male lovers, and a woman called Yidu Neiren wanted to advise her tactfully against such a practice. Yidu Neiren argued that since ancient times, women have been humble and inferior to men, and that only Wu Zetian has become a true "daughter of Heaven". But the woman represents the feminine principle (*yin*) while the man represents the masculine principle (*yang*). If yang is excessively revered, yin will be debased. Only when yang is eliminated, can yin attain its ambition. If you have too many male concubines, she argued, the masculine will flourish and the feminine will decline. Eventually the state will perish. Therefore, you must get rid of your male concubines and rule China independently. "May you live long. The men will decrease day by day, whereas women will monopolise power increasingly. That's my wish". It is hard to determine whether this story is true or not, but it reflects the fact that Wu Zetian's proclamation of herself as empress did challenge the concept of revering men and debasing women. In the post-Tang period, Wu Zetian was regularly censured for her "evil" actions. Until the Ming dynasty the literati and officialdom felt aggrieved that Wu Zetian had ruled over men while high-ranking officials were indignant at "men serving women,"[20] which shows that Wu Zetian's proclamation of herself as empress hit hard at the pattern of traditional gender relations in which men ruled women and women served men.

After Wu Zetian, Empress Wei (of Emperor Zhongzong) and Empress Zheng (of Emperor Xiaozong), including their princesses and female officials, followed the example of Wu Zetian by ascending to the political arena, and harbouring the ambition to become fully-fledged empresses. The involvement of women in political power was a trend in the early and mid Tang dynasty. However, they were thwarted for various reasons. However, by the mid Tang dynasty, such powerful females more or less fade from the political arena. Although this had something to do with changes in the political situation, such as the expansion of eunuch power, the deeper cause lies in the change in the conceptual world of the ruling clique.

In the latter half of the Tang dynasty, after the death of Emperor Xianzong, the prince was too young, and so the palace eunuchs planned to let Empress Dowager Guo appear in court

---

[20] *Gangjian Hepian* (Compilation of Guiding Principles), juan 22.

to attend to state affairs. However, Empress Dowager Guo flatly refused: "Do you want me to follow the example of Wu Zetian? Although the prince is young, we may choose those who are of noble character and great prestige to help him. How can I take part in external affairs?"[21] These words indicate a change in ideas since the early Tang period. The traditional pattern whereby men managed external affairs and women internal affairs resumed. Moreover, empresses and imperial concubines like Wu Zetian who "interfered" in state affairs were later regarded as discourteous and presumptuous. This change corresponded with the gradual rejuvenation of the Confucian ethical code.

In the Song dynasty, the practice whereby empresses came to court to attend to state affairs in place of the emperor still prevailed. The Northern Song dynasty saw Empress Dowager Liu (of Emperor Zhenzong), Empress Dowager Cao (of Emperor Renzong), Empress Dowager Gao (of Emperor Shenzong), and Empress Dowager Meng (of Emperor Zhezong), and, in the Southern Song dynasty, Empress Dowager Yang (of Emperor Ningzong) and Empress Dowager Xie (of Emperor Lizong) all doing so, outnumbering participants in any other dynasty. However, the background and style of their coming in power differed greatly from that in the Tang dynasty.

In the Song dynasty court, centralisation was unprecedentedly strengthened, and the royal family was known for its rigorous domestic discipline. In those days, court rules were strict; regulations governing activities inside and outside the court were clearly demarcated. The situation was quite unlike that in the Tang dynasty when there were few restrictions on men and women, empresses, concubines, female officials and maids of honour associating with court officials and ministers, or even leaving the court, without authorisation. At the same time, the court had strict control over the families of empresses

---

[21] "Hou Fei Zhuan", *Xin Tang Shu*.

and concubines, prohibiting them from interfering in political affairs. Lu Dafang of the Song dynasty once spoke lightly to Emperor Zhezong of the "forefathers' domestic disciplines", pointing out, "since the Three Dynasties (Xia, Shang and Zhou), only your dynasty has survived peacefully both internally and externally for one hundred and twenty years, and this is because the domestic discipline laid down by your forefathers is the best". He pointed out: "In the previous dynasty preposterous things often occurred in the palace chambers. Maids of honour had affairs with court ministers. However, the present dynasty has strict rules, which are seriously and respectfully regarded both domestically and externally. This is the way to manage domestic affairs.... In the previous dynasty, members of the empress' and concubines' families often interfered in political affairs, resulting in failure and unrest. In the present dynasty, members of the empress' or empress dowager's families refuse to meddle in court affairs. And this is the way in which the families of the empress and concubines should be treated". [22] This deprived the empress and concubines in power of secret support from court ministers. In addition, they were also devoid of backing from their families and had no mass support. Therefore, they could not constitute too great a menace to imperial power. The phenomenon whereby family members of the empress and concubines usurped power, as in the Han dynasty, and whereby the empress, concubines and ministers not of the same surname could form a clique endangering royal power, as in the Tang dynasty, had come to an end. At the same time, the empress and concubines who were in power were restricted in all respects by the ruling group in the Song dynasty who were less tolerant of female authority than that of the Tang dynasty. They allowed the empress dowager, within certain permitted limits, to attend to state affairs in place of the emperor accord-

---

[22] "Lu Taifang Zhuan", **Song Shi**. (The History of the Song Dynasty)

ing to the old system but to go no further. When holding a court audience, Empress Dowager Liu (of Emperor Zhenzong) asked the courtier Lu Zong, "What do think of Empress Wu of the Tang dynasty?" Lu answered, "She was a condemned woman of the Tang dynasty, and she almost ruined the state". It is obvious that Lu's remark implied sarcasm. The Empress Dowager Liu once went out on a journey with the emperor, and her carriage preceded his. Lu Zong commented, "Following a son after her husband's death is the correct behaviour for a woman". Hearing this, Empress Dowager Liu ordered her carriage fall behind.[23] Such an incident could never occurred in the Tang dynasty.

The mentality of the empress and concubines themselves greatly differed from that of the authoritative royal women of the Tang dynasty. Most now conformed to convention and dared not manipulate power for personal ends. Once the emperor reached manhood, they would return power to the emperor immediately. They were also circumspect in their private lives unlike their Tang counterparts. With a reputation as "a sage among women", "Empress Dowager Gao was celebrated for strictly upholding women's virtues. When presented with a picture depicting Empress Wu Zetian holding a court audience, Empress Liu threw it to the ground, declaring: "I won't do anything that betrays my forefathers!"[24] It is evident that they adhered to their subordinate gender status, and were devoted to their husbands' families and ancestors. To sum up, female with power in the Song dynasty were many, but they did not threaten male or the Zhao royal family. In *Song Shi* we read: "In its three centuries of rule, the Song dynasty saw no trouble like that created by the Wangs (empress and concubines) in the Han dynasty in terms of external affairs and no disaster like that created by Empress Wu Zetian and Empress Wei in the Tang dynasty in terms of domestic affairs. Is this not an outstanding

---

[23] "Lu Zongdao Zhuan", *Song Shi*.
[24] "Hou Fei Zhuan", *Song Shi*.

achievement!"[25] Both were cases of females in power, but things were quite different in the Song, reflecting the increasingly dominating power of males and the growth in restrictions on women.

(2) Social Participation and Interaction by Women

A traditional pattern of production throughout ancient Chinese history was that women wove while men farmed. In form, women's labour might seem to belong to the category of household chores, but the products of their labour were not only consumed by family members. Most of their products of labour were used to pay taxes to the state or were sold on the market in exchange for daily use. Their products and the farm produces by the males were economically of equal importance. For example, the Tang dynasty farm and bartered corvee labour system stipulated that each couple had to pay annually 2 dan (= 2 hectolitre) of millet, 2 zhang (66 meters) of silk and 3 liang or 150 g of brocade (or 2.5 zhang or 82.5m of gunny and 3 jin or 1.5kg of fibre crops), and do corvee for 20 days (or 60 chi of silk).

Many poems of the Tang and Song dynasties describe this economic burden. Sima Zha's poem *Can Nü* (The Women Making Silk)) contains the following lines:

My home is not rich,
the officials press for payment daily;
the shuttles rattle all night till dawn.
And yet I am afraid I might delay.

In Wang Jian's poem *Dang Chuang Zhi* (Weaving by the Window) we read:

Crickets chirp beneath my wheel, urging me on,
and in two days I have woven one bolt and a half of cloth.
After sending it to the local official I have only remnants.

---

[25] Ibid.

Mother-in-law has no clothes to wear, and neither do I.[26]

Silk and cloth were mainly used to pay taxes, and these became a major source of the state income. Li Gou of the Tang dynasty once described women engaged in the flourishing weaving industry as bustling about as though running away from robbers and having no time to attend to their own thirst and hunger. All women but the pampered and delicate were engaged in such work.[27] It was women's industry that caused the weaving industry to thrive in south-eastern China. It is evident that women's was an important part of social production.

In addition, women were also involved in such handicraft industries as embroidery, shoe production, porcelain manufacture and engraving. Together with the male sex, they undertook such heavy tasks as farming and firewood collecting. When war broke out and men went off to battle, women became the main labour force in society and bore the heavy responsibility of sending in taxes. Owing to a shortage of able-bodied men, women also had to do corvee labour of all kinds. Du Fu's famous poem "Shihao Li" (The Magistrate of Shihao Village) describes how during the social unrest at the time of the An Lushan and Shi Siming rebellions in the mid Tang dynasty, all able-bodied men in Shihao village were captured and inducted into the army, while even old women were rounded up to do corvee labour for the army. This demonstrates that women's work was social labour in the same way as men's work.

In the Tang and Song dynasties, especially the Song, the most remarkable changes that took place in society included the development of the commodity economy, the flourishing of cities and the rise of an urban citizenry. These changes provided women with more opportunities to take part in social life. To begin with, small- and medium-sized businesses emerged based on women's trades. The rise of cities and the development of

---

[26] Sima Zha, "Can Nü"; Wang Jian, "Dang Chuang Zhi".
[27] *Li Gou Ji* (Anthology of Li Gou).

commerce gave women ever-increasing opportunities to get jobs or be in business. In the Tang and Song dynamites, women were very actively engaged in commercial activities. In the Song capital, the celebrated commodities and stores included Five Sisters' Fish Custard, Granny Cao's Meat Pie, Ma Wang's Tea Shop, Aunt Wang's Wine Shop, Granny Li's Custard with Mixed Vegetables, Ma Chen's Herbal and Medicine Shop and Ugly Granny's Herbal Medicine Store.[28] Business women were different from farming women or weaving women. The mode of business management determined that they had to leave home and enter society. Moreover, being in business enabled women to support themselves and their families, and they were not necessarily dependent on husbands. The renowned poet Su Shi's father, Su Xun, for example, abandoned his schooling in order to support his family life. Later, his wife nee Cheng sold her own ornaments and used the payment as capital to set up a business. With a few years, Su's family had become rich and Su Xun succeeded in completing his schooling.[29] Their ability to manage themselves independently enabled them to attain a certain position in society.

Urban life differed from that in the country. The centralised population, the rich and active life of the city and the many potential social associations all gave women an arena and a chance to get involved in society. More importantly women of the lower and middle social strata in society were less subject to education in the Rites than women of rich families of the literati and officialdom strata. Therefore, they became a quite vigorous participatory force in late ancient society.

In this period, and especially in the Tang dynasty, women were less restricted in their social interaction. In upper class society in the Tang, social interaction was always possible for wives. The wife of high ranking officials often entertained the

---

[28] "Yinshi" (Food and Drink), *Songbai Leichao*.

[29] *Wenguo Wenzheng Wengong Sima Guang Ji* (Anthology of Sima Guang), juan 76.

wives of subordinates. Such social interaction helped her husband handle public affairs and harmonised relations between higher authorities and subordinates, and among colleagues. However, in such social interaction, women still had the status of wife, suggesting subordination to the male sex, but from another perspective, it also showed that the wives of officials did not entirely refrain from meddling in external affairs, for they had some social position and an opportunity for social interaction. Women from the lower social levels were more informal in their social interaction than those from upper class society. In this period, the non-official women had the practice of forming associations. Neighbourhood women volunteered to form "associations of women". These had between twenty and thirty members, who drew up articles of association, gave funds for activities and elected an administrative manager. They would hold regular Buddhist services and conduct other activities. The very purpose in forming an association was "to support those who are in danger and to help those who are in need". If something unforeseen happened to any member, the others were to offer financial assistance".[30] This indicates that the women in the lower stratum of society had their own independent social interaction and mutual aid groups.

As for the interaction between the sexes, the Tang dynasty is recognised as the least restrictive period in Chinese history. From the court down to the commonalty, there were few taboos on contacts between men and women. Empresses, concubines and maids of honour regularly met high officials and even banqueted and entertained them. Empress Wei (of Emperor Zhongzong) of the Tang dynasty played shuanglu, a gambling game, with Wu Sansi, a powerful minister, sitting on the imperial bed, while Emperor Zhongzong stood by, counting the chips for them. An Lushan, a border general, favoured by Emperor

---

[30] Ning Ke and Hao Chunwen, "Women's Farming Associations During the Period from the Northern Dynasties to the Sui-Tang", *Beijing Shifan Xueyuan Xuebao*, 1990:3.

Xuanzong, dined with Yang Guifei, the highest ranking concubine of Emperor Xuanzong, in the rear imperial palace, even staying up until dawn. Yang's younger sister, Lady Guoguo, lived adjacent to Yang Guozhong's mansion. They would communicate at any time of day or night, and even went to court riding on the one horse.

Even fewer restrictions existed among commoners. The famous Tang poet Bai Juyi's poem "Pipa Xing" (The Song of the Lute) describes the story of a merchant's wife, who talks with a group of strangers over a meal on a boat at night when her husband is away on business, and plays the pipa for them. Hong Mai, a Song dynasty scholar nostalgically commented: "Whether a man dated a woman or a woman dated a man in a melon plot or under the plum trees, Tang dynasty people would not find this a matter for derision".[31] However, the Song dynasty did frown upon the common practices of the Tang.

Religious women in the Tang dynasty all the more defied the regulations and commandments, falling into dissipated ways. Li Ye, a renown Taoist priestess and Yu Xuanji were both social celebrities, with mixed widely with officials and eminent persons. They were courted by many talented and romantic scholars who would visit them bringing wine, or going out with them together on excursions, bantering and dallying without any inhibitions. The view developed that Taoist priestesses were "next to prostitutes in their actions".

Social relations between the sexes were more restrained in the Song, as we can see from the above quotation of Hong Mai, but compared with later ages, men and women had fewer taboos in social interaction. Women still went out on excursions together, as on the Lantern Festival, the 15th of the first lunar month, which in the Song dynasty was the grandest occasion, on which, women, rich and poor, were take to the streets to view the lanterns. In the street, men and women were jostle each other

---

[31] Hong Mai, *Rongzhai Sanbi*, juan 6.

in the crowds. The local authorities would arrest hooligans who took the advantage of the occasion to take liberties with women, but many young men and women would also seize the opportunity to get acquainted or date their sweethearts. A well known Song lyric poem (*ci*) titled "Shengchazi: Yuanxi" depicts the mood of a girl dating after dusk with her sweetheart at the Lantern Festival.

Before and after Qing Ming Festival, women also went to the city outskirts for an outing, as did the men, when the grass had just turned green. In the Northern Song dynasty, women in Bianjing, the capital city, and in Luoyang would leave home with them bottles of wine at the Qingming festival. They would occupy a pavilion or terrace in a garden or park, and the appreciate the flowers while eating and drinking. In the Southern Song dynasty, in Lin'an, the capital city, whenever the Qingming Festival was observed, the touring women, who were beautifully dressed and made up, were be seen on the great embankment and on painted boats floating on the waters of the West Lake.

On the whole, the Confucian ethical code was less strictly observed during this period, and there were relatively few taboos on contacts between men and women.

(3) The "Bonds" Guiding Husbands and Wives: Gender Within the Family

In the ethical concept of the ancient family, the women was required to comply with the "three obedience's" (*san cong*) principle, namely: obedience to one's father before marriage, obedience to one's husband after marriage and obedience to one's son after the death of one's husband. Women in ancient times thus always found themselves in the position subordinate to the male sex within the family from the cradle to the grave.

However, while in Confucian ethical code obedience to the father was incontrovertible, both in principle and reality, obedience to a husband, one of "the three bonds" (*san gang*) or guides, could be modified in practice. In some matters the husband and wife would sometimes provide mutual guidance, and filial piety emphasised filial obedience to the mother. While a mother was required to obey her son after her husband's death, this was also designed to provide support for her and obedience to her wishes. In reality, those who showed such filial obedience were often praised by public opinion and commended by the government while those who refused to do so were not only despised but were severely punished by law. In fact, the injunction to "be obedient to one's mother" overwhelmed the injunction to "be obedient to one's son", in terms of both public opinion and reality.

In the historical period from the Sui and Tang dynasties, since the Confucian ethical code was not so actively advocated, the position of women position was not so low and humble. Therefore, the features mentioned above were obvious in gender relations within the family. The tradition of the "tough wife and weak husband"[32] was well established.

Empress Dugu and Emperor Wendi of the Sui dynasty present us with a typical example. It is recorded in history that Emperor Wendi was under the control of Empress Dugu. They were not only called "the two sages" in the political arena, but Emperor Wendi was strictly forced to submit to her will in private life. Although polygamy was prevalent in ancient China and the emperor was permitted to have six concubines, Emperor Wendi had many difficulties in having his way. As a result, his several sons were all born by his wife, which was rare in Chinese imperial history. Once Emperor Wendi chanced to have a conversation with a maid of honour, who was subsequently killed by Empress Dugu when she heard of it. Flying into a rage, Emperor Wendi ran out of the imperial court. Looking up into the sky, he sighed mournfully: "Although I am emperor, I have no freedom!" This emperor was playing his role quite pitifully.

---

[32] Zhang Zhuo, *Chaoye Qianzai*, juan 4.

By the earlier mid Tang dynasty, the "wife fearing" husband had become a common social phenomenon. From the emperor down to the literati and officialdom, "wife fearing" became the order of the day, and monarch and subjects made it widely known without regarding it as a matter of shame. Emperor Gaozong's "feared wife" was grooming herself for the throne, but his son Emperor Zhongzong is even more famous as a "wife fearing" husband. In the presence of him and Empress Wei, an actress sang, "It is a good thing to fear a wife. Outside the court there is Pei Tan (a high official), inside the court there is nobody bu Li the venerable (referring to Emperor Gaozong)".[33] The actress was rewarded for her satire by Empress Wei. Emperor Xiaozong of the Tang was so afraid of Empress Zhang that a poet (Du Fu) wrote ironically, "Empress Zhang is displeased, so the emperor is busy".[34] Among the literati and officialdom, the Duke of Guanguo and Pei Tan, were celebrated for "fearing their wives", a charge against which Pei Tan defended himself: "In my opinion, I have three reasons for fearing my wife: When she was young, she was like a living boddhisattva, so why wouldn't one fear her? When she had matured she was like *Jiuzimomu* (a Buddhist deity), so why wouldn't one fear her? When she reached fifty or sixty, after painting herself up with rouge and powder, she looks like black Jiupantu (also a Buddhist deity), so why wouldn't one fear her?"[35] During the Zhenguan's reign period in the early Tang, Ruan Song, magistrate of Guiyang county, was dismissed from his because of he feared his wife, nee Yan, who was both jealous and tough. Once Ruan Song and his guests were drinking in his parlour. He was in such a merry mood he called in a girl servant to sing them songs. When Yan heard of it, she rushed in with hair in disarray, barefooted and with bare arms. The guests and girl singer were terrified and ran away. Ruan was frightened into

---

[33] Meng Qi, **Benshi Shi** (Poems on Facts).
[34] Du Fu, "Yi Xi" (Recalling the Past).
[35] Meng Qi, op. cit.

hiding under the bed. It turned out that his superior was judging officials, he made the following assessment of Ruan: "The wife is tough while the husband is weak. The wife is hard while the husband is gentle. If a wife cannot be controlled, how can he manage the common people? When a wife refuses to study the Confucian ethical code, how can a husband be energetic?" Ruan thus received a bad assessment and was dismissed from office.[36] What is significant is that this was not an isolated phenomenon. Duan Chengshi, a Tang scholar wrote: "Before the Dali reign period, many wives of the literati and officials were jealous and tough".[37] Obviously, this was also the general mood of the age. Apart from the social cause of the failure to advocate the Confucian ethical code among the people, the prevalent practice had something to do with "women keeping house"[38] and the traditional custom of wives controlling the household in the Northern Dynamites.

In the Song dynasty, the imperial family stressed domestic discipline, and the empress and concubines were strictly restrained. Rarely was the emperor under the control of the empress as in the Tang. Nevertheless, "tough wives" and "fearing wives" could be often found among the literati and officialdom. The phrase "the lioness' roar from Hedong" was frequently used to describe formidable wives during the Song dynasty. This phrase is a line from a poem written by the renowned poet Su Shi who was bantering with his wife nee Liu notorious among contemporaries for being "absolutely fierce and jealous".[39] In many Song biji collections are recorded instances of tough and jealous wives who control their husbands. For instance, Mrs. Xia Yinggong, nee Yang practised "cruel and rigid etiquette and law in the boudoir". When presented at

[36] Zhang Zhuo, op. cit., juan 4.
[37] Duan Chengshi, *Youyang Zazu*, juan 8.
[38] "Zhijia", *Yanshi Jiaxun*.
[39] *Rongzhai Sanbi*, juan 3.

court, she was reprimanded by the empress dowager.[40] Although Shen Kua (1031-1095), author of **Mengxi Bitan** (Essays from the Stream of Dream) was a statesman as well as an accomplished scholar, he was ill-treated in the latter half of his life by his wife nee Zhang, who often gave him a thrashing and scolding. On one occasion she even ripped his beard out.[41] Hong Mai records an instance of the wife of another high-ranking official who was stern and rigid with her husband. When her husband called on his friend who had a concubine for a drink, she went so far as to climb the top of a wall, and let fly a torrent of abuse. The emperor heard of this and removed the husband from office.[42] Tao Gu, a Song Dynasty scholar, records examples in his **Qingyi Lu** of several tough wives and wife fearing husbands. For example, the wife of Lu Shenyan, magistrate of Weishi county, nee Zhu was called "The Rouged Tigress" by local officials and people. Lu was absolutely obedient to his wife and indecisive in political affairs. In the Wu region, Li Dazhuang, a Confucian scholar, was made to sit by his wife with a lamp on his head by way of punishment. Holding his breath, and not daring to stir, he looked like an earthen image. Hong Mai's **Yi Jian Zhi** also records many facts about weak husbands and tough wives, and wives who were regarded as tigresses.

Naturally, the facts mentioned above constitute an abnormal phenomenon, but the fact that records of this sort are so common must reflects a social phenomenon in which the masculine and feminine roles were reversed in many families in those days. It is obvious that the pattern of family ethics which enjoined a husband to guide his wife and a wife to be obedient to her husband, although long established and seemingly unchangeable, broached many exceptions in the social reality of this historical period. The emergence of this state of affairs had specific causes of one kind or another, for example, the wife's

[40]   Yuhu Qinghua, juan 13.
[41]   Zhu Yu, **Pingzhou Ketan**, juan 3.
[41]   Zhang Duanyi, **Gui'er Ji**, juan 3.

higher position in the family. It also demonstrated that the Confucian ethical code was not rigidly in place and that the controls exercised over women were less powerful.

(4) Marriage and Sexual Style

The most outstanding characteristics of the marriage and sexual customs in the Sui and Tang dynasties is that women had a certain initiative and their sense of chastity or virginity was quite thin.

In terms of the marriage form, women had the right to choose spouses, and some parents permitted their daughters to choose mates on their own. Li Linpu, a prime minister of the Tang dynasty, had five daughters, and he had a horizontal window opened up in the wall of his living-room and fitted with crimson gauze so that his daughters could play outside the window and to choose sweethearts for themselves from among the visitors. Li Ao's daughter happened to see the highly commended examination papers of Lu Xu on her father's desk, and she told her maid: "This man is bound to be the top candidate in the highest imperial examinations". When Li Ao got to know this, he chose Lu Xu as his son-in-law to fulfil his daughter's wish.

It was even more evident that a number of women in this period chose to divorce their husbands. It was very common for divorcees and widows to re-marry, and this was not condemned by public opinion. Some women were divorced by their husbands and many couples agreed to divorce. In Tang dynasty law, there is an article on "peaceful divorce", which stipulates: "If the husband and wife cannot live in peace with each other, they must divorce each other, and will go unpunished".[43] This ensured the right of both parties to mutually agree to divorce.

Among the Dunhuang manuscripts there are several exam-

---

[43] "Huhun Lü" (Household and Marriage Laws), *Tang Lü*. (Laws of the Tang Dynasty)

ples of "certificates of release", namely divorce certificates. These state that husband and wife are on bad terms because of predestination. Since they cannot live in harmony and the family property cannot prosper, they are choosing to divorce each other and to try to find fresh partners. Judging from the document, the divorce was willingly entered into by both parties. It is interesting to note that the document congratulates the wife in anticipation of her re-marriage: "I trust that my wife after her divorce will wear her hair elegantly and wear beautiful skirts complementing her graceful bearing. I trust that you marry a high official. Dispel your grief and misgivings and let us never hate and dislike each other. Once we separate, we will both be happy".[44] All this indicates liberal ideas concerning the handling of divorce by agreement and re-marriage of divorced women, and in some senses this was because women did not have a strong sense of obedience to their husbands to the end of their lives. They would initiate divorce when dissatisfied with their marriage.

In the Tang dynasty, many divorces were raised by wives or their families. For instance, Yang Zhijian, a xiucai scholar was poor and so his wife nee Wang went to the local authorities to request a divorce. Yan Zhenqin, the prefectural official granted her a divorce, but he had nee Wang beaten twenty times. He did not blame her for having lost her chastity, but he was furious that a scholar addicted to learning was being deserted. It was said that, thanks to this judgement, no wife was reported to have later deserted her husband in this district.[45] This would also that instances of deserting husbands were probably rare.

Among the Dunhuang bianwen, a popular form of narrative literature flourishing in the Tang dynasty, with alternate prose and rhymed parts for recitation and singing often on Buddhist themes, one can find "Yake Shu", describes a shrew

---

[44] **Dunhuang Ziliao**, (Zhonghua Press, 1961), vol. 1.
[45] Fan Lu, **Yunxi Longyi**, juan 1.

who squabbles with her husband's mother and frequently demands a divorce. "Divorce me and let me marry another man".[46]

It was because of the free passage to re-marriage that a number of women took the initiative in demanding a divorce. Women in this early period not only did not have a concept of obeying a husband all one's life, but the male community also did not regard a women's re-marriage as a disgrace. Even wealthy and influential officials did not avoid marrying divorced women. For example, Song Jing, a prime minister had his son marry a beautiful widow nee Xue. After Wei Ji, a high ranking official died, his wife nee Li re-married another official Wang Jin, who accepted her as his wife. Even the daughter of the great Confucianist Han Yu, who made the revitalisation of Confucianism his mission, got divorced and remarried. And, interestingly, of the 98 princesses of the early and mid Tang periods recorded in the official histories, 27 re-married, and of them, four remarried at least twice. A similar picture emerges of the nobility, and the lower social strata.

A woman's initiative in gender relations and the sense of chastity found expression outside of marriage form in pre-marital and post-marital sexual intercourse, which seems to have been quite common. The female almost always took the initiative and displayed great bravery.

Having been made a concubine and forsaken, Yu Xuanji, the Taoist priestess, not only hankered after love and took many lovers, but she also wrote: "I myself can peep at Song Yu". Here she is referring to the erotic ancient poet and asserting her sexual initiative. In Tang dynasty fiction we read of Bu Feiyan[47], and numbers of other heroines who take the sexual initiative, act bravely and inflexibly, and dare to defy the law and the Rites.

Virginity and chastity were not major issues in the Tang.

---

[46] *Dunhuang Bianwen*, (Renmin Wenxue Publishing House, 1957), vol. 7.

[47] Huangfu Mei, "Bu Feiyan", *San Shui Xiao Du*.

Unmarried women often had affairs with their lovers before they got married. The famous Yuan drama *Xixiang Ji* (The Western Chamber Romance) was derived from *Yuanyang Zhuan*, an autobiographical legend and love story written by the Tang poet Yuan Zhen. The greatest difference between the story on which *Xi Xiang Ji* was based and the drama itself is in the plot. Unlike the play, in the original story Miss Yuanyang, who carries on a clandestine love affair with and loses her virginity to Zhang Sheng, does not insist on marrying him, and finally they marry separately. Thereafter they still meet and contact each other. The pre-marriage loss of her virginity does not bring her any consequences in her married life.

That married women could date their lovers outside of their homes and this practice was more often seen among the nobility in the community. It is well known that Empress Wu Zetian had many lovers, of whom the favourite two Zhangs were introduced to her by her daughter Princess Taiping. On the other hand, Wu Zetian helped find lovers or "private husbands" for her male favourites' widowed mothers. Empress Wei also had several male favourites. Almost all princesses had lovers and more than one. Some princesses would visit their lovers' houses to pay respects to their "mothers-in-law". Many high-ranking women of the literati and official classes were later described as having "licentious behaviour". The highest-ranking imperial concubine Yang Yuhuan's younger sister, Madame Guoguo not only had an affair with the emperor, but had a dubious relationship with Yang Guozhong, brother of the same clan. Surprisingly enough, while Yang Guozhong served as an long-term foreign envoy, he found on his return that his wife was already pregnant. This Tang dynasty practice was later ridiculed as the phenomenon of the "Tang Turtle" (i.e. cuckolds of the Tang dynasty).[48]

---

[48] Cai Dongfan, *Tang Shi Yanyi* (Historical Romance of the History of the Tang), ch. 1.

In love stories of the Tang dynasty, not only did young girls often take the initiative in "offering pillows and mats to have private affairs with men, but empresses and high ranking women would sleep with contemporaries disguised as ghosts and immortals. One story even recounts how the constellation called the Weaving Maid has an illicit affair on earth.[49]

Although all these stories were invented by men of letters, they mirror in a sense the social reality in those days. At the same time, the authors wrote of these women who rebelled against orthodoxy in an appreciative tone, which must reflect social attitudes quite at variance with the Confucian ethical code.

By the Song dynasty, there was some change in a woman's sense of chastity and the general mood of society and signs indicate that the moral code was toughening. What is most striking is that illicit sexual relations were seldom documented among women of the imperial family and nobility. Throughout the Song dynasty, few empresses and concubines or wives of the nobility failed to preserve their chastity. No empress, unlike Wu Zetian, openly kept a seraglio of handsome men.

In marriage, however, women still had a way out. The proposition that wives should obey their husbands all their lives was not strictly implemented and married woman could divorce or remarry. Public opinion remained tolerant and refused to see this behaviour as a disgrace.

There are many instances of female re-marriage in the documentary records. For example, Fan Zhongyan, the great writer of the Northern Song dynasty, lived with his mother who re-married in his childhood. After he became an official, he changed his surname and retrieved his original clan. The prime Minister Wang Anshi's son suffered from a disease, so he re-married his daughter-in-law to a man of good family background. During the reign of Emperor Zhenzong, both Xiang

---

[49] *Taiping Guangji*, juan 68.

Minzhong and Zhang Qixian, the prime minister, wanted to marry nee Chai, the daughter-in-law of the late prime minister Xue Juzheng, which troubled the emperor.

Even Cheng Yi, of the Lixue school, spared no efforts to oppose widows' re-marriage, although his own nephew's wife and niece remarried. In the late Southern Song dynasty, the prime minister Jia Sidao's mother nee Hu re-remarried three times. Hu was welcomed home after Jia became prime minister. Nee Hu was incomparably honourable and on her was posthumously conferred the title "Rouzheng" (Gentle and Upright).[50] It is evident that even by the late Southern Song dynasty, a woman's re-marriage was not regarded as disgraceful conduct entailing the loss of her chastity and virtue. When speaking of Master Cheng's theory that being starved to death is a trifle while losing one's chastity is a serious problem, Zhu Xi of the Lixue school commented, "To my mind, it is high-sounding and impracticable."[51] People in the society of the time generally did not accept it, let alone observe it.

To sum up, in the historical period from the Sui and Tang dynasties to the Song dynasty, women had, to certain extent, the initiative in matters of marriage and love. This indicates that inequality in gender relations and the male monopoly in the relationship and confinement of the female had not yet reached its zenith.

[50] Zhou Mi, *Qidong Yeyu*, juan 15.
[51] "Da Chen Shizhong", *Zhu Wengong Wenji* (Collected Works of Zhu Xi), juan 3.

CHAPTER SEVEN
WOMEN'S STATUS AND GENDER RELATIONS IN THE LIAO, JIN AND YUAN DYNASTIES

Liu Ruzhen

The period of the Liao, Jin and Yuan dynasties is unique in Chinese history, because these three dynasties were successively founded by nomadic peoplesthe Khitan, Jurchen and Mongol peoples, who resided in areas north of the Great Wall. They grew in strength from the 10th to 13th centuries. Their opportunity to seize power in the Central Plain was provided by the disruption, weakening and impoversihment of the Chinese empire. As a result, they took turns to play the role of rulers in the northern part of or the whole of between the 10th and 14th centuries, establishing the Liao, Jin and Yuan dynasties in succession.

China broke up with the decline of the Tang dynasty. Powers within the empire contended fiercely with each other, and border security was neglected. The Khitan, then headed by Yel Abaoji, strengthened itself rapidly and made a series of conquests southward. By 960, northern China was under the control of the Liao, and when the Song dynasty was founded, they could only occupy areas south of the Huaihe River and dream of taking the north, thinking themselves to be its legitimate owner. At the turn of the 12th century the Jurchen along the Heilongjiang River grew increasingly prosperous while the Liao waned. The Jurchen eventually annexed the Liao and drove the Song further south across the Yangtze River. Yet about one century later, the Jurchen Chin also declined, and the Mongols took it in turn to sweep through the whole of China from the northwest with unprecedented violence, annexing the Jin in 1234, and the Song in 1271; hence began the rule of the Mongolian aristocracy over the whole of China. .

In the interval between the Tang and Yuan, northern China witnessed the rule of one nomadic nation after another for over 360 years. The Yuan was the first centralised empire ruled by a minority nationality in Chinese history. With the foundation of the Yuan the nomadic economy and culture were no longer bounded in the areas north of the Great Wall, and they radiated to every corner of the large territory of China.

The Khitan, Jurchen and Mongol peoples underwent a similar course of development when feudal society took form out of tribal slavery, and each of them set up nomadic states before they ruled the Central Plain. They resided in neighbouring areas, and had somewhat similar modes of production and cultural traditions. It was not strange that they shared similarities in national ethos, cultural concepts and the status of the sexes, while the contrasts in these areas with the Hans, who had been living by farming for generations on the Central Plain, were great. The Liao, Jin and Yuan created a special period in China's history, during which nomadic and Han cultures competed with and complemented each other.

As equestrian peoples, the nomads in the north were characterised by martial valour and resourcefulness, and the Great Wall was built to prevent their cavalry from penetrating the Central Plain. When the Mongols founded their great empire across Eurasia, the world witnessed this nomadic cavalry at the peak of its power. Against such a background, the developed both feminine dignity and masculine strength quite different from the Han tradition in which power and the social functions of the genders developed in opposite directions. This was especially the case before the nomads were influenced by Han culture. They had a tradition of prestigious male rulers and strong female rulers. Among them, marriage by capture and polygyny demonstrated masculine strength, and servant-marriage and matri-patrilocality demonstrated female superiority. Some traces of primitive partnership and the maternal clan could still be found among these nomads. However, as the nomadic and Han cultures blended, these traces gradually diminished, and when the Ming dynasty took the place of the Yuan, they finally vanished and the relationships between the sexes returned to the old pattern of the superiority of men over women which had long prevailed on the Central Plain.

1. The Nomadic Economy and Gender Relationships in Politics

(1) The Nomadic Economy and Women's Status

The nomads moved constantly in search of pastures, and this economic compelled them to looting for their life necessities and engage in warfare, which accounted for the military resourcefulness. Their children, both boys and girls, learned to ride and shoot, and all members of the clan, male and female, shared the responsibility for migration and warfare. In their migrations to different pastures, the men would ride ahead to clear the way, and the women would have to dismantle and erect the tents, load and unload the wagons, as well as drive them. In times of wars, the women, together with the old and young, would set up an *ahurq*, a temporary base, fifty or sixty *li* away from the battlefield. The women would be responsible for protecting the supplies and securing the *ahurq*. They played a much more important role than Han women in production and warfare, and were an indispensable link in the nomadic economy.

Nomadic women were both brave and talented in warfare. When Emperor Taizu crossed the Qishui river to attack the

Dangxiang, the Huang-tou and the Choubo of the Shihwei took the opportunity to assault the Khitan headquarters, so "the Empress arranged for troops to await the enemy knowing when they would arrive. Her prowess overwhelmed the neighbouring tribes". ["Hou Fei Zhuan" (Empresses and Concubines), *Liao Shi* (History of the Liao)]

There was no rigid division of labour between the sexes; women were capable of doing whatever the men did. One of Cinggis Qan's laws stated that "when there is compulsory labor, it is the wife who should take her husband's share in his absence".[1] Women could fight on battle-fields and did heavy corvee labour; jobs like grazing, hunting, milling and creaming were, to them, everyday.

The brave and intrepid male rulers of the nomads never considered the opposite sex as weak and inferior. Women's status was determined by their important role in the nomadic economy. They were unmatched by the Han women whose functions were limited within the family.

First, women had equal rights with men to own and inherit property. When Cinggis Qan conferred fiefs, his mother, wives and daughters all received their share. There are records in *Yuan Shi* stating that the fiefs to princesses were increased. In a nomadic family, the property would be divided among the wife and children after the husband died.

Secondly, women took part in all social activities and played an important role. Hunting was the major social activity in nomadic society. The empresses and princesses of the Liao dynasty "were never excluded from the military affairs and hunting".[2] And the Mongol "amirs always set out with the empresses, princesses and the imperial concubines" when hunting.[3] Furthermore, the noblewomen with high rank had a say in important decisions. "Among the attenders" of the Qu-

---

[1] "Hou Fei Zhuan", *Liao Shi*.
[2] **The History of the World Conqueror**, He Gaoji tr., p. 39.
[3] Ibid.

riltai before Temr[4] inherited the throne "were N(a)mbui[5] and her daughter B(a) kjin-qadun, Manzdai, Kukjin-qadun[6] and other qaduns, princes and amirs".[7] After the third successor of Cinggis, Gyk, died, Batu[8] intended to make M(a)nku the heir to the throne, so he sent "messengers to Cinggis' empresses and concubines, Okodei-qan's[9] empresses, concubines and sons, Ikeh-nuyan's wife Siurquqt(a)ni-biki and other princes and the amirs in all the q(a)ums' to get their support. The empresses and imperial concubines played an important part in deciding the candidate for the *qan* at the time of the Mongol Empire.

It was normal for the empresses and the favoured imperial concubines to be involved in the routine affairs of the emperors due to their special residential style. Polygyny was widely practised among the nomads. The emperor's empresses and concubines were fixed in several ordos (tents), with each headed by an empress with the highest rank. There was no separate office for the emperor and he usually dealt with the day-to-day affairs in the ordo occupied by his most favoured wife. Emperor Taizu of the Liao, Yel Abaoji, "received Kun (Yao Kun, the envoy from the Tang) together with his wife" ("Waiguo Liezhuan", *Jiu Wudai Shi*; The Old History of the Five Dynasties: Foreign Affairs). A Western priest who visited the Mongol Empire witnessed Emperor Xian Zong, M(a)nku, "seated with his wife just beside himself in the day time".[10] After the Liao, Jin and Yuan had set up their capitals, luxurious residential palaces took the place of nomadic ordos, and the emperors had their own palaces in which to deal with the state affairs. Whether the empresses and the imperial concubines continued to accompany

---

[4] Qubilai's grandson.
[5] Quabilai's wife.
[6] Jinqin's wife, Chengzong's mother.
[7] Rashid, **Jami'al-Tawarikh**, vol. 2, Yu Dejun and Zhou Jianqi trs.
[8] Eldest son of Suji, who was the eldest son of Cinggis.
[9] Cinggis' second son and successor.
[10] Chritopher Dawson, **The Mongol Mission**.

the emperors in their work remains a question, yet the special residential style was undoubtedly one of the causes of the interference of empresses in state affairs in the Liao, Jin and Yuan.

(2) The Interference of Empresses in State Affairs during the Liao, Jin and Yuan

The interference of empresses in politics reached its climax in Chinese history in the Liao and Yuan.

It was well known that the empresses of the Liao dynasty were heavily involved in political affairs. Empress Dowager Xiao in the novel *Yangjia Jiang* (The Generals of the Yangs) was described as the symbol of the highest authority of the Liao dynasty. Evidence can also be found in *Liao Shi*: "Empress Yingtai struck the Shihwei back, Chengtai (Empress Dowager Xiao) commanded in person in the battle of Chanyuan, and Renyi suppressed the rebellion of Zhongyuan. This was a tradition never heard of in the history [of the Hans]". The Liao empresses exerted an unprecedented influence on Chinese politics.

Empress Chunqing Shul, the wife of Yel Abaoji who had founded the Khitan empire, was a great and wise heroine. She was "decisive and had outstanding abilities" (*Liao Shi*). She accompanied her husband on his expeditions north and south. The Liao Shi states that "when she was with Emperor Taizu on his expeditions, the Empress registered the captured who were good at martial arts, and organized the Troop of Shushan" which was what was probably described elsewhere in *Liao Shi* as "the two hundred of the Empress' command". It was with her troop of "Shushan" that she put up a strong resistance against the Shiwei. Abaoji united North China and performed immortal feats in the history of the Liao, and Empress Shul, as his adviser and assistant, played a very important role.[11]

In 962, Abaoji died of illness, and Empress Shul assumed authority and controlled important military and political matters. She then passed the throne on to her son Yel Deguang (Emperor Taizong) one year later, and ruled the country together with her son. Twenty years later, Taizong died, and she intended to pass the crown to her youngest son Li Hu, so that the rule of mother and son would continue. This did not eventuate because they failed in the struggle against Prince Yongkang for the throne. Thus came the end of the mother-son administration.

Empress Dowager Xiao in *Yangjia Jiang* was Emperor Jingzong's empress[12], Xiao Chuo. Jingzong suffered from a stroke and "was confined to bed most of the time". Xiao Chuo "appeared in the court as a governess, and controlled all national affairs. She meted out severe punishments and launched large-scale invasions of the neighbouring states. When Khitan and Han ministers gathered to discuss state affairs, the Empress had the last say; what the Emperor received was nothing more than her report. After Emperor Jingzong passed away, their 12-year-old son Yel Longx (Shengzong) inherited the throne. Jingzong's dying instruction was that "all decisions on important military and political affairs should be left to the Empress", and so Xiaochuo was legitimised to hold court. After she had ruled the country for twenty-seven years, Empress Dowager Xiao "returned the power to the Emperor" when he was 39, and she "died less than one month later".[13] From the time of Jingzong to Shengzong, Xiao Chuo held the highest authority of the Liao for as long as forty years.

Both Empress Shul and Empress Dowager Xiao were adept

---

[11] Luo Jizu, "Several Stories about Empress Yingtian of the Liao", *Liaoning Daxue Xuebao*, 1985:3.

[12] Fifth emperor of the Liao.

[13] "Hou Fei Zhuan", *Qidan Guo Zhi*. (The History of the Kitan Kingdom)

with both pen and sword. They fought in battles, commanded armies, and improved the administration. Empress Shul strengthened the Khitan empire founded by Abaoji with her son, Emperor Tai Zong[14]; Empress Dowager Xiao made a great effort to put forward a series of reforms to better the administration and develop the economy. She led the country out of depression and into a period of splendour.[15]

It was the custom of the Liao dynasty for "the emperor and the empress to hold court together".[16] When the emperor was too young or too ill to deal with routine work, it was taken for granted that the empress held court; or she could appoint someone else to do it for her. During the time of Xingzong, the Empress Dowager seized control of the court, and assigned all state affairs to her brother Xiaoxian; after Empress Fatian killed Empress Rende and "proclaimed herself to be the Empress Dowager and acted as regent, all rights to deal with domestic and foreign affairs went to her brother'. Xingzong, then capable of governing the country himself, would not resign himself to the fact that imperial power was monopolised by the Empress, so he "put her under house arrest and dethroned her".[17] This was the only case in the Liao dynasty that the emperor and the empress were opposed to each other as a result of over-imperiousness on the part of the latter. Since the empresses' interference in court affairs was accepted as legitimate among the nomads, most of the empresses of the Liao influenced national policies, and it was only when a weak emperor was on the stage at the same time as a strong empress that the empress held all the rights and directly participated in politics.

---

[14] Song Di, "Empress Shul's Political Tragedy in her Old Age", *Beifang Wenwu*, 1985:3.

[15] Zhu Zifang, "On the Reforms of the Khitan Empress Dowager Xiao", *Guangming Ribao*, 1 October, 1989.

[16] "Xiao Pu Zhuan", *Liao Shi*.

[17]"Hou Fei Zhuan", *Qidan Guo Zhi*.

The empresses in the Yuan dynasty outdid their counterparts in any other dynasty in their involvement in politics. The Mongol Empire experienced the rule of thirteen emperors, and during this period, there were as many as eleven empresses who were involved in court affairs.[18]

According to Mongol tradition, the successor of the late emperor was to be decided at the Quriltai, attended by all princes, marquises and aristocrats. The empress was to shepherd the country before the new emperor was selected. Empress Turakineh, Taizong Okodei's wife, "governed the country for as long as four years",[19] and "issued decrees on state affairs"; Emperor Dingzong Gyk's wife[20], Augul-q(a)im(i)s, "and the ministers governed the country";[21] Tolui's[22] wife influenced the politics of the Mongols' Yuan dynasty just as much as those empresses who went in for politics, although she had never obtained the opportunity herself. She was a skilled adviser when Okodei was on the throne, and "most of her advice was accepted". What was most important was that she caused the power of the qan shifted from Okodei to Tolui, using her exceptional intelligence and wisdom. Without her teaching and planning, M(a)nku[23] wouldn't have taken the throne and Qubilai[24] would not have introduced Chinese culture into the Mongols' Yuan dynasty successfully, nor would he have even established the Yuan dynasty. That was why she was considered the wisest and most capable woman in the world by some Western historians.[25]

After the founding of the Yuan dynasty, Qubilai imitated the Chinese practice of selecting the crown prince in advance,

---

[18] Hu Wu, "The Empresses of the Mongol Yuan and Their Involvement in Politics", *Qiusuo*, 1990:3.

[19] "Hou Fei Zhuan", *Yuan Shi*.

[20] Gyk: Okodei's son.

[21] Rashid, op. cit., 2:235, Yu Dajun and Zhou Jianqi trs.

[22] Tolui: Cinggis' youngest son.

[23] Rosaby, *Qubilai-qan: His Life and Times*, (California UP; 1988).

[24] Qubilai: Tolui's second son.

[25] See f.n. 23.

and the Quriltai lost its function in selecting new emperors, although it retained a traditional role. The chances of a vacant throne were greatly reduced, yet the empresses continued their involvement in politics throughout the dynasty. Empress Jabun "was smart and sensitive by nature, and could always understand the essence of things. She rectified national politics and helped avoid policy mistakes, playing a very important role in politics at that time".[26] After Empress Jabun died, Empress N(a)mbui was adopted to fill the vacancy. "Emperor Shizu (Qubilai) was in his old age, and so (the Empress) was heavily involved in politics. It often happened that ministers could not see the Emperor, but they would show the some respect to the Empress as they had showed to the Emperor".

Emperor Shizu adopted Jinqin (honoured by the title of Yuzong) as crown prince, but, unfortunately, he died before Shizu. After Shizu passed away, Yuzong's wife, Empress Kukjin "immediately sent Baryan for Temr ... in order to enthrone him. Before Temr came back, Kukjin-qadun was in charge of all state affairs. She called for a Quriltai when Temr arrived." At the conference, "Temr was confronted by Kanmala who was a couple of years older and his rival for the throne. The extremely witty Kukjin-qadun suggested, "Sitchen, Qubilai, once instructed: he who is well versed in Cinggis-qan's bilik will be enthroned. Now each of you must recite it so that those present can make a sound judgement on who is more proficient".[28] As their mother, she well knew that Temr was very eloquent while Kanmala was a mild stutterer. Through such direct manipulation by Kukjin, Temr ascended the throne.

Chengzong was delicate in health and not able to bear the burden of state affairs after he acceded to the throne, and so Empress Brugan "was in charge. She trusted Qaqasun, and was successful in politics. Her decisions were thought to be fair and

---

[26] "Hou Fei Zhuan", *Yuan Shi*.
[27] Ibid.

just.[29] After Chengzong died, she actively prepared the way to hold court from behind a screen, but Renzong intervened and imprisoned her.

Renzong handed the crown over to his brother Wuzong[30] after his triumph over Empress Brugan, with Wuzong promising to return it to him. An agreement was also reached that the crown should always be passed to the nephew after the emperor passed away. During the reigns of Renzong and Wuzong, their mother, Empress Dowager Dair kept herself well informed of state affairs at all times. Durng the reign of Renzong, Dair colluded with the treacherous court official T(a)mud(a)r and put him under her protection. Their action had unfortunate consequences and they were condemned at court. Yet Renzong "attended upon the Empress Dowager, and never disobeyed her in all his life". According to the agreement, Rezong should adopt Wuzong's son Mingzong as his successor; however, "Mingzong was quite ambitious when he was young while Yingzong seemed more timid", and so the empress Dowager and the treacherous court officials "thought that it would be disadvantageous to them if Mingzong became emperor, so they managed to support Yingzong in his accession to the throne".[31] But Yingzong proved a disappointment to his grandmother, Empress Dowager Dair by not accepting her orders after he had ascended the throne. Despite the obstruction form Dair and her henchman T(a)mud(a)r, Yingzong[32] carried out some great reforms. Dair fell ill from anger and regret, and she died before long. Her three years of interference in the court finally came to an end.

There were frequent changes of emperor after Yingzong, and interference by empresses remained a problem. Yingzong eliminated T(a)mud(a)r and most of his gang, and as a result

28   Rashid, op. cit.
29   "Hou Fei Zhuan", *Yuan Shi*.
30   Renzong, Wuzong: sons of Chengzong's brother Kanmala.
31   "Hou Fei Zhuan", *Yuan Shi*.

was himself murdered by the survivors in the gang. They enthroned Tai Ding, but he died of illness within less than four years. His young son Achakpa then assumed the throne, with Tai Ding's empress acting as regent. Wenzong[33] launched a war to seize the throne, and both mother and son were killed. Wenzong then ascended the throne, but died four years later, and the seven-year-old Ningzong became emperor, with Empress Bdasri acting as regent. Yet the young emperor died only three months after his coronation and Shundi[34] Toqon-temr assumed the crown, while Empress Dowager Bdasri remained regent. After Shundi grew up, she was overthrown and ordered to stay outside the imperial palace.

But emperors could never completely eliminate the empresses' interference in court affairs altogether, even after the exile of the empresses dowager. In the late years of Zhizheng, his second empress became involved in politics. She abetted the Crown Prince to invade Korea to take personal revenge, and colluded with a eunuch called Piao Buhua and the warlord Koketemr to force the Emperor to pass the throne on to the Crown Prince. In the struggle for the throne, the Emperor and the Empress each relied on personal armies, and the ensuing civil war greatly exhausted the country.

In a word, the empresses' involvement in court affairs in the Liao and Yuan dynasties played a special role in Chinese history. Although fewer Liao empresses were involved in court affairs, their contribution was greater than their Yuan counterparts, despite the fact that many more Yuan empresses played an active role in court politics.

The Jurchen also had the tradition of politically active empresses before they founded their empire. Empress Zhaosu of Emperor Jingzu is a good example. "Whenever Jingzu went on expeditions, he would take her with him and listen to her

---

32 Yingzong: Renzong's son.
33 Wen Zong: Wu Zong's second son.

comments on court affairs and lawsuits". "After Jingzu died, Shizu and his brothers always reported to the Empress before they went into battles, and the Empress punished them for every failure and rewarded them for every victory".

Empress Jingxuan is another striking example. "Taizu went to report to the empress before going into battle". "Taizu raised a cup of wine to wish Empress Jingxuan longevity, and escorted her to the door, ... the Empress seated Taizu in front of the generals and asked him to issue orders to them". Among the empresses of Taizu, Shengmu and Guangyi "were skilled in making policy", while Qingxian "was skilled in protecting and helping".[35] The upper-class women of the Jurchen had the right to take part in politics, as other northern nationalities, before they established the empire.

After the foundation of the Jin dynasty, the empresses' involvement in politics greatly reduced as the result of the rapid assimilation of Han culture. On the one hand, most upper-class Jurchen women began to read Chinese books and to follow the traditional disciplines and Rites of the Hans. Of Emperor Xianzong's two empresses, Empress Xiaoyi "was fond of *Shi Jing* and *Shu Jing*, and especially loved the philosophies of Lao Zi and Zhuang Zi. She adopted the natural easy-going attitudes of the Taoists and acted in accordance with the Rites". Empress Zhaosheng "completed reading *Xiao Jing* (The Classic of Filial Piety) within ten days". The Jin empresses were "intelligent, filial to their parents and superiors, kind to the children and subordinates" and "always modest and prudent". They paid as much attention to the Rites as Han women did.

On the other hand, the Jin dynasty emperors were opposed to the empresses' interference in court affairs. Emperor Shizong once stipulated that "the empresses and princesses are forbidden to interfere in politics even when they have high ranks".[36] The

---

[34] Ningzong, Shundi: sons of Wuzong's eldest son, Mingzong.
[35] "Hou Fei Zhuan", *Jin Shi*.

empresses and the princesses were accordingly denied their rights to participate in politics after the Jin was established on the Central Plain. During its hundred years of rule, only two cases of interference were recorded in *Jin Shi*. One was Empress Daoping, Xizong's wife. She "interfered boldly in court affairs, and court officials usually relied on her power to acquire the position of prime minister". She had "Xizong under her control", which angered the Emperor who eventually executed her". The other example was the imperial concubine Li Shi'er who relied on the favours of Emperor Zhangzong to usurp power. Her brothers were "all promoted to important positions, and they formed a powerful clique at court". A villain, Xu Chiguo "obtained the position of prime minister because he had followed her". The clique colluded to edge out the able and virtuous officials, and the court fell into disarray. After Prince Weizhao ascended the throne, he had the concubine put to death.

Unlike the empresses' involvement in the Liao and Yuan Dynasties, the instances in Jin dynastic history are more similar to the female "court intrigues" of the Central Plain. The two cases mentioned above occurred when the empresses were not permitted to participate in politics and imperial power was seized illegally.

(3) Gender Relations in Nomadic Empires

The relationships between the sexes among the nomads developed naturally because of economic and cultural backwardness. Women were not suppressed by laws or rites, and men and women performed their own functions and revealed their own prowess in the social life. The emperor and empress held the highest authority, one acting as master and the other as his assistant; they dealt with state affairs jointly. The imperial power existed as an organism, and the empress would usually stay away from state affairs when the emperor was wise and able, but when the emperor was weak or lacked ability, most imperial power would shift to the empress (or empress dowager). It would solely belong to the empress (or empress dowager) when the throne was vacant. The imperial marriage was thus both a combination of the emperor and the empress, and one of different political powers, interacting and benefiting from each other so that the imperial power would be always in their grasp. Threats from eunuchs or of power monopolisation by high officials, common in Han empires, were thereby greatly reduced. Of course, this is not to suggest that there would never be conflicts between emperors and empresses. Emperors are recorded to have felt discontent with empresses who grab power, and there are also many historical examples of empresses imposing restrictions upon emperors. What was different from the Han empires on the Central Plain was that both phenomena were considered to be the normal struggle for power, and historical records and public opinion of the time shows no tendency to back one particular gender.

On the other hand, we must remember that the nomadic states of the Liao, Jin and Yuan developed under patriarchy. Imperial power was androcentric. Power was normally held by men and passed down the paternal line. It was only when the emperor was too weak or the throne was vacant that the empress was at the helm of the state. It was also rare for the emperor and empress to be equally matched in strength. Furthermore, the empresses' rule was dependent on the emperors, and the empresses in power were merely a bridge connecting the rule of the late emperor with that of the new. This convention did not allow the empresses to replace the emperors totally, regardless of how able and talented they were. The selection of an emperor would only be hastened when an empress was in power and the throne was vacant. That is to say, even in the nomadic states, it was the emperors who were decisive, and the empresses were no more than their assistants, although it was legal for them to share imperial power.

2. Marriage Patterns of the Ruling Nationalities of the Liao, Jin and Yuan

(1) The Fixed Connections by Marriage between the Clans of the Emperors and the Empresses

It was a common practice in the nomadic dynasties for the emperors to choose particular clans and forge long-lasting relationships with them through marriage. The nomads practised exogamy, and it was common for the ruling clan to tighten its relations with other powerful clans in order to enhance their political and military strength.

According to **Qidan Guozhi**, "it was the nomadic tradition that the emperor's clan was only connected with the empress' clans in marriage". The emperor's clan was the Yel clan, and "the empress' clans" carried two meanings. In its broader sense, it referred to the clans of Bali, Yishiyi and Shul, which belonged to the tribe of Xiao, but in a narrower sense to the clan of Shul. "Only the Yel and Xiao clans dealt with state affairs of the Liao jointly". Girls born into the clan of Xiao would be empresses and the boys would marry princesses. These two marriage groups were also powerful in politics. "People outside the clans of the emperors and the empresses had no opportunity at all to hold the power of the state and the armed forces, and control the other tribes".[37] "The clans of the emperors and the empresses shared the power and matched each other in strength; they depended on each other like the lips and teeth to make the state strong. This was a fine way to run a country".[38] The emperors and the empresses shared power, and the most eminent positions in the court were usually occupied by people from these two clans. For example, during the time of Emperor Taizu, the emperor's brother Yel Su was appointed prime minister of the Southern Palace, and the empress' brother Xiao Ludi was

---

[36] "Hou Fei Zhuan", *Jin Shi*.
[37] "Nichen Zhuan", *Liao Shi*.

appointed prime minister of the Northern Palace. It was a practice throughout the Liao dynasty for the members from the clans of the emperor and the empresses to share imperial power side by side.

The founder of the Jin, the Wanyan clan, also had a creed that "women from the ordinary families cannot marry as empresses".[39] Members of the emperor's clan could only choose members from the heading families of the following eight clans: Tudan, Tangkuo, Pucha, Nulan, Pusan, Heshi lie, Wulinda, Wugulun and Peiman. "In ancient times, only those from the clans with an inherited title of duke or marquis and a different family name from the emperor could marry members of the emperor's clan....This is the principle for the emperor's and the princesses' marriages'." The Jin Emperor Zhangzong intended to make Li Shi'er empress after Empress Qinhuai died, because Li "was able to read and write, and was especially capable of figuring out the emperor's intentions and falling in with his wishes". However, it was a "custom passed down for generations" that the members of the emperor's clan could only marry members of the leading families of the eight clans, and the Li family was "quite humble". "The ministers opposed the emperor and the Taijian presented the ministers' opinions to the emperor, so the emperor had to compromise by conferring on her the title of Yuanfei".[40] Yet the discipline of "marrying within the fixed clans" was only applied to the marriage of the emperor and the empress, and there was no such limits in the case of the imperial concubines. Some concubines of Zhaozu, Jingzu, Shizu and Kangzu were from the clans other than those eight.

Cinggis-qan selected the clans which could be connected with the Mongol Golden Horde by marriage in the course of his expeditions. The clans of Qonggirad, Aikiras, Oirat and Onggd

[38] "Waiqi Biao", *Liao Shi*.
[39] "Hou Fei Zhuan", *Liao Shi*.

were all selected, yet not all clans enjoyed the same privilege.

Type 1: "The girls born into the clan will be empresses and the boys will marry the princesses". This was a special honour only for the clan of Qonggirad. The chief of the Qonggirad clan was the first among the Mongols to support Cinggis, and his son followed Taizu on his expeditions and had many brilliant military achievements, so Cinggis conferred the title of Maternal Uncle of the Imperial Family on them and conferred noble titles on them. An imperial edict was issued: "All girls born to the Qonggirad clan will be empresses and the boys will marry princesses. They will receive an edict in the first month of each season every year. This will pass down from generation to generation".[41] The legal wives of the emperors of the Mongol Yuan were almost unanimously from the Qonggirad clan. And all the male members of this clan could marry the princesses of the Golden Horde. If one princess died after her marriage, another princess could be chosen as a replacement. The other clans did have such a privilege.

Type 2: The boys in these clans could marry the princesses, and the girls could be wives of the princes. The clans of Oirat and Aikiras belonged to this type. They were located in the important geographical positions and had made great contributions to Cinggis-qan's unification of the Mongols. But their status was not so high as that of the Qongirad clan. The girls in these clans were mostly married to princes, and the only exception was Sotpala who became the empress of Yingzong. Most girls became princesses: Ailjiqmis of the Auila was married to Ariq-boke, Armukan was married to Minri-timur, Kubak and Auljai were both married to Hulaku, and Orqina was married to Qra-hulaku.

Type 3: The marriages were mainly between the boys of these clans and the princesses. Such clans as Onggd and Uihur were categorised as this type. These two clans belonged to the

---

40 Ibid.

Semu who supported Cinggis in his cause. As a reward, Cinggis betrothed the princesses to the chiefs of these clans, yet the relations could only be maintained in this way. There were a few cases in which the girls from these clans were married into the Golden Horde,[42] but they were only ones among many concubines of the emperors or princes.

The ranks of the empresses and princesses were decided by the position of their clans in politics and military affairs, rather than by their own gifts and looks. The marital strategy in the Liao, Jin and Yuan was vital to the maintenance of their ruling position. Tu Qi once commented that "the imperial clan and the leading clans were connected through marriages so that they were bound together in a common cause and had to share danger and safety; the policies of the Tang dynasty could never be so effective."[43]

(2) The Marriage with the Widows in the Clan in Which Generations Were Not Taken into Account

Marriages with widows in the clan, also known as "continued marriages", were a common practice in the Liao, Jin and Yuan. "When a women was widowed, the men in the clan could marry her",[44] without considering whether they belonged to the same generation. This was a common characteristic of marriages with the widows in the clan, which can be categorised into two types: inter-generational and intra-generational.

The inter-generational marriage with the widows in the clan mainly refers to the marriages with the concubine of one's late father, or one's widowed aunt, which was regarded as a natural thing by the nomads, yet as incest by Central Plain society. After his father died, the eldest son Zongzheng stayed for the

---

[41] *Yuan Shi*, juan 118.

[42] Zhou Qingtao, "The Everlasting Connection by Marriage between the Onggud Clan and the Cinggis Clan", **Essays in Memory of the Foundation of the Mongol Society of China**, 1979.

[43] Tu Qi, *Mengwu'er Shi Ji*.

night with his step-mother Madame Guy who gave birth to a girl later and named it Aseng Niangzi (Epitaph of Yel Shuji). It was nothing shameful in the notions of the nomads to marry one's step-mother and so it was recorded on an epitaph. Furthermore, the Liao emperor sometimes issued edicts urging marriage with one's step-mother. Yel Aongzheng was the eldest son of Prince Qinjin Yel Longqing whose brother was Emperor Shengzong. After Longqing died, "Emperor Shengzong, in his mourning, forced the prince (Zongzheng) to marry the princess (Princess Qinjin). The prince was a man of character and rejected the edict by saying that it was against the divination'. Later, princess Qinjin was married to Liu Erxuan. Yet princess Qinjin was ordered by an imperial edict to be buried in the same tomb with Zongzheng after her death. Thus Zongzheng and Princess were made husband and wife on paper".[45]

The Mongol Yuan was another time in which intergenerational marriages with widows in the clan were prominent. After Cinggis died, his favoured concubine Moge-qadun was married with Okodei who inherited the position of qan, and Chagatai (another son of Cinggis) was also fond of Moge-qadun. Without knowing that Okodei had married her, he sent a message saying, "Of all the mothers and beautiful concubines left by father, give me this Moge-qadun". And Okodei replied, "I have married her; I would have sent her to him if the letter had come earlier; now I can give him another if he likes".[46] The brothers fell over each other to marry the concubines of their late father, and they chose them as if they were carving up property! The marriages with the widows in the clan were so common that even the prestigious Sorqotani (Tolui's widow) could not escape from it. Okodei sent a special envoy to propose to her for his son Gyk after Tolui's sudden death. The wedding didn't take place because Sorqotani politely refused the proposal

---

44 "Hou Fei Zhuan", *Jin Shi*.
45 "Epitaph of Yel Zongzheng".

and Gyk didn't insist.

The Yuan emperors also issued edicts to urge the marriages with the father's concubines. In the time of Shundi, Zhongshu Pingzhang Kukdei's concubine Gao Lishi swore to keep her chastity after he died. The son of his wedded wife Baimaturj "intended to marry her but had no success". He went to the powerful prime minister Baryan for help, Baryan begged for an edict from the emperor which "ordered Baimaturj to marry his father's concubine Gao Lishi".

There were relatively fewer cases of inter-generational marriages with widows in the clan in the Jin, and the recorded cases were mainly in the time before they ruled the Central Plain. After the Jin moved its capital to Beijing, the ruling class was influenced by the morality of the Central Plain, and inter-generational marriages with widows in the clan were gradually proscribed. When Prince Hailing killed his uncle Zongmin, he took his aunt Alan back to his palace and conferred the title of Zhaofei on her in the first year of Zhenyuan. Some ministers presented a memorial saying that "Zongmin was a close relative of the older generation, so it is improper (to marry his wife)".[47] Hailing was forced to move her out of his palace.

The intra-generational marriages with widows in the clan refer to levirates. Yel Zonghan of the Jin first married the widow of his half brother Zongjun, then married the widow of his cousin Zong-Xiong. And Princess N(a)nkiajin of the Yuan was married to the two sons of Alchu in succession. There were many more cases of intra-generational marriages with the widows in the clan, and junior levirates were considered moral even by the Hans. They were so popular among the Han people in the Jin and the Yuan dynasties that it became one of the major patterns of marriage.

There were different causes for the popularisation of marriages with widows in the clan.

---

[46] Rashid, op. cit., vol. 2, p. 245.

First, it was closely related to the distribution of property. The nomadic women enjoyed the same rights to family property as the men. They had the right to inherit the property after the husband died. In this case, if a women was remarried to another clan after her husband died, she would take her share of property with her.

Secondly, when a woman was married to her husband's clan, she was considered to be one of its members. It was important for the prosperity of the clan that the marital relations with the women of other blood be maintained forever to avoid the loss of population of the clan. As a result, "continued" marriages became necessary.

Thirdly, the number of women supported by a clan was regarded by the nomads as an overt expression of its strength and prosperity. In their plundering wars, wives and concubines were looted as property. Cinggis made a rule which stipulated that the number of one's concubines was limited by one's capacity to support them. The more women a clan supported, the stronger it was thought to be. If a clan allowed its widowed women to be taken into another one, "it would be derided as unable to support its women".[48] It was obvious that the popularity of the marriages with the widows in the clan among the nomads was closely related with their notions and customs.

(3) Lawful Polygyny

Polygyny was practised by the Liao, Jin and Yuan. The Hans on the Central Plain had established monogamy as early as the Zhou dynasty, and after that time monogamy with several concubines had been the accepted marriage pattern on the Central Plain.[49] The Liao, Jin and Yuan which arose in areas north of the Great Wall were still in the period of transition from tribal slavery to feudalism when they seized the control of

---

[48] *Yuanchao Mishi* (Secret History of the Yuan Dynasty), juan 1.

[49] Du Fangqin, **Changes in Notions on Women**, (Henan Renmin Chubanshe, 1988).

the Central Plain, and polygyny was still practised by the founders of these three dynasties as a remnant of the earlier communal marriage.

One of Prince Hailing's rules stated that "the officials are allowed to take two sub-wives, and the ordinary people are also allowed to have concubines". The Mongol rulers set no limits on the number of wives and concubines, and men "could marry as many women as they could support".[50] And the situation was similar in the Liao. It was described in the Epitaph of Hanxiao how Hanxiao's grand-father married three women from the clan of Xiao successively. It's a pity that information on the number of wives and concubines permitted by the Liao are not available.

The effect of polygyny on the system of empresses and the concubinage was the co-existence of several empresses at the same time. Emperor Shengzong of the Liao had two empresses, and Taizu had four: Shengmu, Guangyi, Qinxian and Xuanxian; Ruizong, Shizong, Xianzong and Xuanzong in the Jin had two empresses respectively. The Yuan emperors had even more empresses. Cinggis-qan's empresses and concubines amounted to several hundred. Among these empresses and concubines, thirty-eight of them had been listed in *Yuan Shi*. Emperor Taizong of Yuan had six empresses, Dingzong had three, Xianzong five, Shizu eight, Chengzong three, Wuzong five, Renzong two, Yingzong three, Taiding-di ten, Mingzong four, and Shundi four. Wenzong was the only emperor in the Yuan dynasty who had only one empress.

There were some profound social causes for the popularisation of polygyny among the nomads:

First, the nomads were famous for their bravery and resourcefulness at warfare. Quite a number of men lost their lives in frequent wars. The disproportion of men and women in the population made polygyny possible.

Secondly, war and looting increased the disproportion of

---

[50] D'Ohsson, **History of the Mongols**, Vol. 1, p. 29.

the population. The plundering often aimed more at taking property and women than at occupying lands. Cinggis once encouraged his subordinates by saying, "it's the greatest pleasure for a man to defeat and conquer his enemies and stamp them out ... ride their horses, and take their pretty wives and concubines, and let them attend upon him in bed".[51] When he attacked the Xixia and the Jin, and on his expeditions westward, every time he took a town, he would kill all the people in the town, except for the women and the craftsmen. He called this "sacking the town". After the war, the craftsmen would be kept by the state and the property and the women would be given to those who had displayed talent and bravery in war. The result of the plunder was the increase in the number of the wives and concubines of the officers at all levels in each clan, and the emperor was the one who received the most trophies. Most of Cinggis' five hundred wives and concubines were captured in war.[52]

Thirdly, the popularity of the marriage with the widows in the clan was a direct cause of polygyny. The male members, married or not, had the right and the duty to marry the widows in the clan to maintain the property and manpower. It was usual for a nomadic woman to marry two or even three husbands successively. On the one hand, this lead to a dramatic disproportion in the number of husbands and wives; but, on the other hand, it provided those who had no right to get women as trophies with an opportunity to have more wives. The practice of marriages with widows in the clan was one of the important causes why "all men, of the upper-class or the lower-class, have several wives"[53].

Fourthly, the subjective motivation for practising polygyny was the need to multiply the population. Consumed by low

---

[51]   Rashid, op. cit., Vol. 1 (2), p. 256.

[52]   Idem.

[53]   Xu Mengxin, *Sanchao Beimeng Huibian* (Collection of Northern Treaties from Three Dynasties), juan 3.

productivity and frequent wars, the population of nomads was relatively small, and so multiplying the population meant the survival and prosperity of a clan. It was a simple arithmetical law that more wives make more sons. "Cinggis-qan made it a law that jealousy should be shunned so long as one could bring more offspring to the clan".[54]

In a word, polygyny was popular among the Khitayans, the Jurchen and the Mongols. The emperors of the Liao, the Jin gradually abandoned the habit of keeping several empresses at the same time, while it remained a common practice throughout the Yuan dynasty.

(4) The Servant-making Marriage and the Matri-patrilocality

"Servant-making" was another common pattern of marriage among nationalities such as the Wuheng, the Shihwei, the Khitan and the Jurchen.

"After the wedding, (the husband) was to stay with his wife's family for three years labouring as their servant before he could take his wife home". (*Qidan Guozhi*)

"After the wedding, (the husband) was to stay with his wife's family for three years, labouring as their servant, serving food and wine to them before he could take his wife home". (*Da Jin Guozhi*).

The servant-making marriage had long been a tradition of the Liao and Jin, and the ancestors of the Mongols and the Shih-Wei also had a custom that men "first stayed in the wife' home, doing three years' labor"[55] during the Sui and the Tang, and it developed into the custom of matri-patrilocality by the time of Cinggis-qan. The matri-patrilocality, popular among the Mongols, was derived from the servant-making marriage, yet the husbands were no longer treated as servants.

---

[54] *Heita Shile* (Events of the Black Tartars).
[55] "Shiwei Zhuan", *Jiu Tang Shu*.

According to Mongol custom, the father was to propose for his son who had got to the wedding age. If the girl's father accepted the proposal, they would drink to the consent, and there would be a great feast attended by relatives from both parties to celebrate the consent, at which lamb was served. After the feast, the bridegroom's father would go home while the newly-wedded husband would stay in the bride's home.

The story of Cinggis' wedding was recorded in **The Secret History of the Mongols**. His father Yisukai took him to propose to the Qonggrad clan when he was nine years old. Tsajan said to Yisukai after he accepted the proposal, "I will marry my daughter to your son, and your son will stay here as the son-in-law. This is consented to by both families". The acceptance of the son-in-law into the clan was a sign to show the bride's clan's agreement to the marriage, and it was an indispensable stage in a marriage for the bridegroom to stay for some time in the bride's home. The wedding procedure of Cinggis and Borte should be very typical since their fathers were the chiefs of clans. It remained a custom until the Ming dynasty that a girl of a Mongol noble family "would stay in her home" with her bridegroom after the wedding "until they gave birth to a child"[56] Matri-patrilocality was a common marriage pattern among the Mongols.

In both the servant-making marriage and the matri-patrilocality form the husband stayed in the bride's home for a specific period of time, but there was an essential difference between this and the Central Plain custom whereby "the son of a poor family would be married into the bride's home".

(5) Marriage by Capture and Compulsory Marriage

The Liao, Jin and Yuan developed from nomadic states which encouraged militarism and sacking, and marriage by capture was significant before they abandoned the nomadic

---

[56] "Pipei", **Beilu Fengsu** (Customs of the Northern Nomads).

mode of production.

Evidence can be found in *Jin Shi* (juan 68): "Once upon a time, there was a beauty in the Wusazha whose name was Badi Hui. She was captured by people of the Qinglingdong together with people from the Jiangshushui. She gave birth to two girls, one named Dahui and the other Zizai... Zhaozu and Shilu captured them in their plundering. And each took one girl as his concubine".

Three women of two generations, Badi and her two daughters, were thus married by capture.

Accounts can also be found in The New History of the Yuan: Empresses and Princesses. Empress Xuanyi of Liezu, Holawu, was first married to Yikajil(a)tu of the M(a)rkit clan. The bridegroom sent people to escort the bride to the wedding. On their way they came across Liezu when they were going along the Onan River. "Liezu was hunting. When he saw the beautiful bride, he led his people to capture her". Holawu was Cinggis' mother. "When Cinggis had grown up, he married Empress Guangxian, Borte.' Toqto' a who was the chief of the M(a)rkit and the elder brother of Yilajil(a)tu launched an attack and captured Borte, and made her the wife of his brother. Toqto'a said, Yisukai once seized the wife of my brother, and now we eventually take revenge by taking his daughter-in-law". Later, Cinggis allied with Ong-khan and Jamuqeh, defeated the M(a)rkit and retrieved Borte.

The marriage by capture can be classified into two types: those solely for the purpose of obtaining a wife and those for plundering women as well as property. The first type was more primitive and occurred more frequently, but with a relatively small number of women being captured. The second type was not done for the purpose of getting wives: women were captured simply as a special kind of property. In the latter case, women were captured in large numbers. It is recorded in **The Secret History of the Yuan Dynasty** showed that "the three hundred people who once lived densely around Burhan Mountain all perished, and all the women (were captured). Those who could be married were, and others became maid-servants". A number of women were captured and forced into marriage after almost every nomadic war.

The marriage by capture on a large scale disappeared as warfare for loot came to an end after the feudal empires of the Liao, Jin and Yuan were established on the Central Plain. Yet compulory marriages still existed. The compulsory marriages according to imperial edict took place under the cloak of civilisation.

The Khitayans were "obliged to present a report before they got married". (*Liao Shi*) This was the rulers' measure to preserve the traditional customs of the Liao. Marriages were dealt with as administrative affairs and had to be ratified by the emperor. We can see an example of this above in Shengzong's release of an edict ordering Yel Zongzheng to marry his step-mother. Zongzheng disobeyed the emperor's edict and could no longer ask permission to marry other woman, and so finally died without a son.[57] At the time of Taizong of the Liao, an imperial edict was issued, ordering "the administrative agencies to arrange marriages for widowers and widows who cannot support themselves among the Yishi, Pinbei and Tugui".[58] This was compulsory marriage on a larger scale.

The early Mongols worshipped power, and compulsory marriages demonstrate this. Giovanni de Piano Carpini wrote in his account of the Mongols that after a duke was accused of stealing horses and executed, Batu ordered the duke's younger brother to marry his widowed sister-in-law. He called for people to throw the two in bed and forced them to be husband and wife despite their strong protests. Compulsory marriages were common at all levels of society, even after the Mongol ruling class had been greatly influenced by the Central Plain civilisation.

---

[57] "Epitaph of Yel Zongzheng".
Liao Shi.

Another type of compulsory marriage is represented by the marriages between the Qonggirad clan and the Mongol Golden Horde. Weddings were to be held after people received the imperial edicts in the first month in each season every year. These marriages were, however, blessed by the emperor.

Yet another type of compulsory marriage was the custom whereby women were given to meritorious court officials and princes as rewards or gifts. The custom was kept up even after the Yuan united China and the ruling class had no way to capture women in warfare. One of the most important sources for the state of women was the confiscated wives and concubines of officials found guilty of crimes. Many edicts are recorded in Yuan Shi, stating that "so-and-so is to be granted so-and-so's confiscated wife". It was not until the time of Wenzong when the pace of sinification had quickened that the practice of "giving criminals' wives to other people was banned".[59]

The hereditary status system presents another form of compulsory marriage. Qubilai released an edict in the twenty-third year of Zhiyuan (1286), ordering "the officials in the newly subordinate armies should find partners for widowers, widows and orphans suitable in looks and age, in order to build up families" and prevent widows in the army from marrying people outside, thereby avoiding "a gradual reduction in troop numbers because widowers in the army cannot find women to marry". This might be an extreme case, but the regulation itself was compulsory and soldiers could not marry civilians.[60]

Marriage by capture and compulsory marriages existed in different periods, yet they both reflected the nomads' worship of power. In this sense, they were similar.

(6) Women's Status in Marriage

[59] *Yuan Shi*.
[60] *Yuan Dianzhang*.

The Liao, Jin and Yuan were founded by nomads who just entered the class society, and there were faint traces of matriarchy in their social customs, although their lives were violent. Nomadic women had a higher status than Han women in marriage.

First, the upper class nomadic women were representatives of political power in marriage. Nomads usually selected their spouses according to the class they belonged to. The imperial family members selected empresses from the fixed clans, and the other members of the ruling class selected their wives from the noble bureaucratic clans. The social status of a woman's clan was basic and decisive for her marriage and position in her husband's clan. The political significance was important for the ruling class. The purpose of the marriages was to make an alliance of clans, and each party in a marriage represented one political power. Therefore, nomadic women had equal status with men, and an empress, married to an emperor who took the whole world as his own household, usually had the right to participate in politics.

Second, nomadic women were the owners of part of the property in the clan. When a woman got married, she took with her the dowry which could be used jointly by the two parties in the marriage, yet the woman was still its actual owner. The property of the husband would be divided among the wife and the children after he died. Han women never had property rights. A Han woman's property would be taken away by the clan if she remarried after her husband died and had no offspring.

The practice of marriage with widows in the nomadic clan by no means suggested a lower status of women. However, the system of marriages with widows in the clan denied women their rights to make a free choice in their second marriage, and it was virtually a violation of women's rights.

Third, the existence of servant-making marriages and matri-patrilocality was an important sign showing the acceptance of women by society. A man had to reside in his wife's home, as a servant or son-in-law, after he got engaged with a woman, which was a compensation for the wife's family who had given up their daughter. This was a demonstration of women's value and an acknowledgement of the parents' efforts to bring up their daughter. The ceremony of prostrating among the Jurchen was another very typical case. To get engaged, a man would have to go to his bride-to-be's home with money and presents, accompanied by people from his own clan, to present the money and presents and prostrate himself. "All members of the girl's family, old and young, would sit on the kang, while the man and his people prostrated themselves".[61] After the ceremony, the man would stay in the girl's home as a servant. This custom, in some degree, showed women's superiority over men.

Even marriages by capture and compulsory marriages are not directly associated with women's status. For the nomads, capture was as natural as proposing to a future wife. It was a direct reflection of the savagery and power whihc typified the marriages of the early nomads. For example, H(a)mb(a)qai seized Holawu and his wedded wife gave the position to her because she was the daughter of the chief of the Qonggirad and had noble blood. A woman's status in marriage was determined by her blood rather then by the way in which she was married. The main reason most captured wives and concubines had low status was because they were prisoners of war.

On the prairies where the natural circumstances were adverse and the weak became the prey of the strong, survival was the first need of all creatures, including human beings. This is why the nomads worshipped militarism and power, and developed a bold and unrefined character. They emphasised, in their marriages, political and economic factors and fertility. Affection had little part to play. This was the basis for compulsory

[61] *Songmo Jiwen.*

marriages, and the compulsion applied to both sexes; human beings were mated like animals.

Overlooking the surface phenomena in marriage patterns, we can discern that among the nomads who were still in the early stage of patriarchy, women had a much higher status in marriage, as well as politics, economy and other fields, than the women on the Central Plain where the patriarchy was well developed. Yet it was undeniable that even in the nomadic families there existed an obvious inequality between men and women. The practice of polygyny and the absence of polyandry are clear proof of this. Moreover, polygyny was the major marriage pattern. A woman could only be one of the many wives and concubines of a man, and this was true of almost all women. Only a few could be in the position of wedded wife who was relatively equal with the man in politics, economy and family life. Most lower-class women, especially those captured in wars, had neither political support nor property. Their relationship with the man to whom they were married was virtually that of a slave. In the Liao, Jin and Yuan, men's oppression of women in marriage existed even among the ruling nationalities.

3. Cross-influences of Nomadic Culture and Han Culture and Changes in Gender Relations

The ruling nationalities in the Liao, Jin and Yuannamely the Khitan, Jurchen and Mongol, remained a minority of the population. The Han remained the majority. During the four hundred years in which these dynasties ruled China, there were intimate mutual influences between traditional Han culture and the nomadic cultures. The conquering Khitayans, Jurchens and Mongols were actually culturally conquered by the nationality on the Central Plain, and they accepted many philosophical, cultural and political aspects of Han civilisation. At the same time, the Hans, with a relatively better developed economy, experienced changes under the impact of the nomadic cultures. The Han and nomadic cultures infiltrated each other, and a new synthesis characterised the period.

(1) The Cross-influences between Han Culture and Nomadic Cultures

It took a long time for the Hans to accept the nomadic cultures. Beore the Yuan united China, the Song was stalemated with against the Liao, Xixia and Jin in succession. The northern Hans were waging a resistance against nomadic cultures, and they dreamed of reuniting North China under the Great Song Empire. The Liao had to implement out a system of the Two Palaces of the South and the North to rule the Hans and the Khjitayans separately. This policy minimised the cross-influence between Khitan culture and Han culture. Therefore, from the Liao to the mid Jin, the Hans in the north accepted nomadic culture passively, and mostly in the process of marriage. After the Jin took the northern territory of the Song, the Song lingered on feebly, retreating south of the Yangtse River, and for them re-union had become a dream which would never come true. At the same time, the Jin moved its capital southward, and drew more from Han culture, and as greater numbers of Han people accepted Jin rule, the ethnic conflicts abated. On the one hand, most of the Jurchens gave up their own customs to such an extent that after they migrated to the Han-inhabited areas the rulers had to issue decrees calling on the Jurchen to retain their traditions, but most decrees had no effect. On the other hand, the Hans stopped despising and rejecting Jurchen customs, and some Han people began to follow these customs. During the late Jin and the early Yuan many Hans in the North imitated the ceremony of prostrating, until the Mongol rulers order "it to be banned" because "there had never been customs like this among the Mongols".[62] Marriages with widows in the

---

[62] *Yuan Dianzhang*.

clan and the matri-patrilocality among the Han during the Jin and Yuan was a direct reflection of the spread of the nomadic cultures.

The marriages with widows in the clan had appeared on the Central Plain as early as the Xia and Shang Dynasties, but was banned as the moral principles of the Zhou spread because it hadn't taken the factors of generations into consideration. During the reign of the Liao, the Jin and the Yuan, this ancient marital custom which had almost perished on the Central Plain began to revive. The marriages with the widows in the clan included the marriages with one's late father's concubine, aunts, and the levirate and the junior levirate, among which the first three types were forbidden in the etiquette of the Central Plain and were banned by the Mongol rulers during the seventh to the fourteenth year of Zhiyuan to carry out the policy that each nationality "follow its own customs". The junior levirate was common, and cases abound in various Yuan documents. A man, single or married, was allowed to marry his elder brother's widow, and it was considered "hard to equate with cases in which a married man gets another's wife' and is not proscribed by the Mongol rulers".[63]

Unlike the nomadic women, Han women enjoyed no right to own or inherit property, and so marriages with the widows in the clan among the Hans did not serve the purpose of maintaining the property; yet by marriages with widows in the clan, the rich could have more wives and the poor could get married for little or no expense. These were the major reasons for the popularity of marriage with widows in the clan among the Han.

In the mid-Yuan the philosophies of the Lixue or Idealistic School of Confucianism became influential, and more and more Han people rejected the practice of marriage with widows in the clan which was not consistent with the notions of female

---

[63] Idem.

chastity and faithfulness. Emperor Wenzong released an edict in the first year of Zhishun (1330), saying that "those who marry the widows of their elder brothers or their late fathers' concubines, outside their traditional customs, are committing an offence".[64] However, this kind of marriages still existed among the Han people and became a social problem in the early Ming dynasty. One of the laws of the Ming stated: "If one marries his late father's concubines, his aunt and both parties in the marriage are to be executed. A man who marries his brother's widow will be strangulated". (Laws of the Ming: Families and Marriages)

Matrilocality had long been a marriage pattern among the Han of the Central Plain, yet it had been looked down upon since the period of the Warring States, and some grooms who moved into their wives' homes "were even exiled to remote areas" as prisoners until the Sui and Tang dynasties.[65] People would try hard to avoid this if they had no other choice. The tradition remained until the Song in most areas. Yet some areas in present day Sichuan and Hubei provinces were exceptions. "A grown-up son of a poor family would move into his wife's home, and people regarded it as natural". "The wealthy families often accepted their son-in-law into their home, and the poor often left their parents to stay in their wives' homes after the wedding".[66] Matrilocality became a popular form of marriage in those areas.

The bridegrooms of the Khitan and the Jurchen would have to stay in the brides' homes for a certain time. The traditional view of matrilocality on the Central Plain was buffeted when the Liao, Jin and Yuan became masters of the Central Plain successively. During the Jin and Yuan, many cases of the matrilocality emerged on the Central Plain. These included poor families who couldn't afford a wedding for their sons, wealthy

---

[64] *Yuan Shi*.
[65] *Qian Han Shu*.
[66] *Song Shi*.

families who had no sons or whose sons were too young, and
families who thought the grooms were too poor to marry their
daughters. Even some families wealthy enough to afford weddings sent theirs sons into the brides' homes or accept their
sons-in-law into their homes.[67] It was so popular that the Yuan
rulers issued orders to stop the practice: "Wealthy families with
only one son who can afford weddings are not permitted to send
their sons into their brides' homes; poor families with only one
son of marriageable age are not restricted".[68] Matrilocality was
not a special form of marriage practised by a small number of
people in despair. In the eighth year of Zhiyuan, the Yuan
rulers stated in regulations governing wedding systems that "the
number of families in which matrilocality is practised is great,
some people are indeed too poor to afford a wedding, and it will
be hard to stop them from residing in their wives' homes, even
if it is not a traditional custom. These families can be allowed
to act according to the fashion".[69] There were always people
"too poor to afford a wedding", yet it was only during the Jin
and the Yuan that matrilocality became widespread, the most
important reason being the change in people's thinking. Even
Confucius' descendants in the Yuan dynasty, Kong Qi and his
brother, resided in their wives' homes, and the father-in-law of
two famous historians, Su Tianjue and Zhang Delin, was also a
groom living in his wife's home. These practices were simply
impossible at a time when matrilocality was regarded with
contempt. The improvement of the matrilocally residing
grooms and the popularity of the matrilocality were inextricably
related to the impact and influence of the nomadic cultures.

Ruling in the Han-inhabited areas where the economy and
culture were more advanced, the nomads inevitably absorbed
Han culture to strengthen their rule. Yet the degrees of their

---

[67] Wang Xiaoqing, "On the Matrilocality of the Yuan", *Shixue
Yuekan*, 1990:6.

[68] *Yuan Dianzhang*.

[69] *Tongzhi Tiaoge*.

sinification differed regionally.

The Liao carried out the system of Two Palaces, and the Khitans and Hans were ruled separately according to their customs. Sinification of the Khitan was thus relatively slight. Nevertheless, there were many Khitan women who had been quite influenced by Han moral obligations and teachings. When Yel Nu was framed, dismissed and exiled, the emperor persuaded his wife Yixin to divorce him as she was the daughter of a princess, but Yixin replied, "The ties between husband and wife should be maintained till death. I married him when I was a young girl. Now he is in trouble and if I leave him I will offend morality. What difference would there be between me and a beast?" (The History of the Liao: Heroines) This had a very Confucian ring to it!

Of the three nomadic dynasties, the Jin was the most profoundly sinified. Almost all the empresses and princesses followed the moral principles of Confucianism. Empress Qinhuai of Zhang Zong "was refined and virtuous, graceful and solemn", and she "could read and write"; Empress Minghui of Xuan Zong "possessed dignity, and had knowledge about ancient and present times". There were some more outstanding cases: Shi Zong's mother, Empress Zhenyi, shaved her hair and became a Buddhist nun to avoid re-marrying after her husband's death; Shizong's wife empress Zhaode "attended upon her parents-in-law carefully and docilely, managed the family methodically, and her behaviour was quite consistent with the moral principles for women". She drowned herself in a lake to prevent Prince Hailing from having her by force. She was regarded as "a paragon of women", and Shizong left the position of empress vacant for years after he had ascended the throne because "no one could compare with the Empress in virtue".[70] The profundity of the Confucian influence on the emperors and empresses of the Jin can be seen from these examples.

---

[70] "Hou Fei Zhuan", **Jin Shi**.

The Yuan was the dynasty during which the harmony of different races developed to its greatest extent. The powerful and matchless Mongol nobles swept away the regimes in different parts of China like a storm, and divided their subjects into the Mongols, the Semu, the Hans and the Southerners according to the sequence in which these "ethnic" groups were conquered. Thus, people of all nationalities in the former Jin empire in the areas north of the Huaihe River were called Han, even though they could actually be Khitan, Jurchen, Bohai or Korean, as well as Han. As the Yuan rulers had a policy of allowing "each nationality" to "follow its own customs", all Hans could follow Han customs. Thus, most customs of the Khitan and the Jurchen were forbidden, and by the late Yuan, almost all the Khitayans and the Jurchens had been assimilated with the Han people in areas south of the Great Wall. They followed the principles and etiquette of the Hans, and became Hans themselves.

The sinification among the Mongols was unavoidable although the rulers of the Yuan had always emphasised that Mongols "marry within the race" and stressed that "Mongols are excluded" when they released laws and decrees. On the one hand, the Mongol rulers, as a minority nationality, were surrounded by an ocean of Han culture. Since most members of the ruling and other clans "read works by Han sages and scholars for the sake of their administration",[71] it was natural for them to be influenced by the Central Plain's culture. One of the milestones in this process was when Mongol women began to keep their chastity by trying to remain in widowhood after their husbands died.

Princess Luguo Dazhang Sanklagi was Emperor Shunzong's daughter. She was married into the Qonggirad clan in the eleventh year of Dade, at the time of Chengzong. Her husband died less than four years after their wedding. Princess Dazhang

---

[71] *Yuan Shi.*

"kept her chastity by refusing to marry her late husband's brothers, and brought up the children left by her husband". Wenzong summoned the Han scholars Zhao Shiyan and Yu Ji to discussing the matter of conferring a title, "to honour her".[72] It was rare for the nomads to honour a Mongol woman for her chastity, in the way the Hans honoured their heroic women.

Three of the heroic women cited Yuan Shi are of special interest. Tutuni of the Qonggirad clan was widowed when she was twenty-six. The ex-wife of her husband Qrabuqa had two grown-up sons who were still single. They intended to "marry her according to the custom of the clan". Tutuni got furious, "Do you beasts want to marry your mother? How dare you face your father underground when you die?" And she refused them.

Another widow was Jiuqajin whose husband died of disease when she was twenty-six. She "swore not to marry again, and attended her parents-in-law for twenty-five years. On the death of her parents-in-law, she wore dirty clothing and didn't make up, and lived in the mausoleum of her parents-in-law for the rest of her life". The third example is Gka, the wife of the Tongzhixuanzhengyuanshi Luo Wushisan. In the first year of Tianli, Luo was found guilty of a crime and exiled to Hainan, and the emperor presented Gka to Hismulazim Mauqan. Mauqan drove to her house to pick her up in person. Seeing that there was no other way to refuse him, Gka went to the stable and hanged herself.

(2) Cultural Cross-influence and Changes in Gender Relations

Women had quite different status and relationships in the Central Plain and nomadic cultures, but these changed to some degree as a result of cross-influence.

On the one hand, the nomads of the Khitan, Jurchen and Mongol peoples were still at the early stage of patriarchy, and

---

[72] Ibid.

men and women were more or less equal in politics, economy and marriage. These gender relations were observed by the Han people, for whom they offered a breath of fresh air. The Han people first rejected but later followed some nomadic customs. During the acceptance process, gender relations loosened somewhat, which led to matrilocality among the Hans during the Jin and Yuan. This showed that Han women regained some social status.

On the other hand, the modernisation of the nomads quickened after they had been influenced by the more advanced Han economy and culture, yet their absorption of the moral principles of the Central Plain tradition tended to become an obstacle to the natural development of their personality, and women were the most pitiful victims. More and more nomadic women followed the moral principles of classical Confucianism and found themselves increasingly lost. Many became men's shadows' who lived or died with their husbands, and whose sole purpose of life was to bring up the children and wait on the parents-in-law. Undoubtedly this dramatically lowered their status in the society.

We may conclude that the conquest and rule of the nomads over the agricultural nation had a complex influence on the relationships between the sexes throughout society. The impact from nomadic culture enabled Han women to regain some status, but for nomadic women, the rules in the Han-inhabited lowered their status. The is quite different from Eisler's conclusion that nomadic invasions of agricultural nations lower the status of all women.

The nomadic invasions analysed in Eisler's work took place between 5,000 BCE and 2,800 BCE. She believes that prior to that time, the agricultural nations were still at the stage of the matrilineal commune, while the nomads, in their early stages, worshipped the blade which was the symbol of masculine power. When they invaded agricultural society, they broke with their blades the chalice which symbolised the femine power of agricultural society.[73] As a matter of fact, what Eisler analysed is the period when patriarchy was taking the place of the matrilineal commune in Europe, and the invasion of the nomads helped complete this process in agricultural areas.

Yet the case in China was quite different. The transition from the matriarchy to patriarchy took place naturally. The nomads had neither the opprtunity nor the strength to invade and rule the Central Plain until the period of the Wei-Jin and in the Liao, Jin and Yuan dynaties when feudal society had developed into its middle stage because the agricultural empires had been solid and powerful. The nomads' conquest over the agricultural empires in China was one in which nations at the early stage of the patriarchy, whose women had a higher status, conquered another whose patriarchy was well developed and whose women had a lower status. That accounted for the fact that there was no general depreciation of women; instead, some women regained their position in the society.

Of course, what was regained was very limited. The patriarchy in the agricultural areas on the Central Plain had endured for 3,000 to 4,000 years, without any trace of the matriarchy remaining, and the increasing suppression of women in traditional Confucianism enhanced the notion of masculine superiority over women which had become fixed among the people of the Central Plain. What the Hans accepted from the nomads were merely the superficial aspects of the forms of marriage. This is best demonstrated by the fact that they accepted the custom of marriage with widows in the clan but never gave women the right to own property. Moreover, in the course of the change of dynasties from Liao to Yuan and Ming, the status of Han women fell lowered again with the spread of Neo-Confucianism, and even nomadic women were increasingly suppressed by feudal moral principles.

(3) The Legitimatisation of Neo-Confucianism and

[73] P. 45.

the Reinforcement of the Notion of Chastity

The Yuan dynasty served as a bridge in the development of ethics in China. At the one end was Yuan culture: the cultures of the Song, the Liao and the Jin blended together, with the Mongol culture serving as a supplement. At the other end was the Idealist School of Song dynasty Confucianism which was introduced to the north and further developed. Zhu Xi's annotated versions of The Four Books became one of the subjects in the Yuan imperial civil service examinations, and "ideas and words not consistent with those teachings will not be passed".[74] Confucianism which had a tradition of more than a thousand years came into its prime. The Yuan prepared the way for the legitimatisation of the Idealist School of Confucianism by the ruling class in the Ming and the Qing when the shackles of feudal morality and ethics were most rigid.

The Idealist School of Confucianism took form during the Northern Song, and was summarised and further developed in the Southern Song by Zhu Xi. The School spread in the north during the reign of Taizong of the Yuan. In the seventh year of Taizong (1235), Zhao Fu, a scholar from Jianghan, was captured and brought to the capital, where the Mongol rulers built the Taiji Academy and required him to deliver lectures. The Idealist School spread rapidly with much support from the subsequent Mongol rulers. The School theorised and systemized the Three Cardinal Guides and Five Constant Virtues in the classics of Confucianism, made them "heavenly principles", and based them on the principle that it is correct to "extinguish human desires with heavenly principles". Inspired by the theory, women of different nationalities followed "the three principles of obedience and the four virtues" which were regarded as "heavenly principles". They made such a great effort to avoid remarrying after widowhood that some even killed themselves to retain their chastity. For example, Zhao Mei's wife Wang lost

---

[74] *Tongzhi Tiaoge*.

her husband when she was young, and was left with no child. Her parents-in-law persuaded her to remarry. She replied, "It is the virtue of a woman to marry only once; besides, my parents-in-law are still alive, how can I leave them?" Later, her parents-in-law forced her to marry one of her late husband's cousins, and she hanged herself when she considered that this was the only way to refuse.

Another example is provided by the wife of Li Shi'an in Chengdu who was widowed at the age of nineteen. Her brother-in-law intended to marry her, but "she refused by cutting off her hair and ears with a knife".[75] In the eyes of women inspired by the Idealist School, the morale and ethics were so sacred and chastity so precious that they would not exchange them for a second marriage even for the purpose of carrying on the family line. Wang Zhen's daughter declared when she refused to be remarried by her husband's relatives after his death, "it is common that a family is poor and has no offspring, yet it is against moral principles for a woman to marry a second time. If I have to, the only thing I can do is to finish my own life".[76]

On such heroines the Yuan emperors conferred honours, and many men of literature wrote articles and poems to spread their fame. Wang Yun wrote a poem in praise of the heroic behaviour of Wang Zhen's daughter and commented in the preface that "it is obligatory for a husband to marry a second wife, yet it is not righteous for a wife to marry a second husband. This is the manifestation of heaven, and the cardinal principle of the ethics of human beings".

The Idealist School of Confucianism became after several generations of Yuan emperors and scholars promoted it. It became a fashion for Han women to remain widows, and increasing numbers of Mongol women were also influenced by these teachings.

---

[75] *Yuan Shi*.

[76] Wang Yun, "Xiaojie Wangshi Shi Juan Xu", *Qiujian Xiansheng Daquan Wenji*, juan 43.

After Zhu Yuanzhang overthrew the Yuan, a small group of aristocrats escaped to the north with Emperor Shundi of the Yuan and maintained their traditional culture while most of the Mongols stayed on the Central Plain and became the subjects of the Ming dynasty. Their descendants gave up the old Mongol customs and assimilated with the Hans. By the Ming and the Qing, the Idealist School almost became the "national religion" observed by all the people in the country, and "women's virtues" centred around the notion of chastity became the moral principles generally observed by the women of the Central Plain. Gender relationships returned to the Central Plain model.

CHAPTER EIGHT
BRIGHTNESS VERSUS DARKNESS: GENDER RELATIONS IN THE MING AND QING DYNASTIES

Zhao Shiyu

I. The Entangled Skein

(1) Confucianism Kills

The goddess of history is sometimes sentimental and sometimes ruthless. As history entered the latter half of the 14th century and Zhu Yuanzhang drove the Mongolian rulers out of the Central Plain and founded the Ming dynasty, the unruly conventions and customs characteristic of the Tang dynasty did not re-appear in Chinese society. Gone were the days when a girl said a man was good and throw herself into his embrace or when women were strong while men were weak, a social convention which the Neo-Confucian Zhu Xi ascribed to barbarian influence: "The Tang dynasty had its sources in foreign tribes, and it is therefore not strange that women were discourteous." Not to mention such outstanding women as the mother of Emperor Sui Wendi, the queen of the grandson of Tang Taizong, Wu Zetian and Princess Taiping. The important position of women, when compared with early period of the Yuan dynasty, when Mongol women set up yurts, collected saddles, droving carts, milked cows, sheared sheep and made clothes, had been greatly weakened.[1] The intervening five hundred years left only a deep impression of women who died to preserve their chastity and of the abnormal psychology of officials concerning women with bound three-inch feet of women.

The goddess of history is sometimes difficult to fathom. The Song dynasty was a period in which Neo-Confucian received its greatest attention. The rites and piety advocated in the age of Confucius and Mencius and the three cardinal guides and five constant virtues established by Confucius' followers in the Han dynasty were further intensified and made more concrete. The Song philosophers Cheng Yi and Cheng Hao urged people "to preserve the ways of the heaven and eliminate the desires of humans", an injunction that was to have dire consequences for gender relations. Cheng Yi maintained that it was a trifle to starve to death when compared with a major matter such as preserving one's chastity.[2] Another Neo-Confucian philosopher Zhu Xi asked women to cover their faces with scarves when going out, thus imposing further restrictions on women's behavior. The Song historian Sima Guang made a clear distinction between roles and functions of the two sexes when he said that "men are in charge of external affairs, while women are charge of internal affairs. Men are not allowed to enter women's private rooms without reason, while women are not allowed to peep into the man's middle chamber without cause". It is well known that the Song dynasty placed many restrictions on gender relations, especially on the "weaker" sex in terms of ethics, theory, and practice. However, a prosperous economy and urban culture also exerted an influence. *Dongjing Menghua Lu* and the painting *Qingming Shanghe Tu* provide lively scenes of commercial and entertainment activities in which women played an active role. Among women of the upper strata were such well-known female writers as Li Qingzhao and Su Xiaomei, who

---

[1] Zhao Hong, *Mengda Beilu* (Records of Mongolian Nationality).
[2] *Er Cheng Yishu* (Books of Cheng Yi and Cheng Hao) Vol. 22

were also much admired by males. Writers such as Yuan Cai, who wrote **Shi Su** (Worldly Conventions), expressed great sympathy for the miserable plight of women at the time and criticized the drawbacks of the traditional marriage.[3] The many rules and conventions first propounded Cheng Zi and Zhu Xi were not necessarily universally acknowledged and practiced, which is understandable.

With the advent of the Ming dynasty, the Confucian doctrine of the Cheng Brothersi and Zhu Xi at last found fertile soil for growth. In view of the active cultural activities in the Song periods and the disorder caused in the Central Plain by the nomadic culture of the Yuan dynasty, the first emperor of the Ming dynasty, Zhu Yuanzhang, stressed the restoration of the cardinal principles and constant virtues. He encouraged scholars to study the writings of Zhu Xi and to propagate no other theories than those of these two philosophers.[4] Official examinations were based on the writings by Zhu Xi, and Emperor Zhu Li continued his father policies and ordered the compilation by a team of high-ranking scholar officials of **Sishu Daquan** (The Complete Four Books), **Wujing Daquan** (The Complete Five Classics) and **Xingli Daquan** (The Complete Collection of Confucian Doctrines), and urged that these teachings be put into action both in the domestic environment and in state affairs. It was a situation in which "anything counter to the theories of Zhu Xi would be attacked," as Zhu Yizun commented in the early Qing.[5]

Against this ideological background, men of letters in the early Ming dynasty made the pursuit of Confucian doctrines their ideal. Men must be clear minded, must not harbour desire, and must conform with their social position. Women should admire those who would rather die than violate their virtues,

---

[3] See **History of Chinese Women**, Chinese Translation, p. 62, Sanqin Publishing House, 1987

[4] Chen Ding, **Dong Lin Lie Zhuan** (Biographies of Rulers), Vol. 2.

[5] **Dao Zhuan Lu Xu** (Preface to Book of Taoism).

and the emphasis was on only ever having one husband. The noted writers Song Lian and Fang Xiaoru at the beginning of the Ming dynasty wrote in praise about some women who died for their dead husbands or about pious mothers. A woman in Kunshan near Suzhou, called Li Hui, refused to remarry despite the advice of many people. She was commended highly by Emperor Taizu. It was estimated that there were more than 10,000 widows who have left their names in the annals of the Ming dynasty history for dying to preserve their chastity, including more than 300 who became prominent famous. However, the actual figures must have been much higher. According to the statistics calculated by Tang Lixing, in Hexien county, Anhui province, alone, there were 8,606 women who were held up as examples for their deaths designed to preserve their chastity in the Ming and Qing dynasties (up to the reign of the Xianfeng Emperor). Of this, the number of such women in the Qing dynasty was ten times higher than the Ming period.[6]

To what extent were gender relations distorted during the Qing dynasty? The period from the Kangxi to the Qianlong emperors was the heyday of the Qing empire. Like the Ming dynasty in its early period, the Qing very much admired the Confucian doctrines developed by Cheng Yi and Zhu Xi. The Kangxi Emperor personally wrote a preface for *Zhuzi Quanshu* (The Complete Works of Zhu Xi), saying that Zhu Xi propounded uprightness under heaven and the way of the universe. He maintained that Zhu Xi made the biggest contribution to Confucian doctrine after Confucius and Mencius themselves.[7] He hated "false Confucians" and sponsored a debate between true and false Confucians. He went in person to Qufu to pay homage at the temple of Confucius and conferred the title of Upholder of Confucianism on some officials. "To govern the

---

[6] **Merchants and Modern Cinese Society**, p. 154, Zhejiang People's Publishing House, 1993

[7] *Qing Shengzu Shilu* (Factual Records of Qing Emperors), Bol. 249, the first month of the 51st year of the reign of Kang Xi

country, it is of major importance to set the customs and conventions right; to straighten out the ideas of the people, it is important to observe customs and conventions, and to propoagate the Confucian classics."[8] The court would frequently issue decrees commending women for chaste behaviour.[9] Commemorative archways were also erected for chaste women and niches were set aside in family temples to honour such female moral exemplars. Even in family history, much space was devoted to the deeds of these women. According to statistics, it was only after the reign of Kangxi that the number of women who died to preserve their chastity increased sharply. Even during the late Qing when the dynasty was on the decline and persons of insight began to criticize the inequality between men and women, such women appeared in their tens of thousands. In war-ridden modern times, large numbers of women have committed suicide to preserve their chastity. Numerous cases can be found in *Qingbai Leichao* (Record of Social Conventions in the Qing Dynasty). The family of Wang Dingzhi, friend of the noted scholar Yu Yue, boasted four chaste women. But the most illustrative story of chaste martyrdom might be that told in *Rulin Waishi* (The Scholars).[10]

Once there was scholar named Wang Yuhui, who had been a student for more than thirty years. His daughter wanted to commit suicide because her husband died. Her father-in-law and daughter-in-law stopped her, saying that even ants want to live on no matter what the circumstances. But her father Wang Yuhui said: "How can I stop you doing so, since you have chosen to die and that would be something which would go down in the records. Just you go and do it. I will return home right away and ask you mother to say farewell to you". A few

---

[8] Ibid, p.258, the fourth month of the fourth month of the 53rd year of the reign of Kang Xi.

[9] Wang Lin, *Ming Ji Ji Lue* (Outline History of Ming Dynasty, Bol. 14

[10] Chapter 48.

days later, the news that her daughter had died caused the mother to cry so much that she collapsed. Wang Yuhui, however, burst out laughing. "Well done, well done," he exclaimed. But when he went to Suzhou on a sightseeing trip, the memory of his daughter came into his mind when he gazed at the beautiful landscapes. When he saw so many young women in white, he thought of his daughter again and felt so sorry that the tears rolled down his cheeks.

(2) A Faint Light of Brightness

The above story not only reflects the cruelty of the murderous Confucian doctrines in the Qing dynasty, but also the impotence of human nature in the face of moral pressure. Through this incident the author Wu Jingzi was delivering an attack on the realities brought about by Confucian doctrine. Human nature and true feelings can never be totally suppressed or eliminated. Perhaps, even the traditional Confucian doctrines had a veneer of toughness concealing notions of human nature and true feelings.In the late Ming dynasty, the unorthodox thinker Li Zhi was nicknamed a "good women" and a "true man". He maintained that "women with exceptional talents were far superior to men", and cited Cai Wenji and Wang Zhaojun, whom he described as "true men". Such a superficial confusion of sexes perhaps reveals a fundamental understanding of the equality of man and woman.[11] In his set of three collections of short stories titled **Sanyan**, Feng Menglong presented many distinct and vivid images of women. He also collected and compiled folk songs with love as their theme. In the preface to his **Qing Shi** (Histories of Love), he wrote: "The Six [Confucian] Classics teach people by evoking their feelings. **Yi Jing** respects women. **Shi Jing** opens with a poem about love. **Shu Jing** devoted space to the history of a bridesmaid. **Li Ji** clarifies the distinction between normal marriage and elopement. **Chunqiu**

---

[11] See Li Zhi's **Chu Tan Ji** (Miscellaneous Thoughts).

describes in detail the relations between Ji and Jiang families. Surely this is because all feelings derive from the relations between men and women?" He extracted "feeling" from the Six Classics with all the enthusiasm of a Taoist. Had he restored the original features of the classics or was he indulging in well-sustained satire?

Xie Zhaozhi was even bolder. He advocated that, "There is only one father but all men may be a husband". In other words, one has no choice of a father, but a husband may be chosen and there is no need to commit suicide after a husband dies. Not only can a husband choose a wife, but a wife can also choose a husband. He suggested that the biographies of women of virtue should include talented women and their literary pieces.[12]

With the Qing dynasty, anti-asceticism began to grow. Dai Zhen declared that the Song dynasty killed people with Confucianism. Mao Qiling wrote an obituary for a girl who had died because she had been confined in the home, and he criticized the phenomenon of an unmarried girl dying to defend her chastity for her husband to-be. In his **Yuewei Caotang Biji** (Jottings of Yuewei Hut), Ji Xiaolan wrote: "Food and sexual relations are the major desires in human life.... If a man or a girl is infatuated with love and has a lover in his or her heart, it does not violate the doctrines of Rites and it should not tax them theoretically". The scholars Wang Zhong and Qian Dayi raised objections to the relations and position of women in the family and society.

Many novels appeared in the Qing dynasty treating gender relations. Among the most famous was **Honglou Meng** (Dream of Red Mansions) which was sympathetic towards females and **Nuxian Waishi** (History of Women Immortals) which portrays female courage. Li Ruzhen's **Jinghua Yuan** (Flowers in the Mirror) has been described by the 20th century scholar Hu Shi termed as "deserving a glorious position in the history of the

---

[12] Wu Za Zu (Five Major Topics), Vol. 8, Part 4, "human"

rights of Chinese women". Perhaps, the more seriously the relations between men and women were distorted by the traditional system, the more violent the reaction and discontent.

In practice, the attitudes towards gender relations in the Qing were not the same as in the Ming dynasty. In terms of social strata, the controls over women of the upper strata were tighter, but not absolute. Although women were said to have been confined to their homes and there should be no physical contact between a man and a women, except a man and wife, it is not uncommon for laboring women to show up in public and take a man's place in order to eke out a living. Even women of the middle and lower classes had many opportunities to go out, such as during festivals. Individual or organized participation in religious activities and competitions became legitimate social intercourse. There are a great differences from region to region as China is a vast country. Due to historical and traditional forces, the relations between men and women in different regions were quite different.

According to some scholars, the rural society in the Lingnan area was not androcentric. Moreover, in ethnic terms, the Qing was an empire founded by the Manchus. Manchu women did not bind their feet, could go out freely and could even visit theatres and tea houses. When in the 18th century, the British envoy Lord Macartney came to China, he and his colleagues walked the streets of Beijing and were surrounded by women, who exchanged greetings with them and looked them up and down to see what fabrics they wore. Their men folk were also present and showed no anger or jealousy. Such exceptional instances are too numerous to list here, but they present a sharp contrast to the cases of tight control over women.

Here, we can discern two interwoven themes. One is the utter distortion of gender sexual relations and the unrivaled oppression of women. The other is the rising call for the emancipation of women in society, based on an insistence that normal sexual relations are not unnatural. How do we explain this social contradictions?

2. The Cells of Society

(1) The Family: The Dominant Male and Filial Piety

It seems to be an established practice to call families the cells of society. Although it is a correct concept in the restrictive sense, as our colleagues correctly pointed out in their study of the history of family in Europe,[13] we can still use it, because it is a good starting point in analyzing the relations between men and women.

The patriarchal system bonded by blood relations was established in the Western Zhou period, but as some scholars point out the blood relations that maintained the clans were not destroyed when China entered civilised society. "The basic organisational form in agricultural production remained the rural commune which was bonded by blood relations". The patriarchal system of the Western Zhou period was the combination of such primitive blood relations and social classes, with the former intensified by the latter. "In the long course of history, ... the patriarchal system and its vestiges and variations maintained by blood relations have long been retained". The manifestation was the reinforcement of such concepts as the family and family clan and the paternal line principle that was associated with them.[14] This is one of the features of Chinese society that is quite different from Western society and it is this feature that determines the differences in the relations between men and women in the traditional societies of China and the West.

According to the family ethics discussed in this book, the

---

[13] **History of Family in Europe**, Chinese Version, p.4, Huaxia Publishing House, 1987

[14] Feng Tianyu, **History of the Chinese Culture**, pp. 190-290, Shanghai People's Publshing House, 1990

male head of a family enjoyed supreme authority no matter whether we are looking at a nuclear family of two generations or big families with several generations living together or even at a family clan during the Ming and Qing dynasties. This is not simply the result of ethical injunctions and principles. Another important reason is that the male head of a family is responsible for feeding the whole family. In a large family clan, the male head of the clan has even greater authority. He was usually the oldest person of the clan elected according to the principle of blood relations, or was the most reputed gentlemen of the clan. He had the power to rule in internal disputes, was repsonsible for the management and distribution of the shared property, dealt with other family clans and punished those who violated the family clan rules. In a smaller family, as the man shouldered the greater responsibility of supporting his family, his position and authority in the family can be regarded as compensation for his responsibilities. In many families of three or more genera-tions, as the grandfather or great-grandfather retired from the activities of supporting the families and passed the reins on to his sons, their authorities would be lost, even though they were still respected. Those who were responsible for the family's internal and external affairs were the husbands and wives of the next generation. A typical example is the Rong and Ning families described in the classical novel *Honglou Meng*, which showed the positive correlation between authority and the re-sponsibility of supporting the family. Their family position as male head remained by and large the same as in the former generation.

For children, the family position of their mother is obvious and there is no respect for a father who looks down upon their mother. "A strict father but a kind mother" has been a long-standing saying in China. In a family, the children are required to be reverential to both parents. The first emperor of the Ming dynasty once stated: "It is necessary for children to be pious to their parents because they can never return what they have got from their parents. There are no wrong fathers or mothers. All their words and actions must be followed and there should be not the slightest violation. That is filial piety". History books record many instances in which pious sons unstintingly removed organs to save their mothers' lives, and in novels, people beg for their lives usually on the pretext that they still have old mothers at home. The position of the mother next to the head of the household underscores the irreplaceable role of the mother in the family. By managing domestic affairs, women are responsible for the direction the family takes, whether it is the education of the children, the household chores, or production activities. The important position of Sister Feng and the Grandma in *Honglou Meng* is obvious.

The aspirations of a daughter-in-law to become the mother-in-law also indicate the importance of the female family head. According to some scholars, a female family head can even maintain a whole family clan. In Tongtou village in Pucheng county, Fujian province, the Zou family, consisting of five generations and nearly 100 family members, was maintained by a woman family head. Although the older generations managed to old them together, there were growing voices for a split from the grandsons and granddaughters. When the last fe,ale family head died, the family divided into a number of smaller families.[15]

It can be said that the inequality between men and women is more obvious among people of the same generation. The male sons, irrespective of their age, must be subordinate to their father. The mother-in-law may treat the daughter-in-law as a beast of burden. So, among "the three obediences", women were required to obey their fathers before marriage which applied equally to their male counterparts. When it was said that a

---

[15] Chen Zhiping and Cheng Zhenman, "Investigation Report of the Family of Five Generations in the Tongtou Village in Pucheng", carried in **The Society and Rural Economy in Fujian during the Ming and Qing Dynasties**, Xiamen University Press, 1987

woman was required to obey her sons in widowhood it did not mean that her position fell below that of her sons. On the contrary, it meant that they must defend her chastity and help bring up the children. Only the principle of obeying her husband during her married life showed inequality. Such an inequality among people of the same generation begins at birth. In rural China, people call the birth of a son the acquisition of "jade" while the birth of a daughter is getting a "tile". There were also the saying that "a son is a pile of firewood while a daughter is a monetary loss". A daughter is also said to bring harm for three generations.[16]

The custom of female infanticide was therefore common. In Gutian, Fujian province, a family had to "drown the daughter" as it required a huge sum to marry her[17] drowning of female infants child in Fuqing was endemic.[18] In the late Qing period, the instances of drowning female infants increased.[19] **The Annals of Huaxian County** record that the drowning of female infants was prevalent several decades ago but the situation was later eased by making girls child brides.

Such a preference for boys rather than girls became an established idea, an ideological "Einstellung" (mind set) that became part of daily life. For instance, women in Beijing used to have the habit of "feeling the nails" at the Qianmen Gate around the 15th of the first month of the lunar calendar to beg for a birth of a son. In Dapu, Guangdong province, a bamboo pen chip would be used to cut the umbiliacal cord of a son, but a bamboo bellows chip would be used to cut a girl's, indicating that the son would go to school while a girl would only stay at home and cook.

Women used to receive little education before marriage.

---

16 **Annals of Xinhe County**, the Republic of china period.

17 Chen Shengshao, *Wensulu* (Records of Social Conventions), Vol. 2.

18 Zheng Guangce, *Xi Xia Wen Chao*.

19 *Annals of Gaochun County*, the Republic of China period, Vol. 3.

Only girls born in families of the upper strata could receive some education in literature, such as Lin Daiyu in *Honglou Meng*. The collection of poems written by women compiled during the Jiaqing reign of the Qing dynasty contained 375 poems written by women poets and that was a big figure, but meager among a female population of 200 million at that time. Even those people who advocated an education for girls usually had in mind a version of *The Four Books* written especially for women. In the family rules of Yun Chenglin, a local official in Fujian, "girls of over ten years of age are not allowed to return to their mother's home. From the very start, they should not be taught mathematics or writing. What they should be taught is to recite *Xiao Jing*, biographies of chaste women, and all matters concerning weaving, sewing, family affairs, the raising of silk-worms and the making of clothes. If they violate the rules, the mother will be held responsible".[20] In *Nuxian Waishi* we read how the female protagonist Tang Sai read books when young, but not books by Song Confucians. She mocked women who stuck by the rules and wrote martial poems, containing no trace of the temperament of the "weaker" sex. As a result, she was criticized by her relatives, who advised her to "take the four virtues (fidelity, physical charm, propriety in speech and efficiency in needlework) as the main guides and not to play with words, and even less such harsh words". Generally speaking, a woman's education before marriage concerned women's behaviour. This idea was widely accepted by women. On the seventh day of the seventh month of the lunar calendar, women used to pray for homecraft skills. They would try to thread needles in the moonlight or throw needles into bowls of water to see how well their future needle work would be and whether they would be liked by their mother-in-laws. If the results were not satisfactory, it caused great distress.

---

[20] Chen Zhiping, **Family Clan Society and Culture in Fujian over the Past 500 Years**, p. 214, Shanghai Sanlian Bookstore, 1991.

Theoretically, men and women were not allowed to have physical contact except as man and wife, and free physical contact between men and women before marriage was not permitted, even among the male and female members of the same family. However, such rules were impractical even in the Ming and Qing dynasties. There were many exchanges between men and women, and there was no absolute ban on of male and female members of a family mingling. We read of family intimacy in such novels as *Nuxian Waishi* and *Xingshi Yinyun Zhuan*.

(2) The Relations between Husband and Wife and among Other Male and Female Members of a Family

Generally speaking, it was a cardinal principle that a wife obey her husband, is a fact. But on the other hand, it is also advocated by tradition that a husband and wife respect each other. Serious inequality between husband and wife often occurred in families of the upper strata in which one man usually had more than one wife. It also happened in extraordinarily poor families where female infants were drowned and husbands often beat their wives. Family violence was obviously rather common and it was one of the manifestations of strained family relations. Apart from such factors as the husband's external work not proceeding well and the family financial situation being poor, one of the important reasons was the arranged marriage in which the husband and wife could not get on with each other so well from the very beginning.

Another factor causing family violence was extra-marriage love affairs. The novel *Xingshi Yinyuan Zhuan* described in Chapter 19 how Xiao Ya killed his wife and another man Zhao Dashe when he caught them sleeping in bed. The classic novels *Shuihu Zhuan* (All Men Are Brothers) and *Jinping Mei* (Golden Lotus) all described the conflicts resulting from the illicit affairs between Wu Dalang's wife Pan Jinlian and Ximen Qing and how the two collaborated and killed Wu Dalang. There were many such cases in Ming and Qing fiction.

One thing that is not to be ignored is that many cases of family violence were the result of an extremely abnormal psychological state. In his book *Youtianxian-guan Biji*, Yu Yue records how a man named Wang Cheng whipped his wife while joking and suddenly stopped, and violently kissed her, but a moment later, whipped her again and the two had to part company after his mother failed in her attempts at mediation.[21] The novel *Xingshi Yinyuan Zhuan* describes how Xue Sujie maltreated her husband. "A sweeping slap fell on the face of Di Xichen, with a sound so loud that people outside the room thought it was a thunder clap and looked up. ... Sujie gave him two successive slaps, cursing: 'I'll kill you bastard....'" (Chapter 56). Such family violence is not all attributed to social factors.

The scholar Murray A. Strauss made a study of family violence in different cultures and summed up six factors contributing to family violence. They are the duration of family members getting together, the number of activities for common participation and the kind of interests they share, the intensity of centrifugal force, the degree of equality between the two sexes, the degree of privatisation of family property and the degree of social violence.[22] According to these six standards, the amount of violence in pre-modern times was greater than in the modern times and more in times of social upheaval than in times of social stability. This was why there was less family violence during the Ming and Qing dynasties than in preceding dynasties. Of course, the question requires further study.

The relations among family members other than husband and wife demonstrate another feature. There is usually no direct conflict between father and daughter, father-in-law and

---

[21] Peng Wei, **Another World**, Shaanxi People's Publishing House, 1993

[22] Mark Holt, **Changing Families—Transcultural Perspective**, Chinese version, pp. 327-329. Zhejiang People's Publishing House, 1988

daughter-in-law, daughter-in-law and younger brother, and between brothers and sisters. On the contrary, friction and quarrels often occur among female members of the family, such as mother-in-law and daughter-in-law, daughter-in-law and husband's sister, and between daughters-in-law. There is a Chinese saying that, "The old road eventually becomes a river, and a daughter-in-law eventually becomes a mother-in-law". This stresses the displacement of roles in families. It is also rather common for friction to occur between the daughter-in-law and her husband's sister. Such contradictions are very complicated, but I think they reflect the traditional relationship between the sexes. The contradictions between mother-in-law and daughter-in-law involve such psychological factors as the allegainces to son or husband and also the potential power struggle in the family. The contradictions between a married daughter and her brother's wife are the result of the concept that "a married girl is like water poured out", indicating the discrimination against a daughter.

(3) Marriage and Sex

Marriage was guided by the idea that "upon growing up, every male should take a wife and every female should take a husband" and that "it is the mandate of the parents and the words of a matchmaker". But sexual behavior still remained unfathomable. There were also something new. In selecting spouses, male enjoy greater freedom than females. Ximen Qing in the novel *Jinping Mei* is a wastrel with several wives and concubines. Doctor Jiang Zhushan takes advantage of treating a widow patient Li Ping'er to tell her that Ximen Qing would like to marry her. (Chapter 17). Operas such as *Xixiang Ji* (Romance of the Western Chamber) and *Mudan Ting* (Peony Pavilion) all sing the praises of love at first sight and the pursuit of independence in marriage. Such collections of novels as *San Yan* and *Er Pai* advocate that in choosing a spouse, the utmost standard is integrity. A casual attitude is condemned. Feng

Menglong's compiled love songs are even bolder and more open, voicing such determination as "there would be no way of separation unless the heaven is turned into earth."[23] Characters in **Nuxian Waishi** proclaim such ideas as "women should use wisdom to ride over their husbands and manipulate emperors or kings". It criticizes the women in **Mudan Ting** who fell into lovesickness from a dream, saying that such women are useless.

Two stories in the Qing dynasty are also very much illustrative of the changes in concepts. One is about a charming young man in Foshan, Guangdong province. He often attends masked dancing parties and puts on an oyster mask. In Chen village, there is a pretty woman whose husband has just died. Although her mother-in-law orders her to defend her chastity, she is thinking of remarriage. One day, while she was talking with a neighbor, a young man passes by. The two fell in love at first sight. The neighbor sees this and offers to act as a matchmaker. Three days later, the two get married. At the wedding ceremony, when all friends and relatives are present, an old woman appears and flings mud at the grrom. It transpires that she was the young woman's mother-in-law. Toung man announces: "We have a matchmaker. She wants to marry me and I want to marry her. What is wrong? I'm not afraid of you even in court. The old woman is speechless, but accepts some money and goes away. The couple was regarded as a perfect match.

Another story relates how a young man is engaged to a girl.They have a pre-marital affair and she becomes pregnant. The man is frightened away and his parents are forced to look after the girl. When the baby grows up and marries, the man returns and finally marries the mother of his child.[24]

Of course, freedom in love and freedom in marriage did not become the mainstream at that time nor did freedom in sexual

---

[23] Feng Menglong, **Shange, Fenli** (Mountain Songs, Separation).
[24] Ling Li, **Life and Death, Food and Drink, Men and Women: Local Customs of the Qing Dynasty**, pp.155-156, Chinese People's University Press, 1990

behavior. During the Qing dynasty, it was said that when a girl accidentally saw a man passing water down the side of a building, she felt so ashamed that she committed suicide. Chapter 37 of the novel *Xingshi Yinyuan Zhuan* describes a man name Di Xichen who was passing water in a garden when he was seen by a young girl. He was so frightened that he held back half way and ran away, feeling ashamed. He then told his friend that he was afraid that if the young girl told her mother he might have been beaten up or even taken to court. This shows that even men had the same feelings as women at that time.

But the restrictions on sexual behaviour in the late Qing period were somewhat relaxed. Apart from the appearance of a host of novels such as *Jinping Mei*, *Xiuta Yeshi* and *Roupu Tuan* which are filled with descriptive scenes of sexual intercourse, legends and historical anecdotes also included similar descriptions. Pornographic paintings, sexual devices and drugs for stimulating sexual desires filled the market at the time. All strata of society were interested in this fashion, but this does not necessarily demonstrate that men and women enjoyed sexual intercourse equally. It tends to suggest that women were only the play things of men.

The male appreciation of bound feet in the Ming and Qing dynasties suggests the same thing. Pan Jinlian in the novel *Jinping Mei* is noted for her small feet, and the nine standards for beautiful women laid down by Li Liweng at the beginning of the Qing dynasty included bound feet. A book was even devoted to descriptions of bound feet. Gu who was acquainted with Western learning was even of the opinion that "The beauty of Chinese women lies in the bonded feet. After the feet are bound, the blood goes up and the thighs and hips become bigger naturally, thus creating a willowy figure."[25] This explains the distorted aesthetics.

Although sexual desire was openly expressed in the Ming

---

[25] Zhou Zuoren, "On Bound Feet" of **On Tiger**.

and Qing dynasties, it still reflected the inequality in sexual roles. But the changes in social conventions would inevitably stimulate the sexual desires of women that had long been suppressed and unsatisfied. In *Qing Shi*, Feng Menglong includes the following anecdote: "Once there was a woman who was widowed and had preserved her chastity until she was more than eighty. On the verge of dying, she told her daughters-in-law: 'Now I have come to realise that remaining chaste is not easy. When a woman is widowed young, she should remarry. Do not try to preserve chastity'. She then extended her left hand to show a big scar on it, saying that the scar was the result of plunging her hand in a barrel of molten wax to suppress her sexual urges one mid-night. She had never told anybody about this before."

Some women who could not bear the loneliness sought physical contact with men, and it was almost certain that their first encounter would result in an affair. The myth of the Wutong Deity, a belief very common in southern China from the Song to the Qing dynasties, is very illustrative. The Wutong was a deity that could incarnate as a young man who would have sexual intercourse with young women, leading to spiritual breakdown and even death. It was said that if the young women refused, the deity would strip the woman's house bare. At the beginning of the Qing dynasty, Tang Bin destroyed the local Wutong temple, but the common people still believed in the spirit. The existence of Wutong is of course absurd, but the tale sheds light on the spiritual breakdown or illusion caused when the sexual urge was suppressed or overexcited during illicit sexual intercourse.

In general, men had greater initiative than women in sexual behavior. Apart from family life, men could also visit prostitutes. In the novel *Xingshi Yinyuan Zhuan*, Di Xichen is no libertine, but his first sexual experience was with a prostitute. The same book describes how widow Sun Shi has had affairs with men and how her elder daughter also has love affairs with men. When her daughter gets married and it is discovered she is not a virgin, she receives a good beating and is sent back home. Sun Shi verbally abuses him, but the neighbours all rebuke her. "Brother Wei is a good man, hoping to marry a wife who will take a good care of his mother and give birth to sons and daughters. But it turns out that he married a woman like you." Men and women were obviously extremely unequal in terms of whether or not virginity was preserved before marriage

3. General Division of Labor: Relations between Men and Women and Their Social Roles

(1) "Men till, women weave"

The differences in the social roles of men and women or the gender division of labour in social production appeared much earlier than the family roles or the family division of labour. According to archaeological data, historical documents, and modern anthropology, hunting in primitive society was mainly undertaken by men while women were responsible for collecting plants and other food. Later when primitive farming appeared, men played an increasingly important role in daily production. Apart from raising children, women devoted more of their time to household labor, thus leading to the model that prescribed that "men are responsible for external affairs while women, internal affairs." Since the period of the Warring States, the individual household-based production model was basically fixed. As **Lüshi Chunqiu** states: "When a farmer stops farming, people will starve; when a woman stops weaving, people will suffer from cold". Women had an irreplaceable role to play in family production and even in social production.

The book **Changing Families** mentioned above quotes such sociologists as Philippe Aries, Edward Short, Alice Clark, Ann Oakley and E.P. Thompson, saying that family used to be a production unit in the pre-industrial revolution period in Europe. There were not much difference between men, women or children when they were working in the fields. Social life featured close cooperation between husband and wife in family as well as economic life. Women not only participated in the basic economic activities in the home but also took care of the family affairs and children. "Tradition handed down the power to rule a family to the husband, ..., but the power of the husband was restricted due to the importance of women and children in production. Although the majority of wives were subject to beating and abuse, the economic superiority of the husband could in no way totally negate the economic contributions of the wife." In the early industrial revolution period, the production function of the family died out. "For men, this means that they have entered a broader market of jobs while for women, it means that they have to be confined to the home." Becoming housewives marked the start of the inequality between men and women in the modern sense.[26] The above conclusions aside, the description of the economic functions and associated positions of women in Europe in the pre-industrial revolution period is rather similar to that in China during the Ming and Qing dynasties. Although women played an important role in family-based production activities, that in no way changed their subordinate positions at home and in society. But the more important such a role, the more favorable for women to change their subordinate positions and that is beyond question. We know that during the Ming and Qing dynasties, the family textile industry was playing an increasingly important role in society. In Qingping county, Shandong, it was recorded, "women were mainly engaged in textiles, ... they either sold or retained the products. The whole family depended on such products for clothing".[27] In Feicheng, it was recorded, "women are industrious in weaving and spinning. The poor ones can support the

---

[26] See **Changing Families**, pp. 200-212.
[27] **Annals of Qingping County: Mineral Resources**.

family while the richer ones can have more than enough"[28] In Songjiang, it was recorded that "the rural textile industry was very flourishing and the products were noted for their workmanship. During slack seasons, the textiles were produced in tens of thousands a daily. Women also contributed to farming".[29] In Baoshan, we read: "Families that tilled the land and wove fabrics could obtain money with fabrics and offset poor harvests, because they could use the money to buy food".[30] There are numerous instances to list here.

All these accounts reflect the fact that, by spinning and weaving fabrics, women could not only meet their needs in clothing, but also ensure food supplies and pay taxes. In some families, the husbands or sons simply waited to sell the cloths their husbands or mothers wove at midnight and exchanged it for some rice for cooking.[31] In some families, even women took the cloth they wove to the market in the morning to exchange for cotton and then took the thread they span back to the market to sell. According to one account, they never rest and a weaver can make one bolt of cloth a day. Moreover, some people even work all night.[32] This shows that women not only created value but were also out to realize the value of their labour.

According to statistics, during the Ming and Qing periods, about one third of counties or prefectures did not have any family textile industry and the proportion was larger in the Ming dynasty than in the Qing period. People in these areas, due to natural conditions or tradition, did not know how to grow cotton. There were some families that grew cotton but did not practise weaving. In other words, only men tilled the land

---

[28] **Annals of Feicheng County: Local Customs and Conventions.**
[29] **Annals of Songjiang: Local Customs and Conventions.**
[30] **Annals of Baoshan County: Local Customs and Conventions.**
[31] Chang Chunhua, *Hu Cheng Sui Shi: Quge* (Annecdotes in Shanghai).
[32] Zheng De, **Annals of Songjiang: Local Customs and Conventions.**

while women did not engage in weaving. This shows exactly the flow of commodities from the family to market. and the flow of the family handicraft products. On the other hand, it shows that in these areas women of poor families were mostly working together with men.[33] In Fengyang, for instance, it was recorded that "women often worked together with men in miscellaneous jobs".[34] This can be proven by a British diplomatic eyewitness who observed: "Along the way, we saw women sitting in door-wayswith their spinning wheels and ohers working in the fields, harvesting." "Women in the northern part of the country worked in the fields all day long, doing the same kind of rough jogs as their men folk". And, in Jiangxi, "we saw a farmer put one hand to the plough and use the other to toss the seeds while his wife was pulling the plough just like a beast of burden."[35] In many places, women engaged in more than one production activity. In Suzhou, for instance, "people are very industrious. Apart from farming and fishing, men and women work together to process hemp for making caps, to weave cloth, to quarry stones and to make utensils."[36] In Songjiang, "all men and women had made a living by weaving socks since the reign of Wanli of the Ming dynasty and they derive their income from shops".[37] In Taicang, "people in Xijing Town make straw shoes. All the towns folk work day and night, weaving shoes"[38] Women in Huitong county "help their husbands tea picking or collecting tung oil."[39] The women in Xianxian "often weave wheat stalks into hats outside their houses or in the shadow of trees".[40] Women, therefore, just like their husbands, became handicraft

[33] **Annals of Fengxian: Local Customs and Conventions**.
[34] **Annals of Fengtai County: Local Customs and Conventions**.
[35] **Factual Record of the Audience of Emperor Qianlong to British Envoy**, Chinese version, Commercial Press, 1963.
[36] Zhang De, **Annals of Suzhou: Local Customs and Conventions**.
[37] Fan Lian, *Yun Jian Ju Mu Chao*, Vol. 2.
[38] **Annals of Taicang**, Vol. 5
[39] **Annals of Huitong County: Local Customs and Conventions**.
[40] **Annals of Xianxian**.

manufacturers by engaging in various kinds of sideline industries for a living.[41]

Some have scholars correctly pointed out that the traditional division of labor with men tilling the land and women doing the weaving reflected the economic relations combining main economic undertakings with sideline industriess, as reflected in the aid to farming provided by weaving. But in some places, there was not much differentiation with both men and women engaged in growing cotton, or weaving cloth or doing other types of work. They simply worked together, and there was no sideline production to speak of.[42] In such circumstances, when men and women were basically equally engaged in family or social production and in creating wealth and making a living, the social position of women was likely to be improved. We may cite some special cases, such as those "merchant women" mentioned by Tang Lixing in his books. These women were often born into families of business people. They not only brought with them a large dowry and so provided their husbands with commercial capital, but they also helped their husbands pioneer or maintain their businesses. They even had a direct hand in the business operations. In the Qing dynasty, after Wang Shigong, one of the eight biggest salt dealers died, "his wife took up the responsibility for domestic affairs and the business". She was admired by the Qianlong Emperor when she had an impromptu audience with him.[43] This would inevitably lead to the changes in the mind set and behaviour of women. In his *Wuza Ju*, Xie Zhaozhi said that jealous women were everywhere in Xin'an and Pucheng. The reason was that they used to be very poor and the wives were greatly restricted by the husbands. But once they emerged from poverty, they would refuse to be restricted;

[41] Zheng Changgan, **Rural Commodity Economy in Ming and Qing Dynasties**, Chinese People's University Press, 1989

[42] Chen Xuewen, **Commodity Economy in the Late Feudalistic Eriod in China**, p. 53, Hunan People's Publishing House, 1989.

[43]**Qing Bai Lei Chao: Luxuries.**

money had great power or the power fell into the hands of the wife, decision making no longer being in the husband's hands. After the economic position of women rose, they naturally could not bear to see themselves restricted and hoped to improve their position in the family and society. They were therefore called jealous women. At the time, they could break the bonds imposed by Confucianism on their words and actions. For instance, some women, after marriage, "went their own way and often mocked their husbands for their poverty". "They never respected their fathers-in-law, got on well with their sisters-in-law or respected their friends and distributed gifts to those they liked".

Well, then, are these instances contradictory with what we described of women trying to defend their chastity after their husbands died in the Huizhou area during the Qing dynasty? I think, on the one hand, there was only a tiny minority of women who dared to challenge traditional doctrines, and there would be many more such instances during the times of social upheaval as in the mid Ming and Qing dynasties. On the other hand, there were so many instances of women defending their chastity in the Huizhou area showing that it was very common antagonistic behavior or that there were so many business people not doing business, that preserving chastity was advocated in order to keep wives in line. Such instances reflect the fierce struggle between progress and reaction in pre-modern times.

4. Seeking More Space

(1) The Conflict between the Pressures of the Confucian Doctrine and Intrinsic Desires

"Men are responsible for external affairs while women are responsible for internal affairs". This was the model norm defining the roles of men and women in family and society. Although, by tradition, external activities were also not encouraged as reflected in various sayings, men were still endowed with the responsibility of supporting the family. But for women, they were strictly limited to their rooms. It seemed that all social intercourse and outdoor activities by women were banned. Women could contact no other males except their husbands or a few male family members while men could not contact other females except their wives or prostitutes. During the Ming and Qing dynasties, there were many restrictions on the movement of women, especially women of the upper society. When the members of the British missions to China went sightseeing at the West Lake in Hangzhou in the middle period of the Qing dynasty, they found that all the people on the lake were men. "Women did not show up on such occasions." Women of the lower strata, however, had greater freedom, but not without any restrictions. The British envoy said that rural women "went out of their homes to see foreigners out of curiosity, but they were immediately called back by the men of their families, as if afraid of their being seen by barbarians".[44]

Things were not quite so absolute. The facts about shared field labor by men and women already placed them in social intercourse. Their curiosity as mentioned above also drove them into the outside world. As the British envoy recorded, "women appeared both shy and curious. They peeped from doorways or climbed walls to steal a look at us. Some bolder grandmothers even ran up to the river bank, standing even in water with their small feet in order to see us more clearly. But most young women were peeping us from behind flocks of older women folk." The experience of the British envoys on their way to Peking even led one of them to conclude: There was not much ground for the view that Chinese women were shut up in their houses, not allowed to meet outsiders. Among the people surrounding the caravan of the British mission, at least one quarter

---

[44] **Factual Records of the Audience of Emperor Qianlong to British Envoy**, pp. 457, 425.

were women. Such proportions far exceeded that for similar instances. If we say that one of the characters of European women is curiosity, it is correct. I can, therefore, assert that the characters of liking to see things new as was expressed in their faces that we saw as we were passing by them are equally existent quite universally among Asian women.[45]

It is of course not propret to negate the restrictions upon Chinese women merely by quoting the observations of a foreign traveller. But the strong curiosity of Chinese women he pointed out was a fact, and the more and the longer women were isolated from the outside world, the stronger such curiosity would be. In order to satisfy their curiosity, they had to find a reasonable pretext, a pretext that male members of a family would agree to. That pretext was the participation in activities that were religious in nature.

(2) Religious Activities: A Reasonable Pretext

There were by and large three main kinds of religious activities in the Ming and Qing dynasties and women were active participants. One was activities associated with pure spiritual beliefs such as described in Chapter 39 of *Jinping Mei*. Such activities were first only confined indoors, but gradually spread beyond the home. Here is a description of such activities: "The nuns tried to inspire women with such Buddhist theories as "samsara" (transmigration) and "*yinguo*" (cause and effect), and daily, they were induced out of their homes in the name of saying prayers and listening to the singing of Buddhist sutras and receiving ordination, with monks distributing presents".[46] Even these activities had the nature of sightseeing and entertainment. In the Huaiyang area, there was a "Zhaigong-hui", designed as a "pilgrimage to the deity, but its purpose was

---

[45] Anderson, **Record of Visit to China By British Envoy,** Chinese version, p. 98, Commercial Press, 1963.
[46] **Annals of Huzhou,** Vol. 29.

entertainment".[47] The novel *Xingshi Yinyuan Zhuan* speaks of a Taoist nun advising Xue Sujie to go on a pilgrimage "for the purpose of both accumulating happiness and seeing the sights". "There are many big temples and many exciting scenes along the road, which is filled with pilgrims, men and women, and a lot of good things to see. But it is a pity that the road is not long". (Chapter 68). People of the upper strata were opposed to such customs, saying they caused men and women to mix together".

The second category of religious activities was associated with ritual, such as the Buddhist rites during wedding or funeral ceremonies. In Xinxiang, if a daughter paid for the Buddhist rites at a funeral, "she would place a bundle of flowers on the grave in order to attract people".[48] In Huixian, "only on the day when a baby was born or a person died, would the son lead all men and women of the clan to visit the temple of the tutelary deity".[49] During Qingming festival, "newly married women would don their best clothing to sweep the graves of the dead".[50] Women took advantage of such occasions to breathe fresh air, especially during Qingming when they went out enjoying themselves in the name of remembering the dead.

The third category of religious activities was religious festivals. It was these activities that women attended frequently.- There were a dozen such festivals or celebrations associated with different seasons and there were more than one hundred fixed and popular days of memory. So festivals or celebrations were very frequent in a year. Men and women participated in these activities together and many of them were specially arranged for women. In Xiangfu, Henan province, there was a festival to celebrate the birth of Yue Fei. During the celebrations, "rural girls, with their faces covered with dust and women

---

[47] **Rural Customs in Huaiyang**.
[48] **Annals of Xinxiang County**, the Republic of China period.
[49] **Annals of Huixian County**.
[50] **Annals of Xinzheng County**.

dressed in bright colors, all flocked to the temple".[51] In Liuyang, Hunan province, in the first half of the seventh month, all men and women gathered at the Piety Son Temple nearest the city. "The place was so crowded that some people lost their shoes or hair pins and became a laughing stock".[52] In one place in Shandong, "The third of the third month was a temple fair. There were streams of people and the place was so crowded that men and women mixed together".[53] In Nanhui, Jiangsu province, the 12th day of the 4th month was a day to mark the "birth of Mrs. Bai and all the merchants and peddlers gathered at the temple. There was a theatre in the temple. Women were seated on the seats to watch the play. The sons of rich families were mouthing their loud criticisms".[54] In Changxing, Zhejiang province, at the celebrations marking the birthday of Yue Fei, when "women were sent to the temple of Yue to pay homage and night fell, they would sit on the ground in and outside the temple, in a crowd numbering no less than ten thousand. Some people would fight and some got drunk".[55] At Deqing, Guangdong province, dragon boat races were held on the 2nd day of the 5th month, and "men and women would go to watch, and there were many merchants and peddlers at the gathering".[56]

There were also many religious activities especially for women, such as the greeting of the Zigu Deity and the worship of Goddess Mazu. It is interesting to note that the activities women participated in were all associated with the relationship between men and women. The greeting of the Zigu Deity expressed sympathy for a concubine who was persecuted to death by her husband. The *Qiqiao* (literally, "begging for skills") ceremony was another religious activity for women. It was

[51] **Annals of Xiangfu County.**
[52] **Annals of Liuyang County.**
[53] *Xing Shi Yin Yuan Zhuan*, Chapter 73.
[54] **Annals of Nahui County,** Vol. 20.
[55] **Annals of Huzhou,** Vol. 29.
[56] **Annals of Deqing.**

designed for women who feared being looked down upon by their husband's family. If "their figures were too fat or too thin they were mocked" and "young girls were especially afraid of displaying a lack of skill and they often cried because they were too clumsy.Their mothers had to console them."[57] This reflected great psychological pressures.

Among religious activities, the deities that could ensure that women gave birth to male babies were especially patronised, such as Avalokitesvara, princess Pixia in north China, the Golden Flower Lady in Guangdong, Chen Jinggu in Fujian and Zhejiang, and the Flower Lady in Guangxi. Moreover, each locale had its birth goddess. In Changyang, Hubei province, the third day of the third month of the lunar calendar marked the birth of the matchmaking deity and women desiring to give birth to a son all flocked to a local temple fair for the celebration activities.[58] Another example is the Temple of Mrs. Ma at the foot of the Five Dragon Hill in Suichang, Zhejiang province. It was said that endless streams of women went there to pray for the birth of a son, and there was not a single day without visitors. "People went there to pray for the health of their babies and it was extraordinarily effective."[59] There were also such activities in Qishan, Xiguanshan, and Fengxiang in Shaanxi where people held activities to pray for the birth of sons, especially those infertile women who believed they could get pregnant after the prayer ceremony.[60] All these practices reflect the tremendous pressure on women exerted by the doctrine that, "There are three major offenses against filial piety, (not supporting one's parents when they are alive, not giving them a decent burial upon their death, and not producing an heir), of which the last is the gravest offense".

[57] **Annals of Xingyang County, Annals of Xiangfu County.**
[58] **Annals of Changyang County.**
[59] **Annals of Suichang County.**
[60] Gao Zhanxiang, ed, **On Temple Fair Culture**, pp. 223-232, Culture and Art Publishing House

Of course, these activities provided excellent opportunities for women to mix in society. As recorded in *Jinping Mei*, "Hui Lian went together with the others to participate in the activities associated with the god of healing", and "in the course of this activity, Chen Jingji seduced Jin Lian and other women, and got lost walking with Hui Lian". (Chapter 24). Here, the author saw this walking ceremony as an opportunity to show off one's beauty, and this was the general opinion.

(3) Fallen Blossoms: Male Attitudes

It would be entirely unimaginable for males to ban their women from these activities. In the novel, *Xingshi Yinyuan Zhuan*, when Sujie goes on a pilgrimage, her husband accompanies her all the way. *Jinping Mei* also describes how Zhong Yueniang goes to burn incense to fulfill her vows in the company of his brother and two menservants. *Fengsu Tiaoyue* (The Public Conventions) written by Chen Wengong stated that "it is not strange as the men are their relatives".[61] In his "Tiantai Zhile", the Kangxi Emperor said that "men are not ashamed and women seem to not tire", while "the sons and daughters are not ashamed and their relatives do not blame them". Even "families with a good family education encourage their women to go there".[62] The British envoy to China recorded the following experience in China:

Among the people surrounding us, I saw some women. I boldly tried to approach them and said "Hao" and "Jiao" to a few of them. They seemed so startled that they converged to my side and scrutinized the make and fabric of my clothes in a proper and courteous manner. When my carriage began to move, I shook hands lightly with these courteous women and they reciprocated with very graceful warmth. The men among them did not seem to be offended

---

[61] **Annals of Wuxian County**, Vol. 52, the Republic of China period.
[62] **Annals of Shangshui County**.

by my actions. On the contrary, to my judgment, they were extremely satisfied with the way I treated these ladies. In this city, obviously, women were notdeprived of the freedom due to them.[63]

The author arrived at the following conclusion:That Chinese women were strictly confined to their homes spread by he and other authors does not square with the facts. In vast China, the customs and conventions in various places might be quite different. The authority of the husband over his wife may become the master of the freedom of women and it is perhaps necessary to use such authorities or use them out of uninhibition. But I am not hesitant to say that in usual circumstances, women in China have their reasonable freedom.The exchange or social intercourse with women is regarded as a good thing in social life just as in Europe.[64] This conclusion might helped us to arrive at some new understanding of the social intercourse between men and women during this period.

Nevertheless, women engaging in social intercourse during holiday times was regarded by some officials and gentlemen as "tarnishing customs" and the writers of local histories were also ashamed of such happenings, rather than honoured. The annals of Xinchang County record: "In orthodox families, there were strict rules for women and they were not allowed to see people other than their blood relatives. There were no women strolling on the streets; nor were there women engaged in trading and business". The **Annals of Lishui County** during the reign of the Wanli Emperor of the Ming recorded that "women did not go out of their rooms. Instead, they were confined to their homes, spinning and weaving." The **Aannals of Jintan County** during the reign of Emperor Zhengde said: "Women should be ashamed to venture out of their apartments". The **Annals of Qingpu County** during the reign of the Guangxu Emperor,

---

[63] Chinese version, p. 99.
[64] Chinese version, p. 226-227.

quotes Guo Shixiu as saying that "women are clean and beautiful, knowing how to keep the house and no one of them were think of visiting the mountains or temples" In their annals, the Qianlong and Tongzhi Emperors all recorded that "women would not go on outings during the spring and men do not go out in the second month at the time of the birth of the tutelary deity". These examples show that in certain places and at certain times, taboos were in place, but the tone of these accounts indicates that such opportunities for social intercourse were common.

Based on the above descriptions, I believe there were great discrepancies between regions and social groups regarding the degree of freedom women had to venture out, the contacts possible between men and women, and the frequency of such exchanges. Labouring women clearly enjoyed greater freedom than women of the upper strata; women in places where the commodity economy was developed had more freedom than women in backward areas; Manchu women more freedom than women of the Han nationality; and women in places with special traditions had more freedom than women in other areas. But generally speaking, the opportunities for social intercourse between men and women during the Ming and Qing dynasties were not non-existent as has been often asserted. This tallies with a situation in which the traditional social order was gradually disintegrating and social control was gradually losing its effectiveness.

5. Concluding Remarks

(1) Various Interpretations of Complex Times

People maintain that the Ming and Qing periods were endpoints. For people defending the traditions, there were more and more abnormal things and adversities, but for those opposed to tradition, the old bondages were becoming increasingly intolerable. Disputes were heated on many questions such as women and the relations between men and women.

The disputes concerning women in the late Ming dynasty were focused on the following two points: one was the opposition between sentimental women and chaste women, and the other was the opposition between the talents and wisdom of men and women. A large number of conservative thinkers sang the praises of women defending their chastity and said that it was their unshirkable duty to advocate ethics of women, but a number of other thinkers influenced by the commodity economy broke with traditional feelings and reason, and placed sentiment above reason. They also advocated some measure of equality between men and women in terms of talent and wisdom and struck a contrasting tone in a cultural atmosphere imbued with treating women as inferior to men.[65]

Philosophically, such thinkers as Song Lian, Gao Ming and Qiu Suo advocated traditional values; opposed were philosophers such as Li Zhi and Chen Baisha, and novelists such as Tang Xianzu, Feng Menglong and Ling Mengchu. Lu Kun maintained that Confucian doctrines "were strict with women with regard to defending chastity but too lenient to men who abandoned themselves to carnal desire."[66]

Authors of novels and dramas tended to be progressive as they were closer to the broad masses of the people and their ideas were reflected in their works. The novel *Xingshi Yinyuan Zhuan* which appeared towards the end of the Ming dynasty was a social novel devoted entirely to gender relations within and outside marriage. The author, Xi Zhousheng, basically defended traditional ethics, and he lashed out at women who went on pilgrimages. However, he expressed a reasonable attitude towards women when he wrote: "Whether or not a women tries to defend her chastity after her husband dies entirely depends

---

[65] Chen Baoliang, **Silently Dispersed Cloud**, p. 9, Shaanxi People's Education Publishing House, 1988.

[66] *Shenyinyu* (Groaning), Vol. 2.

on her own heart. If she herself refuses to do so, nobody can obstruct her ... Even if you could restrain her physically, you cannot restrain her thoughts. It is better for her to go her own way". He maintained that if women refused to defend chastity and openly expressed it, "outsiders can only mutter". (Chapter 36). This reveals the general attitude towards remarriage and defending chastity. Although the Ming and Qing did much to extol women who defended their chastity and people usually looked down upon a widow who remarried, such an attitude existed and more and more people came to accept such an attitude. In contrast to the late Ming period, the atmosphere in the cultural and ideological fields at the beginning of the Qing dynasty was dull, mainly because the emperors of the Qing staunchly advocated Confucian doctrines and suppressed rival views. During that period, the rulers intensified education in the cardinal principles and constant virtues through the patriarchal system. All literary works with love as the theme written in the late Ming period were banned. "All people who purchase pornographic novels will be brought to court and punished, with all their books confiscated and burnt."[67]

But, this was the eve of modern times, after all. The progressive trend of the late Ming period left a precious legacy, and the old traditional rites and doctrines began to be attacked. In his Shu Xue, Wang Zhong argued that widows may re-marry. After the husband died, it was not necessary that his wife must also die. Young men and women should be allowed to engage in free social intercourse. In his Collection of Qianyan Tang, Qian Dayi asked: "Haven't the sages gone too far in suppressing women? Formulating principles on the relations between men and women not only serves to protect husbands but also wives. There were women who died of depression because they were not liked by their fathers-in-law or mothers-in-law or were

---

[67] **Daqing Huidian Shili** (Cases of Ceremonies during the Qing Dynasty), Vol. 1039.

talked about by their brothers- and sisters-in-law. Some were driven to suicide because of their husbands' violence, drunkeness or infidelities. According to the ancient rites, although there were rules governing divorce, why should husbands be bound by them and not be happy until they had driven their wives into the grave?" Novels in the Qing dynasty inherited the ideological tradition of those of the late Ming period and developed it. The tragedy described in Honglou Meng went beyond the confines of a love story. Its characters Jia Baoyu and Lin Daiyu were no longer the traditional types of talent and beauty. Jinghua Yuan by Li Ruzhen, set against the background of the reign of Empress Wu Zetian in the Tang dynasty, expressed the author's views on bound feet, chastity, education and participation in political affairs. Of course, the end of the tragedy of the main characters shows the impotent resistance of the young people of the upper strata and the tremendous pressure of the old tradition while the ideals in the novel are but beautiful illusions like flowers in the mirror or the moon on the water that cannot be realized. The struggle between brightness and darkness was by no means confined to the intellectual and ideological fields. The common people also actively fought for their rights in everyday life. They fought for free exchanges, free marriage and equality in family and social life between men and women through all forms of activities. These practices were regarded by the guardians of old tradition as "blemishing customs and conventions" and they called for their prohibition. In the early Qing, Tang Pin advised: "Young women should stay in their rooms, learn to apply cosmetics, remain silent and avoid being seen, not even by relatives of the opposite sex. But in Kaiyuan and other temples, some people incite rural women to gather in their hundreds to watch topless people lighting candles on their shoulders and arms in what is called carnal lighting. Day in, and day out, men and women mingle, thus tarnishing the local customs. This is too immoral to witness. If any girl is found engaging in such activities, her father should be imprisoned; if she is a women, her husband should be imprisoned; and if a monk or Daoist is found to have violated the rules, they should be allowed to live in obscurity. If anybody is reported for his or her misbehaviour, he should be severely punished and paraded in public in shackles". The Chen Wengong Public Customs and Conventions state that: "Women should stay in the recesses of their chambers and sit behind a curtain. When going out, they should shield their faces with scarves in order to avoid suspicion and being watched. But some women take pleasure in brazenly wandering around. Young women wear bright and eye-catching dresses, and try to display themselves unrestrainedly.... Monks and nuns come out to greet them and vicious young women surround them, but their relatives have no sense of shame. This truly tarnishes customs. A notice is hereby posted. If any temple is found allowing young women to enter, the monks should be pilloried in front of the temple gates and men and women who are found to have visited temples should be punished".[68] This shows, on the one hand, that the authorities had to resort to legal means to control the free exchange between men and women, which had already broken through the Confucian doctrines and, on the other hand, reflects the attitude of the people.

Many people mistakenly regarded exchanges between men and women as the source of such social evils as illicit love affairs, seduction, elopement and rape. They failed to understand that the exchanges between the two sexes are normal psychological and physical needs. An interdict at the Tiantai Hill in Zhejiang at the beginning of the Qing dynasty was very typical:

Women like frenzied outings. In their beautiful dresses, they gather at Buddhist temples in groups, trying to show themselves off, almost becoming delerious with pleasure. They eat and talk with monks and nuns, seemingly tirelessly, and try

---

[68] **Annals of Wuxian County**, Vol. 52.

to please them with their charm and beauty. Even if there is no love making and no miscreant monks to abduct them, they are still the brunt of accusations and harsh comments. After returning home, they are still lost in the grand occasion, and are unable for forget it. This is also very bad.[69]

The persons who drafted this document failed to understand that everybody loves beauty and women especially desire being appreciated by others, especially males. Women in beautiful dresses feel a sense of self-satisfaction before men. The simple banning of such activities could only end in failure.

China was at that time impatient for a new type of gender relations. Of course, we cannot overestimate women's liberation and the new type of gender relations in the Ming and Qing periods. Not mentioning the influence of the Confucian doctrines by Cheng and Zhu and the great efforts by the rulers to support their doctrines, the obstinate existence of the traditional ideas of treating women as inferior to men that had existed over thousands of years of the patriarchal system could not be eliminated overnight. But it was the darkness before the dawn. In the struggle between light and darkness, the night had not yet retreated, but there was a faint light already over the horizon in the east. The dawn light lay ahead.

(2) Superfluous Remarks

Gender relations during the Ming and Qing periods still serve as an example of how complex history is. Obviously, when human society entered the civilized period in all parts of the world, there remained differences in social status. The inequality between men and women under the patriarchal system is one of those differences, but such differences vary greatly from place to place and from period to period in terms of reasons, processes and degrees. The dominant position of the patriarchal system in the West was perhaps due to the invasion of certain

---

[69] *Tiantai Zhilue* (Outline History of Tiantai).

nomadic tribes, but in China, the emergence and development of the patriarchal system is inseparable from the clan government's order of succession. Even in China where the patriarchal system dominated, there might be diametrically opposed cultural traditions in certain areas, but even in these areas the differences were not absolute. Any attempt to generalize about certain historical phenomena is apt to lead to absurdity. No doubt, for people in real life, any manifestation of social inequality should be eliminated. However, historically speaking, any inequality in any given historical period is devoid of value: civilised society with its inequality is obviously more progressive and more valuable than primitive society with its relative equality. Inequality at a higher level is better than equality at a low level, and inequality at a high level should be replaced by equality at a high level. This is beyond any doubt.

But we should not, for this reason, go so far as to advocate equality at a lower level. Although industrialised society has reduced the traditional functions of families, thus intensifying the inequality between men and women, can we then say that industrialised society is more backward than prehistoric matriarchal society? I am afraid that so many symptoms of the relations between men and women in history cannot be discussed or regarded in the same frame of mind or in an indiscriminate manner.

Take the status system of family. Can we say that the system is especially designed to oppress females? Obviously, it was established to meet the demands of family management and the arrangements for production and daily life. Then we come to the problem of women committing suicide to defend their chastity, a problem that has been regarded as the glaring example for the oppression of women. Many such women committed suicide in the face of threats of violence, and such suicides are quite different from sacrifices for dead husbands. On the contrary, such suicides do manifest a sense of righteousness such as men should also display and such righteousness should be upheld rather than rejected.

The analysis of the relations between men and women during the Ming and Qing periods might arouse many questions and ideas, and the veins of the history of the development of gender relations need to be further delineated. I hope that, through the efforts of all scholars, the solution to these problems will be found. The dawn lies ahead.

MONOGRAPHS

CHAPTER NINE
MONOGRAPH I
GODDESSES WORSHIPPED
BY THE CHINESE

Zhao Zewei

1. Ma Zu

(1) The Name Ma Zu

Ma Zu is the general name of the goddess also called Tian Hou, Tian Fei, Ma Zu Po, Ma Zu, Lady Tian Fei, and Heavenly Saint. In Putian, she was called Mother of Meizhou; in Tong'an, Mother of Yin Tong; in Quanzhou, Mother of Wenzhou. Moreover, she is also called Mother of Peace, Mother of Boats, Mother of the Turtledove, Red-faced Ma Zu, Black-Faced Ma Zu and Lady Shuiwei.

(2) Historical Basis

Ma Zu is reputed to have once been a real person. There is a diversity of views regarding her family origins and date of birth, but most sources say she was born in the third month of the first year of the reign of the Song dynasty emperor, Taizu (960). Her father was Lin Yuan, who served as a xunjian, an official in frontier areas vested with the training of militia and policing authorities, in Putian county, Fujian province. She was the seventh child in her family. Pious believers in Buddhism, her father and mother were kind and generous to people and often offered sacrifices to Avalokitesvara. After giving birth to five girls and one son, they were looking forward to another son.

Her mother, Wang, once heard Avalokitesvara, known in China as the Goddess of Mercy, say to her in dream: "For generations, your family has done good deeds and you deserve to be rewarded". The Goddess then presented Wang with an epiphyllum and a pill. Wang swallowed the pill and became pregnant. When about to give birth, a shooting star swept across the sky, emitting a glowing red light, and all heaven and earth turned dark red. Then, there was a loud crash as rocks went flying into the sea, and an exotic fragrance could be perceived. The girl baby never cried from the time of her birth until her thirtieth day. So she was named Linmo (Silence), and later was called Silent Lady.

Silent Lady was quite different from other children. She was extremely clever and at eight was sent to a private school. At ten, she had a passion for worshipping deities and Buddhas and learning to recite Buddhist sutras, and at thirteen a monk came to her home and presented her with a book called **The Taoist Secret Canon**. She studied and mastered all its secrets. One day, at the age of sixteen, she fell into a deep well. The neighbours came to her rescue, but, to their surprise, she emerged from the well with dry clothes and two long strips of paper on which magic figures and signs were written. From then on, she became even more devoted to study and meditation, and gradually she acquired unusual skills, including healing powers. For this, she was loved by the local people, and soon she became famous.

One day at the age of 19, when she was trying to doze off by the spinning wheel, she had a dream in which she saw her father and brother in a boat about to be overturned by mighty waves. She rushed to the scene, grabbed her brother and father, and swam with them back to the shore. At this juncture, she

suddenly heard her mother calling her. She answered immediately, but on opening her mouth, her brother fell back into
the water again. She suddenly woke up and told her mother
about this, with tears rolling down her cheeks. Her mother
thought it only a dream.

Days later, bad news came. Her father and brother's boat
was overturned and at the crucial moment, a lady came to their
rescue. Her father survived while her brother was drowned.
When she was twenty, a prolonged drought struck the local
area. The wells dried up and all the woods and grass withered.
People and animals died of thirst. The county magistrate asked
Silent Lady to pray for rain. She complied, and It did rain, to
the joy of the local officials and people, who were extremely
indebted to her.

When she was 22, two evil deities arrived from the northwest. One was called Shun Feng'er and the other Qian Liyan.
These two deities rode roughshod over the local people. With a
silk handkerchief, Silent Lady fought the two devils, conquered
them and made them run errands for the local residents.

When she was 26, floods afflicted her area from spring to
summer, causing great losses. People had no food to eat and
nowhere to live. The local officials again turned to Silent Lady
and asked her to drive away the floods. She built an altar and
burned incense to pray for the people. All of a sudden, mighty
winds arose and dispelled the dark clouds. The rain stopped and
the sun came out. A dragon was seen rising from water, fleeing
up into the sky.

These are only some of the good deeds she did on behalf of
the local people, to whom she devoted herself.

She had not married even at the age of 28. On the eighth
day of the ninth month in 987, she said to her father and
mother: "Tomorrow is the Double Ninth Festival. I would like
to climb the hill alone". Her father and mother thought this was
the local custom and so did not stop her. The following day,
after reciting sutras, she farewells her sister and her parents,

saying: "Today, I would climb the hill to realise my dreams. As it is very far away, I will not let you accompany me which makes me feel very sad". Saying that, she boarded a boat and crossed the sea to Meizhou Island. She climbed Meizhou Peak.

At that moment, beautiful clouds covered the skies. In the heavens the laughter of immortals could be heard. Silent Lady stepped onto the clouds as if walking on the ground and rose up into to the sky, in a shining red light. Many immortals came to welcome her and together they flew away.

From then on, although Silent Lady had risen into the sky and had left the mundane world, she still sometimes wandered around the island in a red dress, watching for and rescuing people in danger. The local people called her Ma Zu, and built a temple in Meizhou to remember her. Later, during the Song, Yuan, Ming and Qing dynasties, Ma Zu sometimes rescued people and stories about her have been passed on down to the present. During the Song dynasty, she helped the Song army fight the foreign invaders, and she protected Cao Yun. In the Ming dynasty, she time and again protected court officials on long journeys abroad, and in the Qing dynasty, helped the Qing armies quell a rebellion in Taiwan.

To remember her, the local people constructed temples, but only the people in Putian worshipped her. In the 5th year of the reign of Huizong of the Song dynasty (1123), an official went on a tour of Korea. On the way, he encountered a storm at sea, and under the protection of Ma Zu he was able to return safely. The official reported the incident to the emperor, who ordered more temples built to commemorate her, and from then on, the worship of Ma Zu was officially recognised. When the Song imperial court moved to the south, increasing numbers of people from Fujian joined the army, and she began to attract many followers among the troops. The story of Ma Zu spread with the army. During the Yuan, Ming and Qing dynasties, the rulers, out of the necessity to keep their rule stable, made great efforts to promote the worship of Ma Zu, and henceforth she became one of the influential deities in China.

Beginning in the Northern Song dynasty, all rulers heaped praise on her. By 1875, her title ran to 68 Chinese characters, and she thereby became the female deity with the most titles in Chinese history. The sacrificial ceremonies to her were extended to the imperial court to become some of the most ceremonious events in China.

(3) Memorial Activities in Honour of Ma Zu

The 28th of the 3rd lunar month is the anniversary of her birth and the 9th day of the 9th is celebrated as the day she became an immortal. The celebration of her birthday is most ceremonious.

Every spring and autumn, local officials attend celebrations in her honour. On that day, on the southern table of the main hall is placed the plate of memory and on the northern table are placed cloth, wine sets, pots, kettles and plates, and slaughtered pigs and sheep are displayed. The official overseeing the ceremony in court attire prays in the centre of the hall and the others occupy significant positions.

Locally, in Ma Zu temples homage is paid to Ma Zu on the 15th day of the 1st month of the lunar calendar, but some bigger temples select a day after the 15th and before the end of the month. The custom of paying homage to Ma Zu on the 15th of the 1st month began in the Ming dynasty. On that day, pilgrims stream to the Ma Zu temples, especially in Meizhou. The most famous item in the ceremony are the sacrificial objects consisting of nearly one hundred aquatic products and more than one hundred plates of flowers, in addition to two pots of red and white flowers. The white flowers foretell the birth of boys while the red flowers foretell the birth of girls. Women wishing to give birth to children would pick whatever flowers they liked and put them on their heads. In Wenfeng Palace and Yanning Palace in Putian, people also erect beacon towers made of sugar cane or oranges as sacrificial objects.

In the main hall is placed an extraordinarily large pot of fruit, with a red candle set in the middle. The sugar canes would then be peeled, dyed red and piled up in the shape of a tower. In some places, people placed layers of oranges on a wooden rack and then set a candle in the middle to form a beacon tower.

From the 1st of the 1st month until the birthday of Ma Zu is a traditional time for burning incense. The Ma Zu temples all receive streams of pilgrims escorting a portrait of Ma Zu to its original temple where a grand memorial ceremony is held, with a great fanfare of drums and gongs and fire crackers. When the birthday of Ma Zu approaches, people carry the portrait of Ma Zu in a circuitous procession. It was said that when the Qian-long Emperor travelled south and saw many people carrying the Ma Zu portrait in a procession, he was so pleased he donated his own gown as a gift.

All the memorial ceremonies held both by localities and officials are all designed to pray for the protection of the localities. Believers bring incense and sacrificial objects in memory of Ma Zu, praying for protection against disaster and for peace and good luck.

(4) The Spread of the Ma Zu Cult

Ma Zu is regarded locally as a legend about the Sea God, starting from the Northern Song dynasty. According to historical records, in the year Ma Zu ascended to heaven, the people in her hometown built a temple in her memory, which was later rebuilt into the Meizhou Ancestral Temple. Twelve years later, in the 2nd year of Emperor Xian Ping (999), the first Ma Zu Palace, also known as Pinghai Tian Hou Gong, was built. In the Southern Song and Yuan, Ming and Qing, the rulers all ordered that Ma Zu temples be built in Putian. There are now more than 300 remaining, including 30 built in the Song dynasty, 6 in the Yuan period, 58 in the Ming, 57 in the Qing period and more than 160 in modern times.

Fujian features high mountains, but sea communications

are excellent. To seek safety and defend against evil forces, people all believe in Ma Zu. The belief spread even to other countries. From northern Yingkou to the Beibu Gulf, people in all coastal areas, especially Taiwan, believe in Ma Zu. Believers can even be found in inland cities and towns such as Beijing, Shenyang, Jinzhou, Leshan and Neijiang, where Ma Zu temples can be found.

There are three Ma Zu temples in Macao. The earliest was built in the Ming dynasty, and it was subsequently rebuilt in 1605 and 1629. It was said that Macao was originally called Haojing. The name "Macao" was, in fact, the phonetic transliteration of Mao Zu [Ge] in the local dialect. Misunderstood to be the place-name by the Portuguese, the designation has stuck. In Hong Kong, Ma Zu temples are all called Tian Hou temples (lit., heavenly queen temples). There are altogether more than 60 such temples, averaging one per 17 square kilometres. The oldest is the Beitang Tian Hou Temple at Clear Water Bay. It was built in 1266 or the second year of the Xiancun reign period of the Song dynasty. The temple built before the reign of the Kangxi Emperor at Causeway Bay is also well known. Most early immigrants in Taiwan came from Fujian and coastal areas of Guangdong. The customs of commemorating Ma Zu spread to Taiwan at an early date. During the Qing dynasty, when the imperial court patronised the Ma Zu cult, Ma Zu temples were built throughout Taiwan and the Ma Zu cult became the predominant local belief, which even persists until the present. There are now more than one thousand Ma Zu temples in Taiwan, of which 510 have been listed for priority protection by Taiwan authorities. They include Tian Hou Temple in Taipei, Ci Ceng Gong at Shilin, Ci Yu Gong at Chunan, Nanyao Gong at Changhua, Grand Tian Hou Temple in Tainan and Tian Hou Temple in Penghu.

The Ma Zu cult also spread to other countries with Fujian migrants. There are Ma Zu temples in Southeast Asian countries, Australia, Canada, the United States, Brazil, Argentine,

Norway, Denmark and Africa. There are about one hundred million Ma Zu believers in the world, and Ma Zu has evolved into an omnipotent God from the original Sea God.

Today, the Ma Zu belief, which symbolises the partnership relations between men and women, has evolved its own influential culture and it forms a major link that binds the Chinese people both at home and abroad.

2. Avalokitesvara

(1) Origins

Avalokitesvara in Sanskrit is one of the Boddhisattvas of infinite compassion and mercy. Known in Chinese as Guan[shi]-yin and Guan[shi]zizai, Avalokitesvara is one of the most popular of all Buddhist deities, beloved throughout China.

According to the Chinese sutra titled **Qianshou Qianyan Dabeixin Tuoluoni Jing**, the God of Mercy is in fact an ancient Buddha, earlier than Amitayus, titled "Pure Brightness Tathagata" (Zheng Fa Ming Rulai). The earliest boddhisattva, Avalokitesvara exemplifies that state and is committed to assist every being on earth to achieve emancipation. Another historical record shows that Sakyamuni once said that Avalokitesvara became a Buddha earlier than Sakyamuni himself, and is, therefore, known as Pure Brightness Tathagata. "I serve only as a disciple."

The Lotus Sutra (Chinese: **Miaofa Lianhua Jing**; Sanskrit: Saddharmapundarika-sutra) records that Avalokitesvara is the bodhisattva of infinite compassion and mercy, capable of incarnating himself in innumerable forms and in whatever guise is required to help the suffering. He is worshipped in the belief that assistance and even miraculous rescue will never be denied to any devotee in a situation involving suffering. There are many stories about how the god of mercy rescued people. For instance, when a prisoner recited the sutra, his shackles opened of their own accord, as did the prison gate. Once there was a prisoner who made a self-confession before being beheaded and when he recited the title of the god of mercy, the knife of the executioner split into three. There are also widespread stories about how the god of mercy helped banish evil and bring benefit to ordinary people.

The prototype of Avalokitesvara is a pair of ponies in ancient Indian Brahmanism, known as Asvin, symbolising mercy and kindness. In the 5th century, when Sakyamuni founded Buddhism, Asvin become a Buddha of mercy, known as Hayagriva-Avalokitesvara or Horse-Headed Avalokitesvara. Later, this deity was personified in a male's body. According to the Chinese sutra titled *Beihua Jing*, Avalokitesvara was also a prince, known as Buju, who, after achieving Buddhahood, became the left guardian of Amitabha. Together with Amitabha and the Right Guardian, they are called the Three Saints of the West or the Amita Saints. In the Buddhist frescoes at Dunhuang and famous paintings of the Tang and Song dynasties, Avalokitesvara is presented as a brave man. According to Buddhist theory, Buddhas have transcended the wheel of life and therefore there is no distinction between the sexes. In order to rescue people in difficulties, they may change into the body of either sex necessary to accomplish the task in hand. Therefore, the Southern and Northern Dynasties period, Avalokitesvara was depicted as either gender. After the Tang and Song dynasties, Chinese Buddhism mostly came to present him as female. In the Yuan dynasty, a genealogy was prepared which showed that the god[dess] of mercy was a female. Until the present, Avalokitesvara is more familiar as a pretty lady, with kind eyes and brows, and in princely ornaments, with willow branches in her right hand and a bottle in her left. The attire is entirely Chinese.

(2) Legends Treating Avalokitesvara with the One Thousand Arms and Eyes

The One Thousand Arm and One Thousand Eye Avalokitesvara (Sahasrabhuja-Sahasranetra-Avalokitesvara) is one of the six Avalokitesvaras in the Tantric sect of Buddhism. According to a Buddhist account, as Avalokitesvara vowed to help every being on earth achieve emancipation, one thousand arms and one thousand eyes grew, indicating that he could protect all beings on earth and look in every direction, and hence show great compassion and mercy.

The sculptures commonly seen in temples usually show twenty hands, each with an eye under the two normal eyes and hands, thereby totalling forty hands and forty eyes. Then each of the hands and eyes has a twenty-five sat, that is, forty eyes and forty hands times twenty-five, totalling one thousand. The iconographic connotation is that the goddess is quick of eye and nimble of hand, and can reach everywhere.

The largest timber-carved One Thousand Arm and One Thousand Eye Avalokitesvara in the world is in the Puning Temple in Chengde, Hebei province. It is 22.28 meters high, weighing 122.24 tons. In the Xiangguo Temple in Kaifeng, there is a gold coated wooden sculpture of the deity. Similar sculptures in Suzhou and Dazu, in Sichuan province, are all well-known.

A legend concerning the One Thousand Arm and One Thousand Eye Avalokitesvara recounts how, a long time ago, there were three pretty daughters of the Wang family in Miaozhuang, called, in declining order of age, Miaoyin, Miaoyuan and Miaoshan. The eldest and the second daughters were married when they came of age, but the third daughter was a devotee of Buddhism and she harboured the idea of becoming a nun in violation of her father's will. The father was so infuriated that he ordered his daughter to kill herself. However, the sword, rather than cutting her throat, broke into one thousand pieces. The vicious father ordered some people to strangle her to death, so that her soul would be consigned to Hell, but the King of Hell revived her on a lotus flower on Mt. Putuo because her heart was filled with compassion. She subsequently began to punish evil and relieve people of their misery. It was said that her birthday was the 19th of the second month, her enlightenment day the 19th of the 6th month and the day of her Nirvana the 19th of the 9th month. Several years later, her father fell seriously ill and death was imminent. Only medicine made from the hands and eyes of his daughter could save him, and so his daughter gouged out her eyes, cut off her hands and prepared a pill for her father, which saved his life. Wang Miaozhuang, feeling conscience-stricken, regretted his past evil deeds, and in order to relieve his conscience, he ordered a portrait of Avalokitesvara with all eyes and hands displayed to remember her daughter. The aged sculptor was hard of hearing and mistook his words "all eyes and hands" to mean "one thousand hands and one thousand eyes", the two phrases being very similar in spoken Chinese, and so fashioned the One Thousand Arm and One Thousand Eye portrait of Avalokitesvara.

(3) Avalalokitesvara as a Bestower of Offspring

The portraits of Avalokitesvara we usually see in temples depict a boy on her left side and a girl on the right side. The boy is named Sudhana, one of the Buddhas. According to Buddhist scriptures, Manjusri once lived in a forest east of Fucheng. At the time, an elder in Fucheng had five hundred boys, of which Sudhana was one. He was so named because all kinds of precious treasures naturally emerged at the time of his birth, but Sudhana very much looked down upon wealth. To him, everything in the world was void, and so he vowed to become a Buddha. Later he became a disciple of Manjusri. He then went south and visited some fifty-three Buddhist instructors until he met Samantabhadra, who made him a Buddha.

The portrait of Sudhana on the left side of Avalokitesvara draws on materials from stories about him receiving the teaching of Avalokitesvara. After the Yuan dynasty, his portrait was officially placed on the left side of the deity Avalokitesvara, but ordinary people were not concerned with the origins of the portrait.

Local Chinese people also worship Avalokitesvara as a bestower of offspring, believing that she can confer pregnancy, promote birth and protect children. **The Lotus Sutra (Saddharmapundarika-sutra)** states that if a woman wants to give birth to a boy, she should worship Avalokitesvara and give birth to a wise boy; if she wants to give birth to a girl, she will have a pretty girl. This is the basis for local people revering Avalokitesvara as a bestower of offspring.

(4) Thirty-three Physical Attributes and Thirty-three Representations

According to **The Lotus Sutra**, Avalokitesvara incarnated in innumerable forms and in whatever guise was required to help the suffering. There are altogether thirty-three forms of images. They are:

1. Buddhakaya (body of Buddha)
2. Pratyeka-buddha (body of pratyeka)
3. Body of Sravaka (hearer)
4. Body of Prasenajit
5. Body of Sakra-devanam Indra
6. Body of Avalokitesvara
7. Body of Mahaisvara
8. Body of Heavenly General
9. Body of Vipasyn
10. Body of lesser king
11. Body of an elder
12. Body of layman
13. Body of Zai Guan
14. Body of Brahman
15. Body of Bhiksu (mendicant)
16. Body of Bhiksuni (nun)
17. Body of Upasaka

18. Body of Upasika
19. Body of elder woman
20. Body of lay woman
21. Body of woman Zai Guan
22. Body of Brahman woman
23. Body of a boy
24. Body of a girl
25. Body of heaven
26. Body of a dragon
27. Body of Yaksa
28. Body of Bandharva
29. Body of Asura
30. Body of Garuda (King of birds)
31. Body of Kinnara (heavenly musicians)
32. Body of Maharaja
33. Body of Vajradhara

In conformity with these thirty-three bodies, local people drew thirty-three pictures of the deity, called the Thirty-three Avalokitesvara, but not all the representations come from these bodies. Most of are single pictures, and some are three-dimensional sculptures. All were handed down in China in the form of pictures and small sculptures. The thirty-three representations are:

1. Willow Avalokitesvara
2. Dragon-head Avalokitesvara
3. Sutra-reading Avalokitesvara
4. Halo Avalokitesvara
5. Playing Avalokitesvara
6. White-clad Avalokitesvara
7. Lotus Avalokitesvara
8. Soaked Avalokitesvara
9. Medicine dispensing Avalokitesvara
10. Ulam Avalokitesvara
11. Dewang Avalokitesvara

12. Avalokitesvara gazing at the moon reflected in the water
13. Leaf Avalokitesvara
14. Green-neck Avalokitesvara
15. Great virtue Avalokitesvara
16. Life prolonging Avalokitesvara
17. Treasure Avalokitesvara
18. Rock Avalokitesvara
19. Clean Avalokitesvara
20. Aru Avalokitesvara
21. Leaf-clothed Avalokitesvara
22. Amoti Avalokitesvara
23. Glaze Avalokitesvara
24. Oyster Avalokitesvara
25. Sgrolma Avalokitesvara
26. Six Hour Avalokitesvara
27. Puci Avalokitesvara
28. Avalokitesvara as a bride
29. Avalokitesvara with palms together
30. Yiru Avalokitesvara
31. Advaya (identity of all things) Avalokitesvara
32. Lotus-holding Avalokitesvara
33. Drop of water Avalokitesvara

Besides, there was the Offspring-bestowing Avalokitesvara.

(5) Sites of Avalokitesvara Woship

Putuo Mountain in Zhejiang, Mount Wutai in Shanxi, the Jiuhua Mountains in Anhui and Mount Emei in Sichuan are the four most famous sites for Buddhist services held for Avalokitesvara, Manjusri, Ksitigarbha and Samantabhadra.

Putuo Mountain is an islet of the Zhoushan Islands belonging to Zhoushan city, Zhejiang province. It covers 12.76 square kilometres, and is one of the most famous Buddhist island sites.

Legend has it that once during the Tang dynasty, a Japanese monk came to Wutai Mountain, and there he found a beautiful and lively portrait of Avalokitesvara, which he wanted to take home. Without permission, the monk took the portrait away and boarded a boat to Japan. On his way to Putuo Mountain, a hurricane blew up, and on the sea numerous iron lotus flowers appeared, obstructing his way. The Japanese monk was suddenly awakened to his wrong-doing. He confessed to Avalokitesvara and vowed to stay on the mountain to mend his ways. No sooner had he finished than the hurricane died down and the sky cleared. The Japanese monk stayed there and build the first temple, known as the Temple of the Reluctant-to-Go Avalokitesvara.

After the Northern Song dynasty, the worship of Avalokitesvara began to catch on. The number of temples increased and monks flocked to the mountain. In 1214, the Southern Song dynasty officially proclaimed that Putuo Mountain was devoted to the worship of Avalokitesvara. During the Ming and Qing dynasties, great efforts were made to construct temples, and there are now three big temples, eighty-eight nunneries and one hundred and twenty eight thatched temples on Putuo Mountain. At the peak period, the number of monks and nuns swells to as many as four thousand. There were three major ceremonial occasions, i.e., the birthday anniversary of Avalokitesvara on the 19th of the 2nd month, the enlightenment day on the 19th of the 6th month, and the Nirvana anniversary on the 19th of the 9th month. On these three occasions there are crowds of pilgrims, with worshippers also coming from South Korea, Japan and Southeast Asian countries. It has become the largest international service of Buddhism in modern times.

The three best known temples are the Front Mountain Puji Temple, the Back Mountain Fayu Temple and the Fuoding Mountain Huiji Temple. Other historical sites include Purple Bamboo Forest, Luojia Mountain, Chaoyin (Tidal Sound) Cave, Fanyi (Supreme Sound) Cave, Tai Zi Tower and Qian Bu Sha

(Thousand Pace Beach).

The great passion and mercy of Avalokitesvara are well expressed in literature, and it was as a symbol of justice, equality, mercy, tolerance, wealth and fertility that ensured the popularity of her cult in China.

There are numerous Avalokitesvara temples. Apart from Putuo, there are Southern Putuo Temple in Xiamen, Fujian province, Tanzhe Temple in Beijing, Qixia Temple in Nanjing, the West Park in Suzhou, Lingyin Temple in Hangzhou and Longshan Temple in Taipei.

3. Other Goddesses

(1) East and South China

Jiangsu, Zhejiang, Fujian, Jiangxi, Anhui, Guangdong and Guangxi in East China and South China are the original Wu and Yue culture areas, which are quite different from the Central Plain regional cultures. The social status of women in the south used to be higher than that of women in northern China as they were active in social production and often replaced men in all kinds of economic activities. So female worship became one of the main features of the local cultures in these areas.

Xin Qi Niang is a female deity worshipped by people in Fujian, Guangdong and Jiangxi to the present day. Xin was once the wife of a soldier, and during the Five Dynasties period, she travelled with her husband to Ninghua county, Fujian province, where she died of illness and was buried. She was later described as a deity that could oversaw childbirth and brought good local weather conditions. For centuries , she was worshipped in these areas.

Lady Lin Shui is another female deity with most followers in north-eastern Fujian and southern Zhejiang. She was once a village witch, said to be capable of summoning rains and winds and forecasting the future. She later became married and got pregnant, but died in labour. Upon her death, she vowed to become an immortal to protect women in childbirth. Local people portray her as a deity responsible for protecting women in labour and bestowing children on women, protecting babies and conquering evil. It is said that she is part of a line of thirty-six female deities who assist Lin Shui in her fight against evil and protect the people. Local people erect portraits of her in the home and burn incense to her in the morning and evening. After the cult spread to Taiwan, local people built many temples to her and the cult has been flourishing for several centuries.

Lady Jin Hua (Gold Flower) is worshipped by people around Guangzhou, where there are many temples to her memory. The largest is the Jinhua Temples in the Henan district of Guangzhou city, where more than 80 deities, including 20 female deities, are venerated. It is said that Lady Jin Hua was once a daughter of the Jin family. At 10, she became quite a famous witch, often coming to the rescue of women having difficulties in labour. In the 22nd year of the Hongwu reign (1389) period in the Ming dynasty, she was drowned in a lake, but her body did not decay and remained fragrant. A portrait of her appeared beside her corpse, and local people later built temples in her memory. Women who want to give birth go to the Jinhua Temple for pray, and the cult continues to this day.

Apart from the goddesses mentioned above, there are other deities, including Ma Xian Gu in Zhejiang, Long Mu in Guangxi, Qi Xing Nai and Jiu Xian Nai in Fuzhou. These deities are venerated for their feminine features of selflessness, mercy and kindness.

(2) The Central Plain Area

The vast north China plain, extending from the Great Wall in the north to the Huaihe River in the south, from Hangu Pass in the west to the East China Sea in the east, is one of the birthplaces of Chinese civilisation. Influenced by northern Chinese culture, the local people mostly worshipped male deities that represented power and strength, but there are also a few female goddesses that are widely venerated in the area.

There are many temples to goddesses in this part of the country. Among them, Wang Mu Niangniang or Xi Wang Mu is the most venerated and there are many historical records concerning her. The cult of Xi Wang Mu dates back to early totemic worship. The prototype resembles a cross between an animal and a human being, with tangled hair and tiger's fangs, and was said to be a ferocious deity in charge of killing and dispelling disasters. She lives in an idyllic grove of jade trees in the Kunlun Mountains. In her possession is the elixir of longevity. With the spread of the cult, Xi Wang Mu's status was also elevated; she emerged from her cave and evolved into a leader among female deities, and eventually became the wife of the heavenly emperor, having the function of protecting the peace. The legend concerning the banquet she staged at which the divine peaches of immortality were eaten also became widespread.

Another goddess of North China in modern times is the Goddess of Taishan. There is a diversity of views on the origins of this feminine deity. One view is that she was originally the daughter of Emperor Dong Yue and lived on Mount Taishan. Another view was that she was one of the seven immortals sent by the Yellow Emperor to greet a Buddhist monk from the West at Taishan. Still another legend had it that she was a local girl called Shi Yuye who lived during the Han dynasty and that she became an immortal at Mount Taishan. The cult began in the Northern Song and Ming dynasties, when she was given the name Bixia Yuanjun. Local legend has it that the goddess can promote female fertility and protect children. She can also pray for rain. There is a temple in her memory at Mount Taishan. There are also some temples to the goddess in other parts of North China.

From history, we know that the Chinese people, with time-honoured cultural traditions, have always appreciated nature and have sought to transform nature through the world view based on the balance between Yin and Yang and the integration between Heaven and Man. This concept has been reflected in religious beliefs. In order to balance the relations between strong males and weak females, the Chinese people venerated goddesses with feminine characters and social functions, such as Avalokitesvara and Ma Zu, in addition to the masculine deities representing power and authority. Since ancient times, in both the Central Plain areas or East and South China and other places, the industrious and kind people have piously worshipped kind and merciful goddesses in order to acquire firm beliefs and the courage to conquer all difficulties. The worship of goddesses which symbolize propagation, peace and male-female partnership relations has become an indispensable component of the fine traditional culture of the Chinese nation.

MONOGRAPH II
CHANGES IN WOMEN'S STATUS
AS REFLECTED
IN ANCIENT CHINESE LAW

Zhang Zhijing

The ancient Chinese legal system boasts an extraordinarily long and unbroken history. Founded in the Western Zhou dynasty, perfected at the height of the Tang dynasty and terminating in the late Qing dynasty, it operated for four millenia. During this extended period of evolution, it underwent various changes and revisions, thus providing us with a paradigmatic model with unique "oriental" features. An investigation of women's status in ancient China with reference to selected examples from the records of ancient Chinese law will help to map the vicissitudes in gender relations in Chinese history.

1. Civil Law

(1) Marriage

Monogamy

The ancient Chinese system of customary morality unfailingly advocated monogamy, as is evidenced in the following quotations from the Confucian classics: "The beginning of the way of a gentleman can be traced to the alliance between a wife and her husband. Its ultimate form can be found in the correspondence between Heaven and Earth"[1]; and, "What the emperor is to the empress the sun is to the moon, and yin to yang. Just as they need each other, so they complement each other".[2] An analogy is here implied between heaven-earth and sun-moon alliances, on the one hand, and wife-husband union, on the other. As the heaven has only the earth, and the sun one moon, so a man may have but one wife. As neither polygyny nor polyandry was tolerated by customary morality, bigamy was proscribed by law as early as the Spring and Autumn and the Warring States periods. **Fa Jing** (The Canon of Laws), the source of later feudal codes, stipulated that any man who possessed two concubines, in addition to a wife, was to suffer the penalty of having his left ear clipped, that if he had two wives he was to suffer capital punishment, and that a woman who had a second husband was to have her womb destroyed.[3] Laws ranging from the Qin and Han dynasties to the Ming and Qing dynasties invariably inherited the proscription against polygyny and polyandry. It is no longer possible to check relevant provisions prohibiting polygamy in the now lost Qin and Han legal codes. "Huhun" (The Statutes on Family and Marriage) in *Tang Lü* (The Tang Code), however, state in clear terms:

> The punishment for anyone who takes as a wife a second woman when he already has a wife is one year's penal servitude. The punishment for the woman is to be reduced by one degree. The punishment for anyone acquiring a second wife by fraud is one and half year's penal servitude. The woman shall not be held culpable; and both the man's original and later marriages are to be dissolved.... The punishment for wives and concubines who take it upon themselves to run away from their husbands and subse-

---

[1] **Zhongyong** (The Doctrine of the Mean).
[2] "Hunyi" (Marriage), **Li Ji**.
[3] "Xingfa Zhi" (Legal Treatise), **Jin Shu**.

quently re-marry is to be increased by two degrees.

The same procedure was followed in the Tang dynasty. A proscription against ousting sons-in-law for new ones was recorded in "Xingfa Zhi" (Legal Treatise) in *Yuan Shi* (The History of the Yuan Dynasty). Ming and Qing statutes on marriage also stipulated that

> in case any married man should marry a second woman, he shall receive 90 blows of the heavy bamboo. His second marriage is to be dissolved.... Any woman who runs away from her husband without his awareness of the escape shall receive 100 blows of the heavy bamboo. Her husband will be free to sell her to another man as a wife. If she re-marries after her escape from her husband, she is to suffer the penalty of strangulation.

In Ming and Qing times, as an exception to prescribed monogamy, a man who took as wives two women in order to perpetuate sacrifices to the ancestors of two collateral families of the same clan was not culpable. To safeguard the sanctity of monogamy, provisions were installed in the Ming and Qing codes prohibiting the substitution of concubines for wives, as well as disruption of the hierarchical relation between wives and concubines:

> Any person who treats a concubine or a maid as his wife shall be sentenced to two years of penal servitude. Any person who takes as a wife a concubine, a female of tenant status or a maid, shall be sentenced to one and half year's penal servitude; and these women shall be restored to their former and proper positions.[4]

Women were required to conform strictly to monogamy. Not only were they forbidden to marry more than one husband, but they also had to endure stringent restraints on their freedom to re-marry when bereft of spouses. Beginning in the Sui

---

[4] "Huhun" (Statutes on the Family and Marriage), *Tang Lü*.

dynasty, the law imposed compulsory obligations on women of specified social strata to strictly adhere to monogamy. The imperial edict issued in the sixteenth year of Emperor Kaihuang of the Sui dynasty proclaimed that "wives of officials above the seventh rank are not permitted to re-marry after the decease of their husbands; concubines of officials above the fifth rank are not permitted to re-marry after the decease of their husbands". There were no legal prohibitions against re-marriage in either the Tang or the Song dynasty, although there were edicts to the same effect during the reigns of the Tang Emperor Xuanzong and the Song Emperor Renzong. The Yuan code, in contrast, provided clear regulations in this respect. Women whose husbands had been enfeoffed by the Emperor belonged to a different class from ordinary people. Once they had dignities conferred on them, they were not allowed to re-marry when their husbands died. This was to become established as the norm.

Women of the official class who showed disregard for these regulations always had their titles revoked, became liable to punishment, and faced dissolution of their second marriages.[5] The Yuan norm was adhered to by the Ming and Qing statutes which provided that "if a lady [a wife of an official above the seventh rank] honoured with a title by an imperial order should re-marry following the decease of her husband, she shall merit one hundred blows of the heavy bamboo, be deprived of her title and face the dissolution of her second marriage". A female commoner was required to serve a mourning period of three years before re-marrying another man. Otherwise she would be sentenced to "three years of penal servitude". If she were a concubine, her punishment was to be reduced by three degrees, and her second marriage was to be dissolved.[6] If a husband went missing, his wife would have to wait for a legally specified period of time before re-marrying someone else. As an example,

---

[5] *Yuan Dianzhang* (Institutes of the Yuan).
[6] "Huhun", *Tang Lü*.

Ming Huidian (Collected Institutes of the Ming Dynasty) recorded the following: "Any woman whose fianci fails to marry her without due cause five years after betrothal, or any woman whose husband is absent for three years after leaving his family, shall be granted a license to marry another after a hearing before the authorities".

Legal prohibitions against a man marrying a second wife when he already had one did not stop him leading a polygamous life, as monogamy in the patriarchal society only required that a man keep but one wife in form, that is to say, he was allowed only one main wife in order to maintain the distinction between direct lineal descent through the wife and secondary descent through the concubine. With such honourable excuses as maintaining prosperity at home and peace in the nation, as well as expanding the family tree, a husband was entitled to marry concubines in addition to his formal "main wife". In reality then he was practising a one-husband-one-wife-many-concubines system. Indeed, the higher a man's position in society, the nobler his rank in the hierarchy, the greater the number of concubines he was allowed to possess.[7] This was fully endorsed by both the ethical code and the law. Beginning in the Tang dynasty, limits were applied to the number of concubines officials and aristocrats were allowed to keep:

A blood prince is allowed to keep two ladies with noble titles as well as ten concubines. An heir apparent to the throne, a prince in possession of a fief, or an official of the first rank is allowed ten concubines. The allotted number is to decrease by ranks down to the level of three concubines

---

[7] According to "Hunyi", *Li Ji* and *Gongyang Zhuan,* a king in the pre-Qin period was entitled to six empresses, three ladies, nine consorts, twenty-seven titled ladies, and eighty-one concubines; a vassal king, one wife and ninety concubines; a lord, one wife and two concubines; a noble, one wife and one concubine; a commoner, one wife and one husband.

for an official of the fifth rank.[8]

Prior to the Song dynasty, monogamy was widely practised among commoners. However, the Ming code not only specified the number of concubines members of the imperial family, aristocrats, and officials were entitled to, but it also included the unprecedented regulation that "any childless commoner above the age of forty was allowed to take one concubine".[9] In this respect the Qing code followed the Ming code in broad outline, but it relaxed requirements for marrying concubines, paying no attention to whether a husband was childless. Moreover, it disregarded age criteria. On the issue of concubines, the judiciary adopted a policy of non-intervention.

The development of the legal code from the Tang to the Qing saw an increase in liability for polyandry from three years' penal servitude to strangulation, with a corresponding decrease in liability for polygyny from one year's penal servitude to ninety blows of the heavy bamboo. Imperial edicts prohibiting widowed wives and concubines of deceased high ranking officials from re-marrying resulted in formal legal provisions. Legal restrictions on adoption of concubines also gradually diminished until they were abolished. These changes clearly demonstrate that ancient Chinese marriage law established and consolidated male privilege regarding the number of marriage partners. Consequently, the adoption of concubines became a widespread social phenomenon affecting all classes, both high and low.

"Seven misdemeanours meriting dissolution of marriage" and "offences against social correctness."

In ancient times, a woman once married became detached from her father's clan and joined that of her husband's. In turn, she became a possession of her husband's clan. It followed that the right to initiate a divorce belonged to the husband. To

---

[8] *Tang Liudian* (Six Institutes of the Tang).
[9] "Hulü" (Statutes on the Family), *Ming Lü* (The Ming Code).

embody the notion that "a husband is justified to re-marry, whereas a wife has no excuse for a second betrothal", the law bestowed upon a husband the right to desert his wife. In point of fact, the right to divorce did not belong exclusively to a husband, in that his parents and some of his senior relatives could oversee to dissolution of his marriage.

Since a wife was a property of her husband's family, they were entitled under legally prescribed requirements to dismiss her as wife. The prescribed reasons that formed the grounds for divorce were called the "seven misdemeanours". There were a number of legal strings attached to the "seven misdemeanours", which were called the "three excuses for retention". The "seven misdemeanours" and "three excuses for retention" used to be part of the code of behaviour dictated by customary morality, which was then subsumed under the law after the Han dynasty. *Tang Ling* (The Tang Code) prescribed as follows:

> Any man who seeks to divorce his wife will have to produce evidence of the "seven misdemeanours": failure to bear a male offspring, looseness and idleness, failure to perform filial obligations to parents-in-law, quarrelsomeness, thievery, jealousy, and incurable or contagious sickness.... Even though a wife may be guilty of these seven offences, she cannot be dismissed if she has any one of the following excuses, i.e., if she has served the required period of mourning for her deceased parents-in-law, if her husband was poor and low when she first married him but is now rich and pre-eminent, or if she now has no natal family to return to after being sent away from her husband's family which had formerly admitted her...

This practice was to be followed by succeeding dynasties. Relevant legal provisions in the Yuan, Ming, and Qing dynasties differed from those of the Tang and Song only on the point concerning the "three excuses for retention". However, "where a woman is either adulterous or incurably sick, these rules for retention do not apply".[10] What this exception meant is that once a wife was incurably sick or committed adultery, she could not refuse divorce initiated by her husband even though she had the aforementioned excuses for retention. This practice was to serve as a model for succeeding dynasties. Relevant provisions in the codes of the Yuan, Ming, and Qing dynasties differed from those of the Tang and Song dynasties only in the exception clause concerning the "three excuses for retention". Under the Tang and Song codes, an adulterous and incurably sick wife had to be dismissed from her husband's family. The Ming and Qing laws prescribed that only an adulterous wife be divorced, as we can read in this contemporary sub-statute: "Women guilty of any one of the 'seven misdemeanours' who are yet able to cite one of the three excuses for retention may not be divorced, except those guilty of adultery".[11]

In addition to the "seven misdemeanours" meriting dissolution of marriage, a number of offences classified as being opposed to "social correctness" were listed as compelling reasons for the dissolution of a marriage. These were legally prescribed reasons for compulsory divorce. When such offences had been detected, the state was to take both mandatory measures to dissolve the affected marriage and punitive actions against concerned parties should they have failed to dissolve their marriage voluntarily. "Offences against social correctness" are obviously different from the "seven misdemeanours" because the "seven misdemeanours" formed only the grounds for a husband to divorce his wife while it remained his prerogative to decide whether she would indeed be divorced. "Offences against social correctness" which compelled the dissolution of marriage were first seen in the Tang code and inherited by succeeding dynasties. "Huhun" in *Tang Lü* stipulated: "Where offences against social correctness are committed, the wife and husband concerned shall be divorced. Any person who disregards this order shall be sentenced to one year's

---

[10] "Huhun", *Tang Lü*.
[11] "Hulü" (Statutes on the Family), *Qing Lü* (The Qing Code).

penal servitude". According to **Shuyi** (The Commentary), the following constituted offences against social correctness deserving compulsory divorce: assault by a husband on his wife's parents and grandparents; homicide by a husband of his wife's maternal grandparents, paternal uncles and their wives, brothers, paternal aunts, and sisters; killings occurring among paternal grandparents, maternal grandparents, paternal uncles and their wives, brothers, paternal aunts, and sisters of both a husband's and his wife's families; either assault or verbal abuse by a wife on or by her husband's paternal grandparents and parents; assault leading to injury by a wife by her husband's maternal grandparents, paternal uncles and their wives, brothers, paternal aunts, and sisters; fornication between a wife and her husband's relatives above the fifth degree of mourning, or fornication between a husband and his wife's mother; and, intended homicide by a wife of her husband.

Apart from divorce on grounds of the "seven causes" and "offences against social correctness", divorce effected by a husband and his wife of their own free will was also provided for, as is evidenced in the following statute: "Divorce on the grounds of incompatibility between a husband and his wife is free from legal penalty".[12] Moreover, the law in the Yuan, Ming, and Qing dynasties provided that the authorities imposed a divorce order in the following cases: a husband forcing his wife into prostitution,[13] a husband selling and lending his wife[14], a husband raping his

---

[12] "Huhun", **Tang Lü**.

[13] **Yuan Dianzhang** records the statutory provisions: "If a husband for gift-money tolerates the prostitution of his wife or concubine, his marriage to his wife or concubine is to be dissolved". And: "If a husband forces his wife and concubine to become prostitutes in order to profit from the earnings, his wife and concubine are to be sent back to their natal families".

[14] "Diangu Qiqie" (Statutes on Selling and Letting of Wives and Concubines), **Ming Lü Li** (The Ming Statutes and Sub-Statutes); "Diangu Qiqie" (Statutes on Selling and Letting of Wives and Concubines), **Qing Lü Li** (The Qing Statutes and Sub-Statutes).

wife's close relatives, or a husband's father raping the wife.[15] The legally prescribed reasons for divorce, both the "seven misde-meanours" and "offences against social correctness", testify to the low position women held in Chinese society. It was entirely a husband's prerogative to act on "seven misdemeanours" as the grounds for dissolution of his marriage. Even though she could plead the "three reasons for retention", once she was found to be an adulteress a wife was nonetheless abandoned by the law and left to her husband's mercy. Among different categories of off-ence against "social correctness" it was only with respect to the second category that a wife and her husband were treated equally by law which required reciprocal responsibilities of them both. In the other categories, heavier legal obligations were put on a wife than on her husband. Only when a husband perpetrated assault on his wife's paternal grandparents and parents did he then become guilty of an offence against social correctness, whereas a wife's verbal abuse of, as well as physical assault on, her husband's paternal grandparents constituted the same offence. Similarly, fornication between a wife and her husband's relatives above the fifth degree of mourning was considered an act against "social correctness", whereas unless it happened between a husband and his wife's mother fornication between the husband and his wife's relatives was not considered such an offence. What merits special attention is the fact that a wife's intention to kill her husband was an "offence against social correctness", while a husband's similar intention against his wife was not mentioned in the same statute as a similar offence. That survival of a marriage hinged entirely on the will of the husband should offer us a clear enough glimpse

---

[15] "Xingfa Zhi", **Yuan Shi** contains the following passage: "Punish-ment for attempted rape of either a daughter or son by one's own wife's previous marriage and consummated rape of one's wife's daughter by a previous marriage is 170 blows of the heavy bamboo and dissolution of marriage with his wife". And: "Where a father attempts to seduce the wife of his son, whether the liaison is consummated or not, the wife shall be sent back to her natal family".

into the way in which the law extended protection over a husband's prerogative in divorce. It was only in the compulsory dissolution of a marriage executed by the authorities that a meagre measure of protection of women's interests was found.

(2) The Family

Title of Master of a Family

Derived from marriage, the family, as the object of direct governmental control in ancient China, comprised a head of the family and family members. As a head of the family was the family's figurehead and administrator within the family, the sole holder of this position had to be one senior male member, as asserted in the following maxim: "The father is the master of the family. One master means rule, two masters mean chaos. From time immemorial it has never been witnessed that a family can last long when two masters are competing for dominance".[16] Under normal circumstances, a female senior family member could not be appointed master of a family. People in ancient times believed that "when the hen crows in the place of the rooster, the family is on the decline; when the wife usurps the place of the husband, the state is about to perish".[17] It was also believed that "women do not lead but are led".[18] Consequently, a female senior family member could become the head of a family if it had no male members left, but then only as head of the "female household". In a typical patriarchal family, the master of a family wielded absolute power over all family members, not even excepting his spouse. While it is true that the legal codes of successive dynasties always mentioned grandfathers, grandmothers, fathers and mothers together, and required that offspring equally obey both, and, moreover, provided identical punishments for off-

---

[16] "Zhi Shi" (On How to Act as an Official), *Xun Zi*.

[17] Apocryphal Kong Anguo annot., "Mushi", Shang Shu.

[18] *Guliang Zhuan*, entry of "Second Year of the Reign of Yin Gong".

ences against them, they were not held in equal esteem.[19] This is because within a family the father's power was supreme, whereas the mother was to "be loved but not revered". Moreover, whether a woman could continue to hold her title as mother in a family depended upon the will of the father and grandfather. To sum up, the possibility for a female senior member to become master of a family was next to nil. As the spouse of the master of a family she, too, would have to obey the master.

Property rights

In ancient times, family property was owned jointly by all family members. The right to dispose of it, however, belonged exclusively to the master of the family. Family members, male and female alike, were not allowed to take it upon themselves to use it, benefit from it, or dispose it. Even the mistress of a family, entrusted as she was by the master with the duty to run family affairs, nonetheless administered them by proxy and was not supposed to act beyond her authorised power. The laws of successive dynasties provided severe punishments for unapproved use of family property by family members, including wives and concubines.[20] The Qing code stipulated in very specific terms: "Within a family, all lands and grains are to be managed by the master; all properties and money are be controlled by the master". A wife not only had no right to own property of her own family, but also had to ask for permission from her husband and her deceased husband's adult son to dispose of property she had inherited or brought at the time of

---

[19] "Ming Li" (General Principles and Terms), *Tang Lü* (The Tang Code); *Song Xing Tong* (Compendium of Song Criminal Law); "Ming Li", Ming L Li (The Statutes and Sub-Statutes of the Ming); "Ming Li", Qing L Li (The Statutes and Sub-Statutes of the Qing).

[20] "Huhun", *Tang Lü* includes the following: "The punishment for appropriation of family properties by servants and juniors living in the same household is ten blows of the light bamboo for any stolen property worth ten bolts (*pi*) of cloth, to be increased by one degree for every extra ten bolts. The punishment, however, shall not exceed 100 blows of the light bamboo".

marriage from her natal family, as the latter property had also become jointly owned by her husband and herself. The laws of successive dynasties provided differently for the disposal of a wife's dowry when she was divorced from her husband. In the Han dynasty, "a woman dismissed from her husband's family shall leave with her dowry", i.e. a divorced woman was permitted to take her dowry with her.[21] This regulation was followed by those of succeeding dynasties until the Yuan when the law stipulated that "her dowry and other properties are to be left at the disposal of her former husband. She is not allowed to take them with her when she leaves her former husband's family".[22] The Ming code copied the Yuan provision until the Qing dynasty when it was revised in *Xingbu Xianxing Zeli* (Regulations issued by The Board of Punishments): "Where a wife and her husband divorce on grounds of their incompatibility, her clothes and other objects which still exist shall be returned to her upon witness. Penalty shall be meted out in accordance with relevant statutes where a squabble breaks out between the two sides over the said property". If a wife re-married or died, this property would be inherited by her husband's family, as was provided for example in the Song dynasty *Hu Ling* (Ordinances on the Family): "When a wife dies, her natal family is prohibited from demanding properties, maids, and servants that had been brought into her husband's family". "Huyi" (Household Corvee) in *Qing Lü* (The Qing Code) stipulated: "When a widow re-marries, properties of her late husband and her dowry for her first marriage shall be left at the disposal of her late husband's family". The only legal protection a woman could expect over her dowry and property was a clause which reads as follows: "Her husband's brothers shall equally divide all lands, houses, and properties except those from her natal family".[23] In sum, in ancient China women had hardly any property rights worth

---

[21] "Huozhi Liezhuan" (Stories of Men of Commerce), *Shi Ji*.

[22] *Yuan Dianzhang*.

[23] *Hu Ling* (Ordinances on the Family).

mentioning.

(3) Right of Succession

Family succession and property succession were the two main kinds of succession in ancient times. The objective of the former was to perpetuate sacrifices to family ancestors and continue the family line. The wife's elder son was to succeed in the former case. Women had absolutely no right to succession within this system. In the latter case, the laws of successive dynasties from the Tang to the Qing only acknowledged the right of sons of the wife and the concubine to equally divide the property of the deceased. By custom, a woman had her share in the form of her dowry. A daughter could inherit the estate of her natal family only when its family line had come to a stop (i.e. when no male family member survived and when there was no inheritor from the same clan to which the family belonged), although a married daughter and an unmarried daughter were not to inherit equal shares. For example, under the Tang and Song codes, an un-married daughter was to inherit the estate of her family that had come to a lineal end. Where there was no un-married daughter, a married daughter was to inherit one third of the estate in subrogation after the deduction of mourning service costs. The rest of the estate was to be inherited by any close relative that had lived with the deceased for more than three years. Where there was no close relative, the rest of the estate was to belong to the state.[24]

The Ming and Qing codes provided for inheritance by blood daughters only, making no distinction between an unmarried daughter and a married daughter. Judicial practice, however, still followed the Tang and Song regulations, with the result that a married daughter continued to inherit no more than one third of the estate of her natal family.[25]

Whereas the law affirmed a woman's conditional right to

---

[24] Tang dynasty, *Sangzang Ling* (Ordinances on Mourning and Burial); *Song Xing Tong*.

[25] *Da Ming Huidian* (The Collected Institutes of the Great Ming).

inherit the estate of her natal family, it completely denied her right to inherit her husband's estate. It was her husband's heir who was to inherit his estate. A wife was only entitled to take care of the estate. Although a widow and widowed concubine could inherit her son's or deceased husband's share of an estate, she was required to select an heir from families collaterally descended from her late husband's ancestors. The estate was to belong to the heir. Those few who did not appoint an heir were to keep the estate as "old age maintenance" which could be neither sold nor taken with her should she decide to re-marry. This was made very clear in the relevant provision in the Ming dynasty Hu Ling (Ordinances on the Family):

> Where a woman bereft of her spouse and without a son commits herself to widowhood, she is entitled to her late husband's share of a legacy and is subsequently required to have an heir chosen for her by the head of her later husband's clan from suitable families collaterally descended from her late husband's ancestors. Once she re-marries, the property of her later husband's family and her own dowry shall be left at the disposal of her former husband's family.

2. Criminal Law

(1) Investigation of Punishable Offences
Infanticide of Baby Girls
In ancient times, women were discriminated against from the moment of their birth, as is testified in this song:

> Where a baby boy was born, put him in a cot, swaddle him in finery, and please him with a jade toy.... Where a baby girl was born, put her on the ground, swaddle her in sack cloth, and please her with an earthen tile.[26]

In later times witnessed the abominable practice of drowning baby girls. It was recorded that in the Southern and North-

---

[26] "Xiaoya" section, *Shi Jing*.

ern dynasties noble families were not above it.[27] Presumably it must have been prevalent among commoners. When it came to the Yuan dynasty, a provision against the drowning of baby girls had to be included in the statutes: "if any one drowns a newly born baby girl, half of his property shall be confiscated to entertain soldiers".[28] That should give an idea of how widespread infanticide of baby girls was. Explicit provisions against drowning baby girls are not seen in either the Ming or Qing statutes. Da Qing Huidian (The Collected Institutes of the Great Qing), nonetheless, bears this entry: "the drowning of baby girls has reached epidemic scale. It is now banned categorically by law. Violations shall hence be dealt with severely according to statutes". Infanticide of baby girls remained a social problem during the entire feudal period of China.

Affrays and Assaults between Wives and Husbands Causing Homicide.

In Qin times, a husband enjoyed no absolute privilege in an affray with his wife. As recorded in the Kuaiji Stele and the inscribed bamboo slips, a wife killing her adulterous husband was not punishable by law while a husband who inflicted injury on his shrewish wife's ear by tearing at it was to suffer the penalty of "having his beard sheared". The situation changed drastically after the Han dynasty.

A wife striking her husband, under the Tang and Song codes, was sentenced to one year penal servitude. In case where grievous injuries were inflicted, the sentence was to be increased by three degrees.[29] In Ming and Qing times assault by a wife on her husband came to be seen as an unforgivable felony similar to assault by offspring on fathers and grandfathers. The law accordingly provided that such an assault was automatically punished by 100 blows of the heavy bamboo, that punishment

---

[27] *Yan Shi Jiaxun*.

[28] "Xingfa Zhi", *Yuan Shi*.

[29] "Dousong" (Statutes on Conflicts and Suits), *Tang Lü*; "Dousong Lü" (Statutes on Conflicts and Suits), *Song Xing Tong*.

was to be increased by three degrees above the norm if it resulted in injury more grievous than bleeding and fracture, and that if it caused fatal injury it was deserving of the penalty of strangulation.[30] Besides, assault by wife on husband was in itself reason enough for a request on the part of husband for a divorce. If injuries above bleeding and fracture resulted, it would constitute an offence against social rightness. For a concubine her husband was her master. Penalty for a concubine striking her husband was therefore to be increased by one degree, which means one and half year penal servitude regardless of whether injuries were inflicted. If injuries more grievous than bleeding and fracture were caused, punishment for her would be increased by four degrees than that provided for ordinary offenders to reach up to the category of capital punishment.[31] Abusive language by a concubine against her husband also constituted an offence punishable by 80 blows of the heavy bamboo under the Ming and Qing provisions whereas a wife verbally abusing her husband was not guilty of any offence. Assault on a husband causing his death was punishable by decapitation under all the codes of successive dynasties from the Tang to Qing dynasties. Punishment for premeditated homicide of a husband was increased in the Qing and Ming codes to death by slicing. Punishment for accidental homicide of a husband was two degrees below that provided for premeditated homicide under both the Tang and Song codes, although under

---

[30] "Xing Lü" (Statutes on Criminal Offences), *Ming Lü Li* (The Statutes and Sub-Statutes of the Ming); "Xing Lü" (Statutes on Criminal Offenses), *Qing Lü Li* (The Statutes and Sub-statutes of the Qing).

[31] "Oushang qiqie" tiao ("Assault by husbands on wives and concubines causing injuries" clauses) in *Tang Lü Shuyi* (Commentary on the Tang Code); "Fu Qi Qie Lou Xiang'ou bing Sha" tiao ("Affrays between husbands, wives, and concubines leading to death" clauses) in *Song Xing Tong* (Compendium of Song Criminal Law); "Qiqie ou fu" tiao ("Assault by Wives and Concubines on Husbands" clauses) in *Ming Lü* (The Statutes and Sub-Statutes of the Ming) and in *Qing Lü Li* (The Statutes and Sub-Statutes of the Qing).

the Ming and Qing codes it was still punished under the same statute without mitigation.

Punishment for assault by husbands on wives was diminished by two degrees as opposed to that provided for ordinary affrays causing injuries.[32] It was generally accepted in the Ming and Qing society that husbands striking wives was a justifiable measure required for good housekeeping comparable to fathers and grandfathers scolding and striking children and grandchildren. The law therefore provided that unless it caused significant injury assault on wife was not chargeable and that it was subject to punishment two degrees less than the norm if it caused significant injury and only when the wife personally lodged a complaint with the authorities.[33] A divorce may be requested on the grounds of an assault by husband on wife causing significant injury with the proviso that both parties involved had to agree to it. Assault on a wife by her husband causing her death was punishable by strangulation under the codes of Tang, Song, Ming and Qing dynasties. Homicide of a wife with intent was punishable by decapitation.[34] Homicide of a concubine was punishable by exile under the Tang and Song codes, 100 blows of the heavy bamboo and 3 years penal servitude under the Ming and Qing codes. Accidental homicide of wives and concubines was free from legal penalty under any one of the codes.[35] Beginning in the Tang dynasty, however, a husband who killed

---

[32] "Dousong", *Tang Lü*; "Dousong Lü", *Song Xing Tong*.

[33] "Xing Lü", *Ming Lü Li*; "Xing Lü", *Qing Lü Li*.

[34] "Dousong" (Statutes on Conflicts and Suits), *Tang Lü*; "Dousong Lü" (Statutes on Conflicts and Suits), *Song Xing Tong* (Compendium of Song Criminal Law); "Xing Lü", (Statutes on Criminal Offenses), *Ming Lü Li* (Statutes and Sub-statutes of the Ming); "Xing Lü", *Qing Lü Li*. (Statutes and Sub-statutes of the Qing)

[35] "Dousong" (Statutes on Conflicts and Suits), *Tang Lü*; "Dousong Lü" (Statutes on Conflicts and Suits), *Song Xing Tong* (Compendium of Song Criminal Law); "Xing Lü", (Statutes on Criminal Offenses), *Ming Lü Li* (Statutes and Sub-statutes of the Ming); "Xing Lü", *Qing Lü Li*. (Statutes and Sub-statutes of the Qing)

his wife with intent was either acquitted or given reduced punishment under the extenuating circumstances that the wife had committed adultery" or "had reviled her husband's immediate senior family members". As an example, the Yuan Code for the first time in Chinese legal history permitted the husband to kill his adulterous wife with the provision "the husband shall kill his wife if she shall resist his arrest when he catches her at an act of adultery"[36]. *Ming Lü* contains further provisions which read as follows: "A husband shall be acquitted who instantly kills his adulterous wife or concubine when he personally discover her with her paramour at the site of the adulterous act.... A husband who takes it upon himself to kill his wife or concubine because she uses abusive language against his parents and grandparents shall be sentenced to 100 blows of the heavy bamboo. If a wife or concubine commits suicide because her husband has beaten or reviled her, the husband is not culpable". The Qing code, providing as it did a penalty of strangulation for a husband beating to death or killing with intent a blameless wife, nonetheless leaves the husband an opportunity to escape the penalty in the name of "remaining at home to care for parents or perpetuating sacrifices to ancestors". This means that a husband who qualified for this category may settle a matter of uxoricide with enduring 40 blows of the heavy bamboo and two months wearing of the cangue.[37] Although wives and concubines both belonged to the female sex, they were absolutely different in their social status. The concubine was subject to the wife's control. The wife injuring or killing the concubine was as guilty as the husband injuring or killing the wife. The punishment for her infliction of injury on the concubine was two degrees less than that for an ordinary offender and was not applicable unless the concubine personally brought an accusation before the authorities. The punishment for her killing the

---

[36] "Xingfa Zhi", *Yuan Shi*.

[37] "Fanzui Cunliu Yangqin" tiao (Clause on "Clemency for offenses on grounds of remaining at home to care for parents"), *Qing Lü Li*.

concubine was strangulation; if the killing was accidental then no punishment was provided.[38] In contrast, the concubine who beat or reviled the wife was subject to the same punishment as awaited the wife who beat or reviled the husband.

Selling of Wives and Concubines

Wife-selling, which existed as early as Zhou dynasty, was prohibited by promulgated laws of successive dynasties. The relevant passage in "Guangwu Ji" (Chronicle of Guangwu) in *Hou Han Shu* reads as follows: "An imperial edict was promulgated in the 3rd month of the second year of Emperor Jianwu's reign: wives and sons who have been sold shall be free to return to their parents' families. Any person who dares to apprehend and detain them shall be arraigned according to relevant statutes". Under the Tang code, any person who took to wife a married woman and any person who married her to another was sentenced to two years penal servitude, which was reduced by two degrees if the woman in question was a concubine. The marriage was to be dissolved. The Yuan code contained the first provision which categorically forbade selling and letting of women as wives: "selling and letting of wives and concubines for profit is prohibited. Any person who marries his wife for money to another shall be sentenced to 67 blows of the heavy bamboo. The gift-money shall be confiscated".[39] The Ming and Qing codes followed suit and stipulated that "where a person sells for profit his wife or concubine to become another's wife or concubine, he shall be sentenced to 80 blows of the heavy bamboo. Where a person sells his daughter to become someone's wife or concubine, he shall suffer the penalty of 60 blows of the heavy bamboo. Where a person pays to marry someone's wife

---

[38] "Dousong" (Statutes on Conflicts and Suits), *Tang Lü*; "Dousong Lü" (Statutes on Conflicts and Suits), *Song Xing Tong* (Compendium of Song Criminal Law); "Xing Lü", (Statutes on Criminal Offenses), *Ming Lü Li* (Statutes and Sub-statutes of the Ming); "Xing Lü", *Qing Lü Li*. (Statutes and Sub-statutes of the Qing)

[39] "Xingfa Zhi", *Yuan Shi*.

in full awareness that she is already married, he shall suffer the same punishment". Beginning in the Yuan dynasty, however, the law allowed a husband to sell his wife to someone else if she was guilty of having pursued unlawful sex or having falsely alleged to have had unlawful sex forced upon her, or if she tried to run away from her husband's family. The provisions cited below are very illustrative:

1) In case of adultery, the male offender and the female offender shall receive the same punishment. Any child born of the liaison shall be left with the male offender to bring up. The female offender shall be left for her husband to sell. The husband may keep her if he so wishes.[40]

2) If a wife being frustrated in her attempt to run away from her husband brings false accusations of felonies against her husband with the authorities, she shall receive the same punishment as would be provided for the felonies she has falsely accused him of and may be sold by her husband to become another's wife.[41]

Unlawful Sex

By unlawful sex is meant fornication between men and women outside wedlock. It is a category of offence that was established from times immemorial and punishable under the laws of successive dynasties. Unlawful sex may be broadly divided into fornication, seduction, and rape. Voluntary sex outside wedlock was punishable by one year penal servitude for both man and woman and by two years penal servitude for a married woman under Tang and Song statutes.[42] The same offence was punished less harshly under the Yuan, Ming and Qing Codes. The Qing Code, for example, provided 80 blows of the heavy bamboo for voluntary fornication and an increased

---

[40]"Xing Lü", *Ming Lü Li*.

[41]"Xingfa Zhi", *Yuan Shi*.

[42] "Za Lü" (Statutes on Miscellaneous Offenses) in both *Tang Lü* and *Songxingtong*.

90 if the fornicator was a married woman.[43] Both unmarried and married women could be guilty of this crime, although married women were subject to harsher punishment. Seduction referred to fornication effected in a site to which a male fornicator allured a female fornicator. This offence was not listed in either the Tang code or the Song code. Relevant statutes and sub-statutes in the Ming and Qing codes provided the same 100 blows of the heavy bamboo for women guilty of this crime regardless of their marital status.[44] Relevant provisions in the Ming and Qing codes stipulated that any married woman who committed adultery or consented to unlawful sexual allurement could be sold by her husband to another, though not to her paramour, to become the latter's wife. It was still permissible for the husband to keep her as wife.[45] As for rape, punishment provided for this offence was one degree harsher than that for fornication with consent. The violated woman was not culpable.[46] The punishment for this offence became more severe in the Ming and Qing dynasties. Rape was punishable by strangulation, attempted rape by 100 blows of the heavy bamboo plus exile at a distance of 3,000 li. The woman was not culpable. However, the official "Xiaozhu" (Small Commentary) on the Qing code maintained that for conviction of a rape four conditions must be met: symptoms of violation, unavoidable circumstances, presence of an ear witness, and injury to the victim's body and tears in her clothes. "If, however, an attempt with use of force at the beginning led to fornication with consent in the end, it is not to be counted a rape", i.e. even though the aforementioned conditions were met, it would still be dealt with as fornication had the woman succumbed without further contention once an intercourse was consummated. Un-lawful sex between relatives was viewed by ancient Chinese as

---

[43] "Xing Lü", *Qing Lü Li*.
[44] "Xing Lü", *Ming Lü Li*; "Xing Lü", *Qing Lü Li*.
[45] "Xing Lü", *Ming Lü Li*; "Xing Lü", *Qing Lü Li*.
[46] "Za Lü" in both *Tang Lü* and *Songxingtong*.

a "bestial act", the punishment for which as provided by law was much heavier than that for ordinary sexual offence. Punishment for fornication with paternal grandmothers of collateral families belonging to same ancestors, sisters of paternal grandfathers of collateral families belong to same ancestors, wives of paternal grand uncles of collateral families belonging to same ancestors, sisters of paternal uncles, sisters of mother as well as wives of younger brothers and wives of sons was exile at a distance of 2,000 li for both parties. Rape of aforementioned relatives was punishable by strangulation.[47]

In ancient China women since birth were condemned to the extreme extent that their lives were hardly secure with the result that legal provisions had to be made forbidding the drowning of baby girls. When they grew up to become wives, they were subjected to the power of their husbands and had to unconditionally perform obligations of chastity and conjugation. In an affray between wife and husband, the law invariably leaned in favour of husband.

The principle of meting different penalties to wife and husband for the same offence was seen in operation. A wife who strikes her husband is punished more heavily than the norm, whereas a husband who strikes his wife is punished less than the norm. Moreover, a wife is automatically punished by law if she strikes her husband, regardless whether she inflicts an injury, whereas the vice versa situation does not constitute a crime of assault unless it results in injury. In the Ming and Qing times only when assault by husband on wife results in a significant injury, and only if the wife personally lodges a complaint with the authorities, will the husband then incur penalty. Laws in the Yuan, Ming, and Qing dynasties accorded husband the right to sell wife to become another's spouse or to take wife's life under the circumstances of wife having committed adultery or reviled husband's direct lineal seniors means that the hus-

---

[47] "Za Lü" in *Tang Lü*.

band was empowered by the law to dispense with the life of enabling husband to exercise state power under specified conditions. This undoubtedly represents the culminating point of the expansion of the husband's power.

Group Culpability and Judicial Protection

As early as the Qin dynasty a system of group culpability was instituted. It was after the Tang dynasty that this system came to perfection. Under this system, people could become implicated in an offence simply because of their consanguine ties to the offender. A woman, whether married or unmarried, used to be automatically implicated in felonies deserving of group punishment perpetrated either by her natal family or her husband's family. It was during the Wei-Jin period that her marital status was taken into account: "an unmarried woman shares the penalty that befalls her parents' family; once married, she shares her husband's death sentence".[48] Punishment provided for women implicated in high treason meriting group punishment varied in successive dynasties. The punishment provided by the legal code of the Han dynasty for a wife and concubine implicated in her husband's high treason because of their conjugal ties, like that for his parents, sons, blood brothers and sisters was death and exposure of her corpse in the market place. In Wei-Jin period, wives of criminals sentenced to death for heinous offences, as a penalty, were forcibly sent to military camps. The Tang legal code provided slavery for the mother, daughter, wife, concubine, and sister of any one guilty of plotting high treason and great subversion. In less grave cases, it was exile at a distance of 3000 li for the mother, wife, concubine, and daughter.[49] The Ming and Qing legal codes provided authorised slavery irrespective of circumstances for mothers, daughters, wives, concubines, sisters, and wives and concubines of sons, of criminals guilty of plotting high treason

---

[48] "Xingfa Zhi", *Jin Shu*.

[49] *Han Lü* (The Han Code), cited in *Tong Dian* (General Institutes).

and great subversion. In addition, the Ming and Qing statute on high treason and great subversion also stipulated that "wives and concubines [were] to accompany their husbands on their military exiles to the frontier.[50] In successive dynasties from Han-Tang to Ming-Qing, women implicated in crimes of plotting high treason and great subversion were consistently subject to punishment except when they were above sixty years of age and when they were handicapped. Conversely, where a woman was convicted, penalty for her offence stopped with herself, implicating none of her relatives.

While a woman could be implicated in crimes perpetrated by members either of her natal family or of her husband's family, she could also enjoy a number of judicial privileges and claim the benefit of belonging to a elite class because of her father, brother, or husband. As recorded in *Zhou Li*, "titled husbands and titled wives are exempt from personal attendance to court proceedings". The Tang dynasty continued to honour this practice and went on to establish "eight categories qualified for consideration"[51] in statute form with an attendant system of

---

[50] "Xing Lü", *Ming Lü Li*; "Xing Lü", *Qing Lü Li*.

[51] "Mingli" (General Principles and Terms) in *Tang Lü* contains the following explanation: The eight categories in question are members of the imperial family, descendants of former imperial households, persons of great merit, persons with great capabilities, persons with past contributions to the state, diligent persons, guests, dignitaries. Sentences of persons within the aforementioned categories when they are found guilty of an offense are to be memorialized to the Emperor for consideration with a view of possible reduction. Once a reduction is granted, any punishment below exile is to be diminished by one degree. Where any one of the ten abominations is perpetrated, this rule of consideration does not apply.

consideration[52], reduction, and monetary redemption[53], which was to be adhered to in later dynasties. These provisions allowed certain women offenders to benefit from such privileges as exemption from and reduction of punishment which were extended from their fathers, brothers, and husbands. For example, officials above the seventh grade and paternal grandparents, parents, brothers, sisters, wives and children and grandchildren of officials above the fifth grade, when found guilty of crimes meriting penalty below exile, could expect a reduction of their punishment by one degree.[54]

Under the statutes on group culpability and judicial protection, women either endured penalties or enjoyed privileges, both of which were derived from their special ties with men. Their personalities in consequence were totally absorbed into their relations with such males as their fathers, brothers, and husbands to the effect that they held no independent positions of their own.

---

[52] "Mingli" in *Tang Lü*. contains the following explanation: Where a crime punishable by death is committed by a relative above the third degree of mourning of a concubine of the heir-apparent, or by a grandson, as well as by a relative above the second degree of mourning of one qualified for consideration, or by an official above the fifth grade, his case shall be memorialised to the emperor. When he commits a crime punishable by penal servitude, he shall have his punishment reduced by one degree. The rule, however, does not apply in cases of perpetration of the "ten abominations", consanguine implication in crimes of plotting high treason and grand subversion, homicide, commission of sexual offence and theft within the culprit's own district of jurisdiction.

[53] "Mingli", *Tang Lü* contains the following explanation: Where a crime meriting punishment no heavier than penal servitude is committed by one qualified for consideration, memorialisation, reduction, or by an official above the ninth grade, or by a paternal grandparent, paternal parent, wife, son or grandson of an official whose grade entitles him to the reduction of penal punishment, the punishment for the crime shall be reduced by one degree.

[54] "Mingli", *Tang Lü*.

3. Procedural Law

(1) Right to Suing

In the bamboo slips of the Qin dynasty we read the stipulation that "a wife who reports her husband's crime to the authorities shall not incur penalty". This shows that in Qin times the law would allow the wife to bring an accusation of her husband's wrongdoing before the authorities and would on that account let the wife off with impunity. Beginning in the Han dynasty, however, in accordance with Confucian doctrine, close relatives were prohibited from revealing the crime of one of their family members, that is to say, with the exceptions of rebellion and high reason relatives within certain degrees of kinship are permitted to conceal the crime of one of their members. Behaviours contrary to this principle would be seen as criminal. Different degrees of punishment were meted in recognition of intrafamily hierarchy, wherein seniority invariably takes precedence over juniority. Husbands were accorded by the law the same treatment as dominant senior members of the family, whereas wives were considered similar to subordinate junior members. An imperial edict promulgated in the fourth year of the reign of Emperor Xuandi in the Han dynasty pronounced: "Henceforth, sons, wives, and grandsons who conceal wrongdoing of their parents, husbands, and grandparents shall not incur penalty. Parents, husbands, and grandparents who conceal wrongdoing of their sons, wives, and grandsons, thus incurring capital punishment shall be memorialised to the imperial court for examination by the legal commissioner".[55] This announcement amounted to relegating wives to the class of sons and grandsons and assigning husbands to the same class as parents and grandparents. With the exception of rebellion and high treason, wives reporting crimes of husbands were guilty in the eye of law and severely penalised under the codes of all the dynasties. The Tang Code stipulates that a wife who

---

[55] "Xuandi Ji" (Chronicle of Emperor Xuan), *Han Shu*.

brings an accusations of her husband's wrongdoing before the authorities is subject to two years penal servitude the same kind penalty as awaits her if she brings an accusation of wrongdoing of her own parents.[56] Under the Ming and Qing Codes, she is to suffer ever harsher punishment of 100 blows of bamboo and three years penal servitude and the ultimate punishment of strangulation if such accusation proves false.[57] By way of contrast, according the same rule as regards parents reporting their offsprings' wrongdoing, punishment for a husband who brings an accusation of his wife's wrongdoing before the authorities is reduced by two degrees, as is evidenced in the provision found in the "Dousong" (Conflicts and Suits) section of *Tang Lü* (The Tang Code) that "in the case of a husband falsely accessing his wife applicable punishment for false accusation shall be reduced by two degrees".

While women had the obligation to conceal wrongdoing of their relatives, they had only limited right of prosecution. The codes of imperial China which often put them under the same category as the senile, the juvenile and the invalid stipulated that women had to have their suits brought by their family members. Thus, women in principle were not allowed to bring suits on their own. No case would be filed otherwise. The Ming Code, for instance, stipulates: "a woman may not bring suits concerning marriage, estate, and family property. She may do so only when she is widowed and without a son. She may present a bill of complaint on her own if she personally suffering wrongs has no agent ad litem to bring a suit on her behalf". The Qing Penal Code has the following in the item concerning offences committed by women: "Where a woman submits a bill of complaint, if it bears either the name of her agent ad litem nor the signature of a head of thousand households to vouch for its truthfulness, it shall be rejected and returned to her

---

without a perusal".

(2) Preferential Treatment Accorded to Women in Judicial Procedure

Interrogation

The Ming and Qin Codes stipulate that women are not to be interrogated except in cases of sexual offences, burglary, and homicide and that their sons, nephews, and brothers shall be interrogated in their stead.[58] The Tang, Ming and Qing Codes provide not only for exemption of women with privileges of petition, application for re-deliberation, and commutation from torture during interrogation, but also for suspension of such torture on women convalescing within a period of one hundred days after childbirth.[59]

Conviction and Penalty

Ancient Chinese laws have provisions which mete out punishment on males for offences committed by female relatives. Under the Ming Code, for instance, the master of a family was to be penalised for sacrilegious act perpetrated by any women of his family.[60] An article from the Ming Code reads as follows: "Where a woman is found guilty of kidnapping persons or kidnapping persons for the purpose of selling, her husband shall be punished instead. If a woman guilty of this offence has no husbands, she shall be personally penalised".

Imprisonment

Under the Ming and Qing codes, pregnant women offenders of serious crimes may be spared the wearing of chains.[61] The Qing code stipulated that unless convicted of sexual offences and offences worthy of capital punishment, when they shall be imprisoned, female perpetrators of miscellaneous offences were to be placed on probation supervised by their hus-

---

[58] "Xing Lü", *Ming Lü Li*; "Xing Lü", *Qing Lü Li*.

[59] "Duanyu" (Statutes on Trial and Imprisonment), *Tang Lü*; "Xing Lü", *Ming Lü Li*; "Xing Lü", *Qing Lü Li*.

[60] *Tang Lü*", *Ming Lü Li*; "Xing Lü", *Qing Lü Li*.

[61] "Xingfa Zhi", *Han Shu*; "Duanyu", *Tang Lü*.

MONOGRAPHS 447

bands. Those without husbands were be entrusted to their relatives within the five degrees of mourning and their neighbours for supervision. During their probation they must be forever ready to report to local magistrates. In no way were they to be indiscriminately taken into prison.[62]

Execution of Sentences

Female offenders serving sentences of penal servitude were subject to less harsh labor than their male counterparts.[63] Under the Jin code, monetary redemption for female offenders were reduced to half the amount for male offenders.[64] Under the Tang Code, an exile sentence on woman would be commuted to blows of the bamboo, after which she would be permitted to remain at her native domicile. Female convicts guilty of homicide were not subject to removal from her native district once pardoned in an amnesty.[65] The Ming and Qing codes contain an even more lenient provision that women could have their sentence of penal servitude and sentence of exile commuted to 100 blows of the bamboo and have the remainder of their sentence redeemed with money.[66] Successive codes from the Tang to Qing dynasties also provide for suspended execution of capital punishment as well as light and heavy bambooing for pregnant women till after 100 days of their labor.

The aforementioned provisions on female offenders were drafted out of humanitarian concerns. The provision that sentences were to be delayed for pregnant women until 100 days after childbirth was clearly adopted in consideration of female physiological conditions. The same provisions, however, also stand in testimony to female subordination. For instance, the provision that apart from those guilty of sexual crimes and felonies punishable by death female offenders were to be placed

---

[62] "Xing Lü", *Ming Lü Li*; "Xing Lü", *Qing Lü Li*.
[63] "Xingfa Zhi", *Han Shu*.
[64] *Taiping Yulan* (Taiping Imperial Encyclopedia)
[65] "Mingli", *Tang Lü*.
[66] "Mingli", *Ming Lü Li*; "Mingli", *Qing Lü Li*..

under their husbands' probationary supervision rather than imprisoned amounts to an affirmation of the right of custody husbands hold over their wives.

4. A Brief Inquiry into Women's Subordinate Position

We are able to make following observations on the basis of the above cited legal literature.

In the first place, a huge gap of inequality exists between rights and obligations enjoyed and undertaken respectively by men and women. With respect to marriage, the laws of successive dynasties forced women to perform their obligation of chastity, demanding that they stay loyal towards one husband throughout their lives and never leave them as their lords. On the other hand, the same laws entitled men to keep concubines and to dismiss their wives, thus encouraging men to possess as many women as they could. Concerning the family the laws imposed restrictions on women to become ruling masters of their families. Moreover, the laws deprived women of right to own family properties by means of insisting that all properties were owned by all family members and all properties were owned by wives and their husbands. With reference to inheritance, the ancient laws denied women the right to inherit their husbands' properties and to participate in the distribution of properties of their natal families except when their natal families came to a lineal end with no male family members surviving them, in fact the only time when they were allowed on prescribed conditions to inherit properties of their natal families. In matters of criminal and judicial law, a double standard punishment system was instituted, which always provided heavier punishment for wives as opposed to husbands for the same offence respectively perpetrated. Besides, under the ancient criminal law, a husband was granted the power to sell his wife to another in marriage or simply to take her life if she was guilty of a serious misdemeanour. Under the system of associated culpability and related privilege, women either suffered harsh penalties or enjoyed extra-judiciary privileges according to their relation with concerned male parties. In these matters ancient laws always operated in reference to and in favour of the male. Even women's judicial rights were curtailed. In sum, the laws openly upheld superiority of the male over the female and maintained the rule of the husband. It followed that although women were life-breathing individuals like men they possessed no independent personality and were forever kept in subordination to men, as is indicated by the line: "a woman is subject to her father' will when in her natal family, to her husband's will after marriage, to her elder son's wish after the decease of her husband. A woman should never act on her own but should always obey another".[67]

In the second place, as time drew gradually towards the closing days of the feudal society, women's subordination to men became ever more entrenched. The legal codes of the Yuan and Qing dynasties, especially that of the Qing, contributed most to this development. The legal code of the Qin dynasty still installed a number of provisions on equal rights between men and women. The Han dynasty, however, represented a turning point, when women's subordination to men was entered into the law and was to be perpetuated in the legal codes of later dynasties. Throughout the long time from Hang dynasty to the Ming-Qing period, which witnessed continuous progression of social history, legal restrictions on women became more and more stringent. For example, punishment for "any woman's escape from her husband's family ... leading to her re-marrying another person" was raised from three years penal servitude in Tang dynasty to strangulation in the Ming and Qing dynasties.

---

[67] *Guliang Zhuan*, see: entry for "Second Year of the Reign of Yinggong".

Indeed, the regimes founded by the Yuan and Qing nomadic peoples created new measures to cement women's subordination to men. For example, the Yuan dynasty witnessed for the first time in Chinese history the authorisation of a husband either to kill his adulterous wife or to sell her to another person to become the latter's wife, in effect putting into a husband's hand his wife's life. As another example, the Qing code provided that a woman who ceased to resist once a rape on her was consummated would still be punished as for fornication. This was a hitherto unknown provision, indicating that in Qing dynasty even more rigorous requirements were made on feminine chastity.

The law without doubt helped to safeguard the aforementioned gender relation that was based on superiority of the male over the female. The reason why the laws went all out to uphold male dominance in gender relation is to be found in the unique nature of the ancient legal system of our country. Firstly clan hierarchy and autocratic monarchy were the twin pillars supporting the ancient legal system. If we look down the whole time corridor of 4000 years Chinese history, the political systems that come into our vision are invariably the two models listed above. The long period when slavery obtained, especially Western Zhou dynasty, was characterized by a hierarchical clan system. As for autocratic monarchy, it was initiated by Ying Zheng the Emperor of the Qin dynasty and was followed and strengthened by later dynasties until the later years of the Qing dynasty. In spite of their differences in the underlying economic infrastructure and the way of manifestation, the two systems shared the same spirit. That is to say, the principle of clan hierarchy characterized by "affection toward kindred" and "respect toward the honourable" ran through the whole feudal period. "Affection toward kindred" was an expression of the principle of patriarchal hierarchy, which demanded that "the father be benevolent, the son filial, the elder brother kind, the younger brother respectful, the husband amiable, and the wife compliant". "Respect toward the honourable" was an expression of the principle underlying the feudal system of social differentiation, which demanded absolute obedience of inferiors to superiors. Under the influence of patriarchal hierarchy, a system of clan-state symbiosis came into being, which stressed "harmony between the family and state" and "oneness of the patriarch and the Emperor". Therefore it is only to be expected that males held exclusive power on every level of the system from the family to the government. The law, constantly seen as the king's way to conduct his administration, held it as its fundamental mission to maintain male dominance in social and political spheres. Following the law in importance was the was Confucianism, which was the soul of ancient Chinese legal system. In the Han dynasty, the great Confucian Dong Zhongshu started theorisation and theological reform of the original thinking of the Sage. He put forward the idea of "moral indoctrination first punitive action second". For him, morality was the embodiment of the will of the Heaven in human society. Under his theorem:

> The superiority of *Yang* and the inferiority of *Yin* have been prescribed by Heaven.... The relationships between the emperor, the father, and the husband on the one hand and the minister, the son, and the wife on the other are all derived from that between *Yin* and Yang.... The emperor is *Yang*, the minister *Yin*; the father *Yang*, the son *Yin*; the husband *Yang*, the wife *Yin*. [Therefore], *Yin* is the complement of *Yang*, the wife the complement of the husband, the son the complement of the father, the minister the complement of the emperor.[68]

This tenet was later summarised by Ban Gu in the Eastern Han period in the following words: "Ruler guides subject, father guides son, and husband guides wife".[69] The so-called "three cardinal guides" and "five constant virtues" [benevolence, right-

---

[68] *Chunqiu Fanlu*.
[69] *Baihu Tongyi* (Universal Principles of White Tiger Hall).

eousness, propriety, wisdom and fidelity] formed the backbone of the Confucian ethical code and were held by the Han rulers as a spiritual standard, which in turn determined the course of legislation and political practice of the government. From then onward till the last years of the Qing empire, successive regimes observed this moral code and in practising it refined its operational procedure. In the periods following the Tang dynasty in particular, the Confucian code of morality became established as the principle for legislation, the standard for trial, and the criterion for penalty with the effect that the legal code and the Confucian moral was merged into one. Under such circumstances, it was hardly surprising that males came to rule over females.

What merits attention in this connection is the way Confucian system of "three cardinal guides" and "five constant virtues" as an ideology reinforcing the patriarchal state should have stressed the correspondence between the family and the state thus effectively locking women's status with state politics. In this way, so long as the monarchy survived, the rule of the husband would never perish, and women's subservience would never come to an end. The laws from the Qin-Han to the Ming-Qing became increasingly hard on women in proportion to the never-ceasing growth of the power of the monarchy and the constant refining of the Confucian moral code. Among the legal codes of successive dynasties, those formulated by the Yuan and Qing national minority rulers proved to be more thorough going in implementing Confucian ethical code than the majority Han rulers. Apart form the increasing consolidation of the monarchy, there was another explanation for this phenomenon, i.e. the influence of the culturally more advanced Confucian ethical code. As Marx pointed out, "barbaric conquerors were forever to be conquered by the more advanced culture of the people they had conquered. Such is the universal truth of history".[70] Moreover, the Yuan and Qing rulers realized that they had to depend on Confucian morality to consolidate their rule over the overwhelmingly vast numbers of the Han Chinese. The Manchu aristocracy proved to be much more sober, sensitive and successful than their Mongol counterparts on the appropriation of the Han culture for their own benefit. As a result, "it was not the earlier Han Chinese regimes but the Manchu rulers that created the orthodox Confucian body politic par excellence. Never before in Chinese history had Confucian values become so imbedded and so widespread as in the Qing dynasty".[71] Besides, the Mongols and Manchus, being warlike and backward nomadic peoples, could not have refrained from resorting to drastic and barbarous measures in the process of switching their crude native culture to the feudal ethics of Confucianism.

The gender relations as have been outlined in the foregoing review of Chinese legal history coincides with the historical pattern of power relations teh American thinker Eisler has observed in her study of Western society. Both have presented a picture of male rule and oppression of the female. It can be concluded therefore that both Chinese and Western societies have experienced a historical phase which is described in her terminology as one of power relationship. Human beings are but one kind. Just as we had the same past, so we shall face the same future. If mankind cannot start their pursuit of an intra-familial partnership by eradicating family oppression and violence, they will not be able to eliminate violence and oppression in society at large or stop wanton destruction of nature. In other words, only through an evolution from the patriarchal system of male oppression of the female to a new partnership system of sexual equality can mankind create a future of mutual prosperity.

---

[70] **Selected Works of Marx and Engels**, vol 2.

[71] He Bingdi (Ho Ping-ti) "The Importance of the Qing in Chinese History" in **Translated Research Papers on the Qing**, 1 (1980).

MONOGRAPH III
PEKING OPERA: A WINDOW ON CHANGES IN CHINESE WOMEN'S SOCIAL STATUS (1790-1937)

Huang Yufu

Peking Opera is an important part of Chinese traditional culture. After the Four Big Anhui Troupes (*Si Da Huiban*)[1] came to perform in Beijing in 1790, Peking Opera gradually took shape and developed into an excellent artistic form. With its varied and interesting repertoire, highly difficult and graceful movements, colourful and gorgeous costumes, agreeable and pleasant singing, and wonderful and exaggerated make-up, Peking Opera, contributed to by outstanding artists for generations has fascinated millions both inside and outside China for generations. It is not only a gem of Chinese traditional culture, but also a world treasure. For more than a century, many scholars, both in China and overseas, have taken an interest in this old theatre form. Many studies of it have appeared, and these explain its unique jargon and terminology, roles, styles of performance, origins, development, and great practitioners. In short, every aspect of Peking Opera as an art form has been explained in detail.

This article, however, will examine Peking Opera from the new perspective of sociological and gender studies, taking Peking Opera as a socio-cultural phenomenon and tracing its development as a social history providing a key to understanding the

---

[1] Hui Opera (Anhui Opera) was a local regional opera.

changes in Chinese gender relations.

Such a study is possible because Peking Opera, like other art forms, is derived from life, reflects life, and has been deeply rooted in social life since its inception. It would be not exaggerated to say that almost every significant social change and major social custom in Chinese history has found its expression on the Peking Opera stage, while all dominant social values and role expectations have been advocated in its plays. The prevailing views concerning gender relations in feudal China, such as the view that men are superior to women and that men are stronger than women, were fully displayed in this old art. What is worth mentioning here is that Chinese women's social status and the changes in it have been not only reflected in the plays, but also in the relations between men and women in Peking Opera circles, as well as between actors/actresses and those on the outside. These characteristics make it possible to take Peking Opera as a window on the changes in the social status of Chinese women.

Due to limited space, this study does not claim to present a complete picture of the history of Peking Opera. Instead, it consciously limits its discussion to the period from 1790 to 1937, i.e., from the birth of Peking Opera to the beginning of the War of Resistance Against Japanese Aggression (Marco Polo Bridge or Lugouqiao Incident), with special emphasis placed on the period between 1900 and 1937. The reason for this lies in the fact that during the years between 1900 and the War, many significant changes took place in China. For example, from the point of view of women's studies, in this period, along with the dissemination of the bourgeois democratic ideology and the demise of feudal rule, the feudal codes of ethics which had oppressed and restrained Chinese women for thousands of years was fiercely attacked. At the same time a preliminary feminist movement arose and there was some improvement of women's status. The changes in Chinese women's status were reflected clearly in Peking Opera. Moreover, this was also a period when the art of dan (female roles) underwent a great development and women began to enter the world of Peking Opera.

Peking Opera is an art so popular among people in many districts in China that it is also called Guoju (National Opera). However, this study is further limited to a discussion of the activities of actors and actresses in Beijing, because Beijing is where Peking Opera originated and the outstanding representative actors playing female roles, the Four Famous Dan, appeared.

I. Peking Opera in Its Early Days: A World of Men

In 1790, in order to celebrate the eightieth birthday of the Qianlong Emperor, the Four Big Anhui Troupes came to perform opera in Beijing. After combining artistic elements drawn from northern Kunqu Opera in that city, Bangzi-qiang (Clapper Opera) which originated in Shanxi and Shaanxi provinces, and Hanju (Han Opera) from Hubei province, they gradually developed a new type of opera with the special characteristics of the capital, i.e. Peking Opera. After that time, this new opera form was disseminated throughout the country and it became widely popular.

One of the important characteristics of Peking Opera in its early days was male domination of the art form. All people in Peking Opera circles, whether they be playwrights or performers, musicians or make-up artists, were men. As for the characters in plays, all roles, regardless of sex or age, were acted by men. Women were simply excluded from Peking Opera. At that time, the traditional theatre training schools would not enrol female students, neither would actors have female apprentices. Women were deprived of all opportunities to be trained as actresses.

Not only were women deprived of the opportunities to learn and play Peking Opera, but also of almost all opportunities to enjoy it. Until the early 20th century, there were four main venues where performances of Peking Opera could be seen: 1. The Forbidden City. Since Peking Opera was extremely popular with China's emperors, it was often performed in the palace for the emperors' and empresses' enjoyment. Occasionally, relatives of the emperors, high ranking officials and their families could also go to see performances. 2. Private functions. People of imperial lineage, high officials, and rich merchants might hold private functions and banquets at which troupes were invited to play. Among the audience, there might be women. 3. Every year, on the occasion of religious festivals, temples with stages might invite troupes to play. Such performances were called *xianghui xi* (performances for incense gatherings), and usually women would attend and also make donations which were an important source of temple revenue. 4. Popular theatres. Prior to 1735, women were permitted to enter theatres. In 1735, a scholar named Lang Sumen submitted a written statement to the Qianlong Emperor, saying that women entering theatres was an offence against decency. The Emperor then issued an edict decreeing that women were no longer permitted to go to theatres.[2]

Since very few women had the honour of being able to enter the Forbidden City, or to attend private functions, and because performances in temples were few, the great majority of women hardly ever had the chance to see Peking Opera.

Although women were completely excluded from the world of Peking Opera as playwrights and performers, and had hardly any right to be in audiences at performances, it was impossible to remove female roles from the stage completely. However, in the early years of Peking Opera, female roles were, regrettably, mostly minor roles. In Yang Jingting's **Dumen Jilue** (Chronicle of the Capital) and **Huatian Chenmeng Lu** (Chronicle of Mun-

---

[2] The famous actor, playwright and theatre critic Qi Rushan mentions seeing women in Peking Opera audiences in his "Female Audiences over the Recent Century", in **The Complete Works of Qi Rushan**, (Taibei, 1961), pp. 1644-1646.

dane Dreams and Dazzling Heavens) and Zhu Jiajin's *Qing Shengpingshu Dang'an Xinji* (New Compilation of Archives of the Qing Court Theatrical Office), 147 plays were recorded which were performed between 1845 and 1861. Moreover, Su Yi in his **A Survey of Two Hundred Years of Peking Opera** recorded 538 plays performed in 1861-1911. Table 1 is a gender analysis of the leading roles in these plays:

**Table 1 Sex of the Leading Roles in Plays Performed
Between 1845 and 1911**

Sex of leading role	1845-1861		1861-1911	
	No. of plays	(%)	No. of plays	(%)
Male	72	49	323	60
Female	36	25	111	20
Male & female	20	13	89	17
N.a.	19	13	15	3
Total	147	100	538	100

Resources:
1. **The History of Peking Opera**, Vol.1, 1990, pp. 80-90.
2. **A Survey of the Two Hundred Years of Peking Opera**, 1989, pp. 132-135.
3. **A Dictionary of Plays of Peking Opera**, 1989.

Table 1 shows that in these two periods, the proportions of plays with males in leading roles were 49% and 60% of the total repertoire respectively, while those with female in leading roles were 25% and 20% respectively. This difference is mainly due to the fact that in the early days of Peking Opera, most plays took political, historical, or military events as their themes (for instance, there were 36 plays adapted from the novel *Sanguo Yanyi*, translated into English as **Romance of the Three Kingdoms** created and acted by Lu Shengkui, 1822-1889), while

Chinese women were long excluded from political life in society and maintained a marginal position in history.

An analysis of female characters in leading roles in plays performed in 1845-1861 shows that among them, about 34% were "silly women", such as Deng's wife in **Paying a Visit to the Mother of the Son-in-Law**, evil or licentious women, such as nie Wang in **Tale of Poisoned Tea** or Zhao Yu in *Liangding Ji* (Story of Two Nails), or sirens who bewitch men, such as the Fox Spirit with Nine Tails in *Qingshi Shan* (Mount Bluestone) and Goddess Jellyfish in *Sizhou Cheng* (Sizhou City). Usually they were played by huadan[3] or wudan.[4] The social prejudice which maintained that women instigate trouble was fully played up in these dramas. The leading female roles in about 31% of the repertoire were virtuous wives, wise mothers or ladies ready to die to preserve their chastity, such as Wang Chun'e in *Sanniang Jiao Zi* (The Third Mistress Teaches Her Son), Xueyan in **Shentou Ci Tang** (Assassinating Tang Qin), or Dou E in *Liuyue Xue* (Snow in Midsummer). These characters were usually played by qingyi,[5] the ideal image of Chinese women and the rule for whose performance was "not to show the feet while walking, nor to show the teeth while smiling". A small number of plays (about 20%) featured women with outstanding military skills in leading roles. However, most portrayed women were of very low origins, such as Yang Paifeng in **Yanhuoju** (The Poker), or members of the greenwood, such as Sister-in-Law Gu, Sun Erniang and Hu Sanniang in Nü Sanzhan (The Battle of Three Women). These roles were played by wudan. In their performances, the martial skills were best displayed when the characterisation was to a great extent neglected.

---

[3] Huadan, a role genre in Peking Opera, usually very lively, rude, unreasonable or licentious women.

[4] Wudan, a role genre in Peking Opera that features acrobatic and martial arts routines.

Qingyi, a role genre, usually depicting the virtuous wife, wise mother or chaste widow.

In short, during the century or so after the birth of Peking Opera, men dominated and monopolised this theatrical form. This situation did not change until the end of the 19th century.

2. Changes in the Status of Women in Peking Opera.

By the late 19th century and early 20th century, spectacular changes had taken place in the status of women in Peking Opera, which broke the monopoly males exercised over this field. The changes could be mainly seen in the following aspects:

(1) Women Enter the World of Peking Opera as Audiences

It was in 1900 that women in Beijing could go to theatres to see Peking Opera performed. The well-known playwright and critic of Peking Opera Qi Rushan wrote: "In 1900, the Eight Power Allied Forces occupied Beijing. At that time, all theatres were open to women, because it was inconceivable for foreigners to prohibit women from entering theatres. So women enjoyed themselves watching Peking Opera for more than one year. However, the greater part of the female audience were women from the rank and file of society. Those from honourable families would not deign to visit theatres.... In 1902, the Allied Forces withdrew from the capital, and Beijing was once again under the rule of the Chinese government. Women were subsequently excluded from theatres until the foundation of the Republic of China."[6] Table 2 shows the process of women's going to the theatres.

---

[6] Qi Rushan, op. cit., p. 1646.

Table 2 Sex Composition of Audiences in Theatres in Beijing (1790-1937)

Time	1790-1900	1900-1902	1902-1912/3	1912/3-1914	1914-1937
Audience	m.	m.f.a.	m.f.a.	m.	m.f.b.

m. = male only; f.= female only; m.f.a. = male and female audiences seated separately. Usually women's seats were on the second floor, while men's seats were on the first floor.; m.f.b. = male and female audience seated together.

Sources:
1. Qi Rushan, **The Complete Works of Qi Rushan** (1961), pp. 1644-1648.
2. Takeo Tsuji, "A Pioneer for Co-acting by Actors and Actresses", *Shuntian Shibao* (Shuntian Times), 28 January 1930.
3. Ma Shaopo, Zhang Lihui et. al. eds., **History of Peking Opera**, vol. 1, pp. 186-187.

The opening of theatres to female audience offered women opportunities to see Peking Opera. However, before 1914 when the first Western-style theatre in Beijing, The First Stage (*Diyi Wutai*) was built, women had been seated on the second floor while men were seated on the first. They had been not allowed to sit together with the male audience, including even their father, brother, husband or son. The First Stage was different from traditional theatres, with a line of "boxes" (*baoxiang*) in the front row on the second floor, which was convenient for the audience. ("Boxes" were separated groups of seats for families and their friends, with usually five or six seats in each group.) It was after 1930 that men and women could sit together outside the "boxes". The author consulted Master Cheng Yujing, who was a senior actor playing female roles, and he recalled, "In the late Qing dynasty, women were not allowed to go to the theatres. In 1912, women could enter theatres, but could not sit together with men. They sat in the 'boxes'. When I played in the 1920s, women were still sitting in 'boxes', usually with family members or close friends, among whom there might be men. The seats on the first floor were called the 'pool' (chizi) and no women sat there. So it was in the late 1920s or early 1930s that men and women could sit together outside the 'boxes'. As far as I can remember, in the early 1930s, many students went to the Jixiang Theatre, and I saw girls sitting side by side with boys".[7] Moreover, on 28 January 1930, an article written by a Japanese columnist Takeo Tsuji was published in **Shuntian Times**,[8] and in it he strongly appealed for the authorities to extend permission for male and female audience members to sit together outside the "boxes" in theatres. This further proved that women and men were not able to sit freely until the early 1930s. In spite of all these restrictions, women could enjoy themselves in theatres at last. Having been deprived of the right for more than one hundred years, women in the capital crowded into theatres with great enthusiasm and soon became an important part of the audience. Although they could not quite understand the minutely studied airs of Peking Opera, they took great interest in the beautiful appearance and colourful costumes of the characters, and female roles precisely met their needs in these aspects. In a sense, the enlargement of the female audience promoted the flourishing of the art of female roles.

(2) Women Entered Peking Opera as Students.

There have been mainly two ways for people to become actors/actresses of Peking Opera: one is to enter training schools, the other is to formally acknowledge a particular artist as one's teacher. However, until the early 20th century, women had been deprived of the right to learn Peking Opera. Table 3 shows the process of theatre training schools to enrol female

---

[7] Author's interview with Prof. Cheng Yujing, 9 Oct., 1994.

[8] Takeo Tsuji, "A Pioneer of Coacting of Actors and Actresses", **Shuntian Shibao**, 28 January 1930.

students.

Table 3 Sex Composition of Main Theatre Training Schools
of Peking Opera in Beijing

1790-1880	1880-1917	1917-1937
?-? Shuangqing (m)	1882-after 88	1917-19 Binqing (m)
?-? Xiaohechun (m)	Xiaorongchun (m)	1930-19 China Theatre Training School (m+f)
?-? Xiaofusheng (m)	1889-? Xiaojili (m)	
?-? Xiaojinkui (m)	1889-? Xiaodangui (m)	
1862-73 Quanfu (m)	1889-? Xiaoyucheng (m)	
?-1877 Deshengkui (m)	1889-? Xiaofushou (m)	
?-after1880 Sizhentang (m)	1904-07 Changchun (m)	
1904-12 Xiliancheng (m)		
1909-14 Sanle (m)		
1912-48 Fuliancheng (m)		
1914-16 Zhengle (m)		
1916-19 Chongya Society (f)		

Key:
   m—male students only; f—female students only; m+f—coeducation.

Sources:
   1. Zhang Geng et. al. eds. **Traditional Opera and Chinese Folk Art Volume, Encyclopaedia Sinica**, p. 486.
   2. Ma Shaopo and Zhang Lihui et. al. eds. *Zhongguo Jingju Shi*, (1990) vol. 2, pp 47-51.
   3. Su Yi, **A Survey of Two Hundred Years of Peking Opera**, pp. 204-209.
   4. Wu Tongbin and Zhou Yaxun, **A Dictionary of Peking Opera**

Knowledge, pp. 286-290.

Table 3 shows that the first training school for actresses was set up in 1916, and it was in as late as 1930 that the first coeducational institution of Peking opera was established, i.e. China Theatre Training School. We could see that women had much less opportunities than men to learn Peking Opera. While women had few opportunities to enter theatre schools, and they had much more difficulty in personally accepting actors as their teachers. At that time, many actors strictly adhered to the old tradition and refused to have any female students. The first actor who formally accepted actresses as his students was the highly creative actor Wang Yaoqing (1881-1954). In 1927, he accepted his first female student Li Huiqin,[9] so as to break down the old convention which had existed for about one century. Wang Yaoqing had many students during his lifetime, among whom there was no lack of outstanding actresses. Many other actors followed his example and took actresses as their students. For instance, in 1927, Mei Lanfang (1894- 1961) accepted Xin Yanqiu (1910-   ) as his first female student who was voted in as one of the four best actresses in 1930.

The more opportunities women had to go to theatre school after the beginning of the 20th century was a reflection of the advocacy of women's education in the larger society, and the acceptance of female students by actors who ventured to break with the old convention was a sign of a decrease in the discrimination and prejudice against women among Peking Opera actors. The better training in schools and the guidance of distinguished actors proved to be favourable factors and prerequisites for the emergence of numerous excellent actresses.

(3) Women Entered Peking Opera Circles as Actresses.

It was in 1874 that women began to play Peking Opera.

---

[9] Author's interview with Prof. Cheng Yujing, 2 December 1994.

Being unable to earn much money through performances, a second-rate actor of clown (*chou*) roles named Li Mao'er bought some girls from poor families in Anqing, taught them some pieces of Anhui Opera and Peking Opera, and told them to perform in teahouses or at private functionsin Shanghai. This was the first female troupe playing Peking Opera.

Table 3 shows that the first training school for actresses was set up in 1916, and it was as late as 1930 that the first coeducational institution of Peking Opera was established, i.e., the China Theatre Training School. We can see that women had far fewer opportunities than men to learn Peking Opera. While women had few opportunities to enter theatre schools, they had many more difficulties.

It was much later that women began to play Peking Opera in Beijing. As Xingshi wrote in an article titled "*Kunling Kaishi Zhi Ping Zhi Leli*" (A Short History of Actresses' Coming to Beiping) (1930), "In 1912, actresses began to play in Beiping.... In the dismal days after the 1911 Revolution, people in Beiping were so scared that there was an extremely bleak scene on all sides. Zhao Zhi'an was then in charge of internal affairs. In order to calm public feeling, he partly lifted the ban on performances. Yu Zhenting, the fifth son of Yu Senior (Maobao), nicknamed Earth Monkey (Tuxing Sunzhe), thought this was an excellent opportunity. He invited actresses to play in order to attract audiences by being different. He submitted a report to the police, which requested lifting the ban on actresses' playing in Beiping. The requirement approved, he built a theatre at Xiangchang, so actors and actresses began to co-act there, like those in other cities in the country...".[10] This shows that actresses began to play Peking Opera in Beijing around 1912.

It is beyond doubt that the appearance of actresses was a great shock to the world of Peking Opera which had been

---

[10] *Xiju Yuekan* (Theatre Monthly), (1930), vol. 3, no. 1, pp. 1-4.

dominated by men for so many years, and the former gradually became a threat to the latter. As Wangxi Gezhu wrote in his "Nan-n Lingren Heyan Shihua" (History of the Co-acting of Actors and Actresses) (1939), "In 1912, actors and actresses began to co-act in Beijing. People thought it strange while the curious ones flocked to it like ducks to water.... At that time, all performers in the Xiliancheng troupe were male actors. Whether in the performances by themselves or in their co-acting with actors from other troupes, no actresses were to be found on stage. Even the theatres in which they played were not open to female audiences. The convention in Peking Opera circles in these early days was thus evident, but later the co-acting of actors and actresses became a fashion. Theatres with actresses would be always filled to capacity while those with interesting plays acted by male actors only would, no matter how excellent they might be, have small audiences. In order to adapt to this situation and make a livelihood, the Xiliancheng troupe invited actresses to attract audiences".[11] This shows that by then actresses had become a force that could no longer be neglected.

However, it was by no means all plain sailing for women entering the field of Peking Opera, and the co-acting of actors and actresses, which was so important for actresses who had not yet made a foothold for themselves, had to break down many barriers. Only after repeated setbacks was co-acting realized. Co-acting was important because:

(1) In female troupes, all the roles regardless of gender were played by actresses. Although women had advantages in acting female roles, they encountered many difficulties in playing male roles, especially roles such as jing (painted face, usually speaking and singing in an extremely loud and gruff voice) and chou (clown). The co-acting would help them give full play to their strong points while avoiding their shortcomings.

---

[11] **Shiri Xiju** (Ten Days of Theatre), (1939), no. 55, p. 19.

(2) In the early days of the 20th century, actresses had only just embarked on careers in Peking Opera, and they had very limited artistic attainments and experiences. Co-acting was a good opportunity for them to learn from actors so as to improve their own performances.

(3) By the early 20th century, there were many male actors who enjoyed a great reputation among audiences. Co-acting with them was a shortcut for actresses to become well-known.

Table 4 shows the covoluted development of co-acting:

Table 4. The Development of Co-acting in Beijing (1790-1937)

Time	1790-1912	1912-1913	1913-1930	1930-1937
Co-acting	No	Yes	No	Yes

Sources:
1. Zhou Mingtai, *Wushinian Beiping Xiju Shiliao*, (1932), vol. 4, no. 9, p. 15.
2. Takeo Tsuji, op. cit., **Shuntian Times**, 28 January 1930.

Between 1912 and 1913, some actors and actresses in Beijing co-acted for several months. However, co-acting was soon prohibited. In accordance with the prohibition by the authorities, actors and actresses were not supposed to act in the same troupe, not to mention acting in the same play. The excuse for this ban was that the co-acting was an offence against public decency, but it actually reflected the conflicts and competition between men and women in the field of Peking Opera. An article published in the **Shuntian Times** on 6 February 1930 pointed out: "After the founding of the Republic of China, there was co-acting in some troupes in the capital. However, since the audience tended to pay more attention to the good looks of the actresses than the artistic skills, actors gradually found it difficult to keep a foothold for themselves. Such being the case, some actors tried to persuade the authorities to ban co-acting on the pretext of upholding a good social climate. As a result co-acting was prohibited for as much as seventeen years after 1913"[12] Jiang Shangxing also dicussed the prohibition in 1913 in his **What I Saw and Heard of Peking Opera over the Past Sixty Years** (1986). He wrote: "After the Revolution of 1911, the market in Beijing was depressed for a time. In 1913, Yuan Shikai became president, Tang Shaochuan (alternate name Shaoyi) set up a cabinet, and Zhao Zhi'an (alternate name Bingjun) was placed in charge of the Ministry of Internal Affairs. In order to prosper the market and boost popular morale, he lifted the ban on co-acting. However, these happy days soon passed. Several famous actors submitted a joint letter to Zhengle Yuhua Hui, the predecessor of Liyuan Gonghui, the Guild of Actors, saying, 'Co-acting is an offence against decency and should be banned'. The Police in the capital approved this suggestion and issued an order halting co-acting within a definite time limit. After that, actresses had to leave Beijing one after another."[13]

The discrimination against women in Peking Opera circles can also be seen in the fact that some actors simply refused to co-operate with actresses. Chuiyun Gezhu in his "Nling Jiuhua (Anecdotes Concerning Actresses) (1932) recorded how Tan Xinpei (1847-1917), honoured China's leading actor refused to co-act with an actress in Tianjin in 1912: "When Tan Xinpei learnt that he was going to play **Silang Tan Mu** (Silang Visits His Mother) with an actress as his partner, he sighed, saying, 'I am so old and have played Peking Opera all my life. How could you ask me to co-act with an actress? I would never do that'.' Then the manager of the troupe had to ask another actor to be

---

[12] Anon., "Hope to the Coacting of Actors and Actresses", **Shuntian Shibao**, 6 February, 1930.

[13] Jiang Shangxing, **What I saw and Heard of Peking Opera in the Past Sixty Years**, (Shanghai: Xuelin Chubanshe, 1986), pp. 171-172.

his partner".[14] This is only one example of the deep prejudice some actors harboured against actresses.

In spite of all this prejudice and discrimination, women's entry into the field of Peking Opera had become an irresistible trend. By the 1920s, actresses had made considerable progress, and, among whom, many were studying very hard and had made brilliant artistic achievements. As Zhucun pointed out in his "The Masculinised Actress Xue Yanqin", "the performances of actresses used to be not worth mentioning because their singing and dancing were often not in accordance with the required tunes and rhythms, and their acting was often sluggish. Yet, in recent years, many excellent actresses equal to those famous actors have appeared".[15] The outstanding skill of actresses gradually won audience recognition. In 1930, the authorities lifted the ban on co-acting, and co-acting thereafter became more and more popular while many actors, including some renowned ones, were willing to have actresses as their partners. For example, the young actress Xin Yanqiu co-acted with Yang Xiaolou (1878-1938), a well-known actor who enjoyed a reputation equal to that of Mei Lanfang and who was honoured with the title of Master of Wusheng[16] Roles. According to the theatre advertisements in the **Shuntian Times**, in January and February 1930 Xin Yanqiu and Yang Xiaolou co-acted on as many as eleven occasions.[17] It is clear that by the 1930s women had appeared as partners of men on the Peking Opera stage.

Not only did women become men's partners in Peking Opera circles, but they also began to develop a competitive relationship with the latter. By the 1920s-1930s, being very active on stage, some actresses such as Xue Yanqin (1906-1986), Zhang E'yun (1912-   ), Xin Yanqiu, and Meng Xiaodong (1907-1977), were enjoying great popularity and were much

---

[14] *Xiju Yuekan*, September 1932, vol. 3, no. 12, pp. 1-2.

[15] *Beiyang Huabao*, 20 July 1929, p. 2.

[16] *Wusheng*, a type of male role specialising in acrobatics.

[17] *Shuntian Shibao*, 1 February-31 March 1930.

admired. They endeavoured to perfect their skills, learnt from others modestly, made great efforts to stage new plays of their own, and did their best to create new artistic styles. Their popularity could even match that of their male counterparts. As You Tian wrote in "Jujie zhi Xin Zoushi" (New Trends in Drama) in 1928, "At a time when audiences value the good looks of women, actresses already have an advantage over actors. Moreover, some actresses have recently striving to perfect their art and can stand up any actor as his equal. They are really very promising."[18] Table 5 statistically shows the number of times actors and actresses performed in 11 theatres in Beijing between January and March 1930, from which we could see how active actresses were on the Beijing stage.

Table 5. Number of Performances by Actors and Actresses (January 1-March 31, 1930)

Sex of Lead Role	Male (%)	Female (%)	Both (%)	Total (%)
No. of Performances	136 (36)	233 (61)	11 (3)	380 (100)

Source:
Shuntian Times, 1 January-31 March, 1930
* The 11 theatres in Beijing were as follows: Jiaxiang, Amusement World in the South City, Zhonghe, Kaiming, Guangdelou, The First Stage, Sanqing, The First Building, Fushoutang and Qingle. Amateur performances were not included.

The actresses had not only worked very hard to improve themselves artistically, but they also participated in social activities with enthusiasm. This can be seen very clearly in their participation in benefit performances for disaster victims in 1930. In that year, serious drought, locust plagues, floods and

[18] *Beiyang Huabao*, 7 March 1928, p. 2.

epidemics ravaged Shanxi and Shaanxi provinces. As a report in the Shenyang newspaper **Shengjing Times** on 28 January 1930 described, "The havoc and loss caused by the disaster were very serious in the Weihe River valley with Xi'an in Shaanxi province a the centre. It is the most dreadful calamity since the dire disaster of 1876-1877. According to an estimate by a member of the Huayang Stricken Areas Relieving Association who witnessed the conditions in the distressed areas, at least two million people starved to death in 1929, and still another two million might be on the verge of starvation before the next harvest.... As far as I know, in more than one village, not a single soul is to be seen ... bodies of those who have perished from cold and hunger can be found everywhere along the road...".[19]

At that time, many actors held benefit performances to aid people in these areas. Among them were the Four Famous Dan, the well-known actor playing laosheng Yan Jupeng (1890-1942),[20] and the Great Master of Wusheng Yang Xiaolou. Actresses also took an active part in such activities. For example, in July 1930, actresses gave a benefit performance at the Jixiang Theatre, and "distributed their pictures among the audience right after their performance. Yang Juqiu sold ten fans painted by herself for more than 30 yuan and donated the money to the distressed areas."[21] In August 1930, Cheng Yanqiu, one of the Four Famous Dan, held a benefit performance at the Zhonghe Theatre", and contributed all of the 1,448 yuan earned to the Committee for Relieving the Stricken Areas in Shaanxi Province. The total costs of 183.42 yuan (including 34.2 yuan for the stage and 149.22 yuan for the backstage) was paid

---

[19] "The Conditions of the Disaster in Shaanxi and Shanxi Provinces —the Latest Report by Huayang Stricken Areas Relieving Association", **Shengjing Shibao**, 28 January, 1930.

[20] Laosheng, a type of male role with a beard, usually playing men in their middle or old age.

[21] "A Chronicle of Events of Actors and Actresses in Beijping", *Xiju Yuekan*, (1930), vol. 3, no. 1, pp. 9-10.

by Mr. Liang Huating, the manager of the theatre. All actors ... as well as the costume renters gave their services voluntarily." In the same month, the renowned actress Xin Yanqiu "held a banquet at Xinfenglou and made arrangements for a benefit performance".[22] The net income was 1073.3 *yuan* (including 1000.8 *yuan* for the tickets and 20 *yuan* contributed by a Mr. Zhang, minus 7.5 *yuan* for the tickets of the "boxes" on the second floor). All the money was given as a donation. The 268.3 yuan paid for the stage and the backstage as well as the payments for the musicians, make-up artists and those who took care of the costumes for amateurs (except Ms. Baofen and Ms. Huizhen) was contributed by Xin Yanqiu."[23] It was indeed something rare and deserving praise that actresses could make such efforts to promote the public good given the historical circumstances.

The achievements of actresses and their enthusiastic participation in social life enhanced their reputations inside and outside the Peking Opera world, while many succeeded in winning over actors and musicians to their cause. In October 1930, **New Beijing Daily** sponsored a poll to select "The Famous Actors and Actresses in Beijing and Tianjin". According to a report in Xiju Yuekan (Theatre Monthly), "First, a chairman and chairwoman were elected. The former was Cheng Yanqiu who received 6,889 votes (published in New Beijing Daily on Oct. 15),[24] the latter was Xin Yanqiu with 12,875 votes (published on 16 October)".The influence of actresses was self-evident from these figures. The observation was made that "*Yin* (female) is rising while yang (male) is falling in Peking Opera".

(4) The Increasing Importance of Female Roles in the Peking Opera Repertoire.

Male roles were the major roles in Peking Opera from its

22 Ibid., (1930), vol. 3, no. 2, p. 2.
23 Ibid., p. 9.
24 Ibid., (1930), vol. 3, no. 1, p. 8.

inception, but this was changing by the early 20th century owing to the contribution of Wang Yaoqing who vigorously reformed the singing modes, the style of performance and the very appearance of female roles, thereby improving their status within the repertoire. With the appearance of the Four Famous Dans headed by Mei Lanfang, the art of female roles had made much more progress. The importance of female characters in plays increased greatly. As a pamphlet which Mei Lanfang (1918) edited and which was published by the Mei Society in Shanghai put it, "Recently, female roles have become the main force in Peking Opera in Beijing. The Shuangqing Troupe simply cannot survive without Mei Lanfang. It seems to the author that the greatest change around the 1930s was the decline of male roles and the growth of female roles. The highest position had been occupied by laosheng for many years. Since Tan Xinpei, generations of excellent actors have appeared and the laosheng role has always been the mainstay of troupes. As for the *qingyi, huadan,*[25] *xiaosheng,*[26] *heitou,*[27] and *laodan* roles, these have been merely minor or auxiliary roles. However, after the death of Tan Xinpei, Mei Lanfang took advantage of the situation at a time when the laosheng roles suffered a disastrous decline and female roles began to occupy a leading position. It seems that Tan Xinpei was the last hero of laosheng and it fell to Mei Lanfang to open up new prospects for Peking Opera. It is Mei Lanfang's good looks, intelligence, creativity and initiative that have made female roles the backbone of Peking Opera while male roles have been reduced to a position below that of the qingyi roles. Only one favoured by Heaven

---

[25] Huashan, a type of female role created by Wang Yaoqing and developed by Mei Lanfang. It combined the styles of *qingyi, huadan* and *daomadan.*

[26] *Xiaosheng*, a type of male role depicting young men.

[27] *Heitou*, painted face.

could have such tremendous power".[28]

Since the beginning of this century, the images of women on the stage have greatly changed. Among the female leading roles in the 83 plays created between 1917 and 1937, 28 (34%) have depicted women searching for love or happiness, as in *Huo Xiaoyu* and *Renmian Taohua* (Face and Peach), 24 (25%) have depicted wise mothers, virtuous wives, or ladies prepared to die in order to preserving their chastity, as in *Lüzhu Zhuilou* (Lüzhu Jumping Down from the Top Floor) and *Qing Shuang Jian* (Blue Frost Sword), 10 (12%) have depicted heroines, as in *Shen Yunying* and *Hongxian Dao He* (Hongxian Steals the Box), 7 (8%) have depicted persecuted women, as in *Huangshan Lei* (Tears in the Barren Mountains) and *Honglou Er You* (The You Sisters in the Red Mansions), 6 (7%) have depicted silly women, vicious shrews or sirens, as in *Bao Si* and *Yu Xiaocui*, and 5 (6%) have depicted goddesses, as in *Luoshen* (The Goddess of Luo River) and *Tiannü San Hua* (The Maiden in Heaven Scattering Flowers). It is obvious that, in comparison with the female characters in the earlier days of Peking Opera, women's images on the stage during this period were more positive on the whole. Such women were either beautiful and affectionate, sensible and wise, had supreme talent and learning, or were highly skilled in the military arts. Even the sirens tended to be kind and tender, while goddesses were an embodiment of beauty. One thing that should be noted here is that many new plays in the repertoire voiced protests about the maltreatment and persecution of women.

In short, in the early 20th century, women's status was improved both on the stage and in the circle of Peking Opera and this improvement was closely related to the changes in the social status of Chinese women.

---

[28] Shanghai Meishe ed., "A New Era of Peking Opera" in **Mei Lanfang**, (1918), p. 33.

3. Observing the Changes in Chinese Women's Status through Peking Opera

Being an artistic form, Peking Opera to a great extent reflected social life. Peking Opera circles were a cross-section of society and changes within them can be regarded as a microcosm of the changes in the larger society.

Bourgeois democratic ideology began to spread in China in the late 19th century. Although the bourgeois reformists did not explicitly advocate equality between the sexes, they did regard the development of women's education and the abolition of foot binding as component parts of the "innate rights of human beings" and they bitterly condemned the feudal code of ethics for its cruelty to women. Kang Youwei (1858-1927), for example, wrote "A Memorial to the Throne on the Abolition of Female Foot Binding" which he submitted to the Guangxu Emperor in 1898. In it he cited the disastrous consequences of foot binding for women, their offspring, the nation and the country.[29] Liang Qichao (1873-1929), in his article "On Setting up Female Schools", discussed the significance of women's education for "defending the nation and protecting our offspring". From the beginning of the 20th century onwards, the bourgeois revolutionaries further appealed for equality between men and women as well as women's rights, calling for women's participation in the democratic revolution to overthrow the rule of the Qing dynasty. It was with the development of the bourgeois revolution that female schools were recognized by the imperial government in 1907. More female primary schools were set up and Chinese women's primary education began to develop slowly. During the bourgeois revolution, a number of progressively-minded women made their contribution. And after the revolution's success, they claimed the female right to political participation. For example, on 11 March 1912, the

---

[29] Kang Youwei, "Memorial to the Throne in 1898", 1898, pp. 43-45

senate of the provisional government in Nanjing promulgated a provisional constitution, the second chapter of which provided that, "All people of the Republic of China are equal, regardless of their race, class or religion".[30] However, not a word was mentioned concerning equality between the sexes. As a result, a crowd of indignant feminists burst into the senate, "broke the glass and kicked down the guards' security screens".[31] After the May Fourth Movement in 1919, the feudal ethics was attacked even more violently while the ideas of women's emancipation spread more widely in society. Marital autonomy, women's employment and economic independence, women's education, women's political participation, freedom of social contact between men and women, and the call for a ban on prostitution all became contentious social issues which gave rise to much discussion. In 1920, Beijing University pioneered enrolling female students and became the first coeducational university set up in China. In some cities, women's organizations were very active.

All these facts demonstrate that Chinese women were looking for a new social role for themselves and seeking to establish a new type of relationship with men.

Although most initiators of the movements mentioned above were progressive-minded intellectuals and the main body of feminists were educated women in the big cities, this trend towards women's emancipation did have a great influence on Chinese society, and Peking Opera circles were no exception. Being an artistic form born in feudal China, Peking Opera had the clear stamp of feudal society on it, and it became an instrument to propagandise the feudal code of ethics especially as they applied to gender. One may say that the social values of the patriarchy found their expression both in Peking Opera

---

[30] Li Xin ed., **History of the Republic of China**, (1982), vol. 1, p. 436.

[31] Chen Dongyuan, **A History of the Life of Chinese Women**, (1975), p. 360.

circles and in the many old regulations governing the genre. However, change had begun to take place in the late 19th and early 20th centuries. The appearance of female audiences, the better training of actresses, the active participation of actresses in artistic as well as social activities, the development of the cooperation and competition between actors and actresses, the beautification of female characters, and the praise of love in plays created in this period—all these changes showed the influence of the endeavours to realise equality between men and women. The changes in Peking Opera can be considered, to a certain extent, to be a projection of the historical changes in Chinese society on this traditional art.

In the same way in which Chinese women did not achieve thorough emancipation, neither did they achieve full equality with men in Peking Opera circles. Although there were a lot of excellent actresses in this period of whom some became quite famous, and there were signs that they were well-matched with their male counterparts, and, moreover, actresses have natural advantages in portraying female roles, most of them, most had fairly ephemeral fame. They could not ultimately displace the Four Famous Dan. Almost all actresses had brief careers. The main factors leading to this situation were:

(1) Social factors.

Before 1949, the social status of both actors and actresses was very low, while that of the latter was even lower than that of the former. Actresses confronted every kind of discrimination and humiliation. Actresses were subject to bullying and were sometimes even forced to be the concubines of warlords, officials, gangsters or rich men. For women, it was by no means easy to withstand this vicious power. Some yielded to the pressure and gave up their careers, and became playthings of the rich and powerful soon after they began their rise to fame. Others would not degenerate and contend for their fate very bitterly. Others were driven from the stage, in order to preserve their reputation and dignity.

(2) Family factors.

When an actress married, she was generally expected to renounce her art, and become a virtuous wife and wise mother. For many Chinese men, it was a disgrace if his wife appeared on stage. Generally speaking, a husband would not allow his wife to continue her career as an actress. Many actresses left the stage immediately after marriage. Such cases were too numerous to be enumerated.

(3) Factors involving women's expectations.

Many actresses regarded being a good wife and mother as an ideal goal. In spite of their deep love for their art, their contemplation of uncertain futures in their careers caused many actresses to lose their self-confidence and choose an uninteresting but comparatively safe course through life. Many sought to find a decent husband while still young and pretty, and it was quite common to find that no sooner had an actress begun to enjoy some reputation than she got married and retired from the stage.

(4) Physiological factors.

Ageing, marriage, child-bearing, and breast-feeding all posed problems for an actress' long-term career. Although the effects of these physiological factors might vary from person to person, for some actresses, these were really unfavourable factors.

These then are the main reasons why many promising actresses, even actresses with great achievements, left the stage early. Of these reasons, the social factors were the most important. Family factors and expectations all ultimately derive from social factors. This reflects the historical fact that in male-dominated Chinese society prior to the 1930s, although the status of Chinese women had somewhat improved, as a gender group, women still suffered rule and oppression by men, as well as their expression in political power, clan authority, and religious authority.

CHAPTER TEN
THE WOMEN'S MOVEMENT AND WOMEN'S LIBERATION IN CHINA

Lü Meiyi and *Zheng Yongfu*

1. The Brewing of the Modern Chinese Women's Movement

The women's liberation movement is a social revolution for the purpose of improving women's social status, recovering their social rights and realizing their value as "social beings". Charles Fourier pointed out: "The development of a specific historical epoch can always be judged by the degree of freedom women attain, for the triumph of humanity over beastliness of mankind is most manifest in the relations between women and men, females and males. The degree of women's liberation is the natural yardstick for the general liberation". Marx and Engels praised that statement as being "most to the point."[1] The world-wide women's movement began along with the bourgeois revolutionary movement. It was marked by women's issues appearing on the agenda of history as major social issues which drew increasingly extensive attention in society, and by women beginning to take an active part in the movement and putting forth their justified demands for their own interests. The rise of the women's liberation movement on the one hand required the growth of social productive forces to a degree which would

---

[1] **Complete Works of Marx and Engels** (People's Publishing House, 1965), Vol. Two, pp.249-250.

be able to provide a material basis for women to return to the mainstream of society, and, on the other hand, it requires mankind, women included, to be able to reassess the value of their own being. When mankind reached the capitalist stage, human society more or less possessed those two conditions.

Strictly speaking, the women's liberation movement in China began to gather momentum after the bourgeoisie appeared on the historical stage. Nevertheless, the 1840 Opium War broke open the tightly closed door of the feudal kingdom and the country was thus gradually fettered to the chains of international imperialism, which determined the advanced nature of the women's movement in China. In a sense, the Kingdom of Heavenly Peace movement, long known in English as the Taiping Rebellion, the women's schools and societies opposing feet binding sponsored by Western missionaries, and the early propaganda of the Modernisation Movement all served to accelerate the passing away of the old and the emergence of the new. The last two factors in particular prepared the conditions for the growth of the women's movement in China.

(1) The Impact of the Movement of the Kingdom of Heavenly Peace

The Movement of the Kingdom of Heavenly Peace broke out with mighty force in 1851. The leader of this movement Hong Xiuquan had certain vague ideas regarding sexual equality. He believed that, "Most men in the world are my brothers; most women in the world are my sisters"[2] He suggested that people in the ranks of the armies of the Kingdom of Heavenly Peace address one another as brothers or sisters in disregard of rank.[3] This idea stemmed from the simple Christian belief that

[2] "The Kingdom of Heavenly Peace" in **Collections of Archives of Modern Chinese History** (Shanghai Publishing House, 1955), vol. 1, p. 87.

[3] **Simplified Archives of the Kingdom of Heavenly Peace** (Zhonghua Shuju, 1962), vol. 6, p. 393.

all people are equal before God, the egalitarian thinking of Chinese peasant uprisings, and the Confucian concept of universal unity. That great uprising waged by Chinese peasants introduced quite a number of enlightened policies on women's issues. One of them was the establishment of special women's camps, women's schools and women's armies, as ways to attract women into the rebel army and engaging in productive labor to support the uprising. This move enabled large numbers of women to leave their homes and form their own organizations to contribute to the peasant war. Secondly, the uprising introduced a whole series of women's official ranks, official examinations for women and women's ranks of nobility, which provided a structure for women's participation in social and political activities. Thirdly, women were on the same footing as men in the distribution of land. Fourthly, attention was paid to the education for women. Fifth, the movement abrogated certain customs and habits considered detrimental to women such as foot binding, prostitution, the male right to have concubines and the trade in maid slaves. All this dealt a telling blow to the old conventions in the Kingdom of Heavenly Peace.

However, even the leaders of the Kingdom of Heavenly Peace were unable to free themselves entirely from feudal ideological fetters when it came to women's issues. After the Heavenly Capital was established, Hong Xiuquan's somewhat vague concept of equality between men and women did not develop. If anything, it waned. In his "Poems for Children" published in 1852, Hong even advocated the ethical notion that a woman should "be obedient in three ways (namely, to obey her parents before marriage, her husband after marriage and her sons after her husband's death) and should not contradict her husband". Hong and his peasant comrades proved to be unable to break out of the limitations of their class and times. Therefore the women's liberation movement vaporised in the wake of the failure of the peasant war. Peasant uprisings did not exert a direct influence on the women's movement in China.

(2) Western Missionaries and Women's Enlightenment

After the two Opium Wars, the Western colonialists won the privilege to freely preach religion in China, and there were eventually more then 3,200 missionaries of the Catholic, Protestant and the Orthodox Eastern Churches in the country. Quite a number of them were colonialists clothed in missionary robes, but some of them were sincere propagandists for capitalist culture. A fact worth noting is that a considerable number of the Protestant missionaries were women and some of them had even been influence by the women's emancipation movement in the West. Their concern for women's issues in China first found expression in the newspapers they ran. In their articles published in those papers, they denounced foot binding and the practice of drowning female infants and advocated a school education for women. Some articles carried in **The Universal Journal** reported on the development of women's education and women's participation in social work in Europe and America. News of the women's movement in the West, sporadic as it might be, began to reach the Chinese public.

What is more worth noting is that the missionaries sponsored the establishment of schools for women and societies calling for a moratorium on foot binding. The English Society for the Promotion of Education for Oriental Women in 1844 sent Miss Aldersay to Ningbo to run a women's school there. Statistics show that by 1877 the Protestants had set up 82 women's day schools and 39 women's boarding schools in China with a total enrolment of 2,101; and the Catholic churches ran even more women's schools in China.[4] The direct aim of those missionary schools for women was no doubt to spread the influence of the church, but they also served to disseminate Western culture in China and set an example for running

---

[4] **A Chronology of Education in Modern China** (Shanghai Education Publishing House, 1982), p. 37.

education for women in this country.

In order to oppose the practice of foot binding, Western missionaries in China formed the Natural Feet Society, the first of its kind in China, in Xiamen in 1875. Some women missionaries and Christians headed by an Englishwoman Mrs. Archibald Little (Alicia Bewicke) formed a Natural Feet Society in Shanghai in April 1895. This society exerted fairly extensive influence among the Chinese public as well as high ranking Chinese officials. The missionaries' efforts in running women's schools and advocating natural feet mainly influenced religious circles, but they set an example in initiating a women's movement in China, and providing Chinese modernisers with inspiration.

(3) A Rethink Based on Comparisons: The Modernisers' Early Attention to Women's Issues

A very active force in the Chinese ideological field in the period from the early 1860s to the mid-1890s were the proponents of modernisation, who were generally interested in and knowledgeable concerning the status of women in Western countries. Wang Tao, He Qi, Li Gui and many other modernisers had visited Britain and France on study tours, while Zheng Guanying and others had undertaken serious studies of Western society. They admired the fact that equal attention was paid to issues of both men and women in Western countries, that women's education enjoyed equal status as that for men, and that there were no concubines in Western societies. By comparing Chinese society with Western society, they came to ponder women's issues. Their first discovery was that women's issues were "vital for the prosperity and strength of a nation".[5] With this as their point of departure, the modernisers concerned themselves with education for women, running women's

---

[5] Chen Zhi, *Fuxue* (Studies on Women's Issues), *Yongshu* vol. II of Supplementary Edition.

schools, opposing foot binding and advocating monogamy. They urged that "funds should be raised extensively to set up more schools for women by emulating what they do in the West;" and "the ban on foot binding should be reiterated and carried out in one year."[6] Some people criticized the feudal ethical code and pointed out that "the cardinal principle that a husband as the guide for his wife is in fact a selfish position borrowing from the power of the emperor."[7]

The observations and thinking of the early proponents of the modernisation movement already showed signs of bourgeois democracy. Unfortunately, the outcry was rather weak since it was uttered by a very limited number of people. This, plus the divorce of theory from practice, meant that the movement failed to arouse a significant reaction in society at large.

2. The 1898 Modernisation Movement and Enlightenment for Women

(1) The View of the Proponents of Modernisation

During the 1898 modernisation movement, the theories of evolution and civil rights spread from the West to the Orient and became a theoretical weapon for the bourgeois proponents of the modernisation movement. Inspired by the concept that everybody was born with immutable human rights, they unequivocally advocated equality for men and women which constituted the nucleus of the outlook on women of the bourgeois modernisation movement.

Kang Youwei, a recognised leader of the Modernisation Movement, completed his book "A Complete Book on Practical Theory of Public Rights" in the 1890s. He wrote: "The equality

---

[6] Zheng Guanying, "Women's Education," in **Shengshi Weiyan** (Alarming Statements in a Prosperous Era), juan 3.

[7] Song Shu "On Chastity," **Liuzhai Biyi** (Humble Discourses in Liuzhai Studio).

of mankind is like a geometrical principle", and "all men and women all have their own independent rights". "Should men act as the cardinal principle for women, it would be against the geometrical principle and humanity".[8] Liang Qichao announced that "women are entitled to their own rights".[9] Tan Sitong in his book *Ren Xue* (On Benevolence) pointed out: "Men and women are both the finest beings on earth, both have limitless potential for achievements," and should enjoy "equal rights".[10] Yan Fu, who studied in England, reached his conclusion after making a comparison between China and foreign countries that "Chinese women are generally inferior to men, not because they are inferior in intelligence, but they are inferior owing to artificial means".[11] In other words, the inequality and social difference between men and women were man made. They were in consensus that "equal rights for men and women first gained ground in America and then spread to Japan", which made "America rise in triumph" and "Japan grow strong".[12]

(2) Opposition to Foot Binding and Setting up Women's Schools: The Starting Point of the Women's Movement

After the 1894 Sino-Japanese War, the Western powers scrambled to partition China, posing an unprecedented danger to the Chinese nation. In order to salvage the nation, the

---

[8] **A Complete Book on Practical Theory and Public Rights**, in **Collected Works on the Study of Chinese Culture** (Fudan University Press, 1984), no. 1, pp. 324-348.

[9] Liang Qichao, "Trial Articles of Association for Women's Schools," in *Yinbingshi Heji* (Collected Works of the Ice-Drinking Studio), (Zhonghua Shuju, 1989), vol. 2.

[10] *Renxue* (On Benevolence), pt. 2.

[11] "On Setting up Women's Schools in Shanghai," *Guowen Bao* (National News Journal), Jan. 10 -11, 1898.

[12] Liang Qichao, "Announcement of Setting up Women's Schools," **Selected Works of Liang Qichao**, (Shanghai People's Publishing House, 1984), p. 52.

bourgeois proponents of modernisation launched the Reform Movement of 1898. As part of the modernisation movement, the women's movement emerged in the Chinese political arena for the first time in history.

With opposition to foot binding and the establishment of women's schools as a starting point, the modernisation movement's proponents intended to push the women's movement in China by advocating the emancipation of both the limbs and thinking of Chinese women. They launched a large-scale propaganda drive stressing the drawbacks of foot binding. They pointed out that foot binding was "fettering half of our 400 million compatriots and rendering them disabled and useless", which "should be one of the main reasons for the weakness of our country".[13] They strongly denounced foot binding as a suppression of human rights "achieved by destroying the limbs and spirit of women", and that "women with their feet bound lose their capacity for self defence as well as the basic condition for economic independence".[14]

They also energetically advocated the setting up of societies boycotting foot binding. Kang Youwei sponsored a society of boycotting foot binding in his native Nanhai in Guangdong province first in 1883 and then in 1895. The Shunde County Society for Boycotting Foot Binding was set up in 1897 in Guangdong province. In that same year a National Association for Boycotting Foot Binding was set up in Shanghai. The articles of association stipulated: "All members of this society shall not have their daughters' feet bound and any applicant for admission to this association shall not have a wife with bound feet".[15] The Shanghai Association for Boycotting Foot Binding made a great impact across the country and it was estimated

---

[13] Quoted from recollections by Kang Tongbi, *Zhongguo Funü* (China Women), 1957:5.

[14] "A Critique of Advocates of Foot Binding," *Xiang Bao* (Hunan Journal), no. 15.

[15] Liang Qichao, see f.n. 9.

that its membership grew to some 300,000.[16] Later, associations opposing foot binding were set up in Guangdong, Hubei, Hunan, Macao, Fuzhou, Tianjin and Sichuan. A similar association was formed by overseas Chinese in Singapore. These activities signalled winds of progress in Chinese society. Newspapers carried prescriptions for medicinal foot baths and some shoe shops sold shoes for freed feet. Women's schools offered priority for admission to those with natural feet, while radical intellectuals vowed to marry only women with natural feet.

The advocates of the modernisation campaign also attached special importance to the development of education for women as a means for national salvation. They were aware of the fact that "those countries most developed in women's education are the most powerful ... when women's education declines, mothers cannot educate their children properly and the result is an increase in the numbers of ignorant people and a decrease in intelligent people; in the latter case, it is be a blessing if a nation can even survive".[17] They believed that women were "born with the right to a school education" which could not be taken from them under any pretext.

At the peak of the reform and modernisation drive, the first women's school run by Chinese was set up in Shanghai on June 1, 1898. The school was housed in a temple in the southern part of Shanghai. Jing Yuanshan was the founder and Kang Youwei, Liang Qichao and other leaders of the modernisation movement made generous donations. The official name of the school was the School of the China Society for Women's Study. It was also known as the China Women's School or Jingzheng Women's School. The influence of the school spread fast. Suzhou, Songjiang and Guangdong and many other places followed suit and set up schools. Although the Jingzheng Women's School

---

[16] "Some Advice on Foot Binding," *Wanguo Gongbao* (Global Journal), July 1901.

[17] Li Youning and Zhang Yufa, **Archives of the History of Modern Chinese Women's Liberation Movement**, (Taibei), p. 555

was forced to close down after the failure of the 1898 political reform, the setting up of a women's school by Chinese broke with feudal taboos that dominated traditional education, the significance of which cannot be evaluated too highly.

(3) The Initial Awakening of Chinese Women

Inspired by the 1898 movement for modernisation, some Chinese women became active. They were mostly family members of the advocates of the modernisation movement or educated women with a leaning toward that movement. Among them were Kang Youwei's daughters Kang Tongwei and Kang Tongbi, Liang Qichao's wife Li Huixian, Kang Guangren's wife Huang Jinyu, and Tan Sitong's wife Li Gui. They were among the most active elements in setting up societies for women's studies and women's newspapers. Late in the summer of 1897, the China Society of Women's Study was founded in Shanghai thanks to the assistance of the Modernisation Movement's proponents. Li Gui and Huang Jinyu were on the Board of Directors. This was the only women's organization among the dozens of societies at the time. The China Society of Women's Study in the main did two important things during its short existence, namely the board of directors of the society took part in raising funds for the establishment of a women's school and joined in the administration of the school, and the society published the first women's newspaper *Nüxue Bao* (Journal of Women's Studies) in modern China.

Nüxue Bao, the organ of both the China Society of Women Study and the China Women's School, published its first issue on 24 July 1898. On the editorial board were Kang Tongwei, Li Huixian, Zhang Yunhua and Qiu Yufang, as well as a number of senior editors. The journal called for national salvation: "Women share the responsibility for the destiny of our country".[18] This awareness of linking the cause of women's

---

[18] *Nüxue Bao* (Journal of Women's Studies), no. 4.

liberation with the destiny of the country was a salient feature of the Chinese women's liberation movement, as well as its starting point. The journal unequivocally publicised the view of the equality of men and women, emphasizing that "Nature gives birth to men and women, and they are born equal".[19] Some articles published by the journal openly proposed that women should be in a position to publicly voice their views on national affairs and urged the institution of a ministry of women's studies which would include twelve public elected women commissioners to be assigned to various provinces. Many writers discussed equal opportunity in education for women and freedom of marriage.[20]

The women's movement during the 1898 modernisation movement attracted the participation of only a limited number of women and the movement was led and even organized by male members of the modernising group. This was an extraordinary phenomenon in the history of the women's movement in China, and it was the result of the ignorance, backwardness and weakness of Chinese women at the hands of prolonged feudalism. The genuine awakening of broad sectors of China's female popualtion would be more protracted.

3. The Women's Movement Inspired by Democratic Ideas

(1) The Emergence of Progressive Women's Groups and the Deepening Understanding of Women's Issues

A group of progressive women emerged in China at the turn of this century. These women had various levels of consciousness on account of their different perceptions of their own status and the national destiny. Some were able to link women's

---

[19] Ibid., no. 7.
[20] Ibid., no. 5.

liberation with the struggle to overthrow the feudal Qing regime, and such women formed the vanguard and backbone of the women's liberation movement. They were also ardent followers, or even leaders in some cases, of the bourgeois democratic revolution at the time. The most outstanding among them was Qiu Jin. She resolutely broke her feudal family and untiringly campaigned for women's liberation. She was one of the earliest members of the Tong Meng Hui (Chinese United League) founded by Dr. Sun Yat-sen and one of the leaders of the Zhejiang Branch of the League and a member of the Department of Commentary of the League. She was killed in the Anhui-Zhejiang Uprising of 1907. In modern Chinese history, Qiu Jin stands as a heroine and exemplary figure of Chinese revolutionary women during the period of the old democratic revolution. Also belonging to this advanced group were Zhang Zhujun, known as "the Liang Qichao of women's circles", and Chen Jiefen who founded the Journal of Women's Studies. There were other women who supported or even took part in the women's movement, but for one reason or another they did not directly participate in the revolution against the Qing regime. Representing this group were Lu Bicheng and her two sisters. They took an active part in running women's schools, newspapers, forming women's organizations and did propaganda work for the cause of women's liberation. They were sympathetic with the democratic revolution and even sided with it, but they did not take a direct part in it. There were still others, mostly wives of high-ranking officials. The limitations of their social status prevented them from taking an active part in the women's liberation movement, but their thinking was in keeping with the pulse of the times. Among them were Shan Shili, who travelled extensively in Europe as a diplomat's wife, and Qiu Binxin, who was a devoted philanthropist and mother of Liao Zhongkai, a leader of the Tong Meng Hui. At the turn of the century a wave of Western democratic theories were introduced among Chinese intellectuals. Together with the theories of Rousseau and Darwin, Western theories on women's liberation also came to China. Inspired by democratic thinking, people in China began to understand women's issues better. Most conspicuous was the change of the old outlook with an emphasis on women's obligations and a greater consciousness of women's rights. In discussing women sharing men's responsibility for the national destiny, people began to pay greater attention to the civil rights of women. They pointed out that "since we are born human beings, we ought to share democratic rights which are sacred and not to be violated".[21]

Progressive thinkers and activists advocated a new bourgeois outlook on the family in a fairly systematic way. They advocated freedom of marriage and opposed arranged marriages, mercenary marriages, and early engagement and marriage. They even urged birth control. Some tackled the women's issue from the economic point of view, pointing out: "When women cannot make money and have no skills, they have to place their happiness and honour in the hands of their husbands and sons", and so women should "try to master skills and become independent economically".[22] Some discussed the issue of women's right of inheritance, pointing out that "women should also be entitled to inherit property as can men".[23] The earliest modern Chinese book solely on women's issues was *Nüjie Zhong* (Bell for Women) by Jin Tianhe which was published by the Datong Book Company in Shanghai in 1903. The book was a comprehensive reflection of the progressive views on women's liberation since the 1898 Modernisation Movement. It won immediate recognition among the bourgeois revolutionaries and broad sections of intellectuals. The book was sold out

---

[21] "Speech by Xu Yucheng to a Women's Gathering," *Zhongguo Xin Nüjie Zazhi* (Magazine of China's New Women), no. 5.

[22] "Advice to My Sisters", **Selected Poems and Essays by Qiu Jin**, (People's Literature Publishing House, 1982), p. 12.

[23] **Women's Tears**, by He Damiu, pp. 13-19, Jingdu Book Company, 1908

soon after it came off the press and became literally a clarion call to Chinese women to rise in defence of their rights.

This period also saw energetic activities by the Anarchists who resolutely opposed the oppression of women in China and sharply criticized the outlook on women held by the bourgeoisie in the West. They raised slogans such as "sex revolution," "revenge by women," "revolution aimed at destroying the family," etc. However, their views were considered to be too radical and utopian.

(2) A Fashionable Cause

It was rather fashionable at the turn of this century to run women's schools and advocate natural feet. Not only the bourgeois revolutionaries, but the constitutionalists as well, joined in the chorus. Even the Qing government and some officials who were pushing a "New Deal" reform and preparing for a constitutional monarchy expressed their support. Therefore the two campaigns developed fairly quickly.

The women's schools were mostly private ones at the time, the most prestigious among them being the Patriotic Women's School and the Wuben Women's School in Shanghai, and the Northern Women's School in Tianjin. People displayed admirable zeal in running women's schools. A most outstanding example was Miss Hui Xing, president of the Zhenwen Women's School in Hangzhou who took her own life in order to raise educational funding in 1906. The Qing government promulgated its first Articles of Association for Women's Schools in the following year. Thus women's education initially won official recognition and government-run women's primary schools and women's teacher training schools were set up one after another in the provinces. The Christian churches in China jointly established the North China Women's Union University in 1905, marking the beginning of higher education for women in China. According to incomplete statistics compiled by the Qing government, there were 308 women's schools (including those run by churches) with a combined enrolment of 14,054 in 1909.[24] There also emerged a wave of women students pursuing studies abroad in Chinese society at the time. Most of them went to Japan, while fewer went to Europe and the United States. There were nearly 100 Chinese women students in Tokyo alone in 1907. They included both those sent by the Qing government and those who went there as self-funded private students. Some of the Chinese women students abroad took an active part in the bourgeois revolution and played a vanguard role in the women's liberation movement. Noted women social activists such as Qiu Jin, Lin Zongsu, Tang Qunying, Li Ziping, Chen Jiefen, Liu Qingxia, Hu Binxia and He Xiangning all studied abroad.

In the period between 1901 and 1905, the campaign for natural feet took on some new features. Firstly, it became increasingly popular. Societies of natural feet spread from cities to the countryside and a rally for opposing foot binding easily attracted hundreds or even thousands of people. By 1904, the governors of 18 provinces had promulgated laws forbidding foot binding. Secondly, there was a sharp increase in the number of women activists who consciously campaigned against foot binding. Madame Gao Baishu organized a natural feet society in Shanghai, marking the first solely women's society for natural feet. The campaign progressed in an unprecedented fashion. In Guangzhou and other advanced centres, over 80 percent of women refused to bind their feet.

The upsurge of the democratic movement at the turn of the century led to a wave of new organizations, newspapers and magazines being established. According to incomplete data, more than 40 women's organizations and more than 30 women's newspapers and magazines emerged in the 1901-1911 period. That was a great advance when compared with the 1898

---

[24] **Chinese History of Education in the Last 30 Years** by Chen Yilin, p.100, Taibei edition

period.[25] The women's organizations in this period became more formal, and were characterized by a fairly comprehensive organization, and clear goals, articles of association and scheduled activities. But they were varied in their respective goals. Some strove to raise women's rights with women's liberation as their ultimate purpose; some were occupied with participation in the political struggle of the time; and still others were devoted to the reform of social conventions or involved in philanthropic undertakings. About half of the women's organizations belonged to the first category. The Society for Universal Love, the Women's Association of Insurance for Developing Education, the Association of Women Comrades of Russia, and the China Women's Society represented different types of women's organizations.

The most influential women's newspapers early in this century included *Nüxue Bao* founded by Chen Jiefen in Shanghai in 1902, *Nüzi Shijie* (Women's World) founded by Ding Chuwo in Shanghai in January 1904, *Zhongguo Nü Bao* (China Women's Journal) founded by Qiu Jin in Shanghai in January 1907, and the *Shenzhou Nü Bao* (Women's Journal of the Divine Land) founded by Chen Zhiqun in Shanghai in 1907. Chinese women students in Japan ran a number of newspapers and magazines, the most influential of which was the *Zhongguo Xin Funü Zazhi* (Magazine of New Chinese Women) established by Yan Bin and Liu Qingxia. This magazine ran to 5,000 copies at its peak.

The development of women's education, the awareness for the evils of foot binding, the formation of women's organizations and the emergence of women's journals were the outcome of the upsurge of the women's movement at the turn of the century, which in turn accelerated the awakening of women in China.

---

[25] See **Women's Movement in China (1840-1921)** by Lu Meiyi and Zheng Yongfu, pp. 170-173, 188-190, Henan People's Publishing House, 1990.

(3) Women in the 1911 Revolution

The 1911 Revolution which toppled the rule of the Qing Dynasty rallied radical Chinese women under the banner of a bourgeois revolution. Women took part in many armed insurrectionist activities organized by the Tong Meng Hui which included smuggling arms, making bombs, sheltering comrades, giving first aid at the front and even assassinating Qing officials.

The Wuchang Uprising broke out on 10 October 1911 and it attracted the participation of women across China in the struggle. Zhang Mojun took part in the planning of the recovery of Suzhou and Yin Ruizhi and Yin Weijun were directly involved in taking Shanghai and Nanjing. Some women took part in front-line first aid work, as for example did Zhang Zhujun, director of the Shanghai Hospital. She led and organized a Red Cross team and went to the front at Wuchang to provide first aid. She herself was wounded.

What was most impressive was the formation of a women's revolutionary detachment. After repeated requests, 19-year-old Wu Shuqing finally won the approval from the revolutionary military government to form a women's revolutionary army in Wuhan. Women in Shanghai organized the Shanghai Women's Northern Expeditionary Suicide Detachment, the Women's Northern Expedition Detachment, the Women's Military Group, the Shanghai Women's National Revolutionary Army and the Women's Martial Arts Tong Meng Hui. Women in Guangzhou organized the Guangdong Women's Northern Expeditionary Army and marched with the Northern Expedition to Xuzhou, participating in the Battle of Shugu.

Many women took part in the work of collecting provisions for the revolutionary army. Women in Shanghai formed the Shanghai Women's Association in Support of the Revolution and an Association of Women of the Divine Land in Support of the Republic. Zhang Mojun and others presented to Dr. Sun

Yat-sen a donation on behalf of women in Zhejiang Province. Undoubtedly, Chinese women made a valuable contribution to the overthrow of the monarchy in China.

(4) Mass Participation in Political Activities

The progressive sector of the bourgeois women in China followed their British counterparts in taking an active part in political affairs when the revolutionary government was being established.

In November 1911 Lin Zongsu in Shanghai officiated over the establishment of the Society of Women Comrades Participating in Politics, which was followed by the Women's League of the Divine Land for Participation in Political Affairs, the Women's Tong Meng Hui, the Association of Women of the Divine Land in Support of the Republic, the Women's Republican Association, the Society for Equality between Men and Women and other women's organizations aimed at taking part in political affairs in Nanjing, Shanghai and other places. Women delegates more than once interviewed Provisional President Sun Yat-sen, and submitted petitions demanding provisional decrees on women's rights to participate in political activities. Sun Yat-sen, in reply, wrote: "Human rights are conferred by Heaven. Men and women are not born different in their ability. Equality and universal justice are universally applicable principles.... It is absolutely a matter of course for women to take part in political affairs".[26] However, the provisional constitution revised by the Provisional Parliament made no mention of equality between men and women, to say nothing of women's participation in political affairs. This enraged progressive women. Tang Qunying, Zhang Hanying and dozens of others on more than one occasion broke into the Provisional Parliament, debated with parliamentary members and even

---

[26] "A Reply to the Women's Association in Support of the Republic," **Complete Works of Sun Yat-sen**, pp. 52-53, Zhonghua Book Company, 1982

smashed some glass windows from 19 March 1912. Public opinion was also stirred up, leading to a great debate on whether women were capable of taking part in political affairs, what should constitute women's political responsibility, and whether women's participation in politics would impair the family and society. The reality was that at the time the majority of the population were doubtful or even negative on the question of women's participation in political affairs.

After the Provisional Government moved to the north, the women's movement in China entered a dark period. When the Kuomintang convened its inaugural meeting in August 1912 in Beijing, Song Jiaoren, chairman of the meeting was defeated by Tang Qunyin and Wang Changguo because the political program of the Kuomintang contained no clause on equality between men and women. The parliament in November of the same year rejected a plea by Tang Qunying and others by majority vote. That was the first setback for Chinese women in their struggle for the right to take part in political affairs.

4. From the Discovery of the Human Being to the Discovery of the Female: The May 4th Movement and Women's Liberation

(1) The New Culture Movement at Its Early Stage Deepens Understanding of Women's Issue

After Yuan Shikai founded his northern warlord (Beiyang Junfa) regime, an adverse current emerged, and in order to overcome this reactionary tide, Chinese ideological and cultural circles launched a new enlightenment movement, the New Culture Movement. At the early stage of this movement, women's issues became a focus of attention. While during the 1898 campaign and the 1911 revolutionary period people's attention was concentrated on women's obligations and rights, attention during this new period was paid more closely to the liberation of the personality of women. Just as some critics point out that "the discovery of the human being is applied to women, which leads to the discovery of the fact that women are also human beings; when women discover that they are also human beings, all sorts of problems emerge".[27]

Many people pointed out that women's issuesboils down to the question of whether a woman should have an independent personality. The ready answer was, "Women should have their independent personality because they are part of the 'human race' ." "The tragedy for women in history has been that the personality of women is not complete or there is no women's personality".[28] Regarding the hotly debated issue of chastity, some people pointed out that "the question of personality is more important than that of chastity" but those who expect women to die for the sake of chastity "are heartless proponents of chastity" "which is tantamount to the crime of murder".[29] The advocates of the New Culture pushed for the institution of new ethics which would recognise and respect "the independent personality of the individual which would not have being subsidiary to others as the prerequisite". They poignantly criticized the thesis that the husband is the cardinal principle of the wife, pointing out: "If that is true, then the wife would be subsidiary without any independent personality".[30] The New Culture Movement touched on almost all aspects of women's liberation. Li Dazhao, Chen Duxiu, Lu Xun, Hu Shi, Wu Yu and many others displayed an irreconcilable attitude towards feudalism in their criticism of the old ideology, ethics and culture. Their efforts helped further spread a better understanding of the bourgeois outlook on women's issues.

---

[27] **The Discovery of the Female Sex** by Shu Wu, pp.4-5

[28] "The Question of the Personality of Women", No. 2, Vol. 1, **New Wave**

[29] **Writings by Hu Shi**, pp. 40-41, Vol.4

[30] "1916" by Chen Duxiu, No. 5, Vol. 1, **New Youth** magazine.

(2) Women in the Patriotic Salvation Movement

On 4 May, 1919, a massive patriotic movement against imperialism broke out in Beijing. The next day women students in the city were talking about joining in the struggle. On 7 May, the students of the Women's Higher Normal School and a dozen other women's schools in Beijing formed the Beijing Women Students' Federation and published its "Declaration to All Women in China". This first united action by men and women students took place in Beijing in mid-May. On 19 May, all women students in Beijing joined a general strike by 25,000 students. The students of 15 women's schools gathered in Tian'-anmen Square on 4 June and declared their solidarity with those arrested students. They then marched to the front of the presidential house for a demonstration launched for the first time solely by Chinese women students. Women students in Tianjin set an example for women students across the country. Women students marched at the head of columns in many demonstrations in defiance of arrest and violence by police. The most outstanding among them were Guo Longzhen, Liu Qingyang, Deng Yingchao and Zhang Ruoming. Women students in Shanghai began joining the nation-wide general strike by the students on 26 May. In addition to the students, women workers, some local Christian women's organizations and even housewives and prostitutes were attracted to the political struggle. By early June, the wave of struggle had spread to 89 cities and towns in Jiangsu, Shandong, Hunan, Guangdong, Jiangxi, Zhejiang, Fujian, Anhui, Sichuan, Henan and nine other provinces. Women organized themselves into patriotic organizations, joined demonstrations, took part in agitation, boycotted Japanese goods and went on strike. Their soaring patriotism and deep sense of historical responsibility showed that Chinese women had become one of the principal forces in the patriotic anti-imperialist movement, not just playing a secondary role as they had during the 1898 and 1911 movements.

(3) Under the Banner of Democracy and Science

There were two clear central themes of the May 4th Movement, namely patriotism and opposition to imperialism, and the advocacy of democracy and science. In the anti-feudal enlightenment movement, women's liberation became a focus of struggle. At the time all those in support of the New Culture Movement called for equality between men and women. The women's issue became a heated topic of debate in the media. The patriotic democratic movement waged by students and other young people on the one hand inspired the patriotism of the broad masses of Chinese women and attracted them into the mass movement, and on the other hand it swept away the obsolete conventional concepts from people's minds thus creating good conditions for the development of the women's movement. In the spring of 1919, some students and teachers of Beijing University began cultivating the idea of establishing co-education. A young woman named Deng Chunlan from Gansu province wrote a letter to Cai Yuanpei, president of Beijing University, on 19 May, for the first time in China raising the demand to open the door of the university to women as well as men. In the following spring the university enrolled its first batch of women students, which included Deng Chunlan, Wang Lan and seven others, as auditors in the department of arts. This news came "like a thunderbolt in winter"[31] That summer, the university began enrolling regular freshmen women students as well, and other institutions of higher learning soon followed. Co-education surged forward with seemingly irresistible force. Secondary and primary schools subsequently also instituted co-education. A very prominent slogan during the May 4th Movement was "Openly conduct social contacts". Progressive young people displayed admirable boldness in breaking the obsolete convention that men and women

---

[31] "Story of Co-education in Beijing University," No.1, Vol. 1 of **Youngsters' World**.

should not mix in public. They practised and promoted freedom of social contacts between men and women in the patriotic democratic movement. The New Democracy Society in Changsha, Hunan province, admitted 19 females to its membership and the Society of Awakening in Tianjin was composed of equal numbers of men and women members. They set an example.

"Freedom of marriage" was the most outstanding slogan in the women's liberation movement. More and more people were no longer satisfied with criticising the feudal marriage system. They resisted family-arranged marriages, and walked out of them or even took their own lives to protest the old marriage practices. A bride named Zhao Wuzhen in Changsha killed herself in her bridal sedan to protest the feudal marriage imposed on her by her parents in November 1919. The incident shocked the entirety of Chinese society. Mao Zedong wrote nine pieces in the *Changsha Ta Kung Pao* on the tragedy.

Equal opportunity in employment for men and women also drew wide attention. Progressive educated women vigorously demanded a greater scope of employment for women and equality in job openings for both sexes. Following suits against educational and medical departments, the railway administration and banks also began to employ some women workers.

(4) New Goals and New Probing

Numerous schools of socialism were in vogue during the May 4th Movement. Li Dazhao and Chen Duxiu and some others wrote a series of articles in the media to introduce Marxism and Marxist views on women's liberation. They included "Women's Issues after the War," "Women's Liberation and Democracy," and "Women's Issues and Socialism". Some progressive young people finally chose Marxism, which was of far-reaching significance for the women's movement in China.

As the May 4th Movement drew to its close, "reforming society" became the new goal of the struggle by progressive youth. Because the practice of work-study was in fashion, women's societies for mutual aid in work-study emerged as a matter of course in Beijing and Tianjin. Some young women severed their relations with their families in an attempt to lead a new life through forming societies for part-time work and part-time study. Although they inevitably met with failure, what they displayed was an intrepid pioneering spirit. There were other young women who went abroad to work through their studies. There were a dozen women among the more than 300 people who left Hunan province to study in France. Among them were Xiang Jingyu, Cai Chang, Xiong Jiguang, Wei Bi, Lao Zhanjun and Cai Hesen's mother Ge Jianhao who was already over fifty years old. Some women went to Germany and Russia. The work-study drive helped train a group of talented women and outstanding social activists.

The May 4th Movement, a movement for ideological emancipation of profound significance in modern Chinese history, exerted a tremendous impact on a whole generation of people in China. In view of the women's liberation movement, it not only had of direct results, but also prepared public opinion, and public sentiment, thinking and personnel for a new high tide in the women's liberation movement, auguring the onset of a new era in the women's liberation movement.

5. Chinese Women in the 1920s and 1930s

(1) The Guidelines and Policies of the Kuomintang and the Chinese Communist Party on the Women's Movement in the 1920s

Founded in 1921, the Chinese Communist Party inevitably undertook the historical task of guiding the women's movement in China. Between its second congress in 1922 and fourth congress in 1925, the Chinese Communist Party adopted resolutions on women's issues which laid down the party's basic program and policies for the women's movement. The essential points were: First, the party affirmed that "the emancipation of women goes hand in hand with the liberation of the working class and that only when the proletariat wins political power, can women win genuine emancipation". The party argues that the women's movement should unequivocally put forth the slogan of opposing imperialism and feudalism; Second, it affirmed that the labouring women are at the centre of the women's movement, "striving to defend the interests of women workers"; Third, it made clear the relationship between the movement of working women and the movement for women's rights, the campaign for women's participation in political affairs and the campaign for banning prostitution, as well as the relationship between the women workers' movement and the male workers' movement, and it set forth the principles and strategy for correctly handling those relations. The Communist Party set up a Women's Work Committee after its third congress. The veteran women members of the Chinese Communist Party such as Miao Boying, Liu Qingyang, Guo Longzhen, Xiang Jingyu, Cai Chang, Yang Zhihua, Tan Zhushan, and Deng Yingchao took an active part in the leadership of the women's movement during the early period of the Party.[32]

With the assistance of the Chinese Communist Party, the Kuomintang convened its first national congress in Guangzhou in January 1924, at which it pointed it out in its Declaration that the Party "affirms the principle of equality of men and women legally, economically, educationally and socially, and stands for the development of women's rights".[33] At its second National Congress held on January 16, 1926, the Kuomintang adopted a resolution on the women's movement put forth by Soong Ching Ling, He Xiangning and Deng Yingchao. The resolution pointed out: "While leading women in joining the

---

[32] **Archives of the 2nd to 6th Congresses of the Chinese Communist Party.**

[33] **Selected Works of Sun Yat-sen**, p. 529, Vol.2, People's Publishing House, 1956

national revolution, the Party should pay special attention to women's own emancipation". It pushed for the equality of men and women in law enforcement, property inheritance, marriage, education, employment and wages and the principle of protecting mothers and child workers. The resolution put forth 15 slogans, one of which is "Women should rise immediately to take part in the National Revolution".[34] After its first national congress, the Kuomintang set up a department of women's work and a women's movement committee. He Xiangning, Liao Bingyun, Zeng Xing and Wu Zhimei were elected to leading positions.

The institution of the guidelines for the women's movement by the Kuomintang and the Chinese Communist Party and the formation of cooperation between the two parties served to promote forward the women's movement in a comprehensive way.

(2) The Women's Movement Spurred on by Complex Historical Forces

The women workers movement.

The conditions of Chinese women workers were appalling. Early in the 1920s, the women's workers' movement, as part of the Chinese workers' movement, developed rapidly. In 1922 alone, more than 30,000 women workers from some 60 factories joined the national strike. The main goal of that strike was shorter working hours, opposition to maltreatment of women workers and recognition of the management of trade unions. The women workers' movement ebbed after the February 7 General Strike in 1923 was suppressed. After the Kuomintang and Chinese Communist Party initiated their first period of cooperation, Xiang Jingyu, Yang Zhihua and some other Chinese Communist Party women members went to work among women workers in Shanghai and other major cities,

---

[34] See **Political Weekly**, No. 6-7 issue.

which led to a new upsurge in the struggle waged by Chinese women workers. In the patriotic anti-imperialist movement that broke out on 30 May 1925 in Shanghai, more than 140,000 workers from textile mills and cigarette factories in this largest Chinese city walked out for a general strike, and the overwhelming majority of the strikers were women. Some of the striking women workers even joined the picket lines or did agitation work in the streets. Women workers of cotton mills and cigarette factories in Qingdao and Wuhan also went on strike to show their solidarity with their Shanghai sisters. The general strike in Guangzhou and Hong Kong that took place in June of the same year attracted more than ten thousand women workers and workers' wives in the two cities. Among the organisers of that strike were He Xiangning, Cai Chang and Ou Mengjue who were members of the Women's Work Department of the Kuomintang Central Committee and the Guangdong and Guangxi District Committee of the Chinese Communist Party. A rally of women workers of Guangzhou and Hong Kong was held in Guangzhou on 30 March 1926, at which three resolutions including a new factory act and an act regarding the protection of women workers were passed. Women workers in Shanghai also joined in the third workers' uprising in Shanghai in 1927. This women workers' movement was without parallel in Chinese history.

The campaign for women's civil rights.

Beginning in 1921, there appeared a new wave of women participating in political activities under the impact of the campaigns for "provincial autonomy" and "joint autonomy of provinces". Women's federations, women's leagues for participation in politics and women's associations for promotion of participation in political affairs were set up in Hunan, Guangdong, Zhejiang, Sichuan, Shandong, Jiangxi, Beijing, Shanghai, Nanjing and Tianjin. Under the leadership of Tao Yi and others, women in Changsha organized a demonstration involving more than 2,000 women. Through those untiring efforts,

Wang Changguo, Wu Jiaying and Wang Bihua were elected provincial council members of Hunan and Zhejiang. The campaign for women's participation in political affairs ultimately yielded some positive results. However, when the country was partitioned by warlords at that time, the success already won by Chinese women in politics proved to be only partial and short-lived. Some people maintained that the women's issue in China was not just that of women's participation in political affairs, but that of women's rights in a broader sense. In June 1922, Zhou Min, Zhang Renrui and some other students of the Beijing Women Teachers' University founded the League for Women's Rights. Branches were set up in many other cities. They petitioned Parliament demanding a ban on prostitution, establishment of free women's schools and compensation for those women workers whose interests had been infringed upon.

After the first national congress of the Kuomintang, the campaign for women's rights entered a new stage of development. In 1924 there arose a campaign for the convention of a National Conference which aimed at toppling the warlord regime and convening a national conference to seek national unification. Women activists showed unusual enthusiasm. They formed women's associations for the promotion of a national conference in Shanghai, Tianjin, Beijing and other places. On March 1, 1925, a national meeting for the promotion of a national conference was convened in Beijing. Deng Yingchao and 25 women delegates attended. Thanks to the efforts of women delegates, women's issues were placed on the agenda as a separate item of the meeting. However, the "complementary meeting" called by Duan Qirui later ignored women's rights. More than 40 women's organizations in Shanghai jointly called a Shanghai Women's National Conference on 22 March to voice their protest. The Beijing International Women's Day rally also resolutely opposed the draft resolution of the so-called complementary meeting and demanded female participation in political affairs. The All-China Women's Federation was inaugurated in

Beijing on 29 April. Branches were set up in other places, but the federation was forced to suspend its activities after the May 30th Incident.

Under the sponsorship of some members of the League for Women's Rights, the China Women's Association was established on May 1, 1925. The purpose of the association was the recovery of women's freedom as "human beings" and women's rights to equality in all matters. Zhu Qihui was elected president and Zhang Mojun and Shen Yibin vice presidents. That year, the China Women's Association officially joined the International Women's Association.

The Activities of YWCA.

The China YWCA National Association was one of 27 national affiliates to the London-based World Committee of the YWCA. The council of the China National Association of YWCA comprised 30 women members, mostly Chinese. In addition to religious activities, they paid great attention to the work of promoting public health, education and welfare among labouring women, and health and sports among women students. Their lively and interesting activities drew large numbers of people and they registered some success.[35] Another Christian organization, the China Women's Moderation Society which aimed at better family life also did made some contributions to the women's movement. Liu Wang Liming, director of the Students' Affairs Department of the Society, was a well-known figure in Chinese women's circles.

Women students' movements.

Women students constituted a very lively contingent in political activities during the 1920s. The students of the Zhili (now Hebei) Second Women Teachers School went on strike in March and April 1924 in protest at the firing of some progressive teachers. The students succeeded in forcing the Provincial

---

[35] **Historical Data of Chinese Women's Movement (1921-1927)**, pp. 183-184, People's Publishing House, 1986.

Education Bureau into agreeing to all the demands put forth by the students, which sent a shock wave through society. The students of the Beijing Women Teachers University launched a campaign to get rid of the university president Yang Yinyu in February 1924 because Yang arrogantly interfered with students' freedom, tried to oust progressive teachers and even tried to prevent the students from greeting Dr. Sun Yat-sen to Beijing. The students published declarations and demonstrated in defiance of the threat to dissolve the university. Their struggle won the sympathy of students and women in Beijing and ended in triumph.

The Duan Qirui government savagely suppressed the Beijing patriotic students' anti-imperialist demonstration on 18 March 1926. During the demonstration, Liu Hezhen, chairman of the Students Self-Government Association of the Women Teachers University, Yang Dequn, another student of the university, Wei Shiyi, a student of Yanjing University and Yang Juyi, a student of the Republic University, were shot to death during the demonstration. The incident known in history as the "March 18" massacre shocked the whole nation. The writer Lu Xun praised the victims as true heroines who "dared to face the tragic world and confront the bloody reality".[36] The All-China Women's Federation and the Women's Work Department of the Central Committee of the Kuomintang immediately cabled the entire nation in protest. Women's organizations and other circles in Beijing organized mammoth protest activities. A memorial ceremony was held in Central Park by women's organizations, a hundred schools and more than 400 mass organizations. Some 100,000 people attended.

(3) Women in the Northern Expedition

The revolutionaries launched the Northern Expedition in

---

[36] "In Memory of Liu Hejun," Vol. 3, **Complete Works of Lu Xun**, People's Literature Publishing House, first edition 1981.

July 1926 in order to wipe out the forces of the northern warlords. When the expeditionary army set out from Guangzhou, they were seen off at the railway station by He Xiangning, director of the Department of Women Work of the Central Committee of the Kuomintang, Deng Yingchao, representative of the Guangdong Provincial Headquarters of the Kuomintang, and representatives of various women's organizations. A women's first-aid and propaganda team headed by Gao Tianbo went with the expeditionary army. Guangxi also sent a Women's Northern Expedition Working Team with Guo Dejie as its leader. Led and organized by local women's organizations, women in Hunan and Hubei provinces also took an active part in raising provisions, acting as guides, washing clothes and sending food to the front for the expeditionary army.

Spurred on by the Northern Expedition, the women's movement developed rapidly. Late in 1926 and early in the following year, women in Hunan province first convened a labouring women's congress and then the first provincial women's congress which was attended by delegates from 57 counties. On 8 March 1927, under the leadership of Cai Chang, Director of the Department of Women's Work of the Provincial Government of Hubei, the first provincial women's congress was convened. A representative from the Department of Women's Work of the Third International presented the congress with a banner inscribed with a quotation from Lenin: "Without the emancipation of women, the revolution cannot succeed".[37] The revolutionary war further swept away customs and habits that ravaged women. The number of women who quit binding their feet rose sharply in Hunan and Hubei and 90 percent of women who originally bound their feet in Wuhan turned to natural feet. The Hubei revolutionary government even promulgated "Regulations on Banning Foot Binding for Women". The Xi'an Women's Association for Progress and the Legal Committee of the

---

[37] **Republic Daily** of Hankou, March 9, 1927.

Provincial Government of Shaanxi jointly worked out the "Interim Regulations on Marriage" and rules for their implementation.

From the revolutionary struggles a large group of women cadres emerged. Training courses for women revolutionary cadres were run in many places, notably the political institute run by the Kuomintang in Guangzhou, the women's movement institute in Guangzhou run by the Department of Women's Work of the Central Committee of the Kuomintang and the training course for women functionaries run by the Department of Women's Work of Guangdong Province. After it moved to Wuhan, the Kuomintang Central Committee ran a training course for women party cadres with Soong Ching Ling as its president and Liu Qingyang as its dean. The branch school of the Huangpu Military Academy enrolled 183 women cadets, among whom were Zhao Yiman and You Xi and others of the first generation of women revolutionary officers in China. A group of women cadres was also sent to study at Sun Yat-sen University in Moscow.

(4) Women in the Base Areas during the 10 Years of Civil War

With the failure of the revolution in April 1927, the cooperation between the Kuomintang and the Chinese Communist Party ended. As soon as the right wing of the Kuomintang seized control of the whole country, they lost no time in merging all women's organizations into their system of one-party rule. Women's federations set up at all levels which were changed into Women's Salvation Associations in 1930 and again into women's federations in 1933. Most of the leaders of the women's organizations under the control of the Kuomintang were women's liberation proponents whose activities were handicapped in every way by the authorities. That taught the female masses a lesson by negative example. In the ten-year agrarian revolution, the Chinese Communist Party shifted its focus of work to the countryside and went underground for its work in the cities. When the Party convened its sixth National Congress in June-July 1928, it reiterated its decision that in its future work in the women's movement, the Party's principal task was to win over the masses of working women.

The Chinese Communist Party announced a series of programs and policies aimed at protecting women's rights and improving their living conditions in the various revolutionary base areas in the countryside where women's status was markedly raised. On 7 November 1931, the Central Soviet Area adopted "The Outline Program of the Constitution of the Chinese Soviet Republic" which affirmed the principle of equality of men and women before the Soviet's law. Women enjoyed the right to vote and to be elected. Li Duan'e and Xu Damei were elected vice governors of Hunan-Jiangxi province and Fujian-Zhejiang-Jiangxi province respectively. There were also women leading members elected into the provincial and county governments. In November 1931, the "Land Law of the Chinese Soviet Republic" was adopted, which granted women as well the right to possess and use land. Women in the villages also raised their literacy level in the mass literacy drive. In November 1931 and April 1934, Mao Zedong as Chairman of the Chinese Soviet Republic promulgated the "Marriage Regulations of the Chinese Soviet Republic" and the "Marriage Law of the Chinese Soviet Republic" which announced that "marriage between men and women shall follow the principle of freedom of marriage, all feudal forms of forced marriage and mercenary marriage shall be abrogated and child marriage shall be banned," and "Monogamy shall be practised and polygamy shall be banned".[38] The promulgation and implementation of those two documents dealt the backward marriage system in the countryside a telling blow. Women in the villages began to resist feudal forced

---

[38] **Historical Data of Chinese Women's Movement (1927-1937)**, pp. 151-154, Chinese Women's Publishing House, 1991.

marriage and to fight for marital freedom. During the agrarian revolution, women in the base areas made their contributions to developing production, supporting the Red Army and taking part in the building of the revolutionary power in the countryside. Some of them even added glorious pages to the history of the revolutionary war. Women fighters took part in the noted revolutionary uprisings at Nanchang, Guangzhou and Baise and formed the Red Detachment of Women in Hainan, and an independent women's battalion or regiment under the government of Sichuan-Shaanxi Province and the general command of the Fourth Front Red Army. Heroines emerged during the world famous Long March such as Cai Chang, Deng Yingchao, Kang Keqing and others.

(5) Employment and Marriage Trends among Urban Women

Chinese women in the cities during the 1920s and 1930s took up jobs in increasing numbers and broader scope. It is estimated that women workers in the cities numbered between 500,000 and 550,000 at the time. Among them about 150,000 were in industrially developed Shanghai, mostly in cotton and silk textile mills and cigarette factories. Some of them were employed in the electrical appliance and printing trades. The number of women workers in the traditional handicraft industry also increased.

What is noteworthy is that fact that with the development of society and the economy and the rise of the educational level, spurred on by the women's liberation movement, a stratum of career women appeared in Chinese cities. They included nursery governors, primary and secondary school teachers, college lecturers and professors, librarians, hospital nurses, newspaper editors, translators, lawyers, government employees, typists and stenographers, accountants and bookkeepers, secretaries, waitresses, telephone and telegraph operators, postal workers, and booking office workers. A few became writers, painters, musicians, film actresses, and singers. Despite the small numbers, career women bore the characteristics of a social stratum and acted as the main force in the women's liberation movement. In reality, career women at the time were not only bothered by the conflicts between their career and family chores, but also subjected to all forms of discrimination and harassment by men.

The trend to freedom of marriage became increasingly conspicuous during the 1920s and 1930s, which must be attributed in the first place to the enlightening effect of the progressive thought of the 1911 Revolution and the May 4th Movement. Economic independence and higher educational levels undoubtedly prompted women to have new aspirations in marriage. The general trend was that the divorce rate went up and cases in which the female spouses sued for divorce increased markedly. For instance, of the 174 divorce cases that were brought to Guangzhou courts in 1930, 77% were initiated by women. There were 28 divorce cases in Tianjin between July and December 1930 and 24 were brought by women. Of the 62 divorce cases in Beiping in 1930, women brought 66.1%. In Shanghai there were 370 divorce cases between August and December 1928 and those raised by women exceeded those raised by men by 8.5%. The main reason for women to bring up a divorce suit at the time was either maltreatment by the husband or quarrels.[39]

6. Women and the Women's Movement in the Anti-Japanese War

(1) A Great Unity and the Mobilisation of Women in China

Bent on annexing China, the Japanese militarists first provoked the September 18 Incident of 1931 and then the July 7

[39] See Chapter 6 of Liu Wang Liming's **Chinese Women's Movement** and Chapter 2 of Guo Zhenyi's **Women's Issue in China**.

Incident of 1937, spreading the flames of war from Northeast China to North, East, Central and South China. Everywhere the Japanese invaders went, Chinese women were plunged into unparalleled distress. They not only saw their motherland being tramped upon, their homes burnt down and their families rendered homeless and struggling in starvation, but they also suffered insult, rape and cold-blooded massacre by the Japanese invaders. More than 300,000 Chinese were killed in the Nanjing massacre alone, and at least 20,000 Chinese women were raped.[40] In order to resist aggression and lift the Chinese nation from the abyss of extinction, the broad masses of Chinese women bravely joined the nation-wide War of Resistance.

The formation of a national united front against Japanese aggression gave impact to a new alliance of Chinese women. Between May 20 and 25, 1938, Soong Ching Ling personally invited representatives of the Chinese Communist Party, the Kuomintang, the YWCA and other women's organizations and noted public women figures for a conference at Lushan. Three issues were discussed there. They were: 1. efforts were to be made to bring about an extensive unity of workers of women's movement in various political parties and fractions; 2. a decision to assign the Women Guidance Committee of the New Life Movement National Federation as the national leading organ for women work in the country; and 3. the drafting of a work program for women's efforts in the War of Resistance and national construction throughout the country.

Women were never so organized as a result of the united action of women in the War of Resistance. All kinds of women's organizations provided the power for the mobilisation and organization of women in the nation-wide Resistance Movement. Women's organizations developed from the cities to the countryside, from educated women to labouring women, and

---

[40] **Records of Atrocities Committed by the Japanese Aggressors in China**, pp. 149, 176, Liberation Army Press, 1986.

even from within China to overseas Chinese communities. There were more than 300 women's organizations in the region under Kuomintang control. The China Women's Federation to Show Respect to Resistance Fighters was set up in August 1937. In the following year, a Wartime Children's Nursing Society was set up and the Women's Guidance Committee was reorganised on the basis of the united front to become the national women's organization with dozens of branches and a total membership exceeding one million. At the head of the various women's organizations were Soong Mei Ling, Tang Guozhen, Li Dequan, Deng Yingchao, Meng Qingshu, Cao Mengjun, Zhang Aizhen and other prominent women figures from various political parties and democratic organizations. The wives of many high ranking officials and officers of the Kuomintang chaired various branches of the women's organizations. The three women's organizations worked in close cooperation and in the same city. The China Women's Federation to Show Respect to Resistance Fighters and the Wartime Children Nursing Society functioned until the end of the Resistance War. The Women's Work Committee of the Sino-Soviet Cultural Association had considerable influence both in and outside China although it was not a national women's organization. The China YWCA was the only national organization among the religious women's organizations which took an active part in the War of Resistance. The most numerous were those local women's organizations. In the foreign concessions in Shanghai which did not fall under the Japanese occupation, there were the Shanghai Women's Association for Refugee Relief and the China Women's Society for Moderation affiliated to it, the China Women's Mutual Aid Society, the China Career Women's Club, the Shanghai Women's Movement Promotion Society, the Shanghai YWCA, and the Shanghai Women's League. The women's organizations of Jiangxi Province became governmental departments such as provincial, prefectural and county women guidance offices and women's detachments of local communities. Women's organizations and groups in other provinces were also very active. Among women of the national minorities, there were the Hui Women's Association for National Salvation, the Mongolian Women's Association for National Salvation of the Ulanqab League, and women's associations in Dihua (Urumqi) and Kashi (Kashgar) in Xinjiang. However, it was in the democratic base areas of resistance against Japanese aggression under the leadership of the Chinese Communist Party where women were most thoroughly mobilised and best organized. On International Women's Day in 1938, a women's federation was set in the Shaanxi-Gansu-Ningxia Border Area and a women's federation for national salvation and resistance against Japanese aggression was set up in the Shanxi-Chahar-Hebei Border Area. In those base areas where there were no unified women's federations, there were women's associations of resistance against Japanese aggression, women's associations or women's associations for national salvation. There were underground women's organizations for resistance against Japanese aggression in guerrilla areas and areas under the Japanese occupation. Although the Kuomintang and the Chinese Communist Party differed in their political stands, both did much in mobilising and organising women into the Resistance Movement on the basis of the united front. Thus there appeared a great unity and general mobilisation of Chinese women.

(2) Participation in the Nation-wide Resistance Movement

Chinese women of all quarters displayed great zeal for the Resistance Movement immediately after the September 18 Incident. Women leaders Soong Ching Ling and He Xiangning unequivocally voiced their firm stand for national salvation against Japanese aggression. They personally led the people and women in particular in Shanghai in support of the 19th Route Army in battles for the defence of Shanghai. Meanwhile they exposed the Japanese aggressors' atrocities to world public opinion. The students' movement on December 9, 1936 in opposition of the scheme of "autonomy of the five North China provinces" brought the Chinese women's movement for national salvation to a new height. The Marco Polo Bridge Incident in 1937 which marked the Japanese invasion into North China aroused even more women to participate in all forms of the Resistance Movement. The following were their main activities:

Joining the armed forces.

A large number of women joined the Eighth Route Army and the New Fourth Army and the Communist-led Northeast China United Anti-Japanese Army. Among them emerged many heroines such as Zhao Yiman, Li Lin, Liu Yaxiong and Leng Yun. The women's company of the East River Detachment fought the Japanese invaders bravely and won many battles. Most impressive of all were the Guangxi women students' battalion and the Zhejiang women's battalion that made their names known early in the War of Resistance. The Military Commission of the Kuomintang also organized a Young Women's Army. The militiawomen and women members of the self-defence detachments in the base areas within the Japanese occupied districts constituted a formidable force of resistance which was estimated to reach two million by 1941.[41]

Front-line service and first aid.

Right from the beginning of the War of Resistance, women in the rear areas formed front-line service groups to provide first aid, help with transportation and do instigation work. Among the earliest were the Northwest China Front-line Service Group and the Hunan Women's Front-line Service Group sponsored by the women writers Ding Ling, Smedley and Xie Bingxin. The Shanghai Working Women's Service Group led by Ding Lanqi worked alongside the armed forces for some ten thousand kilometres. Also active in rendering services at the

[41] "The Situation of Women in the Liberated Areas Engaged in Supporting the Front or in the Armed Forces," 3rd issue of 1985 of **Information for the Study of the Women's Movement**.

front were women's groups from Beiping, Shanxi, Sichuan, Yunnan and Guizhou or organized by the YWCA, compatriots in Hong Kong and Macao and returned overseas Chinese from Southeast Asia.

Moral support and contributions.

Collecting contributions to the Resistance Movement and visiting army units in salutation of their heroic deeds became major tasks for Chinese women during the War of Resistance. Under the slogan "The rich contribute money; the strong contribute muscle power", women's organizations sponsored donations of cash, gifts, clothes and encouraged people to buy national salvation bonds to support the Resistance Movement. In 1938 and 1939, the Women's Guidance Committee of the New Life Movement National Federation organized women to make a batch of 100,000 padded uniforms and a second batch of 500,000 padded uniforms for the front. By September 1943, women's organizations had collected donations amounting to 2.6 million yuan (enough to buy 13 fighter planes). Many women contributed their jewellery. Even low-wage women workers and old rag-picking women made contributions. By the end of 1939, contributions made by women's organizations already reached 50 million yuan in value.[42] Overseas Chinese women in Southeast Asia and America, and women in Hong Kong and Macao made major efforts in collecting contributions to the Resistance Movement.

Women's organizations and special salutation groups organized by women's organizations made regular and frequent visits to army units fighting at the front to express an appreciation of their heroism and present them with gifts. They brought to the fighters new clothes, shoes, stockings, towels, soups, food, books and magazines and banners. Some salutation groups brought with them art troupes to stage art performances for the

---

[42] "A Prelude to a General Summary of Women's Work in the Country," **Women's Life**, 3rd issue, Vol. 9.

fighters. Among them were the actresses Chen Bo'er and Wang Yin. Their visits fired the enthusiasm of the fighters.

The rescue of refugee children.

Chinese women displayed a disinterested love for refugee children during the War of Resistance. They rescued some 30,000 homeless children in the period. Many women's organizations set up special rescue teams, transfer posts and some fifty or so kindergartens for homeless children in the rear areas under Kuomintang control and in the Shaanxi-Gansu-Ningxia Border Region. Many women risked their lives to rescue children from the battlefield. Cao Mengjun, president of the Wartime Children Protection Committee personally led a rescue group to the front to bring homeless children to the rear areas.

During the War of Resistance, women took up production posts vacated by men in industry and agriculture. In order to frustrate the Japanese blockade, women joined in the construction of the Burma Road and the Hunan-Guangxi railway. There were numerous cases of mothers sending their sons and wives sending their husbands to the front. In order to defeat the Japanese Fascists, women of all nationalities in China made admirable contributions and untold sacrifices which demonstrated their lofty patriotism.

(3) Debate on the Orientation of the Women's Movement

In the 1930s there rose a world outcry urging "women to go back into the home". After seizing power in 1933, Hitler clamoured that women return to the "Kche, Kirche und Kahn" (kitchen, church and bed) in the hope of solving the problem of unemployment caused by the economic crisis. This adverse current made its impact felt also in China. A prolonged debate on this issue in China involved dozens of newspapers, including **Da Gung Bao** and the "Women's Road" supplement of *Xinhua Daily* in Chongqing, the supplement "New Women" of *Xin Min Bao* and **Woman's Life** magazine in Nanjing. The debate could be divided into two stages. The first stage unfolded around the new version of the doctrine about women's primary qualities as "worthy wives and excellent mothers". The **Echo of Women** magazine in its November 1935 issue focused on the basic concept of the new doctrine of women's qualities as "worthy wives and excellent mothers". The gist of this doctrine was that the family is the basic unit of a society and the quality of being worthy and excellent is essential for a healthy family. While women should be worthy wives and excellent mothers, men should also be worthy husbands and excellent fathers. This specious argument was attacked by some progressive women leaders. Luo Qiong among others in an article pointed out that this argument in essence was a prototype of the "women going back to the home" doctrine, camouflaged with some utopian ideas draw from the old doctrine concerning worthy and virtuous women. They argued that regardless of whether males or females returned to the home, the advocacy of the improvement in family relations behind the closed doors of the home can only benefit the activities of capitulationists.[43] The new doctrine of being worthy and excellent quieted down after the outbreak of the War of Resistance.

The *Chongqing Da Gong Bao* daily carried an article by Duanmu Luxi on 6 July 1940. The author advised women to be content with family life. Yin Ji in an article in the first issue of **Zhan Guo Ce** (War Time Strategy) said: "The real place for women is 'in the home' because they can obtain genuine, biological and lasting equality only 'at home'." Those articles aroused vehement reactions. Women leaders and cultural figures wrote dozens of articles to refute those arguments. Another wave of debate emerged. Deng Yingchao in an article pointed out that the arguments of Duanmu and others involved an extremely important issue, namely the theoretical basis, orien-

---

[43] "From 'Worthy Wife and Excellent Mother' to 'Worthy Husband and Excellent Father'" by Luo Qiong, **Women's Life**, 1st Issue, Vol. 2.

tation, tasks, contents and purpose of women's liberation movement in China, as well as the development and appraisal of the history of Chinese women's liberation movement. She wrote that Duanmu's thinking remained at the level of the "new doctrine" of being worthy and excellent which were advocated several years previously. That argument was a one-sided assessment of the May 4th Movement and the women's liberation movement, represented the pessimism of part of the bourgeoisie, and reflected their lack of thoroughness and resolution on the issue of women's liberation, Deng Yingchao pointed out.[44] In order the clarify the muddled conceptions on the women's issue, Zhou Enlai who was then Secretary of the South China Bureau of the Chinese Communist Party wrote an article in 1942 entitled "On So-called 'Worthy Wives and Excellent Mothers' and Women's Obligations" in which he stressed, "We who stand for women's liberation do not object to the euphonic phrases 'worthy wives or excellent mothers'. But when a 'worthy wife and excellent mother' becomes a fixed expression it actually specifies the fettering of women in a society under male domination and reflects the one-sided wish on the part of males in the old society. The error of the new doctrine of the 'worthy wife and excellent mother' lies in the fact that no matter how you try to explain the expression from the stance of equality of men and women, when you retain this set expression, you become bogged down in the stand for a male-dominated society and perpetuate the old social status of women. That kind of practice can never be proper or logical".[45] Zhou Enlai's article represents the basic view of the Chinese Communists in the debate on the women's liberation movement in China.

(4) The Campaign of Women's Participation in Politics

[44] "A Critique of 'A Little Subdued Azure'" by Deng Yingchao, 7th issue of **Women's Road**.

[46] **Women's Road**, 38th issue.

The fourth session of the first National Political Council was convened in September 1939. Thanks to the efforts of the Chinese Communist Party and progressive elements, a council for the promotion of a constitutional government was established with an aim to urge the government to convene a national congress to adopt a constitution and implement it. This touched off a drive within the united front to urge for the switch over from a military government to a constitutional government.

Women from various quarters in Chongqing held seven forums on constitutional government between November 1939 and March 1940. Among those attending the discussions were representatives of the Women's Guidance Committee, the YWCA, the All-China Women's Federation for Salutation to Fighters of the War of Resistance, the Shanghai-based delegation of the Shaanxi-Gansu-Ningxia Border Region and dozens of other organizations as well as noted female public figures such as Liu Qingyang, Luo Shuzhang, Cao Mengjun, Shi Liang and Zhang Xiaomei. Some female members of the National Political Council held separate discussions on women's participation in political activities and other related issues. Some provinces under Kuomintang control at the request of progressive women also sponsored discussions and lectures on women's participation in political activities. This led to a new drive for female participation in political affairs. At the first and second sessions of the National Political Council, resolutions were adopted on equal employment opportunities for men and women and protection of the rights and interests of women workers. Those resolutions were more or less implemented. But women accounted for only 5% of the members of the National Political Council. Except for a few members of the NPC and of a few provincial and county NPCs, there was virtually no way for the broad masses of women to participate in political affairs. The campaign for women participation in political affairs in fact did not yield what people had expected.

In contrast to the areas under the control of the Kuomintang, however, the drive for women's participation in political affairs was immensely successful in various democratic base areas of resistance against Japanese aggression. People in the base areas, irrespective of class, political party, nationality, sex, and religious belief, all had the right to vote and to be elected. A resolution was adopted a the first Political Council of the Shaanxi-Gansu-Ningxia Border Region in April 1939 which stipulated that, "Women shall account for 25% of the members of the political councils at all levels and all governmental institutions should admit as many women workers as possible".[46] Women of all quarters in Yenan established a constitutional government promotion association which defined its purpose of assisting the government to realise a constitutional government and to fight for genuine equality and other democratic rights for women throughout China. The association wrote a letter to Soong Ching Ling and He Xiangning expressing its support for them as women delegates to the National Congress. When elections were being carried out on the principle of a three thirds system in the Shaanxi-Gansu-Ningxia Border Region, women students from Yenan University were sent to do publicity work among the masses of women in the region. Women in the region, including some illiterate women and women with bound feet, zealously participated in political activities. Nearly one third of the female population went to the polls. The elections produced 17 women members of the regional political council, 176 women members of county political councils, and 2,005 women members of the township political councils. One woman was elected county magistrate and many were elected district and township leaders. Female participation in political affairs also had great success in the Shanxi-Chahar-Hebei Border Region, the Shanxi-Suiyuan Border Region and other base areas.

---

[46] **Liberation**, 68th issue, January 1940.

(5) The Marked Elevation of Women's Status in Base Areas

During the War of Resistance, women in the border regions improved their political status through participation in political affairs and their economic positions through participation in productive labor. They also won better conditions in family relations, which was the result of the implementation of the new marriage regulations and decrees promulgated by the border region governments. The Regulations on Marriage of the Shaanxi-Gansu-Ningxia Border Region were promulgated in April 1939, and similar regulations on marriage were enforced in the Shanxi-Chahar-Hebei Border Region, the Shanxi-Suiyuan Border Region and other base areas. Those regulations embodied a democratic spirit in marriage, particularly protecting the marriage of the military personnel in the Resistance Movement, thus bringing China's legislation on marriage to a new historical stage. In order to safeguard women's rights and interests in marriage and other aspects, the base areas of democracy and resistance against Japanese aggression adopted laws and decrees on women's rights to inheritance. The Shaanxi-Gansu-Ningxia Border Region adopted regulations which stipulated that if a person had a daughter or daughters but no son, the daughter or daughters (irrespective of whether it were one daughter or a number of daughters, or whether married or not), all property of the deceased would be inherited by the daughter or daughters. The base area in Shandong Province stipulated that daughters were entitled to inherit and that unless the heir(s) forfeited the right voluntarily, nobody could hamper or restrict her or their right of inheritance. This was an economic guarantee for the implementation of the marriage regulations.

The marriage system and family relations underwent a very happy change in the democratic resistance base areas thanks to the vigorous growth of production, the development of democracy and the promulgation and propagation of marriage regulations. Women's social and family status improved tremendously in those base areas, which was the envy of progressive women in the areas under the control of the Kuomintang.

7. The Women's Movement during the War of Liberation

(1) Women in KMT Controlled Regions Fought for Peace and Democracy

The victory of the War of Resistance brought infinite joy and hope to the broad masses of Chinese women, but that joy and hope were short-lived. The Civil War broke out in June-July 1946. Chinese women were forced to plunge themselves into the fight for peace and democracy once again.

The China Women's Fellowship was formed on the eve of the V-J Day (15 July 1945) with Li Dequan as chairman of the Council of the Fellowship. There were branches in Shanghai, Chongqing, Nanjing, Beiping and Hong Kong. The independent Women's Fellowships in Yunnan, Chengdu, Guilin and Kowloon maintained a relationship of sister-bodies with the China Women's Fellowship. The CWF published its "Statement on the Current Situation" on 25 January 1946 in which it raised various political demands: an end to the Civil War, reorganisation of the government, guarantee of the basic rights of women and the people, and issues related to the National Congress. As an important women's organization in the KMT controlled region fighting for peace and democracy, CWF ran **Modern Women, Women of Our Time, Sichuan Women** and other magazines which voiced most distinctly the aspirations of Chinese women for peace and democracy. Following the bloodshed of December 1, 1945 in Kunming, Women's Fellowships everywhere mounted large-scale solidarity demonstrations. The China Women's Fellowship and its Yunnan branch contributed 100,000 yuan and 167,000 yuan to the striking students respectively. The Shanghai

Women's Fellowship and 51 other mass organizations there organized 30,00 women in collecting signatures for peace and 50,000 people in demonstrations for peace in May 1946. Lei Jieqiong, a member of the students' delegation demanding for peace and Pu Xixiu, a woman reporter with the students' delegation, were wounded in the Xiaguan incident in which the students' delegation were beaten up by KMT armed police and soldiers.

The tide of the students' movement surged high after the KMT unleashed the Civil War across the country. Women students fought shoulder to shoulder with their male school mates in the fight to oppose American imperialism and atrocities. They demanded an end to hunger and the Civil War, denouncing the US attempt to prop up Japanese militarism. Women workers in the KMT controlled region launched fights to protect their factories and then to resume production after V-J Day. They fought for democracy and peace, and opposed the Civil War. From June 1946 on, women workers in Shanghai launched a number of large-scale fights against the US-Jiang reactionaries. Professional women in the KMT controlled region also waged various struggles. Women teachers in Shanghai, Chengdu and elsewhere, taxi dancers in Shanghai, Guangzhou and other cities, and women bank clerks in Shanghai and Anhui also joined in the fight against the Civil War, political persecution and hunger.

(2) Women's Organizations and Women's Movement in Liberated Areas

After the Civil War broke out, **Liberation Daily**, the Communist-led daily newspaper in the liberated area published an editorial on 8 March 1947 which mentioned major tasks for women in the liberated areas, namely, participation in the war, the land reform and the production drive, fighting for the independence, peace and democracy of the motherland, and the emancipation of women.

Together with women in the old liberated areas, those in the newly liberated areas gradually organized themselves. Women's federations were first established in Harbin and Nenjiang Province in 1946. In the following year, Cai Chang was appointed secretary of the Women's Committee of the Northeast China Bureau of the Chinese Communist Party. Later women's committees were set up under the Chinese Communist Party provincial committees of Songjiang, Longjiang and Hejiang. The establishment and consolidation of women's leading organs and women's organizations in the old and new liberated areas served to lay a foundation for further development of the women's movement.

Between July and September 1947, the Chinese Communist Party called a national land conference at Xibopo in Hebei Province. The "Outline of China's Land Law" adopted at the conference stipulated that land in the countryside shall be distributed equally among the population irrespective of sex or age. The masses of women in the liberated areas took an active part in the land reform through which Chinese women for the first time in history won possession of land, something long dreamed of.

Enlightened women in the countryside vied to join the peasants' associations and poor peasants' leagues. Young men joined the army or went to the front to aid the armed units. Women left behind broke with the old conventions and enthusiastically took part in farm production and handicraft production. Their efforts not only aided the revolutionary war but also helped raise the social-economic position of Chinese women.

Women fighters were very active in the field armies of the Chinese People's Liberation Army during the war of liberation. They fought beside their male comrades and laid down lives for the final victory in the people's revolutionary war.

(3) The First Chinese Women's National Congress

Exchanges between Chinese women and women of other

countries developed rapidly after the end of World War II. Delegates from 41 countries gathered in Paris for an International Women's Congress on 26 November 1945. Chinese women and women students in Europe sent a ten-member delegation to the congress. On the invitation of the International Democratic Women's Federation, the standing organ of the Congress, the Chinese liberated areas elected Cai Chang and Deng Yingchao as members of the IDWF Council and Ding Ling as alternate member of the Council. Deng Yingchao planning to attend the first council meeting in May of the following year but was blocked by the KMT authorities.

An International Women's Conference was held in October 1946 on the proposal to set up a relevant women's organization under the United Nations. Having received invitations to the conference, Soong Ching Ling and Deng Yingchao solicited opinions extensively among Chinese women in preparation for the occasion, but again Deng Yingchao was blocked from attending the conference by the KMT authorities. Li Dequan who was then in the United States accepted the request to attend the conference. She made a speech at the conference which drew the attention of those present.[47] In February 1947, Cai Chang in the capacity of a council member, attended the council meeting of the International Democratic Women's Federation held in Prague. She delivered a speech entitled "The Chinese Women in the Struggle for Independence, Democracy and Peace" at the meeting. In the following year she led a Chinese women's delegation to the Second International Women's Congress held in Budapest and was elected vice president. At this point, the women's movement in China joined with the international women's movement.

In September 1948, the Central Committee of the Chinese Communist Party called a national conference on women's work

---

[47] **Historical Data of Chinese Women's Movement (1945-1949)**, pp. 53-77, Chinese Women's Publishing House, 1991.

in Pingshan County, Hebei province, at which it was decided to establish a national women's organization. The First Chinese Women's National Congress was convened on 24 March 1949 in the Huairentang Hall in Zhongnanhai, Beiping. The congress adopted "The Articles of Association of the All-China Democratic Women's Federation". Joining the All-China Democratic Women's Federation as affiliates were the Women's Federation of the Chinese Liberated Areas (Preparatory Committee), the women's federations of various provinces, the China Women's Fellowship, the China Women's Moderation Society and the All-China YWCA. He Xiangning was elected Honorary President at the first Executive Council meeting, Cai Chang was elected president and Deng Yingchao and Li Dequan vice presidents. That congress was important for it inspired Chinese women from all walks of life to seize the final victory in the people's revolution and greet the birth of a New China. It was the landmark of the start of a new historical stage in the Chinese women's movement.

8. The Historic Emancipation of Chinese Women

On October 1, 1949, the People's Republic of China was founded. The establishment of a socialist system in China marks the greatest and most profound change in Chinese history. In the past 40 years and more, Chinese women have traversed a significant journey on their road to emancipation. The fundamental change in the social status of the Chinese women has drawn the attention of the whole world.

(1) Legislation on Women's Issues and Rights

The recognition and guarantee of women's status and rights through state legislation has been the most distinct feature of the women's movement in China. The Constitution of the People's Republic of China unequivocally stipulates: "Women in the People's Republic of China enjoy equal rights with men in all spheres of life, in political, economic, cultural, social and family life". In addition, the State has promulgated a dozen basic laws such as the Marriage Law, Election Law, Inheritance Law, Civil Law and Criminal Law and 40 sets of administrative statutes and regulations and more than 80 sets of local regulations. The "Law of the People's Republic of China on the Protection of Women's Rights and Interests" was promulgated in 1992, and it furnishes a fundamental guarantee for the realization of the equality of men and women, the protection of the specific interests of women and the prevention of the humiliation of women. Soon after the founding of the People's Republic, the Chinese government relied on its political power to wipe out prostitution, and other ugly phenomena left over from the old society, within a very short time. Over the past several decades, the law and the government of China have always served as the most powerful backing of women's rights and interests. To protect the interests of women, the Judicial Committee of the National People's Congress has a special team on women's and children's affairs and the State Council has set up a Women and Children's Committee. All government agencies, enterprises, undertakings and mass organizations must uphold and protect the lawful rights and interests of women and children in accordance with the law.

(2) All-Round Improvement of Women's Status

On the basis of equal rights with men to own property and the right to work, Chinese women have constantly improved their economic position through extensive participation in social productive labor. In the Land Reform that was carried out between 1950 and 1952, women with no or insufficient land throughout rural China obtained their share of land on an equal footing with men. With the recovery and development of the economy, more than 70% of rural women and many urban housewives engaged in productive labour during the first Five-Year Plan period. The annual rate of growth of the number of women workers outstripped that of men workers by 23.7%.[48] Today women workers account for 44% of total employment in China, while the rural female work force accounts for about half whereas urban women workers constitute about 38% of the payroll. The scope of women's employment has also become increasingly diverse and shows a steady rise in technical and professional levels. In 1993, professional women accounted for 36.8% of technical personnel in enterprises. The number of women experts, professors, entrepreneurs and model workers has constantly been on the increase. Equal pay for equal work for men and women has been introduced virtually in all trades. The state has given special protection to pregnant women and nursing mothers. Women workers enjoy a paid maternity leave which has been extended from the original 56 days to a period ranging from three to six months. Most state-owned enterprises have set up creches and kindergartens for the convenience of their women workers.

Women's participation in political affairs, as an important component of the country's democratic development, has made considerable progress. The ratio of females in the National People's Congress, the supreme organ of power, has risen from 12% at the first NPC in 1954 to 21.03% at the 8th NPC in 1993. Soong Ching Ling and He Xiangning were once Vice-Chairpersons of the NPC Standing committee. Women also occupy leading posts from that of Vice President down to grass-roots government agencies. In 1994 there were 16 women ministers and vice ministers, 18 provincial governors and vice governors, and more than 300 mayors and vice mayors. The All-China Women's Federation and women's federations at all local levels are supervising government administration at all levels, a unique form of female participation in political affairs with Chinese characteristics. The state of affairs when the broad

---

[48] **Am Introduction to the Study of Women's Issue**, p. 154, North Women and Children Publishing House, 1987.

masses of women were barred from social life is virtually a thing of past. Women are now making their presence felt in all spheres of education, science and technology, culture, health, and sports, and bringing their talents and intelligence into full play. Chinese women have made amazing achievements in the most advanced branches of science and technology, international sports and art.

The development of education for women and the improvement of women's educational levels have created basic conditions for women's participation in social life in China. In Old China nine out of every ten women were illiterate. Three nation-wide literacy drives were launched within a few years beginning in 1952 and as many as 1.6 million illiterate women learned to read and write. The illiteracy rate among Chinese women today has dropped to 32%. The education of women has received particular attention and made rapid growth. School attendance of school age girls has reached 96.2% and women students accounted for 43.1% and 33.7% of the student body at secondary schools and colleges respectively in 1992. The All-China Women's Federation has launched a sustained campaign of educating women in self-respect, self-confidence, self-improvement and self-reliance, which has greatly raised Chinese women's cultural qualities and confidence in themselves so as to keep abreast with the times. With their social status greatly risen in all spheres, Chinese women are appearing on the historical stage with an entirely new outlook.

(3) The Improvement of Marriage and Family Life

The first law promulgated by the new People's Republic was "The Marriage Law of the People's Republic of China", which is a further improvement on those marriage laws of the former Soviet Region, border regions and liberated areas. It lays down the fundamental principles of freedom of marriage, monogamy, equality between men and women and the protection of women and children. It guarantees freedom of marriage, divorce and remarriage. At present 74% of the marriages in China are decided by young people themselves or by themselves in consultation with their parents. The traditional patriarchal family is being replaced by the modern family based on equality and love and a new type of family relationship is being established. Women have won the right to possess and inherit family property and have gained the basis for economic independence as a result of their participation in labor or employment. With household chores gradually being taken up by the service trades in society, the time career women in the cities spend on household chores every day has been cut back to 3.75 hours, which is nearing the level of developed countries. Chinese women have freed themselves of the fetters of the old-tyle family which reduced them to domestic slaves and child bearing machines.[49]

(4) New Features of the Women's Movement

The women's movement in socialist China has its own features. First, the interests of the Chinese Communist Party highly conform with those of women. The Party is a representative and guardian of women's interests. Therefore you cannot find conflicts of interest between the masses of women and the authorities. Rather, the Chinese Communist Party has always been the leader of the Chinese women's movement. Second, women's organizations are highly unified. Although there are women's national, regional and industrial organizations, such as women workers' committees, women scientists' fellowships, and YWCA, they are mostly affiliates of the All-China Women's Federation. ACWF is the most authoritative and comprehensive women's organization in the country. The Chinese Communist Party and the people's government exercise leadership over the women's movement via ACWF which acts as the spokesperson for all women in China. No other women's organization in the

[49] A white paper entitled **The Status of Women in China** published by the Press Office of the State Council of the People's Republic of China, June 1994.

country can substitute for ACWF. Third, China has always followed closely the improvement and elevation of women's status in the world at large. China has taken a clear-cut stand in its support for the UN regarding its strategy of improving women's status. The Chinese government has taken a positive stand on this issue by actively signing all international conventions and pacts aimed at protecting women's interests and opposing discrimination against women. Chinese women have established friendly cooperation with women of other countries and persisted in upholding equality, progress and peace in all bilateral and multilateral activities along the road of common progress together with their sisters throughout the world.

The Chinese women, along with their motherland, have gone through many vicissitudes over the past 40 years and more. They have shed sweat and blood in the socialist revolution and construction and in the wars of self-defence. Meanwhile women's social status has undergone a historical change, but China is currently at the initial stage of socialism, its economy remains to be developed, and the heavy cultural sedimentation over thousands of years is still making itself felt in many ways today. Signs and traces of discrimination against women and inequality between men and women are to be found in society as well as in family life. Although legislation in favour of women's interests has made marked progress in recent years and there are a series of such laws and statutes, it is an arduous task to translate the laws on equality of men and women into reality. For example, some departments, regions and units still show their preference for men in student enrolment and workers' employment. Labor protection and insurance remain a problem in some enterprises, especially those foreign-invested and privately owned enterprises. Occasionally women are still victims of infringement on the person in marriage and family relations. Certain ugly social phenomena and crimes are showing a growing tendency. There are still 80 million Chinese on the poverty line and about 60% of them are women and children.

It remains an arduous task to lift them out of poverty. While the country's economy is in the course of transition, some women are employed in irregular economic departments characterized by low wages, long work hours and the absence of employment security and labor protection. These include small peddlers, household maids and day workers. Incomplete data of 1990 show that of the 180 million illiterates in the country, women accounted for 70.1%. It is still a hard job to eliminate all forms of violence against women. According to statistics for 1991 and 1992, Chinese public security departments solved than 50,000 cases of abduction of women and children and handled dozens of felonies in which women were cruelly injured or killed. These problems have attracted the close attention of the Chinese government, and concrete plans and measures have been worked out to cope with them.[50]

Looking back at history, we are proud of the road of emancipation the Chinese women have traversed. Looking ahead, we are inspired to continue our struggle for an even more brilliant future for women's emancipation.

---

[50] "Report of the People's Republic of China on Its Implementation of the Foreseeing Nairobi Strategy for Improvement of Women's Status", **China Women Journal**, Oct. 12, 1994

CHAPTER ELEVEN
RELATIONSHIPS BETWEEN THE SEXES IN THE NEW AGE OF REFORM AND OPEN POLICY

Huang Dezhi and *Feng Chunfeng*

1. Marriages in the Social Transformation in China

A profound change has taken place peacefully and gradually in our country since the late '70s. The planned economy which had got rigid was questioned and challenged for the first time in the 30 years, and the market economy which had been despised and rejected gradually appeared in people's life. The economic reform and the open policy marked a transformation from the "traditional" society to the "modern" one in China. Since the effectuation of the reform and the open policy, our society stepped into a period of overall transformation, a transformation from the planned economy to the market economy, from a closed and semi-closed society to an open one, from a traditional ethical society to a modern legal one. Changes occur inevitably in such a time in people's notions and values, which are certainly reflected in marriages and families. Indeed, a family is a society in miniature; it presents in every detail the progress and achievement, the difficulty and conflict in the history of social development.

The transformation from the traditional society to the modern one is a hot topic in the study of developmental sociology. The starting point of the transformation can be traced to a time much earlier than the late '70s. The gradual changes to the modern society appeared in as early as the beginning of the century, and were accelerated after the foundation of the new China. Yet the modernization of our society was delayed due to the restrictions of the international political environment and the interference of the ultra-Left policies, and we have to make every effort to catch up since the late '70s. The economic reform in the recent 10 odd years has broken the unitary planned economy and established a multiplicate socialist market economy market economy. And consequently, the relationships in families tend to grow multiplicate. What's more, the public media which function as a cultural medium and carrier of information across the boarders have brought marriages and families to all kinds of impacts, social, economic and cultural, from inside and outside of the country.

There is no clear-cut division between "tradition" and "modernity", the terms are relative. From the point of view of marriages and families, the traditional society during the three decades from the foundation of the new China to the reform and open policy can be characterized as the following: first, the living conditions in most areas were maintained at the subsistence level with a backward economy and a low productivity; second, the education was underdeveloped, and women had especially less education and participation in the social activities, the fertility kept high; third, the society was closed up, less information from outside was received, and people's thoughts and behaviors were firmly limited by the traditional native concepts; fourth, there was less democracy and personal freedom, most people's personal life, especially that of women, was heavily influenced by politics.

In the traditional society mentioned above, the major function of marriages was to produce offspring and to support the family members financially, that's why the marriages have been called by our sociologists "the birth commune" or "the economic community" in which personal affections and psychological needs played little part; and it was the fact for decades that marriages submitted to politics. Most marriages in the urban and rural areas of our country had been maintained by several ties: one was to give birth to and bring up children: one couple would have several children, and they would be so old when their youngest child became self-supporting that a divorce became unnecessary and unlikely. The nest one was economy: a large family with three generations would live on a very small income, their clothing, food and housing could only be provided by the family, consequently, the relationships between husband and wife, parents and children and other relatives were close, they depended on one another to survive, which made the independence of the individuals impossible. Another one was the belief in "being faithful to each till old and gray" in marriages which had been deep-rooted, and it was especially common for a woman to follow her husband no matter what has lot was. And marriages were greatly influenced and controlled by parents and other seniors. Still another tie was politics which had been a very important factor: he partnership was regarded as the relationship between comrades, as well as husband and wife; and divorces were seldom allowed if not for the "contradictions between classes" or "the basic conflict of interest". For instance, during the "Cultural Revolution", the court would conduct courses to those couples who asked for divorces, in which the works by Chairman Mao such as Dealing with the Contradictions among People Properly and Serving the People, and other political documents would be read. This is a case in point to demonstrate the relations of politics and marriages and families.

In a word, marriages in the traditional society were restricted by the outside ties. As a matter of fact, marriages were decided by factors such as the political background, the family origin, the financial condition, the registered permanent residence and the housing condition, and etc.; marriages arranged by parents and match-makers, or even ratified and assigned by organizations were common, and individuals had little room for choice. And once a marriage had been set up, the spouses should be faithful to each other and live together till old and gray, it was extremely rare and difficult for them to part halfway. That accounts for the fact that marriages in the urban and rural areas of our country remained to be super-stable during the 30 years from the foundation of the People's Republic of China to the late '70s, the divorcing rate was too low for the government to make statistics.

The tide of reform surging up in the late '70s dramatically accelerated the development of the economy in China and changed the way of living, the way of behaviors and the values of a generation in China.

The social and economic reform would lead to changes of marriages and families for sure. Some of the backgrounds for these changes are: first, the birth control policy carried out in the '70s achieved great success in the early '80s; more than 90 per cent of younger couples in the urban areas have only one child. As a result, the significance of children as a tie to connect husband and wife has been reduced. Second, the economy develops rapidly, people (including women) have had much more income; the pace to socialize housework has been quickened, more and more food and clothing have been provided directly by markets, the economic tie between spouses has loosened. Third, under the open policy, the public media have been opened up, and the outside information surged into the country and brought a shock to all the traditional concepts which had long controlled people's thoughts and behaviors, people have had a stronger sense to marry the partner of their own choice, and marriages can be hardly controlled by the outsiders. Fourth the political ties restricting marriages have virtually disappeared, people's private life has completely separated from politics, and marriages no longer undergo any political examinations, and divorce has nothing to do with one's political manifestations. Fifth, the effectuation of the second

Marriage Law after the reform and open policy made these changes legitimate. Compared with the first Marriage Law, the second one put more emphasis on the affective factors in marriages. People not only have a right to make their own choice when they get married, but they have a right to decide on a divorce when the marriage breaks up. Divorce is no longer regarded as a "mischief by the thoughts of bourgeoisie".

Marriages and families in our country are undergoing a revolution of shifts of functions. And the main characteristics of this revolution are: families are changing from the birth communes and "economic communities" to "psycho-cultural" communities in which personal needs, above all, affective needs of partners are satisfied; people's freedom of choice and autonomy in marriages have been increased, with the compelling factors from outside weakened; the political flavor in family life has been reduced, while the privacy has been emphasized; partnership has become the assist of a family, the psychology, education and morale of the spouses have had a decisive influence on marriages and families; the sense of democracy and equality in families has been increased, with a relative weakening of the authority of the head of the household; the concepts of values in marriages, sex, employment and the ways of living have greatly changed, and the "generation gap" in families becomes very obvious.

The results of the surveys conducted by the Institute of Marriage and Family of Beijing in 1989 can partly demonstrate the characteristics of the above changes. One survey to 977 married young people showed that only 4.7 per cent of marriages were arranged by parents or older generations; as to the conditions of choosing a spouse, the most important one was that "the other party should be a person of good characters"; 80 per cent thought that the first motive of marriage was "to seek a person who can share the feelings"; 20.2 per cent thought that "children play little part in maintaining the partnership" (the actual number of people who agreed on this point may be greater for the fact that they are greatly influenced by the traditional ethic values and dare not, or will not, speak it out); 36.5 per cent often take recreations or travel with their spouses. It is hard to see the extent of changes before and after the '80s for lack of data. Yet what is obvious is that the psychological, affective and cultural factors in marriages are more emphasized than in the traditional marriages which were maintained by the external factors such as "the kids, the notes, the houses, the faces and the maintenance". "Lack of love", "being different in characters", "lack of common interest", and "the unhappy sexual life" have been mentioned as grounds for divorces, which showed the needs of the married couples to the "modernized" marriages.

In another survey to 1,509 people, 34.7 per cent didn't agree to the making-do-with-it marriages; 57.2 per cent agreed to the democracy in families; only 1.9 per cent too it as the purpose of their marriages to give birth to children. When asked about the freedom of choosing partners, 79 per cent of male questionees and 83 per cent of female questionees thought that it is all right to love one who has had a partner to marry with although who has not got married yet; 17.4 per cent even thought it acceptable to be in love with a married person. 49.7 per cent thought the pre-marriage sexual intercourse is acceptable and 40.2 per cent took sex as a "personal matter".

A survey to 144 married questionees under 35 in the fields of culture, education and public health service, or the departments of administrative management and commerce on the notion of "extramarital affairs" showed that approximately 70 per cent regarded the extramarital affairs as a natural tendency and should be tolerated; 36.5 per cent admitted having the extramarital sexual intercourse. This would be just incredible during the period from the '50s to the '70s.

A survey to 166 divorcees showed that 70 per cent of them received high school or higher education; 94 per cent got divorced during 1986 to 1990, which means that the rise of the divorce rate in the late '80s is more obvious than that in the early '80s; 73.6 per cent divorcees got married after 1979, that is, their marriages lasted less than 10 years. As for the causes of divorce, 50 per cent stated an improper choice of partners before their marriages, and 20 per cent admitted that they had fallen in love with someone else.

The changes in marriages and families have two sides just as anything else. They have brought about a great challenge and some confusing problems.

"Confusing" is a word in point to describe people's mind. To most people, the confusion of marriages in the transformation is caused, above all, by the conflict between the unified thinking set and the multiplicity of life in reality.

The unified social life had been emphasized for a long time since the liberation of the country, the term "multiplicity" had almost disappeared. The political slogan and military principle of "unified thoughts, unified pace and unified action" used to dominate people's thoughts, words, behaviors and life style, thus formed a unified and stereotyped life style in which men and women, the old and the young, wore the same clothes, had the same things for their meals, and read the newspapers and magazines of the same contents; they seemed to have had the kind of identity and equality which existed only in the primitive communism. Of course, it was partly because the multiplicity was a luxury and was not allowed in a society in which the productivity was so low that a low wage system had to be carried out and the supply of commodities had to depend on the tickets in order to satisfy the basic need to survive of most people. And the unified model of marriage and family was a matter of course in such situations.

Yet the multiplicate market economy has taken the place of the unified planned economy since the '80s, and the introduction of the foreign techniques and management methods under the reform and open policy inevitably brought in the concept of competition and multiplicity. A very obvious fact in the recent

10 years is that the economy has been multiplicate, the state-owned, the collective-owned, the private-owned, the joint-venture and the foreign-funded enterprises are all legal members in the big family of "socialist market economy". People began to differ from each other in their thoughts, words and behaviors and life styles, and are classified into different levels due to the differences in their education, profession and income. The concept of social stratification has been accepted by people.

In a word, everything in the social transformation indicates that it is an unchangeable tendency for the multiplicity to take the place of the unification, and every one has to find out his new position in the new coordinate, and diversity is inevitable. When it comes to marriage models, those arranged by parents or even by abduction and the mercenary marriages still exist in the remote countryside. They are, of course, illegal, yet they are hard to be banned by laws. On the other hand, "single nobles" and "the common law marriages de luxe" emerged in metropolises, which are extraordinary yet hard to get restricted by unified regulations. Between these two extremes of backwardness and outstripping, there are various styles of marriages and families. Nevertheless, the habitual force has had a deep-rooted influence on people's mind. Some people refuse to accept the multiplicate situation and grumble against fate and blame upon other people, they criticize on everything, recollecting the unification of the old days, and feeling ill at ease with the reality. They get confused and puzzled in the colorful world of multiplicity and can't find their own positions. Others simply run after the "modern" life style, neglecting their conditions, only to find themselves unable to deal with it. These phenomena are also caused by the influence of unification. The pressure from the public media is apparent, which press people to compare and compete. This "confusion" can be seen in marriage crises ranging from extramarital affairs, divorces to forced delicacy.

There are also conflicts between the ideal marriages and the practical conditions. Some people don't understand that they can only be in certain positions on the "coordinate of the transformation" due to all kinds of objective or subjective factors for the time being or even for quite a long time, they are unsatisfied with what has happened to them and can't help emulating the "ideal" model which is a long way from them. And the "fashionable" models in the public media have stimulated the impractical dreams and made some people neither satisfied with the existing condition nor able to reach the ideal land. Some people in present China still can't get rid of the constrains such as the houses, the notes and the kids, etc. while choosing the partners in marriages or keeping their marriages going. According to the ideal standards of marriage as a psycho-cultural group, their marriages are not so satisfactory, their families not so happy; however, they can't afford a divorce and a new choice, and the prospect after the divorce may not be so bright, it might even worse than it is now. That's why there are many do-with-it marriages and maintenance marriages. These couples are torn by the ideals and realities, they're full of hesitation and confusion. This kind of marriages is quite normal during the social transformation. It is better to help them adjust the partnership and solve the family problems to get a better life than to persuade them running after an impractical "ideal kingdom". They need the sincere care and effective help of marriages consultees, social workers and even lawyers.

2. The Employment of Women during the Social Transformation in China

The deepening of the economic reform and the overall effectuation of the open policy have brought great changes to the employment of women since the '80s. First, the range of jobs open to women has been widened and the rate of employment increased. The reform and open policy vitalized the national economy, and the new enterprises and the town and township enterprises developed rapidly, which provides an excellent chance and circumstance for women to find jobs in a wide range and become independent economically. The changes of the public notions brought about by the changes of economy and the development of education make it possible for women to have a higher position in families and to popularize education among women. Second, the competition and efficiency asked by the market economy challenged the employment of women which was guaranteed by the "equalitarian policy" of the planned economy during the decades after the liberation. Under the circumstances, and with the influence of the traditional notions, they crisis in the employment of women occurred: many women lost their work, and women have less chances in the recruitment of workers, cadres and students.

Nevertheless, the situations diverse a lot in different regions, and in rural and urban areas.

The gradual format on and development of the market economy since the '80s has improved the productivity, and profound changes in social life and the adjustment of the trade structure provide an enormous space and excellent opportunities for women in towns and cities to go out of housework and find jobs. Not only has the employment of women made great strides forward in the traditional trades such as textile, transport, post and telecommunications, commerce, education, public health and welfare, women have also had a wide participation in the new trades such as finance, real estate, electronics and fashion, they have played an outstandingly important part in the tertiary industries such as the garment industry and catering trade. According to the data from the population census in 1982 and 1990, the rate of increase of in employment of women during these eight years is 162 per cent in the field of finance and insurance, 154 per cent in the real estate service, 79.6 per cent in commerce and catering trade, 78.6 per cent in organizations and offices, 42.7 per cent in the field of public health and welfare, 27 per cent in industry. Textile industry has long been a kingdom of women, its development provides women with more job opportunities, 31.6 per cent of the increased number of workers in textile industry are women

The competition of the market economy has freed women from the restrictions of the traditional notions. They have gone out of housework's and taken the positions of directors or managers; in the areas where the reform and open policy has been carried out earlier, these women directors and managers have showed up in a strong lineup. Relying on their own talents, they have overcome their inferiority complex and fought against the bias from the society, and ascended to the administrative levels where competitions are fierce. They are trying to fulfill their selves. Ninety-seven ordinary women workers in the 28 experimental enterprises for reform were promoted to the positions of managers and leaders after a fierce competition in Liaoning province in 1992.

The economic reform in the countryside expands the farmers' lebensraum. On the one hand, they enjoy the right to arrange the agricultural operation and production and the agricultural products; on the other hand, they are no longer bound to the land; instead of working on the field all their life, they have got the opportunities to enter the secondary and tertiary industries. The contract system of responsibility linked to production and the town and township enterprises provide the women in rural areas with a lot of opportunities and channels for employment.

Women have become a laboring force absolutely necessary in the rural household productions after the reform. Since the effectuation of the contract system of responsibility linked to productions, women's responsibilities of taking care of the crops and other plants in the collective labor in which they had little right to speak in the production and operation nor had they any right to arrange the products, have shifted to taking part in the whole process from growing to gathering in, and they have been in charge of the household breeding and raising. And in the meantime, they are the main participants in developing the town and township enterprises, the trades they widely enter such as the food industry, the garment industry, the braiding industry, the toy industry, the electronic industry, the traditional craft and the hospitality industry are the supporting parts in the town and township enterprises. The rate of employment of women has been rising, and women have played an important part in creating values and earning foreign currencies. Women's independence in economy greatly promotes women's liberation and overall development.

The development of the market economy also brought some problems to women. The principle of competition and the seeking of efficiency broke the tenderness of the equalitarianism in the planned economy. The fossilized system can hardly resist the impact of reform, and women are the first to feel this impact. That some women have to go off their posts has become an outstanding problem in the process if reforming the operational mechanism and shifting the functions of the enterprises, and it has caused difficulties for women in the recruitment of workers, cadres and students. According to incomplete statistics in the old industrial base of Liaoning province, the number of women in the province who had to go off their posts is 420,000, which is 56 per cent of the total number of the off-post workers, and 10 per cent of the total number of the women workers. And what's more, the crisis and unstability also occurred in the women leader group. The rate of women in the leader group dropped to a level even lower than that before the "Cultural Revolution".

Problems also exist among the women in employment. In the urban areas, women are mostly in the labor intensive enterprises or those where women's patience and carefulness are needed. They only occupy a small portion of posts in the fields of high technology and in the high administrative departments; while in the towns and rural areas, women mainly work in the breeding and raising of, say, chickens, cattle and pigs, or take care of crops and plants, and it is men who take the main responsibility in the planting. Women are responsible for the family security whereas men decide more on commodity production. Women take more charge in the labor intensive activities and the time of labor has been increasingly extended, whereas men mainly conduct the technique intensive activities such as purchase and sale. The traditional notion of "men doing business and women housework" still have a great influence on the employment of women, although those women in the more developed areas have different chances from those in less developed areas. In the more developed areas, women get more chances to take part in the non-agricultural production and are no longer bound to the land, however, they are constrained by some conditions, for example, they can only work in the nearby labor intensive town and township enterprises, under the condition that housework be not delayed. And usually they get lower wages and are more difficult to be promoted to administrative positions. In the less developed areas, women can hardly part with farming or housework. Most workers from the country are men, part of them are unmarried women, while married women are usually bound to the household and can't leave their villages. Yet the married men are hardly burdened with their families, they can be on the way to anywhere at any time. Women are usually more passive due to their aptitude and the influence of the families, although some did move out of their villages with the men after the men had taken a firm stand. The model of "men doing business and women housework" is till quite influential.

Employment is an important way to improve women's status, the increased employment of women after the reform and open policy may make it possible to improve women's economic and social status, and is quite effective. But the co-existence of employment and unemployment of women and the fact that the level of jobs women get is usually low showed that to create a partnership equal to both men and women, it is necessary not only for women to improve their own aptitude and level of education, but also for the society to have a change on its notions and eliminate some of the traditional customs. It is la long way to go in China.

3. The Sexes in Families during the Social Transformation in China

More opportunities for women in employment means more economic independence for them; they no longer completely depend on parents and men, and have had more saying their marriages. Yet marriages is just a start point for families, in the final decision on family properties and distribution of housework that really show the status of men and women in families, in which the traditional type of "men doing business and women housework" still plays a great part, it is even overwhelming in some areas.

The rights of men and women on family properties changed greatly since the liberation, especially after the effectuation of the reform and open policy. The relevant surveys showed that the husband and the wife shared the right to make important decisions (those on the types of production, selecting and building houses, buying the expensive goods and production tools, and investment and loan) in quite a number of families. yet the ratio of the families is high in which men make most decisions on family properties. The number of families in which decisions are made jointly increases with the descending of the age under 35. That is to say, women have had a say in family decisions after the liberation, especially the reform and open policy, although men still have a much greater right on family properties.

On the other hand, women have quite a right to budget the routine expense, but they spend more money on their clothing and cosmetics whereas men invest more on developing and improving their personal qualities. Men have a higher level of consumption than women, while women's control of daily expense is mostly limited within housewifery's, which is another demonstrations on the influence of the notion of "men doing business and women housework".

Women are usually the main doers of housework. According to two surveys in Hebei province in 1992, it is lamely women's task to take care of kids, do washing, cooking, shopping and sewing, etc. while men mainly do some heavy labors such as buying coal and some clumsy items. It is men who decide what to grow in the land, whether to adopt new technology and how to assign the tasks. Another survey in towns showed that women spent 4.38 hours per day on housework, while men only spent 2.17 hours, which is much less, although men did do some housework; in the countryside, the average time women spent on housework was 5.18 hours as against 2.24 hours of men. The time women spend on housework is almost twice as much as that of men. This is, of course, an effect of the traditional notions. 57.7 per cent of our public thought men have a higher status in the social concept, 51.1 per cent supported the idea that men should mainly contribute to the society while women mainly to families, 72.8 per cent thought that "the husband success is also that of the wife's, so the wife should support her husband whole-heartedly". And there once even appeared the argument that "wives should go back into families", which reflected the conflict between the double role of the working women and their confusion. How to deal with the relationships between housework and profession still remains to be unsolved when housework are not highly socialized yet.

Women are forced to take most of the low-leveled family obligations and housework, there is virtually no difference on this point in both urban and rural areas. Lack of free time for women directly leads to the fact that they are not able to receive the equal education with men. The inequality exists in the right for men and women to receive education.

Girls dropping from schools virtually doesn't exist in cities and towns and some developed areas due to the development of economy and the effectuation of birth control policy, boys and girls can get equal opportunities on education. Yet girls get much less opportunities in higher education because of the difficulties of finding jobs after their graduation; there much less girl students in colleges and universities. The adult females also get less opportunities for education than men. Influenced by the traditional notion of "men doing business and women housework", women usually sacrifice themselves to "guarantee of success of her husband and her son" in the commence practice of "guaranteeing one member's success in a family of two". Efficiency has been taken as a standard of value in the market economy, in such a situation, the barriers which prevent women from having education come both from the society and family, such as too heavy a burden of housework and lack of free time, and from individuals. A survey in Hebei province showed that 49 per cent of surveyed women didn't show their clear attitude to education, 38 per cent didn't intend to have education. Women's role in the traditional notion in families and the society is to be an understanding wife and loving mother; the idea that the husband's honor is the wife's pride makes women sacrifice themselves for the success of their husbands, they would rather give up their own opportunities of success to submit to their husbands' needs.

In the poor and remote mountain areas, men and women get quite different opportunities to receive education, the number of girls dropping from schools is several times higher than that of boys. The data from the population census indicate that girls took up 86.4 per cent in the total number of the children ranging from seven to eleven who have dropped from schools, and two thirds of illiterates in our country are female, most of who reside in the remote poor mountain areas. And it is a general idea along these women that "boys will be sent to

schools and girls will stay home when money is not enough".
This idea directly influences the younger generation due to the
mother's function and position in daily life, thus formed a
vicious circle of "poverty—difficulty in going to school—low
education—high fertility—poverty". And women lacking education and training are not likely to get themselves improved,
which leads to the difficulty in finding jobs and a lower social
status. It is very important to make a change on the traditional
notions and liberate women from housework and give them an
equal right to receive education. The Communist Party of
China and Chinese government have been carrying out the
Project Hope—a project in which city dwellers contribute to
help the children dropping from schools in the remote areas—to
solve this problem.

CONCLUSION

Min Jiayin

The Variations of *Yanggang* and *Yinrou*—Gender Relations and Social Models, written jointly by the members of the Chinese Partnership Research Group, has the title **The Chalice and the Blade in Chinese Culture—Gender Relations and Social Models** in its English translation. It is on these titles that I will base my summary of the achievements of the group, while at the same time I will draw some tentative conclusions, and express my own views briefly.

1. The Chalice and the Blade in Chinese Culture

(1) Similarity with European Culture

A matriarchal society which may be symbolized by the chalice in the hands of goddesses once existed in prehistoric China, just as it did in Europe. Yet there were no "matriarchs" through whose rights women dominated and oppressed men. Partnerships were maintained between the sexes, although goddesses were enshrined and worshipped.

Many ancient writings can be found in China which record a time when "a man knew his mother without knowing his father" and when a husband resided with his wife's family. Also, children adopted their mother's family name—the Chinese character *xing* (family name) is an associative compound formed by combining the element meaning "woman" and the element meaning "bear". The character itself carries some shade of the matrilineal system, for which further evidence is provided by some family names passed down from ancient times which also contain the element meaning "woman": Ji (姬), Jiang (姜), Yao (姚), Si (姒), etc.

In ancient Chinese legends (dating from the Old Stone Age), Nü Wa, who created man from mud and who smelted stones of five colors to repair the sky, was confirmed to be a female deity, while nothing about gender is mentioned in the legends of Youchao, who taught people to build tree houses, Suiren, who invented the method of making fire by drilling wood, or Shennong, who initiated farming and Chinese herbal medicine. However, these names are very likely to represent the deification of matriarchies. There co-existed in Chinese myths and legends goddesses and gods. One brick sculpture in relief dating from the Han Dynasty portrays the deities Nü Wa and Fuxi, who, with human heads and serpent bodies, were supposed to be the first ancestors of human beings. They mated with their tails tangled together, which presents vividly the partnership between men and women.

Judging from the funeral objects excavated from over 7,000 Stone Age burial sites, women had a social status slightly higher than men; yet the tools buried with the dead indicated a slightly higher status of men in production. So, on the whole, men and women had an equal position. What is most intriguing are the statues of nude females—the Venuses of China—excavated in Liaoning, Hebei and Shanxi provinces during the 1970s and 1980s. Lining them up, we may have a picture of the pedigree showing the evolution of the prehistoric Chinese goddesses —from the small goddess of fertility to the tribal goddess, then to the images of a group of goddesses which came in life-size or even two or three times larger. These statues are a deified reflection of the matrilineal commune.

Full-scale villages have been unearthed at the site of the Yangshao culture—one that is unanimously thought to have been a matriarchal society by archaeologists and historians in China. They show a well-developed architecture, agriculture, animal husbandry, fisheries, and weaving and painted pottery skills. Art was well on its way to maturity, but there are no signs of weapons or war. That was indeed a time of peace and tranquility, a time symbolized by the chalice in the hands of goddesses.

The ways of living and marriage in a matriarchal society are preserved in different degrees in more than a dozen ethnic minorities in the vast southeastern mountainous areas of China, and also on Hainan and Taiwan islands. The system of "visiting marriage" carried out among the matriarchies of the Naxi nationality in Yongning County is of particular value. The sexual partnership (the relation of A'xiao), which, solely based on sex, was not restricted by the economic conditions, and in which men and women made their own choices and were on an equal footing, is a living specimen of the partnership in the ancient matriarchal society. It reveals to us a society, gender relationship and marriage system which are completely different from the present patriarchal ones in which men dominate women and monogamy is the rule.

(2) Differences Compared to Europe

About 4,000 years ago China turned into a patriarchal society, which can be symbolized by the blades in the hands of male warriors, as was the case in Europe. Women's status suffered a dramatic decline as the patriarchs dominated and oppressed women, and it became an unalterable principle that man was superior to woman. However, the "historical failure of women" and the dramatic change in the status of and the relationships between the sexes in China was not caused by the invasions of the barbarous and violent nomads; instead, the patriarchy, the patriarchal society and the dominator model took shape in the process of a gradual evolution, although the male physical power and forcefulness, the blade and war, did play a decisive role.

So far, Chinese archaeologists have not found any signs indicating nomadic invasions on any great scale which could

have been the force replacing matriarchy with patriarchy between 5,000 BC and 3,000 BC. We may conclude from the
ancient documents, archaeological finds and modern scholars'
studies that Chinese society evolved into a patriarchy during the
period 3,000 BC to 2,100 BC, which coincided with the time
when the Five Chieftains—Huangdi, Zhuanxu, Diku, Yao and
Shun appeared as the leaders of the tribes in China. Yet these
all took their family names from their mothers, and their sons
"were born from the same father and had different family
names", according to the Dialogues of the States. This ancient
record tells us that Jin, the father of Huangdi and Yandi, was
married to a princess of the tribe of Youqiao. His son Huangdi
was born of a girl named Ji; hence Huangdi's family name was
Ji. His son Yandi was born of a girl named Jiang; hence Yandi's
family name was Jiang. Huangdi had 25 sons who took 12
different family names. And the cases were similar with the
other four chieftains. Moreover, the power of all the chieftains
was passed to their ablest successors, chosen according to the
non-hereditary principle, instead of to their own sons. These
contradictions reveal the transformation from a matriarchy to
a patriarchy: men had assumed a major role in both production
and war, although the matrilineal system was still adhered to in
reproduction (marriage and the family) and the inheritance
system.

What is worth noting is that it was war—men's business
—which hastened the transformation from matriarchy to patriarchy in China. First, there was the war between the tribes of
the half-brothers Huangdi and Yandi. The latter retreated to the
east after his defeat and united with the Dongyi tribes. Later,
Chiyou, a descendant of Yandi, led his tribe in rebellion against
Huangdi. Moreover, the war against the barbarian Miao tribes
in the south took place in the times of the legendary emperors
Yao and Shun. Another war broke out some ten years after the
last of the Five Chieftains, Yu, had passed his power and
position to his chosen successor Boyi, when his own son tried

to seize power. As a result, Qi established the Xia Dynasty, the first empire in China's history to carry out the hereditary principle, from which time dates the beginning of patriarchal society in China and the decline of women's status. Qi replaced the notion of "sharing the power to control the world" with that of "holding the power within one household."

(3) First Patriarchal Model

Chinese civilization was born in the valleys of the Yangtze and Yellow rivers, with agriculture as the base and with animal husbandry as a complement. The first dominator model in China, which was developed and improved during the Xia, Shang and Zhou dynasties (2,100-221 BC), was the patriarchal system in which the patrilineal blood line was to bind together the small states of different regions. And it was within this 2,000-year period that monogamy and the patrilineal family with the principle of the inheritance going to the eldest son of the lawful wife became stereotyped.

As the first empire in China, the Xia Dynasty and its civilization were a mystery due to the dearth and confusion of evidence until the publishing of the first monograph on Xia history by the young historian Chen Shengyong.[1] With Chen (1994) as a reference, we may draw the following conclusion on that part of the history and civilization of the Xia that concerns our topic: Zuo Qiuming's Commentary on the Spring and Autumn Annals (the Zuo Zhuan) says that "sacrifice and war were the greatest events of a state". Excavated at the site of the Liangzhu culture[2] (in present-day Yuhuang County, Zhejiang

---

[1] Chen Shengyong, **The Rise of the First Chinese Empire—Decoding the Origins of Chinese Culture and the State**, Hunan Press, 1994.

[2] The author of this article refers to the **History of the Shang Dynasty** by Peng Bangjiong, published by Chongqing Press, 1988, the first dynastic history of the Shang ever published in China. The book is reliable for it is based on the data of the inscriptions on bones and tortoise shells, and excavated articles.

Province) were numerous battle-axes symbolizing the power to command and control the armies during the Xia Dynasty, according to ancient documents. Also discovered were the nine tripods used in the sacrifices which connected Heaven and human beings, the monster design (a god with a human body and an animal face), long hollow pieces of jade with rectangular sides, known as cong, semi-ring-shaped jade pendants, known as huang, black elongated pointed tablets of jade held in the hands, known as *gui*, the altar for sacrifices to the God of the Land and a jade board inscribed with the Xia calendar. These finds disproved the previous belief that the first native Chinese civilization—the Xia civilization—originated in the Yellow River Valley. Other theories held that "the Xia tribe originated in the lower reaches of the Yangtze River", and "the Xia civilization derived from the prehistoric civilization in Southeast China". The Xia were a farming tribe good at growing rice, raising silkworms and weaving silk, making and using bamboo articles, and sailing boats.

Studies by modern geologists show that there were many instances of the sea invading the plains of East China in prehistoric times. One such incursion lasted a long time at the end of the Liangzhu culture, around 3,000 BC, due to global climatic variation. The rise of the sea level is described in the Book of Mencius: "In the time of Yao the sea washed back and flooded China". The delta of the Yangtze River became a vast body of water, and people were forced to move to higher ground. According to the historical documents, Yu's father Gun was ordered to take charge of harnessing the rivers and other waterways. He failed in trying to block the rivers and was killed. After that, his son Yu was ordered to continue the endeavor, and he succeeded by adapting the method of dredging, whereupon he became the successor of Shun. There is a story in the Book of Master Zhuang which goes as follows: "Yu wielded a wooden spade himself, and kept dredging all the rivers and waterways. His long exposure to the wind, the rain and the parching sun roughened his body. Finally he helped thousands of tribes settle down." It is also recorded that he passed his home three times without entering it during the 13 years he spent battling the floods. This account extols Yu's capacity to endure hardships and his virtue of selflessness, by which he won the love and respect of the various tribes of China at that time and was able to organize their able-bodied men to tame the rivers. They showed masculine strength in both intelligence and physical power in the struggle to remold Nature. It was this battle to harness the rivers that prepared the way for the great change of replacing matriarchy with patriarchy after Yu's death.

Xia Yu and his son Qi established the monarch as a dictator, based on the power they exerted over the people in the fight to harness the rivers. The Xia hou was the commander who monopolized the powers of religion, the military and administration in his own hands. It had been decided that the eldest son would succeed to the throne. At the same time the capital of the state had been built, hereditary officials appointed, tributes and taxes collected, the army, the prison and the criminal law established, rituals formulated and music composed. However, the male dominator social model was just in its initial stage and was neither perfect nor stable. It drifted unsteadily in antagonistic natural and social surroundings. Qi passed the crown to his son Taikang before he died, which led to a rebellion by his other five sons. During the 500 years of the Xia Dynasty there were 17 monarchs over 14 generations. They moved the capital as many as 13 times, which has resulted in the failure by archaeologists to locate them with any certainty.

The ancestors of the Shang Dynasty (1,700-1,100 BC) arose in the area of the middle and lower reaches of the Yellow River. They were a semi-agricultural and semi-nomadic tribe who migrated eight times before they overthrew the Xia and established the Shang Dynasty. They lived by growing drought-resistant crops such as broomcorn, millet and wheat, and raising cattle, horses, pigs and sheep. After the Shang state had been established by military force, the title of prince was conferred on those who were from the same family as the ruler patrilineally as well as on deserving retainers from other patrilinear families, and the people were divided according to the regions to which the officials were assigned to rule them. The percentage of the cases in which the throne was passed from the elder brother to the younger brother was around 50, and it was usually passed to the son of the elder brother in case of the subsequent death of the younger brother. The central government was reinforced, the position of xiang (prime minister) was instituted to assist the monarch, and a regular army was organized which was mainly comprised of chariots and cavalry. People at that time had a deep belief in the supernatural, and nothing could be done before a divination was held: "The gods appeared at the rituals." Clear class divisions appeared, and slave labor was widely used. Bronze wares were produced and used on a wide scale. The capital was moved five times in the early Shang, and it could be said that there was no fixed capital until Pangeng made the final move to Yin (the present-day Anyang, Henan Province).³ The Zhou Dynasty (1,100-256 BC) was set up by a semi-agricultural, semi-nomadic tribe which was a mixture of the Huaxia, the Rong and the Di tribes. They lived on the upper and middle reaches of the Yellow River and had migrated more than a dozen times before they overthrew the Shang Dynasty. The Zhou rulers, who established their capital on the site of present-day Xi'an, perfected the first dominator model in China—patriarchal feudalism. "Patriarch" is explained in The Origin of Chinese Characters as a temple to honor the ancestors, and the character standing for the ancestor in Chinese in turn has been textually proved to mean a sacrifice to the male genitals. In addition, the original meaning of "feudal-

---

³ See **History of Chinese Civilization**, Feng Tianyu, He Xiaoming, Zhou Jiming, Shanghai People's Press, 1990, pp. 196-209.

ism" in Chinese is to "confer the territory and establish a state". So, combined together, "patriarchal feudalism" means "to sacrifice to the same male ancestor and confer the territory within his blood lineage to establish states". This was realized as follows: The monarch who owned the territory and the people referred to himself as the "Son of Heaven", and the throne was passed only to the eldest son of the lawful wife, who would in turn pass down legitimacy to the eldest son of his lawful wife, who would be the major forefather. The other sons of the lawful wife and those of the concubines to whom the titles of duke, marquis, earl, viscount or baron would be conferred, depending on status and age, would be the minor forefathers. However, on their own territories, where they had the right to confer the titles of qing and daifu, they would be the major forefathers.[4] At the beginning of the Zhou Dynasty there were 53 princes from the imperial family and another 18 princes from other families. The princes from outside the imperial family were sent to the remote areas. Hence a hierarchical system was completed in which the enfeoffment was hereditary and according to the blood lineage of the male ancestors. The system lasted almost 300 years, until the Zhou capital had to be moved eastward to Luoyang in 770 BC under pressure from the incursions of the nomadic tribes of the Rong and the Di.

The Xia, the Shang and the Zhou existed both diachronically and synchronically. There were dozens of patriarchal tribes in China which established "states", and the rulers of these three dynasties did no more than take the leading position in the alliance of the tribes, depending on their superior military force. Nevertheless, there did exist a relation of evolution in all aspects among them, and there are such records in the ancient documents as "The setback of the Xia, which was not long

---

[4] After the transfer of the capital to Yin (Anyang in present-day Henan Province) by King Pan Geng, Shang also called itself Yin.

before that of the Yin[5], could serve as a warning to the latter", "The Yin revolutionized the Xia" and "The Zhou undertook a reform although it was an old state". The replacement of one with another was regarded as a revolution, a revolution realized not only in completing the patrilineal system, or in the perfection of the patriarchy, or even not only in the gradual formation of China as a state, but also in ideology: the Xia people believed in the "Mandate of Heaven" and the Shang people in "spiritual Beings", while the Zhou people, abandoning both the previous beliefs, believed in "human ethics". Finally, it was a revolution realized in the change of gender relations.

The ancestors of the three dynasties were all born of women who were made pregnant by gods, according to the ancient legends, which may serve as evidence that they were living in a matrilineal society. The patrilineal system took the place of the matrilineal system in the early Xia, when women lost their priority over men by having offspring and inheriting property. There were no fixed spouses for a long time among the Shang, although one did have a partner who was superior in status to the others. Monogyny was not instituted until the 12th ancestor Shiren. The concept of valuing boys did not take shape until the Shang Dynasty, when the custom of drowning girl babies emerged, which led to a disproportion of the genders. The average life span of men was longer than that of women. However, women still had rather high social status, judging from the funereal objects from that time which have been excavated. Instead of sacrificing to the gods of Heaven and the Land and the Spiritual Beings, the Zhou rulers only sacrificed to their male ancestors. At the same time, the female ancestors were excluded or reduced to a secondary position. Women were deprived of their right to inherit property in the patrilineal inheritance system. And they were forced out of politics by the social division of labor under which "men take charge of affairs

---

[5] **Historical Records**: The First Emperor of Qin.

outside the household and women the domestic affairs" and "men do farming, while women engage in spinning and weaving". Those women who did otherwise would be sneered at as "the hens that announce the coming of the morning." And the saying that "women are disastrous" was spread through the stories about the fall of the Shang and the Zhou because of King Zhou's infatuation with Daji in the Shang Dynasty and King You's infatuation with Baosi in the Zhou Dynasty. The practice of concubinage emerged, and the principal wife and the concubines had different statuses, which brought about inequality of women in sexual life. Women's status suffered an overall decline.

(4) The Second Patriarchal Model

The emergence of a centralized autocratic monarchy, the Qin, from the chaotic state of the wars among the feudal lords during the period of the Warring States marked the formation of the second patriarchal model in China. Before long, the Oriental dominator model in China was formed in the Han Dynasty, with the governmental system of a centralized autocratic monarchy combined with a patriarchal system. This was much stronger than the male dominator model in the Indo-European culture and so was the oppression of women.

The patriarchal system, under which states in different regions were established according to paternal blood lineage disintegrated after several generations because of the chaotic wars among the feudal lords and the abandonment of the rituals and music due to the unbalanced development of the economy and military force in different states and power struggles within each state. The Zhou emperor was the Son of Heaven and the major forefather in nothing more than name. So the Eastern Zhou, the period after King Ping's eastward migration, was also known as the period of the Warring State.

The splits and wars lasted as long as 500 years during the period of the Warring States. Philosophers of different schools traveled from state to state, lecturing, arguing and interfering in politics. This was known as the period when "One hundred flowers bloomed and one hundred schools of thought contended". The golden age of philosophy in China coincided with that in Ancient Greece in the Indo-European culture both in time and academic accomplishments.

The seven major states during the period of the Warring States, rose to prominence and fell, one after the other. The state of Qin on the loess plateau in the Northwest, whose ancestors had been nomads, settled down in houses and farmed fertile lands after they took Feng and Qi, where the Zhou originated, and forged sharp weapons after they learned metallurgy from the Zhou. Yet Qin was behind the other six states in the development of the patriarchal system, which accounts for its easy adaptation of the new theories of the Legalist thinker Han Feizi; one of his students, Shang Yang, was appointed prime minister of the state and introduced overall social reforms, whereupon Qin became rich and powerful. Eventually, it annexed the other six states and unified China in 221 BC, establishing a centralized autocratic monarchy.

After the unification of the territory of China, the ruler of Qin unified the household register, the system of military service, roads, currency, taxes and the written language throughout the empire. The country was divided into prefectures and counties, all placed under the control of the officials sent by the central government according to the new laws. On top of a pyramid-shaped bureaucratic hierarchy was the monarch, Qin Shihuang, who grasped all the power in his own hands: "The affairs of the country, big or small, were all decided by the Emperor."[6] He organized manpower from all over the country to build the Great Wall in order to keep out the northwestern nomads. Qin Shihuang thought that the second dominator model he established would last forever, yet his

---

[6] **Book of Changes**: Kun: The Record of Wenyan.

empire collapsed like a house of cards during a peasant rebellion soon after his death because his radical policies had alienated the populace at large. The path of a cultural type similar to that of ancient Rome stopped there and then. Today we can only recall his glory, his dignity and his militarism from the battle array of the terra cotta army excavated from the mausoleum of Qin Shihuang in Xi'an.

Learning a lesson from the rapid decline of the Qin Dynasty, the Han Dynasty combined the two dominator models. On the one hand, "Han inherited the Qin system" of the centralized autocratic monarchy, setting up schools and holding imperial examinations to select competent officials at all levels whose positions were not hereditary; on the other hand, there were only 15 prefectures which were directly ruled by the court, the other territories being bequeathed to the nine princes outside the imperial family and the 143 marquises who had achieved military glory in the setting up of the dynasty. When the central government was adequately consolidated, the princes outside the imperial family were wiped out, and the territories were re-distributed among the princes within the imperial family. What was more important was the derivation of the patriarchal clan system from the patriarchal system: the descendants from one ancestor would live together, with some fields as the public property of the clan. There would be an ancestral temple for sacrifice to the common ancestor of the clan, and a genealogical record of the family history. Hence an Oriental despotism was established in a combination of the centralized bureaucracy and the patriarchal system which was isomorphic at both levels of the country and the family. It was more complete and much stronger than that in Indo-European culture, and lasted a longer time. Burdened by the "three big mountains" of political power, clan power and the authority of the husband, just as Mao Zedong once pointed out, Chinese women were oppressed more severely and had a lower social status than their sisters in most parts of the world.

(5) The Confucian Classics and the Bible Play Similar Roles

The Confucian scholars who explained the Book of Changes in terms of yin and yang defined men as the latter. They were supposed to stand in a high place, side by side with Heaven, the ruler and the father; and women, as yin, were in a lower place, standing side by side with land, the minister and the son so that it would fit into the patriarchal dominator model. Emperor Wu of Han trusted in the great Confucian scholar Dong Zhongshu, who proposed the theory of the Three Cardinal Guides and Five Constant Virtues, and the superiority of men over women became an orthodox teaching. The Confucian philosophical classics in Chinese culture played a role similar to that of the Bible in the Indo-European culture in setting up an irrational, unequal gender relation, but Chinese women were placed in a much lower position.

We have discussed the process by which the concept of yin and yang was introduced into the Book of Changes in the prelude. What I would like to add to that is that "there were different divinations in ancient times and during the three dynasties," according to the ancient documents. The hexagram kun (☷) or female was followed by the hexagram qian (☰) or male in both the book Lian Shan of the Xia Dynasty and the book Gui Zang of the Shang Dynasty, which demonstrated that those two dynasties were the products of matriarchal society, in which women had a higher status than men. The Book of Changes is the most ancient book of divination passed down till today. It is said to have been compiled by the founder of the Zhou Dynasty, King Wen, when he was imprisoned by the Shang ruler. At that time, a patriarchal society had come into being, and that was why kun and qian were reversed. Deviating from the dialectical thought of "sticking to yin and valuing weakness" advocated in the book of Laozi, the authors of the Commentaries emphasized that the superior man should devote himself to ceaseless activity. It also justified the domination of yang as the way of Heaven, the husband and the sovereign, who were superior to the yin, which submits in a lower place as "the way of the earth, the way of the wife, and the way of a minister."[7] It further pointed out that "a fight is unavoidable if yin is in doubt about yang;"[8] that is, a fight would break out should the inferior be discontented and try to promote themselves into the place of yang, and thus ominous. In fact, the authors tried to avoid the struggle through the dichotomy of the fixed positions in order to "reach the supreme harmony" and maintain "the great unity."[9] Being reconstructed by the authors of the Commentaries with the Daoist concept of yin and yang, the Book of Changes was turned into metaphysics to maintain the patriarchal system and men's superiority over women. The Han Dynasty reached its peak at the time of the Emperor Wu, who "banned all the others of the hundred schools but Confucianism" and put his trust in the master of Confucian classics Dong Zhongshu, who further systematized the Confucian philosophy, emphasizing yin and yang and the Five Elements and made it the official ideology. He discussed gender relations: "Everything is composed of smaller parts, and there must be a higher part and a lower part in each combination." "The righteous relationship between a ruler and a minister, a father and a son a husband and wife should correspond to the way of yin and yang. A ruler is Yang while a minister is Yin; a father is Yang while a son is Yin; a husband is Yang while a wife is Yin." "Yang is superior to Yin," so a ruler is a cardinal guide to a minister, a father a cardinal guide to a son, and a husband a cardinal guide to a wife. "These three cardinal guides may be

---

[7] See Note 6.

[8] The Similarities and Differences between the Book of Changes, The Commentaries and the Dialectics of Laozi.

[9] Luxuriant Dew of the Spring and Autumn Annals: the Basic Meanings.

got from Heaven."[10] He also named the five Confucian ethical categories—benevolence, righteousness, propriety, knowledge and sincerity—the Five Constant Virtues, which were combined with the Three Cardinal Guides to define women's status and regulate women's actions.

The social model, the ideology and the gender relations of feudal China had taken shape by and large by the Han Dynasty (the Western Han, 206 BC-25 AD), and were adapted in the following 2,000-odd years of more than ten dynasties with only slight variations. Women were barred from receiving education, taking the imperial civil examinations and acting as officials, which is evidence of the further decline of Chinese women's status in the Han Dynasty. The confinement of women began: eunuchs were widely employed in the imperial palace; women alone were demanded to be chaste, and those who were chaste were honored by the court. The Biographies of Heroines by Liu Xiang and the Seven Commandments to Women by Ban Chao restrained women's actions through praise or criticism.

(6) The Protracted Antagonism between Farming Tribes and Nomadic Tribes

The matriarchal society at the two extremities of Eurasia evolved into patriarchal society, and the patriarchal system of the dominator model was created in both places in succession; the partnership between the sexes turned into men's domination of women. This was the rule of social evolution, although the evolution happened in different times along different routes, and different social models developed from it. The characteristics of this in Indo-European culture and Chinese culture were,

---

[10] For nearly 2,000 years, the "Commentary on the Book of Changes" was believed to be Confucius' work, but research findings by contemporary scholars have refuted this view but proved it to be the work of some Confucian scholars living in the Qin and Han dynasties. Therefore the book's back role of advocating male supremacy should be be attributed to Confucius.

first of all, decided by the different geographic conditions. In China, the struggle between farmers and nomads lasted 2,000 years, in which the northwestern nomads, who had fleet horses and strong cavalry forces, were superior in military achievements, while the ethnic Han in the southeast, who were economically and culturally more advanced, were superior in political achievements.

According to modern evolutionist theories, the evolution of a complex system may carry some non-decisive features: two systems with the same initial conditions may be driven into different paths of evolution at a mutational junction due to enlarged fluctuations. After a period of time, the conditions of these two system will be quite different.[11] Eurasia is the largest continent and is split up by the Pamirs, the Ural Mountains and the Siberian forests, which accounts for the separate evolution in the ancient Indo-European culture (the European culture) and the Chinese culture. The initial conditions based upon which the two cultures developed—the natural geographic environments—differed. Therefore, it is no surprise that they evolved along different paths, although the direction and the process were rather similar.

The European Continent, more like a extended peninsula, is only one fourth of the Asian Continent in area, although there is more pasture for grazing than in Asia at the same latitudes, and it is warmer and more humid. I think this may account for what has been described in the book The Chalice and the Blade by Riane Eisler: the Kurgans on the grand prairies in northeastern Europe developed their patrilineal society during the period 5,000 BC-3,000 BC. They had a strong military force and swept with the blade over the matrilineal society in southern Europe. The latter was wiped out, for, being located in a much smaller area, it had no room for maneuver.

---

[11] **Evolution—The Grand Synthesis**, Ervin Laszlo, Shaambhala Publications, Inc; 1987, pp. 43-47

East Asia, excluding the Arabian Peninsula, the Indian Subcontinent and the Indo-China Peninsula, is more than twice as large as the European Continent. The southeast monsoon from the Pacific Ocean brings monsoon rain to the East Asian Continent and causes a gradual decline of annual rainfall from the coastal lands in the southeast to the inland areas of the northwest, ranging from a high of 2,000 mm in the coastal lands to a low of 5.9 mm in the inland areas. Divided by the 400mm isohyet (fig.17), there is a humid farming zone to the southeast and a dry grassland zone to the northwest.[12] However, both sides have a climate not so agreeable as that of Europe. It is cold and dry in winter in the northwest, and overly hot and humid in summer in the southeast. Thus, affected by the harsh natural environment, the nomads in the northwest of the East Asian Continent developed much more slowly than those on the European Continent, so slowly that they were not strong enough to sweep over the vast East Asian Continent. And the farming tribes in the southeast were not able to develop a rice civilization in the middle and lower reaches of the Yangtze River until Yu the Great led his people to tame the rivers and the other watercourses. As a result, atrilineal society emerged 1,000 years later on the East Asian Continent than on the European Continent. The farming tribes which grew rice, raised silkworms and used bamboo articles gradually formed patriarchal societies when people, mainly men, were organized to fight floods. In the light of these considerations, we may see the different economic bases from which Chinese culture and European culture originated.

Sima Qian formulated a rule in Chinese history as early as in the Han Dynasty: "More often than not it was the southeasterners who initiated a cause, yet it was the northwesterners who finally succeeded."[13] Testing it with the data of the Xia, Shang,

---

[12] See Note 3, pp. 96-98.
[13] **Historical Records**: Chronological Table of the Six States.

Zhou, Qin and Han dynasties, as well as the following dynasties, we find this to be absolutely true. The Xia, living on farming and rising in the southeast, was replaced by the Shang, which rose in the northwest and developed both farming and grazing. The Shang was again replaced by the semi-farming, semi-nomadic Zhou Dynasty, which had once mixed with the nomads like the Rong and the Di. The Zhou, in its turn not long after that, was wiped out by the Qin, which ad its power base in the west, "a remote small country which was compared to the nomads like the Rong and the Di and rejected by the tribes in China."[14] A war between Chu and Han broke out after the demise of the Qin, and again it was the Prince of Han, Liu Bang, who occupied the northwest and defeated Xiang Yu the Conqueror, who occupied the southeast. The conclusion may be drawn from the historical data that the semi-farming, semi-nomadic races, among which the patriarchal dominator model was more advanced, imposed their culture and social model on the farming races, whose system of patriarchy and dominator mode was underdeveloped. And that the Zhou, the Qin and the Han successively conquered Wu, Yue and Min in the southeast, Jing and Chu in the south and Bashu in the southwest, and expanded their territories was undoubtedly a process in which the blade smashed the chalice and, when it came to gender relations, replaced the matriarchal partnership with the patriarchal dominator model. It was only because of the vastness and the varied topography in south China that some matrilineal tribes, hidden in the vast mountains or on remote islands, were able to more or less preserve their social models and cultures till today.

The physiocrat theory of economics began to form in the Han Dynasty, when the Chinese, who called themselves the Han race, gradually dropped the combined emphasis on both farming and grazing and took new directions which put crop plant-

---

[14] See Note 12.

ing in first place, followed by spinning and weaving, and then animal husbandry. It was their ideal that everyone should have enough food and clothing, live in peace and enjoy his work in which "men do farming and women weave." Animal protein was greatly reduced from people's diet with the shrinking of fisheries and animal husbandry. As a result, the Hans of later generations have been rather physically fragile, although quick in mind and flexible in the limbs. What's more, the Hans put political achievements above military achievements, resulting in the fact that in a society falling into different strata, such as scholars, farmers, workers, merchants and soldiers, the soldiers were in fact nothing more than armed farmers. In contrast to this, every nomad was a soldier, and grazing their herds in their daily lives on horseback was, at the same time, a kind of military training. Therefore, it was extremely difficult for the Hans to cope with the protracted military confrontation with the northwestern nomads in defense of their own culture, social structure and way of life.

Despite this, the Hans, depending upon the Great Wall, succeeded in preventing the nomads from overcoming them. There were two great victories over the powerful nomads: one was during the Han Dynasty, when the Huns were driven into Europe, which led to a great migration of the races in Europe; the other was during the Tang Dynasty, when the Turks were defeated and migrated to Asia Minor. And there were three times when the Hans and the nomads came to a north-south stalemate, with the Yangtze River as a natural boundary: the first time was during the Northern and Southern Dynasties, following the Han Dynasty; the second time was in the period of the Five Dynasties and the Ten Kingdoms, after the Tang Dynasty; and the third and last time was in the Southern Song Dynasty, when a prolonged war had been fought against the Liao, the Jin and the western Xia in the north. And finally there were two crushing defeats, after which the Hans were ruled by other races: first by the Mongols, who founded the Yuan

Dynasty, then by the Manchus, who founded the Qing Dynasty. In terms of figures, the scores would be 2:0, 3:3 and 0:2—the Hans' luck deteriorating from victory to draw and finally to defeat.

Two factors that had much to do with the performance of the Hans in their military confrontation with the nomads from the north were martial arts (*wushu*) and horses.

Not all Hans were turned into soldiers, yet it was also the case that most of the Han people, especially most Han farmers, who constituted the overwhelming majority of the population, practiced martial arts. A kind of body-building sport and entertainment in movies and television programs, martial arts (*kongfu*) was once a sort of skill to protect their homesteads and country in ancient China. The farmers who practiced martial arts daily were quite effective in combat after some training. Unfortunately the popularity and the spirit of the Chinese martial arts have been declining in China over the last 2,000 years.

Chariots and cavalry played the same role in battles in ancient times as tanks and mobile troops in modern times; they were overwhelming in battles against infantry. Chariots had been widely used since the Shang Dynasty, hence the infantry of the northwestern nomads were no menace at all. Yet the Hans' advantages were gone after the nomads developed their cavalry. The Chinese were forced to learn from the nomads. This led to the military reform during the period of the Warring States, in which "King Wuling of the state of Zhao issued an order to popularize nomadic-style clothing, and the skills of riding and shooting. That was the first recorded cavalry in Chinese history. The vast areas at the foot of the Yin Mountains and the Helan Mountains (including the present-day Hebei and northern Shanxi provinces) is a natural pasture where fleet horses have long been raised. And the area to the south of the Qin Great Wall was part of the territory of the Han. There were lots of horse experts among the Qin, among whom were Bole, who was good at identifying pedigree horses, and Jiu Fanggao, who was an expert at appraising horses. The rulers of the Han Dynasty put great store by horse breeding. They also began to use saddles to make riding more convenient, which made it possible for them to send several hundred thousand cavalrymen to fight the "battles across the desert". During the Northern and the Southern Dynasties Chinese were the first to invent stirrups, which increased the flexibility and effectiveness of cavalry, making the rider and the horse a united whole. According to studies by Dr. Joseph Needham, stirrups greatly changed the situation of warfare after they were introduced into Europe. The significance of horse-breeding in politics reached its peak in the Tang Dynasty. Horses of fine breed were imported from Central Asia. Portraits of six of Emperor Taizong's best war-horses were carved on his tomb according to his will, which were known as "the Six Handsome Horses at the Zhao Tomb". It was by depending on powerful cavalry that the Tang defeated the Turks. In the Song and Ming dynasties, horse-breeding declined, and the areas for stud farms for fine-breed horses were all occupied by the northern nomads. So the part of the Great Wall built in the Ming Dynasty was several hundred li further inland than in the Qin Dynasty, accounting greatly for the conquest of the Song Dynasty by the Yuan and the Ming Dynasty by the Qing.

The Hans had a special way of "overcoming strength with flexibility" although they had been conquered by the nomadic Mongols and the semi-farming, semi-nomadic Manchus and fell under their rule for 350 years altogether. The Hans overcame the military achievements of the conquerors with their cultural achievements, and the conquerors were themselves finally conquered. The Mongols, who carried out a policy of a hierarchy of races as a strict precaution against any resurgence of the Hans, began to adapt the Han system, including political and tax policies, rituals and laws, Confucianism, the imperial examinations and language under the reign of Kublai Khan. The

Mongols had deeply assimilated the culture of the Hans by the time they returned to the Mongolian grasslands after their empire across Europe and Asia had fallen. As for the Manchus, who were underdeveloped culturally and a small minority of the population, they took pains to find ways to rule the vast land of China. One of their methods was to adapt and absorb the Han culture. The founder of the Qing Dynasty, Emperor Kangxi, and Emperor Qianlong set good examples. They studied Han classics, poetry, calligraphy and painting so well that they themselves became masters of these arts. When the Qing Dynasty was overthrown 250 years later, at the beginning of this century, the Manchu language, spoken and written, had virtually disappeared.

So, the Chinese culture on the East Asian Continent differs from the European culture not only in origin, economic base, social model, and evolutionary path, but also in the outcome of the prolonged struggle against the force of the blade of the northern nomads. The ethnic Han, a farming race, was never conquered culturally, and, of course, was far from being eliminated. On the contrary, this culture has not only been kept intact, but has virtually assimilated those of a dozen nomadic races that invaded China.

(7) The Four Cycles

Chinese history in the 2,000 years since the Han Dynasty has traversed four cycles of rulers of the Han—a nomadic ethnic group—the Han—a nomadic ethnic group again, and so on. In its development, the ruling mode has been continuously fortified by a combination of three major philosophies—Confucianism, Daoism and Buddhism. Neo-Confucianism, which was the outcome of the amalgamation of the above three philosophies, has served to fetter the freedom of Chinese women. With the onward progress of Chinese feudalism, the female sex in China found its social status constantly deteriorating. Nevertheless, the rulers of the nomadic ethnic groups, who were much less advanced than the Hans in their social and cultural civilization, instilled into the relations between the sexes some remnants of their matriarchy, thus somewhat relaxing the bonds on the women and breathing some romance into the relations between the sexes.

Mencius, however, foresaw the rhythm of Chinese history when he said: "A new king is bound to rise in 500 years."[15] The development of Chinese history after him proved his prophecy to bw correct. Luo Guanzhong, author of The Romance of the Three Kingdoms, wrote: "The general historical trend is division after a long period of unity, and unity after a long period of division." Lu Xun had a more poignant remark. He said: "There were times when the desire to be slaves could not be realized and times when the position of slaves was secure."

The first cycle (25 A.D.-581 A.D.) began with the Eastern Han, and continued through the Three Kingdoms period, the Wei, the Jin and the Northern and Southern Dynasties to the Sui and the Tang—a cycle of unity-division-unity.

The country was divided for some 300 years in between, when the region north of the Yangtze was occupied by the nomadic ethnic groups of the Xiongnu, Jie, Di, Qiang and Xianbei. The five dynasties under the rule of Hans were forced to the south of the Yangtze. The downfall of the centralized Han regime and the dominating position of Confucianism was shaken. Intellectuals turned to Xuanism, which was a school of metaphysics characterized by nihilism and liberalism. Meanwhile Buddhism spread to China from India and Daoism developed. All this, coupled with the influence of the way of life and customs and habits of the nomadic ethnic groups from the north, gave rise to a multitude of ways thought and philosophies in Chinese society and culture.

On the question of the relations between the sexes, the patriarchal ethics founded in the Han Dynasty was on the

---

[15] See "Gongsun Chou, Mengzi".

decline in this period, and females occasionally outshone their male counterparts in talent and ability. Here and there the female sex revealed its disgust with the practice of polygamy and there was no lack of activities seeking sexual freedom and equality in sexual activities. On the other hand, people began to attach importance to appropriate social status in marriages and extravagance in wedding ceremonies. This tendency led to marriages solely arranged by the parents, and in extreme cases families of the same social status even arranged engagements of their children before they were born. Rich families took in courtesans.

The second cycle (581 A.D.-960 A.D.) began in the Sui and Tang dynasties, and continued through the Five Dynasties and Ten Kingdoms to the reunification under the Song Dynasty.

The rulers of the Tang Dynasty came from the military aristocracy in Northwest China. They had the blood of nomadic ethnic people running in their veins and they carried on the influence of the latter's culture. The Great Tang was a powerful empire with its doors wide open to all of its neighbors in the world at that time. Therefore, it had brisk economic and cultural exchanges with its neighboring countries. Whenever the Tang regime declined, as a rule peasant uprisings broke out, ethnic groups in the outlying regions invaded and the country was again torn apart into warring states. The central region experienced five short-lived dynasties, whereas the surrounding regions were partitioned into ten small kingdoms. The founding emperor of the Song Dynasty Zhao Kuangyin, formerly a general, did not have much trouble in seizing state power in a military coup. For fear his subordinate generals might do the same to him, he deprived them of their military power and put himself at the command of the entire military establishment. Both the Tang and Song dynasties chose officials through the imperial examinations. The fact that success in the imperial exam meant an immediate surge in rank and wealth drove people to pursue book learning to the neglect of martial arts.

The resultant phenomenon was that during those dynasties culture was highly developed, whereas the state suffered a dearth of military talent. After Shi Jingtang seized[16] prefectures in what are today's Shanxi and Hebei provinces during the Five Dynasties, the Song Dynasty, because of its lack of military strength, was forced to pay an annual tribute of a large amount of silver to the northern nomadic tribes as the price for peace.

Women still enjoyed fairly high status during the Tang-Song period, as the society was still rather permissive. Females at that time could travel and go hunting on horseback and take part in business activities. They had a measure of initiative on the question of marriage. Women could attend sacrificial ceremonies to ancestors and even participate in politics. One woman even ascended the throne in the Tang Dynasty. Meanwhile, however, Han Yu and some other outstanding scholars advocated a restoration of the Confucian ethics. By the Song Dynasty a group of Neo-Confucianists held sway in the ideological realm. They advocated "Maintaining the law of Heaven and suppressing worldly desires." With the adage "Rather starve to death than lose one's chastity", they condemned remarriage by widows. The male sex began to extol virginity, and women with bound feet began to be considered beautiful. Gradually women of the Han nationality lost the ability to dance.

The third cycle (960 A.D.-1368 A.D.) began with the Song Dynasty and continued through the Liao, Jin and Yuan regimes of the nomads to the Ming Dynasty, when national reunification was once more achieved under a Han ruler.

The Song Dynasty marked the turning point of the decline of the dominance of the farming Han nationality. The Qidan (Khitan) nationality founded their political power, under the title of the Liao Dynasty, north of the Huai River. Then the Nuzhens founded their Jin Dynasty north of the Yangtze, and finally the mighty Mongols ruled over the whole of China as

---

[16] "Plain Questions", "The Yellow Emperor's Internal Classic".

the Yuan Dynasty. The Han people for the first time in history were ruled over by an ethnic group from the north. That marked the beginning of a merger of the northern and southern cultures and the spread of Zhu Xi's Neo-Confucianism to the north. Zhu's Collected Commentaries on the Four Books became the emperor-authorized textbook and standard reference for the imperial examinations. Thus Neo-Confucianism was not only a school of thought but the official ideology and virtually a national religion. The Confucianist ethics became "the Law of Heaven" serving as the criteria for truth.

The Qidans, Nuzhens and particularly the Mongols were warlike nomads with a way of life entirely different from that of the Hans. Among them were found the remnants of matriarchal influence. For example, women worked shoulder to shoulder with their men, rendered their support in wartime and took an active part in politics. There was still a partnership in the relations between the sexes. Unfortunately when they moved to the hinterland of China they readily accepted the culture of the Hans, including the Confucian yardsticks for the behavior of women.

The fourth cycle (1368-1912) began in the Ming Dynasty, through the more than 250 years under the Manchu Qing rule up to the founding of the Republic of China, which was another domination by the Hans.

The Ming Dynasty was founded on the basis of peasant uprisings, but founding emperor Zhu Yuanzhang was originally a bandit. His rule was ruthless, and that style was passed down to his successors. So the Ming Dynasty was marked by a highly centralized state power, the slaughtering of meritorious officials and generals, a luxurious life in the palace, seizure of power by eunuchs, palace intrigues and literary inquisitions, all of which were carried out to the extreme. The Manchus were originally part of the Nuzhen tribe, originating in Northeast China. It was the tide of history that gave it an opportunity to sweep down across the Great Wall with their cavalry in eight divisions, each under a distinctive banner, and found the Great Qing Empire. In order to rule over the majority Hans, the minority Manchus resorted to high-pressure policies and national oppression. Therefore, both the Ming and the Qing represented the most perfect mode of the Chinese-style domination with the most savage suppression of individuality. The imperial-authorized Neo-Confucianism became a tool that distorted human nature and served as a sword that kills without spilling blood.

The regime of the two dynasties of the Ming and Qing carried the male chauvinism and dual personality and double criteria advocated by Neo-Confucianism to the extreme. While men recited quotations from the Four Books as a means of achieving officialdom, fame, position and wealth, women on the other hand were confined to the women's quarters and made to read books that taught them to be docile and subservient to their fathers, husbands and sons. The imperial court issued citations on "chaste" women who would rather die than remarry after the death of their spouses. Meanwhile men were free to lead a loose life. Prostitution, and pornographic literature and art were rampant. In addition to the old dictums for women such as "Obey your father and elder brothers at home, obey your husband after marriage, and after your husband's death obey your son" and "Women should abide by the strictures on ethics, language, appearance and skill required of women", there were two more new fetters for women, namely, "Ignorance is a fine quality for women" and "women should be confined to their quarters".

With the growth of a commodity economy and the emergence of many bustling towns, however, an urban ideology began to develop during the Ming and Qing dynasties. With the introduction of new thinking from the West, people began to voice women's protests, some of which took the form of writings. Among them were the works by Li Zhi and Dai Zhen, who criticized the Neo-Confucianism of Song and Ming times, and advocated equality for men and women alike—an indication of the light at the end of a long, dark tunnel.

(8) The Women's Movement as a Component of the Chinese Revolution

The earliest Christian missionaries came to China in the middle of the Ming Dynasty. Their arrival marked the beginning of the clash and merging of Western culture and Chinese culture. Beginning with the Opium War of 1840, Chinese society endured periodic upheavals every five to 10 years. In other words, there would break out a war, uprising, revolution, unrest or reformist campaign every five to 10 years. The enlightenment and liberation of Chinese women ultimately constituted a component of the Chinese revolution. The shackles that bound Chinese women for 4,000 years were smashed one after another. Equality between men and women, with equal pay for equal work as the central link, has become the state policy of New China.

Chinese culture is a culture that has evolved independently in the secluded environment of the East Asian continent. It is the most developed culture in the region, radiating far and wide. Militarily, China met challenges and even defeats, but culturally it has never met any serious challenge. The only major clash between the indigenous culture and a foreign culture was that following the introduction of Buddhism from India, which however was peacefully assimilated by Chinese culture.

Western culture (European culture, to be more specific) is alien in nature to Chinese culture. It is the industrial civilization of modern times, which is at a higher plane of historical evolution as compared with Chinese culture. When Western culture invaded China in all realms of military science, commodities, way of life, literature and the arts, technology, science, philosophy and religion it constituted a challenge from a more developed civilization without precedent in history. Clash, resistance and repulsion have taken place together with assimilation, adaptation, alienation and merger. In the broad sense, we find that the Chinese social system, which served as the "manifestation" of Chinese culture, lost its stability in the world surroundings. This instability took the form of periodical upheavals and random selections from among the numerous trajectories at the junctions of abrupt changes—departing step by step from the cycle that had made Chinese society stagnant and entering a new trajectory of evolution.

The events cited below clearly show the periodic upheavals China has experienced in the past half a century, at intervals of every five to 10 years:

1840	Opium War
1851	The Taiping peasant uprising
1856	Second Opium War
1862	The Westernization Movement
1874	Japan's Occupation of the Ryukyu Islands
1883	Sino-French War in Vietnam
1895	China-Japan Naval War
1898	The Reform Movement
1900	Boxer uprising and invasion of the Allied Army
1911	The revolution that toppled the Qing regime
1919	May 4 Movement
1924	First revolutionary civil war
1927	Second revolutionary civil war
1937	War of Resistance against Japanese Aggression
1945	Third revolutionary civil war
1949	Founding of the People's Republic of China
1956	The Socialist Transformation Campaign
1966	The Cultural Revolution
1976	April 5 Movement and downfall of the Gang of Four
1981	Adoption of policies of reform and opening to the outside world
1989	The Tiananmen Square Incident

Over the one and a half centuries encompassing the events

listed above, the Chinese women's liberation movement has been characterized by: first, that it has always been a component of peasant uprisings, reformist movements, the old and new democratic revolutions and the socialist revolution launched by the Chinese people; and second, that it started from minor acts such as the "Natural Feet" movement and schools for women, then to opposition to forced marriage arranged by parents, opposition to child marriage and advocacy of monogamy, and finally reached the stage of women's participation in politics and equality for all through legislation.

Three things stand out in our discussions on those one and a half centuries. One was the 1911 revolution that toppled the Qing regime and together with it ended for good the centralized feudal monarchy which had been closely related with the patriarchal system. In its place was set up a new party politics whereby the patriarchal system lost its political legitimacy. Second was the "May 4 New Culture Movement" of 1919, during which people advocated the adoption of democracy and science from the West and put forth the slogan of "Down with the Confucian Shop!" It also marked the abolition of the old-style written language and the imperial examination system, and an end to the domination by Confucianism of Chinese culture. And the third was the founding of the People's Republic of China in 1949, which marked the establishment of a new democracy and the recognition of Marxism-Leninism as the guiding thought that stands for equality for all and equal pay for equal work. All these new ideas were legalized by specific provisions of the Constitution and the Marriage Law. The Chinese women at last won emancipation.

2. The Chalice and the Blade in Chinese Culture

I agree with Riane Eisler's quotation of the view of Western academic circles that there is a paradox in Chinese culture. On the one hand, the social mode of patriarchal rule that determined the low status of women in China has been much stronger and longer than that in Europe, and on the other, Chinese culture displays a greater measure of femininity than European culture.

The first part of the Conclusion to this book which I have written discussed the first half of that paradox and I am going to discuss the other half in this second part. One thing I would like to make clear is that, just as I pointed out in the Foreword, the *yin* and *yang*, and their derivations *yinrou* and *yanggang* are conceptions peculiar to Chinese culture. Yanggang and *yinrou* retain some similarity with the ideas of the chalice and the blade in European culture, but they are not identical. When we are discussing the subject of "The Variations of *Yanggang* and *Yinrou*—Gender Relations and Social Models in China" we refer to the variation curves of those two interacting elements in Chinese culture. And what is noteworthy is that the so-called "equilibrium between *yin* and *yang*," or "mutual complement of *gang* (hardness, muscularity) and *rou* (soft, femininity)" or "*yanggang* and *yinrou* in harmony" so much emphasized in traditional Chinese culture has been rarely found in Chinese history.

(1) The dialectics of *yin* and *yang*

The foreword of this book touches upon the process of how the concepts of *yin* and *yang* have evolved in Chinese culture, whereby we come to know that the concepts of *yin* and *yang* have become categories to a degree similar to that of the "way" in Chinese philosophy. This pair of categories of *yin* and *yang* are extensively used in Chinese meteorology, earth science, military science, architecture, the arts and literary theory, and particularly conspicuous, and most successfully, in the theory of traditional Chinese medicine.

The traditional theory of *yin* and *yang* holds that *yin* and *yang* are mutually contradicting and interdependent at the same time. "*Yin* and *yang* have the same roots," and "the way of *yin* and *yang* are interdependent, without the one, the other will not exist." The definition of *yin* and *yang* is infinite just as "there is *yin* in *yang* and vice versa," and "yin and *yang* are infinite, they can be counted in tens, or hundreds, or thousands or tens of thousands."[17] Yin and *yang* may be transformed into each other as "when *yang* grows to the extreme, it becomes *yin* and vice versa"[18] and "when *yin* triumphs, *yang* is sick; when *yang* triumphs, *yin* is sick", "when *yin* is damaged, *yang* is affected, and the same with *yang*", and "too much emphasis on *yin* makes it turn into *yang*, and vice versa".[19] The ideal state of *yin* and *yang* is an equilibrium between them and in harmony, which is called he, which means harmony in English. The book of Laozi says: "Everything has *yin* and *yang* on each side, which interact to reach harmony,"[20] and the book of Zhuangzi has it that "the intercourse between the two gives birth to everything."[21] And the extreme of he is divine—"the blur of demarcation between *yin* and *yang* is divine," and "the state of infinite changes is divine."[22] On the other hand, when there is disharmony between *yin* and *yang*, it is "sickness"[23] for "when the two exist in harmony, the body is healthy; when the two depart, the body is dead; when the two are not in harmony, it is sickness; when the two are diametrically contradictory, life is in danger."[24] Therefore medical treatment is aimed at restoring the harmony of *yin* and *yang*, or in other words, "It is to try to watch *yin* and *yang* and to readjust them with the aim of achieving a harmony."[25]

---

[17] Ditto.

[18] Ditto.

[19] "Discourse on the Yue", "Discourse on the States".

[20] Chapter 42 of **The Book of Laozi**.

[21] "Tianzifang", "Zhuangzi".

[22] "Plain Questions", "The Yellow Emperor's Internal Classic".

[23] "A Discourse on Tracing Back to the Medical Classic" by Wang Lu.

[24] "Principles and Prohibitions for the Medical Profession" by Yu Chang.

[25] "Plain Questions", "The Yellow Emperor's Internal Classic".

If we translate the above-mentioned medical theory of *yin* and *yang* into a mathematical diagram (fig.14), *yin* and *yang* are represented by the coordinate axes of x and y, and the space between the two curves in the coordinates represents the state of the human physique. Since there is no mention of waxing (excess) of *yin* and waxing (excess) of *yang* simultaneously, the upper right-hand part forms a blank. According to the life and death manifestation in a mathematical diagram x --› 0, y --›0, the lower left shows an arrow pointing to the origin of coordinates, which represents death. The diagram falls into nine divisions:

Symbol	Name	Formula
A	*yin* & *yang* in equilibrium	x=y=n
B	waxing of *yang*, normal *yin*	x›n, y=n
C	waxing of *yin*, normal *yang*	x=n, y›n
D	waning of *yang*, normal *yin*	x‹n, y=n
E	waning of *yin*, normal *yang*	x=n, y‹n
F	waxing of *yang*, waning of *yin*	x›n, y‹n
G	waxing of *yin*, waning of *yang*	x‹n, y›n
H	waning of *yin* and *yang*	x‹n, y‹n
J	perish of *yin* and *yang*	x--›0, y--›0[26]

A in the center of the diagram represents the equilibrium of *yin* and *yang*, which is the goal of good health people crave. Around A are C, D, E, F, which are in a lop-sided imbalance, showing light ailment. F, G, and H farther out from A show three states of serious illness. A physician's work is to pinpoint the position of the imbalance and to bring the state to A with medicine.

---

[26] See "*Yin* and *Yang*—Air and Variation" by Yang Xuepeng, pp. 173-174, Science Press, 1993, Beijing

My view is that the Confucian analogy of *yin* and *yang* in Chinese culture at large to the gender relation in human society and its emphasis of "respect for *yang* and debasement for *yin*" is an erroneous theory that created a basis for the oppression of the female sex and caused serious repercussions in history. Nevertheless, the dialectics of *yin* and *yang* as two opposites, particularly the attention paid to the seeking of an equilibrium between the two as a way to attain good health and longevity is something worth carrying forward. This theory of *yin* and *yang* can be applied not only to the study of the mechanism of the human physique and the cultural phenomena of society, but also to the concept of partnership and the theory of cultural transformation.

(2) The dialectics of *yanggang* and *yinrou*.

There are numerous fuzzy concepts extensively used in Chinese culture, and a case in point is the concept of *yin* and *yang*. We may have virtually come to the exact meaning of *yin* and *yang* after we have compared and studied all the discussions of those two ideas by our predecessors, and equally with the concepts of *yanggang* and *yinrou*.

Yanggang and *yinrou* are used first of all to define the quality of a person. A *yanggang* person is strong, brave, extrovert, enthusiastic, enterprising and creative, good at logical thinking, just-minded and with a strong sense of responsibility. This is the positive side. The negative side of *yanggang* is crude, cruel, robust but muddle-headed, predatory and disruptive. A person of *yinrou* is tender, modest, introvert, sensitive, good at perceptual thinking, good at imitating, sympathetic, etc. The negative side is timid, weak, sentimental, indecisive, conservative and self-exclusive. Therefore there is *yin*nish *yang* in *yanggang* and *yang*ish *yin* in *yinrou*.

Generally speaking, *yanggang* refers to the quality of the male sex, whereas *yinrou* refers to that of the female sex. However, the two are not independent of each other in reality, but a unity of opposites. After Zhang Xianliang published his novel **The Other Half of Man Is Woman** the idea caught on among the Chinese people. I understand the statement to have two meanings. First, it means that man in society can never live without his other half—his woman. Second, half of the quality of a man is that of woman. This is also true for women. Every woman also has her other half containing the quality of a man. The point is that it differs from person to person how much of the qualities of the opposite sex he or she has.

King Ba of Western Chu no doubt was a typical *yanggang* soldier in Chinese history. But when the remnants of his army were besieged by the enemy at Gaixia, he chanted an impromptu poem to his beloved concubine Yuji lamenting "Oh! What can I do, my dear Yuji! What can I do, my dear Yuji!" While chanting, tears rolled down his cheeks. It was recorded that all his followers were moved and could not bring themselves to look at him. The dauntless hero revealed his tenderness typical of *yinrou* at that moment.[27] Li Qingzhao of the Song Dynasty, a poetess known for her tender emotions, has been extensively quoted by her lines "Do not say it's not sorrow. A westerly wind's rolling up the curtain and my figure is leaner than the daisy". This is typical of *yin*rou. But she also has lines like this: "Live the life of a hero and die the death of a hero. Whenever I recall Xiang Yu, I hate to cross to the east of the Yangtze". This obviously is the quality of *yanggang* that many strong men may admire.

The coexistence of *yanggang* and *yinrou* in a person is manifested mainly in the quality, but not outer appearance. For instance, a person of *yanggang* may not be heavily built and have a fierce look. Lu Xun, a literary giant in the history of Chinese literature, was small, fragile and sickly. However, he was a man of admirable *yanggang*. Mao Zedong praised Lu Xun like this: "Undoubtedly, Lu Xun's bones were supremely hard;

---

[27] "The Story of Xiang Yu", "Book of History".

he had no slavish traits or weak bones whatsoever". Lu Xun wrote a short poem in which he said: "A hero may not necessary be ruthless and a stout man may have a tender heart for a child; the beast that raises a tempest with its roar may look at its cubs tenderly". He likened a strong man with the quality of *yinrou* to a tiger showing its love for its cubs. On the other hand, the quality of *yinrou* may not necessary be the monopoly of the female sex. For there is no lack of robust men carrying swords all day long who are cowards in their innermost hearts.[28] It is even more complex when we come to discuss *yanggang* and *yinrou* as two cultural qualities. Yin and *yang* in traditional Chinese medicine are fuzzy concepts of infinite variations. In diagnosis, a traditional Chinese physician employs the four methods of looking, smelling, questioning and feeling the pulse. The information he collects through those four channels are fuzzy. Based on these fuzzy values, the physician judges the state of health of the patient and tries to restore the physique to the state of equilibrium of *yin* and *yang*, i.e. the healthy state. We are now using the two derivatives from *yin* and *yang* —yanggang and *yinrou* as two collective, fuzzy and infinite variations of cultural qualities. We may diagnose a cultural phenomenon to determine its fuzzy value of *yanggang* or *yinrou*. Based on that, we are able to advance a proposal for the attainment of a new equilibrium needed for cultural evolution and the creation of a new and still healthier culture.

If we are obliged to interpret the categories of *yanggang* and *yinrou*, we may say that *yanggang* is a cultural quality that upholds the quality of muscularity, militancy, active participation in social life, the conquest of nature, accomplishment in career, inventions and discoveries, the belief in the evil nature of human beings and the suppression of evil by evil means, the quality of simplicity and plain living, a strong willpower and open mind. When carried to its extreme, a culture of *yanggang*

---

[28] "The Story of Marguis Huaiyin", "Book of History".

may lead to aggression, predatoriness and disruption of nature and society, and ultimately to its own destruction. On the other hand, a culture of *yinrou* upholds femininity, rule by reason, a pessimistic approach toward life, submission to conventions, the belief in the fine nature of human beings and the correction of evil by persuasion, the quality of ornateness and elegance, and self-seclusion. When carried to its extreme, a culture of *yinrou* may lead to social stagnation and helplessness in the face of foreign aggression and natural adversities.

Therefore we should not lop-sidedly admire a culture of *yanggang* or *yin*rou. What should be appreciated is a harmony of the two elements in a culture. Take the Chinese art of calligraphy, for instance. Among the masterpieces, the tablet inscriptions about Zhang Qian and those on sacrificial vessels have the beauty of *yanggang*, whereas the inscriptions on the tablets of the obituaries to Cao Quan and Cao E have the beauty of *yinrou*. They have neither attained the highest level of beauty of the calligraphic art. When Wang Xizhi wrote his Preface to the Orchid Pavilion Collection a masterpiece was produced. The work is praised for its superb blending of bold heroic strokes and refined graceful strokes to convey the harmony of *yanggang* and *yinrou*.

(3) Daoist Culture and Matriarchal Society.

Mr. Wang Bo of the Department of Philosophy of Beijing University has written a brilliant essay on Lao Zi and the culture of the Xia Dynasty.[29] Based on his studies of the archaeological findings of the Xia culture, he has come to the conclusion that the Daoist culture which upholds femininity stems from the culture of the Xia, Yue and Chu, which were matriarchal societies. The article describes the rites of the Xia described in the Book of Rites and adds sporadic descriptions of the rites of the Xia from other books. Then the author

---

[29] See "Philosophical Studies" No. 1, 1989.

discovers the following features of the Xia people: (1) Love of the color black (2) Esteem for honesty and credibility, (3) Advocacy of kindness, (4) Frugality, (5) Love of water, and (6) Love of simplicity and plain living. All these coincide with what Laozi advocates.

The article also cites scores of examples to show the inclinations of the people of the Yue which the author finds identical with the thinking of Laozi. I would like to quote a few here: (1) Lao Zi: "The Way of Heaven—what a similarity between it and the bending of a bow! If it is too high, lower it; if it is too low, raise it; if it is too long, cut it short; if it is too short, add to it. The Way of the Heaven is to cut short that which is too long and add to that which is too short." Discourse on the States: "The King (of Yue) says: 'In the State of Yue I let the rich live in peace and let the poor have more, subsidize the needy and take from the surplus so that both the rich and the poor benefit from me.'" (2) Laozi: "To assist the king by Dao (the Way), it will not do to use military power to rule over the world ... weapons are not auspicious tools, not gentlemen's tools, and must not be used unless under extraordinary conditions. It is far better to rule with benevolence." Discourse on the States: "Valor runs counter to ethics; the weapon is a lethal tool; ... scheming against ethics originates in man and kills man." (3) Laozi: "The Dao of the sage is to strive, but not to fight." Discourse on the States: "Fighting is the meanest of behavior." Why this identity? This is because the Yue were the descendants of the Xia. In the Records of the Historian, in the chapter titled Story of Gou Jian, the King of Yue has this to say: "Gou Jian, King of Yue, his ancestor was the offspring of Yu and a younger son of Shao Kang, King Houdi of Xia, who was enfeoffed to Kuaiji in charge of the sacrifices to King Yu."

The article then discusses the legendary Goddess Nü Wa, who was the creator of the universe, and her husband Fu Xi. The author found that in ancient southern China the matriarchal tribes worshipped the snake as their totem, which was the god of the Xia people. The Xias were concerned with Heaven, a proof of which is in the book Liezi, which describes the people of Qi worrying about the collapse of Heaven. Among ancient Chinese philosophical works, only the Book of Laozi contains a fairly developed theory of the universe. Its central category, Dao, has been interpreted as being of the feminine sex: "Naught, the origin of the universe; Being, the mother of everything." According to the Explanation and Study of Principles of Composition of Characters by Xu Shen, the character " 始 shi" means the origin of the female. So it is clear that "shi", like " 母 mu", refers to the female sex. Therefore, Dao is actually a philosophical category derived from a divine creator.

Finally, let us observe how Laozi describes the ideal society: "A small state with a small population, using no extravagant utensils, its people cherish life and hate to travel far. They have boats and sedan chairs but seldom use them; they have weapons and armor but nowhere to display them. People have returned to the state of making knots for the keeping of records. With fine food, good clothing, quiet residence and happy customs, the people of various states live side by side and may hear the barking of dogs of neighboring states, but they never communicate with each other." We come to a similar description by Zhuangzi, another patriarch of Daoism. He writes: "In the days of Shen Nong, people slept in their own houses and walked about in their own places. They knew their own mothers but not their fathers. They lived with deer, they fed on the food they grew and wore the cloth they wove, and harbored no ill will against one another. This was indeed a supremely ethical society."[30] This peaceful picture of a farming matriarchal society is a precise representation of the society of the Xia, as is manifest in Lu's Almanac, which says: "There were ten thousand states during the reign of Yu, and the number came to three thousand and more during the reign of Tang. None

---

[30] "Zhuangzi".

remain today." When we put the above-mentioned together against the background that both the authors of the Book of Laozi and the Zhuangzi, namely, Li Dan and Zhuang Yin, were natives of the southern State of Chu, the picture becomes clearer:

The tribe of Xia represented by Yu rose in the lower reaches of the Yangtze as a purely farming group. Even up to the time when Yu led his people in combating floods some 21 centuries before Christ, it remained a union of numerous matriarchal states leading a peaceful life. The Xia people cherished an ultimate concern for the universe. They worshipped the Divine Creator Nü Wa and her brother-husband Fu Xi, who were a reflection of their own gender partnership in the divine land. The Xia people held their mothers in esteem, and the female sex enjoyed a high status. They lived in a marshy land of rivers and lakes, and were good at swimming. They used tensile bamboo extensively and wore soft silk. Yu led them in dredging waterways to divert floods. This success convinced them of the truth that the best approach toward life was to obey the law of nature. Yu had the fine qualities of industry, modesty and frugality, which ultimately became the national character of the people of Xia. After the fall of the Xia Dynasty, the culture of Xia was retained among the people of Yue, who were in charge of making sacrifices to the memory of King Yu. The culture of Yue spread to its neighbor the State of Chu, and a native of Chu by the name of Lao Dan extoled that national character in his book and evolved his Daoist philosophy that upholds femininity. Zhuangzi developed the theory of Lao Dan. We may venture to say that the philosophy of Daoism stems from the matriarchal society of the southern Xia nationality living in the Yangtze basin and that Daoist philosophy was a philosophy of the matriarchal society or a philosophy of the female sex.

Daoism later developed into a religion and a culture which has retained the quality of *yin*rou. That is why Daoism has always enjoyed the favor of women in Chinese history. The Han Dynasty in its early years used the Daoist philosophy to rule the country with great success during the reigns of Emperor Wen Di and Jing Di. The Empress Dowager Dou, who played an important role in that period, was a devout worshipper of Daoism. Later, Daoism as a religion was active in admitting female believers. According their doctrine, those who succeeded in their self-cultivation could ascend to heaven as immortals. The book Register of Transcendents Gathered at Yongcheng, written by Du Guangting of the Tang Dynasty, recorded 36 immortals of the female sex, including Nü Wa, the Heavenly Queen Mother of the West, King Yao's wife E Huang and daughter Nu Ying, Chang E who flew to the moon after taking a dose of longevity medicine, and the fairy lady of mount Wushan and the two fairy concubines of the Xiang River mentioned in Elegies of Chu. The goddess Bixia Yuanjun worshipped by people in the north and Goddess Ma Zu, worshipped by people in the south since the Song Dynasty are female immortals created under the influence of Daoism. When Wang Jianzhang of the Qing Dynasty compiled his Stories of Immortals through the Ages he cited 145 female immortals (fig.21).

(4) *Yanggang* and *yinrou* in the culture of Confucianism differ from those of Daoism.

The Confucian culture stems from the semi-farming, semi-nomadic tribes of the Zhou, which was a patriarchal society. As we have discussed previously, Confucian culture upholds patriarchal authority, patriarchy and the patriarchal social model, and furnishes a philosophical basis for male chauvinism. Therefore Confucian culture is one of *yanggang*, which is manifest in the Confucian advocacy of active male participation in social affairs, that men should have the valor to "die for justice." Furthermore, Confucianism should be held responsible for the ugly practice of slighting women and drowning female infants, because Confucius once said, "It is women and villains who are difficult to keep."[31] And Mencius said, "The number one of the three types of unfilial behavior is lack of descendants."[32] Yet, we would be mistaken if we thought Confucian culture were characterized only by the quality of *yanggang*. The quality of *yinrou* is also obvious. First, Confucian culture after all is a culture based mainly on the Han people, who go in mainly for farming. Second, this had much to do with the personality of Confucius. Like Socrates, Christ, Sakyamuni and Laozi, Confucius was a modest, mild-tempered and well-read person. From his statements and behavior recorded in the Analects, people can see that he believed that human nature was kind and that he took benevolence as the highest criterion of ethics. He advocated universal love and "All are brothers within the four seas." He also advocated forbearance, proposing to forgive a person who has admitted and corrected his mistake. He says, "Help others accomplish what you yourself want to accomplish, and help others reach a goal you yourself want to reach," and "Do not do unto others what you do not want others to do to you." This has the element of altruism. He urged parents to be kind to their children, children to be filial to their parents, elder brothers to be affectionate to their younger brothers and sisters and the younger brothers to respect the elder brothers as a way to realize family harmony. He attached great importance to rites, advising people to be gentleman-like by strictly abiding by rites. He advocated the doctrine of the mean and was opposed to going to the extreme. On the question of dealing with the bellicose nomadic neighbors, he advocated a policy of persuasion and appeasement, saying, "When those afar are not reconciled, try to attract them with a mild policy. When they come, try to pacify them."

After nearly 2,000 years of advocacy of respecting Confu-

---

31 "The Annotated Analects of Confucius," Vol. 932.
32 "Commentaries on the Thirteen Classics".

cius and reading the classics, the introvert, conservative and modest personality of Confucius to a considerable degree has evolved into the Chinese national character. His *yinrou* character has added an element of *yinrou* to the Confucian culture and, by and large, to Chinese culture.

(5) The Yinrou Character of Buddhism.

When Sakyamuni created Buddhism he intended to help the Indian people free themselves from the misery of living, old age, illness and death, for the people there under the heavy yoke of caste, hostile climate and diseases were generally pessimistic and weary of life.

Buddhists take the passive approach toward life by leaving their families and the hustle and bustle of society and hiding themselves in quiet temples for self-cultivation in the hope of reaching nirvana, the highest state that transcends life and death. Buddhists follow asceticism, refrain from killing, theft, lust, loose language and drinking alcohol, and forsake all enjoyment, honor and wealth. They try to guide the human desire to introverted self-study so as to suppress the urge to seek worldly things. Buddhists believe in the life cycle of heaven—human society—beast kingdom—starvation—hell. They believe that a man who did evil in his previous life will suffer in his present life and if he does kindness in his present life, he will ascend to heaven in his next life. Therefore, Buddhism teaches people to be reconciled to fate and accept every setback without resentment, revenge or resistance. Finally a Buddhist must be kind and benevolent to all, good and evil, human beings and beasts. All this shows that Buddhism is a religion of *yinrou* in nature.

Matriarchy was fairly well developed over a long period of time in Indian society. Following their invasion, the Aryans established a social model characterized by a caste system and Brahmanism. The emergence of Buddhism was a form of passive resistance. Buddhism in its primitive form advocated equality irrespective of caste, wealth or sex. Unfortunately, when

Buddhist scripts were translated into Chinese, the passages containing the doctrine of equality were left out. One Buddhist sect, the Secret Sect, advocates indulgence in sex, believing that the orgasm in sexual intercourse is the ultimate relief. In addition to Tibet, this sect of Buddhism was also introduced to inland China during the Northern Song. When it became too unbridled, a Song emperor banned it. However, Buddhism, for its *yinrou* quality, runs counter to Confucianism, which is in the main of *yanggang* quality. Buddhism primarily reveres no king or father, and its converts do not marry or raise children. This runs counter to Confucianism, which advocates that to have no offspring is a kind of unfilial behavior. If men all go to live in the temples, who will take an active part in social life and work for the emperor and the country? Therefore, Buddhism met resistance and repulsion time and again after it was introduced typical Buddhist practises spread far and wide and a Zen Sect, characterized by internal experience and relief and full of philosophical thinking—a highly developed and localized Chinese-style Buddhism—was born. This Zen Buddhism caught on quickly among Chinese intellectuals in the olden times. Thus the quality of *yinrou* was greatly increased in Chinese culture.

(6) The Rise of Neo-Confucianism and Its Model of Man.

Neo-Confucianism was a philosophical school popular from the Song through the Yuan, Ming and Qing dynasties. It focused on the discussion of principle and force, mind and matter. It was also known as the philosophy of the Dao (ethics) because it upholds the traditional ethics of King Yao, King Shun, King Tang, King Wen, King Wu, the Duke of Zhou, Confucius and Mencius. Neo-Confucianists styled their philosophy "the philosophy of the sages". Its nucleus is the thinking of Confucius and Mencius, but it also assimilates Daoist thought about the evolution of the universe and Buddhist thought concerning self-cultivation by reflection. Indeed it is a hybrid of Confucianism, Taoism and Buddhism. Neo-Confucianism in its narrow sense was the philosophy advanced by the Cheng brothers Cheng Hao and Cheng Yi of the Northern Song Dynasty and Zhu Xi of the Southern Song Dynasty, which holds "heavenly reason" as the ultimate category—an objective idealism. Neo-Confucianism was upheld as the orthodox ideology by later feudal rulers.

Reason in Neo-Confucianism became "heavenly reason", or absolute or objective truth. Based on reason, Neo-Confucianists advanced the logical structure of "reason—force—matter—reason", of which the last reason was the "rite" between the emperor and subjects in a centralized monarchy, the "rite" between husband and wife, and the "rite" between brothers. So the "rites" which Confucianism had advanced as ethical rules were elevated to "heavenly reason". This reinforced rule by "rites", recognizing only the existence of human relations and negating individuality. The subject and individuality of man thus disappears behind social status. "The man of higher position may reprimand a man of lower position, the elder may reprimand the younger, the nobler may reprimand the humbler. Even if the reprimand is mistaken, it is in line with the rites. If the lower, the younger or the humbler argues with reason, even if correct, it is in violation of the rites."[33] Deeply influenced by ascetic Buddhism, Neo-Confucianism pits "heavenly reason" against "human desire". Zhu Xi says, "When heavenly reason exists there is no room for human desire; when human desire triumphs heavenly reason vanishes."[34] The Cheng brothers also say, "After human desire is suppressed heavenly reason stands out". And thus was derived the theme of "self-restraint and restoration of the rites". As the Cheng brothers say, "Self-restraint helps get rid of selfishness and makes restoration of

---

[33] "Annotations to Expressions in 'Mencius'" by Dai Zhen.
[34] "Classified Sayings by Master Zhu Xi" Vol. 13.

the rites possible."[35] Therefore the man molded by Neo-Confucianism is no long the subject of cognition and practice, but subject of ethics. Yet the inborn desires and emotions of a person cannot be suppressed, much less eliminated. Such desires and emotions keep stirring within a person, giving rise to the dual personality of the hypocrite.

From the very beginning, Confucianism was torn by controversy over the modeling of the "internal sage" and the "external king". By assimilating "thinking in solitude" and "the mind giving rise to everything" of the Zen Sect's way of self-cultivation, Neo-Confucianism integrated Mencius' theory of man being kind by nature and the theory of cultivating force. So it stands firm for the "internal sage" and excludes the "external king". It advocates the theory that "Everybody from the Son of Heaven (the emperor) down to the common folk should perfect himself through self-cultivation."[36] That was the way of internal perfection to become a sage, and having become a sage it is undoubtedly possible to "manage the home, run state affairs and rule the country well". Scholars of the Han nationality during the Song and Ming dynasties were devoted to self-cultivation and internal perfection more than administration of state affairs. They attached greater importance to the status of a sage than to worldly official positions. In their daily behavior, they "buried themselves in their studies and devoted their time to discourses on philosophical terms" "giving the least consideration to the prosperity of the state or the livelihood of the people."[37] And in the event of a natural calamity or foreign invasion, they "had no other recourse than to lay down their lives in recognition of the emperor's favor."[38] That is the cultur-

---

[35] "Letters of the Cheng Brothers".

[36] "Annotations to the Four Books".

[37] "Elementary Studies of History" Vol. 89 of the "Department of History," and the "Ji Mei Lu" Vol. 61, "List of the Complete Library of the Four Branches of Books".

[38] "Concentration on Study" by Yan Yuan.

al background from the fall of the Song to the Yuan and the fall of the Ming to the Qing.

(7) The Decline of *Yanggang* and the Rise of *Yinrou* among Chinese Males.

Up to the Qin Dynasty, Chinese males possessed the yang-*gang* quality because they had not experienced heavy pressure or oppression spiritually. Their ideal was to be militant, trustworthy and ready to die an honest death. Zuo Qiuming in his Commentary on the Spring and Autumn Annals, in the entry concerning Duke Xiang's 25th year, recorded this story: After Cui Shu, a minister at the court of the State of Qi, killed his master Duke Zhuang of Qi, the imperial historian wrote "Cui Shu killed his sovereign", and he was executed by Cui Chu for telling the truth. His two younger brothers succeeded to his position as the grand scribe one after the other, and they also recorded the event faithfully. They too lost their heads. Then the third younger brother succeeded to the position, and again he wrote the same. Cui Shu had to give in. The story did not stop here. A man by the name of Nan Shi, on learning that three historians had been executed for telling the truth, wrote the words "Cui Shu killed his sovereign" on a bamboo splinter and took it to the court. On his way he was told that the statement had been accepted into the annals of Qi. He was satisfied and returned home. That was the spirit of the intellectuals in those days.

The book Strategies of the Warring States records that the emperor of Qin wanted to exchange a piece of land 250 km in diameter for the small state of Anling. The king of Anling did not agree and sent a man of no official rank by the name of Tang Ju to negotiate. The emperor of Qin said to Tang: "Aren't you looking down on me by refusing my offer? Haven't you heard about the wrath of an emperor?" Tang replied: "Yes, when the emperor is angry, a million may die and blood may spill over a thousand li." "But," he added: "have you ever heard about the wrath of the common folk? That may lead to the death of two persons, and blood spills over only five steps, but the whole nation may have to wear mourning. That might happen today." With that, he drew his sword. The emperor of Qin turned pale and consoled Tang, and dropped his idea of taking the small state of Anling. That was the style of a diplomat of that time.

Zuo Qiuming has another story under the entry "Second Year of Duke Xuan": Duke Ling of Jin was a tyrant. His minister Zhao Dun remonstrated with him on many occasions, but the duke would not listen. Instead, he hated Zhao and sent Chu Ni to murder him. Early in the morning Chu Ni went to Zhao's house. The door was already open. Zhao had already dressed in his official robes ready to go to court. Since it was still early, he sat in the hall taking a rest, with his eyes closed. Chu Ni retired exclaiming, "The man who is serious about his duties is a good official for the people. It would be disloyal to harm a good official. But I would be unfaithful if I refused to carry out the duke's order. I would rather die than to commit either of these errors." He then beat his head against a tree until he died. He was just an assassin, but how honest, reasonable and gentleman-like he was!

Instances like those cited above were by no means rare. One can find many in Chinese annals. That was the reflection of the spirit of Chinese males in those days. We find many similar stories in the Records of the Historian. Those upright men ready to take their own lives in defense of their honor were very much like Japanese warriors in later times.

And this militancy can still be found in the male sex during the Han and Tang dynasties. The supreme value for men during the Han Dynasty was meritorious deeds on the battlefield. The Romance of the Three Kingdoms abounds in deeds of great valor and wisdom. By the time of the Northern and Southern Dynasties large numbers of upright men of the Han nationality were slaughtered. Those who survived the massacres fled to the south in the first wave of refugees in Chinese history. In southern China, with a mild climate and rich natural resources, people led a comfortable life for nearly two centuries, occupied by discussions on the philosophy of Laozi and Zhuangzi, metaphysics and Buddhism. Gradually the quality of *yinrou* began to penetrate into the spirit of Chinese males (fig.20). The Tang Dynasty was founded by militant nobles from the Northwest and the early Tang reached its zenith of cultural and military accomplishments. Intellectuals of the Tang period did not lack the quality of yang*gang* and militancy. The huge number of poems singing the praises of heroic deeds at the frontiers render ample proof of this spirit. Li Bai, the great poet of the Tang, was a gallant sword-bearing poet. Du Fu, another great poet of the Tang period, wrote many poems eulogizing just wars against foreign invasions. Even Jia Dao, known for his painstaking way of composing poems, had a poem entitled "The Swordsman", which has these lines: "Ten years spent on grinding a sword, its blade never tested. I show it to you. Are there any wrongs to be righted?"

Late in the Tang Dynasty, the Han people were beaten for the second time by nomadic tribes from the north. Many fled to the south and stayed there for half a century. By the time the Han people rebuilt a dynasty, the Song, neither the state strength nor the national spirit could match those of the mighty Tang. The history of the Song Dynasty was one of successive defeats, appeasement, negotiations for peace and retreats southward in the face of advancing enemies. With the southward retreat, the economic and cultural focus moved southward too. The ruling class was once more able to lead a corrupt and extravagant life in hiding.

The Song Dynasty was the most conspicuous turning point in Chinese culture and history. Prior to the Song, the Han people were capable of resisting the invasion of the nomadic ethnic groups from the north. But they could not do that after the Song, and twice lost their state power. Before that, China was leading the world in economy, science and technology, and culture, but after the Song Dynasty China's position declined continuously. Before the Song both Chinese culture and males had displayed yang*gang* quality, whereas after that the yang*gang* quality gradually gave way to that of *yinrou*. Chinese women did enjoy a certain cultural room to move before the Song, but after that Neo-Confucianism was on the rise and Chinese women's position declined further.

The period of the Song Dynasty in China coincided with the middle period of medieval Europe, when European culture nursed the stratum of knights who, bubbling with an adventurous spirit, aspired to conquer the world. Japan, China's neighbor to the east, cultivated a stratum of warriors by its martial spirit, a spirit brimming over with the quality of yang*gang*. Those warriors succeeded in urging their emperor to introduce a cultural reform and catch up with China, and later launched the Meiji Reform in their determination to catch up with the West. The negative side of that spirit was that with it Japan launched aggressive wars. Chinese culture cultivated intellectuals with too much *yinrou* and too little yang*gang* who were unable to defend their motherland and homesteads.

The Chinese literati were a particular social stratum who aimed at reaching officialdom through education and success in the imperial examinations. A high official position meant a high salary and the amassing of a fortune through extortion. With that fortune, one bought land and became a rich landlord with a stable income. The rich landlords had their children well educated and so that they could seek success through the imperial examinations to reach officialdom likewise. Thus, there emerged families belonging to the literati stratum from generation to generation. Families like this were strongholds of the patriarchal system. When young men from such families failed on their way to officialdom or when the family was stricken by ill fate and lost their high official position, the young people of these families would become poor petty intellectuals. Therefore literati is a sweeping term that covers all Chinese intellectuals. Despite their failings, the literati were the salt of the Chinese nation.

Chinese intellectuals from the middle-high to the lower levels during the 800 years between the Song through the Qing bore the following features: (1) They cared for book knowledge and slighted sports, and generally had rather weak physiques. They read books, wrote poems and essays all their lives, seldom or never indulging in physical exercises, to say nothing of going to the battlefield. To them, the examination room was their battlefield. Their typical image was "a white-faced gentleman with not enough strength to catch a chicken". (2) They cared only for book knowledge to the neglect of social practice. Their motto was "Every trade is low, except book reading", and "There are treasure stores in books; there are beauties like jade in books". In their eyes, soldiers were on the lowest rung of the social ladder, scientific studies were crude craftsmanship and commerce was money-seeking selfishness. They were described by other people as "having four weak limbs and being incapable of telling wheat from rice". (3) They were bookworms swallowing knowledge raw and whole. They spent the prime of their lives devouring the Confucian classics and wrote examination papers "just speaking on behalf of the sages" in a rigid stereotype of the eight-legged essays, revealing little of their own thoughts. Their nickname was "bookworm." (4) They were introvert, sentimental and weak-willed. In contrast to the bold and heroic style of the poetry of the Tang Dynasty, poems of the Song period were mostly sentimental, ornate and pessimistic. The heroic, open-minded poems of Su Dongpo and Xin Qiji were rarities. After the emergence of Neo-Confucianism, the intellectuals fell into the habit of suppressing their emotions, and made their every act and move in compliance with conventions and family disciplines. They were weak not only in their physiques but also in their will power and emotions. (5) They professed to be above worldly considerations and tended to shirk responsibilities. Even the advanced elements among them were inclined to take the road of passive resistance in the face of evil forces, or to hide themselves as hermits, indulge in wine, bury themselves in studies of the past, divert their interests into calligraphy or painting, become Buddhist converts or just keep themselves away from those they despised.

Men with such an effeminate quality, or men of the *yinrou* quality, certainly cannot shoulder the responsibility of propping up society. So it was only natural for the men from the upper class of the nomadic ethnic groups from the north to take up the ruling positions. That was precisely the situation in the Ming, Yuan and Qing dynasties, after the Song. The founding of the Yuan and Qing dynasties marked the fourth and fifth defeats of the Han people by the northern nomads. In the wake of the downfall of the Song and the Ming came large-scale massacres in which those Han men with yang*gang* took the brunt. Under ideological enslavement for a total of 350 years during the Yuan and the Qing, the yang*gang* quality of men of the Han further dwindled. What made things even worse was that the Chinese culture during the Yuan Ming and Qing gradually become a "soy sauce pot" as the Taiwan writer Bo Yang describes it. Even leaders of peasant uprisings or military leaders of the brave nomadic tribes could not avoid corruption within three generations once they were bogged down in this "soy sauce pot." Let us look at the Qing emperors. The first two or three generations displayed an ability to bring prosperity to the country, but the descendants kept becoming weaker and living shorter lives generation after generation. The last but one emperor of the Qing Dynasty, Emperor Guangxu, was too young and too weak-willed. The reformist drive he supported lasted no more than 100 days. The child emperor succeeding him was just a puppet in the hands of the Japanese.

This waxing of *yinrou* and waning of yang*gang* phenomenon can be found in almost all of the typical works by modern Chinese writers. The most typical is Jia Baoyu, the main male character in the novel A Dream of Red Mansions. He lived amid maids and sisters, was soft-spoken, fine complexioned and had the mentality of a woman. Wu Qingzi, in his The Scholars, portrayed all sorts of intellectuals who were pedantic, poor and ambitious for position and honor. The most tragic of all is Fan Jing, who is beside himself after learning the good news that he has succeeded in the provincial official examination. The hapless, desolate scholar Kong Yiji in a short story by Lu Xun is so miserable that he has never succeeded in the official examinations, and, after he is caught stealing books he is beaten up. Zhou Ping in the drama Storm, written by Cao Yu, Jue Xin in Ba Jin's Family, Spring, and Autumn, Qi Ruixuan in Lao She's Four Generations Under One Roof and Fang Hongjian in Qian Zhongshu's novel A Town Besieged are representatives of another category of Chinese intellectuals. They are born into patriarchal families but they have one thing in common—all have weak will power. They fall in love with their fathers' young concubine, cousin or maid servant or with somebody else's wife, but none of them dare to speak out, to pursue their love or to resist the patriarchal, and all come to tragic ends. Wu Sunfu in Mao Dun's **Midnight** is a national capitalist with a Western education, but he also has weak bones, a legacy of traditional Chinese culture, that lead him to financial ruin.

All of those personalities suffer from the same ailment —the ailment of cultural deficiency called "waxing of *yin* and waning of yang." But this phenomenon occurs only among the educated males of the middle and upper classes in Chinese society.

(8) Heroines with the Quality of Yanggang in Chinese Culture

Chinese culture in the Ming and Qing dynasties suffered from an ailment marked by the decline of both *yin* and yang. That is to say that in the upper classes the phenomenon was the decline of *yang* (males) and the rise of *yin* (females) and in the lower classes it was the decline of both sexes, because the women of the lower classes were the most oppressed members of society.

People during the Ming and Qing dynasties made unhealthy demand of the female sex. The criteria for a beautiful woman were: a face in the shape of a watermelon seed, a pair of thin, curved brows and small round eyes, a small mouth, sloping shoulders, willowy waist and feet no longer than three inches —the picture of a sick woman exuding tenderness and love. That was the manifestation of a waning of both *yin* and *yang* among women in Similarly, a culture of deficiency in both *yin* and *yang* is about to perish. The traditional Chinese culture did die, and together with it died its patriarchal system and social model based on the patriarchal family and suppression of women by men. When we look at the waning and waxing of that culture and the curves of the changes of the gender relations, we can hear the groans and cries of numerous Chinese women buried under the ruins. But we should not forget that there has been no lack of heroines with the quality of yang*gang*. They uttered a eulogy of female vitality and added a powerful note of yang*gang* to the main tune of *yinrou*.

Notable among them were Wu Zetian, a beautiful and talented woman who actually ruled the nation during the Tang Dynasty for half a century; Hua Mulan, who performed military service for her father and did meritorious deeds on the battlefield; Mu Guiying, who took command of an army and defeated the invading nomads from the north; Li Qingzhao, who was an expert in music, poetry and the ancient inscriptions on stone tablets and bronze utensils; the courtesan Du Shiniang, who threw her casket of priceless jewelry into a river, thoroughly exposed the lover who had betrayed her and drowned herself by leaping into the river; the sing-song girl Li Xiangjun, who denounced traitors and spilled her blood on the folding fan she presented to her former lover; Huang Daopo, who renovated the spinning wheel and brought about a revolution in cotton spinning and weaving in the Songjiang area (near present-day Shanghai); Zhu Yingtai, who disguised herself as a man in order to pursue her studies in Hangzhou and took her life in the fight to win freedom of marriage; Qiu Jin, who dared to sever ties with her feudal family, went to study in Japan, joined the revolution and died a heroic death; and Liu Hezhen, Zhao Yiman, Liu Hulan, Sister Jiang, and many others, who bravely laid down their lives for the revolution and the war of resistance against Japanese aggression.

After the Duan Qirui military government fired upon demonstrating girl students in Beijing in 1926, Lu Xun wrote a moving article entitled In Memory of Miss Liu Hezhen. The concluding passage of that article best describes the caliber and spirit of those heroic Chinese females:

"What a soul-stirring greatness it was when three women calmly moved about in a shower of bullets which have been invented by civilized people! ... It was last year when I first saw how Chinese women did things. Although they were few, I could not help but applaud their competence, resolution and unflinching spirit. And this time they helped one another amid a hail of bullets in total disregard of their own safety; this is proof enough of the bravery of Chinese women which still exists despite all sorts of schemes and oppression over the past several thousand years.... Those who have survived will see in the bloodstains a dim hope; true warriors will march forward even more dauntlessly."[39] In fact, the Chinese people have never forgotten these legendary heroines. Their deeds have been retold by people from generation to generation, irrespective of whether the tellers were men or women, and represented in dramas, films, operas and music. This shows that the Chinese people aspire after equality between men and women and a partnership between the sexes. The last two lines of the Song of

---

[39] "Complete Works of Lu Xun" Vol. III, p. 277, People's Literature Press, Beijing, 1987.

Mulan are: "The buck's feet are nimble and the doe's eyes are glazed; the pair talk side by side, who can tell which is which?" What a vivid description of harmonious gender relations. Toward the end of the folk tale of Liang Shanbo and Zhu Yingtai, the sky clears up after a thunderstorm and the souls of the recently deceased young couple become a pair of butterflies flying up from their tomb—representing the longing of the Chinese people for the ideal gender relationship.

(9) Some Explanations of the "Waxing of *Yin* and Waning of *Yang*" Phenomenon in Present-day Chinese Sports and Film Circles

In the concluding chapter of this book we cannot avoid dealing with the phenomenon of "waxing of *yin* and waning of yang" in present-day Chinese sports and film circles—a topic much talked about among the Chinese for years.

By the "waxing of *yin* and waning of yang" we mean the phenomenon that the female sex outshines the male sex among the Chinese people, and to a very considerable degree indeed. And this is particularly true in sports circles.

For many years Chinese women table tennis players and tennis players have ranked first or second in the world, and the Chinese women's volleyball team won five world titles in a row. Chinese women basketballers have been among the top teams in the world, and in the newly emerging women's soccer, Chinese women are among the top four in the world. Chinese women gymnasts and divers have won many gold medals. In those sports which require speed and stamina, such as swimming, Chinese women won the largest number of gold medals at the last world championships. Even in the track events, at which the Chinese are not particularly good, Chinese women have won a number of world records in long- and medium-distance races. Meanwhile, Xie Jun is the reigning world women's international chess champion.

On the other hand, Chinese sportsmen have maintained a

glorious record for years in only one sport—table tennis. Chinese men have lost their superiority in badminton, although they still can win some medals in swimming and gymnastics. Chinese men are still rather weak in those events which call for sprinting and stamina, and cannot even qualify for many track-and-field events of the Olympic Games. Chinese men have never reached the semi-finals of the basketball world championships or the quarter-finals of the world volleyball championships or even qualify for the world cup soccer events as a team from Asia.

In the election of the ten best Chinese athletes some years ago, no male athletes were selected. By coincidence, it has been impossible to choose the best male lead in the election of best film actors and actresses for many years. The most outstanding film actors lack manly qualities. On the other hand, there have been enough female candidates for best film actresses every year. This is indeed a phenomenon of the "waxing of *yin* and waning of yang."

People in China have written quite a number of articles trying to find an answer to this phenomenon. This author would like to say a few words on this.

Chinese cuisine has long been recognized as one of the best in the world. For thousands of years the Chinese people did not have freedom of thought, but they have been free to cook as they liked. So they could divert part of their talents to cooking and created many schools of culinary art renowned for their taste, flavor and variety. But is Chinese cuisine scientific and nutritious? I, as a Chinese, dare not give a definite answer. The philosophy of Chinese culinary art comprises the three elements of "color, aroma and taste". Conspicuous by its absence is the mention of nutrition. Most of the Chinese people eat rice as their staple food, but rice has a lower nutritional value than wheat or potatoes, not to mention milk. The area of grassland in China is next only to that of Australia, but it is far from fully exploited for animal husbandry. The average European or

American drinks about 100 kg of milk a year, and the figure in India has risen to 65 kg, whereas in China the average per capita consumption of milk is only one kg a year. The Chinese physique is naturally deficient in calcium. What is more, the Chinese like to cook fresh vegetables till most of the vitamins are cooked out of them. The serious deficiency of calcium and vitamins in Chinese food obviously has been one reason for the absence of a strong physique among Chinese men.

The problem in education is even more serious. China is practicing a "one family, one child" policy. The result is that the only child in a family is likely to be spoilt, as the parents and grandparents pamper the child as a "little emperor". Teachers in primary and secondary schools in China get relatively low pay, work long hours and do not have a very high social status. Teaching, therefore, is not an attractive career, particular to males. All the people working in nurseries and kindergartens are women, and 80% of primary school teachers and 70% of junior middle school teachers are also women. This means that most Chinese boys grow up mainly in the embrace of female adults, which is an environment very much like that of Jia Baoyu in A Dream of Red Mansions. In China only a small percentage of the graduates from senior middle schools are admitted into colleges. So the college entrance examination has become a fierce battlefield every summer. Meanwhile, the rigid demands of the college entrance examinations have a negative effect on the country's educational policy, which in theory places equal importance on moral, scholarly and physical education for the all-round development of the student. But the reality is that the college entrance examinations cover six subjects with a total of 600 points as full marks, and there is simply no scope for checking the moral and physical education of a college applicant. Since the success of a secondary school is gauged by the number of its graduates admitted into colleges, secondary schools vie with one another to increase the burden of study, and parents trying to get their children admitted to colleges try in every way to get their children to take extra courses. The result is that the satchels of primary and secondary school students keep growing fatter and heavier. Physical culture is therefore virtually squeezed out of the curricula. Very often the sports ground of an urban secondary school is used to build more classrooms. As a result, among the primary and secondary schools, there is a high percentage of plump students, bespectacled students and effeminate boys. And many students have high grades but are incompetent at their daily routines. A recent authoritative report indicates that 32% of secondary school students in China display abnormal psychological behavior—depression, irritation, loss of interest in studies, and unrequited love.[40] When we view the problem in the perspective of Chinese culture as previously discussed, it will be easy to see that the lop-sided composition of the Chinese diet and the problems in Chinese education stem from traditional Chinese culture. The one-sided emphasis on farming to the neglect of animal husbandry dates from the Han Dynasty, and the overemphasis on book knowledge to the neglect of practical skills can be traced to Confucius. The emphasis on learning to the neglect of the martial arts and the substitution of the examination hall for the sports ground and battlefield began in the Song Dynasty. The imperial examination through the eight-legged essays, that required only learning by heart without creativeness, began in the Ming Dynasty. Effeminacy among Chinese males also began in the Song Dynasty. Therefore, a fundamental solution to the problem should be sought in a "cultural transformation."

As we mentioned above, the cultural transformation in China began in the middle of the Ming Dynasty, when Western missionaries started to arrive. And this trend assumed a certain scale during the 1911 revolution and the May 4th Movement. Clashes with and assimilation of Western culture have never

---

[40] "Beijing Evening News" p. 12, Jun. 13, 1995.

ceased in China, giving rise to cycles of upheavals every 5 to 10 years. The Yan'an culture was born in the people's revolution under the leadership of the Chinese Communist Party and the guidance of Marxism-Leninism. Soviet Russian culture made an all-out advance into China during the 1949-1960 period. Since the "Cultural Revolution" (1966-1976) Chinese culture has experienced invasions of Japanese culture and the cultures of Hong Kong and Taiwan. Present-day China has become a juncture of many cultures. Cultural transformation in China has traversed the greater part of its journey, but it has far from reached its destination. Its various components have still not developed to reach their proper proportions. In connection with our topic, the emancipation of women and equality between the sexes have become true in the cities and reached a fairly good standard in the greater part of the countryside. But there is a problem peculiar to Chinese culture, albeit secondary in importance, i.e. the ascendancy of *yinrou* and decline of yang*gang* among Chinese males. That problem has not drawn adequate attention, and naturally has not been reversed. This problem is manifest particularly in sports circles, the film industry and even among some singers.[41] That is not a phenomenon of the "waxing of *yin* and waning of yang", as analysed above, but a phenomenon of "normal *yin* but waning of yang". The problem of the trend toward effeminacy among Chinese males was first raised by a female college student by the name of Fan Yang. Soon after her graduation from college, she wrote a book titled, **The Decline of Yanggang—A Comment on the Waning of the Manly Quality among Chinese Males with Reference to Jia**

[41] The author once invited some European friends to dinner. After the meal, the author played a cassette of a Chinese male singer known in China for his yang*gang* quality. But surprisingly, the European guests were convinced that it was a female singing. After listening to the tape a second time, they still stuck to their opinion. This incident might serve as an example of the *yinrou* quality of Chinese males.

Baoyu's View on Gender Relations.[42] Near the conclusion of the book, Miss Fan raises a provocative topic—"The Emancipation of Chinese Males". She writes: "Those who are the most profoundly influenced by the traditional culture need thorough emancipation. Once the Chinese women unbound their feet, they walked out of their homes and made big strides forward, full of vigor and vitality. Yet our males think that nothing binds them and that they have nothing to be freed from. But, in reality, they walk timidly and simperingly. Compared with their foreign counterparts, they are 'castrated', coquettish, sentimental and poor-spirited, as if they cannot display their manliness without resorting to inflating themselves. Isn't it a tragedy!?

"The renaissance of China, to a great degree, depends on the emancipation of Chinese males!"

3. Fine Conditions Exist for the Cultural Transformation and the Realization of a Good Partnership Between the Sexes in China

Historical Research, in its fourth issue of 1994, published an article titled "On the Question of the Gender of Legendary Kings in Ancient China", by Professor Li Hengmei. The author points out that although among primates such as baboons, apes, gibbons and chimpanzees the females are in charge of nursing children and the males in charge of seeking food and protecting their territory, among the Iroquois, Hopis and Zunis of North America and some tribes in Africa which are still at the stage of matriarchal society, the chief of a clan is always a male and the females and males live in a natural partnership. But under the matriarchal system, real power is not in the hands of the females.

The author then proceeds to determine that in ancient

---

[42] Published in Beijing, 1988, International Cultural Publishing Corporation.

China, even if it was a matriarchal society under the Five Kings, the supreme rulers of the time, namely the Five Kings, were definitely males.

The article cites convincing proof to support its views, which coincide with those I touched upon earlier in this concluding chapter. Then how was the patriarchal social model evolved?

Riane Eisler's book and this book tell us that the hierarchical order or hierarchy as the embryonic form of the patriarchal social model first existed in the armed units of men of nomadic ethnic groups or the sub-military organizations of water-control bodies of men of farming groups, which through certain forms of "revolution" or "coups" were imposed on the whole group and forced it to be organized after the pattern of a hierarchical system. Men of strong build, good at fighting and with merits in battle held power-vested positions on various rungs of the hierarchical ladder. These men had a redistribution of the women, captives (women at first), property and land, and passed these down as patrimony. In order to ensure the purity of the genealogical line, it was necessary to monopolize a woman (wife) or several women (wife and concubines), suppress them and shut them up. Males obtained power, property, land and sexual freedom in the new social relationship, whereas the females lost power, property, land and sexual freedom. That was the beginning of the male domination of the female.

Through long and large-scale wars, the social model of patriarchy was imposed on most of the matriarchal societies. Later this new social model developed into a more perfect and stable feudal and Christian hierarchy in Europe and a centralized, patriarchal officialdom in China. In order to justify and perpetuate patriarchy and make people forget goddesses and the partnership between the sexes in the matriarchal society, a religious myth of a god in the form of a male was created in Indo-European cultural circles, and a philosophy of exalting *yang* and degrading *yin* was created in Chinese cultural circles.

The social model characterized by male domination and its culture, which have lasted for 5,000 years in Europe and 4,000 years in China are nearing their end. In Europe, religion has long been separated from government and a democracy of independent legislation, administration and judiciary has replaced feudal dictatorship, agricultural society has given way industrial society, the women's liberation movement has made great progress in the last century and the entire society is in transition to a post-industrial society—the information society. This is a new social and cultural transformation.

What will be the social structure in the information society? In October 1989 the author arranged a high-level seminar in honor of Mr. Ervin Laszlo, an advisor to UNESCO and member of the Rome Club, who was visiting China at the invitation of the Chinese Academy of Social Sciences. Touching on the structure of future society, Mr. Laszlo advanced a new term —"holarchical system", which, he said, was coined by him together with other systematologists in New York in 1986. The author, acting as Mr. Laszlo's interpreter at the time, asked him what the difference was between "holarchical" and hierarchical. Mr. Laszlo thought for a while and said that a "hierarchical system" might be termed a "multi-level command system" because it denotes only the downward flow of information, while a "holarchical system" may be considered as a "multi-level participation system" because it denotes information flow in all directions.[43] I would like to add the point that the relationship between participants on an equal footing is partnership. If we combine Laszlo's theory of "multi-level participation" with Eisler's concept of "partnership" and theory of cultural transformation we may come to this conclusion: The whole world is undergoing a new cultural transformation—from the industrial society to the information society, from a multi-level command

---

[43] See "Speeches on Systematological Philosophy" by E. Laszlo, translated by Min Jiayin, pp. 220-222, CAAS Press, 1991

system to a multi-level participation system, from a gender relationship of male domination over the female to a gender relationship of partnership in which men and women will be equal partners in competition as well as cooperation in all spheres, political, military, economic, social, cultural and the family.

I will refrain from anticipating how this will be accomplished in Europe and other parts of the world. I only want to point out that so far as the field of discussion of this book is concerned, there exist favorable conditions in China for the requisite cultural transformation and establishment of a new, partnership-like relationship between the sexes.

(1) For the first time in its history, China has become a conjuncture of a multitude of cultures. World history tells us that a nation meeting such an opportunity generally achieved a high degree of civilization, or even a new civilization such as those of Ancient Greece, Medieval Arabia, Renaissance Europe and modern Japan and the United States. As long as China persists in its policy of reform and opening to the outside world, the progress will lead to the emergence of a highly developed civilization, entailing a new gender relationship.

(2) The social structure in China has undergone a significant change, and this change will continue. The centralized planned economy has given way to a system that combines a market economy with a planned economy. Considerable progress has been made in the ongoing political restructuring focusing on a simplification of the administrative institutions, the vesting of greater autonomy in local governments, the separation of the ruling political party from governmental administration and the severing of governmental departments from state-owned enterprises, a system of employment and tenure for government functionaries, the two-way selection of personnel by the employer and the employee at the same time, etc. And it is certain that the orientation of the political reform will be toward the pattern of "large society with a small admin-

istration" and multi-level participation.

(3) Confucianism as the theoretical basis for patriarchy and male domination of the female, after repeated critiques, has lost its original economic and social foundations. Therefore, even if there is a revival of Confucianism it cannot be an overall reinstatement of it to a dominating position. The Confucian theory of male supremacy has been cast into the dustbin of history for good.

(4) Marxism-Leninism and Mao Zedong Thought, which have replaced Confucianism in China, stand for sexual equality and take women's emancipation as a component of the revolution led by the Communist Party, emphasizing that the emancipation of women must start primarily in the economy through the realization of equal pay for equal work, and men and women should take an active part in economic competition on an equal footing under conditions of a market economy. This has furnished correct guidance for the women's movement in China.

(5) The Chinese people have lived for half a century under the slogan and in the social reality of equality of men and women, and have fundamentally formed a new cultural tradition. The specific content of equality between the sexes has taken the form of laws and government decrees which are being applied by the law enforcement departments. The All-China Women's Federation and its local organizations have been active in upholding Chinese women's rights and interests, and pushing the women's liberation movement forward.

(6) Nine-year compulsory education is being implemented throughout the country. This, plus the "Hope Project", which aims at helping school drop-outs (mostly girls) in poor areas return to school, offers a guarantee for the attainment of a junior middle school education for the great majority of women in the future and an ability to compete with men on an equal footing in social activities.

(7) The policy of family planning based on "one family, one

child" has been implemented firmly as a state policy. This, plus the fairly complete institutions of child care such as creches and kindergartens, will ensure that Chinese women will have ample time to pursue careers.

(8) Chinese culture has been endowed with its own theory for reaching an equilibrium and the harmony of *yin* and *yang* through self-readjustment on its ultimate aesthetic principle of an integration of yang*gang* and *yinrou*. This traditional philosophical heritage naturally provides a theoretical basis for the Chinese people to achieve equality of the sexes and the establishment of a new partnership between them. With this basis and the identification of the mainstream ideology with contemporary culture, the concept of partnership and the theory of cultural transformation which Eisler advances will certainly merge smoothly into Chinese culture.

There will be no serious obstacles in urban China in the way of the establishment of a new partnership between the sexes and the continuation of cultural transformation, but there will be greater difficulties in this respect in rural China.

Vast rural China, with its huge population, is unevenly developed economically. The countryside of the open coastal region is already fairly better off, whereas many poor households in the remote rural areas in inland Southwest, Northwest and Central China are still struggling on the starvation line. Generally speaking, one finds much more serious remnants of the patriarchal system and feudal superstition in the rural areas than in the cities. For instance, the idea of male superiority may occasionally lead to the drowning of female infants, there are more girl school dropouts than boy dropouts, commercial marriage and the kidnapping of women for sale still take place, and male chauvinism in family life with the male members doing no household chores—all these are rare in the cities now they are not uncommon in the rural areas. All these problems have to be resolved through economic development, education for all and the raising of the cultural level of Chinese farmers. But with the rapid development of township industry and the urbanization of the rural areas, and the spread of television and other mass media, these problems will be resolved.

The establishment of a new partnership between the sexes signifies by no means a return to the old partnership under the matriarchal system. The new partnership will definitely assimilate many positive elements from the old gender relations which have developed over thousands of years, but it will also resolve many new problems cropping up under the new circumstances. For example, a recent article in the journal China Population proposes that in naming newborn babies the family name of the father be given to a boy and the family name of the mother be given to a girl, or a combined family name adopting both the family names of the father and the mother be given to both boys and girls. This is a good idea promoting the equality of men and women and may solve some new problems arising from the "one family, one child" practice. Some propose that the personal name be extended from the present normally two to three or even four characters as a solution to the problem of too many people having the same or similar names.

To sum up, while the Chinese people are building socialism with Chinese characteristics under the leadership of the Chinese Communist Party, the country is still undergoing a social transition, as well as a cultural transition. Nevertheless, with the eight favorable conditions we have mentioned above, China is expected to advance to the forefront of the world in building a new partnership between the sexes and bringing about an equilibrium between *yin* and *yang* and a harmony of yang*gang* and *yinrou*.

EPILOGUE

It was already June 18, 1995 when I completed the 35,000-word Conclusion to this book. I heaved a sigh of relief —happy that a complex and strenuous project was finally drawing to an end. This book, both the Chinese and English editions, will be off the press in August to greet the convocation of the World Women's Conference to be held in Beijing.

The China Partnership Research Group was set up just a year ago. Thanks to support and assistance from many organizations and friends in China and the United States, it has been possible to streamline the work on the two editions almost simultaneously. For instance, when the first 260,000 words of the Chinese scripts were through second copy reading and my Conclusion was almost completed, one third of the English translation of the book had been polished by Mr Bruce Gordon Doar on his computer and the printed version was on the desks of Ms Riane Eisler and Mr David Loye on the other side of the Pacific.

In addition to the names of the advisers, writers, translators, copy editors and editors we have mentioned in our acknowledgment, I would like to express my thanks to Mr Zheng Wenlin, Director of the China Social Sciences Publishing House and Mr Lü Zhanghua, Vice-Director of the China Social Sciences Publishing House, Mr Zhao Zhigang, General Manager of the Beijing Tianlong Science and Technology Company, and Ms Xie Lihua, member of the Editorial Board of the "Chinese Women's Newspaper", for their invaluable support. I would also like to express my gratitude to the many accomplished experts and scholars who have helped me solve many questions with admirable patience and/or lent me valuable reference books and their own works. They are: Mr Huang Xinchuan of the Asia & Pacific Institute under the Chinese Academy of Social Sciences, Mr Zhang Zhiyan and Mr Sun Jing of the Institute of Philosophy of the Chinese Academy of Social Sciences, Mr Peng Bangjiong of the Institute of History of the Chinese Academy of Social Sciences, Mr Wang Xuetai of the Institute of Literature of the Chinese Academy of Social Sciences and Mr Fang Litian of the Chinese People's University.

The book was translanted by 11 people and then the translation was checked and copy-edited and photoset. Unfortunately, owing to my lack of experience, I neglected the translators to use a unified word processing software, which inevitably resulted in many shortcomings of the print format. I hope my readers will forgive my inexperience and the inconvenience I give them. In order to rush out the book before the World Women's Conference in Beijing, our specially invited Mr Huang Jisu, English editor of Social Sciences in China Press and the director of the photosetting department of the Beijing Foreign Languages Press did a wonderful job. I would like to take this opportunity to express my gratitude for them. Finally I must thank my wife Tian Xiaoqi, without whose sacrifice in shouldering all the household chores I would not have had so much time to complete this project.

We would also like to express our appreciation for the valuable support which the Threshold Foundation, the Namaste Foundation, Kobert Graham and Elinore Detiger gave us through the Center for Partnership Studies, U.S.A.

When we are through with the studies, discussions and writing, I feel this book may have broken some new ground in the following aspects: It is not merely a history of Chinese women, but a history of gender relations in China in the perspective of the cultural and social history of China; by grasping the two cultural qualities of yanggang and yinrou, the book may have grasped the mainstream of Chinese culture, which has further aroused Chinese academic circles' attention to the cultural differences and clashes between Chinese farming nationalities and nomadic nationalities in history and which provides an initial explanation of the "paradox" in Chinese culture noticed by Westerners, as Ms Riane Eisler mentions in her book; it reminds Chinese males of their weaknesses and urges them to rebuild an image of yanggang; and, most important of all, it may impress upon the Chinese people the concept of partnership in gender relations and in the ongoing cultural transformation in China.

Finally I would like to say, on behalf of our writing group, that the first fruit of our research has met with an invaluable opportunity—the convocation of the World Women's Conference in Beijing. It is our hope that the more than 30,000 representatives at the conference and the 4,000 reporters covering it will carry this book to all parts of the world, thereby enhancing the world's understanding of the Chinese people, Chinese women in particular, an understanding of their past, present and future, and the challenges they are facing, and thereby inspire people, particularly women, of all countries, to join hands with the Chinese people in their forward march in the common struggle for the establishment of a new partnership between the sexes. Of course, we sincerely hope to hear comments and views on this book and welcome your support for our future research work.

Min Jiayin
China Partnership Research Group
June 18, 1995   Beijing

GLOSSARY OF HISTORICAL TEXTS

Baihu Tongyi	Universal Principles of the White Tiger Hall
Baihu Tong	Comprehensive Discussions in the White Tiger Hall
Beilu Fengsu	Customs of the Northern Nomads
Benshi Shi	Poems on Facts
Chu Ci	Elegies of Chu
Chunqiu Fanlu	String of Pearls of Spring and Autumn Annals
Chuogeng Lu	Records Made When Stopping Ploughing
Da Qing Huidian	The Collected Institutes of the Great Qing
Da Ming Hudian	The Collected Institutes of the Great Ming
Dadai Liji	Recorder of Rites Compiled by Dai the Elder
Diwang Shiji	The History of Emperors and Kings
Du Yi Zhi	Annals of Marvels
Dufu Ji	Records of Jealous Women
Dumen Jilue	Chronicle of the Capital
Fa Jing	The Canon of Laws
Fang Bao Ji	Anthology of Fang Bao
Fengsu Tiaoyue	Public Conventions
Fengsu Tongyi	A Comprehensive Discussion of Customs
Gangjian Hepian	Compilation of Guiding Principles
Guanzi	Works of Master Guanzi
Guige Sishu	The Four Books for Women
Guo Yü	Discourses on the States

Han Lü	The Han Code
Han Shu	The History of the Han Dynasty
Hanfeizi	Works of Master Han Fei
Hanshi Yizhuan	Han's Commentaries on the Book of Changes
Hanwu Neizhuan	The Inside Stories of Emperor Wudi of the Han Dynasty
Heida Shilue	Events of the Black Tartars
Honglou Meng	Dream of Red Mansions
Hou Han Shu	The History of the Later Han Dynasty
Hu Ling	Ordinances on the Family
Huatian Chenmeng Lu	Chronicle of Mundane Dreams and Dazzling Heavens
Jia Fan	Family Norms
Jing Hua Yuan	Flowers in the Mirror
Jinping Mei	Golden Lotus
Jiu Wudai Shi	The Old History of the Five Dynasties
Jiu Tang Shu	The Old History of the Tang Dynasty
Jiuchao Lue Kao	Laws of the Nine Dynasties
Jizhong Zhushu Jinian	The Bamboo Annals from the Tumulus at Ji
Kuodi Zhi	A Comprehensive Geography
Laozi Zhu	Annotations of Laozi
Laozi	Works of Master Laozi
Lienü Zhuan	Lives of Honorable Women
Lingwai Daida	Replies from the South
Liuyue Xue	Snow in Midsummer
Lun Heng	Discussions Weighed in the Balance
Lunyu	The Analects
Luoshen Fu	Prose-Poem to the Nymph of the River Luo
Lüshi Chunqiu	Master Lü's Spring and Autumn Annals
Mengxi Bitan	Essays Written on the Stream of Dreams

Mengzi	Works of Master Mengzi
Ming Lü	The Ming Code
Mozi	Works of Master Mozi
Mudan Ting	Peony Pavilion
Mutianzi Zhuan	The Biography of Emperor Mu
Neize	Domestic Principles
Nü Lunyü	Women's Analects
Nü Jie	Instructions to Women
Nüer Jing	Classic for Women
Nüfan Jielu	Account of Female Norms
Nüxian Waishi	Histories of Women Immortals
Qian Han Shu	The History of the Former Han Dynasty
Qianjia Shi	The Poetry of a Thousand Poets
Qidanguo Zhi	The History of the Khitan Kingdom
Qing Lü Li	The Qing Statutes and Sub-statutes
Qing Shi	Histories of Love
Qingbai Leichao	Records of Social Conventions in the Qing Dynasty
Qingshi Shan	Mount Bluestone
Ren Xue	On Benevolence
Rulin Waishi	Scholars
San Wu Lie Ji	Histories of Prehistoric Legendary Tribal Leaders
Sanchao Beimeng Huibian	Collection of Northern Treatises from Three Dynasties
Sanguo Zhi	The History of the Three Kingdoms
Sangzang Ling	Ordinances on Mourning and Burial
Sanniang Jiaozi	The Third Mistress Teaches Her Son
Sanzi Jing	The Three Character Classic
Shang Shu	The Book of Documents
Shangjun Shu	The Book of Lord of Shang

Shanhai Jing	The Book of Mountains and Rivers
Shentou Ci Tang	Assassinating Tang Qin
Shi Fan	Norms for the Age
Shi Jing	The Book of Songs
Shi Su	Worldly Conventions
Shi Ji	The Records of the Historian
Shu Yi Ji	Accounts of Marvels
Shu Jing	The Book of Documents
Shuangding Ji	A Story of Two Nails
Shui Jing	The Book of Waters
Shuihu Zhuan	All Men Are Brothers
Shuowen Jiezi	An Etymological Dictionary of Chinese Characters
Silang Tanmu	Silang Visiting His Mother
Sishu Daquan	The Complete Four Books
Sizhou Cheng	Sizhou City
Song Xingtong	Compendium of Song Criminal Law
Song Shi	The History of the Song Dynasty
Songqin Yanli	Paying a Visit to the Mother of the Son-in-law
Su Shuo	On Customs
Sui Shu	The History of the Sui Dynasty
Sunbin Bingfa	Sun Bin's Martial Art
Sunzi	Works of Master Sunzi
Tang Lü	The Tang Code
Tang Liudian	Six Institutes of the Tang
Tangshi Yanyi	Historical Romance of the History of the Tang
Taiping Yulan	The Taiping Imperial Encyclopedia
Tong Dian	General Institutes
Wei Shu	The History of the Wei State
Wu-Yue Chunqiu	Spring and Autumn Annals of the Wu and Yue States

Wudai Shi	The History of the Five Dynasties
Wujing Daquan	The Complete Five Classic
Xiao Jing	The Classic of Filial Piety
Xin Tang Shu	The New History of the Tang Dynasty
Xingbu Xianxing Zeli	Regulations Issued by the Board of Punishments
Xingfazhi	Legal Treatise
Xingli Daquan	The Complete Collection of Confucian Doctrines
Xingshi Yinyuan Zhuan	The Predestined Marital Disaster
Xixiang Ji	The Western Chamber Romance
Xunzi	Works of Master Xunzi
Yangjia Jiang	Generals of the Yangs
Yanhuoju	The Poker
Yanshi Jiaxun	The Family Instructions of Yan
Yaocha Ji	A Tale of Poisoned Tea
Yi Jing	Book of Changes
Yi Li	The Book of Rites
Yinbingshi Heji	Collected Works of the Ice-drinking Studio
Yiwen Zhi	Records of Literature and Art
Yiyu Zhi	Annals of Outer Regions
Youyang Zazu	The Youyang Miscellany
Yuan Dianzhang	Institutes of the Yuan
Yuan Shi	The History of the Yuan Dynasty
Yueling	Monthly Ordinance
Yuewei Caotang Biji	Jottings of Yuewei Hut
Zhongyong	The Doctrine of the Mean
Zhou Yi	The Book of Changes of the Zhou Dynasty
Zhou Li	The Rites of the Zhou Dynasty
Zhuangzi	Works of Master Zhuangzi

Zhushu Jinian	The Bamboo History
Zhuzi Quanshu	The Complete Works of Zhu Xi
Zhuzi Yulei	Quotations from Zhu Xi
Zizhi Tongjian	Comprehensive Mirror for the Aid of the Ruler
Zuo Zhuan	Zuo Qiuming's Commentary on the Spring and Autumn Annals

A BRIEF INTRODUCTION
TO CHINESE PARTNERSHIP
RESEARCH GROUP

The Chinese Partnership Research Group is a non-governmental and non-profit academic research body, embracing representatives from many institutes and disciplines. It is based in the Chinese Academy of Social Sciences. It conducts research independently under the guidance of the relevant institutes of the Chinese Academy of Social Sciences and the Center for Partnership Studies in California, co-directed by Prof. Riane Eisler and Prof. David Loye.

With reference and comparison to the research on gender relations and social evolution in the Indo-European world undertaken by the U.S. cultural anthropologist Riane Eisler in her **The Chalice and the Blade**, the group has set out to make a thorough study on the gender relations and the evolution of social models from the prehistoric age to the contemporary period in China and probe the profound implications, and universality and adaptability of the "partnership concept" and the "cultural transformation theory", in order to make the "partnership concept" known to the Chinese public and make it a new concept in handling the relations between men and women and those between friends, companies, groups and countries, to advance the cause of women's emancipation, and create a social model in which men and women enjoy equal partnership.

It conducts social surveys, sponsors seminars and organises the compilation, translation and publication of books. It applies for and receives financial aid from foundations at home and abroad, and receives donations from other organizations and individuals for the purpose of its academic research.

Liaison person: Min Jiayin, Zip Code:100732, Address: Institute of Philosophy, Chinese Academy of Social Sciences, Beijing, Telephone: 8610-5021887, Fax: 8610-5137826.

The Chinese Partnership Research Group is composed of researchers accepted and recruited in light of the needs of research subjects. To date, apart from having translated and published The Chalice and the Blade in Chinese, the group is conducting a research project to be published under the title **The Chalice and the Blade in Chinese Culture—Gender Relations and Social Models**. The book will appear in both Chinese and English editions and be presented at the International Exhibition of Books on Women to be held in Beijing in September 1995, as a contribution to the '95 World Conference on Women.

EDITOR-IN-CHIEF,
WRITERS AND EDITORS

Min Jiayin

Editor-in-chief, male, MA in philosophy, research fellow and deputy director of the Section of Marxist Philosophical Principles of the Institute of Philosophy of the Chinese Academy of Social Sciences, member of the International Research Group of General Evolution and a consulting editor of **World Futures**, the journal of the group. Major works include **Evolutionary Pluralism** and **The Cultural Circle of Chinese Characters**.

Cai Junsheng

Male, senior research fellow of the Institute of Philosophy of the Chinese Academy of Social Sciences. Major works include **The Formation of Human Societies and the Formation of Primitive Society** and **The Leap of Civilisation: The Formation and Development of Social Information**.

Jiao Tianlong

Male, MA in history, assistant research fellow of the Institute of Archaeology of the Chinese Academy of Social Sciences, and head of the Shandong Archaeological Team. Major works include Prehistoric Culture from the End of the Pleistocene to the Beginning of the Holocene in the Area South of the Five Ridges and On the Neolithic's Features and Its Initial Signs.

Du Jinpeng

Male, research fellow of the Institute of Archaeology of the

Chinese Academy of Social Sciences, and head of the Henan Archaeological Team. Major works included A Study of Bronze Jue Vessels of the Shang and Zhou Dynasties and A New Study of the Chronological Problems of the Xia and Shang Cultures.

Du Fangqin
Female, MA in literature, executive director of the Women's Study Center of Tianjin Normal University and research fellow. Major works include **Changes in Women's Concepts** and **Chinese Women and Development**.

Sun Xiao
Male, MA in history, research fellow of the Institute of History of the Chinese Academy of Social Sciences, well-versed in the study of the in Qin and Han dynasties. Major works include **A Brief History of Chinese Marriages** and **The Teachings from the Mind-Study**.

Pan Shaoping
Male, MA in history, official in the Personnel Bureau of the Chinese Academy of Social Sciences. Major works include **A Study of Currency in the Wang Mang Interregnum** and **A Summary of Studies on China's Qin and Han Dynasties**.

Gao Shiyu
Female, professor, director of the Section of Ancient History of the journal **Historical Research**, produced by the Chinese Academy of Social Sciences. Major works include **Women in the Tang Dynasty** and **The Life of Women in Ancient China**.

Liu Ruzhen
Female, MA in history, editor in the Section of Ancient Culture of the Science Press. Major works include **The War between the Two Capitals of the Yuan Dynasty and the Problem of the Chronology of the Middle and Late Yuan Dynasty** and **A Study**

of Jiang-Zhe Province in the Yuan Dynasty.

Zhao Shiyu
Male, MA in history, associate professor of the Department of History of Beijing Normal University, scholar of folklore of Ming and Qing dynasties. Major works include Biography of Dorgon, the Imperial Regent and King of the Early Qing and **An Outline Cultural Geography of China**.

Zheng Yongfu
Male, MA in history, professor of the Department of History of Zhengzhou University, scholar of the ideological history of modern China and modern Chinese women's history. Co-author of **The Chinese Women's Movement** and **Modern Chinese Women's Life**.

Lu Meiyi
Female, associate professor of the Department of History of Zhengzhou University, scholar of the history of the modern Chinese political system and modern Chinese women's history. Co-author of **The Chinese Women's Movement** and **Modern Chinese Women's Life.**

Zhao Zhewei
Male, BA in English and literature of Beijing Second Institute of Foreign Languages and LLB of Beijing University. Co-author of **Encyclopedia of Securities' Practice** and **A Study of Civil Cases Concerning Foreign Elements**.

Zhang Zhijing
Female, LLB, assistant professor of the Department of Law of China University of Political Sciences and Law, scholar of history of ancient China's legal system. Co-author of **China and Foreign Legal Cultures** and **History of Ancient China's Legal System**.

Huang Yufu

Female, senior research fellow of the Center for Documentation and Information of the Chinese Academy of Social Sciences, sociologist. Major works include **Human Being and Society: Socialisation in America** and **Sex Education in the West.**

Huang Dezhi

Female, editor of the Chinese version of **The Chalice and the Blade in Chinese Culture: Gender Relations and Social Models**, and senior copy editor of the Philosophical Editorial Section of the Chinese Publishing House of Social Sciences.

TRANSLATORS, POLISHER
AND EDITORS OF
THE ENGLISH VERSION

Translators:

Chen Simin

Graduate School of Chinese Academy of Social Sciences (Chapter 6)

Huang Jisu

Editorial board of the English edition of the journal "Social Sciences in China" (Chapter 3)

Huang Jue

English Department of Beijing Tourism Institute (Chapter 7, Chapter 11, part of Conclusion)

Jin Shaoqing

Department of Home News for Overseas Service of Xinhua News Agency (Chapter 8, Monograph I)

Liu Bingwen

China School of Journalism (Chapter 10, part of Conclusion, Epilog)

Mo Runxian

Institute of Archaeology of Chinese Academy of Social Sciences (Chapter 2)

Shen Lin

Department of Drama and Literature of Central Drama Institute (Monograph II)

Shi Yang

Department of Home News for Overseas Service of Xinhua

636

News Agency (Introduction and Addenda)
Wang Jinhe
Department of Home News for Overseas Service of Xinhua
News Agency (Chapter 1)
Yang Pinquan
Institute of History of Chinese Academy of Social Sciences
(Chapters 4, 5)

Polishers:
Mr. Bruce Gordon Doar
(The whole book except Conclusion and Epilog)
Mr. Paul White
(Conclusion and Epilog)

Editor of the English Edition:
Mr. Huang Jisu

Editor-in-Chief:
Min Jiayin
Institute of Philosophy of Chinese Academy of Social Sciences

Managing Editors:
Song Lidao
Philosophical Editorial Section of the Chinese Publishing
House of Social Sciences
Feng Chunfeng
Philosophical Editorial Section of the Chinese Publishing
House of Social Sciences

(京)新登字 030 号

图书在版编目(CIP)数据

阳刚与阴柔的变奏: 中国历史上的圣杯与剑: 英文版/
闵家胤主编.–北京: 中国社会科学出版社, 1995.8
　ISBN 7-5004-1741-1

　Ⅰ.阳… Ⅱ.闵… Ⅲ.性别差异–关系–性社会学–东西文
化–对比研究 Ⅳ.C913.14

中国版本图书馆 CIP 数据核字(95)第 13106 号

中国社会科学出版社出版发行
(北京鼓楼西大街甲 158 号)
北京兆成印刷厂印刷　新华书店经销
1995 年 8 月第 1 版　1995 年 8 月第 1 次印刷
开本: 850×1168 毫米 1/32　印张: 20.625　插页: 4
字数: 300 千字　印数: 1—5000 册
定价: 50.00 元